OREGON
HANDBOOK

OREGON
HANDBOOK

STUART WARREN & TED LONG ISHIKAWA

MOON
PUBLICATIONS INC.

OREGON HANDBOOK

Published by
Moon Publications, Inc.
722 Wall Street
Chico, California 95928, USA

Printed by
Colorcraft Ltd.

Please send all comments,
corrections, additions,
amendments, and critiques to:

**STUART WARREN &
TED LONG ISHIKAWA
c/o MOON PUBLICATIONS, INC.
722 WALL STREET
CHICO, CA 95928, USA**

Library of Congress Cataloging-in Publication Data

Warren, Stuart, 1949-
    Oregon Handbook / Stuart Warren & Ted Long Ishikawa.
        p.   cm.
    Includes bibliographical references and index.
    ISBN 0-918373-50-6 : $12.95
    1.   Oregon—Description and travel—1981- —Guide-books.   I. Long
Ishikawa, Ted, 1958-   . II. Title.
F874.3.W37   1991
917.9504'43—dc20
                                                90-24664
                                                CIP

Printed in Hong Kong

Although the authors and publisher have made every effort to ensure that the information was correct at the time of
going to press, the author and publisher do not assume and hereby disclaim any liability to any party for any loss or
damage caused by errors, omissions, or any potential travel disruption due to labor or financial difficulty, whether such
errors or omissions result from negligence, accident, or any other cause.

```
OREGON HANDBK
LONG TED     TS MONB  Q      $12.95
06/17/91     IBCOE K34140TN        1
285557       0-918373-50-6
             PO NUMBER 31191
C
```
****

To Mr. Ed Hardy, who always said we could.

CONTENTS

MAPS

MAP SYMBOLS

FREEWAY
MAIN HIGHWAY
SECONDARY ROAD
UNPAVED ROAD
FOOT PATH, TRAIL
STATE BORDER
OTHER BORDER
TUNNEL
PASS
RAILROAD
BRIDGE

INTERSTATE HIGHWAY
U.S. HIGHWAY
STATE HIGHWAY
LARGE CITY
SMALL CITIES & TOWNS
MOUNTAIN

WATERFALL
WATER
SKI AREA
POINT OF INTEREST
N.W.R. NATIONAL WILDLIFE REFUGE
N.P. NATIONAL PARK
S.P. STATE PARK

CHARTS

ACKNOWLEDGEMENTS

Oregon Handbook began in Alaska when Moon's editor-in-chief emeritus and esteemed author Deke Castleman grabbed Stuart and said, " Oregon needs a good book. Just get it down, man." Shortly thereafter " it" got under way and was carried to conclusion largely because of Taran March, the best editor we've run into (and who we hope won't notice that we end with a preposition). We had the facts, Taran, but you helped make them sing. Thank you from us and your favorite state, Oregon. We're also indebted to Rhys Thomas and Theo Trimmell for their wise and witty sidebar about the Oregon Country Faire. However, the biggest contribution to *Oregon Handbook* came at the 11th hour when Dave Johnson, the most respected environmental journalist in the state, stepped in to help cover the other side of the mountains.

Moon's man-with-the-golden-hand Bob Race deserves kudos for his maps and illustrations, as does Anne Hikido for graphic layout, and Anne Long for artistic brilliance. Special thanks to Jennifer and Elliot Gehr for their help on the prehistory section, and also to Bill and Dierdre Dant for their insightful comments about Portland and the north coast, which prevented those sections from reading like a telephone directory. Sawako Ishikawa, Rebecca Singer, Rhys and Maria Thomas, Bruce Bush, Henning Larson, and Marty Immerman all played significant parts in bringing the project to fruition.

In addition to the " Beast of the East," we thank Number 95, " Old Blue," for schoolin'; The Bob, The Big Man, and Larry for being straight shooters; Duke Dunnell for esprit de corps; Bowl-of-Rice for teaching us how to avoid black holes; and The Prez for sage advice. We'd also be remiss if we didn't give a nod to the college boys and overly articulate Bill " for inducing a more sanguine outlook," and to Ralph and April, looking hopefully over our shoulders as we wrote. Last but not least, our gratitude goes out to our parents for their unwavering encouragement which sustained us through many long months of work.

ILLUSTRATIONS

Anne Long: 1, 8, 9, 10, 11, 12, 14, 15, 43, 216, 261, 307, 371, 385, 400
Bob Race: 7, 13, 31, 35, 38, 113, 153, 208, 277, 400

IS THIS BOOK OUT OF DATE?

We strive to keep our books as up to date as possible and would appreciate your help. If you find that a resort is not as we described, or discover a new restaurant or other information that should be included in our book, please let us know. Our mapmakers take extraordinary effort to be accurate, but if you find an error, let us know that as well.

We're especially interested in hearing from female travelers, RVers, outdoor enthusiasts, expatriates, and local residents. We are always interested in hearing from the tourist industry which specializes in accommodating visitors to Oregon. Happy traveling! Please address letters to:

Stuart Warren & Ted Long Ishikawa
Moon Publications, Inc.
722 Wall St.
Chico, CA 95928, USA

ABBREVIATIONS

B & B—bed and breakfast
BLM—Bureau of Land Management
CCC—Civilian Conservation Corps
FSR—forest service road
NFS—National Forest Service
NRA—National Recreation Area
NWR—National Wildlife Refuge
ORE (plus number)—state highway
pp—per person
RV—recreation vehicle

INTRODUCTION

Theodore Winthrop, a mid-19th-century adventurer and novelist from New England, made the following observations at the end of his journey to the Oregon Territory:

> Our race has never yet come into contact with great mountains as companions of daily life, nor felt that daily development of the finer and more comprehensive senses which these signal facts of nature compel. . . . These Oregon people, in a climate where being is bliss—where every breath is a draught of vivid life—these Oregon people, carrying to a newer and grander New England of the West a full growth of the American Idea . . . will elaborate new systems of thought and life.

What this boils down to in the language of today is that "these Oregon people" know how to live. Modern travelers to the state will tell you that nowhere in the country has civilization meshed so peacefully with the environment. Recycling and mass transit maintain a beneficent quality of life in the cities, and vast tracts of preserved land attest to Oregonians' appreciation of their gem-like coastline and snowcapped mountain ranges.

Most of these trophies of the good life didn't come easily. Just as it took Oregon Trail pioneers many months to cross 2,000 miles of forbidding deserts and treacherous mountain passes to reach the promised land, Oregonians have sacrificed much to blaze trails in the thickets of environmental legislation and jurisprudence. And while the dilemma of one person's conservation being another's unemployment has been a continuous fact of life here, the debate has never raged more fiercely than it does at present. Inevitably, the outcome will bring more change and the regrettable passing of a way of life for many. But as the Millenium approaches, one fact becomes clear: if Oregon has erred on the side of conservation, it has at least preserved an increasingly valuable and vanishing commodity: namely, its natural resources. The proof is here for you to see.

THE LAND

GEOGRAPHY

The Overview

If Oregon were part of a jigsaw puzzle of the U.S., it would be a squarish piece with a dip in the center of its top. To the west is the Pacific Ocean; to the east is the Snake River and Idaho. Up top, much of the northern boundary between Oregon and Washington is defined by the Columbia River; the southern border is comprised of the state lines of California and Nevada.

If this puzzle also depicted the vertical relief of topographic features, it would show broad columns of mountains dividing the coast from the inland valleys, as well as peaks cutting off western Oregon from the central and eastern parts of the state. East of the highest central range a broad plateau predominates, broken up in the northeast where mountainous features reassert themselves. In the southeast, many lakes provide the major discontinuities in the least mountainous expanse of the state.

The Peak Experience In Western Oregon

Moving west to east, let's consider the major ranges, beginning with the Coastal and Klamath mountains. The Klamaths comprise the lower quarter of the state's westernmost barrier to the Pacific; the eastern flank of this range is generally referred to as the Siskiyous. As we move north, the Oregon Coastal Mountains, a younger volcanic range, replaces the Klamaths. The highest peaks in each of these cordillera barely top 4,000 feet and stand in between coastal plateaus on one side and such agricultural centers as the Yamhill, the Willamette, and the Rogue valleys on the other. East of these valleys there are dormant (as of this writing) volcanoes. Known collectively as the Cascades, two of the largest of these peaks average almost 11,000 feet above sea level.

Contrasts In Eastern Oregon

Beyond the Cascade's eastern slope, one finds semiarid high desert conditions contrasting with the Coast Range rainforests and the mild, wet maritime climate which characterizes much of western Oregon. The contrast is repeated in the northeast, where the 10,000-foot elevation of the

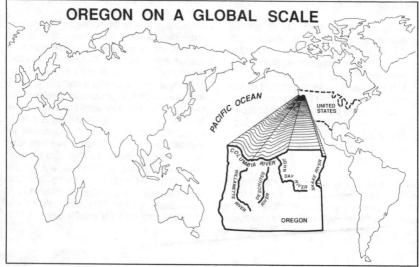

OREGON ON A GLOBAL SCALE

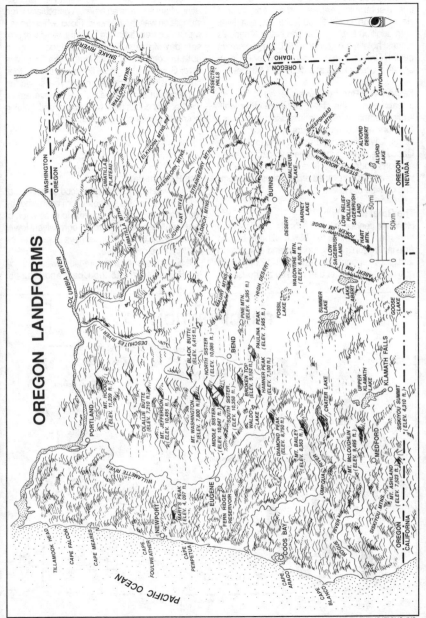

OREGON LANDFORMS

© MOON PUBLICATIONS, INC.

snowcapped Wallowas lies less than 50 miles from a subtropical enclave—the hot dry floor of Hells Canyon, about 1,300 feet above sea level.

In addition to Hell's Canyon being America's biggest hole in the ground (7,900 feet maximum depth), Oregon also boasts the continent's deepest lake: Crater Lake at a depth of 1,962 feet.

Last Of The Red-hot Lavas

In each part of the state, there are other well-known remnants of Oregon's cataclysmic past. Offshore waters here feature 1,477 volcanic islands. Lava fields dot the approach to the High Cascades. East of the range a volcanic plateau supports cinder cones, lava caves, and lava-cast forests in the most varied array of these phenomena outside of Hawaii.

The Great Meltdown

However pervasive the effects of volcanism here they must still share top billing with the big Ice Age in Oregon's topographic grand epic. When that glacial epoch's final meltdown 12,000 years ago unleashed water dammed up by thousands of feet of ice, great rivers were spawned and existing channels were enlarged. A particularly large inundation was the Missoula Flood, which began with an ice dam breaking up in the vicinity of present-day Montana. Before it subsided, it carved out the contours of what is now the Columbia River Gorge. Other glacial floodwaters found their outlet westward to the sea, digging out silt-ridden estuaries in the process. Pacific wave action washed this debris back up onto the land, helping to create dunes and beaches.

CLIMATE

The Rainshadow

Oregon weather is best understood as a series of valley microclimates set apart from each other by mountain ranges. Moving west to east, each of these valley zones records progressively lower rainfall levels until one encounters a desert in the eastern side of the state.

It all begins when moisture-laden westerlies off the Pacific slam into the Coast and Klamath

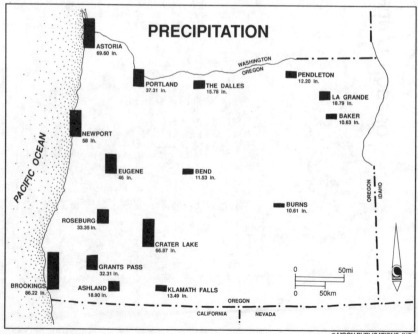

PRECIPITATION

ASTORIA 69.60 in.

WASHINGTON
OREGON

PENDLETON 12.20 in.

PORTLAND 37.31 in.

THE DALLES 15.78 in.

LA GRANDE 18.79 in.

BAKER 10.63 in.

NEWPORT 58 in.

PACIFIC OCEAN

EUGENE 46 in.

BEND 11.53 in.

OREGON
IDAHO

BURNS 10.61 in.

ROSEBURG 33.35 in.

CRATER LAKE 66.87 in.

GRANTS PASS 32.31 in.

BROOKINGS 86.22 in.

ASHLAND 18.90 in.

KLAMATH FALLS 13.49 in.

0   50mi
0   50km

OREGON
CALIFORNIA   NEVADA

The painted hills of John Day Fossil Beds National Monument

PHOTO BY OREGON TOURISM DIVISION

ranges. As the clouds climb higher they drop their moisture in the form of rain or snow. That is because rising air cools 3° F every 1,000 feet, and cooler air can't hold as much moisture as warm air. As a consequence, coastal rainfall often exceeds 80 inches a year, while the Willamette and other inland valleys on the other side of the mountains usually record half that total. The rainshadow effect is repeated when the Cascades catch precipitation from eastward-moving cloud masses; consequently, the other side of this range often records annual rainfall totals below 10 inches. This dryness is contrasted by the western Cascade and Coast Range where precipitation commonly exceeds 100 inches.

Western Oregon

Oregon's location equidistant from the equator and the North Pole subjects her to weather from both tropical and polar air flows. This makes for a pattern of changeability where calm often alternates with storm and extreme heat and extreme cold seldom last long. (Coastal conditions will be treated in detail in that region's chapter.)

If there is one constant in western Oregon, it is cloudiness. Portland and the Willamette Valley get only about 45 percent of maximum potential sunshine; more than 200 days of the year are cloudy and rain falls an average of 150 days. While this might sound bleak, consider that the cloud cover helps moderate the climate by trapping and reflecting the earth's heat. Daily fluctuations in temperature average only 15° F here;

differences between the average temperatures of the warmest month, July, and the coldest one, January, are only about 20°. Best of all, there are only an average of 44 days below freezing. Thus, the region, despite being on a more northerly latitude than parts of Canada, has a milder climate. Except for mountainous areas, snow usually isn't a force to be reckoned with here. Another surprise is that the average annual rainfall of 40 inches is often less than totals recorded in New York, Miami, and Chicago.

While Portland and the Willamette Valley share mild climates, with wintertime highs of 45° and average summertime mercury readings between 65° and 75°, their weather differences are worth noting. Portland is affected by icy winds coming out of the Columbia River Gorge, originally derived from frigid Rocky Mountain air. At these times, the otherwise mild Portland climate experiences uncharacteristic frosts.

The Willamette Valley is affected by temperature inversions. In winter, for example, warm air above the valley walls holds in the colder air below, resulting in enduring, but not endearing, fogs. In the southern valleys, fog has a more positive manifestation, as it helps to counterbalance the region's long dry season. It should also be mentioned that Ashland and Medford can sometimes record half the yearly precipitation of their neighbors to the north, as well as higher wintertime and summertime temperatures. At the same time, these inversions can cause unwelcome pollution to linger.

In much of western Oregon, the day-night differences in temperature are seldom extreme because of cloud cover and vegetation. Both act to keep the air cool and moist during the day and trap heat at night.

Eastern Oregon

By contrast, the scorching deserts of eastern Oregon can give way to cold temperatures at night. This is because clear skies and a dearth of vegetation facilitate the escape of heat.

Mountain areas also experience extreme diurnal ranges. Thin mountain air does not filter out ultraviolet radiation as effectively as denser air at lower elevations, thereby accentuating the sun's force. At night, chill spreads quickly through this thin air.

The saying "only a dude or a fool predicts mountain weather" can apply with equal force to Oregon's high desert, where snow has fallen every month of the year. Sudden storms and cold affect both desert and mountain areas even in midsummer.

Choose Your Poison

What eastern and western Oregonians have in common is a tendency to poke fun at the others' climate. West of the Cascades, the reigning opinion seems to be that it's so dry in the Oregon desert that the jackrabbits pack canteens. In like measure, the dry-siders will assure you that people in western Oregon don't tan, they rust. A quick look at the extremes of rain, heat, and cold will set the record straight.

As the rainiest places in the state don't have weather stations, we'll have to accord the dubious distinction for precipitous precipitation to a "non-community." West of Salem, nestled high in the Coast Range, is Valsetz, a tiny lumber town that once was. Until the town's demise in '85, its 129.9 inches yearly average (with their record 161.4 inches compiled August '73 to July '74) was the highest in the state, although rainfall in the surrounding mountains and over maritime locations commonly exceeds 150 inches. Then too, the typical winter storm season on the coast usually sees 100 mile-per-hour gales and 12-foot waves near Cape Blanco, Cape Foulweather, and at the mouth of the Columbia River near Astoria. And if that's not enough, the *1989 World Almanac* cites Eugene as having the highest relative humidity air on a monthly basis of any place in the U.S.

Statistics from the other side of the mountains make it clear that the sectional debate over whose climate is worse can best be summed up by the phrase, "choose your poison." To wit, Pendleton and Prineville have both recorded 119° F days. Two other eastern Oregon communities, Seneca and Ukiah, share the distinction for the lowest temperature, -54° Fahrenheit.

Such statistics should be viewed in their proper context. These climatic aberrations are not the reality that most Oregonians experience. In fact, the extremes of wind, rain, heat, and cold affect less than one percent of the population, leaving the vast majority in mild, temperate conditions.

FLORA AND FAUNA

FLORA

Trees

Oregon is known for its forests. The mixed conifer ecosystem of western Oregon boasts such record specimens as the 302-foot Finnegan's Fir in the Coast Range outside Coos Bay, rated the nation's largest Douglas fir by the American Forestry Association based on height, diameter, and crown size. Jumbo-sized western hemlock and Sitka spruce also exist in between Oregon's shoreline and the mid-Cascades. Within this region, the evergreen forest of the wet lowlands is the most productive belt of conifers in the world. This woodland carries up to 1,000 tons of plant matter per hectare and sometimes more.

While the record ponderosa pine outside Bend, the tallest Sitka spruce anywhere off U.S. 26 near Cannon Beach, the world's largest cypress in Brookings, and a bevy of similar distinctions might also rate a nod from the *Guinness Book of Records,* the rainforest-to-desert diversity here is straight out of *Ripley's Believe It Or Not.* With only seven percent of the rainfall experienced by Coast Range forests, 24,000 square miles of eastern Oregon's desert is largely sagebrush and juniper.

Tree lovers will also be taken by such arboreal aberrations as southern Oregon's redwood groves, the huge ponderosa pines in the middle of Christmas Valley desert, and fall color in Portland and Willamette Valley towns from deciduous trees planted by early pioneers. A particularly striking natural display along the McKenzie River mixes red vine maple and sumacs with golden oaks and alders against an evergreen backdrop.

Trees To Know In Oregon, published by the Oregon State University Extension Service in Corvallis, is an excellent aid to tree identification as well as a compendium of useful facts. Oregon schoolchildern first learn to distinguish between fir, spruce, hemlock, and ponderosa pine by a memory device. The needles of a fir are flat, flexible, and friendly. Spruce needles are square, stiff and will stick you. Hemlock needles have a hammock-like configuration, and the crown of the tree is curved like it's tipping its hat. Finally, the ponderosa pine's plate-like bark is also distinctive.

Flowers And Fruits

The state of Oregon has forever been associated in the public mind with such sobriquets as the "Emerald Empire" and the "Chlorophyll Commonwealth." While giant conifers and a profuse understory of greenery do in fact surround the state's most populous areas, this ecosystem represents only the most visible part of Oregon's bountiful botany. In between the mist-covered mountains and deserts exist other worlds.

While not as visually arresting as the evergreens of western Oregon, the several varieties of blackberries in the state are no less pervasive. Found mostly from the coast to the mid-Cascades, blackberries favor clearings, burned-over areas, and people's gardens. Some Oregonians swear that they've seen this hardy vine growing on the fenders of cars! It also takes root in the woods alongside wild strawberries, salmonberries, thimbleberries, currants, and salal. Within this edible realm, wild food connoisseurs especially seek out the thin-leafed huckleberry found in the Wallowa, Blue, Cascade, and Klamath ranges. Prime snacking season for all these berries ranges from midsummer to midfall. During the fall, U-pick orchards are also popular. Apples in the Hood River Valley and on Sauvie Island, pears outside of Medford, and all of the above throughout the Willamette Valley are choice pickin's.

Pseudotsuga menziessi,
Douglas fir

Autumn is also the season for those who covet chanterelle and morel mushrooms, particularly after the first rains. This mycological harvest, along with the cutting of ferns, helps many residents of forest communities make ends meet. Maidenhair ferns command an especially high price from florists.

Exempt from exploitation but no less prized are the rare plant communities of the Columbia River Gorge and the Klamath/Siskiyou region. A quarter of Oregon's rare and endangered plants are found in the latter area, 14% of which is in the valley of the Illinois River (a Wild and Scenic River that is a tributary of the Rogue). One of these anomalies, *Kalmiopsis leachiana*, even has a wilderness named after it. Whole volumes have been dedicated to Oregon's singular ecosystems, such as *Rare Plants Of The Columbia Gorge* by Buss Jolley, Oregon Historical Society Press, 1990.

Motorists will treasure such springtime floral fantasias as the dahlias and irises near Canby on I-5, the blue lupines alongside ORE 97 in Central Oregon, apple blossoms in the Hood River Valley near the Columbia Gorge, pear blossoms in the Bear Creek Valley near Medford, beargrass, columbines, and Indian paintbrush on Cascade thoroughfares, as well as Scotch broom, rhododendrons, and fireweed along the coast. And on some of the busiest highways in the state, Willamette Valley daffodils chart a springtime yellow brick road through the heart of the Emerald Empire.

Wildflower lovers will notice that in the country east of the Cascades, the undergrowth is often more varied than the groundcover in the damp forests on the other side of the mountains. This is because sunny openings in the forest permit room for more species and for plants of different heights. And, in contrast to the white flowers that predominate in the shady forests in western Oregon, "dry-side" wildflowers generally have brighter colors. These blossoms must attract color-sensitive pollinators like bees and butterflies. On the opposite flank of the range, the commonly seen white trillium relies on beetles and ants for propagation, lessening the need for eye-catching pigments.

The hand of man has brought Oregon's horticultural highlights to the notice of flower lovers everywhere. Such world-famous displays as the **Hendricks Park Rhododendron Garden** in Eugene, Brookings' **Azalea State Park**, and the **International Rose Test Garden** in Portland all

peak in mid-June. Not surprisingly, nationally known seed companies and nurseries proliferate in the western part of the state.

An especially good book, if you can get a hold of it, is *Wild Flowers Of The Pacific Coast*, by L.L. Hoskin, published by Binford and Mort, 1934. In any case, there is no shortage of good flower books about each specific section of Oregon. Powell's on Burnside St. in Portland has a good collection. Since the color plates in many of these books make them expensive, you'll appreciate the fact that Powell's sells used editions at a discount.

FAUNA

Wildlife

Oregon's creatures great and small comprise an excitingly diverse group, especially in so developed a country as the United States. Oregon's low population density, abundance of wildlife refuges and nature preserves, as well as landforms running the gamut from rainforest to desert explain this variety.

Let's begin our overview from the ground up with the venerable Oregon slug. There are few places on earth where these snails-out-of-shell grow as large and in such numbers. The reason is western Oregon's climate: drier than drizzle but moister than mist. This balance enables the native banana slug and the more common European black slug to thrive while being the bane of Oregon gardeners. When these three- to ten-inch

Felis concolor, *mountain lion*

Eutamias townsendi, *chipmunk*

squirts of slime are not eating plants, you'll see them moving along at a snail's pace on some sidewalk or forest trail.

It's altogether fitting that the continent's fastest land mammal, the pronghorn, also walks the earth here . . . when it's not running, that is. Able to log 40 miles per hour, pronghorns prefer open country east of the Cascades. The low brush there facilitates their excellent vision that can spot predators at a distance. The most dangerous predator of all is kept at a distance by the boundaries of the **Hart Mountain Antelope Refuge**.

In like measure, such tracts as the **South Slough Estuary**, the **Malheur Bird/Wildlife Refuge**, the **Jewell Preserve for Roosevelt elk**, and the **Finley Bird and Wildlife Preserve** provide safe havens for both feathered and furry friends.

While the dominant animals in each of the state's ecosystems are profiled in the chapters which correspond to their habitats, there are certain species whose ubiquitous presence demands an in-depth treatment.

Smaller Scavengers

Many of the most frequently sighted animals in Oregon are smaller scavengers. Even in the most urban parts of the state, it's possible to see raccoons, skunks, chipmunks, squirrels, and opossums. All are frequently encountered in woodsier neighborhoods, often around garbage cans, in parks, and near picnic areas. Urban gardens attract moles and pocket gophers.

West of the Cascades, the dark-colored Townsend's chipmunks are among the most commonly encountered mammals: east of the Cascades, lighter-colored pine chipmunks prolif-

erate in drier interior forests. As for tree squirrels, expect to see the dark brown cinnamon-bellied Douglas squirrel on both sides of the Cascades.

Urban jungles, suburbs, and bush communities throughout Oregon have seen an infestation of opossums. These docile nocturnal marsupials are usually sighted during twilight hours and often as roadkills. Brought by a contingent of rural folk from Arkansas as a food source back in the '30s and '40s, their numbers have increased exponentially. In fact, people are becoming so used to them that the opossum is taking on a new life as a domesticated household pet. Part of their attraction is the fact that they can't get rabies or distemper because their body temperatures are too low. Their ability to grasp objects with their tail and the presence of opposable thumbs make opossums fascinating to watch. Just catch them when they're awake. These nearly blind fruit and carrion eaters spend most of their lives asleep. The fact that oppossums are the only marsupials on the North American continent has further stimulated interest.

Raccoons are not so agreeable. These deceptively cute critters are really vicious scavengers who've earned the dubious distinction of dog-killers. Though no match for many canines on land, they can even the odds by luring a family pet to water to drown. Be especially careful of potentially rabid mothers near cubs.

Big Game And Fellow Travelers

Sportsmen and wildlife enthusiasts alike appreciate Oregon's big game herds. Their habitats differ dramatically from one side of the Cascades to the other, with Roosevelt elk and blacktail deer in the west and Rocky Mountain elk and mule deer east of the Cascades. The Columbian whitetail deer is a seldom seen endangered species that populates western Oregon. Pronghorn reside in the high desert country of southeastern Oregon.

While sightings are rare, the state boasts cougar and wild horse populations. Encounters with these shy creatures will become next to impossible as we approach the Millennium, no thanks to a state-sanctioned cougar hunt in the Cascades and the slow but sure federal auctioning off of the captured wild mustang herd (about 60 strong) who graze in the shadows of the Steens Mountains.

Servus canadensis, *elk*

Beavers In The Beaver State

Castor canadensis, the world's largest rodent, has long been associated with the state of Oregon as a mascot. For good reason: it was the beaver that inspired the fur brigades and spurred the initial exploration and settlement of the state. Apart from its role in bringing Europeans into the wilderness, the beaver merits a special mention for being perhaps the most important animal in Oregon's forest ecosystem. Contrary to popular conception, the abilities of Mother Nature's carpenter extend far beyond the mere destruction of trees to dam a waterway. In fact, the activities associated with lodge construction actually serve to maintain the food chain and the health of the forest.

It all begins when a mated pair (beavers mate for life) pack sticks and mud to dam a river or stream. The resulting pool creates deeper water and the preconditions to building a lodge, constructed in water to protect these ungainly creatures from predation. The beaver's chances for survival are aided by their ability to enter the lodge underwater and stay beneath the surface for as long as twenty minutes. Retractable membranes that protect their eyes and ear flaps enable them to dive comfortably, and a flat rudder-like tail helps them to swim. Add a pair of long sharp middle teeth and beavers are perfectly equipped to cut trees into sticks of exact specifications and float them to the construction site

The resulting lodge, together with the dammed beaver pond, creates a fertile web of life. Aged trees killed by the intrusion of a pond into a forest become homes for millions of insects, which provide food for woodpeckers and many other birds. Fish, turtles, frogs, and snakes soon inhabit the pond and its surrounding environment, and herons, muskrats, otters, and raccoons arrive later as part of the newly emerging ecosystem. Bears, birds of prey, and deer may come to the shore to drink or feed on smaller animals. In like measure, fish may feed on mosquito larvae deposited in the still waters. After the beavers have exhausted the nearby food supply and have moved on, the pond may eventually drain and become a fertile meadow and home to yet other creatures.

The presence of beavers has other positive implications for the nearby human population. In early times, pioneers coveted the fertile soil left from a drained beaver pond. Floods and droughts are tempered in the long run by beaver activities; controlling soil erosion and reducing forest fires are other positive byproducts. All of these benefits result from a beaver complex built of trees that are considered trash species by lumbermen—willow, birch, alder, swamp maple, and certain kinds of pine.

The beaver's belated recognition from scientists as Oregon's forest manager comes along with an increased respect for the complexity of its social order. Despite the traditional rodent propensity for violence when living in close quarters, the beaver is distinguished by a peaceable demeanor. Even though the mating pair and their litter (kits) may be crammed into a small lodge, their ability to cooperate is notable. This seems to be

Castor canadensis, *beaver*

Ursus americanus, *black bear*

due to touching and territoriality. Their instinct to groom one another has a soothing behavioral effect, and information conveyed by imparting their scent to sticks in the pond can serve to ward off other trespassing beavers. Then too, a higher order of rodent is created by the beaver's extra-long lifespan of 25 years. This enables it to socialize its young for several years, thus perfecting an intricate behavioral repertoire. Beavers are widespread throughout the state, though most commonly sighted in second-growth forests after sunset.

Bears
Black bears, *Ursus americanus,* proliferate in remote mountain forests of Oregon. The state's Department of Fish and Wildlife estimates that about 14,000 to 19,000 black bears roam the western Cascades and the Coast Range. Adults average between 200 and 500 pounds and have dark coats. Despite Washington Cascades sightings of the feared grizzly, a species twice the size of the black bear with long three-inch claws and sharper teeth, no encounters have been reported in the Oregon wilderness since 1931.

Black bears shy away from people except when provoked by the scent of food, when they are cornered or surprised, or upon human intrusion into territory near their cubs. Female bears tend to have a very strong maternal instinct that construes any alien presence as an attack upon their young. Authorities often counsel hikers unfortunate or foolish enough to walk between mama bear and her cub to lie down and play dead when she charges. Bears can run faster than the fastest human can sprint on steroids, and their retractable claws enable bears to scramble up trees like squirrels. Furthermore, bears tend to give chase when they see something running.

So if you see a bear at a distance, try to stay upwind and back away slowly. Remember, bears are omnivorous, eating fruits and greens as readily as meat, but it is worth noting that human flesh has no appeal to them. In fact, some studies suggest that our body scent is abhorrent to bears.

Despite a strong sense of smell, bears possess very poor eyesight, which makes an attack by mistake a possibility, particularly when a human-on-the-run evokes the behavior of the bear's prey. Bears can remove a human limb with one swipe of the paw, so an encounter should be avoided at all costs. To this end, campers should place all food in a sack tied to a rope and suspend it 20 feet or more from the ground.

Male bears usually spend all their lives in an area of about two square miles; females may never venture beyond a territory of one square mile. About every third year the female also is accompanied by cubs. Her one to two young, born blind and helpless usually in February, stay with her through the first summer and commonly den up with her the following winter. Humans tend to first see the cubs in the spring, when they are five months old, having no idea that at birth they were small enough to fit into a teacup.

Salmon
"To everything there is a season," and spring and fall are prime times to savor the fate as well as the flavor of the Pacific salmon. During these seasons, Oregon's rivers and streams become choked with spawning fish returning to the exact site of their conception, where they mate and die. As with the eruptions of Old Faithful geyser and the swallows of Capistrano, this poignant dance of death affords a look at one of Mother Nature's time clocks.

The salmon's cycle begins in a freshwater stream when the female deposits her eggs on some coarse sand, and papa fertilizes them in vitro. The bodies of the parents then deteriorate to become part of the food chain for young fish. Prior to their death, the adults starve themselves in their journey upriver from the ocean. The resulting weight loss acts as a deterrent to predators along the way. Thus, the optimum time for a fisherman to reel in something fit for dinner is prior to spawning.

Each species varies in the number of years it remains away from its home stream. Consider that the largest species, known as king or chinook, can spend as many as seven years away from its nesting (and ultimately its resting) place. For smaller species like chum, it is less than half that. Theories about how the salmon's miraculous homing instinct works range from electromagnetic impulses in the earth to celestial objects in the sky, but one thing has been established with certainty—"the nose knows." When salmons' olfactory orifices were stuffed with cotton and petroleum jelly, they were unable to find their spawning streams. The current belief is that baby salmon imprint the odor of their birth stream, enabling them to find their way home years later.

The salmon's traditional predators like the harbor seal, black bear, and herring gull pale in comparison to the threats posed by modern civilization. Everything from phosphates to nuclear waste have polluted Oregon waters, and until recently hydroelectric turbines threatened to block Oregon's all-important Columbia River spawning route. This was remedied when the U.S. Army Corps of Engineers built the fish ladders, a series of concrete baffles, at Bonneville Dam to divert the fish from turbine blades which would chop them to bits. These facilities, together with subterranean fish-viewing windows, offer a special perspective on the spawning phenomenon.

While viewing the salmon's life cycle in various rivers and streams in the fall and spring can be inspiring, most people's interests extend beyond food for the soul. Hence, let's briefly survey what's on the menu.

King or **chinook** salmon—the largest of the species, sometimes weighing in at over sixty pounds. Touted as the best-tasting salmon when caught fresh (especially the spring chinook caught off the Rogue River estuary).

Silver or **coho** salmon—coveted by the Europeans for smoked salmon, it is also known as a fighting fish among sportsmen.

Sockeye or **red** salmon—the "money" fish. Frequently seen in cans, this fish is also smoked and eaten fresh, and commands a hefty price.

Chum salmon—known derogatorily as "dog salmon" because Canadian and Alaskan native people thought them only worthy of being fed to their dog teams. (Be aware that Oregon salmon contain a microorganism poisonous to dogs). Today, this misconception has been replaced by the realization that these fish can be enjoyed canned or smoked.

Birds

Oregon is rapidly gaining a reputation as one of the best birding states. Seasonal variance in populations are often dramatic. Those in the state for

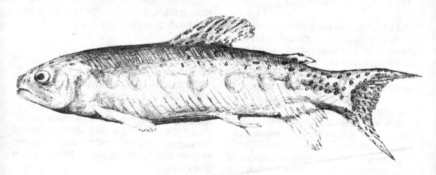

Oncorhynchus tshawytscha, *chinook salmon*

THE SPOTTED OWL—A BIRD IN THE HEADLINES

The Northwest spotted owl is spoken of so passionately in Oregon that newcomers to the state might have the impression that every other person on the street is an ornithology buff. To the environmentalist, the bird represents the "indicator" species of the old-growth Douglas fir forest, an animal whose health and survival is synonymous with an ecosystem that took centuries to develop. To the loggers, the bird is the scourge of the timber industry, a species whose protection will tie up millions of acres of valuable trees, resulting in the loss of tens of thousands of jobs. To the Oregon legislators in Washington, the bird represents a knotty problem, that of balancing the mandates of the 1972 Endangered Species Act and the interests of a public increasingly sensitive to environmental issues with the needs of almost 80,000 people who work in the state's forest products industries.

The points of contention between the two constituencies are better understood when we examine the spotted owl's habits and habitat. In a 150-year-old Douglas fir forest, hollowed-out trees provide ideal nesting areas for these birds. Voles, snowshoe hares, flying squirrels, and other prey of the spotted owl also abound here. A mated pair needs 1,000 acres of old growth forest to feed and reproduce, so the survival of several thousand mated pairs might require that logging of the few remaining ancient stands be stopped. The fact that these forests contain several times more biomass than any other forest in the world makes scientists covet them as a laboratory to study this crucial part of the food chain. They point out that destruction of the old growth forests is like playing dice with Mother Nature. The counter argument contends that one person's conservation is another person's unemployment.

Old growth Douglas fir makes straight-grained lumber with no knots. It is prized around the world as a building material par excellence. With lumber prices up worldwide and the demand expected to increase 300% by the 21st century, the wood represents an economic bonanza. However dire the consequences to the spotted owl, sustained-yield forestry and the environment must be balanced against the consequences of reduced logging: destruction of families, communities, and the state's economy.

If the tangible concerns seem to cast spotted owl defenders as selfish ideologues, consider that an overall shortage of trees and automation in the mills will phase out logging revenues and employment drastically within the decade anyway. Perhaps extending the life of the spotted owl will extend the life of the logging industry.

a long time, or during the interface of seasons, are best able to appreciate the diversity of the influx. For example, in the winter and summer the outskirts of Klamath Falls become inundated with more bald eagles than any place else in the lower 48; other times of year, many of these birds are in Alaska. But southern Oregon hunting season byproducts such as deer carcasses, roadkills, and wounded waterfowl provide a ready food source for migrating carnivorous birds.

Birds of prey, or raptors, abound all over the state. Northeast of Enterprise and near Zumwalt are perhaps the best places to see hawks. Species commonly sighted include the ferruginous, red-tailed and Swainson's hawks. Along I-5 in the Willamette Valley, look for red-tailed hawks on fenceposts and American kestrels, a falcon-like bird, sitting on phone wires. Further south turkey buzzards circle the dry areas during the warmer months. Vultures are commonly sighted a-

Branta canadensis,
Canada goose

bove the Rogue River. Along the lower Columbia east of Astoria, over a hundred bald eagles have chosen to winter there during the past few years; in 1989 the Twilight Eagle Sanctuary was established in this estuary.

Those motoring on Sauvie Island near Portland will be treated to an amazing variety of birds. The northern third of this island is a protected wildlife refuge. More than 200 bird species come through here on the Pacific Flyway, feeding in grassy clearings.

The best inland locations to take in an array of migratory species are wildlife preserves such as Finley and Malheur. The latter is Oregon's premier bird retreat and stopover point for large groups of Canada and snow geese, whistling swans, and pintail ducks. It's also home to the rare sandhill crane.

Apart from great flocks of geese, gulls, and other shorebirds, the species most travelers notice are Clark's nutcracker and the Steller's jay, whose grating voice and large size (for a jay) often commands the most attention. Mountain hikers are bound to share part of their picnic lunch with these birds. The seven-foot wingspan of the great blue heron is also unforgettable.

In terms of sheer numbers and variety, the coast's mud flats at low tide and the tidal estuaries are the best birding environments. Rare species like tufted puffins and the snowy plover enjoy special protection here, along with other types of migratory waterfowl. *Birding In Oregon,* by Fred L. Ramsey (Portland Audubon Society, 1982) will introduce you to the habits and hangouts of Oregon's avian ambassadors and clue you in to where you can break new ground. The author of this book himself candidly admits that much remains to be discovered, especially in the remote northeastern part of the state.

The zeal of **Oregon Birders** (Box 10373, Eugene, OR 97440) is evident from their monthly publications of *Oregon Birds.* In addition to articles on various species and sightings, phone numbers for each part of the state are included for the **Oregon Rare Bird Telephone Network.** Should you see a particular bird of note, you can participate. The U.S. Fish and Wildlife Service has established viewpoints for wildlife and birdwatching at 12 Oregon national wildlife refuges. You can obtain specific information from these branches: Hart Mountain, (Room 308, Post Office Bldg., Lakeview, OR 97630; tel. 947-3315), Malheur (Box 245, Princeton, OR 97721; tel. 494-2323 or 494-2364), Umatilla (Box 239, Umatilla, OR 97882; tel. 922-3232), which serves McKay Creek and Cold Springs, and William L. Finley (Route 2, Box 208, Corvallis, OR 97333; tel. 757-7236), which serves Ankeny, Cape Meares, Oregon Islands, Three Arch Rocks, and Bandon Marsh.

Also of interest to serious birders and naturalists is the excellent *Oregon Wildlife Viewing Guide* put together by Defenders of Wildlife and published by Falcon Press (Box 1718, Helena MT 59624). Not only does this highly regarded resource list wildlife sites and nearby accommodations, but detailed state and regional maps and several guided nature trails offer independent readers the means to design their own wildlife adventure. Proceeds from the book go toward wildlife site maintenance and publications put out by Defenders of Wildlife.

HISTORY

NATIVE PEOPLES

Early Days

Long before the white man came to this hemisphere, native peoples thrived for thousands of years in the region of present-day Oregon. A popular theory concerning their origins maintains that their ancestors came over from Asia on a land/ice bridge spanning what is now the Bering Strait. Along with archaeological evidence, shipwrecks of Oriental craft on the Pacific coast also support the theory that Native Americans had Asian roots. This contention has been further substantiated by facial features and dental patterns common to both peoples as well as isolated correspondences in ritual, music and dialect.

Despite common ancestry the tribes on the rain-soaked coast and the Willamette Valley lived quite differently from those on the drier eastern flank of the Cascade Mountains. Tribes west of the Cascades enjoyed abundant salmon, shellfish, berries, and game. Great broad rivers facilitated travel, and rain-forests ensured that there was never a dearth of building materials. A mild climate with plentiful food and resources allowed the wet-siders the leisure time to evolve a startlingly complex culture. This was perhaps best evidenced in their artistic endeavors, theatrical pursuits, and in such ceremonial gatherings as the traditional potlatch, where the divesting of one's material wealth was seen as a status symbol. Dentalia and abalone shells, obsidian blades, and hides were especially coveted. Later on, Hudson Bay blankets were added to this list.

an Umpqua Indian

Chinook, an amalgam of Indian tongues with some French and English thrown in, was the common argot among the diverse tribes that gathered in the Columbia Gorge during solstice. It was at these powwows that the coast and valley dwellers would come into contact with their poorer cousins east of the Cascades. These dry-siders led a seminomadic existence in order to follow the game and avoid the climatic extremes of winter and summer in their region. Subsistence needs were thus pushed to the fore in their cultures while recreational endeavors were limited.

The introduction of horses in the mid-1700s made hunting, especially for large bison, much easier. In contrast to the 100- by 40-foot longhouses of their west-of-the-Cascade counterparts, extended families in the eastern tribes inhabited pit houses when not hunting. Hunting necessitated caves or crude rock shelters.

Twelve separate nations populated Oregon. Although these were further divided into eighty tribes, the primary allegiance was to the village. The "nation" status referred to language groupings such as Salishan and Athabascan. Tribal names such as Calapooya, Alsea, or Shasta Costa were usually from a word in the local argot for "the people," or it was derived from what the neighboring tribe called them. On occasion, white explorers bestowed a name upon the particular native grouping. An example of this was the "Rogue" Indian appellation. According to one theory, this name came from French fur trappers who referred to the troublesome thieves as "les coquins," which was translated as "the rogues." Another theory was that Rogue was inspired by euchre beds in the river described as "rouge" by French trappers and subsequently misspelled. Across the region, many Indians were united in their worship of Spilyai, the coyote demigod. Spilyai, as well as many other figures, animal and human, formed the subject of a large body of folk tales which explain the origins of the land in ways that are both entertaining and insightful.

The White Man

The coming of the white man meant the usurpation of tribal homelands, exposure to diseases of civilization like smallpox and diphtheria, and the passing of a way of life. Violent conflicts ensued on a large scale with the influx of settlers seeking missionary work and government land giveaways in the 1830s and '40s. In the 1850s, mining activity in southern Oregon and on the coast incited the Rogue River Indian Wars, adding to the strife brought on by annexation to the U.S.

All these events compelled the federal government to send in troops and to eventually set up treaties with Oregon's first inhabitants. The attempts at arbitration in the 1850s added insult to injury. Tribes of different, indeed often incompatible, backgrounds were rounded up and grouped together haphazardly on reservations, often far from their indigenous surroundings. In the century that followed, the evils of modern civilization destroyed much of the ecosystem upon which these cultures were based. An especially regrettable result of settlement was the decline of the Columbia River salmon runs due to overfishing and loss of habitat through pollution. This not only weakened the food chain, but made the spiritual totem of the many tribes along the Columbia an expendable resource.

For a while, there was an attempt to restore the balance. In 1924, the government accorded citizenship to Indians. Ten years later, the Indian Reorganization Act provided for tribal guards and prohibited the sale of land to non-Indians. A decade later a court of treaty claims was established. In the '60s, however, the government, acting on the premise that the Indians needed to assimilate into white society, terminated several reservations.

Recent government reparations have accorded many native peoples preferential hunting and fishing rights, monetary/land grants, and the restoration of tribal status to certain disenfranchised groups. Nonetheless, most of the 27,000 native peoples of the region feel they can never regain their birthright.

Archaeological Perspectives

To help measure what we've lost by the passing of the traditional ways, archaeologists have unearthed all manner of native artifacts. One that has evoked considerable controversy is a site found at Fort Rock, east of the Cascades near Bend. Charcoals from a hearth there are thought to be over 13,000 years old, exceeding earlier estimates of the period of human presence in the region by about 4,000 years. A sandal found at the same site dated at 9,500 years old had been the previous standard-bearer. Another significant find are 5,000-year-old petroglyphs on the walls

The bicentennial wagon train retraced the pioneers' journey along the Oregon Trail.

PHOTO BY OREGON TOURISM DIVISION

of a cave in the foothills just east of the Willamette Valley. The valley itself boasts perhaps the best-known excavation in the state, due to its location on the site of the Oregon Country Faire near Eugene. Relics there have been dated at 8,000 years of age. Other recent finds include coastal and Rogue Valley digs where 9,000-year-old artifacts have been unearthed. Marine fossils which date back 225 million years were found in eastern Oregon creekbeds.

In terms of written history, a manuscript found in a Chinese monastery could have the distinction of being the first written account of a voyage to our continent. A Chinese navigator, Hee-li, was spirited from offshore Cathay waters by a violent storm. Both captain and crew survived the storm, but were thrown off course during their return voyage by a cockroach lodged underneath a compass needle. Hee-li persisted in following the cockeyed compass in the direction he thought was west, despite sunsets appearing on the opposite horizon. After miles and miles of open ocean, the ship docked in a country of forests towering around a vast inlet which the mariners explored. The manuscript, which was found by American missionaries in Shenshi Province several decades back, also spoke of encounters with red-faced men.

When you add this story to the fossil record, it is clear that while east may be east and west may be west, the two probably *did* meet in the Oregon Country.

The only in-depth overview of Oregon's prehistory currently in print is *Oregon Archaeology*, by Melvin Aikens, obtainable for a nominal fee through the Department of the Interior, BLM, Oregon State Office (Box 2965-825 NE Multnomah St. Portland, OR 97208).

EXPLORATION, SETTLEMENT, AND GROWTH

One theory of how Oregon got its name goes back to an encounter between the native peoples and the Spanish mariners who plied West Coast waters in the 17th and 18th centuries. Upon seeing the abalone shell earrings of the coastal Salishan Indians, the sailors exclaimed, "Orejon!" ("What Big Ears!"). This was later Anglicized to Oregon. A less fanciful explanation has it that the state's name was inspired by the English word "origin," conjuring the image of the forest primeval. In any case, Spanish, English, and Russian vessels came to offshore waters here in search of a sea route connecting the Atlantic with the Pacific. Accounts differ, but the first sightings of the Oregon coast have been credited to either Spain's Juan Cabrillo (1543), or the English pirate Sir Francis Drake (1579). Other voyagers here of note included Spain's Vizcaino and de Alguilar (1603) and Heceta (1775) and England's Cook and Meares during the late 1770s, as well as Vancouver (1792).

Sea otter and beaver pelts added impetus to the search for a trade route connecting the two oceans. While the existence of a Northwest Passage turned out to be a myth, the fur trade became a basis of commerce and contention between European, Asian, and eventually American governments. The pattern was repeated inland when the English beaver brigades eventually moved down from Canada to set up headquarters on the Columbia near present-day Portland.

American Expansion In Oregon

The Americans first came into the area when Robert Gray sailed up the Columbia River in 1792. The first American overland excursion into Oregon was made by the Corps of Discovery in 1804-07. Co-captained by Lewis and Clark, the expedition trekked across the continent to the mouth of the Columbia and back to St. Louis. Dispatched by Thomas Jefferson to explore the lands of the Louisiana Purchase and beyond, the expedition threw down the gauntlet for future settlement and eventual annexation of the Oregon territory by the United States.

Lewis and Clark's exploration and mapping of Oregon wasn't the only impetus to America becoming a two-ocean power. The expedition also initially secured good relations with the Indians, thus establishing the preconditions to trade and the missionary influx. In fact, several decades after the coming of the expedition, the Nez Perce Indians sent a delegation to William Clark in St. Louis to ask for "The Book of Heaven" as well as teachers of the Word.

But before the missionaries came west, there were years of wrangling over America's right to settle in the new territory. John Jacob Astor's Pacific Fur Company was a case in point. The mere threat of British gunboats on the Columbia

In 1807, Meriwether Lewis and William Clark arrived in Oregon along with their Corps of Discovery.

caused the quick abdication of Astor's Company during the War of 1812. It wasn't until the Convention of 1818 that the country west of the Rockies, south of Russian America, and north of Spanish America, was open for use by American citizens as well as British subjects. The following year, the U.S. and Spain signed a treaty which fixed the present southern border of Oregon. With the Monroe Doctrine in 1824 opposing European expansion in this hemisphere, another blow was struck toward removing the shackles of British rule in the Northwest.

During the 1820s, the Hudson Bay Company continued to hold sway over Oregon Country by means of Fort Vancouver on the north shore of the Columbia. Over 500 people settled here under the charismatic leadership of John McLoughlin, who oversaw the planting of crops and the raising of livestock.

Despite the establishment of almost half a dozen Hudson Bay outposts, several factors harbingered the inevitable demise of British influence in Oregon. Most obvious was the decline of the fur trade as well as England's difficulty in maintaining her far-flung empire. Less apparent but equally influential was the lack of females in a land populated predominantly by white trappers and explorers. If the Americans could attract settlers of both genders, they'd be in a position to create an expanding population base which could

dominate the region. The first step in this process was the arrival of the missionaries. In 1834, Methodist soul-seekers led by Jason Lee settled near the Columbia River. Two years later Marcus and Narcissa Whitman's missions started up on the upper Columbia in present-day Washington (until 1853, the Washington area was considered a single entity with Oregon). The missionaries brought alien ways and diseases for which the Indians had no immunity. As if this wasn't enough to provoke a violent reaction, the Indians would soon have their homelands inundated by thousands of settlers lured by government land give-aways.

But it wasn't just the 1843 Organic Act's 640 free acres which each adult white male could claim that fueled the march across the frontier. The westward expansion that Americans regarded as their "manifest destiny" leapt to the fore as a ready solution to the problems of the 1830s. During this decade, the country was in its worst depression yet, with land panics, droughts, and an unstable currency. Despite ignorance of western geography and the hardships it held, the Oregon Trail, a 2,000-mile frontier thoroughfare, was viewed with covetous eyes, especially in Missouri. By 1840, 400,000 settlers had arrived there, tripling the population in ten years. Around Independence, Missouri, the trees thinned, the settlements ended, and the Oregon Trail began.

Over 53,000 people traversed the trail between 1840 and 1850 en route to western Oregon. In 1850, the Land Donation Law cut in half the acreage of the Organic Act, reflecting diminishing availability of real estate. But although a single pioneer man was now entitled to only 320 acres, and single women were totally excluded from land ownership, as part of a couple they could also own an additional 320 free acres. This promoted marriage and in turn families, and helped to fulfill Secretary of State John C. Calhoun's prediction that American families could outbreed the single HBC trappers, thus winning the battle of the West in the bedroom.

The Land Donation Act also stipulated that non-whites could not own any part of the Oregon Territory, enabling the pioneers to seize native people's lands. The act impeded the growth of towns and industries too, as large parcels of land were given away to relatively small numbers of people, which kept the population geographically distant from one another. This was one reason why urbanization was slow in coming to the Northwest.

Early Government And Statehood

Nevertheless, there was enough unity among American settlers to organize a provisional government in 1843. Then, in 1848, the federal government decided to accord Oregon territorial status. With migration increasing exponentially from 1843 on, there was little doubt in Congress about Oregon's viability. Still, it took frontiersman Joe Meek to coalesce popular opinion. He had first performed this role in Champoeg, at the northern end of the Willamette Valley, in 1843 when he boomed out, "Who's for a divide?" . . . the rallying cry for regional confederation. In equally dramatic fashion, he strode into the halls of Congress fresh from the trail in mountain-man regalia to state the case for territoriality.

The Oregon Territory got off to a rousing start thanks to the California gold rush of 1849. The rush occasioned a housing boom in San Francisco and a need for lumber, and the dramatic population influx created instant markets for the agriculture of the Willamette Valley. Portland was located just north of the valley and 110 miles upriver from the Pacific on the Columbia, near the world's largest supply of softwood timber. The young city was in a perfect position to channel goods from the interior to coastal ports. So great was the need in California for food that wheat from eastern Oregon was declared legal tender. The exchange rate started around $1 a bushel and went as high as $6 a bushel. The economic benefits from the gold rush notwithstanding, Oregon lost two-thirds of her adult male population to gold fever. Many of the emigrants returned when the news of gold discoveries in southwestern Oregon came out between 1850 and 1860. The resulting influx helped establish the Rogue Valley and coastal population centers.

However, strategic importance and population growth alone do not explain Oregon becoming the 33rd state in the Union. It was no accident that shortly before statehood in 1859, the Dred Scott Decision had become law. This had the effect of opening the territory to slavery. While slavery didn't lack for adherents in Oregon, the prevailing sentiment was that this controversial institution was neither necessary nor desirable. Because territorial status would be a potential liability to a union on the mend, the congressional majority saw an especially compelling reason to open its doors to this new member.

Economic Growing Pains

During the years of the Civil War and its aftermath, internal conflicts were the order of the day within the state. By 1861, good Willamette Valley land was becoming scarce, so many farmers moved east of the Cascades to farm wheat, where they ran into violent confrontation with Indians over land. In the 1870s, cattlemen came to eastern Oregon, followed by sheep ranchers whose presence precipitated range wars with the cattlemen. Just when it appeared that eastern Oregon land was ripe for agricultural promoters and community planners, the bottom fell out. Overproduction of wheat, uncertain markets, and two severe winters were the culprits. Later on, early 20th-century government land giveaways created further problems by putting a drain on the water table. Thus, the glory that was gold, grass, and grain east of the Cascades was shortlived.

Unlike the downturn east of the Cascades, boom times were ahead for the rest of the state as the 20th century approached. In the 1860s and '70s, Jacksonville to the south became the commercial counterpart to Portland, owing to its proximity to the Rogue Valley and south coast gold fields as well as the California border. During this period, transportation links began to consolidate. The first stagecoach, steamship, and rail lines moved south from the Columbia River into the Willamette Valley; by the 1880's, Portland was joined to San Francisco and the east by railroad. Henry Villard was the prime mover in this effort, eventually dominating all commerce in the Northwest by channeling freight and passengers through Portland and along the Columbia. In 1900, Union Pacific magnate James J. Hill picked up where Villard left off. By selling 900,000 acres of timberland to lumber baron Frederic Weyerhauser at $6 an acre (with the stipulation that Weyerhauser build his mills close by Union Pacific tracks), he hitched the destinies of both men and the region to the iron horse.

Progressive Politics

In the modern era, Oregon also blazed trails in the thicket of governmental legislation and reform.

OREGON—HOTBED OF BIOREGIONALISM

Oregonians often have the reputation of embodying the maverick spirit. This has manifested in Oregon in the form of politicians who don't always vote with a party majority, as well as by the state's unofficial status as a haven to many social, religious, and cultural groups who eschew convention. Therefore, it is altogether fitting to find the only serious American secessionist movement outside of the Southern Confederacy here.

At various times since the 1850s, the people of Oregon and northern California have tried to establish a new state. With common interests unto themselves which transcend state boundaries, inhabitants of this region attempted to secede in 1852 (Shasta), 1853 (Klamath), 1854 (Jackson), and 1941 (Jefferson). This last drive for independence was dramatized by a blockade of U.S. 99 at the Oregon/California stateline. The name of the third president of the United States was chosen because of his vision of America as a self-sufficient agrarian country. This secessionist movement got as far as inaugurating an acting governor, but the outbreak of WW II several days later preempted further action.

These days, southern Oregon is once again a hotbed of bioregional revolt. A more recent impetus to the movement was the 1973 book *Ecotopia* by Ernest Callenbach, which proposed that northern California break off from the rest of the state to join with Oregon as a single republic based on environmental imperatives. Another bioregional manifesto, *The Nine Nations of North America,* divided the continent into nine bioregions on the basis of their cultural, historical, ethnic, economic, and environmental interests. The region north of San Francisco to Vancouver was identified once again as "Ecotopia."

In recent years the Ashland-Jacksonville area, and the surrounding Rogue and Applegate valleys, have carried the torch for bioregionalism, often invoking as a rallying cry the name of the late great state that never was, Jefferson. With a constituency ranging from survivalists and radical environmentalists to just folks tired of big government and bureaucracy, this activist region coalesces the spirit of Jefferson throughout the state.

To keep up on the politics and the patrimony of Jefferson, read the excellent publication put out by the Southern Willamette Alliance. It is distributed free in natural food stores and selected locations throughout the lower Willamette Valley and southern Oregon.

The so-called Oregon system of initiative, referendum, and recall was first conceived in the 1890s, coming to fruition in the first decade of this century. The system has since become an integral part of the democratic process.

In like measure, Oregon's extension of suffrage to women in 1912, a 1921 compulsory education law, as well as the first large-scale union activity in the country during the '20s were red-letter events in American history. This tradition of reform continues to this day with Oregon's bottle bill and progressive land-use statutes.

The 1930s were exciting years in the Northwest. Despite widespread poverty, the foundations of future prosperity were laid during this decade. New Deal programs such as the Works Projects Administration and the Civilian Conservation Corps undertook many projects around the state. Building roads and hydroelectric dams created jobs and improved the quality of life in Oregon, in addition to bolstering our country's defense during wartime. Hydroelectric power from the Bonneville Dam completed in 1938 enabled Portland's shipyards and aluminum plants to thrive. Low utility rates encouraged more employment and settlement, while the Columbia's irrigation water enhanced agriculture.

With the perfection of the chainsaw in the '40s, the timber industry could take advantage of the postwar housing boom. Today, Oregon's resource-based economy has followed a boom-bust cycle. The timber and fishing industries have been especially hard hit by the current era of limits. While Oregon's traditionally humanistic outlook and environmental advocacy have been somewhat tempered by these economic tensions of late, the state still enjoys a reputation of being both progressive and pristine.

ECONOMY AND INDUSTRY

The leading industries within the state are forestry and agriculture, followed by tourism and high-tech enterprises. But these rankings only tell part of the story; the scenario for every sector of Oregon's economy should change dramatically in the coming years.

The ripple effects from the decline in timber will affect many aspects of society in the Northwest. Weyerhauser, Georgia Pacific, and other wood products giants are bracing for a reduction in the allowable cut as well as export restrictions. More timber from private holdings, as opposed to government lands, will be harvested and jobs will shift to the manufacture of secondary wood products such as doors, window frames, laminated beams, and furniture parts.

In agriculture, specialty products have become the fastest-growing business in Oregon. These products include wine grapes, ginseng, organic produce, chanterelle mushrooms, goat cheese, and other fare prized by "foodies." Larger agribusiness entities that rely on grass seed or bulk produce have had problems due to such environmental safeguards as limitations on field burning and bans on certain pesticides. Restrictions on the use of illegal aliens have also depleted a cheap labor pool. Nonetheless, the booming food processing and packing industries in Oregon will continue to thrive.

High-tech industries and tourism are often mentioned as the future moneymakers of the state. Both owe their rosy reputation to being in the right place at the right time. The region's pure water and low utility rates are ideal for chip manufacture; low production costs and a high quality of life has also helped attract the computer industry. In like measure, Oregon is in a perfect position to be "discovered" as a refuge from California's inflated prices and increasing urbanization. The Japanese are also expected to come here to take advantage of world-class *kulturfests* and nature on a grand scale.

Cost Of Living/Shopping Opportunities

Money Magazine considers Oregon second only to Hawaii as the state with the heaviest tax burden. This might be true for folks with high incomes, but the lack of sales tax here, cheap car registration fees, and comparatively low real estate prices act as boons to the average wage earner. Those passing through needn't be concerned with the state's high income tax. Instead, they can revel in the shopping opportunities here, which include an abundance of craft fairs, auctions, and garage sales.

As far as shopping, the profusion of locally made objets d'art available in **Made in Oregon** shops in the larger cities deserves special men-

Oregonians depend heavily on a resource-based economy.

PHOTO BY BUREAU OF LAND MANAGEMENT

tion, as does the potlatch of creations at the Portland and Eugene Saturday markets (for more details, see those travel chapters). Coastal and mountain resort areas also purvey the work of nationally known potters, woodworkers, painters, jewelers, and glass artisans from Oregon. These homemade items often go for quite a bit less than would be charged in out-of-state markets for work of comparable quality. While these "arts" cottage industries don't have the "bottom line" of the large corporations, they are one of the more visible and appreciated forms of economic activity a traveler to this state encounters. The best guide to shopping for indigenous items is *Where to Find Oregon in Oregon,* written and published by Bridget Beattie McCarthy (7277 S.W. Barnes Rd., Portland 97225).

LUMBER

Logging and wood products have historically been the most important industries to Oregon in terms of jobs provided and revenue produced. Currently, there are 79,400 workers employed in logging, sawmills, and paper production, contributing about 3.1 billion dollars or seven percent of Oregon's gross state product. Timber revenues have also contributed millions to state schools and socio-cultural programs. Oregon is the leading supplier of wood products in the nation, providing one-fifth of the country's softwood lumber.

Throughout its history, the Oregon logging industry has been dogged by controversy. In the 1920s, shoddy treatment of workers resulted in the first large-scale unionization in the country and inspired the spadework for the A.F.L.-C.I.O.

Currently, the forestry and economic practices which are the basis of the industry are being questioned. This could result in the reduction of the allowable cut and devastating losses in employment and revenue. Regardless of the imminent ban on logging in spotted owl habitats and the like, the industry will face a slowdown in the '90s simply because of the lack of trees to cut.

The larger implications of the transition from a timber-based economy hinge on the speed and effectiveness of economic diversification. But even with Oregon's impressive gains in tourism, high-tech industries, and specialized agriculture, it will be difficult to replace an industry that has permeated every aspect of Oregon life.

The new forestry orientation has created job opportunities for tree-planters, since the law mandates that for every one tree cut on federally owned land, at least six must be replanted. This line of work is more an athletic event than a career, but you're outdoors and the pay ranges between $10-$20 an hour. With an initial outlay for wet weather gear and camping equipment, you're ready to go. However, you must be willing to submit to slave-driving crew bosses and Forest Service supervisory personnel who are never satisfied with your planting. These jobs are available

a common sight on Oregon highways

PHOTO BY BUREAU OF LAND MANAGEMENT

through the Oregon Division of Employment for those in dire need of short-term employment. You'll work alongside students, Mexican illegals, substance-abusing lifers, and lots of folks who combine an independent streak with a strong back.

AGRICULTURE

In the '30s a Woody Guthrie song extolled pastures of plenty in the Northwest. Five decades later, the pastures are still plentiful, only more so. Oregon leads the world in the production of such varied agricultural commodities as filberts, peppermint, blackberries, several kinds of grass seed, and Easter lilies. The Willamette Valley boasts the most diversified farming region on the planet. In addition to being home to the record-setting crops cited above, the valley was where the Bing and maraschino cherries were developed, and its legendary fertility inspired tens of thousands of Oregon Trail emigrants.

An oft-heard refrain in pioneer days was, "crops never fail west of the Cascades," referring to this verdant region. The Oregon Trail migration and government land giveaways resulted in the settlement of most of the Willamette's good agricultural land by the mid-1850s. In the 1860s, gold rush activity put a premium on eastern Oregon's wheat. Later on, alfalfa, sheep, and livestock diversified farmers' options on the dry side of the mountains. Today, this region's food processing plants have enjoyed a boom, particularly with the potato crop; McDonald's gets most of its spuds for french fries from eastern Oregon, as do several of the leading potato chip and frozen food manufacturers.

The golden age of Oregon agriculture began with the tapping of the Columbia River for irrigation water, enabling large-scale farming to get started. At about the same same time, World War II compelled Oregon to develop her own flower bulb industry, instead of relying upon Japan.

If you're interested in identifying roadside agriculture, certain highways have signs designating individual fruits, vegetables, grains, grass seed of various types, legumes, nursery and flower crops, nuts, specialty crops, and some livestock operations. Look for these signs in Hermiston, Pendleton, The Dalles, Hood River, Madras, Redmond, Medford, Ashland, and Brookings. Agricultural operations are also labeled along I-5 and U.S. 99 in the Willamette Valley, the Sunset Highway between Portland and the coast, ORE 34 from Corvallis to the coast, and ORE 211 out of Molalla.

Oregon grows over 184 different commercial commodities. Agriculture-related employment accounts for 300,000 jobs, with four out of 10 Oregonians involved in getting food from the farm to market. Ony California ranks ahead of Oregon in crop diversity.

In 1989, the leading vegetable crops in the state were onions, sweet corn, and snap beans. The top agricultural revenue producers included such giants as Tillamook Valley Dairy Coop, Norpac (the state's largest farmer-owned food processor), and Fircrest Poultry. In addition, Oregon wineries continued to garner top honors in international competitions, with the bulk of the prizes going to the pinot noir and chardonnay varietals produced from vinifera grapes, which ripen early and benefit from the moist but mild conditions in the Yamhill, Willamette, and Umpqua valleys.

Those in the Northwest looking for short-term jobs might check out the local State Division of Employment offices in the Willamette Valley, southern Oregon, and the Hood River Valley at harvest time. The work is hard and the hours long, but crackerjack pickers can make $50-$100 a day. Seasonal cannery jobs are less plentiful, but also offer a fair wage for hard work.

GOLD AND MINERALS

While not a major economic force in the modern era, gold mining played a pivotal role in the early growth of towns throughout the state. In the decade following the California gold rush of 1849, thousands of miners came into southern Oregon because of gold finds in the Rogue Valley and on the south coast. The boomtown Jacksonville was created in 1851 near a gold-bearing creek, and the Applegate Trail became the low-road alternative to the Oregon Trail for cross-country emigrants. Baker, Jacksonville's eastern Oregon counterpart, was located near the main spur of the Oregon Trail. Both places were reputed to be among the wildest towns west of Chicago during the mid-19th century. In any case, Oregon gold production helped the Union win the Civil War.

miners at the Greenhorn Mine, circa 1913

One stretch of Canyon Creek near Canyon City in the John Day area of eastern Oregon yielded $28 million in gold for Union coffers.

Gold fever abated considerably in the 20th century, except for two footnotes to Oregon's golden decade of 1860-70. During that era, gold strikes launched Jacksonville as a center of commerce. In addition, gold finds were reported in the foothills surrounding Cottage Grove, near the southern tip of the Willamette Valley. This latter discovery by James "Bohemia" Johnson (so-named because of his heritage) in 1863 lay virtually dormant until the early 20th century, due to insufficient technology to mine the million-dollar deposits.

The Bohemia mining country also generated a story, perhaps apocryphal, that part of Cottage Grove was paved with gold-rich gravel from the Row River. So far, no one has been willing to rip up the streets and check. To the south 150 miles, the "streets of gold" story was rehashed with a new twist during the Depression, when residents unearthed tens of thousands of dollars from old claims in their back yards.

In the 1990s, a process which involves the cyanide leaching of gold-laden soils is slated for large-scale implementation in southeastern Oregon, despite the protests of ranchers and environmentalists. Throughout the state, gold is still in "them thar hills," but its price on the world market has to be high enough to make it financially feasible to extract.

Southwestern Oregon is often touted as the part of the state with the most mineral wealth. The only producing nickel mine and smelter in the U.S. is still operating in Riddle, a small Douglas County town off of I-5. In addition to gold and nickel, deposits of copper, chromium, platinum, manganese, asbestos, mercury, iron, molybdenum, zinc, coal, and limestone have been mined in the region. South coast offshore-oil and mineral mining leases have been proposed, but environmental restrictions make such operations more likely off the central coast near Newport.

But when all is said and done, the most mundane minerals and aggregates make the most money. Cement, sand, gravel, and crushed stone account for half the state's mining revenues.

FISHING

The exploitation of Oregon's fishing resources has been an enduring aspect of life in the region for thousands of years. Then as now, salmon has been the most valued species. Native Americans on both sides of the Cascades depended upon it, and commercial fishermen have viewed it as a mainstay for over a century.

The advent of commercial salmon fishing was late in coming due to the pioneer preoccupation with mining, logging, and agriculture. Canning technology and fishing methods first perfected in Alaska made their way down to Oregon in the 1860s in time to meet the demands of emerging domestic and foreign markets. In the modern era, Oregon salmon fisheries have grown into a megabusiness which nets well over a hundred million dollars annually. Still, the future is troubling to contemplate, given the evolution of the industry. At first, fish wheels depleted rivers once so choked with spawning fish that a pioneer pitchfork stuck haphazardly into the water would often yield a salmon. Dam construction and pollution joined overfishing to further reduce the catch. In recent years, Asian drift nets have emerged as the most virulent scourge of all. Northwest fishermen say the 30-mile-long, 50-foot-deep drift nets rake off millions of pounds of baby salmon annually which would otherwise have returned to waters in the American Northwest.

The salmon shortfall and other outgrowths of the drift net debacle have motivated increasing diversification. A caviar industry (derived from Columbia River sturgeon) as well as alternative ocean fisheries have developed. Bottom fishing for black ling cod and rockfish together with the harvest of such long-ignored species as hake, whiting, and pollock have increased in proportion to the decline of salmon, flounder, albacore tuna, smelt, and halibut. Clam, oysters, shrimp, and crab continue to be a strong facet of the industry despite occasional pollution problems. Recently unearthed shellfish middens (mounds) dating back to ancient Indian times indicate that these species were the most enduring part of the Northwest diet.

Well-paid but arduous cannery and fishing-boat jobs are often available for short-term employment in Newport and Charleston.

GETTING THERE AND GETTING AROUND

TOURS

While not for everybody, group travel is the fastest-growing aspect of a fast-growing industry. Those inclined to "do" Oregon by package tour can revel in the fact that Oregon has some of the most modern motorcoach fleets in the country. Recline in the air-conditioned comfort of a Mercedes-like motorcoach as you roll poast the many splendored landscapes of Oregon. A knowledgeable guide gives you the "scoop" on what you're seeing in addition to building your anticipation of cliffside coastal grandeur, a jetboat ride on the Rogue, or a play at Ashland's Shakespeare Festival. Sound idyllic? If so, touring Oregon by motorcoach could well be the mode of travel for you. Superficially, many of these packages may seem spendy but if you compare the price of meals, lodgings, and other services to what you'd pay independently, it's a good dollar value for the upscale traveler. In addition to volume discounts, the tour companies provde the services of a guide to spare you the hassles associated with the logistics and practicalities of travel.

Nonetheless, motorcoach tours are not for everyone. Despite the togetherness that comes from sharing a positive experience with others, younger folks can sometimes feel alienated from the predominantly older clientele and/or constraints imposed by a schedule. On the other hand, there is no better way to survey Oregon in style with a limited amount of time.

The advantages of Oregon tour travel are made manifest by looking at the packages of **Maupintour** (1515 St. Andrews Dr, Lawrence, Kansas, 66046; tel. 800-255-6162) and **Tauck Tours** (11 Wilton Road, Westport, Conneticut, 06880; tel. 203-226-6911). Despite differences in accommodations, routing, and attractions, both itineraries feature a loop from Portland, taking in the best of the coast, the Willamette Valley, a jet-boat trip on the Rogue River, a Shakespeare play in Ashland, Crater Lake, and a Cascades Mountain resort as well as the Columbia River Gorge. Along the way, four- and five-star hotels and restaurants give you the luxurious repose to savor your experiences. To book a tour or request additional information, please contact the companies or see a travel agent.

Tour season in Oregon begins in late May and can run till the middle of September. Before or after that, you're playing dice with the weather. Whenever you go, be prepared for warm and pleasant days all over the state, morning coastal fog, and cool mountain nights.

BY AIR

It is a simple enough matter getting to and getting around Oregon by air and if there is a break in the weather, the views are breathtaking. The main point of entry is Portland International Airport (PDX), which is serviced by 16 airlines. Your travel agent can help you find the best current bargains, and a good weekly overview of airfares is printed in the Sunday travel section of the *Oregonian*. If you have booked and want to reconfirm, or have a question, you can call the airlines on the following 800 numbers: Alaska Airlines, tel. (800) 426-0333; American, tel. (800) 433-7300; America West, tel. (800) 247-5692; Braniff, tel. (800) 272-6433; Continental, tel. (800) 525-0280; Delta, tel. (800) 221-1212 (Portland is Delta's West Coast hub); Eastern, tel. (800) 327-

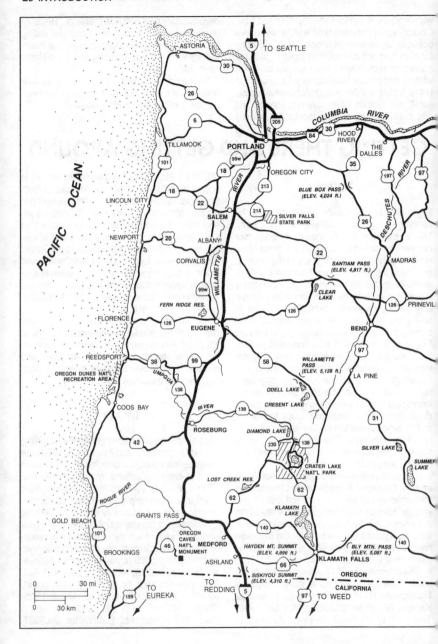

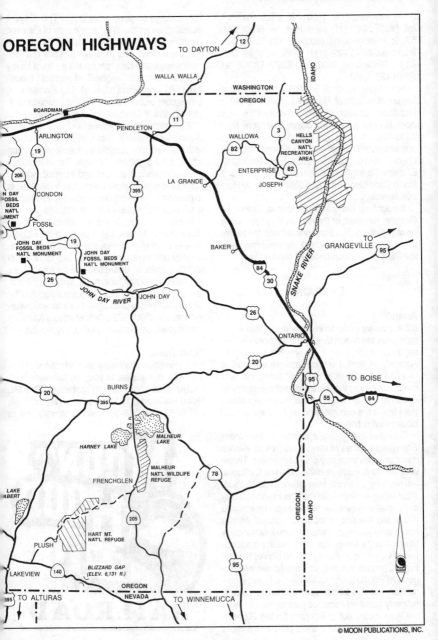

OREGON HIGHWAYS

TO DAYTON

WALLA WALLA

WASHINGTON
OREGON

IDAHO

BOARDMAN

ARLINGTON

19

206

CONDON

FOSSIL

PENDLETON

11

WALLOWA

82

ENTERPRISE

JOSEPH

82

HELLS
CANYON
NAT'L
RECREATION
AREA

LA GRANDE

395

N DAY
FOSSIL
BEDS
NAT'L
MENT

JOHN DAY FOSSIL BEDS NAT'L MONUMENT

19

JOHN DAY FOSSIL BEDS
NAT'L MONUMENT

26

JOHN DAY RIVER

JOHN DAY

26

BAKER

84

30

SNAKE RIVER

TO
GRANGEVILLE

95

26

ONTARIO

20

20

BURNS

395

HARNEY LAKE

MALHEUR
LAKE

MALHEUR
NAT'L WILDLIFE
REFUGE

78

95

TO BOISE

84

55

LAKE
ABERT

FRENCHGLEN

205

HART MT.
NAT'L REFUGE

PLUSH

LAKEVIEW

140

BLIZZARD GAP
(ELEV. 6,131 ft.)

OREGON
IDAHO

95

395

TO ALTURAS

OREGON
NEVADA

TO WINNEMUCCA

© MOON PUBLICATIONS, INC.

8376; Northwest, tel. (800) 225-2525; Pan Am, tel. (800) 221-1111; Piedmont, tel. (800) 251-5720; Southwest, tel. (800) tel. 531-5601; Sunworld, tel. (800) 722-4111; TWA, tel. (800) 892-4141; United, tel. (800) 241-6522; USAir, tel. (800) 428-4322.

Horizon Air, tel. (800) 547-9308, the commuter-league farm club of Alaska Air, connects with a half dozen smaller airfields in the state. Horizon operates commuter prop planes that range from 10 to 40 seats. If you are sensitive to loud noises and pressure change, ask for earplugs when you check in for your boarding pass. Bend/Redmond, Eugene/Springfield, Klamath Falls, Medford, North Bend/Coos Bay, and Salem all enjoy Horizon service.

If your final destination is Astoria, Baker, La Grande, Newport, or Pendleton, there are many private flying outfits that connect with these five municipal airports. Just check the yellow pages or the PDX information booth on the first floor.

BY TRAIN

Amtrak

If the massive increase in Oregon ridership is any indication, the region built by the ironhorse is having a second fling with rail travel. For that matter, Amtrak's expanded service nationwide is starting to ease the stigma of the U.S. being the only major country in the world without a well-developed rail line. So much so that those who plan a train trip in the summer and on holidays should book months before.

Consider that getting a sleeper on the *Coast Starlight* requires reservations five to eleven months in advance any time of the year. Those who take this route northbound from California will see why when the train crosses into Oregon. After riding all night from the San Francisco Bay area, passengers wake up to sunrise over alpine lakes and the snowcapped Cascades. As the tracks take you higher, you can see thousands of treetops in the foreground of dramatic peaks, especially if you're on the right-hand side of the car. From Cascade summit, you head down into Eugene along the beautiful McKenzie River. Commentary over the loudspeaker and on the complimentary handbills enhance your sense of place.

Other routes out of Portland on the *Pioneer* and the *Empire Builder* show off the Columbia River Gorge to good advantage. The *Empire Builder* goes on the Washington side of the river, enabling you to get a full cross-section of Oregon's waterfalls and mountains, while the *Pioneer* westbound runs retrace the paths of Lewis and Clark and the Oregon Trail migrants (paralleling I-84 for much of the way). The *Pioneer* continues from orchard country in the Cascade foothills to eastern Oregon's drier topography.

The trains on these routes are the ultramodern Superliner Coaches. This bilevel train is replete with such people spaces as full-service dining cars and the Sightseers Lounge. The wraparound glass windows in these cars and a smooth ride are conducive to passenger interaction. While food is expensive and selection limited, it's appetizing enough to eat should your own supplies give out.

Regarding costs, trains are usually more expensive than buses, but cheaper than planes. However, as with buses, special airfares occasionally undercut Amtrak. Kids two to 11 travel half fare; children under two ride for free. There are other discounts for groups, seniors, the disabled, and students. The company also advertises special holiday packages. For info and reservations, call (800) 872-7245, or obtain Amtrak's local station number through directory assistance.

Other Trains

If the mystique of a lonely train whistle and vintage rail cars appeal to you, the following trips should avail some golden moments. The **Mt. Hood Railroad** (110 Railroad Ave., Hood River, OR, 97031; tel. 386-3556) was originally built in

1906 to bring lumber out of the Mt. Hood National Forest to Hood River mills. But since 1988 it has been carrying passengers in restored early 1900s coaches through the scenic Hood River Valley to Parkdale. The blossom tours in April are particularly popular, as the train winds through colorful apple and pear orchards on its way up the valley. The 49-mile, four-hour roundtrip (adults $17, seniors $15, ages 12 and under $12) departs Hood River at 10 a.m. and gives you an hour to stretch your legs and shop in Parkdale before retracing its route and returning at 2:30 p.m. A shorter 17-mile, two-hour roundtrip to Odell (adults $10, seniors $8, ages 12 and under $6) leaves Hood River at 3 and returns at 5 p.m. Trains run Wednesday to Friday (Parkdale run only) and weekends (both trips) during the fruit tree blossom season from April 7 through June 3. Thereafter until September 2, the trains run Tuesday to Sunday, both trips every day. September 15 through September 30 the same schedule as spring applies. From October 6 through November 25 both runs go on weekends. Take Exit 63 off I-84 to get to the station.

Oregon Coastline Express (Third St. and Fifth Ave., Tillamook, 97141; tel. 842-2768) makes a four-hour roundtrip (adults $15, seniors $12, ages three to 12 $8) between Tillamook and Wheeler in renovated vintage rail cars with huge windows. Snacks, drinks, scenic stops, and narration further enhance the trip. The itinerary goes from dairy country to the rim of Tillamook Bay, taking in the jetties at Bayview, Rockaway Beach, and Nehalem Bay en route to Wheeler, the turnaround point. The train leaves Tillamook at 8 a.m. and 1 p.m. daily, adding a 6 p.m. sunset run on weekends. This schedule will continue until the end of September when trips are reduced to one per day Mon.-Fri. at 1 p.m. and twice a day on Saturday and Sunday (8 a.m. and 1 p.m.).

BY BUS

Greyhound

Greyhound and its offshoots have regular connections to most population centers in Oregon. "It's offshoots" refers to the slew of smaller companies created in the wake of deregulation and Greyhound cost-cutting. In terms of the consumer experience, all this means is that you might have a bus with a different paint job that uses Grey-

hound terminals and fare structures. Raz, Valley Retriever, Resort Lines, Red Ball, and other smaller companies operate on former Greyhound routes and have information available on their schedules from Greyhound personnel. If present trends continue, Greyhound will soon be operating mostly along I-5 in western Oregon. For an update on local carrier service write to the State Tourism Division (505 Cottage St. N.E., Salem, OR 97310) for the Oregon passenger services pamphlet.

Since routes are continually being dropped and added it's imperative to call the local Greyhound info number to supplement any printed schedule. This is also a good idea given bus travel's high incidence of once-a-day and late-night departures. The lack of terminals in remote locations is another reason to plan your bus trip carefully.

As for comfort, a ride on a Greyhound is good news and bad news. First, the good news: on the West Coast, buses are usually no more than ten years old, which means you can enjoy footrests, reclinable seats, and air conditioning. The majority of folks will also appreciate the fact that there's no smoking permitted on Greyhound while in Oregon. And, should the bus on your route fill up, rest assured the company will put another bus into service. In fact, this extra departure will often run as an express instead of a local, assuming there's a preponderance of passengers with a common destination.

The bad news is not that bad. Too much air conditioning in summer and too much heat in winter can be dealt with by dressing accordingly. The unappetizing fare in many of the terminals can be avoided by bringing your own food.

The ticket prices, while usually twice the cost of the same trip in a compact car with average fuel efficiency, are still not out of line. Even though a special airline fare might occasionally undercut the bus on longer interstate routes, for the most part, the "Hound" is but a fraction of most air tickets. Consider too that half-fare discounts are available to kids five to eleven and to the disabled traveling with an attendant. Another potential discount is the **Ameripass**. This discount program sanctioning unlimited travel for a week is $189, for 15 days $249, and for 30 days $349. It's cost-effective only if you're doing lots of travel in a short time. Also keep an eye out for various promotions which feature low-cost long-distance travel, particularly during the summer. The Ameripass and promotional fares are honored by most of the Greyhound franchises, but all connections should be clarified upon purchase.

A few hints about seating will suffice to ensure a smooth trip. The first and last seats on the bus can be a boon or a bane to your traveling comfort depending on your needs. If a footrest and the ability to recline your seat are important, avoid these locations. The front seats are generally the only seats that lack footrests, and the back ones don't recline. Worse yet, restrooms are in the rear of the coach, which inevitably results in an unpleasant odor on longer trips for those seated close by. Despite these shortcomings, the views out the front windshield are the best to be had, and the back row of three seats on the driver's side offers the most stretching room. For more information, call Greyhound toll-free, (800) 531-5332.

Green Tortoise

One commonly hears the Green Tortoise (Green Tortoise Alternative Travel, Box 24459, S.F., CA, 94127; tel. 800-227-4766) referred to as "the hippie bus." Lest this conjure a seedy anachronism from the '60s, an update is in order. While the Tortoise is not exactly the Orient Express of two-lane blacktop, this mode of travel comes as close to a hotel on wheels as exists in this country. First, imagine a recycled Greyhound with the seats taken out. In their place are foam rubber mattresses on elevated platforms behind a lounge area in the front of the bus. The chairs and tables here are converted to another sleeping area at night. Just bring your sleeping bag.

In Oregon, the fare is usually about 30% less than Greyhound (Eugene to Portland costs $10 Tortoise, $14.50 Greyhound) and might include such amenities as a stop for a home-cooked meal ($3.50 extra) and a hot spring, assuming you're going as far as southern Oregon. Passengers also have the option to pool money for groceries or eat at the restaurants near Tortoise stops. The clientele are a diverse group with surprisingly many Europeans and Australians. It's a rare Tortoise trip that doesn't turn into a party, although alcohol is prohibited. You can also bring your favorite cassettes to listen to on the Tortoise stereo. Another way Tortoise differs from Greyhound is with their policy of stopping at any freeway exit to get on or off for an extra $5. Kids

below four feet nine inches travel for free with an adult. Always reserve trips in advance. In Oregon, the Tortoise only travels I-5, Portland through Ashland, or vice versa.

BY CAR

The automobile remains the vehicle of choice for exploring the state. Oregon is blessed with good roads and light traffic on many thoroughfares. Consider that 141,000 miles of roads and 2.3 million registered cars works out to about 16 cars per mile. But before you jam down on the accelerator, keep in mind that the Man is equipped with the latest in radar technology and sometimes lies in wait out in the middle of nowhere.

Technically, you can only open up to 65 m.p.h. on sections of I-5 and I-84. The rest of the roads in the state have a 55 m.p.h. maximum speed limit. However, most people here seem to cruise at five to 10 miles above the speed limit and usually appear successful in avoiding trouble with the law.

Nowadays Oregon roads are often depicted in TV automobile commercials—the inviting places replete with mountains majesty or cliffside coastal grandeur. In short, welcome to Car Country, where toll roads are the exception, the traffic is light, and the pavement is in generally good condition.

While the roads are beautiful and largely unfettered by rush hour bottlenecks, the motorist must be sensitive to the nuances of the weather. Frequent cloudbursts can cause cars to wildly hydroplane all over the road, thick palls of fog that hang over the Willamette Valley can cause multicar pile ups, and the icy mountain roads of the Cascades and eastern Oregon also claim their share of victims. From late fall to early spring, expect snow on the Cascade mountain passes and I-5 through the Siskiyous; snow tires and/or chains are often required. Those who foolishly venture forth illegally and get stuck/caught are summarily issued steep fines. Another thing to remember in the winter Cascades is your **snow park permit.** Without the daily sticker or season pass in your left-hand window, a car left in a snow park area will also receive a hefty ticket.

Finally, keep in mind that there is bound to be lots of sand and gravel on the road, because the state does not use salts or other chemicals to melt snow and ice. The ground-up pumice from nearby lava deposits comes in many colors and provides great traction, but it sure can scratch up the paint on your car if you tailgate. Also, give oncoming trucks a wide berth to avoid the sand blasting likely to follow in their wake.

Gas is readily available on the main western routes but can be a little trickier proposition on the more remote east side, especially after 5 p.m. Oregon is one of the few states in the Union that *does not* have self-service gasoline outlets.

Renting a car is no problem, assuming you have a credit card. The rental chains (Avis, Budget, Dollar, National, and Thrifty) have outlets in Portland and many other population centers. You can also flip through the yellow pages and try to save some bucks with an independent operator. But while *you* may not care about the way the Rent-a-Dents and Ugly Duckling Rent-a-Cars look, they're not the vehicle of choice to impress your date. Another thing to consider is that the major chains have more service centers to assist you in the event of any mechanical problems. And while it costs a little more, it is always a good idea to spend a few extra bucks on insurance.

BY BICYCLE

If you like to pedal on your own two wheels, the good news is that Oregon is user-friendly to bicyclists. With special bike routes in cities like Eugene, Medford, and Portland, Oregon has given the right of way to cyclists. In the wake of the oil shocks of the 1970s, the Oregon legislature allocated one percent of the state highways budget to develop bike lanes and encourage energy-saving bicyclists. In addition to establishing routes throughout the state with these funds, many special parks were developed with bicycle and foot access specifically in mind. For example, minutes away from Eugene's downtown is the Willamette River Greenway bikepath system, which winds through a string of parks. Oxygen-rich air from the vegetation and the peaceful gurgling of the Willamette make a pleasant change from the fumes and roar of traffic. A decent biker could easily beat a car across town during rush hour using the bicycle network.

Oregon is user-friendly to bicyclists.

A similar respect has been granted to the cyclist on the open road. According to the Oregon *Motor Vehicles Handbook,* a bicycle has the right of way, which means that cars and trucks are not supposed to run you off the road. Nonetheless, remember that there are always motorists whose concepts of etiquette vis-à-vis bikers were formulated elsewhere. Play it safe out there: wear a helmet and reflective clothing, keep close to the right of the road, and always have a light at night. While most of the drivers will give you a wide berth and slow down if necessary in tight spots, rush hours, traffic patterns, and circumstance can change that.

The *Oregon Bicycling Guide* is distributed by the Oregon Department of Transportation (State Highways Division, Salem, OR 97310) and is a good pamphlet to have around to help plan a bike trip. This publication includes statewide maps of bike trails and routing suggestions as well as listings for rental/repair shops and bike touring groups. Be aware that transporting your own machine cross-country can sometimes be a problem, as every carrier has its own set of rules and regulations. If you're not strapping your 10-speed to the roof of the car, check with the carrier to make sure that you are within the allowable parameters.

Fortunately, there are some companies that offer pre-planned group bicycle trips, with everything from the bicycle to the meals and lodging included. **Tour Oregon Style** (Box 987, Oregon

City, OR 97045; tel. 655-2831) has a deluxe seven-day coastal bicycle trip that traverses spectacular U.S. 101. All you have to do is pedal; they take care of the rest. The cost is $299 per person, and a small discount is given to groups. **Bicycle Adventures** (Dept. K, Box 7875, Olympia, WA 98507; tel. 206-786-0989) offers a longer Oregon/Washington package.

WHAT TO TAKE

Without belaboring commonsensical considerations, a few comments are in order regarding the proper apparel for Oregon's rainforest-to-desert diversity.

To begin, remember that this region places a premium on practical and informal dress. A predilection for the outdoors as well as a lack of pretense explain the relative dearth of ties and haute couture even in somewhat formal urban settings.

The Old West is still alive and well east of the Cascades. In the Oregon desert regions, boots are like a second skin. This isn't so much tradition as good sense. It's always advisable to wear boots around horses and when walking in desert-like areas. Durable footwear certainly makes being stepped on or bitten less annoying.

Another concern in the desert is keeping cool. Carry water and wear a shade hat in summer. Cowboy hats work exceptionally well and are in vogue in this region. To avoid dehydration, 7-Up might be your best recourse; it's even better than salt tablets or beer for restoring evaporated sodium rates because alcohol depletes the body's water by accelerating perspiration and elimination.

Finally, remember you're in a territory where severe heat and cold, together with some of the most remote, unpeopled locales in the country, mandate extra precautions. Tell someone where you are going and when you plan to return.

Whether it's the sub-zero temperatures of the desert or the western Oregon mist cutting through your clothes, spare yourself needless discomfort by being prepared. Despite down's superior insulating qualities when dry, it's almost useless when wet because it clumps up and no longer traps air. The synthetic down imitators insulate well and do much better than down when wet, but have a stiffness that bothers active wearers. Nonetheless, given the pervasiveness of moisture here, coats with thinsulate and/or synthetic fleece are becoming more popular than down. A good test of the garment's suitability for vigorous movement is to put it on and quickly raise your fist to your shoulder in an arm-flexing motion. In a better-quality parka, you shouldn't feel insulation material restricting motion at your elbow.

Finally, a word for those who find the lightweight lofting and warming qualities of down hard to kick. These days Eddie Bauer, a well-known Northwest outfitter, has married Goretex to down, so you have a waterproof shell covering a warm insulation layer. Recommended down care for diehards is nothing more than throwing the garment in the washer with powdered detergent, then drying it with sneakers to beat the pockets of down into shape. Do this twice a year to maintain the loft.

ACCOMMODATIONS AND FOOD

FOOD

Oregon's abundance of fresh produce, seafood, and other indigenous ingredients prompted America's apostle of haute cuisine, James Beard, to extoll the restaurants and cooking of his home state. In his autobiography, *Delights and Prejudices,* he implies that Oregon strawberries, Seaside peas, Dungeness crab, and other local fare became his standards by which to judge the culinary staples of the world. This horn of plenty is the basis of a regional cuisine emphasizing fresh natural foods cooked lightly to preserve flavor, color, and texture.

Nonetheless, it *is* possible to have a bad meal in this state. In fact, the quality of the cuisine in some remote eastern Oregon towns is a source of self-deprecating humor for the locals. And as many Yankees will tell you, there is no shortage of bland New England-style clam chowder on the Oregon coast.

Still, with a reasonable amount of discretion, you can dine well at an affordable price throughout most of the state. This does not have to mean McDonald's, either. Because Oregon abounds in places that feature genuine ambience and home cooking at a good value, fast food listings will be kept to a minimum in this book. Budget-travelers might want to bring their own food to places like Ashland and other expensive resort environments.

Also of note are Oregon's liquor laws. Liquor is sold by the bottle in state liquor stores open Monday through Saturday. Beer and wine are also sold in grocery stores and retail outlets. Liquor is sold by the drink in licensed establishments between 7 a.m. and 2:30 a.m. The minimum drinking age is 21. You may legally import one quart into the state.

Throughout Oregon there are stores purveying locally made food products which make excellent gifts. In both Portland and Eugene airports for example, there are mini-malls selling Oregon jams, smoked salmon, hazelnuts, wines, and similar products. Another related development is the popularity of "microbreweries" throughout the Northwest. The trend is so pervasive in Portland that this metropolis is already being touted as "the city that made Milwaukee nervous."

ACCOMMODATIONS

Oregon lodging prices are for the most part significantly lower than those of neighboring California and Washington. Nonetheless, Cascade mountain and coastal resort areas can put a strain on the pocketbook. Fortunately, state park and national forest campgounds proliferate in these areas, mainly as low-cost overnight lodgings in attractive settings. As if by design, the highest percentage of Oregon's 200 state parks surround the high-ticket areas with sites for $5-$10 a night. A few of these have showers. National Forest Service campgrounds are usually comparable in price with more primitive facilities; many of them seem to be chosen for proximity to swimming holes and/or scenic appeal. If creature comforts are a priority, RV parks are often available with such amenities as firewood, laundromats, and showers for about the same price as more basic government sites. All you need is a tent. However, private RV campgrounds and their more expensive KOA counterparts tend to be crowded with people and vehicles, inhibiting the enjoyment of nature. A few of these have been treated in this book's listings, but since many of the state and national campgrounds share facilities for this specialized form of travel, we refer those in rolling homes to Mobil and AAA for info on KOA parks and the like.

Advance reservations are required in a number of high-use campgrounds, and are recommended for coastal and mountain resort hotels. "Off-season" specials are another way to beat the crowds and the costs. For example, one often sees room rates cut in half on the coast during the February storm-watching season. The cost-conscious traveler should also keep in mind that there is no shortage of large condos and vacation homes which rent out to large parties who can split costs. If you're looking for a romantic spot for that special occasion or just a place to get away from it all, there are many hotels with aesthetic locations as well as a high level of comfort and service. A compendium of these is published by Graphic Arts of Portland, Oregon and is aptly entitled *Special Places*.

Bed And Breakfast
These bits o' Britain provide a homey alternative to the typical hotel room. Ashland and the coast lead the state in bed and breakfast establishments, but the idea seems to be catching on everywhere. And why not? Whether it's a glass of sherry by a crackling fire to warm up returning Ashland theatre-goers, or a huge picture window on a Pacific storm, these retreats can impart that extra-special personal touch to the best the state has to offer.

If a turn-of-the-century Victorian or an old farmhouse doesn't give a B&B an extra measure of warmth, the camaraderie of the guest and the host family usually will. Most B&B's restrict kids, pets, and smoking in deference to what are often close quarters. Private baths are also sometimes in short supply. Offsetting any potential intrusions on privacy is an included full or continental breakfast, sometimes in bed. And in Oregon, it has become customary to see homemade jams and breads as well as a complimentary glass of a local wine for a nightcap. For complete free listings of B&B's in Oregon write to the **Oregon Bed and Breakfast Directory** (230 Red Spur Dr., Grants Pass, OR 97527).

CAMPING AND WILDERNESS TRAVEL

Oregon has more state parks than any place else in the country, as well as a natural environment suited to all manner of recreational activities. With a coastline that is largely owned by the public, the nation's first scenic highway in the Columbia Gorge, and the country's fifth national park at Crater Lake, the land ethic was given eloquent voice here. In order to keep Oregon the way it is, here are some suggestions:

• Stay on the trails so as not to increase the rate of erosion or destroy such fragile vegetation as alpine wildflowers.

• Avoid digging tent trenches or cutting vegetation.

• Camp several hundred feet from water sources.

• Bring a tool to dig a latrine and make it four to six inches deep.

• As for trash, if you pack it in, pack it out. Leave nothing but footprints.

• Avoid feeding wild animals so as not to inhibit their natural instinct to fend for themselves.

EQUIPMENT AND RESERVATIONS

As noted before, clothing in layers of polypropylene, wool, and Goretex are the best choices on most Oregon camping trips. Lightweight down vests

are always appreciated for their warmth and make great pillows. Those camping in the Columbia Gorge as well as the Coast and Klamath ranges during early spring might bring along rain pants. Danner boots made right in Oregon are tailored specifically to the state's rainforest, alpine, and desert regions. Whatever brand of boot you buy, it's a safe bet that waterproofing will be useful here.

Lightness, durability, and water-resistance are also the predominant criteria in choosing tents and sleeping bags. Neophyte hikers are reminded that tents and bags should be as compact as possible. These considerations compel the selection of down as the preferable "fill" for sleeping bags, even though these bags can be faulted for becoming useless when wet. Nonetheless, their lightness, warmth, and compressibility supercede the higher resistance to moisture of synthetic fill. To make sure down retains its advantages, bring along a foam mat or Therma-Rest inflatable pad in a Goretex stuff bag. The inflatable pad provides extra insurance for a comfortable night on the damp uneven terrain in many locales.

While it cools down significantly at night almost everywhere in Oregon during the June to October peak hiking season, the diurnal ranges are the most pronounced in the high Cascades and in the Wallowas, necessitating heavier fill in your sleeping bag. By contrast, the Willamette and southern Oregon valleys along the I-5 corridor sometimes experience daytime heat continuing into the night; at such times a down bag becomes a sweat lodge. Regardless of the kind of bag you choose, it should have a waterproof cover.

In like measure, tents should have rainflaps. Dome tents are the best choice, given their ease of setup and lightweight construction; waterproof ones go for a little over $100. Probably the best selection in the state is available at the REI Co-op in Portland's Jantzen Beach Mall, just off I-5 near the Columbia River.

As long as we're on the subject of camping-gear outfitters, it should be mentioned that Oregon is one of the best places in the world to purchase equipment. First of all, Portland, Bend, and the two college towns of Eugene and Corvallis boast many stores and equipment manufacturers that cater to the the Oregonian love affair with the outdoors. Since these purchases tend to run into higher figures wherever you shop, Oregon's comparatively low overhead and lack of sales tax helps keep costs down. Look for mark-downs on items with "blems" or cosmetic defects, as well as "annex" stores selling same or close-out items. If you need a high level of sophistication in your gear, chances are you'll find state-of-the-art within the Beaver State.

One item many travelers might have to purchase "on-site" will be fuel for cookstoves, since its transport is prohibited on commercial airlines. White gas is the best, but for flexibility, bring a stove that uses a variety of fuels. Propane rates highly with many campers because of its low cost and compatibility with other camping implements. Stoves are very important to have on many treks because of the shortage of dry firewood.

Flashlights, lanterns, and waterproof matches are essential for comfort and safety. Common-sense items like water purification tablets, sunscreen, a canteen, a Swiss army knife, cooking and eating utensils, freeze-dried food, maps and compasses, plastic bags, and nylon twine will also ensure a bon voyage. Finally, a safety kit containing iodine, chapstick, diarrhea medication, aloe vera, aspirin, antibiotics, and bandaids is also a good idea; add eye drops, antihistamine and/or allergy medicine if you're camping in or near the Willamette Valley from April till July.

Camping Reservations

Reservations are accepted at 13 high-use state park campgrounds in Oregon from Memorial Day through Labor Day. These reservations are not necessarily required, but are advisable given heavy saturation levels, particularly at the coastal sites. Applications can be procured by mail or in-person from the State Park Headquarters (525 Trade St., Salem, 97310, tel. 378-6305), as well as at Department of Motor Vehicles offices, Police stations, and chambers of commerce throughout the state. In addition, you can get them from the particular park. As far as returning the application, hand delivery to the park being reserved is discouraged due to limited staff or absence of personnel manning the entrance booth. Instead, send a $13 check or money order which covers the park fee ($9), plus processing ($4) to State Park Headquarters. You're limited to three separate residential dates per envelope. The parks included are as follows:

Coastal locations: Harris Beach near Brookings, Sunset Bay near Coos Bay, Honeyman near Florence, Beachside, Beverly Beach, and South Beach near Newport, Devil's Lake near Lin-

With the most state parks in the nation, Oregon offers great odds of finding the perfect campsite.

on the trail through the
Green Lakes basin

PHOTO BY OREGON TOURISM DIVISION

coln City, Cape Lookout near Tillamook, and Fort Stevens near Astoria.

Non-coast locations: Cove Palisades near Culber, Detroit Lake near Detroit, Wallowa Lake near Joseph, and Prineville Reservoir near Prineville.

For camping-related agencies such as the U.S. Forest Service and Dept. of Fish and Wildlife, etc., see "Information," p. 41.

HEALTH AND HELP

EMERGENCY SERVICES

Throughout Oregon dial 911 for medical, police, or fire emergencies. Isolated rural areas often have separate numbers for all three, and they're listed under "Services And Information" in each section of this book. Then too, one may always dial zero to get the operator. Most hospitals offer a 24-hour emergency room. Oregon's larger cities maintain switchboard referral services as well as hospital-sponsored free advice lines. Remember that medical costs are high here as in the rest of the U.S; emergency rooms are the most expensive. However, the Oregon Public Health Departments in major cities offer low-cost inoculation and testing for certain infectious diseases.

HEALTH HAZARDS

Hypothermia
In this part of the country, the neophyte hiker should be alerted to problems with hypothermia—when your body loses more heat than can be recovered and shock ensues. In fact, the damp chill of the Northwest climate poses more of a hypothermia threat than do colder climes which have low humidity. In other words, it doesn't have to be freezing in order for death from hypothermia to occur; wind and wetness often turn out to be greater factors in putting a person at risk. Runners who neglect to dress in layers in the cold fog of western Oregon often contract low-level symptoms during the accelerated cooling off period following a workout. You might also consider that 85% of hiking-related fatalities are due to this malady. Before we discuss lifesaving procedures, let's describe the preconditions to contracting hypothermia.

The affliction sets in when the core temperature of the body drops to 95° or below. One of the first signs is a diminished ability to think and act rationally. Speech can become slurred and uncontrollable shivering usually takes place. Stumbling, memory lapses, and drowsiness also tend to characterize the afflicted. Unless the body temperature can be raised several degrees by a knowledgeable helper, cardiac arrhythmia and/or arrest may occur. Getting out of the wind and rain into a dry warm environment is essential for survival. This might mean placing the victim into a pre-warmed sleeping bag, which can be prepared by having a healthy hiker strip and climb into the bag with his or her endangered partner. Ideally, a groundcloth should be used to insulate the sleeping bag from cold surface temperatures. Internal heat can be generated by feeding the victim high carbohydrate snacks and hot liquids. Placing wrapped heated objects against the victim's body is also a good way to restore body heat. Be careful not to raise body heat too quickly, which could also cause cardiac problems. If body temperature doesn't drop below 90°, chances for complete recovery are good; with body temperatures between 80° and 90°, victims are more likely to suffer some sort of lasting damage. Most victims won't survive a body temperature below 80°.

Tangible measures you can take to prevent hypothermia include eating a nutritious diet, avoiding overexertion followed by exposure to wet and cold, and by dressing warmly in layers of wool and polypropylene. Wool insulates even when wet and polypropylene tends to "wick" away moisture from your skin. Body heat is lost up to 20 times faster when damp, so polypropylene makes a good first layer. Goretex and its counterparts like Helli Hansen or other new "miracle" fibers make for more comfortable raingear than nylon because they don't become cumbersome and hot in a steady rain. Finally, remember that at least 30% of radiated heat leaves from the head, so wear a hat.

Frostbite
This is not generally a major problem until the combined air and windchill temperatures falls below 20°. Outer appendages like fingers and toes are the most susceptible, with the ears and nose running a close second. Frostbite occurs when blood is redirected out of the limbs to warm vital organs in cold weather, and the exposed parts of the face and peripherals cool very rapidly.

Mild frostbite is characterized by extremely pale skin with random splotchiness; in more severe cases, the skin will take on a gray, ashen look and feel numb. At the first signs of suspected frostbite, you should warm the afflicted area. In more aggravated cases, immerse hands and feet in warm water between 108-113°. Do not massage or risk further skin damage. Warming frostbitten areas against the skin of another person is suitable for less serious frostbite. The warmth of a campfire cannot help once the skin is discolored. As with hypothermia, it's important to avoid exposing the hands and feet to wind and wetness by dressing properly.

Poison Oak

Neither the best intentions or knowledge from a lifetime in the woods can spare the western Oregon hiker at least one brush with poison oak. In this writer's experience, 90% of the afflicted

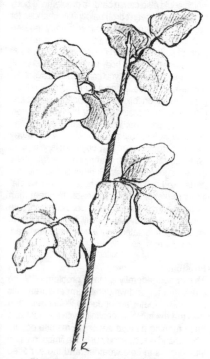

Rhus diversiloba, *the infamous poison oak*

campers knew to look out for the three shiny leaves, but still woke up the next morning looking like a pepperoni pizza.

Since the plant seems to thrive in hardwood forests, it's always a good idea to wear long pants, shirts, etc. on excursions to this ecosystem. Major infestations of the plant are seldom encountered in the Coast Range. In the fall, the leaves are tinged with red, giving the appearance of Christmas decorations. Unfortunately, this is one gift that keeps giving long after the holidays. Even when the plant is totally denuded in winter, the toxicity still remains a threat. Whatever the season, fair-skinned people tend to be more prone to severe symptoms. Shots are of course the most efficient way of dealing with poison oak symptoms.

When you know that you've been infected, try to get your clothes off before the toxic chemical permeates your garments. Follow up as soon as possible with a cold bath treated with liberal amounts of baking soda or chlorox, or a shower with lots of soap. If this doesn't stop the symptoms, cooling the inflamed area with copious applications of aloe vera or calamine lotion is another recourse. Clay has been known to be effective in drawing out the poison. In emergency situations, cortisone cream might kill poison oak but it's said to take lots of healthy cells along with it, too. Some tree-planters talk about immunities built up by eating poison oak honey and drinking milk from goats who graze on the weed. Health food stores now sell a poison oak extract which if taken over time prior to exposure is said to mollify the symptoms.

Allergies

Even if you come out of the forests unscathed, Willamette Valley-bound travelers during springtime might have to confront another pernicious health hazard: perennial allergic rhinitis. With the world's highest volume of grass seed produced between Salem and Eugene, allergy-susceptible visitors should expect some sneezing and wheezing as well as itchy eyes during the June-July pollination season. In addition to grass seed, the earlier bloom of various ornamentals throughout western Oregon might occasion such discomfort.

As allergy shots are not always practical, antihistamines are often resorted to as a short-term remedy for those passing through. Unfortunately, such side effects as depression and sleepiness have been attributed to antihistamines. Lately, many Willamette Valley doctors have been prescribing Seldane, an asthma medicine. This prescription drug (available over the counter in Canada) combats allergic reactions without side effects. Many health food stores offer herbal remedies, but they usually fall short of the quick relief demanded by travelers. Finally, honey from the area of the offending allergen taken regularly several months prior to the allergy season is often mentioned as a folk remedy.

Beaver Fever
Folk remedies just won't do it for that other hiker headache, "beaver fever." Medically known as *Giardia lamblia,* it occurs after drinking water—even from cold clear streams—contaminated by parasites from beavers and muskrats. Boiling water for 20 minutes is the most common prevention. Should that prove inconvenient, try better living through chemistry: apply five drops of chlorine, or preferably iodine, to every quart of water and let it sit for a half hour. Also available are water pumps that filter out giardia and other organisms, but they cost about $60. Potable water is also achieved by purification pills, assuming you're willing to shell out about $35 for products like First Need. However, these chemical approaches are less reliable than boiling.

MONEY, MEASUREMENTS, AND COMMUNICATIONS

MONEY

The prices listed for hotels, meals, and attractions were current at press time, but they will undoubtedly increase due to inflation. But while the rates are not absolute, they should nonetheless prove useful in comparing prices between establishments.

In any case, you'll need Uncle George or plastic to make your transactions in Oregon, and foreign currency can be exchanged at most major banks throughout the state. Canadian coins in particular are considered by many merchants as the bane of existence, and they will not accept them. Banks also turn up their noses at Canadian silver, because it costs them more in shipping and handling than it is worth. So if you happen to bring a pocketful of Canadian change to Oregon, your best bet is to "sluff" it off on a parking meter, a video game, or maybe a laundromat dryer.

But the presidents on your greenbacks aren't the only ones smiling, because Oregon is one of a handful of states in the country that *does not* have a sales tax. Many visitors take advantage of Oregon's generally low prices and lack of sales tax to purchase big-ticket items to take home. You will find, however, that room taxes vary from about 5-12 percent, depending on the locale.

MEASUREMENTS

Oregon has been slow to join the World Community and adopt the metric system. You may see some aberrations now and then, like a bank sign giving the temperature in Celsius, or perhaps liter-sized containers at the supermarket, but basically, Oregon clings to the English system. To aid the traveler not familiar with the English system, we have included a conversion chart in the back of the book.

COMMUNICATIONS

Most post offices are open between 7-9 a.m., and close between 5-6 p.m. In some of the larger cities, you will find main branches open on Saturday. Sometimes local drugstores or card shops have a postal substation where you can purchase stamps or mail packages within the country, but you'll have to go to a full-fledged post office to mail items to foreign addresses. If it happens to be Sunday and the post office is closed, you can often get stamps from grocery stores and hotels for little or no markup. Oregon also has many Federal Express, UPS, and other private shipping companies operating across the state to complement government services.

Oregon (so far) has only one area code, (503), but with the dramatic increase in the number and use of fax and other high-tech communications equipment, this is bound to change eventually. We have not included the area code on our telephone listings for this reason. For long-distance calls within the state, dial one before the seven-digit telephone number. For now, any out-of-state call into Oregon is prefixed by **503.** For directory assistance in Oregon, call 1-555-1212; for Oregon information from out of state, call 1-503-555-1212.

The two largest circulation dailies in the state come out of the most populous cities, Portland and Eugene. Both the *Oregonian* and the *Eugene Register Guard* have gained a bevy of Pulitzers and other awards. In general, the *Guard* has less columns generated by wire service and stringers than does the *Oregonian*. The result is a big-town paper with a charming small-town feel. The *Oregonian's* "Arts And Entertainment" section each Friday and its *Northwest* magazine on Sundays are of special interest to the traveler.

The *Oregonian* is statewide in distribution, while the *Guard* is carried in newspaper dispensers as far away from Eugene as Coos Bay. The editorial content of each paper is mostly middle-of-the-road, but can be activist on environmental issues. While this last assessment would be challenged by residents of different parts of this politically diverse state, an equal amount of letters to the editor from the extreme right and the extreme left each day indicates a measure of balance.

Portland and Eugene also dominate the broadcast media serving far-flung rural communities by means of electronic translators. What is especially noteworthy throughout the state is tremendous support of listener-subscriber public TV and radio. Many Oregon-generated shows, news blurbs, and features are carried by out-of-state public radio outlets.

Since the demise of *Oregon Magazine, Pacific Northwest Magazine* is the closest thing to a regional monthly. Travelers will find the magazine's yearly restaurant poll and destination pieces useful and entertaining.

INFORMATION

For a full list of books, maps, and pamphlets on Oregon national parks and forests write to: **Pacific Northwest National Parks and Forests Association,** Forest Service/Park Service Outdoor Recreation Information (1018 1st Ave., Seattle, WA 98104; tel. 206-442-0170). Another good source of useful information is the *Explorers Map Of Oregon,* available at Exclusive Maps LTD, (Suite 369, 1430 Willamette St., Eugene, OR 97401, tel. 935-7499; $7.50). This map depicts hot springs, fossil beds, caves, gold mining areas, remote beaches, wild areas, Indian village sites, artifact sites, abandoned historical places, petroglyph and pictograph locations, gem, mineral, and precious metal sites, stage and immigrant routes, 19th-century fort locations, Indian travel routes and battlegrounds, anomalies and curiosities, and notes on the state's history and prehistory.

Accommodations And Chambers Of Commerce

The **Oregon Tourism Division** (595 Cottage St., N.E. Salem, OR 97310, tel. toll-free inside Oregon 800-547-7842 or outside Oregon 800-233-3306) will send you a full list of local chambers of commerce and tourist information offices upon request. They also feature many well-produced free pamphlets on different regions, seasons, and activities. Especially recommended are their winter/fall activities booklets and the regional loop tour brochures. The **Oregon Motor Hotel Association** (12724 S.E. Stark St., Portland, OR 97233, tel. 255-5135) has a good set of lodging listings across the state.

The following information centers can be reached by toll-free numbers, and they have a wide variety of information available on their respective locales. The **Bay Area Chamber of Commerce** (50 East Central St., Coos Bay, OR 97420; inside Oregon tel. 800-762-6278, outside 800-824-8486); the **Eugene Springfield Convention and Visitors Bureau** (305 West 7th St., Eugene, OR 97401, inside Oregon tel. 800-452-3670; outside 800-547-5445); **Gold Beach-Wedderburn Chamber of Commerce** (510 South Ellensburg St., Gold Beach, OR 97444, from inside Oregon only 800-452-2334); **Grants Pass**

Visitor and Convention Bureau (Box 970, 1439 Northeast 6th, Grants Pass, OR 97526, outside Oregon tel. 800-547-5927); **Lincoln City Chamber of Commerce** (Box 787, 3939 Northwest U.S. 101, Lincoln City, OR 97367, inside Oregon tel. 800-452-2151), **Pendleton Chamber of Commerce** (Box 1446, 25 Southwest Dorion St., Pendleton, OR 97801; inside Oregon tel. 800-452-9403, outside 800-547-8911); **Southern Oregon Reservation Center** (Box 477, Ashland, OR 97522, inside Oregon tel. 800-533-1311, outside 800-547-8052); and **Seaside Chamber of Commerce** (Box 7, 7 North Roosevelt St., Seaside, OR 97138, from Oregon only tel. 800-452-6740).

Finally, one all-inclusive number merits special mention. First, **Overnight Success** (tel. 800-365-6343, open daily 8 a.m.-11 p.m.) is a free service that lists 2,000 lodgings. Info is available on motels, hotels, resorts, condos, bed and breakfasts, ranches, inns, and RV parks. Callers state destination, accommodation features desired, and price range. Then the computer does the rest, and will give you phone numbers of properties that match your specifications.

Camping, Hiking, And Hunting

The **Oregon Guides and Packers Association** (Box 3797, Portland, OR 97208, tel. 234-3268), has the scoop on outfitting just about any kind of adventure you can imagine. Whether you want to pack llamas into the Kalmiopsis Wilderness, shoot the rapids of Hells Canyon, or take to the Cascades on horseback, you'll find a listing here for something interesting to do in Oregon.

Oregon State Parks (in Portland and out-of-state tel. 238-7488, rest of Oregon 800-452-5687, Mon.-Fri., 8-4:30) provides info on campsite availability and other recreation information. Remember that while campsite reservations can't be made through the center, they can be canceled there. The **National Forest Service** (tel. 800-283-CAMP, Mon.-Fri., 9-6; Sat.-Sun. 9-2) has a nationwide reservation and information center. There is a reservation fee in addition to regular campground fees ($6 for reserving family sites, $10 for reserving group sites). Campsites can be booked up to 120 days in advance for single family sites and 360 days in advance for group sites. Campgrounds in the Willamette, Umpqua, and Suislaw national forests are Oregon's bailiwicks covered in this program.

The **Oregon Parks and Recreation Division** (525 Trade St., Salem, OR 97310, tel. 378-6305), the **U.S. Bureau of Land Management** (Box 2965, Portland, OR 97232, tel. 231-6273), and the **U.S. Forest Service** (Box 3623, 319 S.W. Pine St., Portland, OR 97208, tel. 221-2877) have free information and maps on specific recreation areas and preserves under their respective auspices. Hikers can benefit from *An Oregonian's Trail Sourcebook,* published by the Oregon Student Public Interest Research Group, or OSPIRG (1536 S.E. 11th, Portland, OR 97214, tel. 231-

4181). If you are interested in fishing, contact the **Oregon Department of Fish and Wildlife** (506 S.W. Mill St., Box 59, Portland, OR 97207, tel. 229-5403). Nonresident fishing licenses are $4 (for one day), $18.50 (10 days), or $30 (year). Salmon or steelhead licenses run $5.50 for every 10 fish caught, 40-salmon/steelhead annual limit. Hunting licenses are available at the same address. A nonresident license is $100.50, deer tags are $75.50, and elk tags are $165.50. Game tags are needed prior to the first day of hunting season. Apply early since availability is limited.

Skiers can benefit from info put out by the **Pacific Northwest Ski Association** (Box 34481, Kirkland, WA, 98083, tel. 206-822-1770).

THE OREGON COAST

INTRODUCTION

The Oregon coast is one of those blessed corners of the earth where you come upon a little piece of paradise wherever you go. The south coast is a world apart, with a landscape dominated by dense evergreen forest parting to reveal black-sand beaches and exceptional rock formations. One often gets the feeling here that sheep and cattle outnumber people.

The central coast is a land of superlatives, boasting such features as the largest oceanfront dunes in the world, the highest coastal viewpoint accessible by car, and the only mainland sea lion rookery located in the lower 48 states. In addition, *The Guinness Book of World Records* recognizes Oregon's other coastal claims to fame like the smallest navigable harbor and the shortest river in the world.

The north coast can be billed as "the real end of the Oregon Trail." Although that famous frontier wagon road ends inland, the pioneering spirit that it connotes is on display here by the sea. Lewis and Clark, John Jacob Astor, and the legions of settlers who conquered the wilderness are commemorated in the landmark buildings and historical placards of Astoria, the oldest city west of Missouri. In like measure, many of the works in north coast galleries draw inspiration from these same historical antecedents.

While each part of the coast possesses a distinct regional flavor, together they have one thing in common. Whether it's virgin beachfront, a lofty promontory, or simply a cozy bed and breakfast, each section of Oregon's seascape will leave you hungering for more.

THE LAND

The Oregon coast includes 362 miles of rainforest, sand dunes, high-rise basalt headlands, and tidal pools showcasing marine worlds in miniature. This scenery is broken up by over a dozen major rivers, which flow past mountain barriers to the sea. The estuaries of these rivers offer resting places for migratory waterfowl as well as a thoroughfare for spawning fish. They cut through the Klamath Mountains in the southern quarter of the region and bisect parts of the Coast Range in the north.

Of the two ranges, the Klamaths are much older, dating back 225 million years. By contrast, the Coast Range, beginning near Coos Bay, emerged from the sea between 20 and 50 million years ago. The mountains of each of these coastal cordillera rarely exceed several thousand feet in elevation. The uplifts that created both the Klamaths and the Coast Range also left black-sand beaches and offshore volcanic plugs, as well as headlands made of erosion-resistant basalt lava.

A look at the globe offers a bird's-eye view of this dramatic meeting of rock and tide: the 6,000 miles of water lying between Oregon and Japan are largely unfettered by archipelagoes and reefs—the longest stretch of open ocean on earth. This impression of remoteness and isolation is compounded by the fact that Cape Blanco stands as the westernmost point in the contiguous United States. Finally, this extraordinary region is roughly equidistant from the equator to the north pole. It all adds up to a complex interplay of climatic and geologic forces which have orchestrated nature on such a grand scale.

CLIMATE

Coastal rain or shine begins with the Japanese current. This offshore system of tepid water evaporates up into billowy cloud masses which are blown inland by the Pacific westerlies. If these clouds don't drop their moisture over the water or on the shoreline, chances are good the Coast Range's lower temperatures will create condensation and rain. This translates into a 166-inch annual maritime rainfall, with as much as 150 inches over the mountains.

But generalized regional precipitation totals tell only part of the story. Brookings, with a yearly average of almost 74 inches, and Tillamook, with 94 inches, demonstrate the south-to-north variance. Halfway up the coast, Coos Bay's rainfall totals hover around the 60-inch mark. If this sounds foreboding, remember that almost all of these totals are racked up during the winter months. Keep in mind, too, that in the midst of this gloom, midwinter dry spells with 60°-plus temperatures commonly occur. These respites also serve to thaw coastal habitués used to temperatures in the 40s . . . not that they need it! With infrequent freezes and rarely recorded snowfall, Old Man Winter definitely pulls his punches here. In fact, Coos Bay is often touted as having the mildest (in terms of absence of extremes) year-round climate in the United States.

Here's a little tip for those looking to take advantage of midwinter lulls in the gray wetness which hangs over much of western Oregon. Should you be inland during a rainy spell, keep an eye on satellite photos on TV or in the paper. By the time a major storm reaches the interior, there is often a respite between fronts at the coast. By anticipating the approach of a "blue hole," you can time your visit to coincide with the arrival of nice weather, shortlived as it may be.

In general, count on good weather for traveling mid-April through mid-September, with a preponderance of daytime highs in the 60s. Within this period, there might be enough June gloom to dis-

PHOTO BY LINCOLN CITY VISITOR AND CONVENTION BUREAU
the view from Cascade Head:
a picture-perfect slice of the Oregon coast

may travelers used to simmering southland beaches, but storm-watching is an acquired taste. An added plus is that when summertime inversions drive the temperature readings up east of the Coast Range, the heat will draw cooler maritime air to the shore. While the mountains often lock in these welcome fronts, it can sometimes cause coastal fog and overcast conditions to linger. Nonetheless, respite from the characteristic morning fog banks in summer is often only minutes away upriver on one of the many tidal estuaries.

Finally, newcomers to the region should remember that the icy temperatures of the coastal waters (40-45 degrees) make the beaches more valued for beachcombing than for swimming. Ironically, 20-30 miles offshore, the warming effects of the Japanese current create subtropical conditions.

FLORA AND FAUNA

Sandwiched between the mountains and the sea are predominantly mixed conifer forests of Douglas fir, spruce, cedar, and hemlock. Due to the construction industry's penchant for Douglas fir, which they replant assiduously, this tree predominates. The conifers are broken up by pockets of alder, oak, swamp maple, and myrtle trees. A largely edible understory of thimbleberry, salmonberry, blackberry, and salal are interspersed among the ferns and mosses which carpet the forest floor. Apart from Brookings's Azalea Festival and Florence's Rhododendron Festival, coastbound travelers come to take in such horticultural highlights as the insect-eating Darlingtonia plant and the myrtle tree, said to be native only to the Holy Land and southern Oregon. Serious botanists might search out the pine mushroom, exclusive to the Oregon dunes and Japan, or probe the Kalmiopsis Wilderness near the south coast, habitat to many rare plants.

Such eclecticism is paralleled in the animal kingdom. Consider, for example, the nutria and the boomer. The nutria was brought to Oregon in the 1930s from South America to be raised for its fur. After numerous escapes, this furry rodent was able to breed in the wild and establish a niche in the woodlands of the Coast Range. The boomer is another distinctive resident of this ecosystem. Similar in appearance to a beaver (minus the flat tail), the predilection of this primitive rat species for eating Douglas fir seedlings has made it the scourge of the timber industry. Currently an open season encourages hunting of both these varmints.

Other coastal critters include muskrat, raccoon, Roosevelt elk, blacktailed deer, bald eagles, and an impressive array of anadromous fish, shore birds, and migratory waterfowl. Regional estuaries and the Oregon dunes are the best places to take in this wildlife show. Another distinctive resident of coastal forests is the giant Pacific salamander. This stout mottled creature grows to a length of more than one foot, and is said to pro-

rhododendrons,
another coastal treat

PHOTO BY TED LONG ISHIKAWA

duce dog-like yelping and snapping sounds. Sightings are rare, but hikers occasionally encounter them around stagnant pools in the Kalmiopsis.

HISTORY

In 1542, Spain's Juan Rodriguez Cabrillo sailed into what is now southern Oregon waters. Sixty years later, Sebastian Vizcaino came to the same area, but also failed to lay claim for the armada. A succession of Spanish, English, American, and Russian explorers followed in search of whales, sea otters/beaver pelts, and hides for the tallow trade. But the major impetus for exploring this coast was the quest for the mythic Northwest Passage—a sea route connecting the Pacific with the Atlantic. While written histories vary as to the exact dates and locations of these excursions, hundreds of shipwrecks remain as evidence of the exploratory zeal of past centuries. At the northern edge of this rock-studded graveyard for ancient mariners, the fur-trading center of Astoria was established in 1811. Several decades later, gold mining near the Rogue River drew more settlers to the south coast. It was a later gold rush, however, that had the greatest implications for the development of the region.

In 1849, the influx of prospectors into California's Sierra Nevada occasioned a housing boom in San Francisco, port of entry to the gold fields. The demand for Coast Range timber and foodstuffs from Oregon's inland agricultural valleys allowed downriver Pacific ports like Astoria and Newport to flourish. As a result, the coastline of California's friendly neighbor to the north was able to develop the necessary economic base for it to prosper and endure.

The exploitation of coastal resources was so successful that Governor Oswald West had to spearhead legislation restricting beachfront development in 1913. This set the tone for future preservationist measures in the state. Today, Oregon has more state parks than any place else in America, with the majority of these located on the coast.

WHALEWATCHING

Whalewatching trips serve each part of the coast from December into the early spring. Wherever and whenever you go, dress warmly, take pre-

cautions against seasickness, and expect to get wet if you go out on deck. By land or by sea, early morning hours are best because winds cause whitecaps later in the day. This inconvenience can be made up for the instant you see one of these benign monsters come up for air. The sight of a mammal as long as a Greyhound bus breaking water has a way of emptying the mind of mundane concerns. Wreathed in seaweed and sporting barnacles and other parasites on its back, a 50-foot long, 50-ton California gray whale would look more like the hull of a ship were it not for its sadly expressive eyes.

Further empathy might be engendered upon learning of these mammal's human-like propensities. Some whale birthings have been observed which included the help of whale "midwives" pushing mama above the surface of the water so that baby could be born into the air. If "airborne" whales seem implausible, consider that according to recent research, whale language could be the most sophisticated in the animal kingdom.

Though the latter tendencies might endear these cetaceans to some people, it is their homing instinct which makes it possible to enjoy whalewatching on the Oregon coast. Coastal headlands and beaches provide excellent vantage points from which to spy on the 12,000-mile roundtrip December-to-May migration of the California gray whale, particularly in midwinter. This yearly pilgrimage ranges between Baja and the Arctic, the longest migratory movement by land or sea of any animal. Along the way, the whales search for tiny shrimp-like amphipods, their major food during this time. The southward migration along the Oregon coast lasts until early February, although the migration peaks the last week in December. Whales migrating northward can be sighted off Oregon from March through May.

The following listing gives a cross section of excursions from each part of the coast. Booking info is also available from local Greenpeace chapters in Portland, Eugene, and other major cities. Greenpeace, in conjunction with Newport's **Marine Science Center,** has helped stimulate whalewatching awareness. The Marine Science Center is an extension of Oregon State University, which supplies trained volunteers to staff vantage points from 10 a.m.-1 p.m. each day between December 26-January 1. Look for the big sign that says Whalewatching Spoken Here. For additional info, contact Hatfield Marine Science

Center, Newport, 97365; tel. 867-3011, ext. 226. On the envelope write "attention: whales," and include a self-addressed stamped envelope. You'll receive a list of charter operators as well as background information.

By Land

Cape Arago State Park, west of Coos Bay, has a promontory with a commanding view of the ocean that is excellent for whalewatching.

The Reedsport Chamber of Commerce, located where ORE 38 and U.S. 101 intersect, offers directions to the whalewatching platform across the road from the **Umpqua Lighthouse** in Winchester Bay. The two-tiered platform overlooks the Umpqua River estuary where whales are often sighted. Seven placards here describe whale habits and habitat. Two jetties provide reference points for directing the observer's gaze.

Rockwork, a pullout just north of the sea lion caves, offers a magnificent view of Heceta Head, as well as frequent spottings of whales, sea lions, and an assortment of sea birds.

Three miles south of Yachats, immediately after Devil's Churn, there is a sign for **Cape Perpetua Drive.** Follow the steep and windy road up the highest coastal drive in Oregon to the parking lot on top of Cape Perpetua. From there, take the quarter-mile hike on the famous **Trail of the Whispering Spruce** to the old Coast Guard lookout. On a clear day, you can see 150 miles north, south, and west. If there are whales out there, this is one of the best places to spot them. In 1988, Cape Perpetua led all other sites in total sightings. Nearby is Cape **Perpetua Visitor Center,** where you can whalewatch and stay dry behind picture windows. Locals say that sightings of these leviathans can occur any time of year. This has been the case since the mid-'80s between Cape Perpetua and Otter Crest.

At **Depoe Bay,** in addition to the natural blowholes in the lava rock that shoot up a 30- to 50-foot fountain of water when the tide is right, the lucky visitor is often treated to the sight of whales coming up for air just offshore.

Cape Meares State Park lies 10 miles west of Tillamook on a headland that features a lighthouse built in 1896, as well as great views. If you happen to get rained out, take a look at the Octopus Tree, a Sitka spruce of gargantuan proportions located a short walk away from the parking lot.

By Sea

Dick's Sporthaven Marina (Box 2215, Harbor, 97415; tel. 469-3301) offers two-hour trips beginning in January that cost about $30. Reservations necessary.

Betty Kay Charters (Box 5020, Charleston, 97420; tel. 888-9021) features three-hour trips on weekends December through January and during part of the spring. Depending upon the size of the boat, the cost ranges from $15-20. Reservations are essential. **Bob's Sport Fishing** (Box 5457, Charleston, 97420; tel. 888-4241) hosts three- to four-hour trips in December and January for $20. Reservations required. **Charleston Charters** (Box 5032, Charleston, 97420; tel. 888-4846) runs three-hour trips for $15, beginning in December. Reservations recommended.

Cape Perpetua Charters (839 S.E. Bay Blvd., Newport, 97365; tel. 265-777) has daily two-hour trips for $15 beginning in mid-December, depending upon weather and the number of passengers. **South Beach Charters** (Box 1446, Newport, 97365; tel. 867-7200) operates two-hour trips daily from mid-December to May for $16, reservations required. **Newport Tradewinds** (653 S.W. Bay Blvd., Newport, 97365; tel. 265-2101) offers two-hour trips December through June for $20, reservations recommended. **Newport Sportfishing** (1000 S.E. Bay Blvd., Newport, 97365; tel. 265-7558) runs daily two-hour trips departing at 10:30 a.m. and 1 p.m. from mid-December through May. Adult fare is $15, children $10; reservations are recommended.

Oregon Natural Resources Council from Portland (Attn: Michael Carigan, 522 SW 5th Ave., Suite 1050, Portland, 97204; tel. 223-4012/800-827-9001), or from Eugene (1161 Lincoln St., Eugene, 97401; tel. 344-0675) is a coalition of 90 conservation organizations that have put together a series of two-hour trips. Beginning in mid-December and continuing each weekend (Saturday and Sunday) on through mid-April, these charters depart from Newport at 10 a.m. and 1 p.m. The cost is $20 for adults, $15 for children 12 and under. A naturalist gives an informative and entertaining presentation before sailing. Advanced registration is required.

Dockside Charters (Box 1308, Depoe Bay, 97341; tel. 765-2545) has hourly trips daily, year-round depending upon sightings. Cost is $5; please call ahead. **Deep Sea Trollers** (Box 513,

Beachcombers should take advantage of Hug Point State Park at low tide

PHOTO BY OREGON TOURISM DIVISION

Depoe Bay, 97341; tel. 765-2705) features hourly 45-minute trips, beginning after Christmas, for $5. Please call ahead. **Tradewinds Ocean Sport Fishing** (Box 123, Depoe Bay, 97341; tel. 765-2345) has 45- to 90-minute trips beginning in December. Cost is $5 for adults, $3.50 children, and kids six years and under ride for free. **Oregon Museum of Science and Industry** (4015 S.W. Canyon Road, Portland, 97221; tel. 222-2828) offers two-hour tours departing from Depoe Bay, depending upon availability of boats, weather, and number of people. A naturalist is on hand to give a presentation. Cost is $18.50, reservations required.

By Air
The **Astoria Flight Center** offers a 40-minute flight for $40 in a Cessna 150. Two or three people can charter a Cessna 172 for $65. Departures are from the Port Astoria airport in Warrenton. Call 861-1222 for information.

Aurora Aviation (tel. 222-1754 in Portland/6-78-1217 in Aurora) offers charters from Aurora, south of Portland, at $89 an hour (minimum of three passengers) or $260 an hour (minimum of six passengers). Flying time to the coast is approximately 45 minutes.

McKenzie Flying Service in Eugene (tel. 688-0971) has whalewatching flights that begin and end in Newport with departures also from Eugene or North Bend. Hourly rates, excluding flight time to the coast, are $65 per person in a Cessna 172, $47 in the C-206, $73 in the C-182, and $105 in the C-340.

BEACHCOMBING

The Beach: Contours And Character
For most Oregon visitors who travel west of the Coast Range, life is a beach. Despite Pacific temperatures cold enough to render swimming an at-your-own-risk activity, the cliffside ocean vistas, wildlife, and beachcombing make the coast the state's number-one attraction. With rare exception, all beaches in Oregon below mean high tide are owned by the public. These beaches are generally separated by basaltic headlands, volcanic plugs which remain after wind and sea erosion have worn away the softer surrounding earth.

Black sand, high in iron and other metals, is common on the coast, particularly south of Coos Bay. There was also enough gold in the black sands to spur a flurry of gold-mining activity on the south coast 130 years ago. These days, mining companies are eyeing the shelf off the south coast for possible exploitation of ilmenite, magnetite, chromite, zircon, garnet, gold, and platinum. Scientists have known for decades of the placer deposits of heavy minerals washed ashore on prehistoric beaches thousands of years ago when ocean levels were much lower. These beach sands now lie submerged. A study based on Rogue River and Cape Blanco offshore sands have indicated a significant presence of precious metals there.

Speaking of sand, the Oregon coast has 40 miles of dunes, about 32,000 acres, the largest oceanfront collection in the world. Some hills top out at several hundred feet high. Oregon's Sahara is located between Coos Bay and Florence. Many coastal travelers will notice European beach grass covering the sand wherever they go. Originally planted to inhibit dune growth, the beach grass has solidified into a ridge behind the shoreline, which blocks the windblown sand from replenishing the rest of the beach. In some places, highways are in danger of being engulfed by the dunes.

Throughout your coastal travels, you'll notice names like Oswald West, Samuel Boardman, and Henry B. Van Duzer adorning the names of state parks and highways. These state government officials were the prime movers in preserving the land, building the highways, and establishing the state park system.

Flotsam And Jetsam

One of the first things a newcomer to the Oregon coast notices are the huge piles of driftwood on the beach. Closer inspection usually reveals other treasures. Beachcombers particularly value agates and Japanese glass fishing floats. The volume and variety of flotsam and jetsam here come courtesy of the region's unique geography. Much of the driftwood, for instance, originates from logging operations located upriver on the many waterways which empty into the Pacific. In addition, storms, floods, rockslides, and erosion uproot many trees which eventually wash up on shore.

The Japanese fishing floats are swept into Oregon waters when the Kuroshio Current takes a southerly turn. These balls of ornate green and blue glass sometimes require over a decade to reach the Oregon coast after breaking free from fishnets thousands of miles across the sea. In addition to driftwood and floats, shells, coral, sand dollars, starfish, and other seaborne trophies can be best culled from the intertidal zone on south coast beaches. Unfortunately, the more settled

and accessible north coast has slimmer pickin's due to the larger population of resident beachcombers and the higher visitor influx. December to April are the best months to find agates, jaspers, petrified wood, and a variety of fossils. At that time, the gravel bars covered by sand in summer are exposed. Clamming in the tidal flats and crabbing in the estuaries are also popular, but check carefully for conditions.

Consult a tidal chart any time you anticipate an extended beachcombing excursion. Half a dozen people perish here yearly from being washed off a beach, a jetty, or outcropping. Tide charts are usually available from chambers of commerce as well as from sport and bait shops.

While you may not always come across a 100-foot long kelp or a message in a bottle, you'll probably find beachcombing on the Oregon coast to be its own reward.

PRACTICALITIES

Accommodations

Coastal accommodations run the gamut from humble fishing lodges to a bona fide five-star resorts. In between are condominiums rented as guest rooms, bed and breakfasts, and conventional motels. Air conditioning is a rarity in these establishments, as is direct access to the beach. The latter is due to the strict land-use statutes against building on the beach. Getting to the beach, however, seldom involves more than a five-minute walk. Rates tend to be much lower in the winter, with special weekend getaway packages quite common during the February storm-watching season. Rather than give several seasonal rate changes, coastal accommodations listings will instead indicate a range.

Food

Oregon coast cuisine boasts such delicacies as Dungeness crab, razor clams, Yaquina Bay oysters and bay shrimp, as well as world-famous salmon.

Let's start with the bay shrimp as an appetizer. While a hasty visual appraisal of an Oregon shrimp cocktail might prompt an unfavorable comparison to the larger Gulf prawns, these savory morsels prove that good things come in small packages. Expect them to be in season during August. Another coveted crustacean is the

Dungeness crab. The firm texture of this species in peak season (March or October) has been compared to that of Maine lobster.

Speaking of which, those used to *Homarus americanus* from the East Coast will be disappointed by the oversized crayfish passed off as lobster on some menus. Nevertheless, the freshwater "crawdads" here are exported all over the world. Oregon's Yaquina Bay oysters are also considered gourmet fare. Razor clams are another indigenous shellfish which for many is an acquired taste. Once you get past their rubbery consistency, however, you might enjoy this local favorite.

Spring chinook salmon (May) from the Rogue River estuary seems to be a "can't miss" item for almost everyone. While red snapper would normally also merit such an assessment, this is not always the case, due largely to a case of mistaken identity. In contrast to the red snapper found on Southern and Eastern menus, this Pacific version is a bottomfish. The brown widow rockfish and its several counterparts which receive the red snapper designation out here have a similar consistency, but more of a fishy taste than their East Coast cousin.

Nightlife

With the exception of the **Otter Crest Jazz Festival** and an occasional big-name rock band playing in Bandon or Newport, there are only taverns and lounges for those interested in stepping out

after dark. Taverns sell beer, often cheaply, and are frequented by the locals. Hard liquor, beer, wine, and live music characterize the lounges. Outside of happy hours, prices are much higher than elsewhere, and when many of the bartenders in these establishments pour, they seem to miss the glass. Nonetheless, a picture window on the Pacific or some other pleasant ambience can make up for a multitude of sins.

Information

All manner of information is available from the **Oregon Coast Association** (Box 620, Newport, 97365; tel. 265-2611 or from Washington, Idaho, Utah, Nevada, and California 800-29-COAST). *Oregon Coast Magazine* (Box 18000, Florence, 97439-1030) is an excellent bimonthly about life on Oregon's western edge. It is sold all over the state. A new offshoot of this magazine, *Oregon Coastal Getaways* (same address), has more destination pieces than its parent publication.

Bus Service

The Oregon coast enjoys **Greyhound** service along the length of U.S. 101. Buses leave Portland twice daily, linking up with the coast at Lincoln City and heading south to Brookings. Stops en route include Lincoln City, Newport, Florence, Reedsport, Coos Bay, Bandon, Port Orford, Gold Beach and Brookings. The 10-hour trip from Portland to Brookings sees few terminals in these towns, but that's a small inconvenience for the

The trick to successfully negotiating U.S. 101 along Oregon's coast can be summed up in two words: slow down.

chance to enjoy this scenic drive. The stretch between Gold Beach and Brookings offers the best views from a bus window. The north and central parts of U.S. 101 do not lack for viewpoints, however, and although going by bike or car affords more flexibility, bus travel has its own advantages, the major one being that it frees you from driving in order to take in the views. Then, too, a bus window affords a greater field of vision with an elevated carriage and wide windows.

In addition to Greyhound's trunk route from Portland, coast-bound travelers can to hook up to U.S. 101 by several other ways. From the Willamette Valley, **Valley Retriever,** a Greyhound subcontractor, runs a Corvallis to Newport bus which makes three round trips daily. Further south, **Raz,** another Hound franchise, rolls along an especially scenic and comfortable coastal access, ORE 126 from Eugene to Florence, and eventually down to Coos Bay. Small bus companies run between Coquille and Roseburg and along ORE 199 from Grants Pass to Crescent City, California, a short distance from the Oregon state line.

Those desirous of reaching the north coast from points inland can take advantage of the Portland-Seaside-Astoria loop. Once on the north coast, Greyhound service is replaced by other alternatives. Local public transportation goes from Tillamook to Astoria, but no public transportation links Tillamook and Lincoln City. **Citizen's Transit** runs commuter vans to and from Portland several times a week from Tillamook. Call 322-3477 for a schedule.

Driving U.S. 101

The independent motorist heading up the coast from California should keep in mind that no vehicular routes access the population centers of Oregon's interior for the first 150 miles of U.S. 101, with the exception of ORE 199 which runs from Crescent City, California to Grants Pass. Another characteristic of this road is heavy summer traffic; you'll have a better chance of passing a slow-moving log truck or a lumbering Winnebago on the four-lane main drag of many coastal cities than on the two lanes of U.S. 101. In any case, be prepared to modify your schedule to accommodate the breathtaking scenery surrounding the road. Also, save time and money by stocking up on groceries and filling up on gas inland before encountering the higher prices endemic to the coast's tourist economy. It also pays to be careful of log trucks doing twice the speed limit on circuitous coastal access roads as well as bicycles attempting to share hairpin turns with large vehicles. Beach loops are often less traveled and offer some good scenery. Finally, keep in mind that the majority of the communities on the coast are "strip towns" along U.S. 101. As such, their simple layout usually renders maps unnecessary.

By Bicycle

While not for everybody, biking the Oregon coast is the surest way to get on intimate terms with this spectacular region. Before going, get a free copy of *The Oregon Coast Bike Route Map* (Dept. of Transportation, Salem 97310, or from coastal info centers and chambers of commerce). This brochure features strip maps of the route, noting services from Astoria to the California border. With info on campsites, hostels, bike-repair facilities, temperatures, and wind speed, this pamphlet does everything but map the ruts in the road.

Rail Excursions

Rail travel became available in May of 1989, courtesy of **Oregon Coastline Express,** (see general Intro, p. 29), with a scenic excursion from Tillamook north to Wheeler, including brief stops in Garibaldi and Rockaway. This is essentially a coastal tourist run, although plans to use the Southern Pacific tracks that run over the mountains could make the line an attractive alternative to two-lane blacktop from points inland. Call 492-9344 for updates.

By Air

Despite a dozen airports on the coast, only the North Bend field near Coos Bay enjoys commercial service. **Horizon,** an offshoot of Alaska Airlines, flies in from Eugene and Portland daily. They fly to these same cities, with occasional through flights to Seattle and isolated stopovers in Salem.

BROOKINGS AND VICINITY

If you cross the state line on U.S. 101 in early summer, the welcome mat of Easter lily blossoms often precedes Oregon's gateway city of Brookings (population 3,400). While the lilies may not carpet these roadsides so extravagantly during the rest of the year, the coast-bound traveler can still look forward to being greeted by mild temperatures and colorful bouquets, even in winter. Enough 60° days occur during February in this south coast "banana belt" town that over 50 species of flowering plants thrive here, along with retirees, sportsmen, and beachcombers. With two gorgeous state parks virtually part of the city and world-class salmon and steelhead fishing nearby, only the lavish winter rainfall that often exceeds 80 inches a year can cool the ardor of local outdoor enthusiasts.

Brookings sits on a coastal plain overlooking the Pacific. The ocean and the Klamath Mountains east of town are linked up by the Chetco River. This river drains part of the nearby **Siskiyou National Forest** and the **Kalmiopsis Wilderness,** renowned for their rare flowers and trees and for possessing some of the wildest country in the U.S. This area enjoys strict federal protection, safeguarding the northernmost stand of giant redwoods as well as the coveted Port Orford cedar. The latter species of strong but pliable lumber can fetch $10,000 for a single tree. Quite fittingly, the Kalmiopsis area is named for the flowering plant that grows nowhere else on earth.

But you don't have to trek miles into the backcountry to enjoy the natural beauty of Brookings and vicinity. Just make your way past the somewhat honky-tonk main drag to **Boardman State Park** north of town, where 11 of the most scenic miles of the Oregon coast await you. Or for a total escape, head down to the harbor to enjoy some of the safest offshore navigation conditions in the region. In short, Brookings is the perfect place to launch an adventure by land or by sea.

BROOKINGS TO PORT ORFORD

© MOON PUBLICATIONS, INC.

HISTORY

What is now the shopping hub of rural Curry County started out as a factory town for the Brookings Box Company in 1914. In the years that followed, lumber, fishing, and tourism became established. If we omit the speculation that the offshore waters here were visited by Cabrillo (1542) and the English pirate Sir Francis Drake (1579), the local event with the most historical significance was the Japanese bombing incident in 1942. On September 9th of that year, a Japanese air raid scorched the treetops of nearby Mount Emily in what the Brookings Chamber of Commerce calls the only wartime air shelling sustained by the U.S. mainland.

Ironically, this frightful episode had two positive outgrowths of enduring significance. First, it sounded the death knell of a secessionist uprising comprised of southern Oregonians and northern Californians. During the '30s, these people wanted to break off from the Union to set up the self-sufficient agrarian state of Jefferson (see "Southern Oregon"). Secondly, the bombing encouraged the

Harris Beach

PHOTO BY TED LONG ISHIKAWA

local lily industry to expand in an effort to make up for the imminent cutoff of Japanese flowers. Today, the area produces 90% of the world's Easter lily crop.

SIGHTS

Chetco Valley Historical Society Museum

This museum (5461 Museum Road, Brookings, 97415; tel. 469-6651) is in an older red and white house built on a hill overlooking U.S. 101 two miles south of the Chetco River. Open Tue.-Sat. 2-6, Sun. noon-6. From November to mid-May hours are Fri.-Sun. 9-5. Admission is free, but donations are always welcome. The structure dates back to the mid-1800s and was used as a stage-coach way station and trading post before Lincoln was president.

Even if you are not one for museums, several exhibits here stand apart from the traditional collections of pioneer wedding dresses, Indian baskets, and spinning wheels. These include a small trunk which came around Cape Horn in 1706, a patchwork quilt dating back to 1844, and an Indian dugout canoe. Should these fail to inspire, an iron casting of a woman's face might do the trick—especially in light of the speculation that this relic was left by an early undocumented landing on the Oregon Coast, perhaps by Sir Francis Drake. Drake has been commonly suggested because of the mask's likeness to Queen Elizabeth.

The **World Champion Cypress Tree** is located on the hill near the museum. The 99-foot-tall

tree has a trunk of more than 27 feet, and has been home to a pair of owls for years.

Quail Prarie Lookout

If you've always romanticized mountain fire lookout stations but have never seen an operating one, visit the Quail Prairie Lookout 17 air miles northeast of Brookings. This is one of the few remaining outposts still staffed on a regular basis each summer during the fire season. As negotiating the forest service roads just west of the Kalmiopsis Wilderness can be tricky, get exact directions to 3,000-foot Quail Prairie Mountain from the Chetco Ranger Station in Brookings.

HIKES AND BEACHCOMBING

Harris Beach State Park

You're driving north along the first 20 miles of scenic U.S. 101 in Oregon, but instead of stopping to take out the camera, you're asking yourself, "So where's the Oregon coast?" It's easy to have second thoughts after a half-hour drive through the "Twilight Zone" of small-town America, with only a few fleeting glimpses of the ocean. And then, at the northern limits of Brookings (across from the State Information Center on U.S. 101), you find your lost picture postcard at Harris Beach State Park. One look at the 24 miles of rock and tide visible from the parking lot promontory should quell any misgivings. The effect can be described as Gibraltar-like and then some.

Besides stunning views, this state park offers many incoming travelers from California their first chance to actually walk on the beach in Oregon. You can begin directly west of the park's campground where a sandy beach strewn with boulders often becomes flooded with intertidal life and driftwood. The early morning hours, as the waves crash through a small tunnel in a massive rock onto the shoreline, are the best time to look for sponges, umbrella crabs, solitary corals, and starfish. Offshore, Goat Island, Oregon's largest seabird rookery, dispatches squadrons of cormorants, pelicans, and other waterfowl who dive-bomb the incoming waves for food.

In addition to beachcombing, you can picnic at tables above the parking lot, loll about in the shallow waters of nearby Harris Creek, or cast the tidewaters for perch.

Mill Beach is the southernmost part of the Harris Beach area. Locals prefer the beach access from downtown, which is easy to bypass. To get there, drive toward the ocean on Center Street in downtown Brookings, make a right at the plywood mill, and stop next to a small ballpark. An unimproved road leads to a hillock from which trails take you down to a beach full of driftwood. Residents say that Japanese fishing floats occasionally roll up onto the beach after a storm.

The Kalmiopsis Wilderness/Vulcan Lake

The lure of untrammeled wilderness attracts intrepid hikers to the Kalmiopsis, despite summer's blazing heat and winter's torrential rains here. In addition to enjoying the isolation of Oregon's largest (180,000 acres) and probably least-visited wilderness, they come to take in the pink rhododendron-like blooms of *Kalmiopsis leachiana* in June and other rare flowers. The area is also home to such economically valued species as Port Orford cedar and *Cannabis sativa*. The illicit weed is the leading cash crop in the state, and its vigilant protection by growers might inspire extra care for those hiking here during the late fall harvest season.

In any case, the Forest Service prohibits plant collection *of any kind* to preserve the region's special botanical populations. These include the insect-eating Darlingtonia plant and the Brewer's weeping spruce. The forest canopy is composed largely of the more common Douglas fir, canyon live oak, madrone, and chinquapin. Stark peaks top this red-rock forest, whose understory is choked with blueberry, manzanita, and dense chaparral. Many of the Kalmiopsis species survived the glacial epoch because the glaciers from that era left the area untouched. This, combined with the fact that the area was an ancient offshore island, has enabled the region's singular ecosystem to maintain its integrity through the millennia. Federal protection, remoteness, and climatic extremes ensure a sanguine outlook for this ice age forest.

Even if you don't have the slightest intention of hiking the Kalmiopsis, the scenic drive through the **Chetco Valley** is worth it. From Brookings, turn off U.S. 101 at the north end of the Chetco River Bridge, follow County Roads 784 and 1736 along the Chetco River for six miles, and then turn right and follow County Road 1909 to its end. Here, a one-mile-long trail leads to **Vulcan Lake** at the foot of Vulcan Peak, the major jumping-off point for trails into the wilderness. Hikers should watch out for the three shiny leaves of poison oak, as well as for rattlesnakes, which are numerous here. Black bears also populate the area, but their lack of contact with humans makes them more shy than their Cascade counterparts.

Streams here in the water-deficient Kalmiopsis are often too warm to quench a thirst. This high temperature can be better appreciated at one of the preserve's many secluded swimming holes.

Here's what to expect on the way to Vulcan Lake. Road 1909 takes off up the mountains past Polliwog Butte and Red Mountain Prairie. The open patches in the Douglas fir reveal a kaleidoscope of Pacific Ocean views and panoramas of the Chetco Valley and the Big Craggies. For the botanist in search of rare plants, however, the real show is on the trail. No matter how expert you might consider yourself, bring along a good plant guide to help you identify the many exotic species here. On the final leg of the hike, sadler oak, manzanita, Jeffrey pine, white pine, and azalea precede the sharp descent to the lake. Despite steep spots, the walk from County Road 1909 to Vulcan Lake is not a difficult one.

If you backtrack from the lake to spur 260 on the trail, you can make the steep ascent over talus slopes and brush to Vulcan Peak. At the top, from an old lookout, a view of Kalmiopsis treetops and the coast awaits.

PRACTICALITIES

Camping

Campers should pick up a **Siskiyou Forest Service** map and literature on fishing at the ranger station in town (see "Information" below). In addition to printed matter about Siskiyou and Kalmiopsis trails for hikers, the rangers there can tell you where to find some good fishing holes on the nearby Chetco River, noted for its good fall salmon runs and winter steelhead.

Harris Beach State Park, two miles north of town on U.S. 101 (1655 Highway 101, Brookings, 97415; tel. 469-2021, $8-10), is open all year, but reservations are definitely necessary in the summer. There are 66 tent sites, 85 trailer/motor home sites (up to 50 feet long), and a special camping area for hikers and bicyclists. Picnic tables and firegrills are provided. Flush toilets, electricity, piped-in water, sewer hookups, sanitary service, showers, firewood, and a laundromat are also available. Whalewatching is particularly good here in January and May.

Loeb State Park is eight miles northeast of Brookings on North Bank Road along the Chetco River. For info call 469-2021 or write c/o Harris Beach State Park. The park is open mid-April to late October, but camping is allowed only during the summer, no reservations necessary. The rate is $7 per night, with 53 sites for trailers/motor homes (50 feet maximum), as well as a special campground for bicyclists and hikers. Electricity, piped water, and picnic tables are provided; flush toilets and firewood are available. The campground is located in a secluded myrtlewood grove on the east bank of the Chetco River, the largest collection of old growth of this species in the state, which imparts a special fragrance to the campsite. Close by is one of the northernmost stands of coastal redwoods. When the south coast is foggy and cold on summer mornings, it's often warm and dry in upriver locations such as this one.

Beyond Loeb State Park is the more primitive **Little Redwood Campround,** but for the price it can't be beat. To get there, go one-half mile south of Brookings on U.S. 101 to County Road 784, then go northeast for seven miles. At Forest Service Road 376 turn northeast and drive six miles to the campground. Contact **Chetco Ranger District,** Box 730, Brookings, 97415; tel. 469-2196 for information. Open late May to mid-September, no reservations necessary. Bargain priced at $4 per night per family, there are 16 sites for tents, trailers, or motor homes (16-feet maximum). Picnic tables and grills are on site, pit toilets and firewood available. Though it lacks showers and other amenities, Little Redwood is located on the main access route to the Kalmiopsis Wilderness, 20 miles away, and is a good spot for fishing during the winter steelhead run.

Accommodations

While Brookings's campgrounds seem preferable as far as taking best advantage of the natural splendor just outside of town, you can always get a roof over your head here, but reserve ahead in summer.

The turn-of-the-century contours of the recently restored **Historical Chetco Inn** (417 Fern St., Brookings, 97415; tel. 469-9984) showcases the aesthetic sensibilities of famed California architect Bernard Maybeck. The "historical" prefix of the Chetco Inn is also justified by its location on part of the site of the Brookings Box Company. If this matters little to you, perhaps the knowledge that the Inn is the most reasonably priced lodging in town ($27-$32) might make a difference. Sitting on a hill in back of the Shell station, the hotel overlooks the town and is close to a shopping center and restaurants.

Holmes Sea Cove Bed and Breakfast (17350 Holmes Drive, Brookings, 97415; tel. 469-3025, $75-85), is a year-round retreat located two miles north of Brookings (turn onto Dawson Road. from U.S. 101). Replete with lushly landscaped grounds and continental breakfast in bed, the Holmeses offer two bedrooms on the lower level of their home and a guesthouse. Below is a private park with picnic tables along a creek by a beach.

Across the street from one another are the **Brookings Best Western Inn** (1153 Chetco, Box N 39, Brookings, 97415; tel. 469-2173) and the **Pacific Sunset Inn** (1144 Chetco, Brookings, 97415; tel. 469-2144). Further down Chetco Avenue (also known as U.S. 101) is **Spindrift Motor Inn** (1215 Chetco, Brookings, 97415; tel. 469-5345). These all run around $40 during the spring and summer and average $10 less in the winter. What you get for your money is a clean garden-variety motel and, for more money, an ocean view.

The **Chetco River Inn** (21202 High Prairie Rd., Brookngs, 97415; tel. 800-327-2688, $60-75) is another more intimate alternative. For somewhat more money, you can escape to your own private forest just 16 miles from Brookings. Its location near prime fishing river frontage makes this place especially popular during the steelhead season on the Chetco. In addition to complete breakfast service, there are picnic lunches and dinners available upon request.

Food

One of the largest selections of seafood in town is available at the **Flying Gull** (1153 Chetco, Brookings, 97415; tel. 469-5700), part of the Brookings Best Western. The **Chetco River House** (243 Chetco Ave., Brookings, 97415; tel. 469-4031) offers fresh seafood in an attractive riverside setting. At the north end of town in a small building which gives the appearance of a drive-in is **Rubio's** (1136 Chetco, Brookings, 97415; tel. 469-4919), one of the better Mexican places along U.S. 101. This will be apparent upon tasting the house salsa and the chile rellenos. The house specialty, seafood à la Rubio, throws together prawns, ling cod, and scallops in a butter, garlic, wine, and jalapeno sauce. In contrast to the tight parking lot outside, the interior of **Pickle Barrel Sandwich and Seafood Company** gives the feeling of space to stretch your legs and relax. The early logging camp decor is supplemented by period photos. Interesting sandwich combinations for lunch and seafood specialties for dinner are reasonably priced and tasty. Try the Garbage Grinder.

If you're interested in stretching a dollar and don't mind stretching your stomach, try **Mama's** (703 Chetco, Brookings, 97415; tel. 469-7611), located close to the Greyhound stop. This is the quintessential Italian bistro complete with a five-foot-tall Mama to heap your plate with copious quantities of northern and southern Italian cuisine. The fettucine Alfredo ($4.75) is excellent, and the homemade ravioli with meatballs should sate even the hungriest hiker.

Events

The **Beachcomber's Festival,** held every March, features exhibits, demonstrations, displays, and slide shows as well as an art competition for the best works wrought from indigenous materials like driftwood, agates, and other beachcomber treasures.

The **Azalea Festival** is an unforgettable floral fantasia that takes place each Memorial Day weekend. Among the activities are a parade, flower display and crafts fair, a five-kilometer run, seafood luncheon, and beef barbecue. Much of the activity revolves around Azalea State Park. This WPA-built enclave features 20-foot-high azaleas (several hundred years old) and hand-hewn myrtlewood picnic tables. Wild cherry and crabapple blooms, wild strawberry blossoms, and purple and red violets round out the bouquet. Butterflies, bees, and birds all seem to concur with locals that this array smells sweetest around graduation time in mid-June.

Easter in July celebrates the blooming of the Easter lilies on July 1st. Brookings holds this event in conjunction with nearby Smith River, California, where many of the festivities are conducted.

Shopping

Of the many stores on the Oregon coast purveying items made of myrtlewood, a local hardwood famed for its fine grain and durability, **Stateline Myrtlewood** (located 25 feet across the California border, open 8:30-5:30 every day except Thanksgiving, Christmas, and New Year's Day) and its parent store, **The House Of Myrtlewood** (Box 457, Coos Bay, 97420; tel. 267-7804) both deserve special mention. Factory tours and an array of quality items ranging from cranberry candy to smoked salmon complement the myrtlewood clocks, bowls, and other handicrafts. Best of all, the friendly staff at both of these stores will gladly answer any questions as well as volunteer all manner of helpful information.

Services

The **post office** (711 Spruce St., Brookings, 97415; tel. 469-2318) is open Mon.-Fri. 9-5. **Greyhound** (tel. 469-3326) stops daily at the corner of Cottage and Pacific.

Wondering about offshore **weather** conditions? The Coast Guard hotline (tel. 469-2242) has the answers. For some fun in the sun, cruise down Easy Street to **Bud Cross City Park** for some **tennis** or a dip in the **outdoor pool.**

The **laundramat** (sic) is located within the Brookings Harbor Shopping Center and is open daily 7 a.m -11 p.m.

Samuel Boardman State Park, the first leg of the "fabulous 50 miles"

PHOTO BY OREGON TOURISM DIVISION

Information

Before you embark on the country's longest (341 miles) designated scenic highway, U.S. 101, stop off at the **Oregon State Department of Economic Development** just north of town (1630 U.S. 101, Brookings, 97415; tel. 469-4117). The facility is open May through November from Tue.-Thurs. 8-6, 9-5 the rest of the week. For additional information pertinent to Brookings and environs, backtrack from the state facility to the south side of the bridge. Here you'll find the town's **chamber of commerce** (97949 Shopping Center Road, P.O. Box 940, Brookings, 97415, tel. 469-3181).

Recreational information, including forest and trail maps, is available at the **Chetco Ranger Station** (555 5th St., Brookings, 97415; tel. 469-2196). The station's advisories include info on the Siskiyou National Forest and the Kalmiopsis Wilderness. It's open Mon.-Fri. 7:30-4:30, but is closed on holidays.

Tours

Strahm's Lilies Farm (15723 Oceanview Dr., Brookings, 97415; tel. 469-3885) offers self-guided tours free of charge 8:30 a.m.-6 p.m. from late June to Labor Day. To get there, turn off of U.S. 101 about a mile south of the Chetco Bridge onto Benham Lane, which curves south onto Ocean View Drive. Look for signs that lead to the greenhouses. The Strahm's friendly presence and their literature should pave the way for a memorable walk down the garden path.

Five-hour salmon and bottom-fishing trips may be arranged through **Leo's Sporthaven Marina** (Box 2215, Harbor, 97415; tel. 469-3301).

NORTH TO GOLD BEACH

The stretch of highway from Brookings to Port Orford is known as the "fabulous fifty miles." Within this bailiwick, some consider the stretch of coastline between Brookings and Gold Beach to be the most scenic in Oregon, and one of the most dramatic meetings of rock and tide in the world. The winding roadbed hundreds of feet above the surf and dramatic offshore rock formations here have been compared to Europe's Amalfi Drive; this is perhaps the most apt in the first dozen miles north of Brookings known as **Samuel H. Boardman State Park.** Of the 11 named viewpoints that have been cut into the highway's shoulder here, the following are especially recommended (all viewpoints are marked by signs on the west side of U.S. 101 and are listed in order of appearance).

House Rock

House Rock was the site of a WW II air-raid sentry tower that sits hundreds of feet above whitecaps pounding the rock-strewn beaches. To the north, you'll see one of the highest cliffs on the coast, Cape Sebastian. A steep, circuitous trail lined with salal (a tart blueberry) goes down to the water. The path begins behind the Samuel Boardman monument on the west end of the parking lot. The sign to the highest viewpoint in Boardman Park is easy to miss, but look for the turnout which precedes House Rock, called Cape Ferrelo (named for Cabrillo's navigator, who sailed up much of the West Coast in 1543).

Thomas Creek Bridge

The highest bridge in Oregon (345 feet above the water), as well as the highest north of San Francisco, Thomas Creek Bridge has been used for many TV commercials. A parking lot at the south end of the bridge marks a trailhead down. Do not take the path you see closest to the bridge because it's too steep. At the south end of the lot,

PHOTO BY FRANK LONG

Natural Bridges north of Gold Beach

the true trail eventually leads down to a view of the bridge on one side and miles of coast on the other. The offshore rock formations here are especially interesting. A few miles down the highway, the **Natural Bridges Cove** sign seems to front just a forested parking lot. However, the paved walkway at the south end of the lot leads to a spectacular overlook. Below, several rock archways frame an azure cove. This feature was created by the entrance and exit of a sea cave collapsing. A steep trail through giant ferns and towering Sitka spruce and Douglas fir winds down for a closer look. Thimbleberries (a sweet but seedy raspberry) are sometimes plentiful. Here as in similar forests on the south coast, it's important to stay on the trail. The rainforest-like biome is exceptionally fragile, and the soil erodes easily when the delicate vegetation is damaged.

Natural Bridge's counterpart is present near the north end of Boardman Park. A short walk down the hillside trail leads you to the **Arch Rocks** viewpoint to see an immense boomerang-shaped basalt archway about a quarter mile offshore. This site has picnic tables within view of the offshore monolith.

Cape Sebastian

Beyond Boardman Park and seven miles south of Gold Beach is Cape Sebastian. This spectacular windswept headland was named by Sebastiano Vizcaino, who plied offshore waters here for Spain in 1602 along with Manuel D'Alguilar. At least 700 feet above the sea, Cape Sebastian is possibly the highest south coast overlook reachable by paved public road. On a clear day, visibility extends nearly 50 miles in either direction. A trail zigzags through beautiful springtime wildflowers down the south side of the cape for about two miles until it reaches the sea. In April and May, Pacific paintbrush, Douglas iris, orchids, and snow queen usher you along. In addition, Cape Sebastian supports a population of large-headed goldfields, a summer-blooming, yellow daisy-like flower found only in coastal Curry County.

GOLD BEACH/ROGUE RIVER ESTUARY

Despite the name "Gold Beach," this town is one part of the coast where the action is definitely away from the ocean. To lure people from Oregon's superlative ocean shores, the nearby Rogue River estuary has been bestowed with many blessings. First, it was the gold-laden black sands which were mined in the 1850s and '60s. While this era gave Gold Beach its name, the arrival of Robert Hume, later known as the "Salmon King of the Rogue," had greater historical significance. By the turn of the century, Hume's canneries had established the river's image as a leading salmon and steelhead stream, a reputation which was later enhanced by the writings of Zane Grey (*Rogue River Feud*). Over the years, Herbert Hoover, Winston Churchill, Ginger Rogers (who has a home on the Rogue), Clark Gable, Jack London, and Jimmy Carter have come here to try their luck. During the last several decades, whitewater rafting and jetboat tours focusing on the abundant wildlife, scenic beauty, and fascinating lore of the region have hooked other sectors of the traveling public.

Today, Gold Beach is a town of 1,500 and the Curry County seat. Besides serving as the south coast tourism hub, a pulp mill and commercial fishing industry make up the local economy here. The seasonal nature of many local businesses creates serious wintertime unemployment. This fact combined with torrential rains drastically reduce the population of Gold Beach from Thanksgiving until spring. Thereafter, the wildflowers and warm weather transform this town into a vacation mecca.

SIGHTS

Driving through town on U.S. 101, just before the road gives way to the bridge, the harbor comes into view on the left. Salmon trawlers, jetboats, pelicans, and seals bobbing up and down will be there to greet you. Across the Oscar Patterson Bridge is **Wedderburn,** a baby sister to Gold Beach. Named for the Scottish birthplace of Robert Hume, its major claim to fame is that it's the home port of the Mailboat, which has been

playing postman to upriver residents on the Rogue since 1895.

At the **Curry County Historical Museum** (920 S. Ellensburg, Gold Beach, 97444; tel. 247-6113), the local historical society has assembled a small collection of exhibits on Indian and pioneer life, mining in the region's golden age, logging, fishing, and agriculture. It's located at the county fairgrounds at the south edge of town. Particularly interesting are a realistic reconstruction of a miner's cabin, vintage photos, and Indian petroglyphs. Open summer May 15 to September 30, Mon.-Sun. 1-5 p.m., winter October 11 to May 15 Fri.-Sat. 12-4 p.m. The admission is free.

Jetboat Trips

The best way to take in the mighty Rogue is on a jetboat ride from Gold Beach harbor. There are several different companies who run this trip, but they all provide comparable service and prices. It's a relaxing and interesting look at the varied flora and fauna along the estuary as well as the changing moods of the river. Most of the estimated 50,000 people per year who "do" the Rogue in this way take the 64-mile roundtrip cruise. This and the more adventurous 104-mile cruise offer a sumptuous lunch at a secluded fishing lodge for an additional charge. Your pilot/commentator usually has grown up on the river, and his evocation of the diverse ecosystems and Indian and gold mining history adds greatly to your enjoyment. Bears, otters, and beavers may be sighted en route, and fishermen will generally hold up "a big one" to show off. Ospreys, snowy egrets, eagles, mergansers, and kingfishers are also seen with regularity in this resting place for migratory waterfowl.

In the first part of the journey, idyllic riverside retreats dot the hillsides, breaking up stands of fir and hemlock. Myrtle, madrone, and impressive springtime wildflower groupings also vary the landscape. Both the 32- and 52-mile trips focus on the section of the Rogue protected by the government as a Wild and Scenic River. Only the longer trips take you into the pristine Rogue Wilderness, an area that motor launches from Grants Pass also do not reach. The 13 miles of this wilderness you see from the boat has canyon walls rising 1,500 feet above you. Geologists say that this part of the Klamaths is composed of ancient islands and sea floor that collided with North America. To deal with the rapids upstream, smaller, faster boats are used which are able to skim over the boulders with just six inches of water between hull and rock surface.

Remember that chill and fog near the mouth of the estuary are replaced by much warmer conditions upstream. These tour outfits have wool blankets available on cold days as well as complimentary hot beverages. Also keep in mind that the upriver lodges can be booked for overnight stays and your trip may be resumed the following day.

Located just south of the bridge over the Rogue, west of U.S. 101 is **Jerry's Rogue River Jetboats** (Box 1011, Gold Beach, 97444; tel. 247-4571/800-451-3645). This heavily patronized company runs trips from May through October. They offer a 64-mile roundtrip and a 104-mile roundtrip, both stopping at Paradise Bar Lodge near Blossom Bar rapids, the turnaround point. The shorter trip (adults pay $25, children four to eleven pay $10) takes six hours and departs daily at 8:30 a.m., also at 2:30 p.m., July 1-Labor Day. The 104-mile whitewater trip (adults $50, ages four to eleven $20) leaves daily at 8 a.m. May to October, with a second trip at noon. Please inquire about other itineraries that may be available. An 80-mile whitewater tour, a one-hour lower Rogue cruise, and an hour-long bay cruise

are among those offered on a "sometimes" basis. Jerry's is noted for personable, well-informed guides.

Rogue River Mailboats (Box 1165, Gold Beach, 97444; tel. 247-7033/247-6225/800-458-3511) is located a quarter mile upstream from the north end of the Rogue River bridge. The rates, trips, and times parallel Jerry's offerings, except for an additional 80-mile whitewater trip (adults $32, ages four to eleven $12) that leaves daily at 8 a.m. and 2:30 p.m. July 1-Labor Day, and the fact that there's not a second 104-mile whitewater trip scheduled daily. Besides human cargo, this boat also carries mail sacks, ensuring a warm welcome in upriver locations.

Court's Whitewater Jetboat Trips (Box 1045, Gold Beach, 97444; tel. 247-4571/247-6504/800-367-5787), which leaves from Jot's Resort at the north end of the Rogue River bridge, west of U.S. 101, has packages similar to the others but gives more of a discount to kids. On the 64-mile trips, ages five to twelve go for $10, and kids under five go for free. On the 104-mile trip, ages six to twelve go for $20, and under five goes for free. Court's pioneered the first whitewater trips here almost 30 years ago.

Beach Access/Auto Tour

Two miles south of Gold Beach there's easy access to a nice beach at **Hunter Creek.** The creek is just off the highway and marked by a sign. From Hunter's Creek you can pick up Hunter's

cruising the Rogue River,
jetboat style

Creek Road, which loops north through the forest, finally following the course of the Rogue back into town. The three-hour drive goes past interpretive markers explaining "our national forest, land of many uses," and is mapped out in a free pamphlet available at the Gold Beach Ranger Station. This map shows locations of several picnic areas and campgrounds.

Other roads less traveled include the old coast highway, which you can pick up across from Sebastian State Park, the Shasta Costa Road paralleling the Rogue from Gold Beach to Galice, and an unpaved road into the Rogue Wilderness from **Agness** (a town upriver on the Rogue) to **Powers.** Despite most of these routes being paved (except the last one), they are all narrow, winding, and not suitable for trailers or motor homes. Maps and directions to these back roads can be obtained from the Gold Beach ranger station.

RECREATION

Local Activities
The **Curry County Fair** (920 S. Ellensburg, Gold Beach, 97444) usually takes place the second week of August. Highlights include Oregon's largest flower show and a lamb BBQ. Contact the chamber of commerce for more information. The chamber can also fill you in on the exact times for the **jetboat races** that take place July Fourth weekend. People line the river for the event.

To get to **Indian Creek Trail Rides** (Box 194 Wedderburn, 97491; tel. 247-7704), follow Jerry's Flat Road one-half mile. Ride along the Rogue on well-trained mounts (one hour $12, two hours $20, family and groups $10 per person). **Gold Beach Summer Theater** (Box 1324, Gold Beach, 97444, or contact the chamber of commerce for the season schedule) is a June to late August tradition that used to attract young thespians from all over the state due to its connection with Willamette University. While this is no longer the case, there is no shortage of local talent who plan to continue the modern eclectic repertoire of light comedy and serious drama.

Tours
Pacific Air Services (tel. 247-2414 days, 247-7853 nights) flies out of Gold Beach airport and offers air tours of the coast. The route might include 325-foot Mack Arch, sea lion and bird rookeries, and a flight through the Pistol River area south of Gold Beach into the wilderness supporting the confluence of the Illinois and the Rogue rivers. Rates are $35 per person for a 45-minute flight, three-people minimum to a plane.

The Rogue-Pacific Interpretive Center (510 Colvin St., Gold Beach, 97444; tel. 247-2732) is a block off U.S. 101 behind the courthouse. This environmental education center offers guided trips which include tidepooling, Indian and pioneer sites, coastal forests, and boat charters. They also have free demonstrations on fishing and Indian life and slide shows on natural history. There are special kids' programs on whales, seals, seashore and forest life. Call them for course descriptions and times.

Outdoor Pursuits
Curry County's only golf course, **Cedar Bend** (Box 1234, Gold Beach, 97444) is located in nearby **Ophir.** Eleven miles north of Gold Beach, pick up Ophir Road off U.S. 101. Follow it to Squaw Valley Road and turn right at the Old Ophir Store and continue until you see the links. It costs $9 for nine holes, $12 for 18 holes.

Well-known **fishing guides** Bill McNair and Denny Hughson can be contacted through Jerry's Jetboats (see above). Most lodgings can also set you up with a guide. For fishing and camping advice and equipment, try the **Rogue Outdoor Store** (560 N. Ellensburg, Gold Beach, 97444; tel. 247-7142).

The 40-mile **Rogue River Trail** offers lodge-to-lodge hiking which means you need little more in your pack than the essentials. These lodges here are comfortably rustic, serve home-style food in copious portions, and run between $40-75. They are also comfortably spaced, so extended hiking is seldom a necessity.

Before you go, please check the Gold Beach Ranger Station on trail conditions and specific directions to the trailhead. Pick up the western end of the trail 35 miles east of Gold Beach, about one-half mile from Foster Bar, a popular boat landing (see "Camping"). Park there and walk east and north on the paved road until you see signs on the left marking the Rogue River Trail. Go in spring before the hot weather and enjoy yellow Siskiyou iris and fragrant wild azaleas. The trail ends at Graves Creek, 27 miles northwest of

the Schrader Old Growth
Trail near Gold Beach

Grants Pass. Be careful of rattlesnakes on the trail. Contact the chamber of commerce for more information on the upriver lodges.

Odds And Ends

The more sedentary nature lover can enjoy watching a sunset over cocktails at the **Beach House Lounge** (1432 S. Ellensburg, Gold Beach, 97444; tel. 247-6626). The huge wall-length window looks out on a wild meadow beyond which the surf breaks on a dark-sand beach. This is also the place to come and rock out later in the evening.

Prehistoric Gardens (tel. 332-4463) unfortunately stands out like a sore thumb on the otherwise unspoiled stretch of U.S. 101, 15 miles north of Gold Beach. Imagine a group of dinosaurs built to exact scale amid giant ferns and towering evergreens. While the setting may be appropriate to the display, the reverse is not true unless you're a kid. Still, the explanatory signs and obvious hard work and care of the the concessioner are easy for anyone to appreciate. Open daily 8 a.m. to dusk, admission $3.50 for adults, students 12-18 $3, children 5-11 $2.

PRACTICALITIES

Accommodations

As with most coastal cities, there is no shortage of places to stay along the main drag, Ellensburg Street (a.k.a. U.S. 101). In fact, Gold Beach offers the largest number and widest range of accommodations on the south coast, with intimate lodges overlooking the Rogue as popular as the oceanfront motels. A discount of 20 percent or more on rooms is usually available during the winter here when 80 to 90 inches of rain can fall.

The cheapest place in town is probably the **Oregon Trail Lodge** (550 N. Ellensburg, Box 721, Gold Beach, 97444; tel. 242-6030). For about 30 bucks you get sanitized Motel 6-type accommodations with room to spare. The **Friendship Inn's** (1010 Jerry's Flat Rd., Gold Beach, 97444; tel. 247-4533) location on the south bank of the Rogue, beautiful rooms, and friendly management can even make you overlook the purple doors here. The rates go between $40-50.

Ireland's Rustic Lodge (1120 S. Ellensburg, Gold Beach, 97444; tel. 247-7718) was started by two women who used to bring meals to the rooms. While this is no longer the case here, the touch of home has not been lost. Many of the rooms have fireplaces, knotty pine interiors, and distinctive decor. Best of all, the grounds are lovingly landscaped with pine trees, flowers, and ocean views. A sandy beach is a short stroll to the west. There are 27 motel units, nine old but well-kept cabins, and cottages which sleep eight each. The rates are as follows: $92 for a cottage, $55-68 for a motel suite, $29 to 53 for a double, $27-37 for a single.

Located on the Rogue River's north bank, **Jot's Resort** (94360 Wedderburn Loop, Box J, Wedderburn, 97491; tel. 247-6676/800-FOR JOTS) can host a full vacation in one compound featuring pool and spa, sports shop, private dock, rental boats, and an excellent restaurant across the street. The rooms here are at a premium in summer when the many luxury motorcoach tours come through. The rates are as follows: $65 for standard view rooms, riverfront condos big enough for six people at $145 and $165. The Rod 'n' Reel across the street features evening entertainment with low-stakes blackjack, a country music duo, and a Big Band dance on weekends.

Tu Tu Tun (96530 N. Bank; tel. 247-6664, May 1-Nov. 1) resort emphasizes the tranquility of an evergreen coastal forest on prime river frontage. The latter actually makes you forget that Gold Beach and U.S. 101 are only seven miles away. This feeling of blissful remoteness is reinforced by the absence of phones and TV. As you sit on your patio overlooking the water, only the sounds of an occasional passing boat may intrude upon your Rogue River reverie. A heated pool and other recreational facilities, the lodge's beautifully appointed interiors, and gourmet meals served family style are other appeals of this acclaimed retreat. Tu Tu Tun has earned four-star and four-diamond awards for excellence.

Spring is the best time to be here, because much of the traveling public is still at home and the wildflowers are in their glory. Pink rhododendrons, native to Oregon, blossom at the edge of the forest in May. While autumn is also beautiful, business meetings in September and October necessitate that bookings be made well in advance for stays after Labor Day. The rates are $120-130 for a suite, $93 for a double, and $90 for a single.

Rogue River Campsites

Campsites east of town along the Rogue and off U.S. 101 en route to Port Orford provide wonderful spots to bed down for the night. Those taking the road along the Rogue should be alert for oncoming log trucks, raft transport vehicles, and other wide-body vehicles

Foster Bar (Siskiyou National Forest, Gold Beach Ranger Station, Box 548, 1225 S. Ellensburg, Gold Beach, 97444; tel. 247-6651) campground is located 30 miles east of Gold Beach on the south bank of the Rogue. Take Jerry's Flat Road east for 30 miles to the turnoff for Agness. Turn right on Illahe Agness Road and drive three

miles to camp. There are 10 sites for tents and RVs. Picnic tables and fire rings are provided. Pit toilets and firewood are also available, but there is no drinking water. No reservations are necessary and the fee is $2 per night. The site is open March to late September. This is a popular spot to embark on an eight-mile inner tube ride to Agness. The rapids are dangerous, so wear a life jacket. You are also within walking distance of the trailhead of the Rogue River Trail (see recreation).

Lobster Creek Campground (contact the Forest Service at address above, tel. 247-7922) is nine miles up Jerry's Flat Road along the Rogue's south bank. This free campground is open year-round and has five camping sites, picnic tables, fishing, flush toilets, but there is no drinking water. Ask the Forest Service for directions to the recently established old-growth trail nearby. It is a gentle one-mile walk through a rare and majestic ecosystem under siege in other forests throughout the state.

Oceanside Campgrounds

Honeybear Campground (Box 97, 134161 Ophir Rd., Ophir, 97464; tel. 247-2765/800-822-4444 ext. 00) is located nine miles north of Gold Beach on U.S. 101 (then two miles north on Ophir Road), but could just as well be in the Black Forest. The owners have built a large rathskellar with a dance floor. Six nights a week during the summer, there are dances here with traditional German music. Locals praise the Honeybear's on-site delicatessen for its homemade German sausage. There are 20 tent and RV sites, picnic tables, flush toilets, hot showers, firewood, a laundromat, and ocean views from $9.50 and up. It's open May to October.

Arizona Beach Campground (Box 621, Gold Beach, 97444; tel. 332-6491) is a combination motel and campground close by a beach with lots of driftwood. It has 31 tent sites, motels rooms, and almost a hundred RV spaces. You can camp on the beach ($12), in an adjoining meadow ($10), or back in the woods by a tiny stream ($8). All the amenities are here, 15 miles north of Gold Beach on U.S. 101, but the closely spaced sites lack privacy. Nonetheless, there are few better places for kids due to a creek running though the site and the proximity of the Prehistoric Gardens (see "Entertainment"). It's open all year.

Food

You can't eat scenery, but Gold Beach restaurants charge you for it anyway. Still, this is one place where the oceanfront and riverside views are often worth it. Then too, there's always the option of cheaper restaurants away from port. Spring chinook salmon, blackberry pie, and other indigenous specialties taste good anywhere.

Ethel's Galley (347 N. Ellensburg, Gold Beach, 97444; tel. 247-7713) is next to the movie theater, and has good American food competently prepared, reasonably priced, and amply dished out. Ethel's blackberry cobbler (in season) and all the pies (fruit, berry, and cream) are worth special mention. Breakfasts are popular (open at 5:30 a.m.), but not available on Saturday or Sunday.

Grant's Pancake and Omelette House (94680 Jerry's Flat Road, Gold Beach, 97444; tel. 247-7208) is located on the outskirts of town along the Rogue estuary. This plain roadside cafe serves up pancakes, waffles, omelettes, eggs, etc. at the kind of prices usually found at Las Vegas casinos and Mexican bus stations. It's open at 6 a.m. every day except Monday. **The Golden Egg** (710 S. Ellensburg, Gold Beach, 97444; tel. 247-7528) at last count offered 27 omelette combinations. Try their Western omelette (bacon, onion, green pepper, and cheese) for $4.75. In addition, pancakes and waffles round out the breakfast menu. Sandwiches and burgers are featured at lunch, with moderately priced steak and seafood the bill of fare at night. The large back room offers a distant ocean view beyond the high school football field.

Spada's (1020 S. Ellensburg, Gold Beach, 97444; tel. 247-7730) has an immense menu with breakfast fare, sandwiches, burgers, steaks, and seafood as well as Italian specialties ranging from cannelloni crepes to New York pizza. In addition to boasting something for everybody, Spada's entrees are very moderately priced, and they have the best cappuccino in town.

As you enter the **Rod 'n' Reel** (on the north end of the Rogue River bridge across from Jot's Resort, Wedderburn, 97491; tel. 247-6823), you'll read a sign which says, You're a stranger here but once. The food and attractiveness of the restaurant as well as the congeniality of the Powers family and their staff make it so. Breakfast, lunch, and dinner are served here. Lunch is an especially popular meal, due in part to the restaurant's proximity to the jetboat docks. The more important reasons include the grilled crab or shrimp sandwiches with melted cheese ($5.95, real yummy), some of the best salmon (baked, broiled, or poached for $8.50) you've ever tasted, an ample salad bar, and excellent pies, notably blackberry and strawberry rhubarb.

The Rogue Landing's (94749 Jerry's Flat Rd., Gold Beach, 97444; tel 247-6031) menu is an imaginative blend of European dishes and standard seafood items. The prices are high for Gold Beach, but the food is excellent and you'll enjoy the best window view of the lower Rogue in town. The **Nor'Wester Seafood Restaurant** (overlooking the boat basin, port of Gold Beach, 97444; tel. 247-2333) is another first-rate dinner house with a picture window overlooking the mouth of the Rogue. There is also an eye-catching raised relief wooden mural of two whales and an impressive freestanding fireplace to add to the ambience. The menu emphasizes the freshest seafood and finest cuts of beef available. As with the Rogue Landing, expect to pay between $15-20 per person for a dinner. There is a seafood market downstairs.

The Chowderhead (910 S. Ellensburg, Box 858, Gold Beach, 97444; tel. 247-7174) serves up ocean-view dining and a menu so imaginative that the Ogden Nash-like monickers on each dish seem appropriate. Consider Mexi-Can (Mexican shrimp and Canadian scallops sautéed in garlic and butter) and the lunch shrimparito (tortilla with shrimp salad, tomato, avocado, and swiss cheese —heated). All orders include serve-yourself red or white clam chowder, both very good. For what it's worth, *Bon Appetit Magazine* considers the Chowderhead "one of America's best restaurants."

Information And Services

The **Gold Beach Chamber of Commerce** (510 Ellensburg, Gold Beach, 97444; tel. 247-7526/800-452-2334 in Oregon, 800-542-2334 outside) is open Mon.-Fri., 9-5, and Sat.-Sun. 10-4. They'll send you a good, comprehensive information folder upon request. The Gold Beach **Ranger District office** (1225 S. Ellensburg, Gold Beach, 97444; tel. 247-6651) offers a free packet on camping and recreation in the district. It's open Mon.-Fri., 7:30-5. The **post office** (Moore St., Gold Beach, 97444, tel. 247-7610) is open Mon.-Fri 8:30-5:30.

The **Greyhound** (310 Colvin St., Gold Beach, 97444; tel. 247-7246) station is a terminal case as far as the health hazards of nicotine are concerned. Across the street is a modern building housing the public library. Comfy armchairs here would make this a perfect alternative waiting room to Greyhound except for the lack of restrooms. Open Mon.-Thurs. 10-8, Fri.-Sat. 10-6.

Stonsell's Coin-Op Laundry is located on U.S. 101 near 8th Street.

Curry General Hospital (220 E. 4th, Gold Beach, 97444; tel. 247-6621) is the only hospital in the county. It coordinates the "Mercy Flight," an air taxi service to Medford, should there be any cases it can't handle.

PORT ORFORD AND VICINITY

As you come up U.S. 101 into Port Orford, it's hard to ignore an immense rock promontory fronting the shoreline. Battle Rock was the focus of a conflict between the local Indians and the first landing party of the white settlers in 1851. When Captain William Tichenor observed the hostility of the natives onshore, he put nine men ashore on the rock due to its suitability as a battle position. These men defended this outpost long enough for Tichenor to return with reinforcements to carry the day. From such inauspicious beginnings, "Port Awferd," as the locals call it, established itself as the oldest townsite on the south coast. Shortly thereafter, the town became the site of the first fort established on the coast during the Rogue Indian Wars. This conflict started as a result of gold miners and settlers coming into Indian lands. As a result of the clashes, hundreds of local natives were sent to the Siletz Reservation near Lincoln City in 1856.

Besides Indian conflicts, Port Orford has other claims to fame. By a quirk of geography, it is both the most westerly incorporated city in the contiguous U.S. and the center of the country, if you include Hawaii. What's more, *Forbes* magazine dubbed Port Orford the "sleeper" of the Oregon coast, ready to be awakened due to its "knockout" view, despite the fact that it's the rainiest burgh on the coast—108 inches annually.

Impressive as some of these geographical calling cards may sound, they have not conferred any great prosperity on the region. Commercial fishing and cedar logging join tourism as the leading revenue producers. Lately, many other eclectic cottage industries have supplemented these larger enterprises of the boom/bust resource-based economy. The outskirts of Port Orford host such diverse undertakings as an escargot-breed-ing farm, llama and sheep ranches, a goat-milk dairy, commercial berry growers, as well as spreads that cultivate Christmas trees and exotic herbs. In addition, diving for sea urchins supplies the Japanese with a popular aphrodisiac and seafood delicacy.

SIGHTS

Humbug Mountain

Some people will tell you that Humbug Mountain (six miles south of Port Orford on U.S. 101) is the highest mountain rising directly off the Oregon shoreline. Since the criteria for such a distinction varies as much as the tides, let's just say it's a special place. Once the site of native vision quests, today Humbug Mountain's shadow reflects upon an Eden-like campground surrounded by myrtles, alders, and maples. Just north is a breezy, black-sand beach. A three-mile trail to the top of Humbug will reward the hardy hiker with impressive vistas to the south of Nesika Beach and a chance to see rhododendrons 15 to 20 feet high. The name Humbug derives from the gold miners who were drawn here in the 1850s by tales of gold in the black sands. These stories, of course, proved to be just "humbug." Perhaps more reliable is the Indian legend which says that if the top of the mountain can be seen, the weather will be good.

Battle Rock State Park

Port Orford has an ocean view from downtown that is arguably the most scenic of any city on the coast. A waterfront stroll lets you appreciate the cliffs and offshore seastacks as well as the unique sight of commercial fishing boats being lowered by crane into the harbor. Here too is the previously mentioned Battle Rock in its own state park. If you can make your way through driftwood and blackberry bushes surrounding its base, you can take the short trail to the top for a heightened perspective on the rockbound coast which parallels the town. You'll also notice the east-west orientation of the harbor. Once you get to the top of the rock, don't think that the battle is necessarily over. Bracing winds will often chill you, and high tides can sometimes render this huge coastal extension an island. The rock is also the focus of a **Fourth of July Jubilee Celebration** which reenacts the historic battle described in this section's Introduction.

Downtown Walking Tour

A brochure obtainable from the information kiosk in the parking lot opposite Battle Rock details *Port Orford's History in Its Architecture* and introduces you to homes from the last century in a nice 15-minute walk. Also at the kiosk you can find out about the famed fishing in the Elk and Sixes rivers north of town. Scuba divers can make inquiries at the info desk about the many

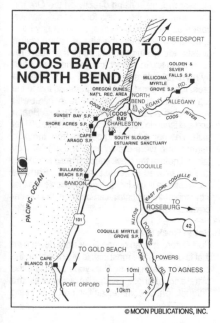

© MOON PUBLICATIONS, INC.

protected coves with water temperatures as high as 50°, which is warm for Oregon's Pacific, and water clarity ranging from 10 to 50 feet in summer.

The Heads

Another shoreline scene worth taking in is located north of town up W. 9th Street at what the locals call "The Heads," featuring a striking panorama from north to south at Port Orford Head State Park, just a short hike away from the parking lot. If you go down the cement trail to the tip of a blustery headland, you look south to the mouth of Port Orford's harbor. To the north, many small rocks fill the water, along with boats trolling for salmon or checking crab pots. On clear days it's said that visiblity extends from Cape Blanco to Humbug Mountain.

Cape Blanco State Park, Hughes House

Eleven miles north of Port Orford on U.S. 101 is Cape Blanco, perhaps the westernmost point of land in the contiguous U.S. (although Californians and Washingtonians beg to differ). Whether or not it rates the nod, the remote appendages of this place will give you the feeling of being at the edge of the continent. From the vantage of Cape Blanco, dark mountains sit behind you and forest almost abuts tidewater. Driftwood and 100-foot-long bull kelp on slivers of black-sand beach fan out from both sides of this earthy red bluff 245 feet above the ocean. Somehow the Spaniards who sailed past it in 1603 viewed the Cape as having a white or "blanco" color. It's been theorized that perhaps they were referring to the fossilized shells on the front of the cliff.

Atop the headland is the oldest and highest lighthouse in continuous use in Oregon. This beacon still uses the same French-made lens that was originally installed in 1870, blinking out a signal every 30 seconds to points 20 miles out at sea Over the years a number of shipwrecks have occurred on the reefs near Cape Blanco. During WW II, Japanese submarines used the beacon as an orientation mark to aim planes loaded with incendiary bombs at the Coast Range. This effort to start forest fires was motivated by the existence of Port Orford cedar trees here which were used as a building material to construct planes. Due to the perennial dampness, the results were negligible.

*the coast south
of Port Orford*

PHOTO BY OREGON TOURISM DIVISION

The vegetation on the state park road down to the beach will attest to the severity of winter storms here. One hundred-mile-per-hour gales (the record winds were clocked at 184 m.p.h.) and horizontal sheets of rain have given some of the usually massive Sitka spruces the appearance of bonzai trees. Lodgepole pine, salmonberry, and bracken fern evoke a southeast Alaska forest.

Near Cape Blanco on a side road along the Sixes River is the **Hughes House,** a restored Victorian home built in 1898 for rancher and county commissioner Patrick Hughes. Owned and operated by the state of Oregon, the house serves as a museum and repository of antique furnishings. The Hughes House is open May 1- Sept. 30, Thurs.-Sat and Mon. 10-5, Sun. noon-5.

Activities

Beachcombing for agates and fishing floats on nearby south coast beaches and searching for the lost Port Orford Meteorite in the surrounding foothills typify the adventures available in the area. The meteorite was found and lost by a government geologist in the 1860s who estimated its weight at 22,000 tons.

Those in search of more conventional pursuits are advised to drive out to 14th or 18th streets to **Garrison Lake.** Boating, water-skiing, and trout fishing are available here. Nearby **Buffington Memorial City Park,** west of U.S. 101, has a dock for fishing or swimming on the lake, plus playing fields, tennis courts, picnic areas, hiking trails, and a horse arena. North of the lake, look for agates on **Paradise Point Beach.** Garrison Lake State Wayside offers access to coastal dunes.

PRACTICALITIES

Accommodations

Port Orford is the kind of place where a room with a view will not break your budget. The **Shoreline Motel** (Box 426, Port Orford, 97465; tel. 332-2903) is across the highway from Battle Rock, has an outstanding view, and offers clean rooms for not much more than $30. **Gwendolyn's Bed and Breakfast** (735 U.S. 101, Port Orford, 97465; tel. 332-4373) is a gingerbread house out of the 1920s replete with period furniture and three bedrooms with brass beds. At $35 for a room with a shared bath, the rates are little more than you'd pay for a cut-rate motel. The owner makes a famous salmon and crab pie. The **Seacrest Motel** (Box C, tel. 332-3040) features views of coastal cliffs and a garden in a quiet location overlooking the ocean. The rates range between $30-40 for a single, and hover around $40-50 for a double. **Home-by-the- Sea** (Box 606, Port Orford, 97465; tel. 332-2855) includes a full breakfast with rates that run between $50-60. The dramatic hillside view of Battle Rock seascape makes for excellent storm-watching here.

Campgrounds

Humbug Mountain State Park (six miles south of Port Orford, tel. 332-6774) features 80 tent sites and 30 sites for trailers and motor homes, and wind-protected sites reserved for hikers and bikers at a buck a night. Flush toilets, showers, picnic tables, water, firewood, and a laundromat are available. The park is open April to October,

THE SEA OTTERS OF CAPE BLANCO

Down on the beach below Cape Blanco, you might see the furry heads of sea otters peering out from above the whitecaps about 200 yards off-shore. The progenitors of this colony were transported here courtesy of the Atomic Energy Commission in 1970. At that time, a planned bomb test in the Aleutians compelled the AEC to move 95 of these animals to this area. In addition to Cape Blanco, they've been sighted south of Port Orford.

Between 1775 and 1823, over 100,000 sea otters were killed for their pelts, many along the Oregon coast. They became the trappings of royalty, selling in Paris for as much as $1,000 apiece. After sea otters were declared extinct south of the Aleutians in 1911, they became a protected species.

Early accounts of the plunder of the sea otter should have brought about their protection long before the 20th century. An early 19th-century Spanish journal describes the colony off of Monterey, California as playful and intelligent. It detailed their ability to dive hundreds of feet down to pull abalone shells off of rocks. This was highlighted by their reemergence on the surface on their backs, shell in paw. Using their stomachs for a table, the seat otters would then hold the shell in one paw, and crack it open with a rock.

In addition to the Spanish chronicler's fascination with their behavior, he noted another similarity to Homo sapiens when mama sea otter was observed putting baby in a cradle of kelp. The account went on to describe the mother's reaction upon returning with breakfast and finding her baby missing: she emitted human-like cries for days on end, eventually starving herself to death.

and an $8 fee is charged. **Cape Blanco State Park** (Box 299, Sixes, OR 97476; tel. 332-2971) can be reached by driving four miles north of Port Orford on U.S. 101, then heading northwest on the park road which continues five miles beyond to the campground. It features 58 sites for tents, trailers, and motorhomes, as well as hiker/biker sites for a dollar a night; picnic tables, water, showers, and a laundromat are available. No reservations are necessary, and a $9 fee is charged mid-April to late September.

Food

While an inexpensive burger or BLT is easy to come by in Port Orford, you'll have to pay for fine dining. Fortunately, "view" restaurants come in all price ranges. The **Wheelhouse Restaurant** (521 Jefferson St., Port Orford, 97465; tel. 332-4605) enjoys a location on Battle Rock Park and has low prices. You can get a decent continental breakfast for $1.75. Burgers, homemade soups, and pies are also available 7 a.m.-8 p.m. daily. The **Golden Owl Deli** (755 U.S. 101, Port Orford, 97465; tel. 332-6592) works well for lunch, featuring diverse sandwiches, or for a late breakfast if you like lox and bagels. It is known for its sandwiches, smoked salmon, excellent coffee, and fine collection of Oregon wines. The sandwiches are large, so the the restaurant lets you order a half sandwich. Try their submarine of turkey ham, two cheeses, lettuce, and tomato for $4.95 (whole) or $2.99 (half). This tiny restaurant is also a feast for the obsessive reader, with interesting slogans and posters adorning the walls. Open Mon.-Sat., 10 a.m.-8 p.m., Sun., 11-5.

The **Truculent Oyster** (236 6th St., Port Orford, 97465; tel. 332-4461) at the south end of town has the nautical atmosphere and fresh fish that one would expect in an Oregon coast seafood restaurant, but also features mild Mexican entrees. Such specialties as oysters sautéed with vegetables and steamer clams run around $8. The house-cut steaks are also very good. The **Peg Leg Saloon** in the same building draws locals here en masse on weekends. **Whale Cove** (U.S. 101 at Battle Rock Beach, Port Orford, 97465; tel. 325-7575) has a fantastic ocean view and, it says, "the only master chef on the Oregon coast south of Salishan." The food lives up to the hype. With such local ingredients as mushrooms, berries, game meats, and seafood, the chef fashions entrees that are light and flavorful. The souffles and too-rich desserts might add a few notches to your belt and some extra bucks to the bill, but they're worth it. The champagne Sunday brunch (10:30-2:30) is highly recommended. Summer hours are 11 a.m.-3 p.m. and 5-10; winter hours are 4:30-9:30 p.m.. After your meal, stop by the **Roaring Sea Gallery** adjacent to the restaurant.

Services And Information

Begin your travels here at **Battle Rock Information Center** on the west side of U.S. 101, (tel. 332-8055). The people here are especially friendly and helpful. The **post office** (Jackson and 7th, Port Orford, 97465; tel. 332-4251) is open 8:30-5:30. The fact that **Greyhound** (1034 Oregon St., Port Orford, 97465; tel. 332-1885) is located at the Port Orford Motel means you needn't worry about hours since there's always a clerk on duty.

BANDON AND VICINITY

In contrast to the glitzy tourist trappings of some of the larger coastal towns, Bandon-by-the-Sea is characterized by the style and grace of an earlier era. The glory that was Bandon is alive and well in Old Town, a picturesque collection of shops, galleries, restaurants, and historical memorabilia. A converted Coast Guard station houses the Coquillle River Museum whose placards tell the stories behind the scenes in this restored neighborhood.

The museum's exhibits also detail other aspects of the heritage of this quiet port city near the Coquille River. While logging, fishing, dairy products, and the harvest of cranberries have been the traditional mainstays of the local economy, in the early part of the century Bandon also enjoyed a brief tourism boom. In addition to being a summer retreat from the heat of the Willamette Valley, it was a port-of-call for thousands of San Francisco-to-Seattle steamship passengers. This era inspired such touristic venues as the Silver Spray dancehall and a natatorium housing a saltwater swimming pool. The golden age which began with the advent of large-scale steamship traffic in 1900 came to an abrupt end following a devastating fire of 1936. The blaze was started by the easily ignitable gorse weed, imported from Ireland (as was the town's name) in the mid-1800s. Dramatic descriptions of the townspeople fighting the flames with their backs to the sea earned the incident a citation as one of the top ten news stories of the year. The face-lift given Old Town decades later and the subsequent tourist influx conjured for many the image of the mythical phoenix rising from its ashes to fly again. On the wings of the recovery, Bandon has established itself as a town rooted in the past with its eyes on the future.

Today Bandon is a curious mixture of provincial backwater, destination resort, and new-age artist colony. Backpackers from all over the world have been flocking to this town of 3,000 in recent years because of its beaches, its cultural and recreational pursuits, and European-style hostelry. They coexist happily with the large population of retirees, award-winning artisans, and locals who seem to have cornered the market on late model pickups with gun racks.

SIGHTS

One of the most appealing things about Bandon is that most of its attractions are within walking distance of each other. In addition, on the periphery of town are a varied array of things to see and do.

West Coast Game Park

Six miles south of Bandon is the West Coast Game Park (Box 1330, Bandon, 97411; tel. 347-3106), the self-proclaimed largest wild-animal petting park in America. There are 450 animals, including bears, tiger cubs, chimps, camels, zebras, bison, and two snow leopards. Along with these exotics you'll also encounter such indigenous species as elk, bears, raccoons, and cougars. Even if you're not with a child, the opportunity to pet a pup, a cub, or a kit can bring out the kid in you. The park is open year-round but call during winter because of restricted hours of operation. Regular hours are 9:30 a.m. to dusk in summer, and 9:30 to 4:30 in other seasons. Adult tickets cost $5, and children get in for $2.75.

Coquille River Museum

The previously cited Coquille River Museum, also known as the Bandon Historical Society Museum (south end of 2nd St., tel. 347-2164), first traces the history of the Coquille Indian tribe and its forebears. The chronology continues with the steamers and the railroads that brought in white settlers. One room is devoted to Bandon's unofficial title as the "Cranberry Capital of Oregon." Black-and-white blowups showing women stooping over in the bogs to harvest the ripe berries are captioned with such *bon mots* as this one from an overseer: "I had 25 women picking for me, and I knew every one by her fanny." Color photos spanning five decades of cranberry festival princesses also adorn the walls. Another room traces "Bandon's Resort Years, 1900-1931," when the town was called the "Playground of the Pacific." The most compelling exhibits in the museum deal with the fires of 1914 and 1936. The museum's hours are Tues.-Sat., 1-4; Fri.-Sun. 1-4 during the winter. There is no admission fee.

Bandon Driftwood Museum, Old Town

Another exposition is Bandon Driftwood Museum, a collection of natural sculptures from gnarly root balls to whole tree trunks. It is housed at Big Wheel Farm Supply store on First Street in Old Town across from the boat basin. The hours are Mon.-Fri. 9-5:30; Sat. 9-5; Sun. 11-5.

Preservation buffs should check out Masonic Hall (2nd and Alabama), one of the few buildings to have survived both Bandon blazes. A photo in the museum shows the same building and surrounding structures on Alabama Street (then called Atwater) circa 1914. The photo depicts boardwalks leading to a woolen mill, old storefronts, a theater, and the Bandon Popular Hotel and Restaurant, outside which a horse and buggy await. This contrasts greatly with the contemporary scene. Today the Minute Cafe and a parking lot sit on the same spot as the classic structures in the photo. Nonetheless, a turn-of-the-century charm still pervades the architecture and ambience of the neighborhood. Housed within many of the Old Town shops and galleries are artisans pursuing such time-honored professions as glassblowing, leathercraft, and pottery.

Wine And Cheese

Nearby these traditional enterprises, you'll find a vintage undertaking of another sort. **The Bandon Tasting Room** (350 2nd St., Bandon, 97411; tel. 347-9129) is a good place to get introduced to Oregon viniculture. In addition to the chardonnay and cabernet of Jonicole Vineyards, the Tasting Room offers generic tastings of other Oregon wines. For an eye-opener, try John Marker's cabernet rosé, "Oregon's breakfast wine." The Tasting Room is a good orientation base from which to embark upon a tour of Umpqua Valley wineries. The storefront here is usually open daily 12-5, but always on weekends all year.

The wine here could be savored best with cheese from the nearby **Bandon Cheddar Cheese Plant** (on U.S. 101 just north of Old Town, Bandon, 97411; tel. 800-548-8961). This is the second-largest cheese factory in Oregon. The famous taste and texture of the Bandon Bar (an eight-ounce hunk) are the result of hand-cheddaring by a master cheesemaker. You can watch the process through a window in the gift store and sample the results, including fresh, squeaky cheese curds, every day of the week except Sunday, 8-5.

Boat Tours

Walk off your wine and cheese at the newly refurbished boat basin just north of Old Town. While strolling the docks here, you can watch locals land salmon, steelhead, and Dungeness crab. The commercial fleet steams into the Coquille River's estuary with holds full of salmon, tuna, or whitefish. If you want to get on the water yourself, the sternwheeler *Rose* (ticket office on Old Town docks, one block north of U.S. 101, Bandon, 97411; tel. 347-3942) will take you upriver to see shipwreck sites, Indian burial grounds, and other local color. Coquille River paddlewheel boats were the only way to Bandon until the road was built in the 1920s. Two-hour sternwheeler cruises leave at 12:30 and 3 p.m. mid-June through September. Call early for reservations on sunny days and weekends. Tickets are $8 for adults, $5 for kids 4-12, and $1 for those under three.

The Beach Loop

Seeing as how U.S. 101 follows an inland path for more than 50 miles between Coos Bay and Port Orford, you'll want to leave the highway in Bandon and take the Beach Loop along the oceanfront. There are several access roads which lead to Beach Loop Drive, each about one-quarter mile from each other. Most of the traffic seems to head west on 1st Street along the Coquille. Another popular approach is from 11th Street which heads toward Coquille Point. On the beach itself are rock formations with such evocative names as Elephant Rock, Garden of the Gods, and Cat and Kittens Rocks. The most eye-catching of all is **Face Rock,** Bandon's answer to New Hampshire's Old Man of the Mountain. This basalt monolith resembles the face of a woman looking at the sky. Indian legends say that she was a maiden frozen by an evil sea spirit. The whole grouping of seastacks looks like a surrealist chess set cast upon the waters.

Despite this array, the beach is surprisingly deserted. Perhaps this is due to the long, steep trails up from the water along other parts of the beach. In any case, this dearth of people can make for great beachcombing. Agates, driftwood, and tidepools full of starfish and anemone are commonly encountered here, along with birdwatching opportunities galore. Elephant Rock has a reputation as the Parthenon of puffins, while murres, oystercatchers, and other species proliferate the other offshore formations in varying concentrations.

ACTIVITIES

Bandon Stormwatchers (Box 1693, Bandon, 97411; tel. 347-2144/347-7246/347-2779) is a group that coordinates activities and natural history seminars out of the Bandon Community Center. The center is located near Beach Loop Drive just north of the Face Rock viewing area.

On Saturday afternoons January through April, show up just before 3 p.m. for meetings.

Bridwatchers flock to the **Bandon National Wildlife Refuge** (a.k.a. the Bandon Marsh) especially in the fall to take in what may be the prime birding site on the coast. Bar-tailed godwits and Mongolian plovers often join the usual assemblage of migrating shorebirds during October. Access is via unmarked trails off River Rd., bordering the Coquille River east of Bandon.

Bandon Beach Loop Stables (tel. 347-9242) is located four miles south of Old Town, just past Crooked Creek State Park. They rent horses by the hour ($10), day, or week for beach trail rides, with lessons available to beginners. In addition, kids can enjoy 15 minutes on a pony for $2 here. Fishing guides and gear can be arranged through **Bandon Bait Shop** (1st and Alabama, Bandon, 97411; tel. 347-3905) across from the boat basin. Clamming and crabbing info can also be procured from the youth hostel.

Just off the south end of Beach Loop Drive, **Bradley Lake** has good trout fishing and a boat ramp. It is protected from ocean winds by high dunes.

PRACTICALITIES

Accommodations
The expression "you can't go wrong" applies for price, view, cleanliness, and whatever else you're looking for in this town. Be aware that Bandon bills itself as "America's Storm-watching Capital,"

Bandon Ocean Wayside

PHOTO BY OREGON TOURISM DIVISION

BANDON ACCOMMODATIONS

Name	Address	Telephone	Price	Features
Bandon Beach Motel	110 11th St. S.W.	347-2103	$30-45	ocean view, restaurant, pets
Bandon Wayside Motel	ORE 42 S.	347-3421	$28-35	restaurant, pets
Caprice Motel	Route 1 Box 530	347-4494	$35-45	kitchenettes, pets, near restaurants and shops
Inn at Face Rock	3255 Beach Loop Rd.	347-9441	$55-105	full-service resort, golf, stables
La Kris Motel	U.S. 101 and 9th St.	347-3610	$28-58	wheelchair access, restaurant, lounge
Lamplighter Motel	40 North Ave.	347-4477	$26-54	kitchenettes, pets
Sea Star American Youth Hostel	375 2nd St.	347-9632	$9.50	ocean view, kitchenettes, laundry, board games, 10-15 minutes of chores required daily
Sea Star Guesthouse	370 1st St.	347-9632	$30-49	restaurant, laundry This is an extension of the hostel with nicer rooms facing the ocean and no chores.
Sunset Motel	1755 Beach Loop Rd.	347-2453	$29-70	wheelchair access, wood-paneled rooms, family suites, ocean views, restaurant, lounge
Windermere	3250 Beach Loop Rd.	347-3710	$35-65	ocean view, quiet, kitchenettes

and special packages are often available October until March.

Bed And Breakfast
Cliff Harbor Guest House (Box 769, Beach Loop Rd, Bandon, 97411; tel. 347-3956) is acclaimed by seasoned travelers as the premiere B&B on the southern Oregon coast. From May to November, reservations should be made two to three months in advance. Casually elegant, this retreat boasts a suite with sitting room and full breakfast for $80, and a self-contained studio with a 180-degree ocean view for $95.

Campgrounds

Bullard's Beach State Park (Box 25, Bandon, 97411; tel. 347-2209) is a great place to spend the night, fish, crab, bike, fly a kite, or picnic. The park has about 100 campsites with some hiker/ biker spaces. To get there, drive north of town on U.S. 101 for about a mile; just past the bridge on the west side of the highway is the park entrance. The beach itself is reached via a scenic two-mile drive paralleling the Coquille River. You'll also see campsites by the river. Electricity, picnic tables, and firegrills are provided. There are also a store, a cafe, a laundromat, an inviting sandy beach, and hiking trails. A side road going out to the north jetty takes you to the octagonal **Coquille Lighthouse** built in 1896. It was abandoned in 1939, but has been refurbished and is open in summer, 12-5, for inspection. Etchings of ships that made it across Bandon's treacherous bar, and those that didn't, greet you as you enter. The fee for camping at Bullard's Beach along the Coquille is $9 a night, and hookups go for $10.

Food

Bandon seems to have quite a few restaurants which serve up specialty dishes that break the mold while not breaking your budget. **Wheelhouse Seafood Grill** (1st and Chicago, Bandon, 97411; tel. 347-7933) deep-fries their fish (they also grill and broil) with a beer batter that doesn't mask the taste of the food. **Andrea's Old Town Cafe** (160 Baltimore, Bandon, 97411; tel. 347-2111) features such items as the restaurateur's home-raised lamb as well as blintzes filled with local raspberries ($4.95). The **Chicago Street Eatery** (130 Chicago St., Bandon, 97411; tel. 347-4215) ladles out a distinctive vegetarian minestrone soup garnished with popcorn that comes with moderately priced hearty Italian entrees. International flavors also predominate at the **Sea Star Coffeehouse** (375 2nd St., Bandon, 97411; tel. 347-9533) with European breakfast plates, croissants, pita sandwiches, fruit dessert crepes, soups, salads, and espresso drinks.

Finally, there is good ol' American food in Bandon. Start the day with excellent $2 breakfasts at the **Minute Cafe** (145 N. 2nd Ave, Bandon, 97411; tel. 347-2707) and diner-style entrees at lunch and dinner. **Bandon Boatworks** (275 Lincoln Ave. S.W., Bandon, 97411; tel. 347-2111) has fresh seafood and steaks for lunch and dinner. For a dinner appetizer, try their squid in the chef's secret recipe batter ($3.50). The Boatworks has views of the Coquille Lighthouse and an intimate lounge with entertainment. A change of pace here is Sunday brunch and Mexican food (dinner only). The restaurant is closed Monday.

Entertainment

Bandon has several theater groups and a well-regarded 350-seat performance center, **Harbor Hall** (325 2nd St., Bandon, 97411; tel 347-4404). Arlo Guthrie, Doc Watson, Jerry Jeff Walker, Bo Diddley, Taj Mahal, and Riders in the Sky have

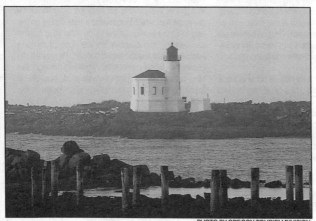

the lighthouse at Bullards Beach

PHOTO BY OREGON TOURISM DIVISION

appeared here along with a local professional repertory group, Encore Presenters. In addition to light comedy and musicals, Encore also presents InsomniACTs, an after-dinner late-night theater with mime, blackout skits, reader theater, dances, etc. The programs of Encore and the other theater groups can be found through the daily paper, *Western World,* and the chamber of commerce.

Less posh, but equally as dynamic as Harbor Hall/Encore Presenters, is the Breuer Building's (1st St. in Old Town) **Whimsical University of Bandon.** This is a loose (in more ways than one) gathering of artists, writers, craftspeople, and actors who generate a constant flow of outrageous art shows, performance pieces, and poetry readings.

For nightlife, there's **Lloyd's Lounge** and the **Pastime Tavern** located side by side on 2nd Street. Lloyd's sells hard liquor, has weekend bands, and dancing as well as low-stakes black-jack. The Pastime features Rainier beer on tap at 60 cents a glass and 80 cents a pint as well as a good jukebox.

Events

The biggest weekend for Bandonians comes in mid to late October when the **Cranberry Festival** brings the whole town together in a parade, crafts fair, and the Bandon High Cranberry Bowl in which the local footballers take on traditional rival Coquille High.

During the Christmas holiday season, the merchants of Old Town and fisherfolk deck their stores and boats with white lights in the traditional **Festival of Lights.** Particularly striking is the Coquille Lighthouse lit up like a multicolored Christmas tree.

On Memorial Day, the Bandon Storm-watchers organize the annual **Wine and Seafood Festival.** On the same weekend, competitors in the

CRANBERRIES

From the vantage point of U.S. 101 between Port Orford and ten miles north of Bandon, you'll notice what appears to be reddish-tinged ground in flood-irrigated fields. If you get close, you'll see cranberries, a small evergreen that creeps along the ground, and sends out runners that take root. Along the runners, upright branches six to eight inches long are formed on which pink flowers and fruits develop. These berries are maintained in bogs to satisfy their tremendous need for water and to protect them against insects and winter cold. Bandon leads Oregon in this crop, with an output ranking third in the nation. Oregon berries are often used in juice production by Ocean Spray because of their deep red pigment and high vitamin C content.

It is possible to arrange a visit to see some of these bogs. The most interesting times fall during the late autumn harvest. Call Alene Kent (tel. 347-3184) to watch the "wet-pick" harvest and Bobbie and Ed Aasen (tel. 347-3230) who "dry-pick" their bogs. Contact the Bandon Visitor Center for other leads to receptive growers. A sweeter encounter can be found at **Cranberry Sweets** (1st and Chicago Streets, Bandon, 97411). Herein are confections ranging from cranberry fudge to cranberry truffles. Sugar fans will be glad to know it's open seven days a week, 9-5.

Oregon bogs were producing wild cranberries when Lewis and Clark first traded with the Indians for them in 1805. Shortly thereafter, cultivated bogs were developed in Massachusetts, which like Oregon has acid soils with lots of organic materials conducive to berry production. By the California gold rush of 1849, East Coast growing and harvesting techniques had transformed Bandon's marshes into commercial cranberry bogs. In the years to come, much of the modern equipment for harvesting these bogs was developed in Bandon. Wet-picking, for instance, is facilitated by the water reel, which is rotated to create eddies on the bog to shake berries off the vines. After they float to the surface, the cranberries are pushed by long booms toward a submerged hopper. They are then conveyor-belted onto trucks. Walking through the bogs without trampling the berries is made possible by fastening wooden platforms with short pegs to the soles of boots.

Without such innovations, Thanksgiving dinner wouldn't be the same. In order to bring the enormous annual volume of cranberries to the dinner table for the holidays, all these harvesting techniques as well as processing and packaging technology are called into play. Coincidentally, Bandon's berries often join turkeys from the Northwest's leading poultry farms in the Willamette Valley and southern Oregon for that traditional November repast.

sandcastle contest create amazing sculptures out of sand, water, and imagination. This takes place on the beach off Beach Loop Drive at Seabird Lane. Construction starts a 9 a.m.; judging is at 1 p.m. Call 347-9616 for more information. A fish fry is the big event of Bandon's **Fourth of July.** Later, at dusk, fireworks are launched across the Coquillle to burst above the river.

Services And Information

The **Bandon Chamber of Commerce** (2nd and Chicago, Bandon, 97411; tel. 347-9616) has an authoritative 63-page guide and a large annotated pictographic map of the town. The **post office** (one block east of U.S. 101, Bandon, 97411, tel. 347-3406) is open Mon.-Fri 9-5. **Greyhound** (Bandon Book and Stationery, 610 2nd St., Bandon, 97411; tel. 347-3324) is only one block from the hostel. It's open Mon.-Sat., 9-5:30. *The Western World* (1185 Baltimore St., Box 248, Bandon, 97411; tel. 347-2423), is a useful compendium of cultural/recreational goings-on here. **Southern Coos General Hospital** (640 W. 4th, Bandon, 97411; tel. 347-2426) features an ocean view that in itself is therapeutic, as well as an emergency room and facilities for coronary/respiratory care.

NORTH FROM BANDON

You can escape the tedium of U.S. 101's inland route to Coos Bay by taking the Seven Devil's Beach route a few miles north of Bandon. This road will eventually get you to Coos Bay by way of Charleston, a fishing village which sits closer to the ocean than its larger neighbors to the east of U.S. 101. En route, beaches, state parks, and an estuarine preserve make the drive interesting.

Whiskey Run

The first beach encountered is Whiskey Run, whose ore-bearing sands spread gold fever down the south coast in the early 1850s. As many as 2,000 miners worked here until a storm washed away the deposit. Other forms of beachcombing at Whiskey Run and on the beaches to the north are still thriving, however. Agate-hunting, after a season of winter storms, and clamming make these solitary shorelines ideal places to forget the cares of the world. The only reminder of humankind is a life-affirming one. The sight of a

wind-energy farm's pinwheels above the beach is evidence of the continuing effort to find alternatives to fossil fuels. Enough energy is generated here to supply several hundred Oregon homes.

South Slough Estuarine Preserve

From the beaches, the road climbs northeastward toward the South Slough Estuarine Preserve, whose visitor center displays and trails can make an hour pass profitably. The center looks out over several estuarine arms of Coos Bay, the largest nautical harbor between San Francisco Bay and the Columbia River. These vital wetlands nurture a vast web of life which is detailed by the placards captioning the center's exhibits. The northbound traveler's first annotated graphic introduction to the coastal ecosystem is presented by the "10-minute trail" in back of the visitor center. The various conifers and the understory are clearly labeled along the gently sloping half-mile loop. Branch trails lead down toward the water for an up-close view of the estuary itself. Down by the slough, you may see elks grazing in marshy meadows and bald eagles circling above while Homo sapiens harvest oysters and shrimp in these waters of life.

Charleston

From South Slough, you drive four miles on Seven Devils Road into the little town of Charleston, which makes few pretensions of being anything other that what it really is—the third largest commercial fishing port on the Oregon coast. Four processing plants here can or cold-pack tuna, salmon, crab, oysters, shrimp, and other kinds of seafood. The town might occasionally smell of fish, but the few restaurants and lodgings here are a good dollar value. Moreover, a post office, a laundromat, and a visitor info center are all conveniently crammed together on the main street, the Cape Arago Highway.

Sunset Bay, Shore Acres, And Cape Arago State Parks

There is a portion of this road which heads south and west of Charleston to some of the most idyllic beaches and interesting state parks on the coast. Pick up this stretch of highway close by the junction of Seven Devils Road. Among the several beaches on the road to Cape Arago, **Sunset Bay State Park** is the big attraction. This is because its sheltered shallow cove is warm and calm enough for swimming, a rarity in the Pacific north of Santa Barbara, California. In addition to swimmers, divers, surfers, and boaters, many people come here to watch the sunset. Close by the park is one of three golf courses within a 10-mile radius. A four-mile cliffside trail from Sunset Beach south is the best way to appreciate the seastacks and islands between here and Cape Arago.

Enough islands are visible less than a mile south at **Shore Acres State Park**, however, to fill an afternoon. The setting of the park is the grounds of a lumber magnate's turn-of-the-century estate. Formal oriental gardens here are in themselves compelling attractions, but the headland's rim is actually more dramatic. Whitecaps appear to hang suspended upon contact with the rock embankments at the base of Shore Acre's sandstone cliffs. The orange, brown, and buff-colored strata of these escarpments heighten the visual effect. Although the original Simpson mansion burned to the ground in 1921, the grounds

are still kept up by the state, which was ceded the land by the family. A restored gardener's cottage with antique furnishings sits in back of the gardens. It is open for exhibition only from Dec. 9-31, with music, entertainment, and refreshments. The history of the Simpsons is really the history of the Coos Bay/Charleston/North Bend area, and is captioned beneath period photos in the observation tower and in a small enclosure at the west end of the floral displays. Also in the gardens, note the copper egret sculptures and the greenhouse for rare plants from warmer climes.

A few miles south is **Cape Arago State Park**. Locals have made much of the fact that it was a possible landing site of the English pirate Sir Francis Drake in 1579, and have put a plaque here commemorating same. Such speculation is not just confined to this part of the south coast. At any rate, beachcombers can make their own discoveries in the tidal pools which abound here. (For more information on Cape Arago, see "The Bay Area" following.)

THE BAY AREA:
COOS BAY, CHARLESTON, NORTH BEND

The towns around the harbor of Coos Bay refer to themselves collectively as the "Bay Area." In contrast to their namesake in California, the Oregon version is not exactly the Athens of the state. Nonetheless, the visitor will be impressed by the area's beautiful beaches, including the largest oceanfront dunes in the world, as well as scenic and historic state parks. Because much of this natural beauty is on the periphery of the industrialized core of the Bay Area, it's easy to miss. All the motorist sees entering Coos Bay/North Bend on U.S. 101 are the dockside lumber mills and foreign vessels anchored at the world's largest lumber port.

The historical antecedents for this scene were laid over a century ago when the region's mills supplied lumber to a gold rush-era housing boom in San Francisco. Heading up this effort was Simpson's lumber company, and later on, the family shipping concern. By the turn of the century, Simpson ships were hauling lumber to 11 nations. Also during that time, companies such as Weyerhauser were building their mills by the Union Pacific tracks here. Today, the Bay Area is in transition along with other western Oregon towns dependent upon tim-

ber. The region's wealth of diversions and what is probably the mildest weather of any major city in Oregon is being promoted to draw tourists and retirees, and to recruit new businesses.

SIGHTS

Along The Coast

To many people, an estuary is a place where you get a boat stranded in a gooey mudflat. More often than not, however, the mix of freshwater and saltwater represents one of the richest ecosystems on earth, capable of producing five times more plant material than a cornfield of comparable size while supporting great numbers of fish and wildlife. The south slough of Coos Bay is the largest such web of life on the Oregon coast. **The South Slough Estuarine Preserve Visitor Center** (off Cape Arago Highway on Seven Devil's Road in Charleston, tel. 888-5558) will help you coordinate a canoe trip through the estuary and offers guided hikes as well. Paralleling the drive to the visitor center is the **estuary study**

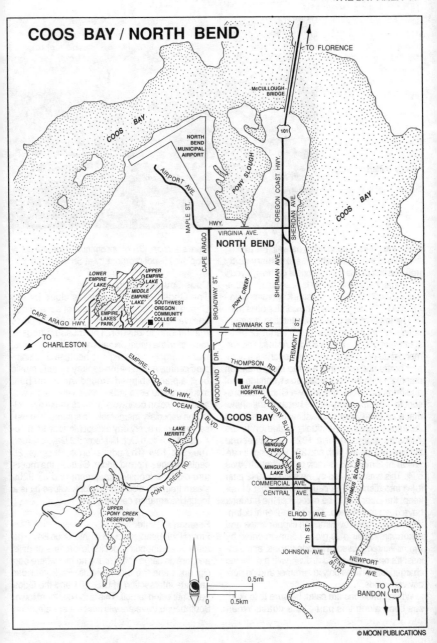

COOS BAY / NORTH BEND

TO FLORENCE

McCULLOUGH BRIDGE

COOS BAY

NORTH BEND MUNICIPAL AIRPORT

101

PONY SLOUGH

AIRPORT AVE.

MAPLE ST.

OREGON COAST HWY.

SHERIDAN AVE.

COOS BAY

HWY.

VIRGINIA AVE.

NORTH BEND

CAPE ARAGO

SHERMAN AVE.

BROADWAY ST.

PONY CREEK

LOWER EMPIRE LAKE

UPPER EMPIRE LAKE

MIDDLE EMPIRE LAKE

EMPIRE LAKES PARK

SOUTHWEST OREGON COMMUNITY COLLEGE

CAPE ARAGO HWY.

NEWMARK ST.

TREMONT ST.

TO CHARLESTON

EMPIRE-COOS BAY HWY.

WOODLAND DR.

THOMPSON RD.

OCEAN BLVD.

Bay Area Hospital

KOOSBAY BLVD.

COOS BAY

LAKE MERRITT

PONY CREEK RD.

UPPER PONY CREEK RESERVOIR

MINGUS PARK

MINGUS LAKE

10th ST.

COMMERCIAL AVE.

CENTRAL AVE.

ELROD AVE.

7th ST.

JOHNSON AVE.

EVANS BLVD.

ISTHMUS SLOUGH

NEWPORT AVE.

TO BANDON

101

0   0.5mi
0   0.5km

© MOON PUBLICATIONS

Oscar Patterson Bridge

tuary and offers guided hikes as well. Paralleling the drive to the visitor center is the **estuary study trail**, the first of a large network of pathways you'll encounter here. The center is open daily in summer 8:30-4:30. In the off season, it operates Mon.-Fri. 8:30-4:30, Sept.-May. The admission is free.

The jewel of the previously detailed "tremendous trio" of Oregon state parks about 12 miles southwest of Coos Bay is **Shore Acres.** This former estate of Louis J. Simpson began as a summer home and grew into a three-story mansion complete with an indoor heated swimming pool and large ballroom. Originally a Christmas present to his wife, Shore Acres became the showplace of the Oregon coast, with formal and Japanese gardens eventually added on to the 743-acre estate. After a 1921 fire, a second smaller (two stories high and 224 feet long) incarnation of Simpson's "shack by the beach" was built. This was acquired by the state in 1942 after it fell into disrepair. Because of the cost of upkeep, the latter had to be razed, but the gardens have been maintained. The international botanical bounty culled by Simpson clipper ships and schooners is still in its glory, complemented by award-winning roses, rhododendrons, and azaleas. It's open year-round till dusk, with a dollar fee charged for vehicles only in summer and on holiday weekends.

When conditions are calm, be sure to look for sea lions along this part of the coast. When there's a storm, it's not uncommon to feel the spray atop the 75-foot promontory at Shore Acres.

Coos County Museum
The Coos County museum is close by the Conde McCullough Bridge, one of several distinctive 1930's-era high-wire acts by Oregon's master bridge-builder. The museum houses more than the usual bric-a-brac from earlier eras, thanks largely to the region's heritage as a shipping center. A turn-of-the-century Regina music box, a piano shipped around the Horn, boat model miniatures, a jade Chinese plaque as well as Coos Indian beadwork/artifacts make this collection especially memorable. In summer, the museum is open every day except Monday from 10-4, Sun 1-4. From Oct. till Memorial Day, it's open Tue.-Sat. 10-4. The admission is 50 cents, 25 cents for ages 12 and under. Outside the museum, old-time logging equipment and a 1920s steam train are also worth a look. Close by is a tourist information center.

Seaman's Center
From North Bend, head south into Coos Bay. The route is an unending dockside detritus of mills and foreign cargo ships giving no hint where one city ends and the other begins. Park your car near the intersection of U.S. 101 and the Coos Bay/Charleston turnoff. This is the center of town. Southbound travelers will notice a storefront on

the right-hand side of the street with an orange model pagoda in the window. Seaman's Center (171 N. Broadway, Coos Bay, 97420) is a cafe/ club where old salts mingle with foreign sailors and anyone else interested in a wealth of sea lore and camaraderie. Model ships made by retired seamen, curios from the back alleys of Oriental ports, as well as coins and curios from the harbor cities of the world fill this treasure chest of maritime memorabilia. What's more, matey, your ears will be filled with some scintillating sagas. Since this center is also founded by an evangelical group, you might also hear the Gospel. The center is open every day after 5 p.m. when ships are in port. There is no admission. Across the street is a tourist information center.

The Harbor: Milling Around

Due to the decline in the supply of lumber and the subsequent mill closures, the Weyerhauser and other forest-product facility tours are currently not operating. But it's still fun to watch the ships docking and the portside wood chip piles growing dozens of feet overnight. The latter are Oregon's number-one forest product export. What had been considered surfeit slivers can now be made into a low-grade paper with the addition of chemicals during processing aboard the Japanese factory ships in the harbor. What's left onshore is often enough "hog fuel"to provide sufficient B.T.U.s to heat a mill. Given the return on these chips, locals call these piles the "million-dollar view." Another roadside perspective on the mills is the sight of "log broncs." These short, powerful boats are highly maneuverable. The broncs evoke the "little engine that could" as they move the floating logjams from the millpond to the conveyors into the mill.

House Of Myrtlewood

To see something closer to a finished product, take the House of Myrtlewood (located just off U.S.101 at the south end of town, Box 457, Coos Bay, 97420; tel. 267-7804) factory tour. Myrtlewood carving is an Oregon folk art with a long history.

In 1869, the golden spike marking the completion of the nation's first transcontinental railroad was driven into a highly polished myrtlewood tie. Novelist Jack London was so taken by the beauty of the wood's swirling grain that he ordered an entire suite of furniture. Hudson Bay trappers used myrtlewood leaves to brew tea as a remedy for chills.

During the Depression years, the city of North Bend issued myrtlewood coins after the only bank in town failed. The coins ranged from 50 cents to $10, and are still redeemable—though they are worth far more as collector items. The House of Myrtlewood tour shows you how an uncut myrtlewood log gets fashioned into bowls, clocks, tables, and other utensils. No admission is charged for this 25-minute guided run through a working factory. After you're done, the store itself is a delight, with Oregon gourmet foods and crafts supplementing the quality woodwork.

Coos Art Museum

The Coos Art Museum (235 Anderson Ave., Coos Bay, 97420; tel. 267-3901) is the Oregon coast's only art museum. It's open Tue.-Fri. 11 a.m.-5 p.m., and on weekends 12-4. Just south of here is the *Marshfield Sun* **Printing Museum** (1049 N. Front St., Coos Bay, 97420; tel. 269-1363) at the junction of Front St. and U.S. 101. This newspaper was in operation from1891-1944. In 1944, Marshfield became Coos Bay. From an old print shop on the first floor, proceed upstairs to vintage photos of early Marshfield and exhibits on printing and newspaper history. It's open June-Aug, Mon., Wed., and Fri, 1-4, and the last Sunday of each month (except December). There is no charge.

Golden And Silver Falls State Park

Twenty-five miles northeast of Coos Bay in the Coast Range is Golden and Silver Falls State Park. Two spectacular waterfalls are showcased in this little-known gem of a park. Getting there involves driving east of Coos Bay along the Coos River, crossing to its north bank, and continuing along the Millicoma River through the community of **Allegany**. To find your way from Coos Bay, look for the Alleghany/Eastside exit off U.S. 101. Beyond Allegany, continue up the East Fork of the Millicoma River to its junction with Glenn Creek, which ultimately leads to the park. The narrow windy roads make this trip unsuitable for a wide-body vehicle. Ignore signs indicating that the bridge is out because the access is always passable.

You can reach each waterfall by way of two half-mile trails. Both 200-foot cataracts lie about a mile apart from one another, and although both are about the same height, each has a distinct character. For most of the year, Silver Falls is more visually arresting because it flows in a near semicircle around a knob near its top. During or just after the winter rains however, Golden Falls's thunderous sound makes it more awe-inspiring. Along the trails, look for the beautifully delicate maidenhair fern. En route, **Millicoma Myrtle Grove State Park** makes a fine prelude or appendix to a tour of the House of Myrtlewood Factory.

RECREATION AND EVENTS

There are two public golf courses in the Bay Area. One, the **Sunset Bay Golf Course** (11001 Cape Arago Highway, Charleston, 97420; tel. 888-9301) is a nine-holer and has been described as "one of the most interesting courses anywhere" by *Golf Oregon Magazine*. The other is the 18-hole **Kentuck Golf Course** (Kentuck Inlet, North Bend, 97459; tel. 756-4464).

Fishing charters, bay cruises, whalewatching, and the like can be arranged through **Charleston Charters** (Box 5457, Charleston, 97420; tel. 888-4846); please call in advance.

The bulk of the Bay Area's special events fall in July and August. The first event of note in summer is the **Oregon Coast Music Festival** (Box 663 Coos Bay, 97420; tel. 269-4150) in mid-July. Coos Bay is the most common performance venue of these south coast classical, jazz, and folk concerts. Tickets cost $8, $6 for seniors.

In late August, the everpresent blackberry is celebrated with the **Blackberry Arts Festival.** Food and winetasting booths and street artists fill the downtown. Picking the fruit itself can best be enjoyed just south of Charleston on the Cape Arago Highway (but everyone has their own secret patch). Avoid picking near roads, as the lead concentrations in the fruits from exhaust fumes tend to be higher.

In mid-September, perhaps the best-known Bay Area personality of this century, Steve Prefontaine, is honored with a 10-kilometer race. Prefontaine was a world-class runner whose gutsy style of running and record performances made him a major sports personality until his death at 24 years of age in 1974. Many top-flight runners pay homage by taking part in the race. For more

information on this and the previous listings, contact the chamber of commerce (see "Information And Services below).

The major airport on the south coast hosts North Bend's **Air Show** (1321-D Airport Way, North Bend, 97459; tel. 756-1723) at the beginning of August. The show itself occurs between 12-3 p.m., but the festival gets off the ground with a pancake feed at 8 a.m.

PRACTICALITIES

Accommodations
Some people take umbrage at the fact that many accommodations here face industrial sites. Nevertheless, there is no shortage of low-cost places to stay and noise is seldom a factor.

Although not blessed with the aesthetic appeal of Bandon's hostel, the **Sea Gull A.Y.H.** (438 Elrod St., Coos Bay, 97420; tel. 267-6114) is inexpensive at $9.50 per nonmember. This includes a sumptuous breakfast and dinner. From the corner of U.S. 101 and the Greyhound station, go toward the ocean on 4th Street to Elrod and the blue church housing the facility. The hostel is open Memorial Day to Sept. 10th, and requires some chores as is customary with all A.Y.H. lodgings.

Over in Charleston is a lodging within walking distance of fishing, charter boats, clamming, and dock crabbing. **Capt. John's Motel** (8061 Kingfisher Drive, Charleston, 97420; tel. 888-4041) is clean, quiet, and has some units with kitchenettes. Close by is a special fish/clam/crab cleaning station and with any luck, your dinner. Staying in Charleston also puts you close to state parks and within easy reach of laundry and postal services as well as temperatures which are warmer than Coos Bay in winter and cooler in summer. The rates run $30-50 in summer and $25-45 in winter; reserve well in advance for July and August.

Situated at a high elevation out of the coastal wind and fog is the aptly named **Highland's Bed And Breakfast** (608 Ridge Rd., North Bend, 97459; tel. 756-0300). The glass and cedar home has a huge deck which overlooks meadows, a river, and thousands of acres of the Coast Range. Breakfast on deck is as much a feast for the palate as it is for the eyes. A few miles from U.S.

101 and nearby sand dunes, beaches, and fine restaurants, Highland's still gives the feeling of being serenely remote. All rooms have antique furniture and private baths (one with a whirlpool tub). There is also an adjoining kitchen and family room with satellite TV and library. The rates are $55-65.

Another spendier alternative is the **Coos Bay Red Lion** (1313 Bayshore Dr., Coos Bay, 97459; tel 267-4141). Red Lion is a luxury chain in the West and in terms of creature comforts, they're hard to beat. Large rooms with immense beds, thick pile carpet, and everything else in the way of little extras are characteristic of these units. The Coos Bay Red Lion is also distinguished by having one of the best restaurants in town, a lounge with quality entertainment, and a happy hour with complimentary hors d'oeuvres. The units closest to the dining room, lobby, and lounge in this two-story motel are often snatched up by tour groups, except for the rooms by the pool. The rates range between $55-85.

Campgrounds

Cape Arago (south of Charleston, tel. 888-5353) has a county park with a few hiker/biker sites with beautiful views at no charge. Even though **Sunset Bay State Park**'s (for reservations write 13030 Cape Arago Highway, Coos Bay, 97420; tel. 888-5353) crowds can make it seem like a trailer park in midsummer, the proximity of Oregon's only major swimming beach on the ocean keep occupants of the 108 tent sites and 29 trailer sites here happy. There's also a laundromat and showers. Sites are $8, RV's $10.

The first campsites encountered south of Charleston on the Cape Arago Highway are found at **Bastendorff Beach County Park** (tel. 888-5353). For $7, 25 tent sites and 30 trailer sites enjoy drinking water, woodstoves, flush toilets, and hot showers (for an extra two bits). Fishing and hiking are the recreational attractions. As with the previously mentioned campgrounds on the Cape Arago Highway, it's open all year.

Food

Oregon's Bay Area abounds in places where your nutritional needs can be met if not in fine style, then at least at the right price. Take the Safeway-Fred Meyer complex (4th and Commercial St., Coos Bay, 97420; tel. 267-3512) across from the post office: between Safeway's salad bar and the fast food places in the pavilion shared by the two stores, you needn't go hungry.

There is also no shortage of seafood places in this part of the coast, but you'll find the freshest, cheapest maritime morsels close by to where they're caught. **The Sea Basket** (Charleston Boat Basin, Charleston, 97420; tel. 888-5711) typifies the good seafood, fast service, and relatively low prices in these parts. Oysters are especially tasty in this restaurant, with two noted breeding farms close by. This and other fish dinners (halibut, scallops, prawns, etc.) with potatoes or rice and salad usually don't run you more than $7. The fluorescent glare above the cafeteria-style tables frequented by fishermen in work-blackened denims may not count much for atmosphere, but you'll leave satisfied. **The Portside** (opposite Captain John's Motel, Charleston Boat Basin, Charleson, 97420; tel. 888-5544) close by has won Silver Spoon Awards from the Diners Club the past three years. Fine dining in Charleston might seem a contradiction in terms, but the chance to select your own lobsters and crabs out of a tank, along with the sight of the fleet unloading other dinners just outside the door, would whet the appetite of any gourmet.

Even though the **Blue Heron Bistro** (110 W. Commercial, Coos Bay, 97420; tel. 267-3933) is located in the heart of downtown Coos Bay, it evokes dining experiences in the San Francisco Bay Area or some other place far from this logging port. This impression can come from opening the door to the restaurant, or opening their menu. The restaurant's tile floors, newspapers on library-style posts, and international posters adorning the walls are in keeping with a European-influenced bill-of-fare. The extensive menu's eclectic array ranges from Greek salad to Cajun-style blackened fish and emphasizes the freshest ingredients and a creative interpretation whenever possible. "Expensive," I hear the reader thinking, but it's not really . . . for not appreciably more money than you'd pay on a high ticket at Denny's, you can enjoy an oasis of refinement in "Timbertown, U.S.A."

The **Coos Bay Red Lion**'s (tel. 267-4141, ext. 305) dining room's extra-thick cuts of prime rib and flambé items prepared tableside are as much a treat to look at as to taste. This restaurant is an "in" place to eat out when there's a special occasion here, so make reservations.

Information And Services

With over 16,000 people, the Bay Area is the population hub of the coast. As such, it has a large array of services available. **Coos Bay Chamber of Commerce** (50 E. Central, Coos Bay, 97420; tel. 260-0215/800-762-6278) is located five blocks west from U.S. 101 off Commercial Avenue. It's open Mon.-Fri. 9 a.m.-7 p.m., weekends 10-4. From Sept.-May hours are Mon.-Sat. 9-5, closed on Sun. North Bend's **information center** is just south of the harbor bridge (138 Sherman Ave., North Bend, 97459; tel. 756-4613). It's open Mon.-Fri. 8:30-5, Sat. 10-3, and Sun. 10-4. From Labor Day to Memorial Day the center is not open on weekends. Another information resource is the **Oregon State Parks** office (115 S. 5th, Coos Bay, 97420; tel. 269-9410).

To get out of town, head to the Tioga Hotel's **Greyhound** depot (tel. 267-6517). The terminal is open Mon.-Fri. 7-4:30, Sat. 7-3, and Sun. 7-8 a.m. If Greyhound doesn't fit into your plans, consider the **North Bend Airport** (1321-D Airport Way, North Bend, 97459). Horizon (tel. 756-2170) flies to or from Eugene and Portland almost every day of the week, and on occasion, to Salem and Seattle. To get to the airport, follow the signs on the road between Charleston and North Bend.

Within the city the Shuttle (tel. 267-4521) offers low-cost transport and scenic/historical tours. There is no set schedule but it's on call 24 hours (roundtrip within the city can be had for $5, and the fare to Shore Acres one way is $7).

The Coos Bay Public Library (525 W. Anderson, Coos Bay, 97420; tel 267-1101) is open Mon-Thur. 1-4, Fri. 10-5, and Sat. 12-5. For **medical emergencies,** Tel-Med (1775 Thompson Rd., Coos Bay, 97420; tel. 269-2313) and the ambulance (tel. 269-1151) will get help fast. Help Line (tel. 269-5910) gives referrals. In a big city, you might occasionally need the **police** (tel. 269-1151). The **post office** (4th and Golden, Coos Bay, 97420; tel. 267-4514) is open Mon-Fri. 8:30-5.

REEDSPORT/WINCHESTER BAY

If you're about to go fishing or coming back from a dunes hike, you'll appreciate a hot meal and a clean low-priced motel room in Reedsport. Otherwise this town of several thousand people might seem like a strange mirage of cut-rate motels, taverns, and burger joints in the midst of the Oregon Dunes NRA.

It originally evolved because of its proximity to the Umpqua River. Jedediah Smith explored this country in the 1820s after the Hudson Bay Company's John McLoughlin theorized that the Umpqua River might be the fabled Northwest Passage. Even though it wasn't, this river is still one of the great fishing streams of the state. Zane Grey avoided writing about it, lavishing the publicity instead upon the Rogue to divert people from his favorite steelhead spots. At any rate, Winchester Bay's Salmon Harbor Marina has given the whole area new life in recent years, following hard times precipitated by the decline in timber revenues. Salmon Harbor sits at the mouth of the Umpqua, the largest river between San Francisco Bay and the Columbia.

SIGHTS

Just south of Winchester Bay is **Umpqua Lighthouse State Park.** Even though the 1893 lighthouse isn't open to the public, there's a county museum (tel. 440-4500) there with marine and timber exhibits, open Wed. through Sat. from May to Sept., 10-5, and on Sun. from 1-5.

Close by the Dunes NRA Headquarters on U.S. 101 south of Reedsport is ORE 38, which takes you inland to Cottage Grove. Oregon's "foremost motorcycle road" (according to Harley Davidson) goes through pastoral countryside along the Umpqua on a well-maintained highway. One highlight is the **Dean Creek Elk Preserve** just outside of Reedsport. There are about 55 head of Roosevelt elk here, the largest species of this animal in the world. They graze the preserve's marshy pastures in full view of the highway. Further east are a number of historical placards by landmarks in the one-time shipping center of **Scotsburg.** Cargo ships from this town supplied San Francisco markets with meat, milk, and produce between 1856 and the early 20th century.

Umpqua River Lighthouse

PHOTO BY OREGON TOURISM DIVISION

PRACTICALITIES

Accommodations

Bargain rooms are easy to find in Reedsport off U.S. 101, but forget about ambience and seclusion. For the latter, check out the small towns close by.

Of the half-dozen motels which sit off of U.S. 101 in Reedsport, the **Fir Grove Motel** (2178 Winchester Ave., Reedsport, 97467; tel. 271-4848) is slightly less expensive, but comparable in comfort to the other lodgings. The rooms go for $34 for a single, $38 for a double, and about $10 less on each rate in winter.

For about the same money, the **Winchester Bay Motel** (4th and Broadway, Winchester Bay 97467; tel. 271-4871) puts you next to the water. Reserve ahead of time in fishing season.

A few miles north of Reedsport in **Gardiner** is another lodging alternative with more character than motel row for not significantly more money. **The Gardiner Guest House** (401 Front, Box 222, Gardiner 97441; tel. 271-4005) is located in a cute, tranquil paper-mill town which sits close by the confluence of the Smith and Umpqua rivers. The 1883 home was built by local bigwig and state Senator Albert Reed, for whom Reedsport was named. The recently remodeled home still has the Victorian "feel" without lacking in modern comforts. Choose between a room with the facility down the

hall for $35 ($45 peak season), or a view room with private bath for $55 ($65 peak). A large home-cooked breakfast is included in the rates.

Gardiner was created in the wake of a shipwreck. The *Bostonian* (owned by Mr. Gardiner) was dashed against the rocks at the mouth of the Umpqua in 1856 and from its remnants the first wooden structure in this area was built. It was soon joined by other white-painted homes and facilities for a port on the Umpqua. While this "white city by the sea" declined in importance when the highway elevated Reedsport to regional hub status, the homes still bear the same color scheme from the earlier era.

Food

Reedsport is not the culinary center of the coast. However, there are some intriguing alternatives in surrounding Dune Country.

Ten miles south of Reedsport is a fisherman's friend, the **Stable Cafe** (at the corner of 8th and Park, Lakeside, 97449; tel. 759-3322). Generous breakfast portions at a good price in an old-time homey atmosphere attract a following to this little diner on the shores of Ten Mile Lakes.

Up the road in Winchester Bay, lunch and dinner at the **Seafood Grotto** also offer the touch of home. This family restaurant relies on the local fleet to supply the ingredients for homemade cioppino, clam chowder, and what might be the best grilled salmon in Dune Country. The menu has a range of prices and selections to suit a variety of budgets and appetites.

Another Winchester Bay restaurant with a following is the **Seven Seas Cafe** (10 4th St., tel. 271-4381). This is where fisherfolk gather for huge helpings of seafood and short-order specialties at low prices. Ship components, navigation charts, and vintage photos provide a backdrop for fish stories and Marilyn's (the proprietress) maritime trivia test. Just walk to the end of "A" dock to climb aboard. It's open after 2 p.m. and closed Wednesday and Thursday.

If you're looking for something to do after dinner in Winchester Bay, check out the dance floor, ping pong tables, pool, and insipid video games at the **Oasis Lounge** (8th and Clearlake St., tel. 271-9976). There's a decent 24-hour restaurant on the premises. As for Reedsport, locals praise the **Windjammer** (1280 Highway Ave., tel. 271-5415) for its seafood and salad bar. Try an overstuffed omelette for breakfast if you're hungry. In addition, the ship models crafted by the owner's son are something to see.

Charters
Winchester Bay has what is probably the cheapest deep-sea fishing outfitter in Oregon. **Main Charters** (4th and Beach Streets, Winchester Bay, 97496; tel. 271-3800) charges around $30 for a full day of salmon or bottom fishing. Call the day before for a full list of departure times and reservations.

Services
The Reedsport chamber of commerce **information kiosk** (tel. 271-3352) is located at the junction of U.S. 101 and ORE 38 just north of the NRA Visitor Center. It's open 10-5 every day, but don't expect lots of help. The Forest Service personnel at the **Oregon Dune NRA Visitor Center** just south on U.S. 101 (855 Highway Ave., Reedsport, 97467; tel. 271-3611) should fill in any gaps. They maintain office hours Mon.-Fri 8-4:30, and weekends 10-5:30. From Labor Day to Memorial Day there are no weekend hours.

DUNE COUNTRY:
NORTH TO FLORENCE

Even though the 47 miles of U.S. 101 between Coos Bay and Florence doesn't overlook the ocean, your eyes will be drawn westward every few minutes. After all, it's not every day that you can see mountains of shifting sand that have swallowed up a giant conifer forest. The largest and most extensive oceanfront dunes in the world are found in this National Recreation Area. Dune NRA headquarters is located halfway in Reedsport, between Coos Bay and Florence. This town of 5,000 people and the nearby fishing village of Winchester Bay have carved out tourist identities as refueling and supply depots for excursions into Oregon's Sahara-by-the-Sea.

These forays can take several forms. While joyriding in noisy dune buggies and other off-road vehicles doesn't lack for devotees, the best way to appreciate the interface of ecosystems is on foot. Dunes exceeding 500 feet in height, wetland breeding grounds for animals and waterfowl, evergreen forests, and deserted beaches can be encountered in a march to the sea. En route you might also come upon the nearly extinct silver spot butterfly and the insect-eating Darlingtonia plant. But most of your attention will probably be focused upon the dunes themselves. How did they come to be in a coastal topography otherwise dominated by rocky bluffs? A combination of factors created this landscape over the past 12,000 years, but the principal agents of dune creation have been the Coos, Suislaw, and Umpqua rivers. The sand and sediment transported to the sea by these waterways are deposited by waves on the flat shallow beaches. Prevailing westerlies move the particulate matter exposed by the tide eastward between one and several yards per year.

Ancient forests lie beneath these dunes, a fact occasionally proven by hikers as they stumble upon the top of an exposed snag. A cross section of sand-swept woodlands from the vantage point of U.S. 101 demonstrates that this inundation is still occurring. Nonetheless, the motorist will have the impression that the trees are winning the battle, as the dunes are only intermittently visible

from the road. A further inhibition to appreciating the range and size of Oregon's dunes is the limited or obscured access from U.S. 101.

The Forest Service personnel at the Dunes NRA Visitor Center in Reedsport can direct you to the best points of entry as well as supply info on camping and hiking in this remarkable landform. One tip you're bound to hear is that the highest dunes can be reached from secluded trails and campsites south of Reedsport. If your interests extend to fishing, boating, and water-skiing, however, **Ten Mile Lakes** and other freshwater paradises encountered en route from Coos Bay (and later on, north of Florence) might divert you from playing in the sand. Many of these lakes were formed when advancing dunes trapped upland streams. Oceangoing nimrods can enjoy the coast's saltwater sport-fishing capital, Winchester Bay, six miles south of Reedsport.

The Dunes NRA is home to over 400 species of wildlife, but the only dangerous animal within this ecosystem is possibly the American teenager. This species migrates here during summer vacation to enact puberty rites or auditory assaults with ghetto blasters. Extreme caution is advised in parking lots or within earshot of dune buggies.

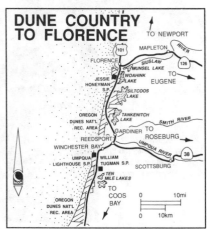

© MOON PUBLICATIONS, INC.

SIGHTS

Begin your travels at the visitor center (855 Highway Ave., Reedsport 97467; tel. 271-3611) where U.S. 101 intersects ORE 38. In addition to the info on hiking, camping, and recreation, the Suislaw Forest Service personnel are very helpful. Next door is a Reedsport tourism info kiosk which can complete an orientation.

Dune Access

The most spectacular dunes landscape can be found nine miles south of the visitor center at **Umpqua Dunes** (at North Eel Campground near Lakeside). After you emerge from a quarter-mile hike through coastal evergreen forest, you'll be greeted by dunes 300 to 400 feet high. It's said that dunes near here can approach 500 feet high and a mile long after a windblown buildup. In any case, be it mountain or molehill, the view here is most photogenic.

Honeyman State Park, ten miles south of Florence, also has a spectacular dunescape and then some. Come here in May when the rhododendrons bloom along the short sinuous road heading to the parking lot. A minute's walk west of the lot brings you to a 150-foot high dune overlooking Cleawox Lake. From the top of this dune, look westward across several miles of sand, marsh, and remnants of forest at the blue Pacific.

The most commonly asked question in the visitor center is, "Where are the dunes?" due to the fact that they are difficult to see from the highway. To answer it for everybody, the National Forest Service opened an overlook about halfway between Reedsport and Florence south of Carter Lake at the point where the dunes come closest to U.S. 101. In addition to four levels of railing-enclosed platforms connected by wooden walkways, there are trails down to the sand. It's only about a quarter mile to the dunes and, thereafter, a mile through sand and wetlands to the beach.

HIKING

A hike through the dunes lets you star in your own *Lawrence of Arabia* flick and moonwalk in the earthbound Seas of Tranquility. The soundtrack can be provided by the 247 species of birds here along with your heartbeat as you scale these elephantine anthills. Deserted beaches and secret swimming holes are among the many rewards of the journey.

Getting Oriented

In order to ensure a bon voyage, it's important to understand this terrain. To begin, carry plenty of water and dress in layers because of hot spots in dune valleys and ocean breezes at higher elevations. Expect cool summers and wet mild winters. While rainfall here can average over 70 inches a year, a string of dry, 50- to 60-degree days in

The dunes stretch for nearly 50 miles along U.S. 101 between Coos Bay and Florence.

PHOTO BY R.W. McLEAN

February is not uncommon. Another surprise is summertime morning fogs brought in by hot weather inland. These fogs, together with the inevitable confusion caused by dunes that don't look much different from each other, make a compass necessary. The lack of defined trails also compels such measures as marking your return route in the sand with a stick. Binoculars help with visual orientation, not to mention the birdwatching opportunities galore. Finally, there are always the sounds of traffic and surf to help you determine the eastern and western extents of this bailiwick.

Prior to setting out, write for or pick up the *Hiking Trails Recreation Opportunity Guide* from the Suislaw National Forest Service, Oregon Dunes National Recreation Area. This and other publications from the National Forest Service will correct the superficial impression that the dunes are just a domain for all-terrain vehicles and campgrounds for day hikers.

Tahkenitch/Three Mile Lakes Trails Loop

Hiking Trails documents several well laid-out trails to overnight destinations far from vehicular vibrations where you may come upon wildlife ranging from black bears to tundra swans. One such overnight excursion is the Tahkenitch/Three Mile Lake Trails Loop, a six-mile jaunt through windsculpted dunes and varied vegetation broken up by lakes, creeks, and a forest. The trail begins at the Tahkenitch Lake campground. To get there, drive seven miles north of Reedsport on U.S. 101 and 100 yards west on Forest Service Road 1090. Tahkenitch means "many arms," which the Salish Indians conjured from the starfish-like extensions of this lake. After a quarter mile of walking, the path splits, with the right fork going to Tahkenitch Dunes. Instead, head west to Three Mile Lake, several miles distant. Past the junction of the two trailheads look for rhododendrons blooming in early June and huckleberries to munch on in late August. Thereafter, the trail to Three Mile Lake alternates between spruce forest with ferns and sorrel and marshy areas with yellow skunk cabbage. The path culminates in a hillock above the lake with the dunes on the right. After a good night's sleep in the sand, continue west through low-lying marshes, shore pines, and small dunes. Once you hit the beach, continue north until you meet the Tahkenitch Dunes Trail close by the mouth of Tahkenitch Creek. From

here head east across the dunes, following the marker posts back.

RECREATION

Riding across the dunes into the sunset on a trusty steed sounds like a fantasy, but you can do it, too, thanks to **C&M Stables** (90241 U.S. 101, Florence, 97439; tel. 997-7540). With rates that work out to $10-12 per person per hour (with discounts for larger parties and off-season excursions), the stables operate seven days a week June through November.

Another option for those who fear to tred is **Dunes Frontier** (83960 U.S. 101, Florence, 97439; tel. 997-3544). This company rents vehicles for travel in specially designated areas within the Dunes NRA. Odysseys, small one-person dune buggies, go for $25 per hour and a $50 deposit. You must be strapped in with a helmet, stay within the marked territory, and be especially careful going uphill. If you lose power on an incline, it's possible to roll over when turning around to go back down. The 20-person dune buggy rides cost $5 for adults, $2.50 for children 6-10 years old, and kids under five ride for free.

The **Dune Mushers Mail Run** is a noncompetitive endurance dog sled run held in March of each year. This is the world's longest organized dry-land run for dog sled teams. It goes most of the length of the dunes from Horsefall Beach in the south, ending in Florence. Call 269-0215 for more information.

CAMPGROUNDS

North Eel Creek

Set along Eel Creek near Eel Lake and Ten Mile Lakes is North Eel Creek campground. The area boasts superlative hiking and aquatic sports as well as a fisherman's favorite, **The Stable Cafe** (on neighboring Lakeside's Main Street close to Ten Mile Lakes) if your breakfast rations run low. The camp is open June to late September at $6 per night with no reservations necessary. Picnic tables, firegrills, piped water, flush and pit toilets service the 52 tent sites and RV spaces. It is close by several other campgrounds ten miles south of Reedsport.

Tahkenitch Landing

Another Forest Service campground close to trails and water sports is Tahkenitch Landing, seven miles north of Reedsport. There are 15 sites for tents or motor homes up to 22 feet long. This place is somewhat primitive with pit toilets and no drinking water, but the price ($2 a night) and proximity to all the amenities at nearby Tahkenitch Lake campground makes it a "can't lose" proposition. The camp overlooks the lake on an open piece of land with picnic tables. For more information on North Eel and Tahkenitch Landing campgrounds, contact **Oregon Dunes Recreation Area** (855 Highway Ave., Reedsport, 97467; tel. 271-3611).

Nearby State Parks

Umpqua Lighthouse and **William A. Tugman State Parks** (Box 94, Winchester Bay, 97467; tel. 271-4118), are five and eight miles south of Reedsport respectively, in the heart of dune country. The Umpqua beacon which bears the name of the river whose mouth it illuminates is a light in the forest for campers who like fishing, boating, swimming, and hiking. Trails from here lead to the highest dunes in the U.S. (elevation 545 feet) west of Clear Lake. From mid-April to late October, 41 tent sites and 22 trailer sites go for $8 per night. Firewood, flush toilets, a laundromat, picnic tables, electricity, and piped water are on-site facilities.

Tugman is a larger campground with 115 sites and a similar range of creature comforts, price, and recreation. It sits on the west shore of Eel Lake east of U.S. 101 across from where the dunes reach their widest extent, two miles to the sea.

FLORENCE AND VICINITY

"Location, location, and location." This tenet of business success also explains the growing appeal of Florence for retirees and vacationers. Many people who could afford to live almost anywhere choose to do so here in between the Dunes NRA and some of the most beautiful headlands on U.S. 101. The fact that Florence is also situated halfway up Oregon's coastal route and a little over an hour's drive from shopping and culture in Eugene has made it a major beachhead of vacation home development in the region. A mild climate, a modern health-care facility, and lower housing prices than would be encountered elsewhere in a comparable setting also explain the influx.

Florence began shortly after the gold rush of 1849 in California put a premium on the lumber and produce upriver from the Siuslaw River estuary here. Several decades later, the town's name was inspired by a remnant from a shipwreck which floated ashore bearing the ship's nom de guerre. The townspeople either recognized an omen when they saw it or just figured they couldn't come up with anything better than "Florence."

SIGHTS

Easy access to beach and dunes is offered by South Jetty Road just south of the Siuslaw River Bridge and Florence proper. While birdwatching opportunities abound in the marshy lakes en route to the beach at all times of the year, the chance to see tundra swans here November to January is a special treat. The six-foot wingspan of this majestic bird is best appreciated with binoculars, and waterproof boots are a must for comfortable hiking in the area.

Siuslaw River Bridge
If first and last impressions are enduring, Florence is truly blessed. From the south, a graceful bridge over the Siuslaw greets you shortly after leaving the city limits. Here, U.S. 101 climbs to dizzying heights above the ocean.

The Siuslaw River Bridge is perhaps the most impressive of Conde McCullough's WPA-built spans. The Egyptian obelisks and art deco styling characteristic of other McCullough designs are complemented by the views to the west of the sand dunes. To the east, the riverside panorama of Florence's Old Town beckon further investigation. Prior to making the turnoff several blocks beyond U.S. 101, you can stop at the chamber of commerce on the highway. Old Town itself is a pleasant restoration with all manner of shops and restaurants along the river. The absence of car traffic is conducive to a pleasant walk after lunch there.

Museums
To fill in the missing captions on the original town site and get some notion of Indian and pioneer life, return to the highway for the **Siuslaw Pioneer Museum** (85294 U.S. 101, Florence, 97439; tel. 997-7884). Open year-round 10-4 every day except Monday, the usual array of artifacts is accompanied by an account of how the U.S. government double-crossed the Siuslaw tribe who sold their land to the Feds and never received the promised recompense.

Another museum in town is the **American Museum of Fly Fishing** (280 Napal St., Florence, 97439; tel 997-6102). Located three blocks north of the Old Town waterfront, thousands of fishing flies are attractively framed here. Next to the tufts of feathers and hair are fish paintings and lifelike wooden amphibian sculptures. This palace of Poseidon is open 10-5 daily with an admission charge of $2.50 for adults; kids under 16 get in free.

Indian Forest
Four miles outside of town is the Indian Forest (88493 U.S. 101, Florence, 97439; tel. 997-3677). When you see a totem pole on the right-hand side of the road, pull into this exhibit of Native American dwellings. A Navajo hogan, an Ojibwa wigwam, a Sioux tipi, and other dwellings are on display here. A kitschy plastic horse and a herd of real buffalo gaze forlornly over this assemblage. It's open daily June to August 8 a.m. to dusk. In May, September, and October, the exhibit is open 10-4. The admission is $3, half that for kids below 18; infants under five get in free.

Fifteen miles east of Florence in the Mapleton area are several cascades on Kentucky Creek and the North Fork of the Smith River. Known collectively as **Kentucky Falls,** they are set in an old-growth forest on a trail kept up by the Mapleton Ranger Station of the U.S. Forest Service (10692 ORE 126, Mapleton, 97453; tel. 268-4473). Contact this office for exact directions or refer to the "Eugene" section for an in-depth discussion.

Darlingtonia Wayside

Several miles up the road from Florence in an area noted for dune access and freshwater lakes is the Darlingtonia Wayside. In a sylvan grove of spruce and alder are a series of wooden platforms which guide you through a bog overlooking the carnivorous Darlingtonia plants, which are shaped like serpent heads. Known alternatively as the pitcher plant, cobra orchid, or cobra lily, the spherical leaf traps insects and digests them. The sweet smell the plant produces invites insects to crawl into the top of the Darlingtonia's serpent-like extension. Once inside, thin transparent "windows" allow light to shine inside the leaf, confusing the bug as to where the exit is. As the insect crawls around in search of an escape, downward pointing hairs within the enclosure inhibit the prey's movement to freedom. Eventually, the tired-out bug falls to the bottom of the stem, where it is digested. The plant needs the nutrients from the trapped insects to compensate for the lack of sustenance supplied by small root systems. If you still have an appetite after witnessing this carnage, you might want to enjoy lunch at one of the shaded picnic tables here.

Sea Lion Caves

Ten miles north of Florence, you'll have an opportunity to descend into a sea cave to observe the only mainland rookery of the Steller's sea lion in the lower 48. Sea Lion Caves (tel. 547-3111) is home to several hundred of this species. These animals occupy the cave during the fall and winter, which are thus the prime visitation times. Otherwise, go a quarter mile past the concession entrance to the "rockwork" turnout where the herd can often be witnessed on the rocky ledges several hundred feet below. Many people snap the picturesque **Heceta Head Lighthouse** across the cove to the north from the turnout. It's said that this is the most photographed beacon in the United States.

Enter Sea Lion Caves through the gift shop on U.S. 101. To the right, tickets can be purchased between 9 a.m.-7 p.m. in summer and 9-4 in winter for $4. Kids 6-15 get in for $2.50, and those under five enter for free. A steep downhill walk reveals stunning perspectives of the coastal cliffs as well as several kinds of gulls and cormorants who nest here. The final leg of the descent is facilitated by an elevator. After disembarking the lift into America's largest sea cave, look for the sea lions to the left from behind a partition. You'll also note a set of stairs on the right. These lead up to a view of Heceta Head Lighthouse through an opening in the cave.

The Steller's sea lions were referred to as *lobos marinos* ("sea wolves") in early Spanish mariners' accounts of their 16th-century West Coast voyages, and their dog-like yelps might explain why. You'll notice several shades of color in the herd which has to do with the progressive lightening of their coats with age. Males can sometimes weigh over a ton and dominate the scene here with macho posturings to scare off rivals for harems of as many as two dozen cows. Their protection as an endangered species enrages many fishermen, who claim that the sea lions take a significant bite out of fishing revenues by preying on salmon. In any case, the sight of these huge sea mammals close-up in the cavernous enclaves of their natural habitat should not be missed . . . despite an odor that can be likened to sweat-soaked sneakers.

PRACTICALITIES

Accommodations

As with Reedsport, there are budget motels on the main drag here, but to experience the coast fully, try one of the romantic getaways between Florence and Yachats.

Campgrounds

Camping here offers recreational opportunities comparable to the Dunes NRA, with more varied scenery.

Carl G. Washburne State Park (c/o The Campground, Florence, 97439; tel. 238-7488) is popular with Oregonians due to its proximity to beaches, tidepools, Sea Lion Caves, and elk. The eight tent sites and 58 RV sites have such modern conveniences as showers, a laundromat, electricity, and piped water. It's located 14 miles north of Florence on U.S. 101 (several miles past Sea Lion Caves), then one mile west on a park road. The fee is $8 for tents, $11 for RVs, and it's open all year. Heceta Head Lighthouse is within state park boundaries, but closed to the public. According to some accounts, Heceta was the first European to set foot in Oregon (in 1774). Beyond Heceta Head is a trail down to the beach at adjoining **Devil's Elbow State Park.** Be conscious of tides here if you climb along the rocks adjoining the beach. Near these campgrounds, Devil's Elbow Tunnel on U.S. 101 is a 600-foot cut through solid mountain.

Alder Lake (Oregon Dunes NRA, 855 Highway Ave., Reedsport, 97467; tel. 271-3671) has dune hiking and access to three lakes. While the

FLORENCE ACCOMMODATIONS

Name	Address	Telephone	Price	Features
Americana Motel	3829 U.S. 101	997-7115	$28-40	kitchenettes, covered pool
Le Chateau Motel	1084 U.S. 101	997-3481	$28-45	restaurant, pool, wheelchair access, laundromat
Gull Haven on the Sea	94770 U.S. 101 (16 miles north of town)	547-3583	$30-65	sandy beach, seclusion, pets, private bath, kitchen privileges, midweek discounts available, reserve early
Silver Sands Motel	1449 U.S. 101 North	997-3459	$30-36	
Money Saver Motel 1	70 U.S. 101	997-7131	$32-40	off-season discounts available, adjacent to Old Town
Park Motel	85034 U.S. 101 South	997-2634	$34-40	restaurant, pets kitchenettes,
Driftwood Shores	88416 1st Ave.	997-8263 (800) 422-5091 in Oregon, (800) 824-8774 outside	$50-120	restaurant, lounge, indoor pool and spa; all rooms have ocean view
Johnson House Bed and Breakfast	216 Maple St.	997-8000	$50-60	antiques in an old Victorian a block from the bayfront, full break fast, afternoon tea, down comforters

smallness of Alder Lake puts a damper on boating and water-skiing, the larger Sutton and Mercer lakes can sometimes look like a set from the rock video "Jetboat Summer." To get here, drive seven miles north on U.S. 101, then a quarter mile west on Forest Service Road 792. Flush toilets, picnic tables, and piped water are available from mid-May to mid-Sept. at the 22 sites for tents, trailers, and motor homes; the fee is $6 a night. Boat docks, launching facilities, and rentals are easily accessible in the area. The only drawback is that Alder Lake, Dune Lake, Sutton Lake, and several other nearby Forest Service campsites don't have showers.

An ideal place to escape from the summertime coastal crowds is the **North Fork of the Siuslaw** campground (write Siuslaw Forest, Mapleton Ranger District, Mapleton, 97453; tel. 268-4473). Chances are you'll see mostly locals here if anybody. From Florence follow ORE 126 about 15 miles to Mapleton to its junction with ORE 36. The latter road will take you 13 miles to County Route 5070. Then its a short drive to the riverside campsite. The fee is $4 between July and early-September.

All of the above sites do not require reservations, but be aware that coastal locations north of Florence fill early on summer weekends.

Food

A famous zen master once said, "If you can make a cup of tea right, you can do anything." The same aphorism seems to apply to clam chowder in coastal restaurants, if three Florence eateries are any indication.

The local **Mo's** (1436 Bay St., Old Town Florence, 97439; tel. 997-2185) is the largest outlet of this famed Oregon chowderhouse, and its fresh fish, fast service, and fair prices make it this neighborhood's most popular restaurant. Try the Lite Lunch Special, which includes three pieces of fresh cod and a cup of clam chowder or shrimp salad for $3.25.

The Bridgewater Seafood Restaurant and Oyster Bar (129 Bay St., Old Town Florence, 97439; tel. 997-9405) features exotic clam chowder with Indonesian clams in keeping with a Banana Republic decor, and the only "fine dining" in Old Town. Of course, this also means the highest prices on the waterfront ($2.75 for a cup of chowder), but to be fair, you're getting what you pay for and then some. The Bridgewater's clam chowder was the recipient of a "People's Choice Award" for the best clam chowder in town several years back. Besides that, if you don't like it, the chowder's free. Fresh fish, often with a Cajun flair, is the star of a menu whose lunch entrees average around $6.50, twice that for dinner. A lower-priced option exists on Wednesdays, winter through early spring, with the all-you-can-eat seafood dinner buffet for $9.95.

Another chowder feted by this award as well as an *Oregon Coast Magazine* 1990 poll is the creamy clam-filled concoction made by **The Blue**

Devil's Elbow State Park north of Florence

PHOTO BY OREGON TOURISM DIVISION

MO'S

Several decades ago Mo Niemi started up a humble fish shanty on the Newport bayfront. Locals extolled her tasty and cheap seafood, especially the clam chowder. Knowledge became more widespread during the filming of *Never Give an Inch*, starring Paul Newman and Henry Fonda. Restaurant scenes from this movie (based on Ken Kesey's *Sometimes a Great Notion*) were filmed here, and the stars soon became restaurant devotees. Over the years other luminaries ranging from Robert Kennedy to Bruce Springsteen joined the club. Soon outlets at Coos Bay, Florence, Lincoln City, and Otter Rock opened up along with an annex to handle the overflow in Newport. Menus are pretty much standard in each restaurant, with fresh fish, clam chowder, and burgers the main bill of fare. Long benches around the kind of tables you'd find in a logging camp cookhouse impart an air of informality to what has become an institution on the Oregon coast.

Hen (1675 U.S. 101, Florence, 97439; tel. 997-3907) at the north end of town. Fourteen finely chopped items go into this beige orange-specked soup. However, as the sign out front depicting a blue hen implies, chicken is the mainstay of this small cafe operating out of a home on the highway. As with Mo's, you may be asked to share your table with the interesting cross section of travelers drawn to this Oregon coastal hub. Prices range between $1.25 and $7.50 here. It's open from 8-8 Mon.-Sat.

Up the road a few miles, it's a safe bet that you'll find the chowder and whatever else is ordered to your liking. That's because **The Windward Inn** (3757 U.S. 101, Florence, 97439; tel. 997-8243) is one of the better restaurants in the state. Without belaboring the critical acclaim and kudos, let's just say this place goes the extra mile. Fresh cut flowers, skylights, a wood-paneled interior, and four separate dining rooms set the stage for an imaginative and extensive menu. For the budget-conscious, the bistro dinners are lighter meals that might forestall your wallet losing too much weight here. A chicken and veal sausage known as *boudin blanc* ($8.50) also makes for an excellent lower-priced alternative to a full

dinner. If you're into a full splurge, go with the fresh mussels broiled on the half shell with Oregon hazelnuts, Oregon peppered bacon, and Tillamook cheddar cheese ($14.75).

After dinner, have dessert at either of **B.J.'s Ice Cream Parlor**'s two locations (2930 U.S. 101 or 1441 Bay St., Florence, 97439; tel. 997-7286). BJ's churns out 48 flavors famous all over Oregon. Full fountain service, ice cream cakes, cheesecakes, gourmet frozen yogurt, and pies complement the cones and cups.

Driving east on ORE 126 en route to Eugene from the coast lets you follow the Siuslaw past isolated farms and lush forests topped by clearcut ridges. Shortly after leaving Florence, you come to **Mapleton**. Set at the base of the Coast Range, it's one of the rainiest burghs in the whole state. It also has two restaurants which'll evoke remembrances of things past.

The Alpha Bit Crafts Cafe (10780 ORE 126, Mapleton, 97453; 268-4311) is only 11 miles outside of Florence, but it exists in a different time and space. Started by a commune in the nearby town of Deadwood, the restaurant serves a varied menu of good ol' American food and vegetarian fare at reasonable prices. The preparations frequently include produce grown on Alpha Farm, and the 20-cent coffee puts the higher priced coastal brews to shame. Occasional live music supplements the soothing sound track which accompanies meals here and the unusual local crafts and fine selection of books makes Alpha Bit the cultural center of Mapleton.

A mile or two down ORE 126 is the **Gingerbread Village** (12300 ORE 126, Mapleton, 97453; tel. 268-4713). This is the kind of place your parents might have taken you when you were a kid . . . you know, a greasy spoon without the grease, serving simple, wholesome meals. While the food here is good enough to get you to Eugene, the gingerbread is unforgettable. Order it warm so the vanilla ice cream on top melts down decadently. Getting this dish to go costs a quarter more ($1.25), but the "boat" it comes in carries a disproportionately larger serving.

Events And Recreation

During the third week of May Florence celebrates the **Rhododendron Festival,** coinciding with the bloom of these flowers which proliferate in the area. A parade, boat and slug races, a carnival, a flower show, and a five kilometer "rhody's run" highlight the festivities. Contact the chamber of commerce for more info.

On July 4th at 2 p.m., the **National Stilt Walking Championship** starts at the corner of Maple and Bay Streets in Old Town.

Ocean Dunes Golf Links (3315 Munsel Lake Road, Florence, 97439; tel. 997-3232) lets you tee off with sand dunes as a backdrop. A manicured nine hole course, a driving range, a full pro shop, and equipment rentals are currently on-site, with 18 holes projected for the summer of 1990. **The Harbor Theatre** (1368 Bay, Old Town Florence, 97439; tel. 997-3361) charges $4 for first-run movies with discounts for seniors and kids. The showtime is 7 p.m.

Information And Services

The **Florence Chamber of Commerce** (270 U.S. 101, Florence, 97439; tel. 997-3128) is located three blocks north of the Siuslaw River Bridge. It's open 9-5. Next door is the **library**, which is slated to be moved to a site close by the junction of ORE 126 and U.S. 101 by 1991. **Peace Harbor Hospital** (400 9th St., Florence, 97439; tel. 997-3128) is open 24 hours. A dozen specialists are represented along with an emergency room. The **post office** (770 Maple St., Florence, OR 97439; tel. 997-2533) is open Mon. to Fri. 8-5. **Greyhound** (2107 U.S. 101, Florence, 97439; tel. 997-8782) is open Mon.-Fri. 9-5, and on Sat. 9-1.

YACHATS AND VICINITY

Yachats (when "ya-hots," you're hot) is an Alsea Indian word which means "at the foot of the mountain," which aptly describes this resort town of 575 people in the shadow of Cape Perpetua. While the native campfires are gone now, ceremonial clamshell middens have been found on area beaches. More importantly, the legacy of the Alsea will live on forever as long as people come here to gaze in wonder at sunsets and at the fury of winter storms.

SIGHTS

Cape Perpetua

The most notable sight near Yachats, indeed on the whole central coast, is the view from 800-foot-high Cape Perpetua. Oregon's highest paved public road this close to the shoreline affords 150 miles of north-to-south visibility from the top of the headland. On a clear day, you can also see 37 miles out to sea. Prior to hiking the trail or driving to the top of Cape Perpetua, stop off at the **Siuslaw Forest Visitor Center** (mile marker 188.5, U.S. 101, tel. 547-3289) on the east side of the highway. A picture window framing a bird's-eye view of rockbound coast along with exhibits on forestry and marinelife begin your orientation to the region here. The center is open 10-5 daily, except Christmas. Personnel at the desk have maps and pamphlets about such trails as Cook's Ridge, Riggin' Slinger, and Giant Spruce, as well as directions for the auto tour to the summit. In addition, they can point the way to tidepools and berry patches.

The awe-inspiring four-mile trail to the cape's summit is of moderate difficulty. En route, placards explain the role of wind, erosion, and fire in forest succession in this mixed conifer ecosystem. Historic events such as the naming of the cape by England's Captain Cook on Saint Perpetua's Day in 1778, and the devastating Columbus Day storm of 1962 are also documented.

At the crest of Cape Perpetua the "Trail of the Whispering Spruce" begins, a quarter-mile loop through the grounds of a former WW II Coast Guard lookout. The southern views from the crest take in the highway and headlands as far as Coos Bay. Halfway along the path, you'll come to a WPA-built rock lean-to which makes a lofty perch for whalewatching. Beyond this ridgetop aerie the curtain of trees parts to reveal fantastic views of the shoreline between Yachats and Lincoln City as far north as Cape Foulweather.

The two-mile drive up the cape is complicated by a not-so-prominent sign on U.S. 101 indicating the turnoff, and a junction in the road midway to the summit which can lead the unsuspecting on a wild ride in the opposite direction. To begin your auto ascent, drive a hundred yards north on U.S. 101 from the visitor center and look for the steep windy spur road on the right. As you climb, you'll notice numbered roadside markers annotated with explanations about forest ecology. Halfway up, you'll come to a Y in the road. Take a hard left and follow the road another mile to the top of Cape Perpetua. If you miss the left turn here and go straight ahead on the auto tour, you'll soon find yourself on an 22-mile paved-over logging route to Yachats. Despite distant shorelines and mountaintops on the horizon, the butchered forests along this blacktopped "cat" trail and signposts bearing Forest Service rationalizations for same might leave you more worried than inspired. Recent clearcuts on the opposite side of this head-

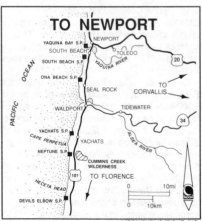

© MOON PUBLICATIONS, INC.

PHOTO BY TED LONG ISHIKAWA
the view from Cape Perpetua

land facing Yachats has prompted many disgruntled locals to refer to Cape Perpetua as "Cape Clearcut."

State Parks, Coastal Waysides

Between Heceta Head and Yachats, state parks and viewpoints abound with attractions. There's so much to see here that keeping your eyes on the road in this heavily traveled section becomes a challenge.

On the way to Cape Perpetua, **Neptune State Park** has a beautiful beach and is close by the 9,300-acre **Cummin's Creek Wilderness** east of U.S. 101. Scenic shorelines can also be found to the south of the cape at **Muriel O. Ponsler** and **Stonesfield Beach** waysides. Close by, there's a chance to explore tidepools and sometimes observe harbor seals at **Strawberry Hill.** Just north from the junction of the Cape Perpetua road and U.S. 101 is **Devil's Churn.** Here, the tides have cut a deep fissure in a basalt embankment on the shore. While watching the whitewater torrents in

this foaming cistern, beware of "sneaker waves," particularly if you venture beyond the boundaries of the **Trail of the Restless Waters.** All along this stretch of the coast, many trees appear to be leaning away from the ocean as if bent by storms. This illusion is caused by salt-laden westerlies drying out and killing the buds on the exposed side of the tree, leaving growth only on the leeward branches.

Just south of Yachats is a short but beautiful beach loop off U.S. 101 where the roadbed sits astride the landscaped grounds of beach houses and a foamy sea. In town the **Little Log Church Museum** (3rd and Pontiac) sits a few blocks from U.S. 101. Clothing and tools from pioneer days and a working pump organ are on display along with period furnishings. The hours of operation are variable, so check the chamber of commerce.

PRACTICALITIES

Accommodations

Yachats area lodgings take full advantage of the dramatic setting in a town they call "the Gem of the Oregon coast." For the ultimate in seclusion, **Oregon House** (94288 U.S. 101, Yachats, 97498; tel. 547-3329), nine miles south of Yachats, overlooks the Pacific from a high cliff. Seven suites with private baths and kitchens, some with fireplaces, as well as one bed-and-breakfast room take advantage of forested walking trails to the beach and a glass-enclosed whalewatching tower. Except in the case of the B&B room, there is an additional charge for full breakfasts. This is the kind of place which is especially cost-effective for groups, with a unit for four at $46 and more spacious units with kitchen, fireplace, dining room, etc. for larger parties costing $66. Ask the hotel proprietors about oceanfront grottoes between here and Sea Lion Caves.

Nancy's Oceanaire Rest Bed and Breakfast (95354 U.S. 101, Yachats, 97498; tel. 547-3782) is another up-close and personal experience of the Oregon coast. Located six miles south of Yachats, you have Cape Perpetua, Strawberry Hill, and other scenic venues right in the neighborhood, and 150 feet from your room is enough beachcombing for a lifetime. Ten Mile Creek, which adjoins the property, brings agates to the shore, and the innkeepers say you can find Indian artifacts along its banks. They'll also share such tidbits as the location of a covered bridge along the Yachats River and prime birdwatching spots just minutes away. This contemporay home features a full panorama of the coast from the deck, a whalewatching lookout in the dining room, and an ocean view in every room. When eggs primavera, shrimp cup toasties, and hot grain cereal greet you in the morning, you just might want to extend your stay. All of the above is yours for $55 May 15-Sept. 15, and $47 the rest of the year.

A little closer to Yachats at the beginning of the beach loop (just south of town and east of U.S. 101) are the **Shamrock Lodgettes** (Box 219, Yachats, 97498; 547-3312). Shamrock's beautiful park-like landscape frames a selection of individual log cabins or more conventional rooms. Stone fireplaces, in-room movies, and ocean or bay views all contribute to a relaxed get-away-from-it-all feeling. The sauna and jacuzzi on the premises also enhance the "mellowing out" process which'll begin as soon as you set foot here. The much requested cabins range between $64-80, while other units start at $50 and go up to $68—a small price for peace of mind.

For those looking for a budget place close to the center of town with some of the comforts of home, try **Rock Park Cottages** on W. 2nd (tel. 547-3214/343-4382), two blocks from the chamber of commerce. Consisting of five cabins right on the beach, Rock Park has to be considered one of the better bargains on the coast. Should weather keep you inside, the wood-paneled walls hold bookshelves with reading matter and board games, and the kitchens are equipped with dishes. The price can be negotiated for multi-night stays, but seems to average around $35 per night for a double, ten dollars less in winter.

The **Fireside Motel** (U.S. 101, Box 313, Yachats, 97498; tel. 547-3636) and the elegant **Adobe Resort** (see "Food" below) both overlook Smelt Sands Beach. If you appreciate all services in one compound, from dining room to gift shop, the Adobe gets the nod, but for less money, the Fireside's smallish rooms have more than enough amenities. In addition to ocean views, many of the rooms also have such extras as refrigerators and fireplaces. Perhaps the most appreciated little touch is the guidebook the management has put together for guest use. It can point the way to some of the area's natural attractions, including Smelt Sands and Cape Perpetua.

Campgrounds

Set along Cape Creek in the Cape Perpetua Scenic Area (Cape Perpetua Visitor Center, Box 274 Yachats, 97498; tel. 563-3211), the Forest Service **campground** here has 37 sites for tents, trailers, or motor homes up to 22 feet long. Picnic tables and firegrills are provided. Flush toilets, piped water, and sanitary services are available, no reservations are necessary, and the $6 fee applies mid-May to late September.

Just south, **Neptune State Park** has several dollar-a-night beachfront hiker/biker sites, and four miles south you can turn east off U.S. 101 and follow Forest Service Road 56 to get to **Ten Mile Creek.** With no reservations and no fee, this small secluded campground has four sites for tents and small RVs. You'll find firegrills, picnic tables, primitive sanitary facilities, but no piped water. It's just 15 minutes off the highway, but feels more remote.

Several miles down Ten Mile Creek is **Rock Creek** (c/o Siuslaw Forest, Waldport Ranger District, Walport, 97394; tel. 563-3211) For $6 a night you get a small out-of-the-way campground a quarter mile from the ocean. Most of the 16 sites are for tents, but a few accommodate small RVs. Firegrills and picnic tables provided; flush toilets and piped water are available.

If you're on a budget, try **Lanham Bike Camp**, which involves a hike in from Rock Creek but doesn't charge a fee. There's everything you need to make it through the night at the 10 primitive sites here, but bring your own water. Each place is open all year and doesn't require reservations.

Food

The eight restaurants in town are able to satisfy a variety of tastes and budgets. Right on the main highway **Yachats Coffee Merchants** (220 U.S. 101, Yachats, 97498; tel. 547-3100) combines reasonable prices, home-smoked meats, fresh seafood, and an array of potent coffee drinks and home-baked items. Try the alderwood-smoked Oregon chicken ($6.45) for dinner or the captain's platter of fish, shrimp, scallops, and oysters ($9.95)—only if you're *really* hungry.

Almost right across the street is **La Serre** (2nd and Beach St., Yachats, 97498; tel. 547-3420). A bright skylit restaurant with lots of plants creates an appropriate setting for cuisine that eschews deep-fat frying and is heavy on the whole wheat.

This may not suggest gourmet continental fare, but somehow La Serre pulls it off. With entrees running the gamut from strawberry-ricotta crepes to char-broiled steaks, the menu manages to please the brie-and-chablis set as well as the health conscious. It's not cheap, but hey, live a little!

A whimsical little place for a quick bite is the **Yachats Pie and Kite Shop** (1250 Ocean View, Yachats, 97498; tel. 547-3360). Crammed in this cheery little hole-in-the-wall are kites from all over the world and tables overlooking the water. After riding the winds, come inside to enjoy great pie (especially the pumpkin), soups, and sandwiches.

On a hill overlooking Smelt Sands Beach is the glass-enclosed **Adobe Resort** (155 U.S. 101, Yachats, 97498; tel. 547-3141) with its semicircular dining room. The setting is a great place to start the day for breakfast or end it with a romantic evening repast. Adobe breakfasts have eye-opening flair as demonstrated by cream cheese pancakes and intriguing variations on french toast and omelettes. Later in the day, the somewhat pricey fare here includes imaginative dishes like Oregon shrimp Sonora style (shrimp, onions, chile, sour cream, and melted cheeses wrapped in a tortilla), and fettucine in a garlic cream sauce with assorted shellfish. After dinner take a drink up to the Crow's Nest Lounge. Make reservations ahead of time in this acclaimed dining room on the north end of town.

Events
During the Yachats **smelt fry** held the second week of July, up to 700 pounds of this sardine-like fish are served on the grounds of Yachats School. Yachats is one of the few (perhaps the only) places in the world blessed with a run of ocean-going smelt. A sizeable run is not always guaranteed, and one year back in the early '80s, the fish didn't come at all. Information is available from the chamber of commerce.

The **Yachats Kite Festival** falls in November when the winds really kick up. Shamrock Lodgettes proprietor Robert Oxley has all the info. Contact him via the hotel or at Box 364, Yachats, 97498.

Services
The **Yachats Chamber of Commerce** (Box 174, Yachats, 97498; tel. 547-3530) has a central location on the highway and a loquacious staff. Ask them about fishing, rockhounding, birdwatching, and beachcombing in the area.

WALDPORT AND VICINITY

Originally a stronghold of the Alsea Indians, Waldport also has had incarnations as a gold rush town and lumber port. In addition, a decade ago it gained an unseemly notoriety for being a hotbed of environmental activism. When locals rallied against the spraying of dioxin-based defoliants in Coast Range forests, Waldport attracted national media attention. These chemicals were used by the lumber industry to eliminate blackberries, vine maples, and other vegetation which impede the growth of the more commercially viable Douglas fir. When the defoliants were linked to abnormally high numbers of birth defects and miscarriages, citizens rallied successfully for a government ban on the toxins.

This otherwise quiet town, whose name in German means "forest port," is today possessed of more mundane distinctions. A chamber of commerce flyer touts Waldport's livability, suggesting that the town's "relative obscurity" has spared it the fate of more crowded tourist towns. This may also be explained by a nondescript main drag that gives no hint of surrounding beaches and prime fishing spots. For those passing through, the town provides a low-cost alternative to the name destinations; in Waldport you won't have to fight for a parking spot or make reservations months in advance.

ACTIVITIES

Waldport's recreational raison d' être is fishing. World-class clamming and Dungeness crabbing in Alsea Bay and the Alsea River's famous salmon, steelhead, and cutthroat trout runs explain the high percentage of visits to the area.

Seal Rock State Park, four miles north of town, attracts beachcombers and agate-hunters as well as folks who come to explore the tidepools and observe the seals on offshore rocks.

Seven miles east of Waldport are the nine square miles of **Drift Creek Wilderness.** Within this area are stands of old-growth forest. Steep ridges and their drainages as well as small meadows make up the topography. The trailhead closest to Waldport is the **Harris Ranch Trail,** which

descends 1,200 feet in two miles to a meadow near Drift Creek. The wilderness is administered by the Siuslaw National Forest Waldport Ranger Station (tel. 563-3211), which can supply specific directions to the different trailheads into this increasingly rare ecosystem (see "Information And Services").

PRACTICALITIES

Accommodations
"Cottage" is a word often heard between Yachats and Waldport. These may be duplex or self-contained cabin-type lodgings generally by a beach. The price ranges between $30-65 for the units with kitchen facilities, fireplaces, and oceanfront locations. Cottages with all of the above include **Deane's Oceanside Lodge** (8800 S.W. U.S. 101, Waldport, 97374; tel. 547-3321), **Terry-a-While Motel** (7160 S.W. U.S. 101, Waldport, 97374; 101, tel. 563-3377), **Sea Stones Cottages** (6317 S.W. U.S. 101, Waldport, 97374; tel. 547-3118), the **Edgewater Cottages** (3978 S.W. U.S. 101, Waldport, 97374; tel. 563-2240), and **Cape Cod Cottages** (4150 S.W. U.S.101, Waldport, 97374; tel. 563-2106).

Camping
Two premium campgrounds sit about four miles south of Waldport on U.S. 101 along the beach. **Beachside State Park** (reserve at Box 1350, Newport, 97365; tel. 563-3023) is located near a half mile of beach not far from Alsea Bay and Alsea River. This is a paradise for rock fishermen, surfcasters, clammers, and crabbers. For $7 a night from mid-April to mid-October, there are 60 tent sites and 20 sites for RVs up to 30 feet long. With all the amenities, including a laundromat and hot showers, Beachside fills fast, so reserve early.

A half mile down U.S. 101 the Forest Service has comparable site offerings at **Tillicum Beach.** Set right along the ocean, the campground is open all year and doesn't require reservations. For $7 a night you have the full range of creature comforts plus ranger campfire programs in summer. Forest Service roads from here access Coast Range fishing streams which are detailed in a Forest Service map. You'll also appreciate the strip of vegetation blocking the cool evening winds which whip up off the ocean here.

Food

Forget fine dining in Waldport. This is an eat 'n' run town. For lunch and dinner, **At'sa Pizza** (Seastrand Mall, Waldport, 97374; tel. 563-3232) is a favorite with the locals. Premium ingredients go into their pizza, calzone, and pasta dishes. The homemade garlic rolls and "grinders" (submarine or hero sandwiches) are great for picnics, and like everything else here are moderately priced. There is also an outlet in Newport (tel. 265-6000).

At the south end of Waldport across from the Visitor Information Center is another local franchise. As with **Leroy's Blue Whale** in Yachats (tel. 547-3397), the **Waldport Restaurant** (tel. 653-3445) is right on U.S. 101. Their all-you-can-eat rib special ($4.95) and fish and chips ($4.25) makes this cafeteria-style restaurant a beachcomber's bonanza.

Also at the south end of town on U.S. 101 is **Moby Dick's Waldport Seafoods** (tel. 563-HOOK). If you're holed up in a cottage with a kitchen or camping, you'll appreciate fresh fish at a good price. The cooked crab here is exceptional attesting to Waldport's status as a leading Dungeness crab fishery, and the smoked fish also makes a great to-go snack.

If you're interested in a unique dining experience, follow ORE 34 along the Alsea River for nine miles to a most unlikely site for a good restaurant. Attached to a trailer court and convenience store is the **Kozy Kove Kafe** (9464 ORE 34, Tidewater, 97390; tel. 528-3251/800-388-KOVE). The dining room and lounge float on a bed of logs by a riverbank and are well placed to observe Australian black swans, elk, and other wildlife. Breakfasts are hearty, and lunch and dinner focus on fresh seafood and steak. There are also Mexican (try the "fajitas with the flame") and Italian entrees to add spice to this retreat from the ordinary.

Information And Services

At the south end of Waldport on the west side of U.S. 101 is the **Visitor Information Center** (tel. 563-2133). It's open 9-4 daily during summer. The **Siuslaw National Forest Waldport Ranger Station** (Waldport Ranger District, Waldport, 97374; tel. 563-3211) can provide information on area camping and hiking. A **post office** (Waldport, 97374; tel. 563-3011) can be found on ORE 34, one block east of U.S. 101. Close by on ORE 34 is the **public library**, which is open Mon-Fri 1-4:30, Sat. 11-2. ORE 34 itself is a scenic 60-mile access road to Corvallis.

Gene-O's Guide Service (Box 43, Waldport, 97374; tel. 563-3171) calls on 35 years of experience to help you reel in salmon and steelhead. **Crestview Hills Golf Course** (1680 Crestline Dr., Waldport, 97374; tel. 563-3020) has nine holes and a pro shop a mile south of town.

NEWPORT AND VICINITY

The discovery of a tiny sweet-tasting oyster in Yaquina Bay during the 1860s was the first major impetus to growth and settlement in Newport. These tasty morsels which delighted diners in San Francisco and at New York's Waldorf Astoria Hotel are almost gone now, but their port of embarkation is still bustling with activity. The shops, galleries, and restaurants along Newport's historic bayfront, together with the Performing Arts Center and quieter charm of Nye Beach, keep up a tourism tradition that goes back over a century. Today, Newport boasts the largest number of oceanfront hotel rooms between San Francisco and Seattle. This can make for traffic jams on holiday weekends, but it's a small price to pay for proximity to some of the coast's best agate-hunting beaches, cultural programs, and restaurants.

SIGHTS

Sea Gulch Trail

In addition to the diverse appeals of Newport, the area is also distinguished by a handful of attractions that skirt the line between the tasteful and the tawdry. This tightrope is skillfully walked at **Sea Gulch** (U.S. 101, tel. 563-2727), a collection of chainsaw sculptures on the east side of the highway five miles north of Waldport. The creator of these red cedar Rodins has a light touch with his sawblades as well as a cartoonist's flair in his art. Western and fantasy themes are humorously hacked out on the quarter-mile Sea Gulch Trail, where anthropomorphic bears and bigfoot vie for attention with cowboys, gnomes, Rip Van Winkle, and Mother Goose. It's open daily from 8-7 in winter, and closes an hour or two later in summer. The admission is $3.50, with discounts for seniors and kids.

Mark O. Hatfield Marine Science Center

Just prior to crossing the bridge into downtown Newport, head east to the Mark O. Hatfield Marine Science Center (Marine Science Dr., Newport, 97365; tel. 867-3011/ext. 226). At the door to greet you is a live octopus in an open tank. You're invited to reach out and touch it, or if you're too squeamish, a giant starfish. Turn left to take in exhibits on estuaries, geology, and other facets of Oregon coast natural history. Aside from the museum, the center is the hub of Oregon State University's research and teaching programs related to marine science. There are free guided walks and lectures by marine biologists every summer in the center's Seataugua program. The museum is open daily 10-4 in winter and 10-6 in summer. There's no admission charge.

Lincoln County Historical Society Museum

After crossing the bridge, a half-hour stop at the Lincoln County Historical Society Museum (545 S.W. 9th St., Newport, 97365; tel. 265-7509) is recommended. It's located a half block east of the chamber of commerce on U.S. 101. The logging, farming, and maritime exhibits (particularly Newport shipwrecks) are interesting, but the Siletz Indian baskets and other Indian artifacts steal the show.

The museum flyer on coast historical sights details the hardships of inadequate housing, insufficient food, and poor medical facilities which plagued the diverse tribes that made up the Confederated Siletz Indian Reservation. These dozen tribes were defeated during the Rogue Indian Wars and other conflicts of the 1850s. In 1856, 2,000 of these coastal natives were marched to a north coast reservation site. En route, they were sometimes forced to stand shivering in freezing rain until the tide moved out, permitting them to cross a beach. It's no wonder that at the end of one year their numbers had dwindled to 600.

The museum is open daily (except Mon.)10-5, June-Sept. and 11-4 Oct.-May. The admission is free. Just north of the log cabin which houses the Lincoln County collection is the **Burrows House.** This is part of the museum and has the same hours, but focuses exclusively on pioneer life. Antique buffs will especially enjoy these exhibits.

The Bayfront

The bayfront is easy to miss, but not if you look for the green marker pointing east at the intersection of U.S. 101 and Hubert Street after crossing the Yaquina Bay Bridge. Several right turns take you down the hill to Bay Boulevard,the bayfront's

Yaquina Bay Harbor, Newport: very much a working neighborhood

PHOTO BY OREGON DEPT. OF TRANSPORTATION

main drag. Forget about parking anywhere here unless you arrive early. Spots close by the boulevard can often be found, however, along the hillside access route to downtown, Canyon Way. Just curb your wheels to inhibit rolling. One of the first things that'll strike you about the bayfront is that it's a working neighborhood. The cries of fishmongers purveying wharfside walkaway cocktails and the smells of fish-packing plants and canneries fill the air as you stroll the boulevard. On the waterfront, you can watch fishermen step off charter boats with their salmon catch and head to Jack's for canning or observe vessels laden with everything from wood products to whalewatchers out in the bay.

The facilities of Oregon's second largest fishing port eventually give way to restaurants, shops, and galleries. Three tourist traps, **Ripley's Believe It or Not**, **The Waxworks**, and **The Undersea Gardens** are also encountered here, but aren't worth the $4 charged unless you have children in tow.

Yaquina Bay State Park

While it's difficult to get a bad meal on the bayfront and there is no shortage of true objets d'art sold here, sooner or later you'll want respite from crowds and commercialism. Relief is just a boat ride away with at least a dozen reputable fishing charter and whalewatching excursion operators here to serve you. Landlubbers are advised to drive under the bridge to Yaquina Bay State Park

for sweeping sea and bay views. There's also the old **Yaquina Bay Lighthouse** (tel. 867-8451), built in 1871 and abandoned three years later. It seems materials intended for lighthouse construction at Otter Crest were mistakenly delivered to this location, which proved to be a poor site. The restored Yaquina Bay beacon, replete with period furniture, is open daily, 12-5, between Memorial Day and Labor Day; the rest of the year it's just open weekends. The chance to hear about the ghost here is alone worth the modest price of admission (50 cents).

Better yet, pick up a reprint of the first written account (1899) of the ghost story at the Lincoln County Museum (see above), then round out your perspective with the century-old pictures on the lighthouse walls, which will convey the bleakness of the treeless, windswept cliff where this lighthouse was erected. This is important because the spit and polish facade of the restoration surrounded by stands of coastal pines would be an inappropriate setting for a ghost story. Without ruining the tale for you, let's just say that if you stand outside the lighthouse on a dark, windy night and hear a maiden's wail, don't linger.

Finally, Yaquina Bay State Park is a good place to have a picnic, or you can descend the trails to the beach and dig for razor clams.

Nye Beach

Another breather from the rampant commercialism on the bayfront and along U.S. 101's business district is Nye Beach. Located a mile north from the bayfront on the western side of U.S. 101 (look for signs on the highway), this one-time favorite retreat for wealthy Portlanders has undergone a revival. Rough times and rougher weather had reduced luxurious beach houses here to a cluster of weatherbeaten shacks until a new performing arts center went up several years back. On the heels of the development of this first-rate cultural facility, the conversion of a 1910 hotel into a kind of literary hostel (see "Practicalities") encouraged other restorations. Culture vultures, beach lovers, and people-watchers will want to come to Nye Beach soon before the shadows of nearby resort hotels grow larger.

Toledo And Sights North

Aficionados of antiquities can head six miles east of town on ORE 20 to Toledo, where "junque" shops abound. This small town's fortunes have risen and fallen with the timber cut. At one time, the world's largest spruce mill was here. In fact, all of the wood for Howard Hughes's *Spruce Goose* was shipped from the Toledo mill. In the era of big timber's swan song, dealers of collectibles have sprouted up to take advantage of coastbound traffic from the Willamette Valley. Most of the antique shops are located on Main Street.

North of Newport is **Yaquina Head Lighthouse.** It is Oregon's tallest and second oldest lighthouse (1873) still in active service, but is closed to the public. However, the **Yaquina Head Outstanding Natural Area** is open during daylight hours, with an observation deck availing views of seals and sea lions as well as shorebirds.

Beaches north of town include **Agate Beach,** famed for its gemstone hunting opportunities, **Moolack Beach,** a favorite with kite-flyers, and **Beverly Beach,** where 20 million-year-old fossils have been found in the sandstone cliffs backdropping the shore.

ACTIVITIES

Sampling Local Fare

Despite the high cost of such local delicacies as Yaquina oysters and Oregon wines, these gourmet treats needn't set you back much if you visit some of Newport's tasting rooms. On the road to Toledo about eight miles east of the bayfront, the **Oregon Oyster Company** (6878 Bay Rd., Newport, 97365; tel. 265-3078) is the only remaining commercial outlet of Yaquina Bay oysters, on sale 9-4 daily. Visitors are welcome to observe the farming and processing of these succulent shellfish. Before you leave, try the smoked oysters on a stick. Wash your oysters down with a bayfront bacchanal, courtesy of **Alpine Vineyard's** (818 S.W. Bay Blvd., Newport, 97365; tel. 265-6843) tasting room, open from mid-June to mid-September.

Fishing Charters

Charter companies here are numerous. In addition to the whalewatching charters (average cost $15 for a two-hour trip) listed in this chapter's Introduction, salmon and bottom fishing average between $30-$40 for a four- to five-hour run. Some local outfits include **Sea Gull Charters** (343 S.W. Bay Blvd., Newport, 97365; tel. 265-7441), **Newport Sportfishing at the Embarcadero Dock** (1000 S.E. Bay Blvd., Newport, 97365; tel. 265-7558), and **Newport Tradewinds** (653 S.W. Bay Blvd., Newport, 97365; tel. 265-2101).

Natural Highs By The Sea

For those who prefer to take matters into their own hands, the **clamming** and **Dungeness crabbing** are superlative in Yaquina Bay. If you haven't done this before, a local tackle shop will rent crabpots or rings and offer instruction. The best time to dig clams is at an extremely low or minus tide. Tide tables are available from the chamber of commerce and many local businesses. And if you're the kind who just likes to watch, **Yaquina Birders and Naturalists** (tel. 265-2965) welcomes newcomers on its free weekly hikes. To really get down, rent diving equipment ($50) and get tips from **Deep Sea Johns** (South Jetty Rd., tel. 867-3742). John can direct you to sheltered coves north of Depoe Bay. Whalewatching and scenic flights can be negotiated with **Bertea Aviation** (tel. 867-7767) at Newport Airport, three miles south of the Yaquina Bay Bridge.

Sports

Swimming and **tennis** enthusiasts are not only served by resort facilities. The city of Newport operates an indoor swimming pool at N.W. 12th Street, (tel. 265-7770). In addition, you can raise a racquet at six public outdoor tennis courts and several privately owned indoor courts. The public courts are located at N.E. 4th and Benton Streets and Bay Creek Road, one block north of the public swimming pool. While its name might evoke visions of that other course on the 17-mile Drive between Monterey and Carmel, the **Agate Beach Golf Course** (just north of Newport on U.S. 101, tel. 265-7331) is more on the order of a nine-hole pitch-and-putt course. True devotees can go 17 miles north to **Salishan Lodge** (tel. 764-3632) to play an 18-hole award-winning course set in the foothills of the Coast Range. The greens fee ranges between $20-30, depending on the time of year.

The Arts

The **Newport Performing Arts Center** (777 W. Olive, Newport, 97365; tel. 265-9231), the coast's largest, hosts local and national entertainment in the 400-seat Alice Silverman Theatre and the smaller Studio Theatre. At the same address is the **Oregon Coast Council for the Arts**, which puts out a free monthly newsletter and has ticket info on the previously mentioned venues, as well as the **Newport Visual Arts Center** (239 N.W. Beach Dr., Newport, 97365; tel. 265-5123).

PRACTICALITIES

Accommodations

The cliché "something for everybody" might literally be the case as far as places to stay in Newport. A vast network of accommodations can be found in every price range here. The following are two places worthy of special mention.

Where else but at an **American Youth Hostel** (212 N.W. Brooks St., Box 164, Newport, 97365; tel. 265-9816) can you find yourself in commodious digs close to the water and two blocks away from the appealing Nye Beach neighborhood for less than ten bucks a night? The check-in time is between 5-10 p.m. The curfew of 11 p.m. and check-out at 10 a.m. are flexible. Kitchen, living room, and piano provide all the comforts of home at what is probably a cheaper price.

The **Sylvia Beach Hotel** (267 N.W. Cliff, tel. 265-5428) combines the camaraderie of a hostel with the intimate charm of a bed and breakfast. Built in the era when the Corvallis to Yaquina Bay train and seven-seater Studebaker touring cars from Portland ferried the newly wed and the near-

ly dead to Nye Beach, this hostelry was considered the height of luxury. Known as the Cliff House and later on as the Gilmore Hotel, even a "Honeymoon Capitol of Oregon" sobriquet could not forestall it eventually being overshadowed by newer, more elaborate resorts. A rebirth as the Sylvia Beach Hotel was expedited by a National Historic Landmark designation and a literary theme which has attracted an enthusiastic following. The 20 guest rooms have been named after different authors and furnished with decor evocative of each respective literary legacy. The Edgar Allen Poe Room, for instance, has a pendulum guillotine blade, stuffed ravens, and who knows what else, given Poe's recurring theme of cementing family relations. The Tennessee Williams Room sets the stage with a ceiling fan, a glass menagerie, and mosquito netting, while Agatha Christie Room drops such clues as shoes underneath the curtains and capsules marked poison in the medicine cabinet.

The Sylvia would be just another cute idea were it not for an imaginative innkeeper who even facilitates guest interactions. This often comes to pass over highly acclaimed nouvelle cuisine in the oceanfront restaurant, **Tables of Content,** thanks to a game called "Two Truths and a Lie." Guests seated at long tables regale each other with several stories, the object being to distinguish which one is true. If this doesn't break the ice, there's hot wine served in the library at 10 p.m., which often leads to conversations far into the night.

Most of the rooms run between $40-60, with oceanfront suites featuring a fireplace and deck going for $80-90. All these rates include a full breakfast. Even if you don't stay here, you're invited to come by for a look at unoccupied rooms whose doors are always left open for this purpose. If nothing else, have a meal at the Tables of Content. There's a nice view of the breakers, good company, and not overly spendy Northwest cuisine.

To get there, turn off U.S. 101 on N.W. 3rd and follow it down to the beach, where N.W. 3rd and Cliff streets meet. Then, look for a large four-story dark-green wooden structure with a red roof on a bluff above the surf.

Campgrounds

Sites at **South Beach** (Box 1350, Newport,

NEWPORT ACCOMMODATIONS

Name	Address	Telephone	Price	Features
Anchorage Motel	N. Coast Highway 1	265-5463	$46-60	ocean view, fireplaces, pets, kitchenettes
B.W. Windjammer Hallmark Resort	744 S.W. Elizabeth	265-8853	$65-85	wheelchair access, ocean view, restaurant/lounge, fireplaces, pets, kitchenettes
City Center Motel	538 S.W. Coast Highway 101	265-7381	$26-36	pets, kitchenettes
El Rancho Motel	1435 N. Coast Highway 101	265-5192	$25-30	pets, kitchenettes, near playground
Embarcadero Resort Hotel	1000 S.E. Bay Blvd.	265-8521	$55-159	bay view, laundry, restaurant/lounge, covered pool, kitchenettes
The Hotel Newport	3019 N. Coast Highway 101	265-9411	$55-80	wheelchair access, ocean view, pool, restaurant/lounge, nonsmoking rooms, live entertainment
Little Creek Lodge	3641 N.W. Oceanview Dr.	265-8853	$65-85	ocean view, fireplaces, kitchenettes
Money Saver Motel	861 S.W. Coast Highway 101	265-2277	$28-65	kitchenettes, laundry, nonsmoking rooms
Moolack Shores Motel	SRN Box 420	265-2326	$62-95	wheelchair access, ocean view, fireplaces, kitchenettes, small and secluded
Newport Motor Inn	1311 N. Coast Highway 101	265-8516	$31	pets, nonsmoking rooms, restaurant/lounge
Park Motel	1106 S.W. 9th St.	265-2234	$34-50	kitchenettes

NEWPORT ACCOMMODATIONS, cont.

Name	Address	Telephone	Price	Features
Penny Saver Motel	710 N. Coast Highway 101	265-6631	$32-36	kitchenettes, nonsmoking rooms, complimentary continental breakfast
Puerto Nuevo Inn	544 S.W. Coast Highway 101	265-5767	$38-100	wheelchair access, fireplaces, pets, nonsmoking rooms, complimentary continental breakfast
Sands Motor Lodge	206 N. Coast Highway 101	265-5321	$28	kitchenettes, pets, nonsmoking rooms, laundry
Shilo Inn	536 S.W. Elizabeth	265-7701	$50-95	wheelchair access, ocean view, pets, covered pool, laundry, restaurant/lounge, complimentary continental breakfast
Surf 'n' Sand Motel	8143 N. Coast Highway 101	265-2215	$47-68	ocean view, fireplaces, pets, kitchenettes
Sylvia Beach Hotel	267 N.W. Cliff St.	265-5428	$50-110	wheelchair access, ocean view, pool, restaurant/lounge, nonsmoking rooms
Tides Inn	715 S.W. Bay St.	265-7207	$25-45	ocean view, pets, kitchenettes
Val-U Inn Motel	531 S.W. Fall St.	265-6203	$50-90	wheelchair access, ocean view, laundry, restaurant/lounge, nonsmoking rooms, complimentary continental breakfast
Viking's Cottages	729 N.W. Coast St.	265-4661	$39-48	ocean view, fireplaces, pets, kitchenettes

NEWPORT ACCOMMODATIONS, cont.

Name	Address	Telephone	Price	Features
Waves Motel	820 N.W. Coast Highway 101	265-4661	$39-48	ocean view, nonsmoking rooms, complimentary continental breakfast
Whaler Motel	155 S.W. Elizabeth	265-9261	$49-68	wheelchair access, ocean view, pets, kitchenettes, nonsmoking rooms complimentary continental breakfast
Willers Motel	754 S.W. Coast Highway 101	265-2241	$30-44	wheelchair access, ocean view, laundry, nonsmoking rooms

97365; tel. 867-4715) and **Beverly Beach** (Star Route North, Box 684, Newport, 97365; tel. 265-7655) state parks could well be the most popular places to stay of their kind on the Oregon coast. The absence of other camping in the area and the special features of each campground explain their appeal.

Beverly Beach's 152 tent sites, 127 RV spaces, and hiker/biker campground are set seven miles north of Newport on the east side of the highway in a mossy glade. Across the road is a tunnel on the other side of which is a beach. **Devil's Punchbowl** and **Otter Crest** are one and two miles up the highway, respectively. All the amenities, including a cafe, are provided for $8 per night, and they're open all year.

South Beach State Park is located two miles south of town along the beach, with opportunities for fishing, agate hunting, and hiking. It has the full range of creature comforts, including a laundromat. It's open mid-April to late October at $7 per night. Hookups at both parks average $9.

Food

This is a town for serious eaters—folks who know good food and don't mind paying a tad more for it. It's also the kind of place where there are wharfside vendors as well as fast-food joints and a 24-hour Safeway (220 U.S. 101, tel. 265-2930) to do it on the cheap. Since you'll probably be spending most of your time at either Nye Beach or the bayfront, eateries in those neighborhoods highlight this section.

The bayfront is where Mohava Niemi, a Siletz Indian, opened the original **Mo's** (622 S.W. Bay Blvd., Newport, 97365; tel. 263-9411) several decades ago. When word got out about the good food and low prices, Mo's small homey place soon had more business than it could handle. In response to the overflow, **Mo's Annex** (657 S.W. Bay Blvd., Newport, 97365; tel. 265-7512) was created across the street. While both establishments feature such favorites as oyster stew and peanut butter cream pie, the Annex bay window has the nicer view.

Champagne Sunday brunch overlooking the bay at the **Embarcadero** dining room (1000 S.E. Bay Blvd., Newport, 97365; tel. 265-8521) lets you fill up on all the breakfast entrees, fresh seafood, and bubbly you can handle for $9.95. This is a good deal in what is otherwise a high-ticket restaurant. Reservations are recommended between 10-2.

Another fancy but flexibly priced alternative is a place which earned the *Pacific Northwest Magazine* best seafood award, **Canyon Way Book-**

store and Restaurant (1216 S.W. Canyon Way, Newport, 97365; tel. 265-8319). Instead of going the haute cuisine route (if you must, the famous baked Yaquina Bay oysters cost $14.95), the budget-conscious might prefer to feast on homemade quiche and croissants from the carryout shop after browsing the wide-ranging selection of travel titles in the front room bookstore. These can be savored with a 45-cent cup of espresso which is somehow five cents cheaper than their regular coffee. In addition to the bakery selections in the carryout shop, there is other low-priced luncheon fare. In the evening, early dinners (available 5-6 p.m. only) for $8.95 almost halve the later menu prices for the same order, and smaller-but-still substantial "light dinners" go for $9.95. You'll also appreciate little extras such as an extensive wine and beer list, outdoor patio dining, and works by local artists adorning Canyon Way's walls.

The **Whale's Tale** (452 S.W. Bay Blvd., Newport, 97365; tel. 265-8660) is another bayfront restaurant that has great food at all meals, but is more cost-effective at breakfast and lunch. Eggs Newport ($5.95) will keep you going all day: local Oregon shrimp and two poached eggs on an English muffin topped with béarnaise sauce and accompanied with home fries.

Night owls will be grateful for the **Pip Tide's Restaurant and Lounge** (8365 S.W. Bay Blvd., Newport, 97365; tel. 265-7797). Besides a 24-hour restaurant, there's low stakes blackjack tables and live rock 'n' roll bands.

Clustered in the small commercial strip along Nye Beach are several dollar-wise and tasty places to grab a bite. Picnickers might want to stock up on homemade bread and fixin's at the **Oceana Food Coop** (415 Coast St., Nye Beach, 97365; tel. 265-8285) and the **Nye Beach Deli** around the corner on N.W. Beach Drive.

Also on N.W. Beach Drive is the **Chowder Bowl** (728 N.W. Beach Dr., Nye Beach, 97365; tel. 265-7477, with another location on the bayfront (434 S.W. Bay Blvd., Newport, 97365; 265-5575), whose clam chowder ($2.50) or salad bar with chowder and garlic bread ($4.95) are favorites with hikers and coast route bikers. But the best deal of all for the trencherperson is the Tuesday night all-you-can-eat fish and chips with salad bar for $8.95. The chowder is also touted as the best in the West by locals. Next door, the **Sand Bar** is a loud and crowded hangout for friendly fisherfolk. Up and over a block to the east is the prominent facade of **Don Petrie's Italian Food Company** (613 N.W. 3rd, Nye Beach, 97365; tel. 265-3663). This place evokes San Francisco's North Beach pasta houses with filling manicotti and fettucine dinners for $6-9. Try the specialty of the house, seafood lasagna.

Events

The biggest bash here is the **Newport Seafood and Wine Festival** which presents these palate-pleasers along with music and crafts on the bayfront. The second event of note is **Loyalty Days and Sea Fair** in early May, focusing on sail-

Devil's Punchbowl

boat races, a chicken feed, and a parade. Call the chamber for updates.

Outside of town, the **Siletz Powwow** takes place on the second weekend of August. It brings together tribes from all over the Northwest to nearby Siletz for a celebration of the reenfranchisement of the Siletz tribe and reservation. Crafts, food, and traditional dancing spice up this event. Siletz can be reached via ORE 20 (Bay Rd.), which will take you to Toledo. At the crossroads, follow ORE 229 eight miles to Siletz. Ask the Toledo Chamber of Commerce (311 N.E. 1st St., Toledo 97391, tel. 336-3183) for more details. This office can also direct you to **Drift Creek Wilderness** access.

Information And Services

The Newport Chamber of Commerce (S.W. U.S. 101, Newport, 97365; tel. 800-263-7844) has lots of literature available. The *Comprehensive Guide to Services* is the most helpful pamphlet of its kind made available by coastal cities. A booklet on agate hunting is also recommended. The office is open daily 8:30-5, except between Nov.-Jan., when there are no weekend hours.

Greyhound (956 W. 10th St., Newport, 97365; tel. 265-2253) handles Hound service along U.S. 101 and the **Valley Retriever** (tel. 265-2253) feeder line service from the Willamette Valley along U.S. 20. **Newport Area Transit** (tel. 265-8088) runs a daily route around the city from 7-7. The fare is 50 cents, and three rides can be had for $1.25. Ask the chamber of commerce for a map.

Given the size of this city, there's more likelihood of calling the city **police** (tel. 265-5352) than in many other coastal locales. Other useful numbers might include **Pacific Communities Hospital** (tel. 265-2244) and the ambulance service (tel. 265-3175). The Coast Guard **weather** phone is tel. 265-5511. The **library** is located on (35 N.W. Nye St., Newport, 97365; tel. 265-2153). It's open Mon. and Weds. 1-8 p.m., Tues. and Thurs. 10-8, and Fri.-Sat. 1-6. The **post office** (310 S.W. 2nd St., Newport 97365; tel. 265-5542) is open Mon.-Fri. 8:30-5.

NORTH TO DEPOE BAY

The expanse of flat beaches and sandstone bluffs north of Newport takes on a more dramatic aspect after you leave the highway at the Otter Crest Loop six miles south of Depoe Bay.

First, the swirling waters of **Devil's Punchbowl** pound out another Oregon Coast rendition of "bubble, bubble, toil and trouble." An urn-like sandstone formation has been sculpted by centuries of tidewater flooding what had been a cave until the roof collapsed. The inexorable process continues today, thanks to the ebb and flow of the Pacific through two openings in the wall of the cauldron. The state park viewpoint sits at a low elevation above the spectacle, giving you a ringside seat on this frothy confrontation between rock and tide. When the water recedes, you can see purple sea urchins and starfish in the **Marine Gardens** tidepools 100 feet to the north. To the south of the Punchbowl vantage point are picnic tables and a wooden walkway down to the beach. In the parking lot in back of the overlook is a Mo's outlet where a seat occupied by "The Boss" himself, Bruce Springsteen, on June 11, 1987, is enshrined.

Further along the loop is the **Inn at Otter Crest,** a pricey condo resort whose **Flying Dutchman** dining room (tel. 765-2111) faces 453-foot **Cape Foulweather** (also known as Otter Crest) to the north. Classical cuisine is served here at dinnertime, and more reasonably priced sandwiches and salads can be enjoyed at lunch. You can call the Inn at the above number for info on the **Otter Crest Jazz Weekend.** This takes place on the first Saturday and Sunday in May, throwing together oldies-but-goodies like Billie Holiday accompanist Jimmy Rowles and new wave musicians of note.

The visibility from atop the cape can extend down to Yaquina Head on a clear day. The view north is another photographer's fantasy of headlands, coves, and offshore monoliths. Bronze plaques in the parking lot tell of Captain Cook naming the headland during a bout with storm-tossed seas in 1778. Comic relief from the coast's parade of historical plaques comes with a tablet bearing the inscription, "On this site in 1897, nothing happened."

The Lookout gift shop on the north side of the promontory is a good place to get Japanese fishing floats for a few bucks or take advantage of the telescopes by the entrances.

From the Otter Crest parking lot, continue north on the loop, whose dips and turns bring the view from the cape into sharper focus. Shortly after this road-less-traveled terminates, U.S. 101 takes you past **Whale Cove.** The tranquility of the calendar photo-come-to-life here is deceptive. During Prohibition, bootleggers used the rocky crescent-shaped shoreline as a clandestine port. More recently, a court decision allowing property owners to restrict access to Whale Cove threatens to undermine public ownership of other Oregon beaches.

DEPOE BAY AND VICINITY

William Least Heat Moon in *Blue Highways* characterized Depoe Bay thusly: "Depoe Bay used to be a picturesque fishing village; now it was just picturesque. The fish houses, but for one seasonal company, were gone, the fleet gone, and in their stead had come sport fishing boats and souvenir ashtray and T-shirt shops."

To be fair, tourists have always come here since the establishment of the town. In fact, for all intents and purposes, the town didn't really exist until the completion of the Roosevelt Highway (U.S. 101) in 1927, which opened the area up to car travelers. Prior to that time, the area had been mainly occupied by a few members of the Siletz reservation. One of the latter group worked at the U.S. Army depot and called himself Charlie Depot. The town was named after him, eventually taking on the current spelling.

Depoe Bay also took on another incarnation as part of the so-called "Twenty Miracle Miles." This bit of hype originally denoted the attractive stretch of rockbound coast near Depoe Bay north to the broad beaches of Lincoln City. Nowadays, the only thing miraculous about the region is that dozens of gift shops selling the exact same merchandise next door to each other survive year after year.

SIGHTS

Depoe Bay is situated along a truly beautiful coastline which cannot be fully appreciated from an automobile. An especially nice perspective is offered alongside the **Channel House Bed and Breakfast** at the west end of Ellingson Street. Just go left up this road where U.S. 101 passes the Channel Book Shop (see "Activities" following).

As you drive over the bridge in town look down to your right to see the world's smallest navigable harbor. This trumped-up distinction is announced by a sign for the benefit of *Guinness Book of World Records* (a tactic repeated later in Lincoln City with its "world's shortest river"). The bridge in between the six-acre harbor and the ocean is a popular spot for whalewatchers December to May.

North of town is **Boiler Bay,** so named because of the boiler remaining from the 1910 wreck of the *Marhoffer,* visible at low tide. This bay is a favorite spot for rock fishing and whale-watching.

OTTER ROCK TO ROCKAWAY BEACH

© MOON PUBLICATIONS, INC.

PRACTICALITIES

Accommodations

Rooms here tend to be priced for tourists instead

DEPOE BAY ACCOMMODATIONS

Name	Address	Telephone	Price	Features
Ocean West Motel	Box 414, Depoe Bay	765-2789	$20-30	ocean view, pets
Arch Rock Motel	Box 21, Depoe Bay	765-2560	$25-40	ocean view, pets, kitchenettes
Four Winds Motel	Box 423, Depoe Bay	765-2793	$25-45	ocean view, pets, free coffee
Beachcombers Haven	7045 Glen Ave., Gleneden Beach	764-2252	$30-50	oceanfront, fireplaces, laundry
Budget Motel	Box 66, Depoe Bay	765-2287	$30-50	ocean view, pets, sundeck, cable TV/Showtime
Holiday Surf Lodge	Box 9, Depoe Bay	765-2133	$30-60	ocean view, motel and cabin units, health club, laundry
Whale Cove Inn	SRS Box 1-X, Depoe Bay	765-2255	$45-95	ocean view, rest/lounge, jacuzzi
Channel House Country Inn with Bed & Breakfast	Box 56, Depoe Bay	765-2140	$40-140	oceanfront, fireplaces, jacuzzi, full breakfast included
Surfrider Oceanfront Resort	Box 219, Depoe Bay	764-2311	$44-62	oceanfront, lounge, covered pool, sauna, and jacuzzi

of dollar-wise travelers. The ocean views are always gorgeous, but the holiday weekend crowds can be oppressive.

Food

Depoe Bay's plethora of places to eat and shop are unequaled on the Oregon coast. However, the numbers drop considerably when you're speaking of *good* places to eat. The following restaurants represent a cross section of the old reliables in the region.

For unpretentious all-American diner food at low prices try the **Whale Watch Inn** (221 S.W. U.S. 101, Depoe Bay, 97341; tel. 763-2623). This cafe juts out over the ocean channel leading to the harbor, making for a great view. Decent coffee

and the specialty omelette (taco meat, hash browns, onions, broccoli, green beans, eggs, and cheese for $4.50) here comprise the quintessential breakfast with "go-power."

The **Chowderbowl** (U.S. 101, Depoe Bay, 97341; tel. 765-2300) serves the same tasty chowder as the Newport outlets. A salad bar, oyster and crab specials, and moderate prices are also here in this "can't-miss" restaurant.

Two miles south of Depoe Bay is a dining room in the **Whale Cove Inn** (Star Route South, Box 1-X, Depoe Bay, 97341; tel. 765-2255) which is everything you could want in a restaurant in this part of the state. If fresh fish innovatively prepared at reasonable prices and a romantic sea coast view don't put a twinkle in your eye, perhaps the Friday night rib special and cozy lounge next door will. Little touches like binoculars at your table and the friendliest waitresses on the coast also rate thumbs up.

The local favorite in Depoe Bay is the **Sea Hag** (5757 U.S. 101, Depoe Bay, 97341; tel. 261-7901). Their seafood hors d'oeuvres (fried whitefish, scallops, oysters, smoked tuna, and boiled baby shrimp) give ample testimony to their claim of "seafood so fresh the ocean hasn't missed it yet." Another popular dish is salmon stuffed with crab and shrimp, baked in wine and herb butter. A lavish salad bar, a Friday night all-you-can-eat seafood buffet, and a recipe for clam chowder feted by the *New York Times* has also generated good word-of-mouth.

ACTIVITIES AND EVENTS

Book Browsing
The largest used book emporium on the Oregon coast is the **Channel Book Shop** (tel. 765-2352), located just south of the bridge, across from the chamber of commerce. The store's five rooms of romance novels, Westerns, travel books, and varied esoterica also functions as the citadel of higher learning in Depoe Bay. In the front of the store, pick up the free map of used book shops on the Oregon coast.

Charleston Charters
With the ocean minutes from port here, catching a salmon or seeing a whale is possible as soon as you leave the harbor. On the way back into port you might see the **spouting horns**, 50-foot "geysers" of sea water that shoot through fissures in basalt when the tide is high. Charters are also popular because of reasonable prices. Fishing trips average around $35 for a five-hour run, and whalewatching excursions run between $5-7. Some companies are **Dockside Charters** (Box 1308, Depoe Bay, 97341; tel. 765-2545), **Deep Sea Trollers** (Box 513, Depoe Bay, 97341; tel. 765-2705), and **Depoe Bay Sportfishing** (Box 388, Depoe Bay, 97341; tel. 765-2382). **Sunset Scenic Flights** (Box 427, Gleneden Beach, 97388; tel. 764-3304) is located at Gleneden Beach airport a half mile southwest of Salishan Resort midway to Lincoln City. Whalewatching and scenic coastline flights of variable lengths depart from hangar number seven.

Events
The **Depoe Bay Salmon Bake** takes place on the third Saturday of September at Fogarty Creek State Park just north of town on U.S. 101. Fresh ocean fish are caught and cooked on the beach Indian style on alder stakes over an open fire and served with all the trimmings ($18 per person). The **Fleet of Flowers** happens each Memorial Day in the harbor to honor those lost at sea. Over 20,000 people come to witness a blanket of blossoms cast upon the waters.

Information And Services
Depoe Bay Chamber of Commerce (Box 21,

the narrow inlet to Depoe Bay, the world's smallest navigable harbor

PHOTO BY OREGON TOURISM DIVISION

Depoe Bay, 97341; tel. 765-2889) offers a lot of printed matter about the town as well as the central coast in general. What's really special about their office is a tranquil back patio overlooking the boat harbor where you can sit and recover from the shop-until-you-drop ambience along U.S. 101.

The **laundramat** (sic) is open 24 hours in the rear lower level of Mall 101 at the north end of town. Also at the north end of town is the **post office** (Depoe Bay, 97341) next to the U.S. Bank. The Coast Guard **weather service** (tel. 765-2122) can be contacted round the clock.

NORTH TO LINCOLN CITY

Salishan Lodge
Seven miles south of Lincoln City on the east side of U.S. 101 is a sign advertising the Salishan Lodge (tel. 800-452-3200). Named for a widespread native tongue in the Oregon territory, this resort is one of a dozen properties in the nation which consistently receives a five-star as well as a five-diamond rating.

Even if you don't stay here, the grounds and facilities are worth a look. The art gallery is free and features the best Oregon artists, and the forested trails behind the golf course (rated among the top 75 in the United States) showcase the rainforested foothills of the Coast Range. A breezeway behind the lobby displays interesting native artifacts and fossils, and the beautifully landscaped grounds look down on Siletz Bay in the distance.

Understated elegance and respect for natural surroundings are encountered at every turn—no high-rise shlocky beach architecture or neon signs here. This low-key approach at top-drawer prices (rooms start at $94) attracts well-heeled nature lovers, corporate expense-account clientele, folks enjoying a special occasion, and serious golfers. You'll also find Mom 'n' Pop from Anywhere, U.S.A. and seminar attendees on winter weekend specials for $50 or less. Despite the fact that the resort does not have oceanfront views or rooms appreciably larger or more ornate than many other places, the house counts are high year around. From attractive cedar-shaked self-contained units in the upper level of the complex to the smaller luxury motel rooms below overlooking the golf course, you'll find nicely appointed interiors in earth colors with no trace of Naugahyde in sight. In addition to the recreational and aesthetic appeals of the resort, the **Dining Room** is also responsible for Salishan's lofty reputation. Consistently touted as one of the top three restaurants in the state, it has become famous for its creative interpretations of seasonal Northwest delicacies and a 20,000-bottle wine cellar.

Salishan celebrated its 25th anniversary in 1990. The essence of its enduring popularity is perhaps best expressed in the words George Bernard Shaw used to describe another palace of poshness: "This is the way God would have done it if only he had the money."

Crafthouses
Just past Salishan on Immonen Road, **Alder House II** is a glass-blowing operation open to the public. The variety of shapes and colors produced are fascinating aspects of this ancient craft which is explained by the artisans. Alder House is open Tue.-Sun., 10-5. A few hundred yards up the road is **Mossy Creek Pottery**. The large win-

dows enable you to watch the proprietors at work, if you're lucky enough to arrive during their irregular working hours. The high-quality creations of both craft houses are on sale at bargain prices. The road to these establishments are indicated by signs on US. 101.

Sometimes A Great Notion

Back on the coast route to Lincoln City, you'll come to the turnoff for ORE 229 along the Siletz River. If you drive down the north side of the river for a few miles, you'll note a Victorian house on the opposite shore that's built to last. A huge porch fronts the river bank, heavily reinforced against the elements. Rather than describe it further, this book defers to its source of inspiration—the first pages of *Sometimes A Great Notion* by Ken Kesey.

Word of mouth has it that the structure was built up to its present specs for the 1972 film *Never Give An Inch,* based on Kesey's novel and starring Paul Newman, Lee Remick, Henry Fonda, and Michael Sarrazen. The plot concerns the never-say-die spirit of an anti-union timber baron, his not-always supportive family, and life in the mythical Coast Range logging community of Wakonda. Much of this movie was shot in this area, with cafe scenes taking place at Mo's on Newport's bayfront.

Drift Creek Covered Bridge

Closer to Lincoln City is another U.S. 101 turnoff, Drift Creek Road, which leads 2 1/2 miles to the oldest covered bridge in Oregon. Oregon features 53 such structures (as late as 1934, there were over 300 before they fell into disrepair). They were built to inhibit the effects of moisture upon the wooden planks and to keep horses from spooking when crossing over water.

LINCOLN CITY AND VICINITY

The Lincoln City area encompasses five towns that banded together for reasons of apportionment and mutual business interests. What "business" means in this case is tourism in its worst conceivable form. In a state known for its appreciation of growth limits and the need for urban planning, Lincoln City's seven miles of shell shacks and "for sale/zoned commercial" signs are an anathema. As if seeking revenge, Mother Nature has visited severe erosion problems on the sandstone bluffs upon which sit many Lincoln City hotels, condos, and business establishments.

SIGHTS

Around Town

The D River Wayside is a state park property where you can watch what locals claim is the "world's shortest river" flow into the ocean. It traverses a 440-foot path from Devil's Lake and despite its unspectacular appearance, was a *cause célèbre* when *Guinness* threatened to withdraw the D's claim to fame in favor of a Montana waterway. Local schoolkids rallied to its defense with an amended measurement, and perhaps the D's title will be restored. In addition to seeing "D"

River flow from "D" Lake into "D" ocean, the beach here is great for kite-flying. The river itself is the point from which the street numbers of the city begin.

In commemoration of the establishment of Lincoln City, a 14-foot bronze statue was donated to the city by an Illinois sculptress. *The Lank Lawyer Reading in His Saddle While His Horse Grazes* originally occupied a city park where Governor Hatfield and actor Raymond Massey came for the dedication. Today the impressive statue is off in a nondescript lot at N.E. 22nd and Quay Avenue (look for the sign on U.S. 101 near the Dairy Queen pointing the way).

With ORE 18 connecting Lincoln City to the Yamhill Valley wine country, its not surprising to find two tasting rooms in town to pique your tastebuds. **Honeywood Winery** (30 S.E. U.S. 101, Lincoln City, 97367; tel. 994-2755) sits across from the D River. Try the blackberry wine from Oregon's oldest continuously operating winery. **Oak Knoll Winery** (3521 S.W. U.S. 101, Lincoln City, 97367; tel. 996-3221) presents its own varietals (try the '85 pinot noir) along with award-winners from other Oregon vintners. The hosts can help you plan a wine country foray, and they sell cases at bulk discounts.

Forested cliffs meet the sea near Lincoln City.

PHOTO BY LINCOLN CITY VISITOR AND CONVENTION BUREAU

OREGON'S CIVIL WAR CONNECTION

Despite the haphazard patterns of growth here, the choice of Abraham Lincoln's name for the city was not made arbitrarily. Shortly after Oregon gained territorial status, Honest Abe was nominated as its first secretary. Even though he declined, his name was affixed to this north coast county in 1867. The choice of the appellation "Lincoln City" a hundred years after his death in 1865 was lent impetus by both the centennials of his passing and of the Civil War's conclusion.

But there were other reasons. In the state of Oregon there's a longstanding tradition of assigning Civil War-era place names to cities and counties. And why not? The major players in America's domestic theater of war had their first curtain calls out west. General George Pickett of Pickett's Charge fame at Gettysburg, General Edward Baker, who distinguished himself at the Battle of Balls Bluff in Maryland; Generals Phil Sheridan and William Tecumseh Sherman, whose marches across the Shenandoah Valley and Georgia were Confederate nightmares; General George McClellan, who preceded Ulysees S. Grant as head of the Union Army; and Generals George Crook and Phil Kearney all served in Oregon. The Southern side was represented at Fort Vancouver near Portland with General Robert E. Lee and the "eyes and ears of the Confederacy," Jeb Stuart.

Primarily, these men were involved in protecting the Oregon Trail settlers, gold mining areas, and trading posts from Indians. When the Civil War drew these men east, much damage was incurred. In 1981, Oregon symbolically and unsuccessfully lobbied for a 1.3-million-dollar reparation for the losses due to the lack of Federal protection. In any case, the aforementioned Civil War generals' presence is still remembered in the names of the Oregon towns of Sheridan, Baker, and Grants Pass, as well as Crook and Sherman counties. Oregon's entry into the Union helped break a tie in Congress on the vote to abolish slavery. It's altogether fitting then that there be a city named for the great emancipator, Abraham Lincoln.

East On ORE 18

Heading east of Lincoln City on ORE 18 takes you on a road framed by the giant fir stands of the Van Duzer corridor. Just prior to heading over this pass through the Coast Range you cross the 45th parallel (it's just outside of Lincoln City by the Devil's Lake Golf Course on U.S. 101, before its junction with ORE 18, indicated by a sign on the highway. At this point you are halfway between the equator and the north pole (every degree of latitude is 66 miles). About a dozen miles east of town is the **Van Duzer Forest Wayside,** a prime spot on the Salmon River for a picnic. The site used to be a post office on an old stagecoach route. ORE 18 continues on through the Coast Range until the greenery of the tall firs gives way to drier orchard country wherein a major percentage of the world's filberts are grown. Roadside stands selling walnuts, cherries, and other crops dot the highway. You'll also see antique stores and tasting rooms as you ease into Yamhill Valley wine country (see "Day-trips From Portland").

PRACTICALITIES

Accommodations

Outside of Portland and Eugene, there aren't any cities in Oregon to rival Lincoln City for sheer volume of creature comforts. There are 1,800 hotel rooms here, and many face the ocean or are close to a beach. The most reasonably priced lodgings, however, are on the noisy main drag in this striptown to end all striptowns. But no matter where you go, you're never far from the madding crowd.

Campgrounds

With plenty of cheap hotel rooms, people camp on the outskirts of town not so much to save money but to get away from the noise and the commercialism. One remote escape is at the previously mentioned **Van Duzer Wayside** on ORE 18. A dozen primitive hiker/biker sites sit in a beautiful forest near the Salmon River at no cost.

More free rustic sites can be found about eight miles north of town and just south of Neskowin. To get there, just look for the "scenic drive" sign east of U.S. 101 and follow County Road 12 for four miles. From there, travel about 100 yards

LINCOLN CITY ACCOMMODATIONS

Name	Address	Telephone	Price	Features
Anchor Motel and Lodge	4417 S.W. U.S. 101	996-3810	$25-45	pets, kitchenettes, non smoking rooms, cable
City Center Motel	1014 N.E. U.S. 101	994-2612	$25-35	pets, kitchenettes, cable
Seagull Beach-Front Motel	1511 N.W. Harbor Ave.	994-2948	$25-120	pets, kitchenettes, wheelchair access, nonsmoking rooms, ocean view
Budget Inn Motel	1713 N.W. 21st.	994-5281	$26-36	pets, nonsmoking rooms
Captain Cook's Motel	2626 N.E. U.S. 101	994-2522	$26-36	pets
Sea Echo Motel	3510 N.E. U.S. 101	994-2575	$28-38	pets, kitchenettes, cable, ocean view
Siletz Bay Inn	861 S.W. 51st. St.	996-3996	$28-125	wheelchair access, fireplaces, cable, ocean view
Lincoln Shores Motel	136 N.E. U.S. 101	994-8155	$30-50	wheelchair access, fireplaces, cable, nonsmoking rooms, ocean view
Edgecliff Motel	3733 S. U.S. 101	996-2055	$30-70	wheelchair access, fireplaces, cable non-smoking rooms, pets, ocean view
Ocean Terrace Condo Motel	4229 S.W. Beach Highway 101	996-3623	$30-75	wheelchair access, pool, restaurant/lounge, nonsmoking rooms, cable, ocean view
Surftides Beach Resort	2945 N.W. Jetty	994-2191	$32-62	wheelchair access, covered pool, restaurant/lounge, live entertainment, ocean view
Char Lu Ocean Front Motel	1605 N.W. Harbor	994-9529	$35-62	pets, kitchenettes, cable, nonsmoking rooms, ocean view

LINCOLN CITY ACCOMMODATIONS, cont.

Name	Address	Telephone	Price	Features
Ester Lee Motel	3803 S.W. U.S. 101	996-2161	$35-91	wheelchair access, fireplaces, ocean view
Sea Gypsy Motel	145 N.W. Inlet Ave.	996-5266	$35-91	wheelchair access, covered pool, cable, nonsmoking rooms
Nendels Cozy Cove	515 N.W. Inlet Ave.	994-2950	$36-84	wheelchair access, pool, fireplaces, complimentary continental breakfast ocean view
Red Carpet Inn	2645 N.W. Inlet Ave.	994-2134	$37-64	pets, fireplaces, covered pool, cable nonsmoking rooms, ocean view
Blue Heron Land Motel/Marina	4006 W. Devils Lake Rd.	994-4708	$39-43	pets, kitchenettes, cable, nonsmoking rooms, river/lake view
Sailor Jack Ocean Front Motel	1035 N.W. Harbor Ave.	994-3696	$39-48	pets, wheelchair access, fireplaces, non-smoking rooms, complimentary continental breakfast, ocean view
Beachfront Motel	3313 N.W. Inlet Ave.	994-2324	$40-60	pets, kitchenettes, wheelchair access, fireplaces, ocean view
Lincoln Lodge Ocean Front Motel	2735 N.W. Inlet Ave.	994-5007	$40-62	kitchenettes, fireplaces, cable ocean view
Sandcastle Beachfront Motel	3417 S.W. Anchor Ave.	996-3613	$40-62	kitchenettes, fireplaces, cable, ocean view
Shilo Inn	1501 N.W. 40th St.	994-3655	$40-100	pets, wheelchair access, covered pool, restaurant/lounge, non-smoking rooms, laundry, ocean view

LINCOLN CITY ACCOMMODATIONS, cont.

Name	Address	Telephone	Price	Features
Sea Horse Oceanfront Motel	2039 N.W. Harbor Dr.	994-2101	$44-76	pets, kitchenettes, fireplaces, covered pool, cable, ocean view nonsmoking rooms
Bay West Motel	1116 S.W. 51st St.	996-3549	$45-70	kitchenettes, fireplaces, cable, river view, ocean view
Coho Inn	1635 N.W. Harbor Ave.	996-3684	$48-52	pets, kitchenettes, fireplaces, cable, ocean view
Nordic Motel	2133 N.W. Inlet Ave.	994-8145	$48-66	kitchenettes, wheelchair access, fireplaces, covered pool
Westshore Oceanfront Motel	3127 S. Anchor Ave.	996-2001	$50-59	pets, kitchenettes, fireplaces, cable, ocean view
Brey House Bed and Breakfast	3725 N.W. Keel	994-7123	$55-65	wheelchair access, fireplace, cable tennis, ocean view
D Sands Motel	171 S.W. U.S. 101	994-5244	$64-80	wheelchair access, covered pool, cable, nonsmoking rooms, ocean view
Palmer House Bed and Breakfast	646 N.W. Inlet	994-7932	$70-85	fireplaces, cable, non-smoking rooms, ocean view
Inn at Spanish Head	4009 S. U.S. 101	996-2161	$78-119	wheelchair access, pool, restaurant/lounge, nonsmoking rooms, laundry, ocean view

west on Forest Service Road 12131 and you'll see the campground set along **Neskowin Creek.** To find out about the trails in the surrounding rainforest, call or write the Siuslaw National Forest (Hebo, 97121; tel. 392-3161). The campground is open mid-April to mid-October—bring your own water or water purification kit. The nearby scenic drive continues up into an area of huge trees captioned by Forest Service placards explaining the ecology. More elaborate camping is available at **Devil's Lake State Park** (write to reserve at 1542 N.E. 6th, Lincoln City, 97367; tel. 994-2002). Sixty-eight tent sites and 32 RV sites are serviced with all the amenities, including showers, a cafe, and a laundromat. The fee is $8 per night mid-April to late October. This campground is just off U.S. 101 at the northeast end of town.

Food

For the most part, eating out at Lincoln City means overpriced hotel dining rooms or roadside dives purveying greasy fish and chips. Here are some alternatives.

The best smoked fish in these parts can be had at **Barnacle Bill's Seafood Store** (2174 U.S. 101, Lincoln City, 97367; tel. 994-3022). The smoked sturgeon here is half the price it is on the East Coast, and although it's not thin-sliced in the style of New York delis, it has a more delicate flavor. Look for a little storefront on the east side of the highway in the middle of town. Another place to graze is the **Safeway** at the northern edge of town in the Lincoln Plaza Mall. Stock up here, too, before heading north on the Three Capes Loop en route to Tillamook.

Mo's (860 S.W. 51st St., Lincoln City 97367; tel. 996-2535) as usual, can be counted on for good clam chowder and full fish dinners in the $6-9 range. You'll find more of the same north of town off U.S. 101 at **Dory Cove Restaurant** (5819 Ogan road, Lincoln City, 97367; tel. 994-5180) near Road's End State Park. The prices are a little higher than at Mo's, but the range of broiled seafood entrees and cheeseburger fantasies make this place the favorite with locals. Another Lincoln City hot spot is **Kips** (next to Safeway 4093 N.W. Logjam Rd., Lincoln City, 97367; tel. 994-3736), specializing in pasta dishes and seafood with an Italian flair. Best of all, the price is right.

A place which appeals to everybody is the **Otis Cafe** (Otis Junction on ORE 18, Otis, 97368; tel. 494-2813), whose innovative variations on American road food have been warmly embraced by everyone from local loggers to yuppies stopping off on the drive between Portland and the coast. Breakfast in this small unpretentious cafe five miles northeast of Otis is such an institution that long waits on the porch are the rule on weekend mornings. The reason why includes the thick-crusted molasses bread that comes with many orders, buttermilk waffles ($2), and their legendary hash browns under melted Rogue Valley white cheddar ($2.75). A half-portion for one dollar less is the equivalent of all-you-can-eat fare, so walk the beach at Neskowin before tackling the

unabridged version. Large portions, low prices, and a culinary touch that turns pork chops and rhubarb pie into epicurean delights are also in full evidence at lunch and dinner (Thurs.-Sun. till 9 p.m.).

The **Bay House** (5911 S.W. U.S. 101, Lincoln City, 97367; tel. 996-3222) is a place food critics have described as "intimate" and "elegant." You might also add "expensive." Dinners can run $30 a person but the poached salmon, sumptuous salads with mounds of sweet bay shrimp, and a Siletz Bay view here might actually be worth it, especially at sunset.

Events And Activities

Several Lincoln City beaches have interesting **tidepools** to explore. Some of the best places in town are north of **Roads End State Park** and at S.W. 11th St. (Canyon Drive Park). There are also intertidal life zones at N.W. 15th St. and at 32nd. A few miles north of Lincoln City (off U.S. 101) on the north bank of the Salmon River estuary is another set of pools to visit. Just follow Three Rocks Road (see "Neskowin Hiking," below). Public telescopes at S.W. 51st St. let you watch a colony of seals offshore.

Lincoln City calls itself the kite capital of the world, pointing to its position midway from the pole to the equator, which gives the area predictable winds patterns. The spring **Kite Festival** takes place Mother's Day weekend; the fall festival is held the last weekend in September. The exact time depends on when the winds are right at the D River Wayside, site of the contest. Call 994-3070/in Oregon (800) 452-2151 for more information. Whenever you come by the D River Wayside, go across U.S. 101 to **Catch The Wind Kites** (tel. 994-9500) for a shop that's bound to set your spirits soaring.

Devil's Lake is the recreation center of Lincoln City. In addition to windsurfing and hydroplaning, eight species of fish can be caught here. Devil's Lake Golf and Racquet Club and picnic tables grace the lake's shores, along with boat-launching facilities. Of the five points of access, East Devil's Lake Road off U.S. 101 northeast of town is the best, offering a scenic route around the lake. Rentals on mountain bikes, canoes, and paddleboats can be arranged at the **Blue Heron** (4006 W. Devil's Lake Rd., Lincoln City, 97367; tel. 994-4708) and windsurfing rigs from **Windsurfing Oregon** (4933 S.W. U.S. 101, Lincoln City, 97367; tel. 996-3157) are also available for

Old growth forest characterizes the flora in the Cascade Head Scenic Research Area near Neskowin.

PHOTO BY LINCOLN CITY VISITOR AND CONVENTION BUREAU

those who want to experience the lake more intimately.

Tennis players can enjoy the public outdoor courts at N.W. 28th. If the weather is bad, play indoors at **Neptune Courts** (tel. 994-8442) and at the **Surftides** (2943 N.W. Jetty Rd., Lincoln City, 97367; tel. 994-2191). These are about half the price of **Salishan** (tel. 764-3633), which averages about $15 per person for about a 75-minute set. Another alternative is Salishan's early morning or late night rate of $7 per person (for more information see "North To Lincoln City" under "Depoe Bay").

Golfers can choose between two nine-hole courses at Neskowin (tel. 392-4120 and 342-2377) 12 miles north of Lincoln City or the 18 holes at the Devil's Lake Club. The small condo-beach house community of Neskowin also has **riding stables** (48490 Hawk Rd., Neskowin, 97149; tel. 392-3277) and a scenic beach to explore. **Proposal Rock,** a high forested butte, sits impressively in Neskowin's tidewater, inviting an assault. Unfortunately, the thick underbrush and undeveloped trails impede in-depth exploration, but the slopes here still have some great hideouts.

Other phone numbers of value, recreationally speaking, include the **Lincoln City Community Pool** (tel. 994-5208), where you can swim for $1.50 and shower for 75 cents, and the **Bijou Theatre** (tel. 994-8255).

Information
The **Lincoln City Chamber of Commerce** (3939 N.W. U.S. 101, Lincoln City, 97367; tel. 994-

3070/in Oregon 800-452-2151) is open Mon.-Fri. 9-5 and on weekends 10-4. The **Greyhound** station (316 S.E. U.S. 101, Lincoln City, 97367; tel. 994-8418) sits behind a bowling alley and is open 9-7. The public **library** can be reached at tel. 996-2277, and the **post office** (Lincoln City, 97367; tel. 994-2128) is two blocks east of U.S. 101 on E. Devil's Lake Rd. It's open Mon.-Fri. 8:30-5.

NESKOWIN HIKING

The tiny family-oriented vacation town of Neskowin has a quiet appeal based on a beautiful beach and two golf courses in the shadow of 1,500-foot-high Cascade Head. When you drive in off of U.S. 101, a deli, a post office, and the **Hawk Creek Cafe** greet you. Behind this small complex are the moderately priced **Proposal Rock Inn** and the **Neskowin Resort.** In deference to the prevailing feeling in Neskowin regarding publicity, it would be inappropriate to elaborate further upon creature comforts. Let's just say you come here more for what's outside your room than what's inside.

Cascade Head Scenic Research Area
This statement is made manifest two miles south of town along the Cascade Head and Hart's Cove trails. The trails fall within the Cascade Head Scenic Research Area, the only region so designated in the United States. It was set aside by Congress in 1974, thanks to the efforts of the Na-

ture Conservancy, and is today a mecca for 6,000 hikers annually. Rainforested pathways and wild-flowered meadows give way to dramatic ocean views on Cascade Head and the Harts Cove trails. The trailheads can be reached on Forest Service Road 1861, an old gravel road west of U.S. 101. Three miles down, there's a fork to a viewpoint where you should bear left. Three-quarters of a mile further on 1861, begin the hike to Cascade Head by a large Nature Conservancy sign, an interpretive map, and a white highway guardrail. Before setting out, pick up a conservancy brochure here which explains the geography and ecology while annotating the views around Cascade Head.

The first part of the trail runs through arching red alder treetops and 250-year-old Sitka spruces with five-foot diameters. The understory of mosses and ferns is nourished by 100-inch rainfalls. In addition, a mind-boggling array of mushrooms come out in the fall. Above the woods is a grassy hillside at the top of which you can look south over the mouth of the Salmon River clear down to Siletz Bay (and sometimes to Cape Foulweather). This climb shouldn't take much more than twenty minutes. From this 1,300-foot aerie, you can descend the long slope toward the sea and then up the 500-foot-high **Pinnacle**, the headland's westernmost thrust. Much of the Pinnacle is fenced off to protect endangered plants and species. The Forest Service and Nature Conservancy fear the onslaught of hiking boots obliterating several rare wildflowers common only to here and Cape Lookout. Originally, these barriers were built by farmers to keep their stock from going over the cliffs.

The effects of humankind were also visited upon the topography around Cascade Head when Indian fires changed the vegetation. The natives burned to provide "browse" for deer and to reduce the possibility of larger, uncontrollable blazes. These manmade alterations were complemented by the inherent dryness of south-facing slopes that receive increased exposure to sun. In contrast to these grasslands, the northern part of the headland is the domain of giant spruces and firs because it catches the brunt of the 100-inch yearly rainfalls and lingering fogs.

Less than two miles from the Pinnacle is Three Rocks Road. En route you descend steep meadows and lose 800-feet in elevation, which might

make the hike back a less than appealing proposition. If you intend a loop and have only one car, you might want to make this hike in reverse order. Whichever way you do it, allow an hour for a one-way jaunt. The access to Three Rocks Road is several miles south of Forest Service Road 1861 on U.S. 101. A midsummer trip to the area is enhanced by purple foxglove blooms breaking up the white yarrow, Queen Anne's lace, and daisies.

Around these parts, there'll be many who'll tell you that Cascade Head is the highest promontory on the Oregon coast rising directly off the shoreline. This is true as long as you accept the figure of 1,770 feet in elevation as its height. Because a height of just over 1,500 feet is just as often reported for Cascade Head, the south coast's 1,756-foot Humbug Mountain might get the nod. One thing is for certain: the silliness of such statistical preoccupations are immediately evident when you're surrounded by the grandeur of either of these headlands.

Hart's Cove

One mile past the Cascade Head trail on Forest Service Road 1861 is the beginning of the trail to Hart's Cove. This five-mile hilly loop can have plenty of mud, so boots are recommended as you tromp through the rainforest. You'll emerge on an oceanfront meadow overlooking Hart's Cove, where the barking of sea lions might greet you. For more info on these trails, write to **Hebo Ranger District** (c/o Siuslaw National Forest, Hebo, 97122; tel. 392-3161).

Sitka Center For Art And Ecology

The region in the shadow of Cascade Head can be explored in even greater depth thanks to the Sitka Center for Art and Ecology (Box 65, Otis 97368; tel. 994-5485). From June-August, classes are offered in art and nature as an expression of the strong relationship between the two. Experts in everything from local plant communities to Siletz Indian baskets conduct outdoor workshops on the grounds of Cascade Head Ranch. Just follow Three Rocks Road along the Salmon River estuary to get to the ranch. Classes can last from a couple of days to a week, and fees vary as well. For complete info, write for a brochure or call the Sitka Center office between 10-5 during the period of instruction, or between 12-4 other times of the year.

THE THREE CAPES LOOP

The Three Capes Loop, a 35-mile byway off U.S. 101 between Neskowin and Tillamook, is considered by many to be the preeminent scenic area on the north coast. While the beauty of Capes Kiwanda, Lookout, and Meares justify leaving the main highway, it would be a mistake to think of this drive as a thrill-a-minute on the order of the south coast's Boardman Park or the central coast's Otter Crest Loop. Instead of fronting the ocean, the road connecting the Capes winds mostly through dairy country, small beach towns, and second-growth forest. What's special here are the three capes themselves, and unless you get out of the car and walk on the trails, you'll miss the aesthetic appeals and the distinctiveness of each headland's ecosystem. The wave-battered bluffs of Cape Kiwanda, the precipitous overlooks along the Cape Lookout highway, and the bizarre octopus tree at Cape Meares are the perfect antidotes to the strip towns along U.S. 101.

SIGHTS

U.S. 101 north from Neskowin passes through pastoral settings befitting Tillamook County's nickname, "the Land of Cheese, Trees, and Ocean Breeze." If you've tasted the world-famous Tillamook cheddar, chances are the mere sight of the cows grazing the lush grasses here will have you salivating. After thoughts of cheese, the realities of trees and ocean breeze will begin to take form on the Three Capes scenic drive turnoff about eight miles north of Neskowin.

Cape Kiwanda And Haystack Rock

Assuming you're not diverted by what some people consider to be the best fishing stream in the state, the **Nestucca River** (noted for chinook and coho salmon and steelhead), the next object of your prolonged gaze will be Haystack Rock. The sight of this 327-foot seastack a half-mile offshore in Nestucca Bay will greet you after you make your way through tiny Pacific City. Your attention will probably then shift to the sandstone escarpment of Cape Kiwanda just to the north of the beach, especially if seas are rough. In storm-tossed waters, this cape is the undisputed king of rock and roll if you go by coffee-table books and calendar photos. While other north coast sandstone promontories have been reduced to sandy beaches by the pounding surf, it's been theorized that Kiwanda has endured thanks to the buffer of Haystack Rock. In any case, hang-gliding afi-

Kite-flyers try their luck on the beach in front of Haystack Rock.

PHOTO BY OREGON TOURISM DIVISION

cionadoes are glad that the Cape is here. They scale the shoulder of the cape by climbing over hundreds of feet of deep sand in order to set themselves aloft off the north face. Most people will probably be content just to look up the coast from here at the knockout view of Cape Lookout or south at the unique spectacle of American fishing dories being launched into the ocean off the beach. The latter practice has been a tradition since the twenties after commercial fishermen took these flat-bottomed boats out to sea when gill-netting was banned on the Nestucca River.

These days outboard motors have replaced oar power, enabling the dories to get fifty miles out to sea from the Pacific City shoreline. If you come here around 6 a.m., you can watch them taking off. The fleet's late afternoon return attracts a crowd which comes to see the dorymen skidding their crafts as far up on the beach as possible to the boat trailers. Other people meet the dories to buy salmon and tuna direct. In addition, this beach is besieged by surfers who enjoy some of the longest waves on the Oregon coast. Other invasions are seen just north of Cape Kiwanda, where squadrons of dune buggies play King of the Mountain outside the town of Sandlake.

Cape Lookout

While the appeals of Cape Kiwanda might be missed by the uninitiated or the sedentary, Cape Lookout can be appreciated by a glance out your car window on the way up to the cape or from beachside picnic tables at the state park in its shadow. However, the two-mile walk out to the tip of the cape should be attempted by anyone in reasonable health. Even if you settle for a mere 15-minute stroll down the trailhead, you'll be able to look southward beyond Haystack Rock to Cascade Head. Giant spruces, western red cedars, and hemlocks surround the gently hilly trail to the tip of the cape. Halfway to the overlook, there are views north to Cape Meares over the Netarts sandspit. A bevy of wildflowers and birds can further enhance your march to the westernmost edge of this headland. Clear days in early April finds hordes of whalewatchers scanning the horizon from atop this 500-foot cliff.

The Cape Lookout trail is marked only by a sign on the highway that says rather cryptically, Wildlife Viewing Area. Such understatement is ironic, given the esteem in which this pathway is held by Oregonians. What the views from Capes Sebastian and Perpetua are to the south and central coasts, the overlooks here are to the northern part of the region. But even if you're not able to make this pilgrimage, the views along the highway to Cape Meares and south to Cascade Head are exhilarating. After a ten-minute drive past the Wildlife Viewing Area, follow the signs to Cape Lookout State Park fronting the beach. A trail beginning at the registration booth eventually leads to a ridge above the ocean. Another trail heads north through a variety of estuarine habitats along a five-mile sandspit separating Netarts Bay from the Pacific. The former is a popular site for clammers and crabbers.

The road between Netarts and Cape Meares heads into the pricey beach house community of Oceanside. Many of the homes are built into the cliff overlooking the ocean, Sausalito style. This trend reaches its apex atop Maxwell Point. From the **House on the Hill** parking lot (see "Accommodations" below), you can peer several hundreds of feet down at **Three Arch Rocks Wildlife Refuge,** part-time home to one of the continent's largest and most varied species of birds. A herd of sea lions also populates this trio of seastacks from time to time.

Cape Meares

With stunning views, picnic tables, a lighthouse, and a uniquely contorted tree a short walk from the parking lot, Cape Meares State Park is the most "user-friendly" site on the Three Capes Loop. The famed octopus tree is less than a quarter mile up a forested hill. The tentacle-like extensions of this Sitka spruce have also been compared to the arms of a candelabrum. Another writer likened this tree to a gargantuan spider in a near-fetal position. The 10-foot diameter of its base supports five-foot-thick trunks, each of which by itself is large enough to be a single tree. An Indian legend about the spruce contends that it was shaped this way so that the branches could hold the canoes of a chief's dead family. Supposedly, the bodies were buried near the tree. This was a traditional practice among the tribes of the area, who referred to species formed thusly as "council trees." Scientists have theorized everything from wind, weather, and insects damaging the spruce when it was young as the cause of its unusual shape. Beyond the tree you can look back at Oceanside and Three Arch Rocks Refuge. The sweep of Pacific shore and offshore monoliths makes a fitting finale to your sojourn along the Three Capes Loop, but be sure to also stroll the short paved trail down to the lighthouse which begins at the parking lot and provides dramatic views of an offshore wildlife refuge (Cape Meares Rocks—bring binoculars to see tufted puffins, pelagic cormorants, seals, and sea lions).

The restored interior of this 1890 lighthouse is Open May-Sept., Thurs.-Mon., 11-6. This beacon was replaced as a functioning light in 1963 by the automated facility located behind it. The free tour is occasionally staffed by volunteers who might tell you about how the lighthouse was built here by mistake and perhaps offer a peek into the prismatic Fresnel lenses. Before leaving the park, be sure to hike 200 yards east of the parking lot into the woods for a look at a giant Sitka spruce. Another giant Sitka is situated in the woods near the park's entrance.

The park was named for English navigator John Meares, who mapped many points along this coast in a 1788 voyage.

PRACTICALITIES

Accommodations
Rooms are where you find them on the relatively unpeopled Three Capes Loop. Here are some choices which give you a window on the sea for an affordable price.

The **Turnaround Motel** (5985 Pacific Avenue, Pacific City, 97135; tel. 965-6496) features units with sitting rooms, cooking areas, and views. Doubles go for around $35. The best deal in the area, if you're fortunate enough to be able to get a reservation, is the **House on the Hill** (Box 187, Oceanside, 97134; tel. 842-6030), located on previously described Maxwell Point. For $45-60 you get the seclusion and cliffside ocean grandeur of this headland. Despite the furniture being more suited to a room in a cut-rate motel, such a location for this price is an incredible bargain.

Campgrounds
Campsites along the loop might offer greater proximity to the capes as well as increased cost-effectiveness for a protracted stay than a room at

PHOTO BY OREGON TOURISM DIVISION
Cape Meares in a benign mood

a motel. Two campgrounds between Cape Meares and Cape Lookout offer centralized locations great views, and more than the usual run of campground creature comforts.

Cape Lookout State Park (contact 13000 Whiskey Creek Rd., West Tillamook 97141, tel. 842-4981) has 197 tent sites and 53 trailer sites as well as special camps for hikers and bikers. Showers, flush toilets, and a laundromat are available here. Reservations are accepted, it's open all year, and the fee is $8 a night.

Happy Camp (Box 52, Netarts 97143, tel. 842-4012) is located a few miles away in Netarts. Stop in at the Schooner Restaurant (see listing below) along the Netarts spit just off the highway for complete directions. There are 30 tent sites and 40 RV sites. All the amenities are available at $7 a night. Reservations are accepted and it's open all year.

Food
A decent selection of roadside stands, moderately priced local hangouts, and fine dining is available along the Three Capes scenic drive. **Wee Willies Restaurant** (6300 Whiskey Creek Rd., Netarts, 97143 tel. 842-6869) has home-baked goodies, grilled crab and Tillamook Cheddar

cheese sandwiches. You can also get chili dogs, hot dogs, burgers and the like. It's located a few miles north from Cape Lookout State Park. Just look for a drive-in secluded among the trees on the west side of the highway.

As you come to the end of Netarts spit after driving the highway from Cape Lookout State Park, you'll see a turnout west of the road with two wide-body mobile homes attached to each other. There is no indication that this is the **Schooner Restaurant and Lounge** (tel. 842-4988) until you come to a sign at the far end of the turnout. The Schooner caters most of the year to a lot of fixed-income retirees as the restaurant's 1950s-style prices attest. In addition to diner food, there's local fish specialties (try the oyster burger, $3.75) and homemade bread pudding and carrot cake for dessert. Fresh cinnamon rolls and the cook's own biscuits and gravy are deliciously filling for breakfast.

If hanging plants, a piano, and Nestucca River frontage don't make you feel at home, the apple pie and other wholesome fare at the **Riverhouse** (34450 Brooten Rd, Pacific City, 97135; tel. 965-6722) probably will. The seafood crepes, burgers, and open-face sandwich combinations are the perfect pick-me-up after a morning of fishing or beachcombing along the Nestucca River estuary. Your bills should run around $6 for lunch and twice that for dinner. Weekends feature the eclectic offerings of live musicians on Saturday night and a wonderful Sunday brunch. Come early, as seating is limited in this small 11-table restaurant.

At first, the weatherbeaten cedar shakes outside **Roseanna's Cafe** (Pacific St., Oceanside, 97134; tel. 842-7351) might lead you to expect an old general store, as indeed it was decades ago. Once inside, however, the lace curtains, fresh flowers, and shocking-pink tableclothes leave little doubt that this place takes its new identity seriously. From an elevated perch above the breakers here you'll be treated to expertly prepared steak and seafood followed by sumptuous desserts. Dishes centered around local oysters and fresh salmon are the specialties frequently touted by the staff. The menu is suprisingly extensive, as is the wine list, but be forewarned—the bills can be high at Roseanna's, so you might just prefer to come for such desserts as blackberry cobbler ($4.50) and watch the waves over a long cup of coffee.

Across the street, the **Anchor Tavern** (Pacific St., Oceanside, 97134; tel. 842-2041) makes great chili if you're seeking a lower-priced alternative.

TILLAMOOK AND VICINITY

Without much sun or surf, what could possibly draw enough visitors to Tillamook for it to rate the distinction of having one of the top three tourism attractions (according to a state tourism survey) in Oregon? Superficially speaking, a tour of a cheese factory in a town flanked by Tillamook Bay mud flats and rain-soaked dairy country shouldn't pull in over 750,000 tourists a year. But as anyone who has driven to Tillamook via the Three Capes Loop, or past Neahkahnie Mountain on U.S. 101 can attest, those tasty morsels of jack and cheddar provide the perfect complement to the surrounding region's scenic beauty.

Aesthetic and gastronomic appeals notwithstanding, Captain Robert Gray was merely looking for safe harbor when he pulled into the area of present-day Garibaldi just north of Tillamook in 1792. Some historians cite this as the first American landing on Oregon soil. In any case, the region whose name in Indian parlance means "land of many waters" has been written up in several other footnotes of history. Shortly after the turn of the century, Tillamook Bay sandspit was the site of a popular resort known as Bay Ocean. Over the years, changes in ocean currents caused the sandspit to wash away and by 1953 nothing remained of the three-story hotel, natatorium, cabins, and private homes here. As any old-timer on the coast will tell you, "Woe betide those who build their castles on the sand." However, many people still choose to construct houses on unstable Oregon sandspits.

In 1933 the Tillamook Burn devastated forests in the Coast Range east of town in what was the worst disaster in the state's history. The blazes raged for four weeks, reducing 500 square miles of old growth to rows of charred stumps. Fires in 1939 and 1945 further ravaged the area. Seedlings planted by a community reforestation effort in the decades that followed has produced an impressive stand of trees in these forests today.

A decade after the burn, the Tillamook blimp hangars, the two largest wooden structures ever built according to *Guinness,* went up south of town. The hangars were built partially in response to a Japanese submarine firing on Fort Stevens in Astoria. Of the five stations on the Pacific coast, the Tillamook blimp guard patrolled the waters from northern California to the San Juan Islands and escorted ships into Puget Sound. Until 1946, when the blimps were decommissioned, naval presence here created a boomtown. Bars and businesses flourished and civilian jobs were easy to come by. After the war years, Tillamook County returned to the economic trinity of "trees, cheese, and ocean breeze" which has sustained the region to the present day.

The old Tillamook lighthouse operated for over 80 years before its closure in 1962.

PHOTO BY OREGON TOURISM DIVISION

SIGHTS

Local Bounty

The traveler heading north towards Tillamook on U.S. 101 encounters sights which might even prove more compelling than the ever popular cheese factory. Start with a field of artichokes, a crop not seen in the United States outside of California. Eleven miles south of Tillamook on U.S. 101, near Beaver Road in Hebo, is a fruit stand purveying the locally grown chokes as well as an astounding variety of herbs, perennials, and fruit. The cherries, marionberries, blackberries, and plums are also recommended, as are the homemade fruit jams. Even if you're not hungry, **Bear Creek Artichokes** (tel. 398-5411; for information write 1604 5th Street, Tillamook, 97141) displays the creations of an enterprising horticulturist who'll be glad to share gardening tips with passers-by.

Munson Creek Falls

Four miles north of the fruit stand on U.S. 101 is a one-mile access road to the highest waterfall in the Oregon Coast Range. Munson Creek Falls drops 266 feet over mossy cliffs surrounded by an old growth forest. A roadside marker on the east side of the highway just past the Pleasant Valley sign directs you up a steep road past a cluster of homes. A very narrow, bumpy dirt road then takes you to the parking lot at the base of the falls. A trail from the middle of the lot provides a good view with a minimum of exertion; to the north of the trail is a steeper route which climbs a quarter-mile up to a perch eye-level with the midway point of the cascade. This is a spectacle in all seasons, but come in winter when the falls pour down with greater fury.

The Hangars

Further north on U.S. 101 you'll see Tillamook's huge blimp hangars east of the highway. A "caboose tour" of this facility is offered by Oregon Coast Lines (see "Getting Around" in the general Introduction). The hangars are where this company refurbishes rail cars for local trips and for the Alaska Railroad. Independent travelers are encouraged to drive up 9-5 p.m. daily and peer inside the 195-foot-high, 1,080-foot-long and 300-foot-wide structures. A single one can hold a 20-story building or seven football fields side by side.

While all kinds of blimp stories abound in Tillamook bars, only one wartime encounter has been documented with certainty. Recently declassified records confirm that blimps were involved in the sinking of what was believed to be two Japanese submarines off Cape Meares. In late May 1943, two of the high-flying craft, assisted by U.S. Navy sub chasers and destroyers, dropped several depth charges on the submarines, which are still lying on the ocean floor. These days you might see smaller blimps in the hangars which are leased by airborne advertising companies and Aerolift, an enterprise which develops dirigibles to gather up timber from remote logging sites.

Tillamook County Pioneer Museum

West of the highway in the heart of downtown, Tillamook County Pioneer Museum (2106 2nd Street, Tillamook, 97141; tel. 842-4553) is famous for its taxidermic exhibits as well as memorabilia from pioneer households. Particularly intriguing are hunks of beeswax with odd inscriptions recovered from near Neahkahnie Mountain (see "Cannon Beach"). It's open Mon.-Sat. 8:30-5, and Sun. noon-5 from April through September. In winter, the hours just listed apply but the museum is closed Monday. Admission is a dollar, $5 for families, and half price for kids 12-17.

Tillamook Creamery

Tillamook Creamery (4175 U.S. 101 North, Tillamook, 97141; tel. 842-4481) welcomes visitors with an imposing parking lot reproduction of the *Morning Star,* the ship that once transported locally made butter and cheese and now adorns the label of every Tillamook product. The quaint vessel symbolizing Tillamook cheesemaking's humble beginnings stands in stark contrast to the technology and sophistication that go into making this world-famous gourmet product today.

Inside the plant, a self-guided tour follows the movement of curds and whey to the "cheddaring table." Whey is drained from the curds, which are then cut and folded. These processes are coordinated by white-uniformed workers in a stadium-sized factory. As you look down on the antiseptic scene from the glassed-in observation area, it's hard to imagine this as the birthplace of many a pizza and grilled cheese sandwich. If you can bring yourself to taste a few samples however, the operation-room ambience will quickly be forgotten. User-friendly informational placards and historical displays also inject a human touch to the proceedings. The latter recount Tillamook Valley's dairy history from 1851, when settlers began importing cows. The problem then was how to ship the milk to San Francisco and Portland. Even though salting butter to preserve it created some export revenue, there remained for ships the difficulty of negotiating the treacherous Tillamook bar. In 1894, Peter McIntosh introduced techniques here to make cheddar cheese whose long shelf life enabled it to be transported overland.

In the early 1900s, the Tillamook County Creamery Association absorbed smaller operations and the modern plant opened in 1949. Today, Tillamook churns over 30 million pounds of cheese annually, including monterey jack, swiss, and multiple variations of their famous cheddar. Pepperoni, butter, cheese soup, milk, and other products are also available at the ice-cream counter, gift shops, and deli. The Tillamook Cheese Factory and visitor center is open daily from 8-8 p.m. in summer and closes at 6 p.m. in winter.

PRACTICALITIES

Food

While not always the height of haute cusine, Tillamook restaurant fare can at least draw on the local bounty from the sea and surrounding farm country. Dungeness crab, bay shrimp, clams, and oysters are indigenous to the area and a burgeoning number of wine and gourmet outlets throughout Tillamook County provide alternatives to the high-priced deli at the end of the creamery tour.

The **Blue Heron French Cheese Factory** (2001 Blue Heron Drive, tel. 842-8281) offers samples of their bleu cheese, picnic fixin's for sale, and wine-tasting from leading Oregon vineyards. Lunchtime sandwiches can be supplemented by locally raised and cured meat from **D's Sausage Factory** (tel. 842-2622) located down the road on U.S.101 in between the Blue Heron and the Tillamook Creamery.

North of town on U.S. 101 **La Casa Medello** (1160 U.S. 101 North, tel. 842-5786) serves lunch and dinner daily, primarily Mexican food geared to American palates at good prices. Full dinners with large portions and a low grease factor go for around $7.

If you're in town for the evening, dinner at **Hadley House** (2203 3rd St., tel. 842-2101) culls fresh ingredients from the Pacific and the pasture. Moderate prices and a pleasant staff also recommend this local favorite across from the courthouse.

Your Tillamook County gourmet tour continues 25 miles north in **Garibaldi**, where **Miller's Seafood Market** (tel. 322-0355) sits on the left-hand side of U.S. 101. Fresh salmon, ling cod, and bottomfish are the specialties here. Garibaldi is a fish processing center, so Miller's selection is both low-priced and fresh.

North of Garibaldi on U.S. 101 is the resort town of **Rockaway.** A walk along the seven miles of sandy beach here could well provide your only respite from 50 miles of inland towns between Tillamook and Neahkahnie Mountain. Another reason to hit the brakes in Rockaway is **Karla's Krabs** (2010 U.S. 101 North, Rockaway, tel. 355-2362). Karla's roadside snack shack exterior in no way suggests that this place catered former Governor Neil Goldschmidt's inaugural or is one of the concessionaires at Portland Trailblazer games in Memorial Coliseum. However, while prices on the menu here bespeak such wallet-stretching influences, the smoked fish delicacies in the display case are worth any asking price. It's hard to resist such exotic offerings as snapper jerky smoked in a honey glaze, alderwood-smoked halibut and prawns, or the extra large Willapa Bay smoked oysters. Picnickers in a less experimental mood might ask for a serving of Karla's mainstays—chinook salmon and smoked sturgeon.

After eating your way up the coast, what could be more fitting than to wash it all down with a local wine? The **Nehalem** (pronounced "Knee-hail-em") **Bay Winery** (34965 ORE 53, Nehalem, tel. 368-5300) produces varietal wines as well as fruit and berry wines (pinot noir, gewürtztraminer, and blackberry). Tour the winery and picnic on the grounds between 10-5 p.m. daily. To get there, look for a ORE 53 sign on the side of U.S. 101 and follow it to the winery.

Camping

Kilchis County Park (tel. 842-8662) has cheap ($5) but primitive sites near a river with good steelhead and salmon fishing. To get there, go up Kilchis River Road about 10 miles northeast of Tillamook. The park is closed September to May.

Information And Services

The **Tillamook County Chamber of Commerce** (3705 U.S. 101 North, tel. 842-7525) is located across the parking lot from the cheese factory. They are open Monday-Friday from 9-5 p.m, Saturday 1-5 p.m. from mid-June to September. This pamphlet-lined shack is also open on Sunday from 11-2 p.m.

The **post office** (2200 1st St., Tillamook, 97191) is open Monday-Friday 8:30-5 p.m.

As of this edition, both RAZ Transit and Citizens Better Transit were bidding on the Beach Bus contract which runs from Portland to Seaside and back via ORE 6 and U.S. 101, serving towns in between. Assuming Citizens retains the contract, getting to Portland will cost $10, under 12 $7.50. Regardless of who the carrier will be, the terminal will remain at the Jiffy Market (604 Main St., tel. 842-5848). Call ahead to clarify exact departure/arrival times.

Other useful numbers include the **Tillamook Crisis and Resource Center** (tel. 842-9486), **Tillamook Ambulance** (tel. 842-4444), the county **sheriff** (tel. 842-2561), and the **Alderbrook Golf Course** (Idaville Road, tel. 842-6413). The latter is located north of town and charges a $12 greens fee.

Events

The **Tillamook County Fair** takes place the second week of August and represents more than three-quarters of a century of tradition. Call the chamber of commerce for more information. The **Dairy Festival** takes place throughout June with rodeos, parades, and evocations of the Swiss-German roots of the region's settlers. Lederhausen, polka bands, sausages, and thousands of cheese-crazed tourists make this a lively celebration of the end of a long rainy season.

CANNON BEACH AND VICINITY

John Steinbeck in *Travels With Charlie* bemoaned how present-day Carmel, California would be eschewed by the very people who gave the town the appealing sobriquet "artist colony." This same thing could well happen to the Carmel of the Oregon coast, Cannon Beach, unless the growth which began in 1980 is slowed. Within a decade, the number of motel rooms here has doubled, as has the number of visitors on a busy weekend (which now averages 10-12 thousand people).

Nonetheless, the broad stretch of beach highlighted by the impressive promontory Haystack Rock still provides a contemplative experience, although you might have to walk a couple of miles from your parking place to get to it. And if you're patient and resourceful enough to find a space for your wheels, the finest gallery-hopping, crafts, and shopping on the coast await. The city is zoned in such a way to keep it small enough for strolling, and a location far removed from U.S. 101 spares it the kind of blight seen on the main drags of other coastal tourist towns.

The hamlet got its name when a cannon from the wrecked U.S.S. *Shark* washed ashore south of the current city limits in 1846. The *Shark* had met its end in the waves of the treacherous Columbia bar while monitoring a territorial dispute with a contingent of English merchant ships.

In 1873, stagecoach and railroad tycoon Ben Holladay helped create the first coastal tourist mecca, Seaside, while ignoring her attractive neighbor in the shadow of Haystack Rock. In the 20th century, Cannon Beach evolved into a bohemian alternative to the hustle-and-bustle of the more robust resort scene to the north. Before the recent era of development, this place was a quaint backwater attracting laid-back artists, summer-home residents, and the overflow from pricier digs in Seaside. Today, the low-key charm and atmosphere conducive to artistic expression are threatened by a massive visitor influx and price increases. While such vital signs as a first-rate theater, a good bookstore, and fine restaurants are still in ample evidence in Cannon Beach, your view of them from the other side of the street might be blocked by a convoy of Winnebagos.

SIGHTS

Neahkahnie Mountain And Oswald West State Park

South of Cannon Beach, north of Manzanita, is Neahkahnie Mountain. The coast highway traces part of the mountain's outlines 700 feet above the Pacific. Nowhere along U.S. 101 is the roadbed so high above an ocean view; soaring another thousand feet above you on the other side of the highway is the peak named for the Tillamook tribe's fire spirit. Nonetheless, keep your eyes on the road until you've parked your car. The area is full of hikers and occasionally, at daybreak or dusk, Roosevelt elk and blacktailed deer.

Scenic turnoffs abound, but take the half-mile trail from the main parking lot at Oswald West State Park (look for signs) to **Short Sands Beach.** This lot is on the east side of the road, where the trail winds down under a culvert beneath the highway. From Short Sands Beach you can pick up the three-mile old-growth-lined Cape Falcon Trail to the highway, or you just might want to linger at Smuggler Cove. Spruce, hemlock,

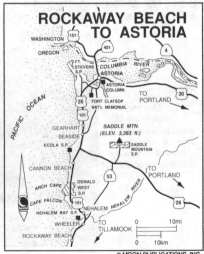

© MOON PUBLICATIONS, INC.

and cedar rainforests crowd the secluded shoreline and it's easy to believe local legends of Spanish pirates burying a treasure along this coast. One legend had the crew of a shipwrecked Manila galleon salvaging their cargo of gold and beeswax (a popular commodity in trade with the Orient) by burying it in the side of the mountain. To deter Indians from the site, the Spanish pirates killed a black man and buried him on top of the cargo. While this account taken from native histories has never been substantiated, a piece of crudely inscribed beeswax retrieved from the Neahkahnie region (on display at Tillamook's Pioneer Museum) keeps alive speculation.

In any case, there is real treasure here today for all who venture into this realm. We have Governor Oswald West's 1913 beach bill to thank for Oregon's virgin shoreline. The 1967 amendment to West's bill protected the dry-sand area of the beach (from the high-tide line to the vegetation line). The spirit of the legislation is honored with the **Matt Kramer Memorial.** Kramer was a reporter whose detailed coverage of the 1967 legislative proceedings produced a groundswell of public support for the bill.

Your return to the highway via the **Cape Falcon Trail** takes you back to a point north of where you parked your car. Die-hard hikers can now elect to trek the **Neahkahnie Summit Trail.** Look for the trailhead just north of the viewpoint honoring Oswald West, marked by a small sign across the highway. It's several miles of steep,

and at times narrow, trail to the top. The summit offers stunning views north to Tillamook Head and south to Cape Meares. In the spring, thimbleberry, wild onions, and foxglove thrive along with other flora. On the way back, retrace your steps or descend the southern route on a one-mile trail.

Entering Cannon Beach

Several miles up from Oswald West State Park's main parking lot is **Arch Cape Tunnel** cut right into the mountain. This marks the end of the state park but not the beauty. On the way into Cannon Beach, views of **Hug Point State Park** and pristine beaches will have you lacing up your hiking boots again. Two miles south of the downtown area, park at **Tolovana Beach Wayside.** Picnic and restroom facilities aren't the only reasons to come here. This is an excellent base from which to walk south three miles to Hug Point (so named because wagons had to dash between the waves hugging the point to get around) or north two miles past Haystack Rock into town. If you are going to Hug Point, you'll appreciate how the knot of beach-goers thins out south of Tolovana. Timing your trek to coincide with low tide will maximize your enjoyment. Not only will it be possible to navigate those areas of beachfront subject to inundation at high tide, but all manner of marinelife in tidal pools will be exposed. At low tide, you'll also see remains of an 800-foot-long, Model-T-sized road blasted into the base of Hug Point, an early precursor to U.S. 101. The cliffs at Hug

The view from Neahkahnie Mt., overlooking the spot of an as-yet-undiscovered treasure supposedly hidden by the crew of a wrecked Spanish galleon

PHOTO BY OREGON TOURISM DIVISION

Point are gouged with caves and crevasses which also invite exploring.

Heading into town on foot from Tolovana is a good idea on holiday weekends when there's a dearth of parking spaces. As you head north, **Haystack Rock** will loom larger. This is the third highest coastal monolith in the world, measuring 235 feet in height. Flanking the mountain are two rock formations known as **The Needles.** These skinny spires had two other counterparts at the turn of the century which were gradually leveled by weathering and erosion. Old-timers will tell you that a trail to the top of Haystack was dynamited by the government to keep people off this bird rookery and away from the intertidal life at its base. It also reduced the number of intrepid hikers trapped on the rock at high tide. Today the area is designated an Oregon Island National Wildlife Refuge and has wilderness status. During the summer, the **Haystack Rock Awareness Program** sponsors free interpretive programs here and evening programs in Cannon Beach; check the chamber of commerce for details. While these talks are interesting, the beach will also speak to you with its own distinctive voices. Don't miss the cacophony of shorebirds at sunset and the winter phenomenon of "singing sands" created by wind blowing over the beach.

The Beach Loop Into Town

Driving into town along the beach loop which branches off U.S 101, you'll pass such destination resorts as the Tolovana Inn, the Surfsand, and the Surfview. Thereafter, the townsite which greets you is more like Cape Cod and Carmel than any other town on the Oregon coast. Wood shingles and understated earth colors predominate the architecture of tastefully rendered galleries, bookstores, and bistros. Throngs of walkers along Hemlock Street, the main drag, also distinguish this burgh from the typical coastal strip town whose heart and soul have been pierced by U.S. 101. You have to go clear to the north of Cannon Beach to find a gas station, and even then you're liable to bypass its stone cottage facade.

Klootchy Creek And Saddle Mountain

From the north end of town, it's not far to the junction of U.S. 101 and U.S. 26. The latter goes 80 miles east to Portland, but many coastal travelers just travel two miles on U.S. 26 to visit Klootchy

Creek Park. In an old growth spruce and fir forest here you'll find the **world's tallest Sitka spruce.** Standing 216 feet high and 52 feet in circumference, it's believed to be over seven centuries old. To find the tree, look for signs on the north side of the highway shortly after leaving Cannon Beach.

Another reason to head east from Cannon Beach is the hike up 3,283-foot Saddle Mountain. To get to the trailhead, take U.S. 26 for 15 miles and turn left on the prominently indicated Saddle Mountain Road. Although it's paved, this road is not suitable for RVs or wide-bodied vehicles. After seven twisting miles, you'll come to the trailhead of the highest peak in this part of the Coast Range. The trail is steep and takes over four hours round trip, but is worth the effort. On a clear day, hikers can see some 50 miles of the Oregon and Washington coastline, including the Columbia River. Also possible are spectacular views of Mt. Rainer, Mt. St. Helens, Mt. Hood, and, unfortunately, miles of clearcuts. If you go between May and August you'll be treated to a wildflower display that is nationally famous among botanists. On the upper part of the three-mile trail to the top, species from Alaska and Canada which pushed south during the last ice age thrive. The cool, moist climate here keeps them from dying out as they did at lower elevations. Some early blooms include pink coast fawn lily, monkey flowers, bleeding heart, oxalis, Indian paintbrush, and trilliums. There are around 2,000 species of flora in all. There are also deer, elk, and black bear in the surrounding forests.

Down U.S. 26 about one mile west of Elsie you can visit **Morris' Camp 18 Logging Museum** (Box 195, Seaside, 97138; tel. 755-2476). Here, the chance to look at steam donkeys and other antique logging equipment breaks up the long drive to Portland.

Jewell Meadow Wildlife Area

Further down U.S. 26, however, is the best place of all to see wildlife. Each fall and winter Roosevelt elk come to the Jewell Meadow Wildlife area. Blacktailed deer might show up in the spring and summer. To get there, take U.S. 26 to the Jewell junction (about 20 miles east of Cannon Beach) then head north on an unmarked state road for nine miles to **Jewell.** Turn west and drive one mile on ORE 202 to parking spaces in close proximity to elk.

the view from
Ecola Point summit

PHOTO BY REBECCA SINGER

Ecola State Park

Ecola State Park is just north of the Cannon Beach townsite. Thick conifer forests line the access road to Ecola Point. This forested cliff has many trails which lead down to the water. The view south takes in Haystack Rock, just over from which the overlapping peaks of the Coast Range extend to Neahkahnie Mountain. Out to sea, the sight of sea lions basking on surf-drenched rocks (mid-April through July) or migrating gray whales (March) and orcas (May) are seasonal highlights. From Ecola Point, trails lead north to horseshoe-shaped **Indian Beach,** a favorite with surfers. Some prefer to drive there as a prelude to hiking up Tillamook Head, considered the region's most beautiful viewpoint by Lewis and Clark (see "Seaside History"). The name Ecola means "whale" in Chinook jargon and was first used as a place name by William Clark, referring to a creek in the area. Lewis and Clark journals note a 105-foot beached whale found somewhere within present-day Ecola Park's southern border, **Crescent Beach.**

From Ecola Point, the historic **Tillamook Rock Lighthouse** sits a mile northwest out to sea. This beacon was operative from 1881 to 1957, despite sustained 100-mile-per-hour gales which frequently pushed seas up and over the 130-foot height of the light. Today it serves as a depository for cremated human remains.

Les Shirley Park

A city park worth visiting is Les Shirley Park. In addition to being the probable location of the whale carcass observed by Lewis and Clark, this place has interpretive signs to explain the interac-

tion of ocean and freshwater that occurs in Ecola Creek estuary. To reach the park after leaving town on the beach loop to U.S. 101, turn left on 5th St. at the foot of the hill. Pass the sign for Ecola State Park; Les Shirley Park is a few more blocks ahead.

PRACTICALITIES

Camping

Nehalem Bay State Park (tel. 308-5943; write: 8300 3rd St., Nehalem, 97130), about 15 miles south of Cannon Beach, offers varied recreation and lots of camping spots. Sandwiched between the bay and a six-mile oceanfront strip are 292 sites going for $9, including some bargain biker/hiker sites and hot showers. Boating, crabbing, and windsurfing in the bay are popular here. Close by is the town of **Manzanita,** where wealthy Portlanders summer. Park amenities include a laundromat, flush toilets, and piped water. No reservations are necessary and it's open mid-April to late October.

At **Oswald West State Park** (tel. 368-5943 or tel. 238-7488; write: 8300 3rd St., Nehalem, 97130) you walk a half mile from a parking lot to campsites in a grove of old growth conifers backdropped by high cliffs. In addition to Short Sands Beach, Smuggler's Cove, and the previously detailed hiking options, surfing and tidepooling can be enjoyed nearby. The State Parks Division supplies wheelbarrows to cart your gear from the parking lot to 36 primitive campsites. Here camping is allowed mid-May to October and costs $7 a night.

Accommodations

If you're not willing to make storm-watching an acquired taste, do not reserve Cannon Beach lodgings from mid-January through early March. During this time much of the annual rainfall total of 80 inches is recorded. Should high room rates or crowds on weekends other times of the year be a deterrent, remember Cannon Beach is only an hour and a half from Portland, perfect for a day trip.

A nice oceanfront family-style lodge is the **Sea Sprite** (write for brochure to Box 66 Tolovana Park, OR 97145; tel. 436-2266). With a beach-front location just south of of Haystack Rock, plus kitchens, TV, and spectacular views, it's not surprising that this place commands $55-120 rates during the regular season. What *is* surprising are off-season discounts of 50% of these rates, Oct.-May, Sunday through Thursday.

Two moderately priced motels close to town but far enough from trafiic for peace and quiet are the **Blue Gull** (632 Hemlock St. Cannon Beach 97110; tel. 436-2714) and **McBee Motel** (888 S. Hemlock St. Cannon Beach 97110; tel. 436-2569). But for somewhat more money than the $30-40 you'd pay at these places, you can get the intimacy and flavor of a bed and breakfast. In Cannon Beach the two-bedroom **Tern Inn** (3663 S. Hemlock, Cannnon Beach; tel. 436-1528) is close enough to the beach for good views. Private baths, private entrances, and full breakfasts with home-baked goodies go for as low as $65 a night. Reserve a month in advance. The **Inn at Cannon Beach** (1116 Hemlock St. Cannon Beach; tel. 436-1392) is a 1910 converted loggers' boarding house with 30 rooms and a small cafe and restaurant on the premises. Full breakfasts are included in the $50-100 per night rates, and lunch and dinner can be enjoyed here apart from the lodging package. Reserve a week in advance.

Food

As you might expect, eating out can get expensive here. However, there are some some ways to beat the costs and if you can't, there are a few justifiable splurges.

The **Mariner Market** (139 North Hemlock St., tel. 436-2412) is an antique-filled grocery that's fully stocked with fresh meat, fruit, and vegetables. The Mariner's prices beat the tab at several other markets in town and it's open 9-9. Before you leave, check out the antique grocery paraphernalia, old-time bottles and containers, and the jewelry and crystal shop upstairs.

The **Lazy Susan Cafe** (126 North Hemlock St., tel. 436-2816) is set back from Hemlock Street in Coaster Square. Just look for Coaster Theater (108 North Hemlock St.) on the west side of the street and go beyond it into the mall. This is *the* place in town for breakfast and lunch. Homemade muffins, eggs Benedict, and the best coffee in town can fuel up or finish off an early morning beach walk. Homemade soups and sandwiches are the bill-of-fare at lunch. With

Short Sands Beach at Oswald West State Park

PHOTO BY OREGON TOURISM DIVISION

prices not going too much beyond $5 for a good-sized meal, the lines can be long on weekend mornings. **Dooley's West Texas Bar-B-Que** (339 North Elm St., tel. 436-1827) serves up mesquite-flavored chicken and ribs in a tasty barbecue sauce.

Morris' Fireside Restaurant (207 North Hemlock, tel. 436-2917) is an attractive log building wherein moderately priced steak and seafood are featured along with "logger" breakfasts. Portions are large and so is the selection. Try the crab and cheese sandwich for lunch and the fresh seafood special for dinner.

Mo's at Tolovana (3400 South Hemlock, new phone listing), formerly Daggatt's, sits next to Tolovana Park and boasts a restaurant site once selected by *Pacific Northwest* magazine as having "the most romantic view on the Oregon coast." Add this to Mo's reliable formula of fresh fish and rich clam chowder at reasonable prices, and you can't miss.

Several afterthoughts deserving of your consideration are the chocolate-covered shortbread at **Cannon Beach Cookie Company** (239 North Hemlock, tel. 436-2832) and the espresso drinks and ice cream across the street at **Osburn's Ice Creamery** (240 North Hemlock, tel. 436-1470). The latter is adjacent to **Osburn's Deli** (tel. 436-2234), featuring $3.50 sandwiches which can make a meal for two. At night **Bill's Tavern** (188 North Hemlock St., tel. 436-2202) is nightlife in Cannon Beach. The woodstove, pool table, and dart board create a friendly ambience and the joint jumps on weekends with live rock bands.

Shopping And Galleries

The preponderance of Cannon Beach galleries and shops are on Hemlock Street. At the north end of town **White Bird Gallery's** (tel. 436-2681) varied arts and crafts are worth a special look. Also on the northern part of Hemlock is a fine kite store, **Once Upon A Breeze** (tel. 436-1112). In the middle of the block is **Cannon Beach Book Company** (tel. 436-1301), the best bookstore on the coast. This is the place to pick up regional titles or a good novel for that rainy weekend.

Events

The half dozen other sandcastle contests which take place on the Oregon coast were given nary a mention in this book, so much do they pale in comparison to the Cannon Beach event. Approaching its third decade, this is the state's first and most prestigious competition of its kind. Tens of thousands of spectators show up to watch 1,000-plus competitors fashion their creations with the aid of buckets, shovels, and squirt guns. This event is free to spectators, but entrants pay a fee. Recent winners included Egyptian pyramids and a gigantic sea turtle. The event usually coincides with the lowest-tide Saturday in late May. Call 436-2623 to find out the exact date of this collapsible art show which takes place a mile north of Haystack Rock. Building begins in the early morning; judging starts at noon.

The **Stormy Weather Festival** in November brings out local artists, musicians, and their creations. Call the chamber of commerce for details. December heralds the annual **Dickens Festival**. Each Friday and Saturday from December 1-16, local thespians don traditional Victorian costumes and perform a Dickensian Christmas play at the Coaster Theater (108 North Hemlock, tel. 436-1242). Other related events such as teas and lamplighting ceremonies usher in the holiday season with a Dickens or Victorian motif.

The Coaster Theater (for information or reservations write Box 643, Cannon Beach, 97110) also features summer plays as well as local and out-of-town shows in winter.

Information And Services

The **Cannon Beach Chamber of Commerce** (Box 64, 201 East 2nd, Cannon Beach, 97110; tel. 436-2623) is open Monday through Saturday 11-5 p.m., Sunday 11-4 p.m. and is occasionally closed on winter weekends. The **post office** (155 North Hemlock, Cannon Beach, 97110; tel. 436-2822) is open Monday through Friday 9-5 p.m. Artists and writers congregate in Cannon Beach for one- or two-week courses in the **Haystack Program for the Arts.** Call the arts office (tel. 464-4812) of Portland State University for more details.

SEASIDE AND VICINITY

Seaside is the quintessential family beach resort. The beach is long and flat, protected from ocean tides by scenic headlands; lifeguards are on duty weekends. In addition, there's beachside playground equipment and the only boardwalk north of Santa Cruz, California. Atlantic City it's not, thank goodness, but the carny motif of the Jersey shore is evoked by the cotton-candy, ferris wheel, arcades, and abundance of tourist facilities. South of town the presence of clammers and waders in the shallows and surfers negotiating the swells also recalls the liveliness of a southern California or Atlantic Ocean littoral instead of the remote peacefulness of many Oregon beaches. East Coast visitors often liken Cannon Beach to Provincetown, and Seaside to Coney Island prior to their decline.

Located in the shadow of majestic Tillamook Head at the mouth of the Necanicum River, Seaside has attracted tourists since the early 1870s when transportation magnate Ben Holladay sensed the potential of a hotel near the water. Train service to Portland helped realize that potential. Prior to being the first coastal resort in the state, Seaside's fame as the end of the Lewis and Clark Trail made it a national landmark. The dynamic duo came here in the winter of 1805-06 and set up a salt cairn, boiling seawater nonstop for seven weeks to produce four bushels of salt for the trip back east.

In recent years, the town has become more than just a retreat for Portland families. Oregon's apostle of haute cuisine, the late James Beard, used to hold a celebrated cooking class each summer here. This opened the door for writers' retreats, art classes, and business conventions. If these occasions or a family outing should bring you to Seaside, you'll enjoy the spirit of fun—just be prepared to swallow hard when you see the bill.

SIGHTS

Downtown Seaside
Sightseeing in Seaside means walking the **"Prom."** This two-mile-long boardwalk extending from V Street to 12th Avenue was constructed in 1921 to replace the rotten planks from an older walk and protect ocean properties from the waves. Beaches along the way offer vantages from which to contemplate the sand, surf, and massive contours of 1,200-foot-high Tillamook Head. Along the Prom is the **Turnaround,** a small traffic circle framing a placard proclaiming this point the end of the trail for Lewis and Clark. Eight blocks south of here between Beach Drive and the Prom is a replica of the Lewis and Clark salt cairn. Running east from the Turnaround, Broadway, Seaside's central traffic artery, goes a half mile to U.S. 101 (Roosevelt) through a mind-numbing array of arcades, game rooms, gift shops, taverns, and a carousel.

If you tire of having a good time on Broadway, make your way to **Seaside Historical Museum** (570 Necanicum Drive, tel. 738-7065) whose Clatsop Indian artifacts will impart more of a sense of history than anything else in town. It's open daily 10:30 a.m.-4:30 p.m.; admission is $1 for adults, 50 cents for children.

Following Lewis And Clark
Just south of Seaside you can walk in the footsteps of Lewis and Clark to **Tillamook Head.** In January 1806 on a quest for a beached whale, Clark found the promontory. He was moved enough by the view to later write about it in his journal:

I beheld the grandest and most pleasing prospect which my eyes ever surveyed. Immediately in front of us is the ocean breaking in fury. To this boisterous scene the Columbia with its tributaries and studded on both sides with the Chinook and Clatsop villages forms a charming contrast, while beneath our feet are stretched the rich prairies.

Prior to setting out, arrange to have a friend drive down to **Indian Beach** to pick you up at the end of this seven-mile, three-hour pilgrimage. Or, you can be picked up another one mile south at the Ecola Point parking lot. To get to the trailhead, drive south of Seaside out Avenue U (Beach St.) past the golf course to Edgewood Street until you reach the parking lot at the end of the road. Nearby is an area known as **The Cove,** frequented by surfers and fishermen. As you head up the forested trail on the north side of Tillamook Head you can look back over the Seaside townsite. In about 20 minutes, you'll be looking down at the ocean from cliffs 1,000 feet above. Several hours later, you'll hike down onto Indian Beach, arriving near the restrooms.

PRACTICALITIES

Whatever your price range, you'll have to reserve ahead for a room in Seaside during the summer. If you do, chances are you'll be able to find the "specs" you're looking for, given the area's array of lodgings; if you don't, come prepared to camp.

Bed And Breakfast
One option especially worth reserving in the so-called "Sunset Empire" are bed and breakfasts. In Seaside, the **Boarding House** (208 N. Holladay Dr., tel. 738-9055) overlooks the Necanicum River. The 1898 Victorian features fir tongue-in-groove walls and beamed ceilings. All rooms have private baths and go for $50-80 a night. Reserve two weeks in advance in summer. The **Riverside Inn** (4305 Holladay Dr., tel. 738-8254) has separate four-room cottages overlooking the river with double occupancy rates ranging from $39-45. Private baths, homemade breakfast, and special discount rates Sunday through Thursday

for stays of three days or more are available October through June. During peak season, be sure to reserve a room a month in advance.

Gaston's Beachside Bed and Breakfast (Corner of I Ave. and the Prom, tel. 738-8320) is the best deal on the Prom. This two-room 1906 home charges $40-50 including a full breakfast. Guests share a bath. **Chocolates For Breakfast** (606 N. Holladay, tel. 738-3622) is a 1921 house with double occupancy rates of $45-65. A river view, chocolate hazelnut croissants for breakfast, and an artsy motif make this place a winner.

If you're in need of a budget room here, the **Holladay Motel** (426 S. Holladay Dr., tel. 738-6529), and the **Mariner** (429 S. Holladay, same tel. as above) offer rooms with facilities down the hall in the $35 range. They share the same management and use of a pool.

Camping
Saddle Mountain and Klootchy Creek parks (see "Cannon Beach"), due east of Cannon Beach on U.S. 26 (the Sunset Highway), make great camping spots.

Klootchy Creek Park (Clatsop County Parks, Astoria, 97103; tel. 325-2631), home of the giant spruce, is 300 yards off U.S. 26. It has nine primitive sites that go for $6 a night. You're paying for proximity to the tree, the beaches, and the civilized haunts of two nearby coastal cities as well as fishing (trout, steelhead, salmon) on the banks of the Necanicum River.

Frederic Remington's depiction of Lewis and Clark meeting an Indian

SEASIDE ACCOMMODATIONS

Name	Address	Telephone	Price	Features
Del Mar Motel	210 N. Downing	738-7622	$25-50	cable TV, pets, kitchenettes, restaurant/lounge, laundry
Country River Inn	1020 N. Holladay Dr.	738-8049	$35-75	wheelchair access, cable TV, restaurant, nonsmoking rooms, river view
Mariner Holladay Motel	429 S. Holladay Dr.	738-3690	$35-45	wheelchair access, cable TV, pool, pets, kitchenettes, nonsmoking rooms
Ocean Vista Motel	241 Ave. U	738-7473	$35-42	cable TV, pets, kitchenettes
River View Inn	555 Ave. G	738-0670	$35-75	wheelchair access, cable TV, kitchenettes, nonsmoking rooms, river view
Royale Motel	531 Ave. A	738-9541	$35-42	wheelchair access, river view
Coast River Inn	800 S. Holladay Dr.	738-8474	$37-69	wheelchair access, cable TV, kitchenettes, laundry, non-smoking rooms
Colonial Motor Inn	1120 N. Holladay Dr.	738-6295	$38-65	cable TV, laundry, nonsmoking rooms, riverview
Driftwood Motel	815 N. Holladay Dr.	738-5597	$38-60	small 10-unit property with a laundry
Hillcrest Inn	118 N. Columbia	738-6273	$38-75	wheelchair access, cable TV, kitchenettes, laundry, nonsmoking rooms
Sundowner Motor Inn	125 Ocean Way	738-8301	$42	wheelchair access, cable TV, pets, kitchenettes, covered pool

SEASIDE ACCOMMODATIONS, cont.

Name	Address	Telephone	Price	Features
Ambassador by the Sea	40 Ave. U	738-6382	$44-95	cable TV, kitchenettes, laundry, pool, nonsmoking rooms, ocean view
White Caps Motel	120 9th Ave.	738-5371	$45-140	pets, kitchenettes, laundry, ocean view
Tradewinds Motel	1022 N. Prom	738-9468	$46-55	pets, kitchenettes, ocean view
Tides Motel	2316 Beach Dr.	738-6317	$47-104	cable TV, kitchenettes, pool, nonsmoking rooms, ocean view
Huntley Inn	441 2nd Ave.	738-9581	$49-66	wheelchair access, cable TV, kitchenettes, covered pool, river view
Oceanfront Motel	50 1st Ave.	738-5661	$53-73	wheelchair access, ocean view
Hi-Tide Motel	30 Ave. G	738-8414	$55-80	cable TV, kitchenettes, pool, covered pool, non-smoking rooms, ocean view
Inn on the Prom	361 S. Prom	738-5241	$55-100	kitchenettes, fireplace, non-smoking rooms, ocean view
Shilo Inn Seaside	East 900 S. Holladay Dr.	738-0549	$55-90	wheelchair access, cable TV, kitchenettes, covered pool, laundry, non-smoking rooms, complimentary continental breakfast
Lanai Condos Motel	3140 Sunset Blvd.	738-6343	$65-75	cable TV, kitchenettes, pool, ocean view

SEASIDE ACCOMMODATIONS, cont.

Name	Address	Telephone	Price	Features
Best Western Seashore Resort	60 N. Prom	738-6368	$66-76	covered pool, ocean view
Best Western Ocean View Resort	414 N. Prom	738-3334	$70-145	wheelchair access, kitchenettes, fire place, covered pool, laundry, nonsmoking rooms, complimentary continental breakfast, ocean view
Seaside Beach Club	561 S. Prom	738-7113	$75-135	wheelchair access, cable TV, kitchenettes, laundry, nonsmoking rooms, ocean view
Shilo Inn-Oceanfront	30 N. Prom	738-9571	$79-169	cable TV, kitchenettes, fireplace, covered pool, laundry, restaurant/lounge, nonsmoking rooms, oceanview

Saddle Mountain State Park (Cannon Beach, 97110; tel. 861-1671) also has nine primitive sites with flush toilets and firewood available. Open from mid-April to late October, these encampments make a good alternative to beachfront parks on cloudy days. Sites go for $7 a night. No reservations are necessary at either campground.

Food

While a stroll down Broadway might have you thinking that cotton candy, corndogs, and saltwater taffy are the staples of Seaside cuisine, there are several eateries here which can satisfy taste and nutrition as well as the broad-based clientele of this beach town. **Dooger's** (505 Broadway, Seaside, tel. 738-3773), a chain with an outlet in Cannon Beach (1321 N. Hemlock, tel. 431-2225), has won acclaim for its clam chowder. Local clams and oysters, fresh Dungeness crab legs, and sautéed shrimp are also the basis of Dooger's do-good reputation.

Equidistant from Seaside and Cannon Beach is a roadside institution since 1938. The **Crab Broiler** (Junction of U.S. 101 and U.S 26, Cannon Beach, tel. 738-5313) has many dishes based around crab and cheese, so how can you go wrong? Mexican flavors predominate at **Christiano's** (412 Broadway, Seaside, tel. 738-5058). Along with chile rellenos and huevos rancheros, such seafood dishes as Mexican prawns (mucho garlic!) and Halibut Ixtapa spice up the menu. Complement it with a marguerita, Mexican beer, or for dessert, a plate of the south-of-the-border custard, flan. If you drive by Christiano's here, there's an outlet in Astoria (144 11th St., Astoria, tel. 325-1816).

Events And Recreation

Seaside predates any other town as a place to have a good time on the Oregon coast. A zoo and racetrack were among Seaside's first structures. Today, the town hosts the likes of the **Miss**

Oregon Scholarship Pageant in July at the Civic Center and the **World Cup Kite Competition** (for stunt kite-flyers) at the Turnaround in October. Contact the chamber of commerce for information on these events.

The story of Lewis and Clark was and always will be Seaside's major event, thanks lately to the **Lewis and Clark Pageant** (783 1st Avenue, tel. 738-0817 or 800-444-6740). This "Journey to the Pacific" takes place in Broadway Park on the east side of town along the banks of Neawanna Creek and tells the story from the time the expedition starts in 1803 near St. Louis, Missouri, to the arrival in 1805 at Fort Clatsop. Showtime is 8 p.m. Thursday, Friday, and Saturday, and 2 p.m. Sunday, July 26 through August 20. Tickets are $7.50 for adults, $6.50 for seniors, and $3 for students age 6-16.

Fishermen don't only come to Seaside for the Necanicum River's steelhead, trout, and salmon. **Carnahan Park** on Cullaby Lake north of Seaside has crappies, blue gills, perch, catfish, and largemouth bass. Just west of Cullaby, **Sunset Lake** adds trout to the list. Boating, swimming, and water sports add to the appeal of Cullaby Lake.

Golfers can escape to public courses south of Seaside (451 Avenue U, tel. 738-5261) and north in the small town of **Gearhart** (Gearhart-by-the-Sea Resort, Marion St., tel. 738-5248). Greens fees are $7 for Seaside's nine holes and $14 for Gearhart's 18-hole course. Gearhart also boasts a quieter beach than Seaside and a bowling alley (Evergreen Lanes, west of side of U.S. 101 just north of the road to downtown) that reportedly serves the best hamburgers and homemade pie around.

Despite the lifeguard stand, don't swim in Seaside unless you're used to the North Sea. Instead, head to **Sunset Pool** (1140 E. Broadway, Seaside, tel. 738-3311). Fees are $2 for adults with discounts for children and seniors. Hours vary greatly, so call in advance.

The Turnaround is the starting point and finishing line for such famed road races in mid- and late August as the eight-mile **Across-the-Sand** beach run and the **Hood-to-Coast Relay** respectively. At the end of each February, the highly regarded **Trail's End Marathon** loops partway to Astoria and back to the Turnaround. Check with the chamber of commerce for details.

Tennis players will find free courts in **Cannon Beach City Park** (2nd Avenue and Spruce St.) with coin-operated lights. In Seaside, the **high school** (1901 N. Holladay Dr.) and **Broadway School** (1120 Broadway) have free courts with lights. There are also free public courts in Gearhart.

The surfing venues north of Tillamook Head, Indian Basin, and near Short Sands Beach in Oswald West State Park can be enjoyed with surfboard and equipment rentals from **Cleanline Surf Shop** (719 1st Avenue, Seaside, tel. 738-7888). Boogie boards and surfboards go for $12.50, wetsuits, boots, and flippers cost $15, or you can spend $25 for the complete package.

Two area bike shops with rentals are **Mike's Bike Shop** (248 N. Spruce St., Cannon Beach, tel. 436-1266) and **Prom Bike Shop** (622 12th Ave., Seaside, tel. 738-8251). Rental fees at these places range between $3-6 per hour. Mike's specializes in mountain bikes which can be returned at a Warrenton outlet.

Birdwatchers revel in **Necanicum Estuary Park** (1900 block of N. Holladay across the street from Seaside High School). Local students have built a viewing platform, stairs to the beach, a boardwalk, and interpretive signs. Great blue and green herons and numerous migratory species flock to the grassy marshes and slow tidal waters near the mouth of the Necanicum River. Occasionally, Roosevelt elk, blacktailed deer, river otters, beavers, minks, and muskrats can also be sighted.

Natural history buffs will also appreciate the **Nesika Program.** "Nesika" is Chinook jargon for "us" and "ours," and the program is a sharing of the north coast environment coordinated by the Seaside Chamber of Commerce (to whom all inquiries should be addressed). To this end, walks, boat tours, and lectures are presented which focus on the history, human and natural, in Clatsop County locales. It takes place through August in venues ranging from Oswald West State Park to the Columbia River. Fees, usually ranging from $5-10, are sometimes charged for the pleasure of being introduced to local plant and bird communities and maritime history by experts.

Information And Services
The **Seaside Chamber of Commerce** (7 Roosevelt, Seaside 97138; tel. 738-6391 or 800-444-

SEASIDE BED AND BREAKFAST

Name	Address	Telephone	Price	Features
Riverside Inn Bed and Breakfast	430 S. Holladay Dr.	738-8254	$39-70	wheelchair access, meals available, river view
Summer House Bed and Breakfast	1221 N. Franklin	738-5740	$45-65	cable TV, fireplace, meals available, non-smoking rooms
10th Avenue Inn Bed and Breakfast	125 10th Ave.	738-0643	$50-55	cable TV, meals available, nonsmoking rooms, ocean view
Walker House Bed and Breakfast	811 1st Ave.	738-5520	$50-60	cable TV, meals available, laundry, non-smoking rooms
The Boarding House Bed and Breakfast	208 N. Holladay Dr.	738-9055	$55-85	cable TV, meals available, fireplace, non-smoking rooms, river view
Gilbert Inn Bed and Breakfast	341 Beach Dr.	738-9770	$60-80	meals available, fireplace, nonsmoking rooms, ocean view

6740 in Oregon) is open from May to mid-September Mon.-Fri. 8 a.m.-6 p.m., Sat. 10-4 p.m., and Sun. noon-4 p.m. In the off-season, the hours are Mon.-Fri. 9-5 p.m., Sat. 10-3 p.m., and Sun. noon-3 p.m. **Greyhound (RAZ)** (9325 S. Holladay Dr., tel. 738-4121) has service to Portland. **North Coast Transit** (tel. 738-7083) has service between Seaside and Astoria with stops at Gearhart and Warrenton. Buses leave from Rexall Drugs (corner of Holladay and Broadway). The **Beach Bus** is run by **Citizen's Transit** (tel.

738-5121) and runs to Tillamook then Portland with 10 stops in between during summer.

A **laundromat** is located on 57 N. Holladay Street and 1st Avenue. It's open daily 6 a.m.-11 p.m. The **police** (1090 S. Roosevelt Dr., tel. 738-6311) are there to help you in the event of trouble. The **post office** (300 Avenue A, Seaside, 97138; tel. 738-5462) is open 8:30-5 p.m. Mon.-Fri. **Providence Seaside Hospital** (725 S. Wahanna Rd., tel. 738-8463) has 24-hour service and an emergency room.

ASTORIA AND VICINITY

Many coastal travelers are aware of Astoria's legacy as the oldest settlement west of the Mississippi whose glory days are kept alive by museums, historical exhibits, and Victorian homes. This often creates the expectation of a "Williamsburg of the West," where the portrayal of heritage is a focal point of the local identity. The reality of modern-day Astoria is more accurately captured in a locally popular bumper sticker which defiantly proclaims, "We ain't quaint!" This city of 10,000 people is still rooted in a resource-based economy whose logging, fishing, and canneries are in decline. The preserved pioneer past and attractive historic homes may soften these rough edges, but not enough to let anyone mistake Astoria for a tourist town.

A maritime flavor dominates the local scene with "old salts" filling many a smoke-filled barroom with stories of ships that didn't make it past the waves and weather of the Columbia bar. Where the River of the West meets the ocean offshore here could well be the biggest widowmaker on the high seas, earning it the title "Graveyard of the Pacific."

Another striking aspect of the town is the pervasiveness of such Scandinavian traditions as public steam baths, lutefish, and smorrebrod platters. Nonetheless, Hollywood has chosen Astoria's picturesque neighborhoods to simulate the all-American city on at least a half-dozen occasions. Given its rich history, this is altogether fitting.

HISTORY

The Clatsop Indians lived in this area for thousands of years before Astoria's written history began. The region was first chronicled by Heceta, a Spanish explorer who sailed near the Columbia's mouth but failed to enter. American presence on the Columbia began with Captain Robert Gray's discovery of the river in 1792, which he christened after his fur trading ship. Thereafter, Lewis and Clark's famous expedition of 1803-1806 incorporated the Pacific Northwest as part of a new nation with their winter encampment at Fort Clatsop south of the present-day Astoria

townsite. In 1811, John Jacob Astor's agents built Fort Astoria—the first settlement west of the Mississippi. Despite temporary occupation by the British between 1813-1818, the fort and a shaky American presence were able to hold on until settlers came to farm the region during the Oregon Trail era of the 1840s.

From that time until the 1900s, emigrants of Scandinavian descent predominated. Commerce grew with the export of lumber and foodstuffs to gold rush-era San Francisco and the Far East. Shipwrecks became commonplace on the treacherous Columbia River bar despite Captain Flavel's pilot service in the 1850s. Later, Fort Stevens was built during the Civil War to guard against a Confederate naval incursion. Salmon canneries became the basis of Astoria's economy during the 1870s, helping it grow into Oregon's second largest city—and a notorious shanghaiing port. Over the ensuing decades, logging, fishing, and shipbuilding coaxed the population here up to 20,000 by WW II.

Near the end of the war, a Japanese submarine's shelling of Fort Stevens made it the only fortification on American soil to have sustained an attack in a world war (this fact is disputed by two locations in California). After the war, the region's fortunes rose and fell with the resource-based economy. In a 1966 attempt to supplement the latter with tourism, the State Highway Division built the 4.1-mile **Astoria Bridge**, connecting Oregon and Washington as the final link in the 1,625-mile-long U.S. 101 (according to *Guinness*, the world's longest three-span, continuous-through-trusses-bridge). The modern era was also characterized by the development of world-class museums and artful Victorian restorations. Unfortunately, preserving Astoria's glory days could not make up for the closing of the canneries and the decline of logging and fishing. Moves to make Astoria a major port of entry for Japanese cars and to begin large-scale touristic enterprises on the waterfront have been suggested as a means to improve the economic climate here. Whether or not Astoria's ship ever comes in, let's hope the unpretentious charm of this hillside city by the sea will not be lost in the process.

THE LAND

The view from **Astor Column** on Coxcomb Hill (for directions see "Museums And Miscellany" below) orients you to the city and the north coast. To the north, note the freighters that are docked on the edge of Astoria's cityscape and the Astoria (to Megler, Washington) Bridge spanning the Columbia. Across Baker Bay to the northwest is Cape Disappointment on the Washington side of the six-mile channel that Robert Gray entered in 1792. Looking over Young's Bay south and west of Astoria, the Clatsop Plains extend to Tillamook Head. Although the 1840s settlers had no luck farming these sand traps, the relative flatness of the terrain lent itself to the building of the region's first road, which U.S. 101 now parallels. The beaches west of the road contribute 95% of the state's harvest of razor clams. Further south, the plains give way to a dense area of settlement around Seaside. Tillamook Head, the coast's northernmost headland then defines a valley cut by the Necanicum River. Fair-weather views reveal Saddle Mountain southeast of this lowland. Clear visibility also treats you to panoramas of Mt. St. Helens and Mt. Hood on the far eastern horizon. A visit to the information booth on top of the hill (open from Memorial Day to the second week of September) and a look at the annotated bronze relief map of the north coast should precede climbing the steps to the top of the column.

The map is found on the entry walkway and notes the distances and directions to such landmarks as Mt. Rainer, Mt. St. Helens, Tillamook Head, and Saddle Mountain.

SIGHTS

Flavel House

Begin your walking tour at the Flavel House (441 8th St., Astoria, 97103; tel. 325-2203) on the corner of 8th and Duane, a right turn off Marine Drive, which is an extension of ORE 30. This splendid Queen Anne-style Victorian mansion was built by George Flavel, whose guiding of vessels across the Columbia bar made him Oregon's first steamship captain and Astoria's earliest millionaire. The home's intricate woodwork, period furnishings, and art along with its extravagantly rendered gables, cornices, and porches rank it with Carson Mansion in Eureka, California as a Victorian showplace. From its fourth-story cupola, Captain Flavel could watch his own sailing fleet and it's said that his wife would keep the light going in this perch when the captain was bringing in a ship. The 14-foot ceilings, Persian rugs, and an international array of tiles are only upstaged by fireplaces in every room framed in exotic hardwoods. Known locally as "the house with the red roof," it has withstood more than a century of storms off the Columbia River estuary. This landmark for incoming ships is now the foremost

one of Astoria's many well-preserved Victorian homes

monument to Astoria's golden age as the leading port in the Northwest. Flavel House is open daily, May to September 10 a.m.-5 p.m., and charges $3 for adults, $2.50 for seniors, and $1 for children 6-12. The admission price includes any two of the three museums operated by the Clatsop Historical Society (see "Museums And Miscellany").

Walking Tour

In addition to the Flavel House, Astoria is home to dozens of beautifully preserved 19th-century and early 20th-century houses. A walking tour of many of them is laid out in a guidebook written by a local historian and is available for $2. After the Flavel House tour, however, most people seem content to forego the purchase and let the architectural scenery do the talking. Just start walking south on 8th Street and turn on Franklin Avenue. Continue east to 11th Street, then detour south a block on 11th Street to Grand Avenue, east on Grand, north on 12th Street, and back to Franklin, continuing your eastward trek. Walk to 17th Street, then south again to Grand, double back on Grand two blocks to 15th Street, then walk north on 15th to Exchange Street and east on Exchange to 17th, where you'll be just two blocks from the Columbia River Maritime Museum. The route will take you past 74 historical buildings and sites.

Columbia River Maritime Museum

From here you can explore the waterfront on an old set of railroad tracks paralleling the rusting ships and moss-draped pilings or proceed directly to the Columbia River Maritime Museum (1792 Marine Dr., Astoria 97103; tel. 326-2323) at the foot of 17th Street. Its roof simulates the curvature of a wave, making it hard to miss the 37,00-square-foot museum. A gigantic 25,000-pound anchor from the U.S. battleship *Indiana* in front of the building is also hard to ignore. This eye-catching facade is more than matched by what's inside. Even if the Columbia River could talk, it would be hard to surpass the eloquence of this museum's historical displays. The eras when Indian canoes plied the Columbia, Lewis and Clark camped on its shores, and dramatic shipwrecks occurred on its bar are recounted with scale models and miniatures of ships and paintings. The chance to peer through a periscope, man the bridge of a WW II destroyer, and enter a Colum-

bia River sternwheeler pilothouse imparts a hands-on aspect to your experience here. Scrimshaw, fishing and cannery artifacts, and sea charts dating as far back as 1587 also highlight your visit.

At the end of your journey through maritime history, tour the 128-foot lightship *Columbia*. This vessel served as a "floating lighthouse" at the mouth of the river to mark its entrance and help many ships trying to navigate the dangerous waters. It was replaced in 1979 by an unmanned, 42-foot-high navigational buoy after almost three decades of service. The museum is open 9:30 a.m-5 p.m. and only closed on Thanksgiving and Christmas Day. Adults are $3, seniors $2, minors under 18 pay $1.50, and children under six get in free.

MUSEUMS AND MISCELLANY

The above walking tour makes for a very full morning. If you get an early start, however, you'll still have time to visit several other Astoria landmarks. Among these Fort Clatsop, Fort Stevens, Astoria Column, and the Maritime Museum are must-see attractions.

Astoria Column

Astoria Column is located a short distance from Marine Drive down 16th Street. You'll go through the southeast residential part of the city before beginning the drive up Coxcomb Hill Road. It's also accessible by city bus (See "Information And Services"). Once atop this 595-foot summit, walk the 166 steps up the 125-foot tower. A frieze depicting major historical events adorns the column's exterior but the real attraction is the view of the surrounding countryside. This column was a joint project of the Great Northern Railroad and the descendants of John Jacob Astor to commemorate a 1926 cross-country rail excursion.

Fire-fighters Museum

Back on Marine Drive is the Uppertown Fire Fighters Museum (30th and Marine Drive, tel. 325-2203). This exposition contains hand-pulled, horse-drawn and motorized fire-fighting vehicles in service from 1877 to 1921. In addition, firefighting memorabilia and equipment from this period are exhibited, supplemented by photos and information about Astoria's major blazes. The museum is operated by the Clatsop County Historical Society and has hours and admission similar to the Flavel House.

Heritage Museum

The Clatsop County Historical Society also operates the Heritage Museum (1618 Exchange Street, Astoria 97103, tel. 325-2203). Several galleries with antiquities, tools, and old photographs depict various aspects of life in Clatsop County. Gallery One deals with the natural history, geology, native American artifacts, early immigrants and settlers in the region, and important natural events. Gallery Two portrays the development of commerce in such enterprises as fishing, fishpacking, logging, and lumber. Gallery Three concentrates on the 22 ethnic groups who came to Clatsop County in search of a better life. The hours and admission here are the same as the Flavel House.

Fort Clatsop

To reach Fort Clatsop National Memorial (Route 3 Box 604FC Astoria 97103, tel. 861-2471), site of the Lewis and Clark encampment, from Marine Drive, head west across Youngs Bay, taking care to stay in the right lane to avoid getting sidetracked by alternate U.S. 101. Lewis and Clark crossed this bay en route to the Fort Clatsop site after their original encampment on the Washington side proved too exposed to the elements. On the other side of the bay look for signs for the Fort Clatsop turnoff a quarter mile past the Fort Stevens State Park sign. Then turn left off the Coast Highway and follow the direction markers. This memorial sits six miles south of Astoria and three miles east of U.S. 101 on the Lewis and Clark River. Although the expedition's story is nicely narrated here with displays, artifacts, slides, and films every day except Christmas, summertime "living history" reenactments are the main reason to come. The winter of 1805-06 put a premium on wilderness survival skills, some of which are exhibited here by rangers in costume, 9 a.m. to 5:30 p.m. daily, Memorial Day to Labor Day. You can see the tanning of hides, making of buckskin clothing and moccasins, and the molding of tallow candles and lead bullets. In addition, visitors may occasionally participate in the construction of a dugout canoe or try their luck at starting a fire by striking flint on steel.

The hands-on experiences complement the following permanent features of Fort Clatsop: a log replica of the original fort (site of living history exhibits); a well-equipped visitors center (check for botanical walks on the bulletin board here); a beautifully landscaped picnic area; and trails that lead from the visitor center to the fort, to the canoe landing, and to a spring used by the expedition in 1805-06. Admission is $1 for visitors 17 through 61, and the ticket is good for seven days. The maximum charge is $3 per family. Visitors under 17 and over 61 enter free. Gates to the memorial are open from 8 a.m. to 8 p.m. during the summer season and from 8 a.m. to 5 p.m. the rest of the year.

Fort Stevens

From Fort Clatsop, retrace the route back to U.S. 101 and the sign pointing the way to Fort Stevens (Fort Stevens Historic Area, Hammond 97121; tel. 861-2000). This Civil War-vintage outpost is situated 10 miles west of Astoria, 15 miles northwest of Seaside on the northwest corner of the coast. To get there, drive through Warrenton en route to Pacific Drive in Hammond, which leads to the Fort Stevens historic area and military museum. The fort was established shortly before the Confederates surrendered at Appomattox on April 9, 1865. Its creation was not the only outgrowth of the Civil War on the West Coast. The year before, Lincoln had created the city of Port Angeles, Washington for "lighthouse purposes." Given the subsequent creation of Fort Stevens shortly thereafter, it's a safe assumption that "lighthouse purposes" also meant being on the lookout for Confederate ships and the British, whom the union feared would ally themselves with the South. This seems more credible when you consider that the last shots of the war were fired by the *Shenandoah* on a fleet of Yankee whalers in the Bering Straits. The June 5, 1865 shelling occurred after the surrender because the Confederate skipper was unaware of the Appomattox treaty signed several months before.

Though Fort Stevens was spared in the Civil War it sustained an attack in another conflict. On June 21, 1942 a Japanese submarine fired 17 shells on Battery Russell, making it the only U.S. fortification in the 48 states to be bombed by a foreign power since the War of 1812. No damage was incurred and the Army didn't return fire.

Shortly after World War II, the fort was deactivated and all armaments were removed.

Today, the site of the old military installation features a memorial rose garden, old photos, weapons exhibits, and maps as well as seven different batteries and other structures left over from almost a century of service. Exploring some of the gun batteries and climbing to the nearby commander's station for a scenic view of the Columbia River and South Jetty are popular visitor activities. During the summer months, guided tours of the underground Battery Mishler ($1.50) and a narrated tour of the Fort's 37 acres on a two-ton U.S. Army truck ($2.50) are also available. The summer programs include Civil War reenactments and archaeological digs; consult the visitors center for schedules. The fort's hours are 10 a.m.- 6 p.m., Memorial Day to Labor Day, and 10 a.m.- 4 p.m. Wed. to Sun during the rest of the year. Except for the tours, admission is free.

Eight miles of bike trails (See "Sports And Recreation" for info on rentals) link the historic area to the rest of the park and provide access to Battery Russell and the 1906 wreck of the British schooner *Peter Iredale* (more remnants of the

PHOTO BY OREGON TOURISM DIVISION
fishing boats at Astoria Dock

ship are displayed at the Maritime Museum). You can also bike to the campground one mile south of the Military Museum.

For those in cars, parking is available at one of four lots about a mile apart from one another at the foot of the dunes. The beach runs north to the Columbia River where excellent surf-fishing, bird-watching, and a view of the mouth of the river await. South of the campground (east of the *Peter Iredale*) there's a self-guided nature trail around part of the two-mile shoreline of **Coffenberry Lake.** The lake also has two swimming beaches with bathhouses and fishing for trout and perch.

Twilight Eagle Sanctuary
Six miles northeast of Astoria in the Burnside area is the new Twilight Eagle Sanctuary (for more info write the Twilight Eagle sanctuary c/o Oregon Eagle Federation, 5873 Estate Drive, Klamath Falls 97601). The 15-acre parcel here hosts 50 eagles during the winter. In addition, there are ducks, Canadian geese, wrens, and songbirds and, on occasion, tundra swans. To get there, drive six miles east of town on U.S. 30 and turn left at Burnside. Another left a half mile later will take you to the viewing platform.

SPORTS AND RECREATION

Fishing
Above and beyond the lure of sport fishing on the Columbia bar, commercial fishing has dominated Astoria more than any other industry throughout its history. Salmon canneries dominated the waterfront at the turn of the century. Albacore and long-line shark fishing put dinner on the table in the '30s and '40s. In the modern era, commercial fishing has turned to sole, rockfish, flounder, and less well-known bottomfish. If it's not enough to watch these commercial operations from the dock, **Tiki-Fleet** (897 Pacific St. Hammond 97121, next to the coin laundry, tel. 861-1201) and **Thunderbird Charters** (tel. 325-7990) will show you where to drop your line for salmon, sturgeon, and bottomfish. Given the retail price of fresh salmon, you could theoretically pay for a charter trip by landing a single fish. Sports anglers can fish for salmon in either salt or freshwater (depending on time of year) or go after trout, bass, catfish, steelhead, and sturgeon in freshwa-

ter lakes, streams, and rivers. Ling cod, rockfish, surf perch, or other bottomfish can be pursued at sea, off jetties, or along ocean beaches.

Astoria Flight Center

Another way to avoid being landlocked is the Astoria Flight Center (tel. 861-1222). One person is charged $40, groups of two or three are charged $65 for 40-minute flights. See the whalewatching section in the Coast Introduction for information on similar options along the coast.

Oregon Coast Trail

More down-to-earth pursuits can be found along the Oregon Coast Trail. It extends from Fort Stevens Park to the area around the Three Capes Lookout. The first stretch extends south along the beach for 14 miles to Gearhart. It's a flat easy walk, and your journey could well be highlighted by a sighting of the endangered silver spot butterfly. It now frequents just six sites, including four in Oregon, with Clatsop County being one of them. The endangered status of this species is protected under law and has stopped developers from building resorts on coastal meadows and dunes north of Gearhart. Look for a small orange butterfly with silvery spots on the undersides of its wings. Call the State Parks and Recreation Division for an up-to-date report on trail conditions before starting out (tel. 800-452-5687).

Tapiola Pool And Tennis Courts

Outdoor recreationists will also appreciate Tapiola Pool (901 W. Marine Drive, tel. 323-7027) and tennis courts at 36th and Leif Erickson; at the grey school, 785 Alameda; and at 6th and Niagara. The latter facility is lit until 10 p.m. Other lit courts are in Warrenton at the corner of Second and Alder streets.

Bike Rentals

Bike rentals are conveniently located next to Fort Stevens State Park historic area (316 Russell Drive, Hammond, tel. 861-0937). Bikes, 10-speeds, mountain bikes, and youth bikes may be rented by the day or by the hour.

Auto Tour

An auto tape tour of the coast is available through **Blue Sky Publications** (P.O. Box 4227 Salem OR 97302, tel. 362-3403). Cassettes include Astoria to Lincoln City and Lincoln City to Brookings, each of which sells for $20. While the commentary sounds like wooden ad copy at times, these tapes have some good information and production values. Other locales covered by the company include Portland and the Columbia Gorge.

PRACTICALITIES

As with the rest of the north coast, bed and breakfasts are the best way to go. This kind of lodging is all the more appealing in Astoria with its picturesque hills framing Victorian neighborhoods.

Fort Columbia Hostel

If a B&B is out of your budget range, try the **Fort Columbia AYH Hostel** (tel. 206-777-8755) across the river in Chinook Washington. Despite charging $7.50 a night for AYH members and $10.50 otherwise, this is more than just another no-frills crash pad for backpackers. The rustic former Army hospital has rocking chairs and couches on a long porch and a fire going on chilly evenings to bring together naturalists, historians, ornithologists, and beachcombers in homey communion. Outdoor barbecue pits on beautiful grounds become gathering spots on warm summer nights. Any misgivings you might have about dormitory-style rooms in a military infirmary are also tempered by 11-foot, tin-tile ceilings evocative of the turn of the century. One private room is available for couples. Reservations are not necessary in this well-kept secret. To get there, cross the Astoria Bridge ($1.50 toll), go two miles west on U.S. 101, and look for signs to Fort Columbia State Park. A Pacific Transit bus goes there for fifty cents from the Greyhound station (364 9th St.) several times a day. Hours of operation are 5 p.m. to 9 a.m. from June to mid-September. As with other AYH hostels, some chores are required.

Bed And Breakfast

Franklin Street Bed and Breakfast (1140 Franklin St., Astoria 97103, tel. 325-4314) is an elegant turn-of-the-century Victorian. Five rooms with private baths and queen beds can accommodate 14 people here. It's a located within walking distance of downtown and a continental breakfast is included in the rates ($50-75 a night, double occupancy). Minimum two-night stay on weekends and advance reservations, ten days in advance, have become necessary due to the popularity of this place.

The **Rosbriar Inn** (636 Fourteenth St. Astoria 97103, tel. 325-7427) is located on a quiet neighborhood street near the Maritime Museum. For $45-$85 nightly (double occupancy) you have a choice of three rooms with baths or seven without (facilities down the hall). In this spacious former convent, a full breakfast on a family-style dining table is also included. Reserve a week and a half in advance during summer.

Camping
With 260 tent sites, **Fort Stevens State Park** (Hammond 94121; tel. 861-1671) is the largest camping facility in the state. The 343 sites for RVs and a special area for walk-in campers and bicyclists ensures that Fort Stevens can accommodate you whatever your mode of transportation. In addition to the usual amenities there's a laundromat and playground. To get there from Astoria cross the Klaskanine River west on Hwy. 30 and take the Hammond Exit four miles to the park. Five miles of ocean frontage and three miles of Columbia River frontage as well as several small lakes here make this *the* place on the north coast for water sports. Add the park's amenities and other natural attractions and you have the perfect base camp to take advantage of the region. Reservations are accepted here and an $8 fee is charged. The state park is open year-round.

Food
If you like good food with a minimum of expense and pretense you've come to the right place. But first, several retail outlets are deserving of mention.

The freshest produce in town is available Tuesday through Saturday at **Columbia Farmers Market** (6th and Bond, Astoria, tel. 325-4045). Just look for a ramshackle yellow house one block off Marine Drive.

As you come into Astoria from the east after crossing the bridge on Marine Drive (U.S. 30), you 'll see a nondescript storefront on the left among the bars and bait shops. Little would you suspect that one of Oregon's most esteemed purveyors of gourmet smoked fish conducts business here. **Josephson's Smokehouse** (106 Marine Dr. Astoria tel. 325-2190) produces a Scandinavian cold-smoked salmon without dyes

or preservatives, so it is seldom sold through retail outlets. Instead, Josephson's caters to mail-order clientele (to order: P.O. Box 412, Astoria 97103) and fine restaurants which serve the product upon arrival. You can buy direct at a cheaper (but not cheap) price than the mail-order rates. Pickled salmon, salmon jerky, sturgeon caviar, and a variety of alder-smoked and canned fish are also sold here.

Oregon's number-one retail chain, **Fred Meyer** (1451 U.S. 101 Warrenton, tel. 861-3003) has a deli that stocks salads, meats, cheeses, french bread, and other takeout items. This store is also known for good deals on clothes, camping equipment, and hardware.

Downtown on the waterfront, **Little Denmark** (125 9th St., tel. 325-2409) serves up generously stocked trays of openfaced sandwiches and Scandinavian pastries (try the ableskiver) Monday through Saturdays 9 a.m. to 3 p.m. On weekdays, imported beer and coffee are served until 5 p.m.. In between bites, you can browse the Danish-style crafts in the gift shop.

Underneath the Astoria Bridge near the water, **Pacific Rim** (229 W. Marine Dr. Astoria, tel. 325-4481) can satisfy your hankerin' for pizza and burgers better and more cheaply than any other place in town. In addition, the low-priced and tasty Italian entrees at this drab cafe might also make you forget seafood temporarily.

If you can't, try the fish and chips at **Ship Inn** (1 Second St., tel. 325-0033). A state travel magazine selected this restaurant as the best pub in Oregon, and another regional publication gave it awards for seafood and business lunches. Even if you 're not hungry, you can always enjoy its scenic waterfront location over English cheeses and imported brews.

The **Columbian Cafe** (1114 Marine Dr., tel. 325-2233) is where the meatless '60s meet '90s Northwest cuisine. The good selection of entrees and fresh catch of the day are all expertly prepared and moderately priced. You may also enjoy the free-flowing political repartee with the staff and regulars in this cramped but friendly place. Next door, the **Border Town Bar** does justice to its name with hefty helpings wrapped up in flour tortillas.

Events
The biggest event in town is the **Astoria Scandinavian Festival** (Box 754 Astoria 97103; tel. 325-6311), which takes place the weekend of

former home of Miss
Nellie Wilson and parrot

June 21st, Friday through Sunday. Local Danes, Finns, Icelanders, Norwegians, and Swedes come together to celebrate their heritage. Costumed participants dance around a flowered midsummer pole (a fertility rite), burn a bonfire to destroy evil spirits, and have tugs-of-war pitting Scandinavian nationalities against each other. Food, dancing, crafts, and a parade brings the whole town out to Astoria High School on West Marine Drive just off ORE 202. Admission is $5 for adults and $1 for children 6-12.

Another fete that might prove enjoyable is the **Great Astoria Crab Feed and Seafood Festival,** held the last weekend in April. Seafood, cookery, wines, crafts, a carnival, and a traditional crab dinner are featured. Admission is $3 for adults, $2 for seniors, and $1 for children 6-12; call 325-6311 for more information.

The chamber of commerce offers a **Victorian homes tour** the second weekend in August. They also coordinate the **Astoria Regatta** in conjunction with this event.

Cultural stimulation can be found on 10th Street at **Parnassus Books** (234 10th St., Astoria tel.325-1363) and the **Ricciardi Gallery** (108 10th St. Astoria tel. 325-5420). Around the corner from the bookstore is **Michael's Antiques and Art Gallery** (1007 Maine Drive, Astoria tel. 325-2350).

Theater

Those interested in a melodrama with historic antecedents might enjoy *Shanghaied,* which is based on Astoria's dubious distinction as a notorious shanghai port during the late 1800s. A local theater troupe, the **Astor Street Opry Co.,** has shows Thursday, Friday, and Saturday nights mid-July through mid-August. Performances begin at 8 p.m. in the lobby of the John Jacob Astor Apartments, a renovated 1920's hotel at 14th and Commercial Street in Astoria. Tickets can be purchased at Paperback Traffic (1015 Commercial St., Astoria 97103, tel. 325-4642) for $5 to $10 or at the box office which opens at 7 p.m. Chase scenes, bar fights, and a liberal sprinkling of Scandinavian jokes will have you laughing in between applauding the hero and booing the villain.

Information And Services

At 10,000 people, Astoria is the largest city and media hub of the north coast. The local newspaper, the *Daily Astorian,* is sold around town and is worth a look if only to get the editorial slant of Steve Forrester. This former Washington correspondent's witty commentary on events local, regional, and national pulls no punches.

Throughout the north coast KMUN (91.9 FM Astoria and Seaside, 89.5 in Cannon Beach) is a public radio station with community-based programming that is especially diverse. Classical, jazz, rock, and folk music, public affairs, radio drama, literature readings and children's bedtime stories, and NPR news will keep your dial glued to this frequency.

The **Astoria Chamber of Commerce** (111 West Maine Drive, Astoria 97103; tel. 800-535-3637 or 325-6311) will send you a free guidebook (write P.O. Box 176 Astoria 97103) to all the sites as well as maps, motel listings, and other visitor information. The facility itself also has generic north coast and southwest Washington materials. It's open daily 8 a.m. to 8 p.m.; from Oct.- April hours are Mon-Fri 8-5 .

To get around town take **TBR Transit** (Greyhound Terminal 364 9th St. at Duane St., tel. 325-3524). A full city loop is made every hour Mon.-Sat. 6:30 a.m.-7:15 p.m. The fare is fifty cents.

To get to Seaside and towns en route, **North Coast Transit** (tel. 738-7083) also leaves from the Greyhound station. It costs $2 to Seaside, $3 roundtrip. Two 2¹/2-hour loops are made in the morning. There are also trips in the late afternoon and early evening. It's important to call here because the schedule is in transition.

To get out of town, **Greyhound,** whose service is through RAZ (364 9th St. Astoria, tel. 325-5641), has morning and evening service to Portland.

The **post office** (Astoria 97103, tel. 325-2141) is located in the Federal Building at 8th and Commercial. It's open Mon.-Fri. 8:30 a.m. to 5 p.m.

Other useful numbers include the county sheriff (tel. 225-2061), the **Coast Guard** and **airport** at Warrenton (tel. 861-2242), and **Columbia Memorial Hospital** (2111 Exchange St. Astoria, tel. 325-4321).

PORTLAND AND VICINITY

In shadows cast by 100-year-old trees and buildings, the new Northwest is taking shape in Portland, Oregon. Here amid greenery seldom seen in an urban environment, high-tech business ventures, a full cultural calendar, and an activist community are carving out a vibrant image. A latticework of bridges over the Willamette River adds a distinctive profile, while parks, malls, and other "people spaces" give Portland a heart and a soul. The overall effect is more European than American, where the urban core is equal parts marketplace, cultural forum, and working metropolis.

Such a happy medium is the result of progressive planning and a fortunate birthright. Patterns of growth in this one-time Indian encampment at the confluence of the Willamette and Columbia rivers were initially shaped by the practical Midwestern values of Oregon Trail pioneers as well as by the sophistication of New England merchants. Rather than the boom-bust development which characterized Seattle and gold rush San Francisco, Portland was designed to be user-friendly over the long haul. During the modern era, such utopian refinements as the most advanced and extensive mass transit systems in the U.S. and an urban plan which places strict limita-

tions on the height of buildings and the space between them were added. In this vein, aesthetically pleasing and historic architecture have been spared during Portland's last decades of growth.

Another blessing is Portland's auspicious location. Even though it sits 110 miles from the Pacific Ocean on the Columbia River, the city's port handles the third largest overall tonnage of foreign waterborne cargo on the West Coast. On the export side, the timber, grain, and produce of eastern Oregon, the Columbia Gorge, and the Willamette Valley frequently depart Portland for Pacific Rim countries. In addition to this commerce on the Columbia, battleships, ocean liners, and other vessels go into dry-dock here for repair and renovation.

Portland's waterways are her lifeblood in other ways. Mt Hood's Bull Run watershed supplies some of the purest drinking water anywhere in the U.S. and the printing, textile, papermaking, and high-tech industries place a premium on Portland's clean-running aqueous arteries. Cheap and abundant power from the Willamette and Columbia rivers' hydro projects has also provided an incentive for many other industries to locate here.

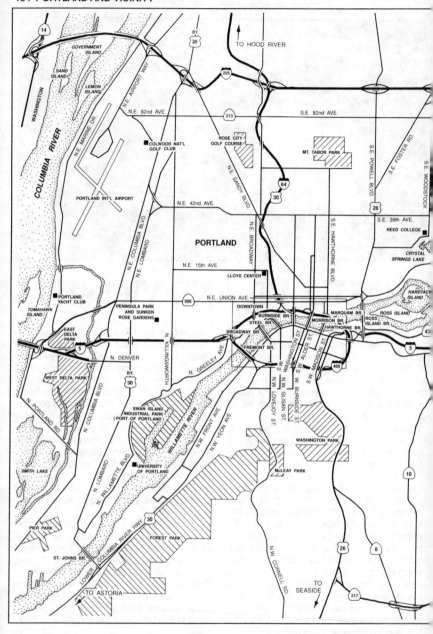

PORTLAND AND VICINITY

© MOON PUBLICATIONS, INC.

The traveler will appreciate Portland's proximity to rural retreats. With scenic Columbia Gorge and skiing on Mt. Hood to the east, and the Carmel of the Oregon Coast, Cannon Beach, to the west, relief from urban stress is little more than an hour away. Other nearby getaways include the wine country and the historic sites of Champoeg and Oregon City. Closer to home, Forest Park is the largest urban wilderness in the country. Washington Park's Japanese and Rose gardens are other internationally renowned places of beauty and contemplation.

The cultural offerings in this city of 432,000 are noteworthy for their scope and excellence. Whether it's the wine, cheese, and camaraderie on first-Thursdays-of-the-month gallery walks or the smorgasbord of live theater and state-of-the-art concert halls, Portland's music mavens and culture vultures enjoy a full table. In like measure, bibliophiles revel in the world's largest bookstore, Powell's, as well as many other outlets for rare editions. The Portland Symphony Orchestra under the baton of James De Priest has also gained an international reputation through its compact disc recordings and world travels. As for pop music, top rock acts regularly hit Portland, while the local pub scene showcases many fine blues and jazz players.

On a smaller scale, readings by local literati Ursula Le Guin and Jean Auel, or an equally prominent visiting author, is a treat for Portland's book lovers. The flame of knowledge is kept burning by Portland's museums. Such arcane exhibition halls as the Portland Police Museum and the American Advertising Museum complement the Oregon Museum of Science and Industry and the Washington Park Zoo. Adding to this array are more movie screens, radio stations, and bookstores than any American city of comparable size.

Nonetheless, there are faint rumblings of trouble in River City. In recent years, Portland has not been exempt from the urban ills of gang warfare, escalating real estate prices, and a sizeable homeless population. Despite these problems, Portland's quality of life is still frequently touted by surveys and media as being unexcelled by few, if any, major American cities. *Newsweek* picks it as one of ten "hot spots" for the 1990s and Allied and United Van Lines said it was the most moved-to destination in the country in 1989. As such, the era of "small is beautiful" may soon be a thing of the past here. Come now and see Portland in its Golden Age.

HISTORY

Sauvie Island northwest of the current city limits was the site of an Indian village whose name inspired William Clark to christen the nearby river the Willamette in 1805. Two decades later, England's establishment of Fort Vancouver across the Columbia brought French trappers into the area, some of whom retired around what would eventually become Portland. The city was formally born when three New Englanders (accounts vary on the number), including a Pettygrove from Portland, Maine and a Lovejoy from Boston, Massachusetts, flipped a coin at a dinner party to decide who would give a name to a 640-acre claim they co-owned. The state-of-Mainer won and decided in the winter of 1844-45 to name it after his birthplace. The original claim is located in the vicinity of Southwest Front Street.

GETTING ORIENTED: PORTLAND NEIGHBORHOODS

Portland's revival picked up steam in the 1970s, turning a city mostly known for rain, roses, and run-down buildings into a showplace of eye-catching art and architecture. Included in this legacy were the renovation of the historic Old Town neighborhood and Pioneer Courthouse Square as well as a law requiring that one percent of construction costs goes towards public art projects.

Before getting started on your travels, here are a few things worth keeping in mind. First, most Portlanders sleep east of the Willamette River. The business district, shopping areas, museums, and theaters west of the Willamette can be easily reached from east-of-the-river residential areas by mass transit. Buses and light rail are preferable to cars because of streets closed to traffic and the dearth of parking in the city. Once you're downtown, Portland's compact beauty invites strolling. So ditch you car, put on your walking shoes, and ride the bus to its point of origin, **Transit Mall,** on 5th and 6th Avenues. This strip of 11 blocks is banned to vehicular traffic other than Tri-Met buses. Bus and light rail travel is free throughout much of downtown (see "Getting Around").

EXPOSE YOURSELF TO ART

The following introduction to Portland neighborhoods is intended to give an idea of how the city is laid out. Obviously, you can't do all of this tour in one day, so slow down and savor each part of town. The bus stops of the most far-reaching and cost effective inner-city transportation system in the nation (according to the American Transit Association) features brick-inlaid promenades and glass-canopied pavilions garlanded with floral displays. But the aesthetics don't stop there. These waiting areas have so many ornate statues and fountains that Portland Mayor Bud Clark exhorts you to "expose yourself to art" here. A famous poster depicts hizzoner flashing the female nude statue *Kvinneakt* (on 5th Avenue between S.W. Washington and S.W. Stark), underscored by the aforementioned invitation. This poster can be purchased by sending a check or money order for $12.50 to Art Flashes, Box 10889, Portland, 97210. It is also available in many shops, bookstores, and galleries around town.

Portland Building

The best-known statue in the city is Raymond Kaskey's *Portlandia,* which ranks right behind the Statue of Liberty as the nation's largest copper sculpture. Located outside Michael Graves's postmodern Portland Building (S.W. 5th Ave. between S.W. Main and S.W. Madison), the golden-hued female figure holding a trident re-creates the Lady of Commerce on the state seal. Locals refer to it as "Queen Kong," and sometimes practical jokers from Portland State University will dangle

PHOTO BY THEO TRIMMELL

Portlandia *beckons passersby.*

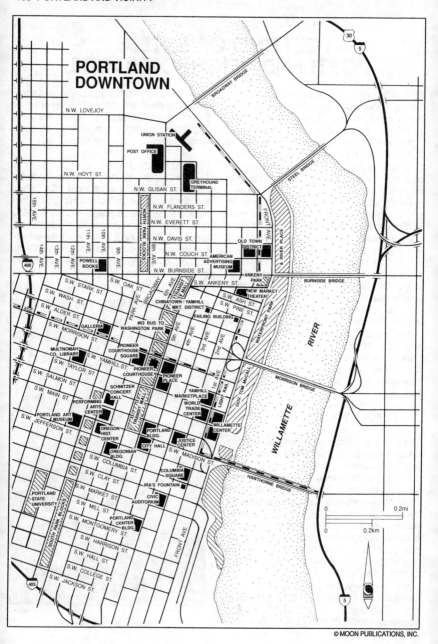

PORTLAND DOWNTOWN

© MOON PUBLICATIONS, INC.

a giant yo-yo from her outstretched finger. Inside the Portland Building on the second floor is the **Metropolitan Center for Public Art** (1120 S.W. 5th Ave., Portland, 97208; tel. 796-5111), where you can pick up a brochure annotating a walking tour of the city's murals, fountains, sculptures, and other art forms.

More graphic evocations of the region are rendered by the 16th-century **petroglyphs** etched into Columbia River basalt at City Hall (east courtyard, behind 1220 S.W. 5th Ave.) and the simulated cascades at **Ira's Fountain.** To get to the fountain, walk down S.W. 4th Avenue to S.W. Clay Street (in front of Civic Center). From the block-long fountain complex, retrace your steps back down 4th to Yamhill Street. If you turn left (halfway between Yamhill and S.W. Morrison), the Northwest motif is maintained by small bronzed beavers and sea lions gathering around a series of pools.

Pioneer Courthouse Square

You are now on the north side of Pioneer Courthouse (555 S.W. Yamhill), the oldest public building in the state, constructed between 1869 and 1873. The classic contours of this gray granite structure contrast with the blue-tiled, mauve-and-beige bon-bon box you saw at the Portland Building. On the first floor of the Hall of Justice is a post office with historic photos on the wall. Period furniture and brass lamps line the hallways on the way to the Ninth Circuit Court of Appeals, located upstairs in room 204. If court is not in session, ask a security guard to let you in to see the Victorian courtroom between 8:30 a.m. and 5 p.m. weekdays.

Two blocks west, outside the front door of the building, is **Pioneer Courthouse Square** (bordered by Yamhill, Morrison, 6th Ave., and Broadway), the cultural vortex of the city. Looking on the south side of the square is *Allow Me,* a life-sized statue of a businessman with an umbrella hailing a cab. Also within the amphitheater-like confines of the square is **Powell's Travel Bookstore** (701 S.W. 6th Ave. at S.W. Yamhill St., tel. 228-1108). Here you can rent the 80-minute narrated *Portland Downtown Discovery Walk* and a tape player for around $10. It traces 90 historic sites within a 20-block radius, complete with sound effects, interviews with local experts, and digressions on architectural subjects.

Diagonally across the square is a 25-foot column known as the **weather machine.** Every day

PHOTO BY TED LONG ISHIKAWA
All roads lead to Pioneer Courthouse Square.

at noon the forecast is delivered by one of three creatures—a dragon if it's stormy, a blue heron in overcast weather, or a sun figure. As if that's not enough, the machine also emits a small cloud accompanied by a fanfare while colored lights display temperature and air quality. The red-bricked square hosts jazz, folk, and other types of music every Tuesday through Thursday from noon till 1 p.m. at the **Peanut Butter and Jam.** On warm spring and summer nights the music and crowds return, augmented by symphony-goers departing the **Portland Center for the Performing Arts** just up Broadway. The Birkenstocks and Goretex of casual Northwest attire mingle easily with business suits here. Should you tire of people-watching, inspect the bricks on the square, each of which bears the name of one of the 50,000 donors who anted up $15-30 for the privilege.

The South Park Blocks And Cultural Attractions

Paralleling Broadway and the square to the west are the south park blocks, created in 1842 and comprising a 25-block spread between Park and

5th avenues. Come here in the fall and you can sense Portland's New England heritage. One hundred-year-old elm trees with their bright yellow leaves line a series of small parks down the middle of Park Avenue. These sentinels tower above cast-iron benches, bronze statues, and neatly trimmed grass fronting the **Portland Art Museum** and the **Oregon Historical Society.** Be sure to check out the murals portraying Lewis and Clark, Sacajawea, fur traders, and Oregon Trail pioneers on the south and west walls of the Historical Center on Main Street. **Portland State University** is on the south end of the park blocks. Sandwiched in between the park blocks and Broadway is the heart of the theater district with the **Performing Arts Center, Schnitzer Hall,** and several smaller theaters nearby. Several years ago, the city increased the number of brighter period-style lamposts here to make it more inviting after dark. To further help the neighborhood realize its potential, there are plans to forge mass transit links to the Greyhound/Amtrak terminals at Union Station in 1991. This would provide easy access to heritage-rich neighborhoods and Waterfront Park on the banks of the Willamette.

DOWN BY THE RIVERSIDE

Old Town And Skidmore

The tile-roofed clock of the **Union Station** on N.W. 6th Avenue has been a beacon since 1890 when passenger trains rolled into the red brick terminal. If you walk southeast from Union Station, you pass through **Chinatown,** a compact area of restaurants and exotic oriental grocery stores. In 1890 Portland had the largest Chinatown on the West Coast. The gargoylish gate at 4th Avenue and Burnside is always good for a photograph. Notice that the male statue is on the right with a ball under its foot, while the female has a cub under her paw. In the spring, the cherry blossoms on 5th and Davis are the highlight of Chinatown. Overlapping this neighborhood are the museums, galleries, restaurants, and shops of **Old Town.** Many of the buildings here date from the 1880s despite Portland beginning four decades earlier. This is because an 1872 fire razed much of what was then the commercial district. Cast-iron buildings with Italianate flourishes went up in the wake of the fire. While a large number of these foundry facades were torn down in the 1940s to make way for a Willamette River Bridge and a waterfront freeway, a few survive in Old Town and the adjoining **Skidmore Historic District.** Old Town runs predominantly north of West Burnside between Front and 4th Avenues.

Skidmore spills over just south of Burnside. These neighborhoods are adorned with antique street signs, newly touched up "old brick," and lots of iron and brass. Despite this ambience, the sights and sounds of traffic and panhandlers on West Burnside might intrude upon your reveries of 19th-century Portland. Nonetheless, these

fall foliage at the south park blocks

PHOTO BY THEO TRIMMELL

the China Gate

PHOTO BY THEO TRIMMELL

street people would fit right into the historical fabric of a century ago, when shanghaied seamen and unemployed loggers were commonplace here. In fact, the term "skid row" is said to have originated in Portland or Seattle. This expression came from the "skid roads" where logs were slid downhill to the waterfront mills. After logging booms went bust, lumberjacks and other folks down on their luck would hit the skids in these parts of town. If you're not careful in the Old Town/Skidmore district after sunset, you too might end up "history."

Just south of Burnside near the Burnside Bridge is the **Skidmore Fountain** (S.W. 1st Ave. and S.W. Ankeny St.), named for a man who intended that it provide refreshment for "horses, men, and dogs." Despite the spouts and animal troughs, the 1888 bronze-and-granite fountain is purely decorative. It does serve, however, as a portal to **Saturday Market** (108 W. Burnside; tel. 222-6072) and to **Waterfront Park,** a mile-long oasis of greenery along the Willamette. The market is an outdoor potlatch of homegrown edibles, arts, and crafts. You can also expect the presence of excellent street performers. The market takes place every Saturday and Sunday from April through Christmas in the shadow of the Burnside Bridge. On Saturdays the hours are 10 a.m.-5 p.m.; on Sundays the market operates 11 a.m.-4:30 p.m.

Across Southwest 1st Avenue and cobblestoned **Ankeny Square** is the **New Market The-**ater, constructed in 1872 as a theater and produce market. Today it houses inexpensive restaurants and boutiques in a three-tiered atrium. Public bathrooms are downstairs and upstairs. Ask a New Market merchant about a key or entrance code.

Two blocks south the **Failing Building** (235 S.W. 1st Ave. and Oak St.) typifies the influences and use of cast iron so popular during the 1880s. Writer Gideon Bosker asserts that you can trace the evolution of American architectural style on a stroll through Portland. This is easy to believe if you turn left on S.W. Oak and S.W 1st, then left again on S.W. Front Avenue to a prime location of elegant restorations. Prior to Portland's era of expressways and bridge-building, this whole neighborhood was filled with cast iron facades and Italianate architecture.

Waterfront Park And Yamhill Historic District
From the Skidmore District, head east to Waterfront Park. En route to **River Place,** an attractive area of restaurants, specialty shops, and boating facilities, you'll pass joggers and the **Salmon Street Springs Fountain.** This is often the centerpiece for one of Portland's many festivals and provides a refreshing shower on a hot day. The fountain water's ebb and flow is meant to evoke the rhythms of the city. Tom McCall Waterfront Park is named for the governor credited with helping to reclaim Oregon's rivers. In the early 1970s it replaced Harbor Drive, a freeway that impeded access to the scenic Willamette River.

Food and local color are found at Yamhill Market.

PHOTO BY FRANK LONG

From the waterfront meander through the **Yamhill Historic District.** The colorful outdoor produce stalls of the **Yamhill Market** on S.W. 2nd recall the farmers' market that once stood on this site. Attached to the produce markets is a multitiered skylit atrium housing retail shops and a slew of short-order ethnic food stalls. Moving north and west towards city center, make your way to the intersection of Washington and S.W. 5th Avenue.

THE PARK AND ENVIRONS

Washington Park

From 5th and Washington board the colorfully painted Tri-Met bus line #63/Zoo/OMSI (Washington Park). The route includes **Washington Park**—the hillside home of the **Rose Garden,** the **Japanese Garden,** and the **Washington Park Zoo.** In addition, there's the **Oregon Museum of Science and Industry,** a historic carousel, the **Western Forestry Center,** the **Hoyt Arboretum,** and nearby, the **Pittock Mansion** (see "Museums And Miscellany"). Clear days can feature views of Mt. Hood and other Cascade peaks from some of these Washington Park aeries.

You can then head a mile downhill on foot or by bus to the **Northwest District** (north of Burnside between N.W. 18th and N.W. 27th Ave.). In the heart of the neighborhood, N.W. 23rd Street, Victorian homes have been remodeled into boutiques to join stylish shopping arcades, book-

stores, restaurants, and theaters. If you continue north for another mile, you'll see **Forest Park** looming over industrial northwest Portland, the largest park within a city in the United States.

The Pearl

Moving east down Burnside you come to a neighborhood which is affectionately referred to as "The Pearl" (north of Burnside to Marshall, N.W. 8th Ave. to N.W. 15th Ave.). Here, old warehouses have been turned into art galleries and antique showrooms. First-Thursday-of-the-month gallery walks feature a catered "open house" at these establishments. On the southern fringe of The Pearl is the largest bookstore in the world, **Powell's Books** (100 S.W. Burnside; tel. 228-4651) on 10th Avenue and Burnside. This is a world unto itself, so further comment is reserved for the listings which follow.

At this point, you've surveyed enough of downtown Portland to get a feel for what goes on west of the Willamette. There are other Portlands worth visiting on the other side of the river. Here are three excursions by mass transit which will offer a gourmet taste of this realm.

LLOYD CENTER

Go to any Gresham-bound MAX (Metropolitan Area Express) station in downtown Portland (pick-up points include Skidmore Fountain-Ankeny Square, and Northwest 1st Avenue and Davis Street in Old Town). Purchase "one-two" zone tickets and head to Lloyd Center. This mall was the world's largest shopping center in 1960 and today boasts over a hundred retail outlets, a newly domed ice-skating rink (**Lloyd Ice Pavilion** 2201, Lloyd Center; tel. 282-2511), and the largest theater in the city (**Lloyd Cinemas,** 4510 N.E. Multnomah; tel. 248-6938) with 10 screens and a neon futuristic interior. Nearby there is also the **Holladay Market** where **Coffee People** (1200 N.E. Broadway; tel. 284-4359) serves up some of the city's best coffee. In the same building, shops selling deli items, baked goods, produce, meat and fish, Mexican food, and pizza make this a favorite eat 'n' run outlet. Despite these attractions, the journey might be better than the destination. The MAX route goes over the Steel Bridge, from which there are great views of the city and river traffic and the spires of the new convention center (see Portland Convention and Visitors Association).

Hawthorne District

Hop a #5 Hawthorne Tri-Met bus from Southwest 5th Transit Mall or from Union Station. This neighborhood (from Southeast 17th to Southeast 55th avenues along Hawthorne Boulevard) recalls the hip gourmet ghettos of Berkeley, California and Cambridge, Massachusetts. Stores purveying records, fine coffees, second-hand clothing, antiques, crafts, and books join cafes and galleries along Hawthorne Boulevard.

A dense concentration of these establishments can be found between 32nd and 39th avenues. Beyond the Hawthorne District looms **Mt. Tabor.** This extinct volcano has drive-up views of Mt. Hood, the downtown, and the lower Willamette Valley. If you don't have a car, a #14 bus to S.E. 60th Avenue will get you close enough to hike the trail to these panoramas.

SELLWOOD

Antique hunters will be drawn from downtown to Sellwood in the southeast of Portland. Once a separate city, it annexed itself to Portland in 1890. To get there from downtown, take bus #65. Over 30 antique stores are spread along 12 blocks straddling a cliff above the Willamette River. As with the Hawthorne District, many of the stores open past 11 a.m. Most Sellwood stores are closed Sunday and Monday.

MUSEUMS AND MISCELLANY

Washington Park,
International Rose Test Gardens

If you're not on a bus you can get here the following ways: follow U.S. 26 west and look for signs, or go west on Burnside a mile beyond N.W. 23rd Avenue, turn right on N.W. Barnes Road, and then make another right turn on N.W. Irving and follow the signs.

The Rose City's welcome mat is out at this four-acre garden overlooking downtown. With more than 400 species it's the largest rose test garden in the country. The blossoms are at their peak in June, commemorated by the Rose Festival (see "Events"), but even if you're down to the last rose of summer, there's always the view of the city backdropped by (if you're lucky) Mt. Hood. The best vantage point for the latter is the east end of the garden along the "Queen's Walk," where the names of the festival beauty contest winners are enshrined (since 1907).

If you enter from the parking lot west of the restrooms near the center of the garden, look for the rose labeled "Fragrant Cloud" to the left of the

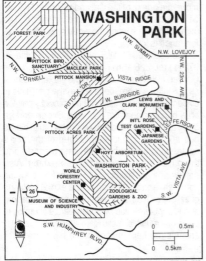

© MOON PUBLICATIONS, INC.

"Methinks of all the flowers, a rose is the finest . . ."

PHOTO BY TED LONG ISHIKAWA

walkway at the beginning of the row. As its name suggests, this is *the* place to stop and smell the roses. On the right-hand side of the walk is the all-star lineup of award winners. This floral fantasia can be enjoyed from dawn to dusk at no charge. And while I promised you a rose garden, leave the roses behind, because the fines for picking flowers here run a steep $250 per rose.

Japanese Gardens
From the Rose Garden head west up the steps that go past the parking lot and tennis courts on the way to the Japanese Gardens (off Kingston Ave. in Washington Park; tel. 223-4070). You can walk up the short but steep road that leads to the Japanese Gardens, or hop the free open-air shuttle that climbs up the hill every 10 minutes or so. The Japanese Gardens so moved the Japanese ambassador in 1988 that he pronounced it the most beautiful and authentic landscape of its kind outside Japan. Ponds and bridges, sand and stone, April cherry blossoms, and a snowcapped Fujiyama-like peak in the distance help East meet West here. This is always an island of tranquility, but connoisseurs will tell you to come during the fall-foliage peak in October. It's open daily in summer 10 a.m.-6 p.m. and thereafter, September 16 to April 4, it's open daily 10-4. The gardens are closed on Thanksgiving, Christmas, and New Year's Day. Admission is $3.50 for adults, $2 for students and seniors; under age three gets in free.

Washington Park Zoo
After the Japanese Gardens, you can catch the zooline train which goes four miles to the zoo. The train costs $2 for adults (ages 12-64, discounts for seniors) and runs 10:30 a.m. to 6:15 p.m. at 40-minute intervals. Figure on 35 minutes for a roundtrip. The ride itself is worth your time if only because the zooliner is a 30-year-old steam engine. But that's not all. The forested ridge defining the route features 112 species of birds, 62 kinds of mammals, and hundreds of plants. During a brief stopover, you may see the five major mountain peaks of the Cascade Range: Rainier, St. Helens, Adams, Hood, and Jefferson. The train may not run when the weather is rainy or attendance is low.

The zoo (4001 S.W. Canyon Road, Portland, 97221; tel. 226-1561) itself predates the Rose Garden (1887 versus 1917) and it exerts almost as ubiquitous a presence within the city. This is evident from a huge elephant prominently painted on a building near the Burnside Bridge and an array of zoo animals depicted on the multicolored bus #63. The city is justly proud of the zoo's award-winning elephant breeding program and the nation's largest chimpanzee exhibit. Also noteworthy are a colony of Humboldt penguins from Peru and an Alaskan tundra exhibit featuring grizzlies, wolves, and musk-oxen. The latter exhibit is supplemented by polar bears swimming in pools of simulated Arctic ice. Whenever possible, animals are kept in enclosures here which re-create their natural habitats. The most recent example is the African Grasslands exhibit which houses impalas, zebras, giraffes, and a black rhinoceros. You also shouldn't miss the zoo's **Elephant Museum,** which takes a lighthearted look at pachyderms. Along with the elephant jokes, elephants in literature and art are depicted with dioramas and masks. A look at the ivory trade injects a somber note into the proceedings.

Compounding the impression that it's all happenin' at the zoo are the free jazz concerts on Wednesday (and bluegrass on Thursday) nights for nine weeks during summer at the amphitheater. Contact the zoo for information on times and the schedule of performers.

The zoo is open May to October each day 9:30 a.m. to 5:30 p.m. The rest of the year, it's open daily 9:30-4. Admission is $3 for adults, $1.50 for children and seniors; under age three, free.

Oregon Museum Of Science And Industry

Across the street from the zoo entrance is the Oregon Museum of Science and Industry (4015 S.W. Canyon Road, Washington Park, Portland, 97221; tel. 222-2828). "OMSI" as it's called is a hands-on interactive museum where you can pilot the wheel of a ship's bridge, gain insight on cardiology from a walk through a giant heart, or coordinate the Gemini space capsule's movements from Mission Control. There is also the **Kendall Planetarium,** the largest astronomical educational center in the state. While much of this is geared to youngsters, it's hard not to find at least several exhibits that'll pique your curiosity. OMSI is open in summer Saturday to Thursday 9 a.m.-7 p.m., Friday 9-8; in winter, Saturday to Thursday 9-5, Friday 9-8. The museum is closed Christmas Day. Get there early on weekends to avoid the crowds. Bring enough money for admission ($5 for adults, $3.50 for seniors and children 3-17) and to cover purchases at the excellent gift shop oriented around science and education. Items like glow-in-the-dark star maps and kaleidoscopes are of exceptional quality.

World Forestry Center

Just over from OMSI is the World Forestry Center (4033 S.W. Canyon Road, Portland, 97221; tel. 228-1367), which offers exhibits on the natural processes of trees, the types of forests in the world, fighting forest fires, silviculture, and timber industry activities. Also featured is the Jessup Wood Collection, within which are displayed examples from the 505 trees native to North America. Dioramas, films, and mechanized exhibits are complemented here by lectures, shows, and spe-

East meets West at the Portland Japanese Gardens.

PHOTO BY OREGON STATE HIGHWAYS DIVISION

cial events. The center's most well-known (and after five minutes, most boring) attraction is a 70-foot talking tree. It's open daily 9 a.m.-6 p.m. in summer, in winter daily 10-5 p.m (closed Christmas Day). Admission is $3; seniors and students get in for half price.

On the grounds is a classic carousel (one free ride with Forestry Center admission ticket), operating only during dry seasons, and a steam engine that began hauling logs in the Coast Range in 1909.

Pittock Mansion

Up the hill from the zoo/OMSI/Forestry Center complex, where Washington Park meets Forest Park, is the Pittock Mansion, tel. 823-4469. Situated at nearly the highest point in the west hills, 1,000 feet above sea level, this French Renaissance mansion completed in 1914 also stands above the rest of the grand edifices in the city for other reasons. *Oregonian* founder Henry Pittock spared little expense in furnishing his 22-room shack with such accoutrements as modern showers with multiple showerheads, a central vacuum-cleaning system, room-to-room telephones, and a Turkish smoking room. The antique furniture, access to Forest Park trails, and fair-weather views of the Cascades also make this place a fixture on many itineraries. Lunch and afternoon tea are available in the Gate Lodge, the former caretaker's cottage, but hours and menu were in transition at press time. Regular tours are conducted (1-5 p.m.) daily except Sunday, and the grounds

are open to the public until dark. The mansion is especially nice to visit when it's bedecked in Christmas finery. Admission is $3 for adults, $2.50 for seniors, and $1 for youngsters ages six-18. Mass transit access from downtown is provided by bus #77 to N.W. Baines and Burnside Street, at which point you'll have to walk the steep half mile up Pittock Avenue.

The Park Blocks

The **Oregon Historical Center** (1230 S.W. Park Ave., Portland, 97205; tel. 222-1741) unfurls a pageant of Oregon's patrimony with artifacts, paintings, historical documents, and vintage photos. There's a permanent display on the second floor which focuses on naval and overland explorers, Indians, and the growth of Oregon communities. Exhibits here include ship models by early coastal mariners, pioneer crafts and tools, and an original 1845 covered wagon. Mundane items like early bicycles, snow skis, and fashions move the time machine into the 20th century. The first floor hosts revolving exhibits. A recent display showed off buttons, posters, and cartoons from American presidential races. The upper floors house a library and photo collection which is open to the public. The center's hours are 10 a.m.-4:45 p.m. Monday through Saturday.

Across the street, the **Portland Art Institute** (1219 S.W. Park Ave., Portland, 97205; tel. 225-2811) can complete a perspective on the Northwest coastal Indians. The masks and totem poles

Simon Benson's drinking fountains are found everywhere downtown.

PHOTO BY FRANK LONG

displayed here are not merely ornamental, being intimate parts of tribal ritual. The totem animals represent archetypal presences in native belief systems and are rendered with loving detail. Other permanent collections include prehistoric Chinese artifacts, tribal art of Cameroon, and contemporary sculpture and painting from around the world. In addition, you can have lunch at the **Ron Paul Cafe** here and listen to jazz Wednesday evenings. Hours can vary so check *Willamette Week* listings or call the Art Institute. Museum hours are 1-7 p.m. Tuesday through Friday (till 9:30 p.m. Thursday), noon to 5 p.m. weekends. Admission is $3 for adults, $1.50 for seniors, and 50 cents for students. Go on the first Thursday of the month between 4 and 9 p.m. for free admission. Take advantage of the Institute's Northwest Film and Video Center's film series (tel. 221-1156) featuring classic and eclectic flicks.

Riverside Museums
The **American Advertising Museum** (9 N.W. 2nd Ave., tel. 226-0000) can just as easily be called the museum of modern Americana. Housed in the former Erickson Saloon Building (dating back to the 1890s), the displays trace the early history of advertising up through the best campaigns of all time. Everything from Burma Shave billboards to Will Vinton's California raisins guide your journey through this visual and auditory feast. Hours are 11 a.m.-5 p.m. Wednesday through Friday, 11-5 p.m. on Saturday, and noon-5 p.m. on Sunday. The admission is $1.50, under 12 free. Around the corner is **La Patisserie** (208 N.W. Couch, tel. 248-9898), a second-floor walkup coffeehouse whose windows overlook Old Town, one of the best people-watching neighborhoods in the city.

The **World's First 24-Hour Coin Operated Art Gallery** (219 Ankeny) can be found near 2nd Avenue, two blocks south of Burnside Street. The bizarre storefront features the "World's Cheapest Psychic" and the Church of Elvis. Drop a quarter in this vending machine to hear from the King from beyond the grave, get "psychic counseling" (as well as "three predictions" and "post-life regressions"), and immerse yourself in various other forms of "erratica." Across the street, the seafood smells of **Dan and Louis Oyster Bar** (208 S.W. Ankeny, tel. 227-5906) and an odd mix of characters from nearby missions and Saturday Market can add to the ambience.

Further east is the **Oregon Maritime Center and Museum** (113 S.W. Front Ave., tel. 224-7724). The Waterfront Park location is appropriate, given the Willamette River docking facilities which used to be here. Handmade ship models, Spanish pieces of eight, sternwheelers, and navigational instruments fill this little monument to Portland shipping tradition. Also, don't miss the sea stories told by the "watchstanders." At any given time, a couple of members of the crew will be on deck, eager to share their stories. The hours in summer are Tuesday and Thursday through Saturday 11 a.m.-4 p.m., and Sunday noon-5 p.m. In winter, it's open Friday and Saturday 11-4 p.m., and Sunday noon-5 p.m. The admission is $2 for adults, 25 cents for seniors and students, under age eight, free.

The **Police Historical Museum** (111 S.W. 2nd Ave., tel. 963-0191) makes the history of law enforcement and the Portland Police Department an entertaining, if kitschy, excursion into the annals of crime control. An outdated display on drugs and their slang names, a homemade weapons exhibit (including jerry-built but nonetheless efficient guns fabricated in prison) join uniforms, badges, and old jail cells in this arcane assemblage. The museum is located in the Justice Center Building on the 16th floor, room 1682. It's open Tuesday to Friday 10 a.m.-3 p.m. and is free. Just up from the Justice Center on Southwest 4th and Main check out the bronze elk. Set in a fountain which had been a trough for horses and pioneers, it now serves as the city's most aesthetic traffic divider.

A fast disappearing aspect of Americana are the vintage carousels on display at the **Carousel Museum** (330 N.E. Holladay, tel. 235-2252). Primal memories can be evoked in adults and passed on to their kids here when visiting the largest collection of its kind in the country. The museum is located near the 7th Avenue MAX station and the admission is $1, free for children six and under.

BEYOND DOWNTOWN

The Grotto (N.E. 5th And N.E. Sandy Blvd., Box 20008, Portland, 97220; tel. 254-7371) is a Catholic shrine whose hand-hewn cavern surrounded by lushly landscaped grounds can in-

bookworm paradise

PHOTO BY THEO TRIMMELL

duce a profound sense of peace no matter the religious orientation of the visitor. Within the ivy-covered fern-lined grotto is an impressive marble
pieta. Outside the 30- by 50-foot enclosure, old
growth firs tower over the 110-foot cliff housing
the shrine. Roses, camellias, rhododendrons and
azaleas, and a cliffside view of the Columbia
River also make this worth the 20-minute pilgrimage from downtown Portland (take Tri-Met bus
#12). It's open daily 9 a.m. to dusk and the admis-
sion is free.

Sauvie Island

At the confluence of the Willamette and Columbia
rivers is the rural enclave of **Sauvie Island.**
Swimming, U-pick farms (raspberries, pumpkins,
strawberries, and apples), and birdwatching on
the Pacific Flyway (eagles, great blue herons,
geese, and sandhill cranes) are some of the activities that can be enjoyed a scant 20 minutes
from downtown (take I-5 north to the Fremont
Bridge, then cross the bridge and look for signs to
U.S. 30 northwest to St. Helens, Linnton, and
Sauvie Island). In addition, anglers come to
Sauvie's lakes and sloughs for panfish and bass
and the Columbia side's sand beaches (check
out **Walton Beach** at end the of N.W. Reeder
Road for swimming) for sturgeon, salmon, and
steelhead; bikers come for the 12-mile biking
loop, and wildlife aficionados come to the northern half to sight red foxes and blacktailed deer.

The more sedate can enjoy fall foliage and the
James Y. Bybee House (Howell Park Rd.,

Sauvie Island; tel. 621-3344). This 1858 farm was
built by Oregon Trail pioneers and is furnished
with pieces from that period. If you're not edified
by reading Sauvie Island's written history dating
back to Lewis and Clark, the Bybee House also
features an orchard with 115 species of apples
brought by the pioneers and a collection of old
farming implements. The house is open June to
Labor Day, Wednesday to Sunday noon-5 p.m.
There is no admission here although Sauvie's
$2.50-a-day per car parking fee might destroy the
island-out-of-time ambience. The island is open
for day use from 4 a.m. to 10 p.m.

Trojan Nuclear Power Plant

About 42 miles west of Portland in Rainier, WA is
Trojan Nuclear Power Plant (Route 2, Box 537;
tel. 226-8510). The dynamics of magnetism, electricity, and nuclear fission are detailed here by exhibits and nuclear engineers. Contact the visitors
center to make reservations for the thrice weekly
tours of the plant; hours are variable. It's all very
clean and comforting yet the issue of what to do
with the nuclear waste and the fact that the plant
sits on the same earthquake fault as Mt. St. Helens breaks through the spit-and-polish facade
like a madman laughing in the night.

Crystal Springs Rhododendron Garden

To the south of the city near the **Reed College**
campus (distinguished for the highest number of
Rhodes Scholars in the United States) is the
Crystal Springs Rhododendron Garden (S.E.

28th Avenue at Woodstock Blvd; tel. 796-5193). Come in April and May to see 600 varieties of rhodies as well as azaleas on seven acres broken up by an island on a spring-fed lake. Even without the 2,500 flowers here, birdwatching and fall foliage encourage a visit. It's free (except for the $1 charge on Mother's Day) and open daily from dawn till dusk.

ENTERTAINMENT

Booklovers' Portland
Powell's Books (1005 W. Burnside, tel. 228-4651) is a Portland institution. Over a million new and used books are housed in a labyrinth of hallways which take up a city block. Helpful staffpeople and maps of the stacks help locate whatever you might be looking for in 50 sections ranging from automobiles to zen. To make it even more appealing, there is the **Ann Hughes Coffee Room** (tel. 228-4651) at the west side of the store which sells espresso drinks, pastries, salads, soups, and snacks. The *New York Times* and other papers on library-style posts and the chance to look over prospective book purchases while sipping coffee makes Ann Hughes (and Powell's) a bastion of civilization in a neighborhood dominated by old warehouses. Free parking in a special garage on the side of the store and actors reading works of favorite authors on Monday night at 7:30 p.m. compound this impression.

The high probability of you being along the waterfront behooves a mention of **Book Port Books at Riverplace** (write to 0315 S.W. Montgomery Suite 340, tel. 228-2665). Although the place is relatively small, the selection is outstanding and the staff extremely helpful. Other noteworthy bibliophilic haunts include the offbeat titles at the **Catbird Seat Bookstore** (913 S.W. Broadway, tel. 222-5817), with a good selection of self-help titles, and **Rich's Cigar Store** (801 S.W. Alder St., tel. 228-1700, and 706 N.W. 23rd, tel. 227-6907) which stocks out-of-town newspapers and magazines from around the world.

Readings And Lectures
Of the many literary events going on in this city, Lit Eruption and Portland Arts and Lectures are the most well-known events on the circuit. **Lit**

Eruption (at Masonic Temple on the South Park Blocks, tel. 223-7692) features several dozen Northwest writers doing readings. There are also a bunch of bookstores with booths. Lectures run from 10-6 p.m. on two days in mid-April.

Portland Arts and Lectures (Schnitzer Hall, 1037 S.W. Broadway, tel. 241-0543) provides a forum for prominent literati, scientists, and other intelligentsia in a half-dozen presentations autumn through winter. The series is usually sold out ($60), but single tickets ($15) may still be available. Call 248-4496 for more information.

Theater
Portland's concentration of first-rate stage productions as well as opera, dance, and other kinds of theater is fast becoming one of the West Coast's worst-kept secrets. With equal doses of tradition and eclectic dynamism, the curtain rises on the most diverse schedule to hit the footlights in any city of comparable size

Headquarters for much of this activity is the **Portland Center for the Performing Arts** (1111 S.W. Broadway, Portland, 97205; tel. 248-4496). Four stages grace this facility; the 3,000-seat **Civic Auditorium,** the 2,776-seat **Arlene Schnitzer Hall** (whose rococco confines evoke a Viennese symphonic hall), 900-seat **Intermediate Theater,** and 350-seat **Dolores Winningstad Theater.** These venues host performances by the Oregon Symphony Orchestra, Portland Opera, Portland Youth Philharmonic, the Oregon Shakespeare Festival, Portland Center Stage, Ballet Oregon, West Coast Chamber Orchestra, Oregon Repertory Singers, Portland Gay Men's Chorus, and Pacific Ballet Theater. Rock, classical, jazz, and country music artists also concertize here. Ticket prices run $10-55 with frequent discounts for seniors and students. You can usually expect to pay around $25 for most events. The free one-hour **tours** of the Schnitzer Concert Hall (11 a.m.-1 p.m. Wednesday and Saturday) are a good intro to Portland's leading cultural center.

The following cross-section of theater groups chart the way to a memorable evening. The **Portland Center Stage Oregon Shakespeare Festival** (1111 S.W. Broadway-Intermediate Theater at Performing Arts, tel. 248-6309) is the outreach of the Ashland company whose Shakespeare series is the most esteemed of its kind in the country. Portland's Shakespeare season features five plays running from November to April. Thus, Shakespeare aficionados can look forward to a different play each month to provide a wintertime counterpart to Ashland's spring, summer, and fall offerings. Ticket prices run $16-22; students and seniors pay $7 on the day of the show.

Storefront Theater (on 1st off of Burnside, tel. 224-4001) presents modern avant-garde plays ranging from whimsical comedies to innovative dramas. Performances are Tuesday through Saturday at 7:30 p.m. and on Sunday at 2 and 7 p.m. Tickets run $12-15, with lower prices on Thursday and Sunday. Senior citizen and student discounts are available. Shows also take place at S.W. 3rd Avenue.

More mainstream fare is the rule at the **Portland Repertory Theater** (25 S.W. Salmon St., Portland, tel. 224-4491). Along with such American classics as *Bus Stop,* the curtain also rises on Noel Coward-type English comedies. Located downtown in the World Trade Center near the waterfront, the rep's convenient underground parking and a technologically sophisticated, intimate 230-seat theater packs 'em in with near sellouts each season. The curtain times are 8 p.m. Tuesday and Saturday and 2 and 7 p.m. Sunday. Half price tickets are available a half-hour before performances.

Due to a funding crunch (as of this writing), Portland's oldest theater company is not functioning. When it's revived, expect children's theater, comedies, and Broadway musicals at **Portland Civic Theater** (1530 S.W. Yamhill, tel. 226-3048). *The Fantasticks, Hair,* and an annual rendition of *Peter Pan* at Christmas typify the productions. Ticket prices range from $13-15 for the Thursday through Sunday performances.

Artists Repertory Theater (1111 S.W. 10 Avenue—Wilson Center YWCA, tel. 242-2400) is a company run by actors whose presentations run the gamut from the classics to modern plays. This is an Oregon version of high-quality off-Broadway theater. The **New Rose Theater** (994 S.W. Main St., in the Park blocks, tel. 222-2487) is also of this ilk. This company is best known for its annual production of *A Christmas Carol* as well as plays by prizewinning authors from all over the world.

For curtain times of all of the above and smaller community-based troupes consult *Willamette Week* (see "Media" in "Information And Services"). The Portland Theatre Alliance has recently announced walk-up windows in the **Galleria Mini-Mall**

(S.W. Morrison at 10th) just west of Pioneer Courthouse Square, offering half-price tickets to live local theater the day of the show. This outlet is open noon-6 p.m. Thurs.-Sat., and noon-5 p.m. Sunday.

Other places to get your cultural fix include **Portland Opera** (1516 S.W. Alder, St., tel. 241-1407) and the **Oregon Ballet Theater** (1119 S.W. Park Ave., Civic Auditorium, tel. 227-6867). Opera tickets range from $18-36 (discounts for seniors and students at dress rehearsals) and ballet admission is $9-30. Finally, the **Oregon Symphony** takes the stage September through June with classical, pops, Sunday matinees, and children's concerts. The matinees are the least expensive ($4-6) of the shows which collectively range $8-28. Students and seniors may purchase half-price tickets one hour before a classical concert.

Galleries
Gallery-hopping on the first Thursday of every month facilitates introduction to Portland's artistic community. More than 30 gallery owners coordi-

PHOTO BY THEO TRIMMELL
*the Intermediate Theater at
the Portland Center for the Performing Arts*

nate show openings, and many offer complimentary refreshments. A free shuttle bus connects gallery districts that evening. The bus has 12 stops and begins its cycle from S.W. 1st and Taylor at 6:30 p.m. When service terminates is according to season so consult *The Downtowner,* which sponsors the service. The Pearl district is a good place to start. Here, warehouses have been converted to artists' lofts and a large concentration of display spaces (see "The Pearl" under "The Park And Environs").

Nightlife

Music and laughs, they're all here in the Rose City, but in varying degrees. To put it more bluntly, jazz is hot, comedy is usually not. In any case, whether it's cooling your heels or dancing up a storm, there's no shortage of night spots. Portland's major comedy club, the **Last Laugh** (426 N.W. 6th Avenue, tel. 295-2844), might suffer from poor acoustics and a lack of intimacy if you sit in the back but the talent is there—besides, it's just about the only game in town. Hours are 6 p.m.-12:30 a.m. daily. Cover charges are $5.50 Sunday through Thursday and $8 Friday and Saturday.

Jazz, Blues, And Rock

Portland has been a prime venue on the West Coast circuit for practitioners of these quintessentially American musical art forms. Several jazz and blues festivals each summer are well attended and you can manage to get an earful on any given many night of the week in Portland night spots all year long. Nationally known bluesman Robert Cray and his locally popular former sidekick Curtis Salgado were weaned on the Portland club circuit, which occasionally hosts the icons of the Delta, Chicago, and Texas-style variations of this music. Performers like James Cotton and Queen Ida have appeared at the **Rose City Blues Festival** (tel. 282-0555) in early July in Waterfront Park (admission free, but donations go to Oregon Food Bank).

The jazz scene here boasts Russian-born pianist Andres Kitaev, the nationally known pianist Tom Grant, and the venerable Mel Brown Sextet with Leroy Vinnegar. You also might appreciate the large number of places in town where jazz is served up with dinner. *Willamette Week* (see

"Media" in "Information And Services") listings and flyers on telephone poles and billboards let you know who's playing and where; also check out *Blues Notes,* a local publication available at bookstores and elsewhere about town. The Friday *Oregonian* features an "Arts and Entertainment" section which also helps you plan your evening out. But the best source of all for jazz information is **Jazz Hotline** (tel. 222-5003). For rock, a free publication, *Live Music,* available in retail outlets, is recommended.

Reggae, blues, and rock lovers can enjoy a variety of local and nationally known artists at these clubs. **Key Largo** (31 N.W. 1st, tel. 223-9919), which is open Monday through Friday 11:30 a.m.-2:30 a.m. and has a $2-8 cover charge; **Starry Night** (8 N.W. 6th Avenue, tel. 227-0071), the **Dandelion Pub** (31 N.W. 23rd Place, tel. 223-0099), and **Day For Night** (N.W. 5th and Davis, tel. 243-2556) are all open nightly. These places may be smoky or sweaty, but are unsurpassed for live acts and the chance to boogie. In like measure, devotees look to the **Pine Street Theater** (221 S.E. 9th Avenue, tel. 235-0027) and the new wave **Satyricon** (125 N.W. 6th Avenue, tel. 243-2380) for inspiration.

The **Portland Art Museum** (1219 S.W. Park Avenue, tel. 226-2811) features top-flight jazz and blues in their museum after-hours concerts. Musicians set up stage in the museum of sculpture court each Wednesday from 5:30-7:30 p.m. Admission is $3.50.

Jazz with Italian-flavored cuisine is presented at these popular nightspots: **Parchman Farm** (1204 S.E. Clay, tel. 235-7831), which is jamming 8 p.m.-1 a.m. nightly, and **Remo's** (1425 N.W. Glisan, tel. 221-1150).

The "in place to be out" is **Brasserie Montmartre** (626 S.W. Park Avenue, tel. 224-5552). Hours for music are 8 p.m.-1 a.m. nightly. Live local jazz is accompanied by magicians and your own artistic creations (crayons supplied free of charge). Light meals are served from 11 a.m.-3 p.m. with a nouvelle French flair and prices reflecting same. A high-ceilinged Paris-in-the-'30s decor makes an appropriate backdrop to this classy spot.

The Hobbit is the home away from home of local favorites, the Mel Brown Sextet with Leroy Vinnegar. Every Sunday from 3:30-7:30 p.m.

there's a jam of other Portland jazzpeople which is broadcast over local radio station KMHD-FM, 89.1 on your dial.

Finally, the **Mt. Hood Festival of Jazz** (Box 696, Gresham, 97030; tel. 666-3810) is *the* event of the year for local jazz lovers as well as connoisseurs from all over the world. Lou Rawls, Count Basie, Stan Getz, Ella Fitzgerald, Wynton Marsalis, and Grover Washington Jr. have graced this event which takes place the first weekend of August at Mt. Hood Community College in Gresham. Two nine-hour concerts make up the schedule. Tickets go around $20 per day and local dining spots cater the affair. Those on a budget should bring a picnic. To get there, take I-84 to the Wood Village/Gresham Exit and follow the signs to the community college.

Cinema

In addition to the previously mentioned Art Institute series and the ten-screen Lloyd Cinema, Portland offers a wide variety of theaters and an equally diverse choice of cinematic experiences.

The **Movie House** (1220 S.W. Taylor, tel. 222-4595) offers wine, cheese (card tables and chess upstairs), and art flicks. Tickets go for $4.50 with discounts for children and seniors. For the price of a pint of microbrew, a burger, or a selection of thick sandwiches, settle into old couches at **Mission Theater and Pub** (1624 N.W. Glisan St., tel. 223-4031) to watch old Marx Brothers and 1940s classic movies at no charge. It's more a tavern than a movie house, but by the second or third mug, you won't care. It's open 5 p.m. to midnight.

KOIN Center Cinema's (222 S.W. Columbia St., tel. 243-3515) marble staircase leads to six screens showing art films and high-quality Hollywood releases. **Cinema 21** (616 N.W. 21st. Avenue, tel. 223-4515) is an old auditorium in the artsy Northwest district showing foreign, experimental, and new wave movies as well as documentaries, cult favorites, and revivals.

The art deco interior of the **Fox Theater** (833 S.W. Broadway, tel. 248-6986) showcases first-run films. Proximity to Pioneer Courthouse Square and the park blocks can make parking difficult but the lovingly rendered roaring twenties motif makes it worth the extra effort. The admission is $5. Another well-preserved screen gem is the **Roseway Theater** (7229 S.W. Sandy Blvd., tel.

281-5173), featuring modern films as well as musicals of the '40s and '50s and a real pipe organ.

Miscellaneous Hangouts

Portland's diverse communities congregate in brewpubs, discos, fern bars, and cabarets.

The **Dakota Cafe** (239 S.W. Broadway, tel. 241-4151) has something for everybody. Disco and R&B recorded music as well as a house band provide background for a yuppies/Bohemians mix. It's open Monday through Friday from 6:30 p.m.-2:30 a.m. and on Saturday and Sunday from 8 a.m.-2:30 a.m.

Produce Row Cafe (204 S.E. Oak St. tel. 232-8355) has 27 beers on tap for a buck a glass and 200 bottled domestic and imported beers. Huge sandwiches are also a good value and feed two people. The cafe straddles the warehouses beneath Martin Luther King Jr. Blvd. and is open Monday through Friday 11 a.m.-1 a.m., Saturday noon-1 a.m., and Sunday 2 p.m.-midnight.

Along with such popular microbrews as Blue Heron Ale and Grant's Ale, brewpubs have earned Portland a good reputation for quality beers and ales. Brewpubs are small friendly beer bars built around custom-made "house" ales. Portland's preeminent brewpub meisters are the McMenamin brothers. The previously mentioned **Mission Theater and Pub,** the **Hillsdale Brewery and Public House** (1505 S.W. Sunset Blvd., tel. 246-3938), and the **Fulton Pub and Brewery (1618 S.W. Nebraska St., tel. 246-9530)** are joined by other McMenamin establishments in Portland, Hillsboro, Gresham, Eugene, and Lincoln City. Such unusual brews as raspberry-flavored Ruby Tuesday, Terminator, Hammerhead, and Mar Bars ales have given this brewpub chain a dedicated following.

The **Goose Hollow Inn** (1927 S.W. Jefferson St., tel. 228-2010) is a popular neighborhood tavern that reflects the personality of the owner, Portland politico Bud Clark. The repartee can be fast and furious here unless it's Sunday, when blues or jazz fills the room 5-9 p.m. However, the management does advertise "quality tunes at a volume you can converse to." With combination sandwiches ranging from $3-6.50 (the best Reuben in town), homemade soup, and the "Goose Hollow Famous Potato Salad," there probably won't be much talking anyway.

RECREATION

Spectator Sports

Portland is more a town for athletes than devotees of spectator sports. Nonetheless, the two stadia in the Rose City draw huge crowds.

In the case of **Memorial Coliseum** (1401 North Wheeler, Portland, 97208; tel. 235-8771), this is entirely understandable given the success of the **Portland Trailblazers,** who nearly won the National Basketball Association championship in 1990. Although the NBA season here is a near sellout, it pays to check out the *Oregonian* sports section for general admission tickets ($7.50-29) which are usually advertised in the middle of the season. If you do get into a game, be sure to enjoy the smoked salmon sandwiches created by the **Karla's Krabs** of Oregon coastal fame (but sold under a different name). The **Winter Hawks** hockey team of the Western Hockey League also occupies the coliseum.

Murrary Kemp Greyhound Park (N.W. 223rd and Glisan St., Box 9, Fairview, 97024; tel. 667-7700) is the only place to see greyhound racing on the West Coast. It's located southeast of Portland near Gresham. The **Multnomah Kennel Club**'s glass-enclosed facility offers beautiful views of Cascade peaks and excellent dining facilities along with pari-mutuel wagering. Evening post time is 7:30 p.m., matinee post time is 1 p.m. The season runs from May through September.

Mention should also be made of the **Portland Beavers,** a AAA farm team that plays baseball in **Civic Stadium** (1844 S.W. Morrison, tel. 248-4345). Tickets are $3-5.

The sport of kings is on display at **Portland Meadows** (1001 N. Schneer Rd., tel. 284-9144) Fri., Sat., and Sunday. A glass-enclosed grandstand with complete food service ensures comfort from October to April.

Hiking

Portland has more urban wilderness than any other city in the country, and as whole books have been written about these retreats, we will have to confine ourselves to just a few hikes and refer the reader to the **Portland Audubon Society Bookstore** (5151 N.W. Cornell Road, Portland, 97210; tel. 292-6855), which has mapped more than 200 urban wildlife habitat sites in Portland, and *A Pedestrian's Portland* by Karen and Terry Whitehill (Mountaineers Books, $10.95). The book outlines 40 walks in greater Portland which the authors divide into six areas. Without doubt, the part of Portland most conducive to a walk on the wild side are the hills behind the Northwest neighborhood. The largest urban wilderness in the world, **Forest Park,** is accessible off I-5 (heading north) by taking the Fremont Bridge into north Portland and turning left at Vaughn Street. Thereafter, if you make a right on Thurman Street and follow it to its end, you'll have reached the portal of Forest Park. The paved walkway at the edge of the wilderness has numerous branch-offs to forested hillsides. Despite scenic beauty, the smells and sounds of Portland's industrial northern extremity can occasionally pierce the tranquility here. Thus, weekends and holidays are recommended for excursions into this preserve.

A scenic adjunct is **MacLeay Park** which can be reached via the Forest Park route and a turnoff onto Cornell Road (instead of Thurman), following it to its end. The Audubon Society Headquarters and bookstore is located near the trailhead. The gentle uphill trail here follows a deep gully paralleling a creek.

Another way to reach MacLeay and Forest Parks is via the 14-mile **Wildwood Trail** which heads north through the Hoyt Arboretum and Pittock Acres before plunging downhill into the parklands below. The trail begins on Canyon Road near the Zoo, OMSI, and Forestry Center. Or, you can drive to the **Arboretum Visitor Center** (4000 S.W. Fairview Blvd.) that's open 10-4 p.m. daily or the Pittock Mansion to begin your descent into MacLeay and Forest parks.

The arboretum is the gem of the Wildwood Trail and covers 214 acres and seven miles of trails, including a one-mile tour through one of the country's largest collections of conifers. On Saturdays and Sundays October through April at 2 p.m., guided tours highlight foliage season. Prime time to come is during the **Fall Festival of Color** weekend around October 20th. Events begin at 9:30 a.m. with a guided one-mile loop (for independents, a comprehensive trail map is available for 50 cents) through more than two dozen species of deciduous trees.

The **Wildwood Trail** is part of a proposed larger network of trails to loop the city. This was originally the brainchild of the Olmsted Brothers (of Yosemite Valley and Central Park fame) at the turn of the century. Their proposed 40-mile loop concept has expanded to a 140-mile matrix. Now the goal is to complete a hiking/biking path connecting parks along the Columbia, Sandy, and Willamette rivers. To find out more, contact the **40 Mile Loop Land Trust** (tel. 241-9105) or pick up a map of the loop at Powell's Travel Bookstore at the Pioneer Courthouse Square (tel. 228-1108).

On the other end of town, another potential component of the loop beckons urban walkers in search of rural pleasures. Snaking along the east bank of the Willamette River between the Sellwood and Ross Island bridges, the **Oaks Bottom Wildlife Park** is a birdwatcher's paradise. Great blue and green-backed herons find this wetland a prime habitat. In winter, a dozen species of waterfowl can be found. Summertime residents include warblers, orioles, swallows, and woodpeckers. Whenever you go, look for wood ducks joining such permanent denizens as beavers and muskrats.

A ridge along Sellwood Boulevard frames Oak Bottoms and offers good views. You can hike into it at the north end of Sellwood Park. After you descend, a loop trail encircles the wetlands, paralleling the bluff on the east side and following the railroad tracks to the west.

Sports

Tennis courts, cycling paths, and lakes for swimming and sailing abound in Portland parks (Portland Parks, 1120 S.W. 5th Avenue, Room 502, Portland, tel. 796-5193). Free swimming pools can also be located by calling this number.

Runners enjoy numerous events, including the well regarded **Portland Marathon** and the **Cascade Runoff.** To find out about these and other events call the **Runner's Hotline** (tel. 223-7867). The **Oregon Runner's Club** (Box 549, Beaverton, 97025-0549; tel. 626-2348) is the second largest club in the county and is glad to recommend the best places to run.

Bipeds in less of a hurry can pick up a free annotated walker's map at Powell's to supplement the one outlined in "Portland Neighborhoods" above. Bikers can procure the *From Here to There by Bike* map at many bookstores in town.

Cyclists looking for organized 30-100-mile rides at a touring pace should hook up with the **Portland Wheelmen Touring Club Hotline** (tel. 282-PWTC).

As for golfers, 20 18-hole courses are within 20 miles of the city, but only half are public. Two of the best are: **Heron Lakes** (3500 Victory Blvd., tel. 289-1818) designed by Robert Trent Jones and 15 minutes from downtown; and **Eastmoreland Golf Course** (24225 S.E. Bybee Blvd., tel. 775-2900). This also has a driving range and the course is near the Crystal Spring Rhododendron Garden. Greens fees average about $13 for 18 holes on public courses in Portland.

EVENTS

The **Portland Rose Festival** (tel. 228-9411) has been the major wing-ding here for nine decades. The Rose Queen and her court (chosen from local high school entrants), sailors and prostitutes, and floats in several parades clog Portland's traffic arteries during this 24-day citywide celebration each June. Air shows, a hot-air balloon classic, the Indy World Series car race, and a pick-up traditional rose show round out the big doin's. The flyer available at the visitor and convention bureau has more on information and scheduling.

Also in June (through mid-July) is **Chamber Music Northwest** (Reed College Commons, 3203 S.E. Woodstock Avenue, tel. 229-4079). Monday to Saturday at 8 p.m. the concert begins and people picnic before. Tickets to this nationally acclaimed series cost $9 and $7.50 for ages 7-14.

In July, the **Multnomah County Fair** (Portland Expo Center, tel. 285-7756) attracts the likes of Johnny Cash, prize bulls, and agricultural exhibits. A carnival midway and food concessions are also fixtures at this event.

An August festival, **The Bite,** (Tom McCall Waterfront Park, tel. 248-0600) lets you sample local culinary specialties of Portland restaurants with the proceeds going to the Special Olympics.

Early September's **Artquake** (tel. 227-2787) takes place in the Center for the Performing Arts and the Park Blocks for three days. Entry fees are negligible (outdoor events free, indoor events $2) to this collage of music, theater, dance, food, crafts, and visual arts.

The Sternwheeler Columbia Gorge *cruises Portland Harbor and the Columbia River.*

PHOTO BY OREGON TOURISM DIVISION

The **Wintering-in Festival** at Howell Territorial Park (Sauvie Island, tel. 222-1741) happens near the autumnal equinox. Enjoy fresh farm produce, crafts, and music at the restored pioneer homestead (see "Sauvie Island" above).

In October, watch the salmon spawn at Oxbow Park in the Salmon River Gorge outside Gresham. Old-growth walks, an eight-kilometer run, and a barbecue as well as arts and crafts round out this fete. To get there from downtown, take I-84 east to the Wood Village Exit. Turn south on Division and east on Oxbow Parkway, then follow the signs to Oxbow Park. There's a $3 parking fee. Call 248-5050 for more information.

The day after Thanksgiving, a Christmas tree is lit in Pioneer Square and a skating rink installed. Skate rentals are available and a small admission is charged . The best Christmas lights display is on Peacock Lane in Southeast Portland; check the visitor and convention bureau for more details.

Tours

In a guide for independent travelers a listing of tours may seem out of place, but sometimes there are organized outings that provide insights unavailable elsewhere.

One such perspective is provided by a harbor cruise on a sternwheeler. This mode of transport opened up the Willamette a century ago and the 49-passenger *Rose* (tel. 286-7673) and the 599-passenger *Columbia Gorge* (tel. 223-3928) today enable you to appreciate the fascinating and otherwise inaccessible (to pedestrians) Swan Island dry dock facilities. Cruise to within 100 feet of the world's largest dry dock, which is actually a huge floating tank made of hollow pontoons filled with an amount of river water proportional to the weight of the vessel. When a ship goes into drydock, the dock sinks and tugs push the ship into place. The dock master then raises the dock by pumping water out over the course of 90 minutes. Most tour intineraries spend 15 minutes here, leaving the bulk of the two-hour itinerary to sightsee the river traffic, seven of the city's 12 bridges, grain terminals, and other facets of this busy port. In addition, there are beautiful views of the skyline. Shipyard sophisticates might want to remember that cruise ships hit the docks here for repairs in May and September, Alaskan oil tankers in summer, and military ships are serviced year-round.

During winter less traffic from pleasure craft make possible unobstructed views, and evenings feature the spectacle of lights switching on for the night crews. Box lunches and dinners are available on some trips. Basic tour costs vary from $7.50-10 depending on the route.

The *Columbia Gorge* departs Waterfront Park (S.W. Front and S.W. Stark, north of the Morrison Bridge) October to mid-June. Departure times are Friday at noon, Saturday at 11:30 a.m., and Sunday at 10 a.m. and 1 p.m. Not every tour takes in the docks, so call ahead for reservations (tel. 223-3928). The *Rose* leaves from Riverplace at varied times; call 286-7673 to check departures. Remember that the scenery upriver (towards Oregon City) is more scenic than the industrial ambience to the north.

Close by Powell's Bookstore is a touring opportunity of special interest on a hot day. The **Blitz-Weinhard Brewery** (1133 West Burnside St.,

Portland, 97209; tel. 222-4351) offers free tours every half hour. Just register at the reception desk. The highlight of the brewery tour is of course the tasting room.

Finally, there is **Gray Line of Portland** (21320 N. Suttle, tel. 285-9845). Gray Line in most cities runs competent tours with experienced drivers. Portland's outfit is no exception. In addition to day-trips to such locales as the Mt. Hood loop, the coast, and the Columbia River Gorge, three- and seven-hour city tours depart April 28 through October 15 at 9 a.m. from major hotels (call ahead to reserve space). The city itineraries concentrate heavily on Washington Park and the scenic West Hills and cost $22 for the full-day trip and $13 for the several-hour loop (half price for children under 12).

PRACTICALITIES

ACCOMMODATIONS

Portland poses no problem for those seeking a reasonably priced overnight. An A.Y. H. Hostel, a traditional city-center landmark, a well-kept standard motel just over the bridge from the urban core, and a bed and breakfast give the bargain hunter a choice of excellent accommodations at half the price of comparable digs in San Francisco.

The **Portland A.Y. Hostel** (3031 S.E. Hawthorne Blvd., tel. 236-3380) is the least expensive ($8.75 members, $11 nonmembers) and one of the best-located places to stay in Portland. It's situated in amongst the restaurants and shops of the Hawthorne neighborhoods and on the bus line (from downtown take Bus #5 to 31st Avenue; from the airport take #12 then transfer to #5). Kitchen privileges and nearby restaurants serving tasty, inexpensive nutritious food less than a block away also recommend it. Hostel hours are 8-9:30 a.m. and 5-10 p.m.; lights out Sun.-Thurs. at 11 p.m. and Fri.-Sat. at midnight. Make reservations for this large rambling white hostelry in summer due to the influx of folks from other countries. A spacious screened-in back porch provides a cool place to sleep in July and August. It should also be mentioned that a day-use fee of $3 is invoked and some chores are required.

Despite a moderate price, the **Mallory Motor Hotel** (729 S.W. 15th Avenue at Yamhill, Portland, 97295; tel. 223-6311 or 800-228-8657) at first glance suggests a luxury lodging, with a lobby boasting ornate plaster, crystal chandeliers, and an elegant skylit interior. The dining room's marble pillars and chandeliers sustain the four-star facade along with the elaborate jungle motif of the **Driftwood Room Lounge.** A location not far from the boutiques of the Northwest districts and the Civic Theater compound the impression of a counterpart to the Benson and Heathman hotels. With an address like this, the Mallory's free parking is also especially appreciated. Only the rather plain rooms might justify prices which range $35-45 for a single and $40-70 for a dou-

ble. If you're lucky enough to score one of the king-sized suites for $65, however, you'll probably walk away shaking your head in disbelief at this lodging value. The staff, who've been there for years, is efficient but more curt than courteous.

The **Jade Tree** (3939 N.E. Hancock, tel. 288-6891 or 800-524-9999) sits tucked away off Sandy Boulevard in Portland's Hollywood district. Proximity to restaurants, movies, shopping, and the bus line (15 minutes from downtown) come along with clean, large well-appointed rooms which go for around $40.

A justifiable splurge is the elegant **White House Bed and Breakfast** (1914 N.E. 22nd, Portland, 97212; tel. 287-7131). Located just off Broadway near an avenue of shops and restaurants, and five to ten minutes from Lloyd Center and downtown, this lumber baron's 1912 mansion has rates ranging from $72-92, double occupancy. The innkeeper's baked scones and other goodies at the included breakfast and tea, together with the complimentary sherry nightcap, impart the touch of home.

FOOD

Portland's renaissance has resulted in the highest number of restaurants per capita of any city in the country. Perhaps more impressive is the fact that you can have a singular dining experience for much less than you'd pay for a gourmet outing in either Seattle or San Francisco. Even the traditionally overpriced bland food served in many hotel dining rooms can often turn out to be affordable and tasty here. Also noteworthy are local chains of ethnic fast food, a profusion of microbreweries, and innovative purveyors of Northwest cuisine. The following cross-section leaves many upscale restaurants to such dining guides as *Portland's Best Places* (Sasquatch Press) and *Pacific Northwest Magazine* (see the general Introduction). What's left are places with personality and a sense of fun geared to the budget of the average traveler.

PORTLAND ACCOMMODATIONS

Name	Address	Telephone	Price	Features
NORTH				
Westerner Motel	4333 N. Interstate Ave.	281-0097	$27-29	cable, pets
Mel's Motor Inn	5205 N. Interstate Ave.	285-2556	$30	cable, pets, kitchenettes
Budget Host Viking Motel	6701 N. Interstate Ave.	285-6687	$30-34	cable, pets, kitchenettes, fireplace, pool, laundry, nonsmoking rooms
Friendship Inn Sands Motel	3801 N. Interstate Ave.	287-2601	$30-35	cable, pets, nonsmoking rooms
Palms Motel	3801 N. Interstate Ave.	287-5788	$30-36	cable, pets
Delts Inn	9930 N. Interstate Ave.	289-1800	$42-50	cable, pets, kitchenettes, laundry, nonsmoking rooms
John Palmer House	4314 N. Mississippi	284-5893	$43-75	restaurant/lounge
Best Western Inn at the meadows	1215 N. Hayden Meadows Dr.	286-9600	$56-95	cable, pets, restaurant/lounge weight room, nonsmoking rooms, complimentary continental breakfast
Red Lion Hotel Jantzen Beach	909 N. Hayden Island Dr.	283-4466		cable, pets, restaurant lounge, pool, live entertainment, river view
Red Lion Inn Coliseum	1225 N. Thunderbird Way	235-8311	$65-71	cable, pets, restaurant/lounge, non smoking rooms, river view
NORTHEAST				
Midtown Motel	1415 N.E. Sandy Blvd.	234-0316	$22-29	cable, nonsmoking rooms, complimentary continental breakfast
Ara-Bell Motel	11324 N.E. Sandy Blvd.	252-6059	$25-40	cable, kitchenettes, laundry, nonsmoking rooms

PORTLAND ACCOMMODATIONS, cont.

Name	Address	Telephone	Price	Features
NORTHEAST, cont.				
Cameo Motel	4111 N.E. 82nd Ave.	774-8876	$25	cable, kitchenettes, laundry, nonsmoking rooms
Cabana Motel	1707 N.E. 82nd Ave.	252-0224	$28-30	cable, kitchenettes, laundry, nonsmoking rooms
States Motel	2620 N.E. 82nd Ave.	255-0103	$28	cable, kitchenettes, pool, covered pool, weight room
Capri Motel	1530 N.E. 82nd Ave.	253-1151	$30-35	cable, kitchenettes, complimentary continental breakfast
City Center Motel	3800 N.E. Sandy Blvd.	287-1107	$30-36	cable, pets, nonsmoking rooms, complimentary continental breakfast
Dune Motel	1525 N.E. 37th Ave.	288-6751	$30-36	cable, pool, nonsmoking rooms, complimentary continental breakfast
Holiday Motel	8050 N.E. Union Ave.	285-3661	$32-38	cable, pets
Jade Tree Motel	3939 N.E. Hancock	288-6891	$34-50	cable, pets, nonsmoking rooms
Carriage Inn	2025 N.W. Northrop	224-0543	$39	cable, pets, kitchenettes, laundry
Chumaree Inn	8247 N.E. Sandy Blvd.	256-4111	$40-99	cable, pool, restaurant/lounge, laundry, nonsmoking rooms
Econo Lodge	518 N.E. Holladay St.	234-4391	$40	cable, pets, pool
Portland/Troutdale Travelodge	23705 N.E. Sandy Blvd.	666-6623	$35-44	cable, kitchenettes, laundry, nonsmoking rooms, complimentary continental breakfast
Execulodge Portland Airport	6221 N.E. 82nd Ave.	255-6511	$55-195	cable, restaurant/lounge, pool, weight room

PORTLAND ACCOMMODATIONS, cont.

Name	Address	Telephone	Price	Features
NORTHEAST, cont.				
Best Western Fortniter Motel	4911 N.E. 82 Ave.	255-9771	$43-53	cable, kitchenettes, non-smoking rooms, complimentary continental breakfast
Best Western Flamingo Motor Inn	9727 N.E. Sandy Blvd.	255-1400	$47	cable, pets, pool, restaurant/lounge, non-smoking rooms, live entertainment
Portland Super 8 Motel	11011 N.E. Holman	257-8988	$47	cable, pets, laundry, non-smoking rooms
Best Western Kings Way Inn	420 N.E. Holladay St.	233-6331	$50-60	cable, restaurant, laundry, nonsmoking rooms
Comfort Inn Lloyd Center	431 N.E. Multnomah	233-5121	$50-67	cable, covered pool, non-smoking rooms, complimentary continental breakfast
Shilo Inn Portland Airport	3828 N.E. 82 Ave.	256-2550	$50-62	cable, pets, kitchenettes, pool, laundry, nonsmoking rooms
Shilo Inn Lloyd Center	1506 N.E. 2nd Ave.	231-7665	$52-58	cable, pets, laundry, non-smoking rooms, complimentary continental breakfast
Execulodge Convention Center	1030 N.E. Union Ave.	235-8433	$62-68	cable, restaurant/lounge, weight room, live entertainment, nonsmoking rooms
Pony Soldier Motor Inn	9901 N.E. Sandy Blvd.	256-1504	$62-71	cable, kitchenettes, restaurant/lounge, pool, weight room, laundry, nonsmoking rooms, complimentary continental breakfast
Travelodge Hotel	1441 N.E. 2nd Ave.	233-2401	$62-85	cable, restaurant/lounge, pool, nonsmoking rooms

PORTLAND ACCOMMODATIONS, cont.

Name	Address	Telephone	Price	Features
NORTHEAST, cont.				
Days Inn Hotel	11550 N.E. Airport Way	252-3200	$63-73	cable restaurant/lounge, pool, laundry, nonsmoking rooms, complimentary continental breakfast
SOUTHEAST				
Del Rancho Motel	7622 S.E. 82nd Ave.	777-3806	$25-37	cable, kitchenettes
Aaron Motel	2724 S.E. 82nd Ave.	771-6460	$26-40	basic
Cascade Motel	10308 S.E. 82nd Ave.	775-1571	$27-37	cable, pets, kitchenettes
Best Value Inn	3310 S.E. 82nd Ave.	777-4786	$29-50	cable, pets, nonsmoking rooms
Unicorn Inn Motel	3040 S.E. 82nd Ave.	774-1176	$30-33	cable, kitchenettes, nonsmoking rooms
Camaree Inn	4512 S.E. 82nd Ave.	774-8876	$30	cable, nonsmoking rooms, complimentary continental breakfast
Chestnut Tree Inn	9699 S.E. Stark	255-4444	$34	cable, kitchenettes, nonsmoking rooms
Powell Motel	6846 S.E. Powell Blvd.	775-0900	$40-75	cable, live entertainment
SOUTHWEST				
Ranch Inn Motel	10138 S.W. Barbur Blvd.	246-3375	$23-28	cable, pets, kitchenettes
St. Francis Hotel	1110 S.W. 11th Ave.	223-2161	$23	laundry
Portland Rose Motel	8920 S.W. Barbur Blvd.	244-0107	$25	cable, pets, kitchenettes, laundry
Sarahan 4th Ave. Motel	1889 S.W. 4th Ave.	226-7647	$30-36	pets, kitchenettes
Sixth Avenue Motel	2221 S.W. 6th Ave.	226-6288 226-2979	$33-50	cable, pets, nonsmoking rooms
Downtown Value Inn	415 S.W. Montgomery Ave.	226-4751	$35-45	cable, pets, laundry, nonsmoking rooms

PORTLAND ACCOMMODATIONS, cont.

Name	Address	Telephone	Price	Features
SOUTHWEST, cont.				
Cypress Inn Downtown Portland	809 S.W. King	226-6288	$43-73	cable, kitchenettes, laundry, nonsmoking rooms, complimentary continental breakfast
Mark Spencer Hotel	409 S.W. 11th Ave.	224-3293	$45-59	kitchenettes, laundry, nonsmoking rooms
Imperial Hotel	400 S.W. Broadway	228-7221	$48-60	cable, restaurant/lounge, nonsmoking rooms, riverside view
Nendels Inn	9900 S.W. Broadway	228-2251	$52-85	cable, restaurant/lounge, pool, weight room, nonsmoking rooms
Riverside Inn	50 S.W. Morrison	221-0711	$63-79	cable, restaurant/lounge, nonsmoking rooms, riverside view
Portland Inn	1414 S.W. 6th Ave.	221-1611	$65-75	cable, restaurant/lounge, pool, weight room, live entertainment nonsmoking rooms
The Greenwood Inn	10700 S.W. Allen Blvd.	643-7444	$75	kitchenettes, fireplace, restaurant/lounge, pool, weight room, live entertainment, nonsmoking rooms

Ethnic Eateries

While not for the faint-of-palate, **Fong Chong**'s (301 N.W. 4th, tel. 220-0235) dim sum is one of the more exotic low-cost dining adventures in the city. It all begins at 11 a.m. every day when steaming carts of Cantonese delicacies come whooshing down the aisles. Even if the mumbled explanations of the barely bilingual staff don't translate, the array of crepes and buns stuffed with chicken, shrimp, pork, and other fillings are so varied and cost so little ($1.20 per plate) that you can't miss. After 3 p.m. the restaurant reverts to unadventurous Cantonese fare off the menu. The adjoining oriental grocery, however, is always fascinating.

Across the bridge to the northeast, near Lloyd Center, **Saigon Kitchen** (835 N.E. Broadway, tel. 281-3669) improves slightly upon Fong Chong's functional decor and replicates the bountiful servings and reasonable prices. Although Vietnamese flavors predominate, Thai dishes like beef in coconut juice and basil leaves ($6.25) and ginger chicken ($6.25) spice up the menu. Dinner combination plates in the $8-10 range might in-

(top) Wizard Island (Oregon Tourism Division); (bottom) the Willamette River at Corvallis (Oregon Tourism Division)

clude such uncommon specialties as squid or tropical fish in garlic sauce or charcoal chicken with lettuce, mint, cilantro, rice papers, and peanut sauce. And don't overlook the fried squid in garlic sauce ($6.25). This restaurant has always been the darling of Portland's alternative weeklies, who rightfully extoll its spring rolls (called *cha gio* in Vietnamese). A serving of three of these at lunch ($2.95) comes to your table all chopped up and ready for dipping into the restaurant's hot sweet fish sauce.

Chang's Mongolian Grill (1 S.W. 3rd Ave., tel. 243-2700; 2700 N.W. 18th Ave., tel. 645-7718; and N.E. 23rd Ave., tel. 253-3535) is based around an intriguing concept which can best be described as Chinese-style burritos cooked-to-order. Each outlet of the chain features a colorful Genghis Khan mural backdropping a stagestruck chef cooking your hand-picked ingredients on a large domed grill. Mooshu pancakes with plum sauce and other condiments are stacked tableside for you to wrap the just-cooked fixin's, and you can return to the grill for as much fresh veggies, thin-sliced raw meats, and fish as you like. Pickled cabbage, soup, and tea come with the meal. All-you-can-eat lunches cost $5 and dinners cost $7.50.

Another outlet of eclectic Asian fare is **Malaka** (825 N.W. Murray Road, tel. 643-6606; 410 N.W. 21st., tel. 223-1290; 635 S.W. College, tel. 223-7266). The proprietors are Malaysian but their food is strongly derivative of Chinese and Japanese cuisines. Especially good is the curry chicken at $4.25, consisting of chicken and potatoes in a spicy curry gravy, with salad, spring roll, and rice. This restaurant can satisfy the healthiest appetite for less than $5 with dishes running the gamut from Cantonese-style dumplings to Japanese tempura.

A good way to judge a Mexican restaurant is by its chile rellenos. If a place can make this popular dish with a light crisp batter so as not to mute the taste of the chile pepper and melted cheese, chances are it can pull off the whole enchilada in fine style. **Chez Jose** (8502 S.W. Terwilliger Blvd., tel. 244-0007) passes this test and probably meets any other standard you might use to judge a Mexican restaurant. You'll also appreciate such touches as being asked if you prefer your order hot or mild as well as the use of Oregon's famous Tillamook cheddar along with the traditional Monterey jack in many recipes. Best of all,

a sumptuous combination plate can feed two people here for $7.50. A new branch is slated to open at N.E. 22nd and Broadway in 1991.

Maya's Tacqueria (1000 S.W. Morrison, tel. 226-1946) offers well-rendered Mexican fast food ranging from chile rellenos to chicken mole enchiladas. The presence of Mexican beer and refrescos and the best array of salsas in Portland also make this elaborate taco stand seem closer to the Guadalajara marketplace than to Pioneer Courthouse Square. On warm days, sit outside to watch passersby and admire the Mayan-style murals. **Santa Fe Tacqueria** (831 N.W. 23rd Avenue, tel. 226-0406) is Maya's outlet in the stylish Northwest barrio.

South-of-the-border flavors are also served up at **Macheesmo Mouse** (723 S.W. Salmon St., tel. 228-3491; 811 N.W. 23rd Ave., tel. 274-0500; 3500 S.E. Hawthorne Blvd., tel. 232-5688; 1200 N.E. Broadway, tel. 249-0002) but with a cooking style that's heart-smart and nutritious. Many items list calorie count and come with brown rice and whole grain tortillas. Thanks to fresh salsa and the Cajun flavors of the restaurant's own Boss Sauce, heathy fast food never tasted this good.

The truly famished will enjoy the $5 all-you-can-eat luncheon buffet at the two-restaurant complex shared by the **Monte Carlo** and **Lido** (1016 Belmont, tel. 238-7627). Lasagna, chicken, and all kinds of salads and pastas find their way onto this spread. Excellent pizza and thick minestrone soup are highlighted at dinner.

Another place for pizza is the **Bridgeport Brew Pub** (1313 N.W. Marshall St., tel. 241-7179). The malt-based pizza crust and out-of-this-world toppings (olives, chorizo, yellow peppers, and eggplant) washed down by the brewery's handmade Blue Heron Ale are a tough combination to beat.

If pizza and a beer are your thing, **Escape From New York** (913 S.W. Alder St., tel. 226-4129 and 622 N.W. 23rd Ave., tel. 227-5423) and **American Dream Pizza** (4620 N.E. Glisan St., tel. 230-0699 and 5020 N.E. 82nd Ave., tel. 255-4360) are frequently touted as the best "by-the-slice" operations in town.

At the edge of Old Town is a Portland institution. *Joie de vivre* is in the air when you step into **Alexis** (215 W. Burnside, tel. 224-8577) but it's not just the retsina, Greek music, and folk dancing that keep people coming back. This is the best Greek food in Oregon. Appetizers like cala-

(top) a pioneer schoolhouse near Zumwalt (Oregon State Highways Division);
(bottom) farm country in Washington County, west of Portland (Oregon Tourism Division)

mari or spanakopita (fried cheese) might start your meal here. You can spend an evening just ordering appetizers and enjoying the crusty bread, but it would be a shame to forgo such entrees as the moussaka and oregano chicken. On weekends this moderately priced taverna features bellydancing and an atmosphere that'll bring out the Zorba in anyone.

Eye-openers

Although lunch is also served at the **Bijou Cafe** (132 S.W. 3rd Ave., tel. 222-3187), it has built its reputation on breakfast. Ordinary breakfast food like scrambled eggs, hash browns, muffins, and oatmeal are done perfectly here with the freshest and most nutritious ingredients. As for the latter, Bijou patrons appreciate the restaurant's emphasis on organic produce and whole grain products for no more than it would cost to eat at a highway truckstop.

The four-course, Jewish-style Sunday brunch has helped establish **Bread and Ink** (3610 S.E. Hawthorne, tel. 239-4756) as *the* gathering place in the Hawthorne neighborhood. The whitewashed walls with lots of windows create a convivial atmosphere for lox, borscht, cheese blintzes, and other delicacies. If this is not the way you choose to start the day, there's always an assortment of homemade breads and imaginative omelettes to sustain you.

Portland's most famous breakfast haunt is the **Original Pancake House** (8600 S.W. Barbur Blvd., tel. 246-9007). This Wed. through Sat. operation has spawned many imitations but the Original is still the greatest. If you're without a car, take bus #38 from downtown. The restaurant opens at 7 a.m. but be there early on weekends. Latecomers should bring a book because waits for seating can be excruciatingly long. Once at the table, the famous apple pancake is a frisbee-sized cinnamon-laced delight for the growing boy or girl. Lighter appetites can choose from among 20 other varieties priced between $4-6.50.

Food Fetishes

Despite the fact that Oregonians often describe **Rose's** as an East Coast-style delicatessen, New York deli mavens will find themselves searching high and low for knishes, kasha, and other standard fare of Jewish soul food. Nonetheless, the tradition of overstuffed sandwiches ($6-9) is taken to a new level here. In a town where, more

often than not, they cut the corned beef with the grain instead of against it, the quality meats piled high on fresh rye (and other breads) will make the most jaded East Coast transplant sit up and take notice. One sandwich feeds two here (try the Reuben), and if you're still hungry, there's always the football-sized pastries in the display case for dessert. And regardless of how you feel afterwards, order some rum balls to go. For hikers going to or from Washington and Forest Hills parks, the west hills outlet (315 N.W. 23rd Ave., tel. 227-5181) is recommended; en route or returning from the Columbia River Gorge, the restaurant at the Menlo Park Shopping Center (12329 N.E. Glisan Street, tel. 224-6545) is closest; coastbound travelers should put on the brakes at the Rose's in the Beaverton Town Square (tel. 643-4287).

If you're looking for good no-nonsense sustenance try **Hamburger Mary's** (840 S.W. Park Ave., tel. 223-0900). Thick burgers with salad fixin's on a whole wheat bun are the specialty, but many come here for great coffee and the chance to create an omelette from two dozen possible ingredients. If it's sunny, you can sit outside this crowded hole-in-the-wall. Inside, a quirky decor which can best be described as '60s flea market chic with lots of plants, and prices as comforting as the good ole American food, awaits.

As you approach **Rimsky-Korsakofee** (707 S.E. 12th Ave., tel. 232-2640) the old red house gives no indications (not even a hand-lettered sign bearing its name!) that this is Portland's favorite artsy hangout and coffeehouse. Only the lines extending out the door on a crowded weekend might convey that the place is something special. Folks come for mocha fudge cake washed down by espresso drinks, live classical music, as well as people and ideas in creative ferment. The atmosphere of a refined house party reigns here from 7-midnight on weekdays and from 7-1 a.m. on weekends.

Hotel Dining Rooms

The two most venerated hostelries in Portland are the **Heathman** (S.W. Broadway at Salmon St., tel. 241-4100) and the **Benson Hotel** (S.W. Broadway and Oak St., tel. 228-2000). In like measure, their dining rooms enjoy a reputation for serving some of the finest cuisine in the region. As in most establishments of this ilk, dinner can be on the spendy side, but this doesn't mean you

the Benson Hotel

PHOTO BY THEO TRIMMELL

have to totally deny yourself the opportunity to break bread in these hallowed halls.

In contrast to dinner checks which can exceed $35 per person, breakfast at the Benson's London Grill is not appreciably more expensive than many places in town, and the few extra bucks are worth it. The experience begins the moment you step into the hotel. The Circassian walnut lining the Benson lobby, together with the marble fireplace and staircase, bespeak the glory that was Simon Benson's Portland in 1916. Benson's legacy also includes the Columbia Gorge Hotel and Scenic Highway as well as dozens of ornate drinking fountains he put up around the city (to promote a teetotaling outlook).

Downstairs from the Benson Lobby, the chandeliered and mahogany-paneled **London Grill** continues Simon Benson's traditions of excellence. Whether it's smoked salmon and eggs (at $7.75, the most expensive item on the menu) or a plate of hangtown fry (an oyster-based omelette for $5.95), the scrumptious food and first-rate service amid plush surroundings give a taste of Portland at its best.

The Heathman Hotel's interior also exudes the understated Old World elegance of the Benson, with generous use of teak paneling and marble. However, the prices in its trendy **Heathman Restaurant** (extolled by the late James Beard) will appeal more to the expense account traveler than to explorers on a budget. The **Heathman Bakery and Pub** (901 S.W. Salmon St., tel. 227-5700) also serves Northwest cuisine in the style of its

parent restaurant but at a fraction of the cost (the restaurant is also called B. Moloch after the caricaturist whose work adorns the walls). The specialty here is gourmet pizza but pasta-seafood concoctions and dishes boasting such local ingredients as hazelnuts, chevre, Oregon lamb, game pâté, and homemade sausage, as well as the in-house Widmer microbrew are also part of the restaurant's identity. Lest this sound like the kind of place where only "yups" come to sup, a $6-10 price range and an informal atmosphere are guaranteed not to scare you away. You can go the takeout route here or have a waitress bring the food to your table after you place your order at the counter.

Seafood

Jake's Famous Crawfish (901 S.W. 12th St., tel. 226-1419) is not just famous for those lobster-like denizens of the Oregon freshwater deep. It is also renowned for the widest-ranging seafood menu in the Northwest and one of the most extensive Oregon wine lists. The largest privately owned fine art collection in the region also graces the mahogany-paneled confines of Jake's. But when all is said and done, it's the local crawfish (available May through September) that put the restaurant's name up in lights. Other specialties include clam chowder, smoked salmon and sturgeon, steamed butter clams, spring chinook salmon, and bouillabaisse. You can also get a good steak here. For the best luck, order one of the two dozen or so specials off the "fresh sheet." Whatever you decide on, leave room for chocolate truffle cake. Getting reserved seating in this 99-year-old landmark is often difficult, but not enough to deter dozens of reservationless people who might wait over an hour for an opening.

Salty's on the Columbia (3839 N.E. Marine Dr., tel. 288-4444) is a great choice for Columbia Gorge-bound travelers. The river frontage and fish-on-ice displays which greet you here set the mood for a seafood feast. Bills can run high so save this one for an occasion. Many fresh specials supplement the menu which offers such imaginative dishes as a Caesar salad garnished with bits of blackened smoked salmon. Rich desserts and a nautical-theme bar well stocked with Northwest microbrews also recommend this place. If it's warm, the outdoor seating above the river is a special treat. When you emerge from the restaurant, fair weather views of Mt. Hood can provide the finishing touch to your dining pleasure.

GETTING THERE AND GETTING AROUND

By Car
Portland sits near Interstates 405, 205, and 84. I-5 runs from Seattle to San Diego and I-84 goes east to Salt Lake City. I-405 circles downtown Portland to the west and south. I-205 bypasses the city to the east. U.S. 26 heads west to Cannon Beach and east to the Cascades.

The parking situation in Portland is good news and bad news. First the bad news. Even though parking meters and day parking proliferate in the city, it's often hard to find an empty spot. The good news is that many of the parking garages accept merchant validation stamps (on the garage receipt) for free parking. As for parking on the street, after 6 p.m. and before 8 a.m. free parking is available on weekdays, and all day Sunday there's no charge.

Information on car rentals can be found in the general Introduction. A reliable cab company is **Broadway Taxi** (tel. 227-1234). Most cabs are required to charge $1.30 for the first mile, $1.40 for each mile thereafter.

By Bus
The **Greyhound** bus station (550 N.W. 6th Avenue, tel. 243-2313) has storage lockers available for 75 cents a day.

The **Green Tortoise** (tel. 225-0310) goes to Seattle (Monday, Wednesday, and Sunday) at 2 p.m. for $15 and to San Francisco (Saturday, Tuesday, and Thursday) at 12:15 p.m. for $49. Departures are from the University Deli on 6th and College.

Amtrak runs *Coast Starlight* trains north and south and *Pioneer* and *Empire Builder* routes east and (inbound) west along the Columbia. Trains depart for Seattle at 8 a.m., 2:30 p.m., and 5:30 p.m. The trip takes four hours and costs $27 one way. Trains depart for San Francisco at 3:05

MAX, Metropolitan Area Express, makes getting around easy.

PHOTO BY THEO TRIMMELL

p.m., arriving at 8:50 a.m. the next day. One-way fare is $119. Trains depart for Salt Lake City at 10:15 a.m., arriving at 5:40 a.m. the next day. For reservations, call 800-USA-RAIL.

By Air

Portland International Airport (general information, tel. 231-5000, ext. 411) is a modern facility served by 16 major airlines. Delta uses PDX as a West Coast hub. Short hops in the Northwest are served by Horizon and United Express. For more information on airlines and rental companies here consult the general Introduction.

Before detailing transportation to the airport, it should be mentioned that an $18 weekly maximum parking fee can justify forgoing a cab to the airport in some cases. A taxi from downtown costs around $20. There are several routes to take and while the cost difference is negligible, going via Columbia Boulevard and cutting through the Colwood Golf Course is usually the quickest and cheapest transfer.

Buses from downtown run from 5 a.m.-12:30 a.m. and leave from S.W. 6th Avenue and Main Street. From the airport outside the baggage claim catch #12. It arrives downtown 40 minutes later via Sandy Boulevard (fare in each case is 85 cents). Buses depart PDX every 15 minutes from 5:30 a.m.-11:30 p.m.

Other ways of getting to town include free hotel courtesy shuttles and the RAZ Downtowner (tel. 246-3301), which stops at the Greyhound station as well as many hotels en route to PDX for $5.

To drive to the city, if you follow the signs to downtown they first go to I-205, then I-84, which brings you to the Willamette River. Take the Morrison Street Bridge across the river to downtown.

Perhaps the most unique feature of PDX is affordable high-quality concession shops. Such Oregon mainstays as Powell's Books, City Kids toy store (high-quality American and imported playthings), Nike, the Real Mother Goose (a combination gallery and crafts store purveying woodwork, jewelry, and singular art pieces), Oregon Mountain Community (camping gear), Van Duyn Chocolates, Made In Oregon (Northwest gourmet food, crafts, books, etc.) and Norm Thompson (the Northwest's answer to L.L. Bean) plus a restaurant where you can get dishes à la Jake's and Timberline Lodge help the state put its best foot forward. You'll be glad to know that each store

must keep its prices identical to downtown outlets. As *Oregonian* writer David Sarasohn put it, "This is the image we want to show the rest of the world. Literate yet playful, athletic but epicurean, and on all occasions wearing natural fibers."

Mass Transit Buses And Light Rail

Begin your orientation to the Tri-Met bus system at Pioneer Square. Here, the Tri-Met office (#1 Pioneer Courthouse Square, 701 S.W. 6th Avenue, tel. 233-3511) is open 9-5 p.m. weekdays. Information can be obtained from Tri-Met drivers, hotel front desks and concierges, or any branch of Willamette Savings. Or, you can call these numbers: recorded information for call-a-bus (tel. 231-3197); all-night information (tel. 231-3196); special needs transportation (tel. 238-4952, Monday-Friday 8:30 a.m.-4:30 p.m.); and bicycle commuter service (tel. 233-0564). Fares range from 90 cents (basic fare) to $1.20 (long trips) and all-day tickets cost $3. These fares also apply to MAX, the light-rail which does not make as many stops. MAX runs every 15 minutes. To ride it to its eastern-most extremity, Gresham, takes 45 minutes and costs $1.20 each way. Buy tickets from machines at MAX stations before boarding. Tri-Met buses require exact change and you can purchase tickets at the Tri-Met office or aboard the area bus.

Passengers in the downtown area can ride free anywhere in the 300-block "Fareless Square." This area is defined by I-405 to the south, West Hoyt Street to the north, and the Willamette River to the east. Thirty-one shelters (color-coded by their region) make up Transit Mall. Southbound buses pick up passengers on S.W. 5th Avenue; northbound travelers board on S.W. 6th Avenue.

Finding Your Way

Before you start muddling your way through downtown, look for some folks wearing green baseball caps and jackets and navy-blue pants. They are part of the **Portland Guides** (tel. 295-0912) program and serve as walking information centers.

If you are not so blessed, the following random observations will help you get the lay of the land. The line of demarcation between north from south in addresses is Burnside Street; between east and west it's the Willamette River. These give a reference point for the address prefixes southwest, southeast, north, northwest, and northeast.

Another useful thing to keep in mind is that avenues run north-south and streets run east-west. The street names on one side of the river are also operative on the other. A series of 12 bridges connect east to west. Almost every downtown address will carry a southwest or northwest prefix.

Other aids to orientation include the fact that Front Avenue is the road nearest the Willamette River downtown and Water Avenue is the nearest on the east side. Thereafter, numbered avenues begin.

The city's major thoroughfares are Grand Avenue, Martin Luther King Jr. Boulevard (formerly Union Avenue), Sandy Boulevard, U.S 26, and S.E. 82nd Street. Expect most streets downtown to run one way, alternating with the next going in the opposite direction. Streets in the Northwest District are named alphabetically (e.g., Burnside, Couch, on through Wilson). The order is broken in these cases: Ankeny Street precedes Burnside in the Southwest District, and Roosevelt and Seed Streets are substituted for "X" and "Y" streets.

Finally, addresses increase by 100, beginning at the Willamette River for avenues and Burnside for streets.

INFORMATION AND SERVICES

Portland's visitor information resources are far-reaching and extensive. Begin at **Portland Convention and Visitors Center** (26 S.W. Salmon, St., tel. 222-2223). This facility sits across Front Street from Waterfront Park's beautiful fountain. In addition to knowledgeable personnel, P.V.C. has the most complete collection of printed traveler information pamphlets in the state. While Portland is naturally the focus of most of these publications, materials about every part of the state fill the racks here. The best free **maps** of the city are available nearby from Powell's at Pioneer Square and from Hertz on the corner of S.W. 6th Avenue and Salmon (tel. 249-5727). The P.V.C. is open 8:30 a.m.-5 p.m.

A local events **hotline** (tel. 233-4444) can supplement the media sources identified below to update you on what's going on, where, and at what time. Other useful numbers include a **Crisis Line** (tel. 223-6161), **Women's Crisis Lines** (tel. 235-5333), **Men's Resource Center** (tel. 235-3433),

Drug Counseling and Intervention (tel. 320-9654), **Health Help Center** (tel. 288-5995), and the **Aging Services Division** (tel. 248-3464).

The hours of the main **post office** (715 N.W. Hoyt St., Portland, 97208; tel. 294-2124) are 8:30 a.m.-8 p.m. Monday through Friday and Saturday 8:30 a.m.-5 p.m.

The **Multnomah County Library** has 15 branches throughout the city with books, films, records, and at some branches, videos available for borrowing. The central branch (801 S.W. 10th Avenue, tel. 223-7201) is a top-notch research facility with a newspaper and periodical section that's well organized and voluminous.

Media

As the media center of the state, a breakdown of Portland broadcast and print journalism is in order.

The *Oregonian* (1320 S.W. Broadway, tel. 221-8327), Portland's only daily, is joined by 16 alternative or community papers which circulate around the city. The Arts and Entertainment section of the *Oregonian* comes out each Friday.

Most useful to the traveler are *Willamette Week* (2 N.W. 2nd Avenue, tel. 243-2122) and two sister publications, *The Downtowner* and *This Week* (6960 S.W. Sandburg St., Tigard, tel. 620-4140). All are free and obtainable at commercial outlets throughout the city and suburbs.

Willamette Week comes out each Wednesday and has the premier entertainment listings in the city and also news, reviews, and comment about a wide range of subjects relevant to visitors. Restaurants, artistic and theatrical presentations, sports, and the local political scuttlebutt are often dealt with in an irreverent, sometimes sardonic tone.

The Downtowner also has extensive listings as well as some reviews and articles, but in a more mainstream, uncritical tone. Read *This Week* for Marilyn McFarlane's "Northwest Discoveries" column which is probably the best weekly travel commentary in the state.

As for radio, Portland's 29 radio stations have something for everybody. Noteworthy on the AM band are a preponderance of call-in talk radio shows. The FM band concentrates more on music, though several listener-subscriber stations do their part to revive the grand old art of conversation with interviews and news commentary. KBOO (90.7 FM) features eclectic community-based programming.

DAY-TRIPS FROM PORTLAND

THE WINE COUNTRY

Although the vinifera grape thrives throughout the interior valleys of western Oregon from the Columbia River to the California border, the so-called wine country is popularly conceived of as just those vineyards west and southwest of Portland. This is where the rich soil and long, warm, gentle growing season have created conditions which sustain the largest concentration of vineyards in the Northwest. The slow-cooling fall days engender a complexity in the regional product by inhibiting high sugar concentrations while maintaining the natural acidity of the grape. In summer, the long sunny days without excessive heat due to Oregon's northern latitude also bode well for the harvest. These factors conspire to produce wines delicate in flavor, low in alcohol, and crisp in finish despite a tendency toward fruitiness.

A free monthly publication, *Oregon Wine* (Oregon Wine Press, 644 S.E. 20th Avenue, Portland 97214), is available in retail outlets throughout western Oregon and can help plan a foray to vineyards throughout the state. In addition, wine and restaurant reports and vintner interviews provide useful information.

With this publication and a preponderance of other literature about wine, it's easy to be overwhelmed. As such, the following wine country ramble concentrates on what most people are looking for—the pick of the harvest. In Oregon that means Yamhill County pinot noir.

More often than not, tasting rooms in Oregon are no-frills makeshift affairs, but that can impart a personal touch which is sometimes lacking with slicker promotion-oriented wineries. Oregon vintners are quick to explain this lack of glitz by saying that they prefer to put their money into the product. After a day along the trails of the pinot noir, you'll happily drink to that!

Getting Started

Before you go, pick up a *Discover Oregon Wineries* pamphlet at the Portland Visitor and Convention Bureau (Salmon across from Waterfront Park) or by contacting the **Oregon Winegrowers Association** (Box 6590, Portland, 97228-6590; tel. 233-2377). This pamphlet includes directions to the state's vineyards, their hours of operation, and a description of each location's offerings. Yamhill County winery visitation facilities and tasting rooms generally are open May to October, 11 a.m.-5 p.m. Those establishments which do not have these hours can usually be visited around Thanksgiving when there is open house in the region. In any case, it's always a good idea to call in advance to confirm hours and other details. Blue-and-white signs are present on 99W and its offshoots to help point the way to such pantheons of pinot as Rex Hill, Veritas, Knudsen Erath, Sokol Blosser, Yamhill Valley, and Amity. All these places have tasting rooms open to the public and accommodate visitors for more of the year than many of their counterparts.

On The Trail Of Pinot Noir

If you look at a globe, you'll notice that U.S. 99W west of Portland shares a latitude in common with the great wine-making regions of the world. While Oregon's Yamhill County (located on the northern cusp of the Willamette Valley) is not yet the Loire Valley of France, its early ripening grapes, notably the pinot noir and chardonnay, regularly vie with the world's best in international competitions. This began in 1975 when an Oregon pinot noir beat out dozens of French Burgundies. The state also gained notoriety for its truth in labeling law which mandates that the varietal grape named on the bottle must be 90% of the pulp used to make the wine in question; other states require just 75%.

Good wine and good food go together, which explains the creation of some surprisingly sophisticated restaurants and bed and breakfasts in this very rural area. Yamhill wine touring has also become popular due to the fact that downtown Portland sits a mere 30 to 40 miles away from the greatest concentration of wineries. Just take I-5 south of the city and go west on U.S. 99W, and within 45 minutes you'll find yourself in the midst of filbert orchards and grapestakes. In terms of distance, this might evoke wine-touring routes from San Francisco to the Napa, Sonoma valleys, but the similarity ends there. Oregon vineyards do not have the elaborate tasting rooms, tours, and on-site restaurants of many of their California counterparts.

Yamhill County Bacchanal

Your Yamhill County bacchanal starts two miles east of Newberg where **Veritas** (31190 N.E. Veritas Lane, Newberg, 97132; tel. 538-0666) and **Rex Hill Vineyards** (30835 U.S. 99W., Newberg, 97132; tel. 538-0666) flank the road. Each winery highlights pinot noir, chardonnay, and riesling. Veritas's 1988 white riesling won the Governor's Trophy as the best wine in the state in 1989. While the Veritas tasting room has a beautiful view of Newberg backdropped by the Red Hills of Dundee, Rex Hill has the more elegant facilities and features pinot gris, a wine not produced outside of Oregon. Also try the '85 pinot noir. Hours at Rex Hill are 11-5 daily, April to December. In winter, it's open 11-5 p.m. Friday-Sunday, February through March. Veritas is open June through August, 11-5 p.m. daily.

Oregon's best-known and greatest producing winery (35,000 cases annually), **Knudsen Erath** (17000 N.E. Knudsen Lane, Dundee, 97115; tel. 538-3318), sits high in the Red Hills of Dundee where it commands an imposing view of local vineyards and the Willamette Valley. To get there, go two miles north from the center of Dundee

until you see a blue state highway sign marking the turnoff near the junction of U.S. 99W and 9th Street. Ninth Street turns into Worden Hill Road, a thoroughfare destined to be lauded as the glory road of Oregon wine, given the legacy of Knudsen Erath. Appropriately, the road looks out over vistas dominated by grapevines. The winery's 1987 pinot noir vintages have garnered medals in competitions all over the world. The tasting room is open 10-6 p.m. daily in summer, 11-5 p.m. Oct. 15 through May 15, and offers cabernet sauvignon, gewürtztraminer, chardonnay, and riesling. Beautiful picnic sites also attract visitors here.

The intersection of Sokol Blosser Lane and U.S. 99W sits about two miles west of Dundee and points the way to a winery of the same name. In addition to their 1988 pinot noir, Sokol Blosser's '87 Redland chardonnay is especially recommended at the tasting room. The latter is open daily May to October, 10:30-5:30 p.m. From November to April, the hours are 11-5 p.m. In addition to a tasting room overlooking a pastoral setting, free tours of the vineyard are given every hour.

You'll find **Yamhill Valley Vineyards** (Oldville Road, off ORE 18, 97128; tel. 843-3100) five miles southwest of McMinnville in the foothills of the Coast Range. This winery's first release, an '83 pinot noir, first distinguished itself at an 1985 tasting of French and Oregon vintages held in

Yamhill County
wine country

PHOTO BY OREGON STATE HIGHWAYS DIVISION

New York City. This wine was also selected as the best vintage wine in Oregon at the 1990 state fair. Yamhill's 1988 Willamette Valley estate-bottled chardonnay took a silver medal there. Riesling and gewürztraminer are also available for tasting May to December, Tuesday through Sunday 11-5 p.m; from January through April, the tasting room is only open weekends 11-5 p.m.

Another Yamhill County vinery that distinguished itself at the 1990 state fair was **Amity Vineyards** (18150 Amity Vineyards Road Southeast, Amity, 97101; tel. 835-2362). Its 1985 pinot noir, Willamette Valley Winemaker's reserve, took a gold medal and the 1989 dry riesling took a silver. An 1989 gewürztraminer from Amity took a bronze in this competition. If you like sweet wines, a late-harvest botrytised riesling here makes an excellent dessert wine or nightcap. The tasting room is open daily, noon-5 p.m. except December 24 to January 31.

Food, Lodging, And Events

McMinnville might be 35 miles south of Portland but make reservations here in advance to dine at one of the best Italian restaurant in the state, **Nick's Italian Cafe** (521 3rd St., tel. 434-4471). A hasty visual impression of the unpretentious decor of this one-time luncheonette may occasion doubts about such an assessment, but any trepidations will be quickly dispelled by the aromas of Nick's hearty fare and a wine list which is both extensive and distinctive. As a host to many wine country functions, Nick is privy to special releases found nowhere else. The latter are fitting accompaniments to such unique culinary interpretations as lasagna with pine nuts, local mushrooms, and dried tomatoes. Green vegetarian spinach ravioli with parmesan and minestrone with pesto are other favorites. The less adventurous will be pleased by the restaurant's famous grilled salmon as well as pastries and desserts made on the premises. A five-course, fixed-price dinner goes for $21 and is highly recommended. Dinner is not served on Monday.

Should you care to extend your stay in the wine country, there is no shortage of bed and breakfasts to accommodate you. Before leaving Portland, consult *Oregon Wine* for a hostelry that can meet your "specs."

The Mattey House (10221 N.E. Mattey Lane, McMinnville, 97128; tel. 434-5058) is one lodging which combines old-world charm, proximity to wineries, and a breakfast second to none. Set in the middle of wheat fields and orchards at the edge of McMinnville, this 1892 Victorian mansion with the big windows looks inviting at the end of a day of wine touring. While some of the rooms may be small or lack private baths, individual phones, and TV, you can't beat the Mattey House for coziness and refinement. Antique furnishings, period wallpapers, and old photographs set the mood for afternoon wine and cheese in the living room. A breakfast of homemade breads and jellies, made with fruits and berries from the innkeeper's own orchard, and smoked salmon and scrambled eggs get your Yamhill bacchanal off to a great start. This fusion of viniculture and Victoriana goes for $50-60 a night. To get there, turn off U.S. 99W between McMinnville and La Fayette onto Mattey Lane and drive until you get to a large oak tree near the house.

Of all the events in the Yamhill wine country and its counterparts, no fete can boast the world-class status of the **Annual International Pinot Noir Celebration** (International Pinot Noir Celebration, Box 1310 McMinnville, 97128; tel. 472-8964). More than 50 American and international pinot noir producers are on hand for symposiums, tastings, and winery tours. Meals prepared by internationally known chefs are also a highlight. The three-day event takes place at the end of July on the Linfield College campus in McMinnville. While the cost of registration ($350) is prohibitive for many, tickets to the final tasting can be purchased separately for $30 from the previously cited address. This epicurean delight takes place on the last day and features a tasting of more than 50 esteemed vintages from around the world.

While harvest festivals, concerts, and other events effectively complement tasting and touring, a drive through the region from mid-September into early October could well offer the biggest treat for the senses. At this time, the sight of multihued grape leaves and intoxicating aromas of fermentation fill the air.

A HISTORY LOOP TOUR

Champoeg State Park

Below Yamhill County, just southeast of Newburg on ORE 219, is Champoeg (pronounced "champooey" or "champooiek"), often touted as the birthplace of Oregon.

Champoeg State Park commemorates the site of the 1843 vote to break free from British and Hudson Bay Company rule and establish a pro-American provisional government in the Oregon Country. To get there from Portland, drive south on I-5 until you see signs for Exit 278. This exit directs you to a rural route which goes five miles to the park visitor center (tel. 678-1251). The 568-acre park is equidistant from Portland and Salem along the Willamette River.

The visitor center has exhibits detailing how the Calapooya Indians, explorers, French Canadian fur traders, and American settlers lived in the Willamette Valley. It's open everyday 9-5 p.m. and there is no admission. The grounds also have several historic buildings. Adjacent to the visitor center is the Manson Barn built in 1862. The Old Butteville jail (1850) and one-room schoolhouse has been moved to Champoeg to also help evoke frontier life. Just west of the park entrance is a replica of the 1852 pioneer house of Robert Newell (tel. 678-5537). Particularly interesting is the second floor of the Newell house, which showcases Indian artifacts and a collection of inaugural gowns worn by the wives of Oregon governors. The house is open noon-5 p.m. Wednesday through Sunday from February to November. Admission is $1.50 for adults, 50 cents for children. The **Pioneer Mother's Museum** replicates the dwellings in the Willamette Valley circa 1850. A collection of guns and muskets from 1775 to 1850 are also displayed. Admission is 75 cents.

During July from Thursday through Sunday, the **Champoeg Historical Pageant** (Box 4567, Salem, 97302; tel. 245-3922) traces Oregon life from statehood to settlement. The spirited drama entitled the *Story of Old Oregon* unfolds at the state park on a set decorated with tepees, pioneer cabins, and a turreted fort; many of the key events depicted actually occurred here. The show starts at 7:30 p.m., but get there at 6:30 p.m. to picnic and enjoy the warmup entertainment. A dinner is available for $3 if you didn't bring your own. Also recommended is a blanket because evenings are often cool here. Tickets are available on site and cost $7.50 for adults, $6.50 for seniors, and $4 for students.

French Prairie Loop

Before leaving Champoeg State Park, pick up a brochure at the visitor center outlining the French Prairie Loop, a 40-mile byway for car and bicycle

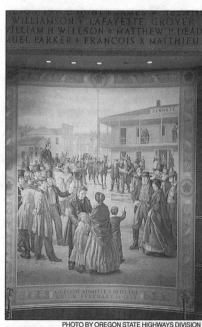

PHOTO BY OREGON STATE HIGHWAYS DIVISION
The 1843 conference at Champoeg marked the beginning of American rule in Oregon Country (from a mural in the state capitol).

touring. French Canadian trappers settled here in the 1820s and '30s to help the Hudson Bay Company establish a presence in the Willamette Valley. During the 1849 California gold rush, wheat and produce from this area were shipped to granaries and warehouses in the area of present-day Portland. Thereafter, the goods were transported to San Francisco.

Churches and buildings dating back to the 19th century have earned **St. Paul,** one of the towns on the loop (ORE 219), National Historic District status. On the east side of the loop, **Aurora** enjoys a similar designation. Oregon's legacy as a haven for utopian communities began here with a Prussian immigrant, Dr. William Keil. He started up a communal colony for Oregon Trail pioneers, naming the town which grew out of it after his daughter. The Aurora colony fused Christian fundamentalism with collectivist principles, garnering distinction for its thriving farms and the excellence of its handicrafts. Despite Aurora's early success, a smallpox epidemic in 1862 and the coming of the railroad to undermine the Willamette River trade in the next decade provided the catalyst for its demise. Keil himself died in 1877 and the struggling colony disbanded a few years later.

The Old Aurora Colony Museum (tel. 678-5754) consists of five buildings, including two of the colony's homesteads, the communal wash house, and the farm equipment shed. It's advisable to call before going, given the great variability of hours according to season. Admission is $2.50 for adults, $1 for children.

The past also lives on in Aurora thanks to two dozen clapboard and Victorian houses as well as 18 antique shops, all clustered along U.S. 99E.

OREGON CITY

History

Further north from Canby on U.S. 99E, the road attractively parallels the Willamette River. Jagged rock bluffs on one side of the highway contrast the smooth-flowing river framed by stately cottonwood and poplar trees. More variety is added by islands in the channel and the broad expanse of 40-foot **Willamette Falls** in Oregon City. As the terminus of the Oregon Trail and the only seat of American power in the territory until 1852, this town is the site of many firsts. Leading off the list is Oregon City's status as the first incorporated city west of the Rockies. Other claims to fame include the West's first mint, paper mill, newspaper, and the world's first long-distance electric power transmission system. The Oregon territorial capital also was the site of the state's first Protestant church and Masonic lodge.

Ironically, a representative of British interests in Oregon Country is credited with starting up Oregon City. John McLoughlin, the Canadian-born chief factor of the Hudson Bay Company, encouraged French Canadian trappers to cross the Columbia River from Fort Vancouver and settle here in the northern Willamette Valley, inspiring the name French Prairie. To further the development of this beachhead of British presence, McLoughlin built a flour mill near Willamette Falls in 1832. He moved down to Oregon City himself in the 1840s and became an ardent supporter of American settlers who wanted Oregon to be independent of England and part of the United States.

McLoughlin's flour mill was the precedent for other uses of waterpower here. It also helped attract pioneers who came over the Cascades via the Barlow Road extension of the Oregon Trail. As a result, Oregon City became a manufacturing center. It's river port thrived due to Willamette Falls impeding the movement of merchant ships further south on the river. Although the development of the railroad and the city of Portland diminished the city's importance, its glory days live on today thanks to a National Historic District status. Buildings which date to back to the mid -19th century exemplify Queen Anne, Federal, and Italianate architectural styles.

Oregon Trail Visitor Center

Begin your day-trip here at the Oregon Trail Visitor Center (500 Washington St., Oregon City, 97045; tel. 657-9336). The terminus of that famous frontier thoroughfare is also claimed by The Dalles in the Columbia Gorge and Independence further south in the Willamette Valley. Different opinions notwithstanding, in 1993 the 150th anniversary of the first wagon trail will be commemorated by another facility in Oregon City. An interpretive center (expanding upon the present one) will be at its heart, focusing on the life of the pioneers after they had completed their transcontinental trek and were about to embark upon farming and settlement. The center is to be accompanied by a working farm modeled after early Oregon agriculture, a theater, and a commemorative square. The other part of the complex is to be a festive center, consisting of restaurants and shops; ask at the existing visitor center for more details. This exhibit will be complemented by expositions at Baker City, Pendleton, and The Dalles.

The current exposition features displays, artifacts, and pictures of covered wagons and trail-weary migrants. Video tapes provide more background on Native American culture, the missionary influx, as well as the incursions of trappers and settlers. Pamphlets with five walking tour itineraries are available here for 75 cents. Admission is $2 for adults and $1.50 for seniors and children under 12. Hours are 10-4 p.m. Tuesday through Saturday and 11-4 p.m. Sunday. The center is closed in January.

Regarding these tours, your historical imaginings of the past are more likely to be stirred by the contours of the town than by the collections within the various exhibit houses. Nonetheless, such repositories of pioneer Americana as the McLoughlin House and the Stevens-Crawford House are worth a gander.

McLoughlin House

Before you begin any explorations, you'll probably encounter difficulties getting around if you don't follow the blue-and-white visitor information signs. Park near the **chamber of commerce** (718 McLoughlin Blvd at 8th St., tel. 656-1619). McLoughlin Boulevard is an extension of U.S. 99E. At the other end of the block from the chamber of commerce is the McLoughlin House (713 Center St., tel. 656-5146) between 7th and 8th streets. This impressive white frame home was moved from its original site down by the river. (Incidentally, the latter can be reached by the stone steps close by the McLoughlin House. Better yet, take a free ride 90 feet down to the riverside commercial district in a huge pink elevator on Railroad Street at the end of 7th Avenue. Gorgeous views of downtown, the falls, and Portland's skyline in the distance are a must-see. The lift operates Monday through Saturday 7-7 p.m.) Despite being the residence of the man touted as the "Father of Oregon," the steep admission ($2.50 for adults with discount for senior and students) at the McLoughlin House might make you expect more than the unexciting collection of original and period furnishings here. It's open Tuesday through Saturday 10-4 p.m., Sunday 1-4 p.m., and closed in January and on holidays. Self-guided walking tour maps are also available here. The McLoughlin House is the starting point of the itinerary.

On the lower terrace is the **Clackamas County Historical Society Museum** (603 6th St., tel. 655-2866) which operates the **Steven-Crawford House** at the same address. It was built at the turn of the century and has two arcane items to complement the original furnishings, dresses, dolls, china, and kitchen implements. The flag flown at Bunker Hill and a copy of the original plat of San Francisco add another dimension to the pioneer themes of Oregon museums. It's open Tuesday through Saturday 10-4 p.m., Sunday 1-4 p.m. Admission is $1.50 for adults with discounts for seniors and children under 18.

Pageantry And Environmental Awareness

Another way to take in the history of Oregon City and the Oregon Trail is at the pageant held at Clackamas Community College from mid-July through the beginning of August (except Sundays and Mondays) at 8 p.m. Tickets are $7.50 with discounts for seniors, children, and families on Tuesdays and Mondays. Fridays and Saturdays, an Indian-style salmon feed ($6.50) starts at 6 p.m., followed by a free pioneer history talk at 7 p.m. Call 657-0588 for reservations (not required) for the show. To get there, take Exit 10 off I-205 and follow ORE 213 south almost three miles to Clackamas Community College.

But that's not all that's happening on the campus. **John Inskeep Environmental Learning Center** (Clackamas Community College,19600 South Mololla Avenue, Oregon City, 97045; tel. 657-6958, ext. 351) is pioneering efforts of a different sort. The 80-acre environmental study area showcases alternative technologies and recycling against a backdrop of ponds, trails, and wildlife. Exhibits on aquaculture, birds of prey, and wetlands are included in this environmental education center's portrayal of Oregon's ecosystems. The latter are supplemented by one of the largest telescopes in the Northwest. Tours and interpretive programs are available at the center on Sunday afternoon. While there's no admission charge, donations are requested. Hours are 9-dusk daily. Adjacent to the Inskeep Environmental Learning Center is the **Home Orchard Society Arboretum,** displaying Oregon's array of fruit-bearing plants.

Food And Lodging

If you need to grab a bite while in town, **Chris' Coffee Shop** (212 7th St., tel. 657-5111) at the foot of the municipal elevator serves the best burgers in Oregon City. The **Fellows House** (416 South McLoughlin) south of the falls serves excellent breakfasts and lunches in the parlor of a restored Gothic Revival structure. This home, built by a ship's captain in 1867, also houses an art gallery and is featured in the National Register of Historical Places.

All of this is only 12 miles away from Portland via I-205.

THE COLUMBIA RIVER GORGE

Portlanders with only a day to show out-of-town-ers what Oregon is all about often head east to the Columbia Gorge. In the 70 miles between Troutdale and The Dalles, the state's pioneer history, rainforest-to-desert diversity, orchard country, and hydropower extolled in Woody Guthrie's "Roll On Columbia" paint a mural-come-to-life of the Oregon experience. The majesty of the river together with dozens of waterfalls coming off the huge basalt cliffs backdrop this pageant of patrimony with the kind of scenery inadequately enshrined in calendar art and coffee-table books.

HISTORY

Artifacts and petroglyphs found in the Columbia Gorge date human presence there back 10,000 years. Further historical perspective is lent by the fossilized remains of mastodons, camels, and ancient horses unearthed near The Dalles. The advent of the white man began with the arrival of the American Navy's Captain Gray in 1792. His ship, the *Columbia Rediviva,* was the inspiration for the name of the river. Prior to this time, British marin-ers Cook (1778) and Vancouver (1792) navigated past the river's five-mile mouth at Astoria but failed to note it, probably because of bad weather. All of these explorers were motivated by a desire to find a transcontinental sea route connecting the Atlantic and the Pacific. The next major incursion was that of Lewis and Clark (1805) who, despite coming by land from the east, were also drawn here in part by the search for the Northwest Passage.

Their journals described "great quantities of salmon" and "a large number of Indians" along the river. It's a good bet that the native population they observed were not just the local residents because the shores of the Columbia have traditionally hosted a gathering of the tribes. Because of this, the indigenous peoples, generically referred to as the Cascades or Chinook tribe, developed a culture with diverse influences. This might manifest in a member of the Cascades clan wearing a Yurok (California) headband, Kwakiutl (British Columbia) sandals, and a Hudson Bay (English) blanket. Even their Chinook dialect became saturated with French and English expressions.

Multnomah Falls in the Columbia River Gorge, America's second highest cascade

PHOTO BY OREGON TOURISM DIVISION

The subsequent decades saw further erosion of the Indian culture. The coming of the trappers during the first part of the 19th century, the missionaries in the 1830s, and the Oregon Trail migrants in the 1840s brought infectious diseases and depleted the salmon as well as other resources in the Columbia Gorge. Steamship transport in the 1850s and the completion of the Union Pacific tracks several decades later facilitated future incursions into this sacred Indian domain so that by the turn of the century, only 30% of the original native population of 5,000 (estimated by early explorers at the turn of the century) remained along the shores of the river.

The Columbia Gorge Scenic Highway

The modern era began with the building of the Columbia Gorge Scenic Highway in 1913. When the project was finished two years later, it was the only paved road in the Northwest as well as the first designated Scenic Highway in the country. It was financed by Sam Hill, heir to a railroad fortune, who wanted to build a road to his Maryhill estate located on the Washington side of the river. Backed by prominent Portland citizens such as lumber magnate Simon Benson, the project also attracted the support of a national group called the Good Roads Committee. Hill recruited engineer Samuel Lancaster for the task and took

him abroad to study the classic roads of Europe. Such inspirations as Bingen-on-the-Rhine in Germany and the Axenstrasse in Switzerland are reflected in the hairpin turns and scenic overlooks of Lancaster's road. Other touches included the dry masonry (without mortar) building techniques of Charlemagne's legions, Florentine viaducts, ornate tunnels, and stone benches. Much of the route was beveled into the steep basalt cliffs in order to highlight a view on every curve.

During the several years of construction, civic groups and convict labor joined road crews to give form to Lancaster's vision. Once completed, it became a tradition for middle-class families from Portland to pile into the Model T for Sunday drives on the Columbia Gorge Scenic Highway. By the '30s, the 73.8-mile thoroughfare became so crowded that a call for a speedier route was enunciated in a state study. Interstate 84 was the result several decades later. While the riverside route of the Interstate didn't lack for aesthetic appeal, Lancaster would have been appalled to see the ensuing neglect and desecration of the old road. Today only one-third of the more than 70-mile expanse remains intact, with the rest consigned to gravel pits, garbage dumps, or simply abandoned. Both state and federal governments have earmarked millions to restore the road to its former glory by the year 2000. The Columbia

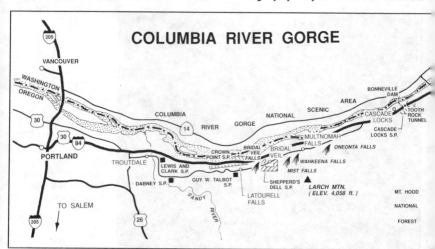

Gorge National Scenic Area Act passed by Congress in 1986 also made provisions for bicyclists, pedestrians, and people in wheelchairs. Thus, the road which started the American love affair with motor touring could well be breaking new ground by the 21st century.

A Damsite Better

Tapping the hydropower potential of the river stimulated Roosevelt to initiate the Bonneville Dam and power project in the '30s. This was the first of many dams on the river, and the undertaking yielded benefits immediately. Besides actively employing thousands during the Depression, the WPA project supplied cheap power to Kaiser's shipyards and Boeing Aviation during World War II. Another Bonneville byproduct was the creation of a 370-mile navigable channel from the Pacific Ocean to Idaho, enhancing commerce at the port of Portland. In the decades that followed, aluminum plants and other industries dependent on cheap power came to the Northwest thanks to Columbia's hydropower. Today the river generates 80% of the region's kilowatts.

Roll On Columbia

The blessings conferred upon the Northwest by the river extend beyond the Columbia's usefulness as an artery of transport and commerce, a major salmon and sturgeon fishery, a source of irrigation water for the surrounding orchard country, and the generator of electricity for the Western United States. The scenic beauty of the waterway and the gorge it occupies have forever drawn admirers of Mother Nature's handiwork. In recent years this influx has increased exponentially due to the popularity of windsurfing and other forms of outdoor recreation. To ensure that the gorge doesn't become loved to death or overdeveloped, the government created the Columbia Gorge Scenic Area in 1986. The latter is an experiment in preserving nature's beauty as well as the region's livelihood. Since there's not enough land for a national park, given the river valley's steep contours filled to the brim with 50,000 residents, this alternative environmental jurisdiction was instituted to monitor growth. Many residents fear the federal government's Columbia Gorge Commission will put a damper on business expansion in the areas outside the dozen small towns here. Already, restrictions on logging and controversies over Indian fishing rights have caused the commission to lock horns with the quintessential dilemma facing Oregon and the whole Northwest: the fact that one person's conservation is very often another's unemployment. Given the economic and environmental microcosm that the gorge has been in the past, it's altogether fitting

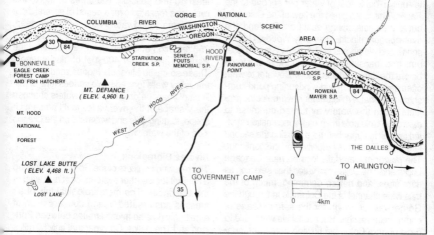

Engineer Samuel Lancaster emulated the dry masonry techniques of Charlemagne's legions.

PHOTO BY TED LONG ISHIKAWA

that this debate now takes center stage along the shores of the Columbia.

THE LAND

As the only sea-level break in the Cascade Mountains, a range extending from western Canada into California, the Columbia River flows 1,214 miles from its source in British Columbia to its mouth at Astoria. In so doing, it carries a quarter-million cubic feet of water per second to the Pacific. This is ten times the flow of the Colorado, but to motorists driving east from Portland, the river appears placid. Now only Woodie Guthrie songs and old photos in Columbia Gorge museums and roadside cafes hint at the river's force before the dams reduced the whitewater to what often seems like a hybrid windsurfing pond-cum-shipping canal. While the four hydroelectric projects along the waterway turned darkness to dawn, the Columbia in an earlier incarnation strutted its stuff in a manner more befitting the second largest and most powerful river on the continent. The power of waterfalls located near Cascade Locks and The Dalles motivated their selection as dam sites, and before damming, much of the mile-wide channel of the Columbia in through the Gorge was too rough for the safe passage of commercial vessels. But even if we were able to gaze upon a Columbia flowing from the mountains to the sea unimpeded by dams or shipping locks, it couldn't begin to approximate what transpired here after dozens of Ice Age inundations.

Missoula Floods

About 15,000 years ago near the end of the Pleistocene Epoch an ice lobe from Canada backed up the water of a lake in the area of present-day Idaho and Montana. When the lake waters rose high enough to breach and wash away the dam, 500 cubic miles of water powered across eastern Washington into Oregon. For at least 40 and possibly 100 times or more, this cycle was repeated over a period of several thousand years. Floodwaters were 1,000 feet deep; where The Dalles are today, they crested almost 750 feet high at Crown Point, and covered the Portland area under 400 feet of glacial runoff. These so-called Missoula Floods scoured away the valley walls formed by volcanoes tens of millions of years before. The flood waters changed the V-shape of the river valley to its present U-shape, forming cliffs and waterfalls on the Oregon side of the waterway.

Diverse Bioregions

The resulting contours of the Gorge have formed a conduit for weather systems east and west of the Cascades. The meteorological mix of air masses has created a high concentration of amazingly diverse microclimates between Portland and The Dalles. Consider that only 50 miles separate temperate rainforests at Bonneville (75-

inch average annual precipitation) from the arid grasslands at Celilo (12-inch average annual precipitation). Several thousands of feet between the highest and lowest elevations in the Gorge also help define one of the greatest range of plant habitats per square mile to be found anywhere in the world. *Wildflowers Of The Columbia* by Russ Jolley, published by the Oregon Historical Society Press, identifies 744 of the area's more than 800 species of flowering shrubs and wildflowers. The region's combination of sun and shade, heat and cold, moisture and dryness, humus soil and rock as well as the juxtaposition of grassland and forest can provide a textbook introduction to most of the bioregions of the American Northwest.

THE COLUMBIA GORGE SCENIC HIGHWAY

With a near total absence of hotels as well as places to camp and eat, the most spectacular section of the Columbia River Scenic Highway is best treated as a day-trip. Beyond Multnomah Falls, creature comforts exist in abundance in nearby Cascade Locks and Hood River.

The Columbia Gorge takes on a different aspect when you depart I-84 and enter the Columbia River Scenic Highway, which begins at Exit 22 at Corbett, 15 miles from downtown Portland. Pull off at the **Royal Chinook Inn** (2605 N.E. Corbett Hill Road, Corbett, 97019; tel. 695-2297) for a look at vintage photos from the era before the dams tamed the torrents and before motorists were able to speed through the region at 65 miles per hour. The Royal Chinook's walls are festooned with shots of Indian fishermen clustered around Celilo Falls (currently The Dalles Dam), Model T's in the foreground of a waterfall, and other poignant images from days gone by. This is also the only restaurant to get a bite at for the next 12 miles of the scenic drive until Multnomah Falls. Their specialty is fresh local salmon. Better yet, get their smoked salmon to go at $12.95 a pound. From the cafe wend your way to the top of the hill. If you bear left and follow the signs for Crown Point and Multnomah Falls, you'll soon experience America's first auto-tour route in all its glory. (If you take the road marked Larch Mountain instead, you'll go 14 miles to an overlook featuring views of the snowcapped Cascades, gorgeous beargrass blossoms in June, picnic tables, and trailheads to the gorge below.)

Vista House

After the Royal Chinook Inn, head first to Vista House at Crown Point, 725 feet above the Columbia. This 1917 structure was built as a visitor

The Columbia Gorge Scenic Highway was the first paved highway in the Northwest.

PHOTO BY OREGON DEPT. OF TRANSPORTATION

PHOTO BY OREGON TOURISM DIVISION
Oneonta Gorge is a cool, moist, and green enclave just down the road from Multnomah Falls.

center in honor of the highway's completion The outside observation deck up the steps from the main floor showcases 30 miles of the Columbia River gorge. Samuel Lancaster is paid homage with a plaque outside Vista House which aptly describes his routing as possessed of "poetry and drama." Photos of the various stages of the road's construction are on display in the main rotunda as well as wildflower cuttings to study. Downstairs is a bookshop and wallboard of printed materials about the gorge past and present.

Waterfalls

From Vista House the next 11 miles feature a waterfall-a-mile, the largest concentration of high waterfalls in the United States. The highest here are Multnomah at 620 feet (the second highest waterfall in the contiguous 48 states) and Latourelle at 249 feet. While all of these cataracts are beautiful and distinctive, the three most majestic falls are, by Lancaster's design, the most visible and accessible from the raod. These include the two just mentioned as well as Wahkeenah Falls.

Latourelle Falls is the first of the big three seen by motorists. A paved 150-yard trail takes you down to Latourelle's base where the shade and cooling spray creates a microclimate for fleabane, a delicate bluish member of the aster family, and other flowers normally common to alpine biomes. The filmy tendrils of water against the columnar basalt formations on the cliffs make La Tourelle a favorite with photographers. Foragers appreciate maidenhair fern and thimbleberries, but hopefully not enough to ever denude the slope. Another trailhead begins in the middle of the parking lot and climbs around and above the falls, though bushes obscure the overhang from which the water descends. You'll probably be more inclined to stop after 50 yards and take in the distant perspective of Latourelle from across the canyon.

Wahkeenah Falls, whose name means "most beautiful," is a 242-foot series of cascades which descends in staircase fashion to the parking lot. To the right of the small footbridge abutting the road is the beginning of the two-mile **Perdition Trail**. This steep path affords views of both Wahkeenah and Multnomah falls. Higher up are panoramic vistas of the Columbia River and gorge. This trail is especially striking in October when the bigleaf and vine maples, cottonwoods, and aspens sport colorful fall foliage. Hikers should also be on the lookout for poison oak, which grows below the 800-foot level in the gorge. A picnic area is north of the Scenic Highway across from the falls.

Multnomah Falls pours down from the heights with an authority worthy of the prominent Indian chief for whom it is named. The half-mile long uphill trail to the bridge should be attempted by anyone capable of a small amount of exertion. Here you can bathe in the cool mists of the upper fall and appreciate the power of Multnomah's billowy flumes. The more intrepid can reach the top of the falls and beyond (see Larch Mountain), but the view simply from the parking lot will be edifying. Placards detailing forest canopies and their understories at different elevations and other aspects of the ecosystem are on display in the first 100 yards of the trail. Look for the image of an Indian maiden's face on the rock behind the falls. Legend has it that she threw herself over the falls as a sacrifice to head off an epidemic. Now when the breeze blows through the water, a silvery stream separates from the upper falls, framing the maiden's form as a token of the spirits' acceptance of her gesture.

The falls area also has a snack bar as well as **Multnomah Falls Lodge** (tel. 695-2376). This magnificent structure was built in 1925 and is today operated by a private concessioner under the supervision of the U.S. Forest Service. A cheery solarium adjacent to a high-ceilinged dining room built from native wood and stone makes a casually elegant setting to begin or end a day of hiking. W.P.A.-commissioned paintings of the Cascades and Columbia Gorge scenes and a menu with such indigenous fare as grilled fresh rainbow trout with two eggs ($7.50) and Caesar salad with smoked salmon ($8.95) also effectively articulate the surroundings.

Recreation
Several activities merit special mention in the gorge. Reasonably priced "flightseeing" is available in a Cessna from the Troutdale airport. Marvin Woidyla offers a Mt. St. Helens excursion which loops back over the gorge, taking in the Bonneville Dam and the waterfalls close up. Reserve by calling 666-2660 and expect to pay around $30 a person in a four-seater plane.

Swimming is safe at historic and scenic **Rooster Rock State Park** (Exit 25 off of I-84 near Troutdale). On summer weekends a dollar parking charge is leveled on each car. West of the parking area is the monolith for which the park is named. Lewis and Clark labeled the cucumber-shaped promontory on November 2, 1805. Playing fields and a gazebo front a sandy beach on the banks of the Columbia here. The water in the roped-in swimming area is shallow but refreshing. A mile or so east is the only nude beach officially sanctioned by the state of Oregon.

Information And Services
Here are some information outlets serving the western part of the gorge.

For travelers not coming into the gorge via I-84 along the river, the **Columbia Gorge Ranger Station** (31520 S.E. Woodard Road, Troutdale, 97060; tel. 695-2276) has maps and infomation on trail locations and recreation opportunities. The ranger station can be reached by taking ORE 30 off of I-84 at the Troutdale Exit. Though this road at first veers from the river, it eventually connects with the scenic highway.

For visitor information of all kinds, the **Gorge Information Service** (tel. 800-222-8611 in Oregon, 800-222-8660 outside of Oregon) has the answers.

Vista House at Crown Point State Park on the Columbia River Scenic Highway east of Troutdale and west of Multnomah Falls (Box 204, Corbett, 97019; tel. 695-2230) offers visitors a *Columbia Gorge Sights and Services* pamphlet, a regional map, and a handbill reviewing the geologic evolution of the Columbia Gorge. Vista House is open 10-6 daily.

The **Multnomah Falls Information Center** (Box 68, Bridalveil, 97019; tel. 695-2376) has a ranger on duty to recommend campgrounds and hikes. You might ask personnel here about such nearby jaunts as Oneonta Gorge (a mile east of Multnomah Falls) as well as Eagle Creek Trail and the Pacific Crest Trail outside of Cascade Locks (see "Hiking And Camping" in "Cascade Locks"). The center's hours are 9-5 seven days

Locals call Vista House the "million dollar restroom."

PHOTO BY TED LONG ISHIKAWA

Indian bivouac and dip-net fishing platform near the Dalles

PHOTO BY KATHY FREEMAN

a week, June through September. Thereafter, call because they vary greatly.

A Portland-based group, **Friends of the Columbia Gorge** (Box 40820, Portland, 97240-0820; tel. 241-3762) offers "Columbia River Gorge Guided Tour" tapes and a map for $21.95. This group also sponsors a free guided hike on weekends in the middle of June; walks are geared to different levels of exertion.

Menucha

"Menucha" means waters of refreshment in Hebrew. This name was given to an estate along the Scenic Highway by Governor Julius Meier (Gov. of Oregon 1930-38) who maintained it as a summerhouse. Today, the 96-acre property houses visual arts, writing, and dance workshops each summer. **Arts At Menucha** (contact the Creative Arts Community, Box 4958, Portland, 97208; tel. 236-4109) sponsors one-week and two-week workshops in August costing $405 and $700 respectively. The package includes the chance to work with eminent masters of such disciplines as poetry, watercolor, maskmaking, and photography while ensconced on the spectacular grounds of the estate (meals and housing included). Studio spaces, meditative gardens, a pool, and tennis courts are at your disposal. Students and instructors eat and interact beyond the confines of the classroom, enhancing the experience. Should money prove a problem, inquire about scholarships and auditing options. The estate can be located by getting off I-84 at Corbett (Exit 22) and proceeding up the hill as if you were going to Crown Point. After turning left drive until you see the Menucha sign on the left.

CASCADE LOCKS

The sleepy appearance of modern-day Cascade Locks belies its historical significance. The town is perched on a small bluff between the river and I-84, and its services and creature comforts are mostly confined to its main drag, Wa Na Pa Street. The shipping locks which inspired the burgh's utilitarian name were constructed in 1896 to help steamboats navigate around hazardous rapids here. Prior to the existence of these facilities, boats had to be portaged overland.

Two events which took place outside the city limits, however, gained the town a permanent place in history books. The first of these claims to fame may not have existed at all, but many reputable scientists now believe an ancient natural bridge once spanned the Columbia's channel for over a mile. According to native oral histories, this formation was destroyed by lava flows from the eruption of two nearby volcanoes. What are believed to be geologic remnants of this event lie just upstream from a modern structure called the Bridge of the Gods in honor of the Indian landmark. The span was raised in 1938 to compensate for a heightened river level due to the Bonneville Dam.

The second event, the construction of the Bonneville Dam in the late '30s, inaugurated boom times in Cascade Locks. Thousands of workers patronized its businesses and set up temporary residence in the area. The dam created 48-mile Lake Bonneville, which submerged the shipping locks. Today you can see Indian dip-net fishermen by the 1896 locks site in the town's riverfront Marine Park. Boom times are gone now but this little town with a dazzling river view and down-to-earth people is a refreshing change of pace from the big city to the west as well as the burgeoning tourist scene and industrial parks of her neighbors to the east. Reasonably priced food and lodging, a historical museum, the Bonneville Dam, and sternwheeler tours together with superlative hiking trails nearby also make for a nice stopover, as long as you don't come during winter. Most of the 75-inch annual precipitation total falls at that time along with ice storms and gale-force winds. Two funnel clouds were even sighted outside of town during the Columbus Day storm of 1962. Such violent weather is not completely devoid of benefits, however. The rains fostered the growth of massive Douglas firs near here and a once thriving timber industry. Nowadays, the winds account for the Columbia Gorge's status as the windsurfing capital of the world, and the tourist-economy's ripple effects are starting to be felt in Cascade Locks.

SIGHTS

Bonneville Dam

The Bonneville Dam (Public Information, U.S. Army Corps of Engineers, Box 2946, Portland, 97208) can be reached via Exit 40 off I-84. The signs lead you under the Interstate through a tunnel to the site of the complex, Bradford Island. En route to the visitor center you drive over a retractable bridge above the modern shipping locks. On the other side are the powerhouse and turbine room. Downriver is the second largest exposed monolith in the world (Gibraltar is first). This 848-foot lava promontory abutting the shoreline is known as **Beacon Rock**. Beyond the generating facilities is a bridge underneath which is the man-made fish diversion canal. These fishways cause back-eddies and guide the salmon, shad, steelhead, and other species past turbine blades. The best perspective on spring and fall movement of spawning salmon upriver can be enjoyed at the visitors center's subterranean fish-viewing windows. Before going there, you'll want to stop for a brief look at the spillways of the 500-foot-wide Bonneville Dam, especially if they're open. While Bonneville isn't anywhere near the largest or the most powerful dam on the river, it was the first project on the leading hydroelectric waterway in the world. Along with its potential for generating 40% of America's power needs, the Columbia's storage of irrigation water and its dam-related recreation sites make the river the most valuable resource in the Northwest—too valuable to be diverted for drinking water in Southern California, despite pleas from Los Angeles politicians.

Benefits notwithstanding, the downside of damming is graphically illustrated by the sight of

Indian fishermen enacting a weary pantomime of their forefathers by the Bonneville spillways. The **visitor center** (tel. 374-8820) is open 10-6 Memorial Day to Labor Day. Ask the Army Corps of Engineers personnel at the reception desk about tours of the power-generating facilities and about public campgrounds, boat ramps, swimming, and picnicing areas. The reception area has exhibits on dam operations, pioneer and navigation history on the Columbia, and fish migration. There is also the opportunity to take a long elevator ride down to the fish-viewing windows. Particularly fascinating are the sight of lamprey eels, which accompany the mid-May and mid-September salmon runs, and the fish-counting procedures. This practice helps determine catch limits on the popular species. Outside the facility there's access to an overlook above the fish ladders. A walkway back to the parking lot is decorated with gorgeous roses from spring into fall.

Retrace your route back to the mainland from Bradford Island and turn right, following the signs to the fish hatchery. This facility is open every day

PHOTO BY U.S. ARMY CORPS OF ENGINEERS, PORTLAND DISTRICT

Fishermen try their luck near the Bonneville Dam spillways.

from 7:30-5. The salmon and trout ponds and the floral displays are worth your attention, but don't miss the sturgeon pools to the rear of the complex. Biologists say the Columbia River white sturgeon, with bony plates instead of scales, has remained unchanged for 200 million years. These sleek black fish can grow as large as 18 feet and weigh 1,200 pounds. Despite being the largest freshwater species in North America, this river-bottom scavenger was largely ignored until the gourmet feeding frenzy of the last two decades put a premium on domestic sources of caviar. When *New York Times* columnist Craig Claiborne pronounced the Columbia's product superior to that of the Caspian Sea, its notoriety was established. In addition, fresh-cooked Columbia River sturgeon is a specialty in the finest dining rooms in the state. Both the Bonneville Dam visitor center and fish hatchery are free of charge.

The Marine Park

Down by the river is the Cascades Locks Marine Park. The highway exit for it is about half-way up Wa Na Pa Street going east. Just follow the signs. Here the sternwheeler *Columbia Gorge* (Box 307, Cascade Locks, 97014; tel. 374-8619) makes it possible to ride up the river in the style of a century ago. River legends and scenic splendor accompany you on a two-hour narrated cruise. This 145-foot, 330-ton replica carries 599 passengers on three decks powered by a paddlewheel. From October through May, the sternwheeler is docked near downtown Portland and cruises the Willamette; from mid-June to the last week of September, riverfront Marine Park is the home port. Port of Cascade Locks also houses the ticket office as well as an information center and gift shop. By the way, here as in the gift shop in Multnomah Falls, you can purchase an excellent local hiking trails map for $1.25. Historic photos of early sternwheelers and 50-cent showers for hikers also make this facility particularly worthwhile.

As for the sternwheeler rides, the current schedule has three cruises per day. At 10 a.m., the cruise focuses on Lewis and Clark; at 12:30 the Oregon Trail is highlighted; and at 3 p.m. turn-of-the-century entertainment is featured. No reservations are needed. The cost is $9.95 for adults, $5 ages four to twelve, and children under four are free. Outdoor and indoor seating and a snack bar ensure a comfortable ride.

BARGES

There once was a little girl who lived in Portland and whose bedroom window looked out over the Columbia River. She loved to watch the boats going up and down the waterway, especially the big barges at night. She spent a lot of time looking out of her window, because she was a very sick little girl. She always wondered where the boats were going and what kind of adventures they would have during their voyages, and she'd dream of going along with them some day. Sadly, she passed away from leukemia at the tender age of ten. But before she departed, she left behind a little song that she made up while watching the barges ply the river. Her friends taught the song to their music teacher, who was able to teach it to other teachers in the school district. "Barges" quickly caught on and spread across the Northwest and to points beyond. Soon the Girl Scouts of America picked up on the song and made it an integral part of achieving a Mariner's Badge.

Nowadays, children on opposite sides of the globe in Europe and Japan sing it. "Barges" is a very special gift for the rest of us that shows us how to see the world through children's eyes.

arr. by Ted Long Ishikawa

Out of my win-dow look-ing in the night I can see the bar-ges flick-er-ing light

Si-lent-ly flows the riv-er to the sea and the bar-ges to go si-lent-ly.

Bar - ges I would like to go with you I would like to sail the o-cean blue

Bar - ges are there treasures in your hold do you fight with pi - rates brave and bold

2. Out of my window looking in the night, I can see the barges flickering light
   Starboard glows green and port is glowing red, you can see them flickering ahead
   Barges I would like to go with you , I would like to sail the ocean blue
   Barges are there treasures in your hold, do you fight with pirates brave and bold

In addition to its regular runs, such events as Sternwheeler Days (see "Events" below), sunset cruises, Father's Day brunches and dinners, a Fourth of July dinner trip to Portland, and a senior barbecue with Western entertainment are scheduled. During the Christmas holidays, the sternwheeler takes part in the Christmas Boats Lights Parade on the Columbia River. Write or call the sternwheeler office for more information about all of the above as well as the new weekend dinner cruises and Labor Day Sunset Dance Cruise (with '50s music). Reservations are needed for all of these special trips.

About a quarter-mile west of the visitor center, **Cascade Locks Historical Museum** (Box 307, Cascade Locks, 97014; tel. 374-8535) is housed in an old lock tender's residence and exhibits Indian artifacts and pioneer memorabilia. Between June and September it's open Mon.-Wed. 12-5, and Thurs.-Sun. 10-5. In May it's open weekends 10-5. Outside the museum is the diminutive *Oregon Pony*, the first steam locomotive on the Pacific coast: its maiden voyage dates back to 1862.

Hikes

Since the **Eagle Creek Trail** is highly recommended by a lot of people, try to avoid peak-use times like summer weekends. This trail begins at Eagle Creek Campground (see "Camping") and goes 14 miles to Wahtum Lake, where it intersects with the Pacific Crest Trail. Along the trail are seven waterfalls, one of which features a perspective from behind the cascade itself. Ideally, this is a two-day backpack, but if you prefer a daytrip, consider Eagle Creek Trail 440 to Punchbowl Falls. It can be reached from the Eagle Creek Campground via Exit 41 off I-84. The four-mile roundtrip to the falls is an easy hike. If you can, come in February when tourists are scarce and stream flow is high.

PRACTICALITIES

Accommodations

This town of 820 people features several reasonably priced hotels. Throughout the Columbia Gorge there is a five-percent room tax. Canadian travelers frequenting the region here can find some of the best exchange rates between the border and Reno. Perhaps the cheapest accommodations from Cascade Locks through The

Dalles can be found at the **Scenic Motel** (Wa Na Pa Street, Cascade Locks, 97014; tel. 374-8390). Located at the eastern end of town, it has about a dozen weatherbeaten bungalows set back from the road on a hill. The small units go for $26.50, and larger units (up to six people) with separate bedrooms and kitchenettes go for $56.50. These rooms may be old and funky, but its a fraction of the price of comparable places at Hood River.

Another bargain is the **Scandian Motor Lodge** (Box 217, Cascade Locks, 97014; tel. 374-8417). A room with a queen bed ranges between $30-40, depending on the time of year and the number of people. A two-bed room averages $5 more. Rooms with a sauna go for $5 more than the two-bed rooms. The units boast a warm Scandinavian decor with wood paneling, air conditioning, and a restaurant and lounge as well as an adjacent laundromat. This retreat fills fast in summer.

Bed And Breakfast

West of Cascade Locks, the only place to stay on the waterfall route of the Scenic Highway is in keeping with its setting. **Bridal Veil Bed and Breakfast** (Bridal Veil, 97010; tel. 695-2333 or 284-8901 from Portland) is a homey country inn with a knotty pine interior, antique quilts, historic photos, and the kind of furniture you used to find in grandma's house. Queen beds, breakfast out on the front porch, and the nearby trails and waterfalls of the Scenic Highway make this worth the $50 rate. Incredibly, this place is only 30 minutes from Portland. From Cascade Locks, backtrack on I-84 then take the Scenic Highway/ Ainsworth Park Exit 35 (past the Bonneville Dam Exit). It's near Bridal Veil Falls State Park on the Scenic Highway. This makes an ideal fall getaway amid a riot of color.

Camping

Camping par excellence is close by town. The **Eagle Creek Campground** (Columbia Gorge Ranger District, tel. 695-2276, or write Mt. Hood National Forest, 31520 S.E. Wooded Road, Troutdale, 97060) is an ideal base camp for hiking. At the seven-mile point of the Eagle Creek Trail (see "Hiking" above) there's a primitive free campground, but it fills up on summer weekends. Back at Eagle Creek, there are sites for tents and RVs up to 22 feet long, with picnic tables, firegrills, flush toilets, sanitary services, and firewood available. It's located in between the Bonneville Dam

Punch Bowl Falls empties into Eagle Creek and is accessible from Eagle Creek Campground.

PHOTO BY FRANK LONG

and Cascade Locks off I-84 and is open mid-May to October. The fee is $5.

Herman Horse Camp (write Mt. Hood National Forest, Troutdale, 97060; tel. 695-2276) is only one-half mile east of Cascade Locks, near the Pacific Crest Trail. It's located a half mile from Herman Creek and is one of three campgrounds in the area. A full array of services including a laundromat, a store, a cafe, and showers are nearby, supplementing the seven tent and RV sites. The availability of piped water, firegrills, picnic tables, and stock-handling facilities are also welcome additions here. It's open mid-May to October with no reservations or fee required. **Cascade Locks Marine Park** (Box 307, Cascade Locks, 97014; tel. 374-8619) has campsites available close by the center of town. The museum and sternwheeler are in the complex, as are tennis courts. Whatever amenities that are not available on site are within walking distance. It's open all year and the fee is $7.

Food

Forget health food and haute cuisine until you get to Hood River. In Cascade Locks, you get downhome country cookin' and lots of it at a decent price.

The Charburger (714 Wa Na Pa Street, Box 366, Cascade Locks, 97014; tel. 374-8477) is located near the Bridge of the Gods at the beginning of town. This is a great place if you're on the go and don't want to spend a fortune for a quick bite. In addition to an extensive salad bar and a bakery, there is a cafeteria line specializing in "home-baked" (and it tastes that way) chicken,

omelettes cooked to order, and other wholesome but unexotic dishes. Prices for a meal generally seldom exceed $5. Other features include a take-out window and a Sunday brunch. The restaurant's outlet in Hood River (4100 Westcliff, Hood River, 97031; tel. 386-3101) is also located at the beginning of town.

The **Cascade Inn** (in front of the Scandian Motor Lodge, see "Accommodations" above, tel. 374-8340) is a neighborhood meat-and-potatoes kind of place where a luncheon crowd of loggers, tradesmen, and secretaries wolf down such overstuffed sandwiches as The Millworker—two beef patties, cheese, bacon, lettuce, tomato, onions, mayonnaise, and relish on a bun. This might not be a "heart-smart" alternative, but you'll leave feeling full and the space inside your wallet should not decrease substantially either. There's a lounge next door.

Information And Services

In addition to the previously mentioned Marine Park Visitors Center, the **Cascade Locks Tourism Committee** (Box 355, Cascade Locks, 97014; tel. 374-8619, ask for Tahoma) can provide help in planning your visit.

Cascade Locks is served by **Greyhound** and the **Amtrak** *Pioneer*. Amtrak can arrange for riders in Portland to be transported to Cascade Locks by an 11 a.m. train in time to catch the 12:30 p.m. sailing of the sternwheeler and to return to Portland by a late afternoon westbound train. The **state police** can be reached at tel. (800) 452-8573.

HOOD RIVER

In the past, Hood River was known to the traveling public primarily as the start of a scenic drive through the orchard country beneath the snow-capped backdrop of Mt. Hood, Oregon's highest peak. Since the early '80s however, the well-heeled adherents of windsurfing have transformed this town into a Malibu-in-the-making. Instead of the traditional dependence on cherries, apples, peaches, and pears, Hood River now rakes in up to $25 million annually from the invasion of "boardheads." A good percentage of this subculture tends to be yuppies able to "drop out" here for extended periods to the tune of $47-85 a day for basic creature comforts (according to a University of Oregon study). The abundance of civilized amenities in the midst of spectacular surroundings complement ideal conditions for this sport. The fury of the winds derives from the heat of the eastern desert drawing in the westerlies. The confining contours of the gorge dam up these air masses and precipitate their gusty release. Because prime time to "catch a blow" is midday, this is also the best time to find a parking spot downtown. City center features an unnaturally high concentration of ethnic eateries, sports equipment shops, and boutiques for a town of 4,500 people. The main thoroughfare, Oak Street, is set on a plateau between train tracks and the riverfront marine park to the north, and streets running up the Cascade foothills to the south. New brick facades dress up old storefronts, and attire on the order of multihued wetsuits and sandals predominates.

The notion that affluent young people in bathing garb would rescue Hood River from cutbacks at Jantzen apparel, Diamond fruit packers, and other economic mainstays seems the stuff of fantasy—like riding the wind on the great River of the West.

SIGHTS

Columbia Gorge Hotel

To ease the culture shock of going from the Scenic Highway and the sternwheeler to the brave new world of windsurfing in Hood River, stop first at the Columbia Gorge Hotel (4000 West Cliff Drive, Hood River, 97031; tel. 386-5366 or 800-826-4027). Take Exit 62 off of I-84 to get there. The hotel is a lovingly preserved memento to the Jazz Age of the roaring twenties, when it was graced by visits from Rudolf Valentino, Clara Bow, and the big bands. Built by lumber magnate Simon Benson (who was also a patron of the Scenic Highway) in 1921, the grounds feature a 207-foot waterfall and the neo-Moorish outlines of a hotel nicknamed the "Waldorf of the West."

Hood River has become the
sailboarding capital of the world.

Glittering chandeliers in the lobby, large wing chairs around the fireplace, and fresh-cut bouquets in the dining room bespeak the refinement of an earlier era. Rates here are high (expect to spend $135-175 a night during peak season, although winter rates are close to half that), but a more romantic retreat would be hard to come by. Spacious rooms with heavy wooden beams, brass beds, fluffed-up pillows, and period furniture clearly demonstrate what was meant by the "good ol' days." The dining room looks east at the Columbia rolling toward the hotel from out of the mountains and west towards alpenglow from the sunsets. Selected in 1990 as "Number One Restaurant in Oregon" by *Pacific Northwest Magazine*, the hotel's fare draws heavily on nature's bounty. Local mushrooms, fruits, and wild game as well as Columbia River salmon and sturgeon are featured prominently here. There is also the "world famous farm breakfast." Imagine four courses running the gamut of American breakfast food served with such theatrical flourishes as "honey from the sky"—Hood River Valley apple blossom honey poured from a height of several feet above the table onto hot fresh-baked biscuits. As they say at the hotel, "you don't just get a choice, you get it all."

The scenic highlights of Hood River are the orchards during the end of the April Blossom Festival and the leaves here during color season in October. To take in the totality of it all, drive to the end of town on Oak Street and bear right on ORE 35 till you see the sign for **Panorama Point** one mile up the road. Vistas here afford a distant perspective on the orchards below Mt. Hood.

Hood River Museum

To learn the history of the region, drive back to the junction of Oak Street and ORE 35, then cross I-84 towards the river. At the intersection turn left and follow the signs to Marina Park and the Hood River Museum (tel. 386-6772). To get there, take Exit 64 off I-84 and follow the signs. Exhibits here trace life in the Hood River Valley from prehistoric times to the founding of the first pioneer settlement in 1854. Thereafter, the area's development as a renowned fruit-growing center is emphasized. Native American stone artifacts, beadwork and basketry, pioneer quilts, and a Victorian parlor set the time machine in motion. The contributions of the Finnish and Japanese communities and World War I memorabilia introduce the first half of the 20th century. Photos and implements related to fruit harvesting and packing methods round out the historical collections on the first floor. Upstairs antique logging equipment, dolls, and remnants of a presentation by local schoolchildren for the Lewis and Clark Exposition in 1905 are on display. At the center of the museum is an attractive open-air courtyard planted with Columbia Gorge flora. From April to autumn, the museum is open Wed.-Sat. 10-4, Sun. 12-4. Other months, the museum is open Mon. and Tues. by appointment. Admission is free.

The "dry" view of the gorge as seen from Rowena Crest.

PHOTO BY REBECCA SINGER

Columbia River Views

Back in town drive up to the offices of United Telephone between Oak and State streets. The lot is restricted to staff vehicles, so park elsewhere and walk to what has to be the most scenic employee parking anywhere. An unimpeded view of the Columbia River, the mouth of the White Salmon River and its deep gorge, the south face of an extinct volcano, and a look up Mt. Adam's western flank are all laid out before you.

The last leg of the Columbia River Scenic Highway can be reached by driving 15 minutes east on I-84 to **Mosier**. At the far end of this small town is a sign pointing the way to the final couplet of Lancaster's poem in stone. While not so spectacular as the earlier route of the waterfalls, this section of ORE 30 still provides a picturesque restful alternative to the Interstate.

Rowena Crest

The highlight of the drive is Rowena Crest. Almost nowhere else can you see both the dry eastern and wetter western faces of the Columbia River Gorge with such clarity and distinction. The dark Columbia River basalt cliffs here are derived from massive lava flows from 15 million years ago. The terracing of the region was due to the action of the Missoula Floods upon Columbia Plateau fault scarps. More information on the geology and ecosystem here is available from a free pamphlet in the drop box on the north side of the highway courtesy of the **Tom McCall Nature Preserve.** This 2,300-acre sanctuary on part of Rowena Crest was created by the Nature Conservancy (1205 M.W. 25th Ave., Portland, 97210; tel. 228-4561) and has trails on the hillsides that are kept open to the public.

These cliffs represented the beginning of the last hurdle facing Willamette Valley-bound Oregon Trail pioneers. After Rowena, the gorge cliffs rose up so high that the pioneers were forced to either build rafts and float the then-hazardous rapids on the river, or follow the Barlow trail around the south flank of Mt. Hood.

Today Tom McCall Nature Preserve is the site of a mid-May pilgrimage by wildflower lovers. Because the preserve lies in the transition zone between the wet west and the dry east, several hundred species and four endemics flourish here. Included in the spring display are yellow wild sunflowers, purple blooms of shooting stars, scarlet Indian paintbrush, and blue-flowered camas. And of course, as with any nature preserve or public park, love the flowers and leave them behind for the next person to enjoy.

ACTIVITIES AND RECREATION

Boardsailing

Boardsailing and vineyard-hopping complement nearby Columbia Gorge hiking and auto touring as well as Mt. Hood skiing. Regarding the latter, the "gorge route" from Portland (I-84 and ORE 35) to Mt. Hood ski slopes is becoming a popular alternative to the more direct ORE 26. Local wags insist the lighter traffic can save as much as an hour on weekends, not to mention the scenic appeals of this route. While this is hard to believe, the crystal paradise created by iced-over waterfalls off I-84 make it a worthy scenic detour.

As for windsurfing, neophytes, adepts, and their fans congregate around the **Hood River Marina** (Exit 64 off I-84). This complex offers a complete package: swimming beach, picnic shelter, concessions, exercise course, and jogging trail. If you've never windsurfed, Hood River has the highest density of shops in the world geared to this sport. They rent equipment and give lessons. For information about sailboarding, wind, and weather, call 387-WIND (9463) or pick up a copy of *Northwest Sailboard* (Box 918, Hood River, 97031). This magazine is available all over town.

Winetasting

Two local vineyards offering tasting and tours are the **Three Rivers Winery** (275 Country Club Road, Hood River, 97031; tel. 386-5433), open 11-5 Mon.-Sat., 1-5 on Sunday, and the **Hood River Vineyard** (4693 Westwood Drive, Hood River, 97031; tel. 386-7772), open 10-5 daily. The microclimate here is similar to that which produces Germany's Rhine wines. In addition to the riesling, chardonnays, gewürztraminer and other white wine varietals, the area is also famous for fruit wines and award-winning pinot noir.

In-town Pursuits

Hood River Golf (1850 Country Club Road, Hood River, 97031; tel. 386-3009) has nine holes and beautiful views of Mt Hood, Mt. Adams, elk, and geese. It's open daylight to dark. Come in fall if only to see the spectacular foliage.

Two worthwhile shopping stops are **Waucoma Bookstore** (212 Oak Street, Hood River, 97031; tel. 386-5353) and the **Fruit Tree** (4140 Westcliff Drive, Hood River, 97031; tel. 386-6688). The bookstore's selection evidences taste and an appreciation of titles relevant to the locale. Added pluses include issues of the *New York Sunday Times,* unique cards, pottery, beautiful music, and gourmet coffee. The Fruit Tree is located on the river side of I-84 and is the perfect place to find a giftbox of Oregon jams, smoked salmon, hazelnuts, and other goodies. They help coordinate shipping right from the store and also have fresh local produce. Try the apple cider. You won't get big discounts on the produce but it's first rate.

PRACTICALITIES

Accommodations

It's hard to find a room in spring and summer in Hood River and the prices reflect it. (By the way, remember to add an eight-percent Hood River room tax.)

Just west of town, however, there are two reasonably priced alternatives in the $30-40-a-night range. The **Vagabond Lodge** (4070 Westcliff Drive, Hood River, 97301; tel. 386-2992) and the **Meredith Gorge Motor Lodge** (4300 Westcliff Drive, Hood River, 97031; tel. 386-1515 or 800-537-5938) have standard motel rooms, many with river views. Proximity to Hood River's **Charburger Restaurant** (4100 Westcliff Drive, Hood River, 97301; tel. 386-3101) is another plus if you like better-than-average American road food at Cascade Locks (rather than Hood River) prices.

"Boardheads" interested in extended stays should realize that rentals go fast and come dearly these days. Nonetheless, the **Inn at the Gorge** (1113 Eugene Street, Hood River, 97013; tel. 386-4429) has a deal after the summer ("when the rain in Portland can give the desert air a yank") which offers rates as low as $275 a month. During other seasons, you'll pay $58-72 a day for private baths and a complete kitchen and living area in each unit. In addition to transfers to and from Amtrak and Greyhound, the innkeepers can provide special windsurfing instruction. This 1908 Victorian home away from home also includes a large and tasty breakfast every morning and has bicycles on hand for guest use. The chamber of commerce has a complete listing of the two dozen other bed and breakfasts in the area which they'll gladly send upon request. Most cost above $60 per day however and may soon run higher.

If the notion of a vintage 1910 hotel appeals to you but you're not prepared to pay Columbia Gorge hotel prices, the **Hood River Hotel** (102 Oak Street, Hood River, 97031; tel. 386-1900) might be your window on the river and on the past. This is not to say that it's cheap, with most of the rooms going for between $70-90 (including a complimentary continental breakfast), but this graceful rendering of memory lane enjoys river views as well as proximity to downtown dining and shopping. If you miss having TV in your room here, the high-ceilinged oak-paneled first floor with adjoining lounge and dining area provides an inviting place to revive the grand old art of conversation.

Camping

Tucker Park (2440 Dee Highway, Hood River, 97301; tel. 386-4477) is a county park campground set along the banks of the Hood River, four miles south of town on ORE 281. Despite a location off the tourist trail, there's a store, cafe, laundromat, and ice machines within one mile. From April to November, five tent and 29 RV sites go for $8 a night. Picnic tables and electricity are provided; piped water, flush toilets, primitive showers, firewood, and a playground are also available.

Viento Park (tel. 235-2205) is eight miles west of Hood River on the river side of I-84. From mid-April to late October you'll pay $7 a night for five tent sites and 58 RV sites. Electricity, picnic tables, and piped water are provided. As with the other Columbia Gorge state parks, there are no reservations accepted.

Sunset Campground is located behind the only laundromat on the west end of Cascade Street in Hood River. In addition to laundry facilities, restrooms and showers can be found in the open area planted with trees which serves as the campsite. There are 16 tent spaces and hookups for seven RVs. Sunset is first come, first served, but call 386-6098 for more information.

Food

The brie-and-chablis set who blow into town during peak windsurfing season have brought sophisticated tastes and higher prices to Hood River. It's still possible however to get a decent

Special events during the Hood River Blossom Festival include an orchard tour aboard the Mt. Hood Railroad.

PHOTO BY MT. HOOD RAILROAD

meal without paying a fortune. Best of all, there's not a town of this size anywhere in Oregon with as consistently good coffee or as many places catering to vegetarians.

A place where you'll see everyone from Columbia Gorge politicos to young mothers with toddlers is the **Coffee Spot** (12 Oak Street, Hood River, 97031; tel. 386-1772). Whether its a cup of premium brew with a spinach ricotta croissant ($1.60) for breakfast, or such imaginative lunchtime sandwiches as cheese and pesto ($2.85 for an ample half sandwich) or tuna, almonds, and water chestnuts ($2.75 for a half sandwich), you can feast for a pittance at this small delicatessen/coffee house. Coffee Spot was chosen as the best "business lunch" in a *Pacific Northwest Magazine* poll.

Locals swear by **Bette's Place** (at the Oak Mall, 416 Oak Street, Hood River, 97031; tel. 386-1880) for breakfast. This family restaurant also specializes in chicken dumplings every other Sunday; seafood and vegetarian fare with orders to go are available. It's open every day except Wednesday. For dinner, **Chianti's Ristorante** (South and Cascade, Hood River, 97031; tel. 386-5737) is another popular gathering spot. Every day between 4:30-6:30 p.m. there's a $6.95 early-bird dinner with salad, pasta, and dessert (kids under 12 eat for half price). Moderately priced pasta dishes dominate the menu and four or five specials are added every night so the "regulars" can enjoy a little variety. Decadent desserts and cappuccino can finish off your meal or become a meal in themselves.

To make your evening an occasion, try **Stone Hedge Inn** (3405 Cascade Drive, Hood River, 97031; tel. 386-3940). This turn-of-the-century house surrounded by a wooded area and gardens has a warm paneled interior that's conducive to leisurely dining. Even "light" dinners here can range between $13-18, but the elegantly presented Northwest cuisine is the best in town. It's open Wednesday through Sunday from 5 p.m. Please call ahead for reservations.

Picnickers are referred to the appetizer and deli section at **Safeway** (419 State Street, Hood River, 97031; tel. 386-1841) and the **Oak Street Deli** (606 Oak Street, Hood River, 97031; tel. 386-6061) for box lunches.

For evening musical entertainment, barbecued burgers, Cajun oysters, and vegetarian munchies washed down by Hood River's award-winning microbrew, Full Sail Ale, head for **White Cap Brew Pub** (506 Columbia Street, Hood River, 97031; tel. 386-2247). Add the panoramic view from the outdoor deck and you have the most laid-back atmosphere in town. Ask about brewery tours and tastings here, too.

Events

The most popular events in Hood River County highlight windsurfing and the seasons of blossom, harvest, and foliage in the orchards.

During April 20-21st, the **Hood River Blossom Festival** showcases breathtaking views of the valley's orchards in bloom. Arts and crafts, dinners, and the seasonal opening of the Mt.

Hood Railroad (see "Information And Services") also can be enjoyed. Contact the Hood River Chamber of Commerce for more details.

The fall counterpart of this fete is the **Hood River Harvest Fest.** On October 20th and 21st, the valley welcomes visitors for two days of entertainment, crafts, fresh locally grown produce, and colorful foliage. Admission is free and the apples and pears are ripe. Regarding fruit, it should be mentioned that Hood River is the winter pear (d'anjou) capital of the world and produces Bartletts, comice bosc, and other varieties at different times of the year. Cherries, peaches, and apples round out the horn of plenty here. Newton pippin apples are another renowned Hood River product. The 15,000 acres of orchards are still the leading economic factor in the county.

Two premier windsurfing events take place on the Columbia in July. The **Columbia Gorge Pro-Am** is the world's largest slalom sailboarding event and traditionally falls between the second and ninth of July. **Hood River Windsurfing** (tel. 386-5787) has all the information.

Another sailboarding spectacular happens July 12-15. The **Gorge Cities Blowout** is a 20-mile open water race from Cascade Locks to Hood River. Call Michael Clark at 667-7778 for details.

Services And Information

The **Hood River Valley Visitors Council** (Port Marina Park, Hood River, 97031; tel. 386-2000) has an extensive array of maps and pamphlets about the area. Take Exit 64 off of I-84 and follow the signs to get here. Down the road is the **post office** (Hood River, 97031).

In addition to **Greyhound** (located at the feed store at the west end of town across the street from Olivia's) and **Amtrak** *Pioneer* service (the depot is just below Oak Street), **Hood River Taxi and Transportation** (315 Oak Street, Hood River, 97031; tel. 386-3355) offers in-city taxi service Sun.-Thurs. 7 a.m.-midnight and on Sat. 7 a.m. to 3 a.m. as well as group van tours. **Hood River County Transit** (1020 Wilson Street, Hood River, 97031; tel. 386-4202) is a local public bus system.

Club Wet Inc. (Box 697, Hood River, 97031; tel. 386-6084) has regular flights to and from Seattle to Hood River airport. Call ahead for reservations and ticketing. The average flight time is one hour.

Hood River Memorial Hospital (13th and May Streets, Hood River, 97031; tel. 338-7889) is open 24 hours a day with a physician-staffed emergency room. **Care Corner** (12th and May Streets, Hood River, 97031; tel. 386-1111) offers immediate care of illnesses and injuries. This facility refers more serious cases to Hood River Memorial.

The **Mt. Hood Railroad** (110 Railroad Avenue, Hood River, 97031; tel. 386-3556, ext. 804) has tours in 1910 passenger cars which traverse the scenic 20-mile valley between Mt. Hood and the Columbia River. See (the general Introduction) for complete information.

THE DALLES

It hits you shortly after leaving Hood River. Scrub oak gives way to sage and the grasslands of eastern Oregon. And then, just as suddenly, there's all the traffic and acrid air of an urban environment. You've come to The Dalles, a place Lewis and Clark in 1805 called the great "Trading Mart of the Northwest." Instead of seeing an Indian potlatch on the Columbia however, the modern scene is 10,000 souls living in the industrial hub of the gorge. While the cherry orchards and wheat fields south of town and the aluminum plants and timber mills by the river are more what The Dalles is about these days than tourism, a complete perspective on the history of Oregon is impossible without a day-trip here.

Shortly after you enter town, stop off at the **Visitor Information Center** (404 West 2nd Street, The Dalles, 97058; tel. 296-2233) and pick up their pamphlets, *The Dalles: Historic Gateway to the Columbia Gorge* and two self-guided *Walking Tours to Historic Homes and Buildings*. The following overview in conjunction with these publications can annotate your day-trip here. As the walking tour showcases churches, homes, and government buildings built between 1859-1929, let's look at those parts of town whose history dates back before that time. Our itinerary will conform to historical chronology.

Seufert Park

Although the visitors center is on the west end of The Dalles, begin your travels six miles east of town off I-84 with the Seufert Park interpretive center, staging area for the free train which tours The Dalles Dam. (For information on this complex call 296-9778.) The train and tour takes about an hour and runs April 14 to June 4, Wed. to Sun. 10-5, with the last train departing at 4 p.m. From June 4 through Sept 3, the hours are 9-6 with the last train departing at 5 p.m. In addition to detailing the workings of the world's fourth largest hydroelectric project, displays and commentary recount the historical importance of this location as a gathering place and gateway for native peoples and pioneer travelers. Just upstream from here was Celilo Falls, where Indians armed with spears and dip-nets pursued salmon for centuries. Although The Dalles Dam ended the fishing frenzy

by submerging the falls in 1957, reminders in the form of artifacts and custom recall its spiritual and mercantile significance in the native tradition. Archaeological finds here from as far away as the Great Lakes hint at the draw exerted by this bartering mecca. Pictures dating back to the early '50s portraying Indians spreading their 20-foot-long dip nets from precarious platforms above the falls will also help the imagination. Finally, you might be treated to this same sight on the Columbia today, albeit with lower water and reduced catch levels. If you can be in this area the first weekend of April, the Visitor Information Bureau can direct you to where the age-old Chinook ritual of welcoming the first salmon upstream takes place. The public is welcome to join the Indians free of charge for salmon cooked over an open fire and served with boiled roots.

Not surprisingly, the Seufert Park interpretive center's emphasis is on the coming of the white man. The arrival of Meriwether Lewis and William Clark was the seminal event in defining another role for the river—transportation for westbound travelers in the Oregon Country. French voyageurs who had passed through at the behest of fur-trapping concerns called these waters near Celilo Falls *La Grande Dalle de la Columbia*—"the Big Trough of the Columbia." From this point, the river was not considered safely navigable. As time went on, the area and the town became known as The Dalles. Oregon Trail emigrants loaded their wagons onto boats after portaging them overland around La Grande Dalle de la Columbia. These portages were later abetted by the first railroad tracks in Oregon, constructed by the Oregon Steamship Navigation Company. Thus, the region near the modern dam site has been the focal point of Oregon native civilizations as well as a pioneer transportation and trade route. Today, the dam itself is the northern terminus of the world's largest intertie power system. Several other important landmarks are back on the other end of town.

Rock Fort

To further stimulate your reverie of the early explorers and for the sake of historical chronology, your next stop might be Lewis and Clark's Rock

old farmhouse (Frank Long)

Fort. After exiting I-84 at Webber Street, take Bargeway Road through an industrial area to the river. A short walk from the parking lot leads you to a historical marker with details of the expedition's 1805-06 encampment. Unlike the more impressive Rooster Rock, Beacon Rock, and other Lewis and Clark landmarks, this site will call more upon your imagination to ward off the sights, smells, and sounds of the surrounding industrial park.

City Park And Fort Dalles

For another less-than-thrilling walk on hallowed ground, proceed to The Dalles City Park at 6th and Union Streets. Pioneer Ezra Meeker placed a marker on this site in 1906 to commemorate the end of the original Oregon Trail. In 1845 Samuel Barlow opened the first overland route to the Willamette Valley here, extending the initial route.

As the final prelude to the walking tour, visit Fort Dalles (for information write: City of The Dalles Museum Commission, Box 806, The Dalles, 97058; tel. 296-4547) at 15th and Garrison Streets. Unlike the preceding points of interest, there's an actual structure here housing memorabilia to help evoke the past. The Surgeon's Quarters, dating back to 1856, serves as a museum for armaments, period furniture, and other pioneer items. In 1850, Fort Dalles was established in response to the massacre of missionaries Marcus and Narcissa Whitman. The Whitman's had attempted to impose the white man's ways on the Indians along with his religion, with unfortunate results. For instance, the natives could not understand the concept of private property and felt that Whitman's whipping those who

inadvertently took what they considered to be communal property was unduly harsh. The last straw occurred when a smallpox vaccine administered by Whitman to Indian and white children killed the native children while the white children were cured. The Indians were further confused and understandably angry when they were told that their offspring's adverse reactions were due to a lack of immunities. Their violent retaliation incited Congress to establish the only military post between Fort Vancouver and the Rockies. The Surgeon's Quarters is the one remaining part of this complex.

Several years later, the establishment of Wasco County in 1859 made The Dalles the seat of a 130,000-square-mile bailiwick stretching from the Cascades to the Rocky Mountains. This was the largest county ever formed in the United States.

Now you're ready to take on the walking tour described in the pamphlet with an understanding of the rich heritage of this gateway to the gorge and the Oregon Country.

A box lunch from the **Dobre Deli** (308 East 4th Street, The Dalles, 97058; tel. 298-8239) is a substantial and cost-effective way to sustain your foray along the path of Lewis and Clark and the Oregon Trail. Call ahead to order their "hearty lunch" consisting of assorted meats (six ounces) and cheeses (three ounces) three slices of bread (wheat, sourdough, dilled rye, or French roll), homemade salad (half pint), and a slice of mousse cake or two cookies. This costs $4.95. For a dollar less, the "petite lunch" serves skimpier appetites. The deli packs each item in large ziplock bags, ensuring freshness, and provides drinks at a nominal extra charge.

(top) Man and beast battle it out at a rodeo in eastern Oregon. (Dave Davidson);
(bottom) the old ghost town of Shaniko in Wasco County (Oregon Tourism Division)

THE WILLAMETTE VALLEY

A 25- to 40-mile wide and 120-mile long fertile river valley bordered by rainforested mountain ranges was the object of Oregon Trail pioneer dreams—a land where crops never failed, a place which offered a second chance, a stage upon which to play out the most cherished economic, civic, educational, and cultural impulses of civilization. One hundred fifty years after the emigrants' epic march across the continent, diversified agriculture, esteemed universities, and cosmopolitan cities fill the Willamette Valley landscape. Covered bridges and historic homes are also here to remind us of the taming of the frontier.

Horn Of Plenty
Prior to the coming of the white man, the Calapooya Indians had subsisted for centuries on game, berries, camas and wapato tubers, and fish. They had never cultivated the soil or logged, save for burning to provide browse for deer and soils for grasses, roots, and berries. Centuries of setting fire to the valley cleared the land of a lot of trees and exposed rich alluvial soils ideal for farming. The first Europeans who came here in the second decade of the 1800s, however, were more interested in the easy money from the fur trade. It fell to the Oregon Trail influx in the mid-19th century to break ground for the present-day agricultural colossus. Today the valley boasts national leadership in everything from berry to prune production. It has carved an identity as the primary source of such specialty crops as English holly, bearded iris, and lily bulbs. Coveted green beans, the highest yielding sweet corn in the U.S., and domination of world markets in grass seed and hazelnuts compound the impression of pastures of plenty.

Now as then, the valley is the population center of Oregon. Eugene and Salem are the second and third largest cities and the region as a whole accounts for over 60% of the state's residents. Nonetheless, you seldom get the feeling of being in a big metropolis, thanks to bike routes, parks, and land-use planning based on environmental imperatives.

The Willamette River
This progressive orientation is embodied in the history of the Willamette River. After the Willamette served as the transport route for valley pro-

duce to Portland en route to gold rush-era San Francisco, prosperity and people coalesced around its shores. By the 1960s, 20 municipalities and over 600 industrial plants along the river had so befouled the waters that Governor Tom McCall described it as an "open sewer." The next decade's Willamette Greenway legislation put 50 million dollars and the efforts of industry toward a cleanup. The results were the first significant salmon spawning runs in 40 years and a spate of riverfront parks and recreation areas.

The coast fork of the river originates south of Cottage Grove; the Middle Fork comes out of the Cascades near Oakridge. They meet each other and the McKenzie River near Eugene. The surrounding valley extends from Cottage Grove to Portland. Since the northern Willamette Valley is within the orbit of Portland, it was treated as part of that section. Further south, Salem, Corvallis, and Eugene have carved a distinct identity as the Emerald Empire.

SALEM AND VICINITY

The used car lots and fast food outlets encountered on the way into Salem off I-5 contrast with the inspiring murals and displays in the capitol building. It's comforting to be reminded in the state house of Oregon's pioneer tradition and proud legacy of progressive legislation. Close by, the tranquil beauty and museums of historic Willamette University also provide a break from the Xerox-copy drabness of a town dominated by gray buildings housing the state's bureaucracies.

odist missionary appellation "Salem." This is an anglicized form of the Arabic "salaam" and the Hebrew "shalom," meaning peace. The surrounding croplands along with Willamette River transport and water power quickly enabled Salem to become the New Jerusalem envisioned by Oregon Trail pioneers. Over the years, the city carved out an economic destiny in government, food processing, light manufacturing and wood products. Today, it has a population of almost 90,000 people, third behind Portland and Eugene.

HISTORY

The Calapooyan name for the locality of Salem was "Chemeteka" or "Place of Rest." Connotations of repose were also captured by the Meth-

SIGHTS

Mission Mill Museum

In 1840-41 the site of the Jason Lee House and

a quiet Willamette Valley country lane

PHOTO BY BRUCE BUSH

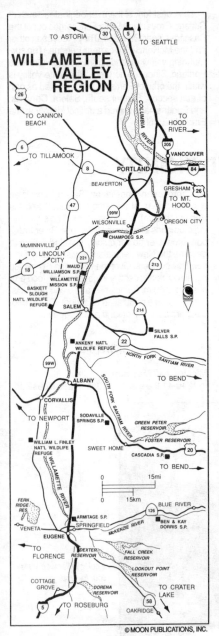

WILLAMETTE VALLEY REGION

© MOON PUBLICATIONS, INC.

Parsonage moved from the Willamette River upstream to Mill Creek, laying the foundations for the present-day cityscape. These structures along with the Boon Home were part of a Methodist mission to the Indians. The reconstructed Thomas Kay Woolen Mill dating back to 1889 is also on the four-acre site of what is now called Mission Mill Museum (1313 Mill St. S.E., Salem 97301; tel. 585-7012). The chance to see the oldest frame house in the Northwest and water turbines converting fleece into wool fabric are interesting, but those with limited time might prefer to come here just to obtain brochures about Salem and vicinity in the reception area in front. There's also a deli and crafts shop in the complex. Hours at Mission Mill are Tues.-Sat. 10 a.m.-4:30 p.m. and Sun. 1-4:30 p.m. in summer. To gain admission to the historic houses or the mill, adults pay $2, students 12-18 and seniors pay $1.50, and children under six get in free. This covers the mill tour or the several houses. For $1 more you can buy an all-inclusive ticket which gets you into everything. Tours of the complex begin every hour on the hour, 10 a.m.-4 p.m. To get there from I-5, exit at ORE 22, go west on Mission Street for two miles to the 13th Street overpass, turn north onto 12th Street, and go west onto Mill Street.

Willamette University

Across the street from the museum is Willamette University (900 State St., tel. 370-6300), the oldest institution of higher learning west of the Mississippi. It began as the Oregon Institute in 1843, a school that Methodist missionary Jason Lee founded to instill Christian values among the settlers. Over the years, Willamette University managed to turn out its share of Oregon politicos, including longtime Senators Mark Hatfield and Bob Packwood. The campus is one of Salem's many oases of greenery that soften the hard edge of a city dominated by government buildings and nondescript downtown thoroughfares. Campus landscape architecture features a Japanese garden, ornate fountains, and a grove of five Sequoias six feet in diameter. This grove, which sits between the state capitol and Collins Hall (home of the science departments), has beside it an Oregon rock of ages. Found atop Ankeny Hill in Salem, the granite boulder floated down from northeastern Washington on an ice raft during the same Missoula Flood which shaped the Columbia River

Gorge 25,000 years ago. This glacial erratic stands as a reminder that the Willamette Valley is largely composed of Lake Missoula sediments. In Collins Hall, crystals and exhibits on Oregon glacial activity as evidence of climate changes join an impressive taxidermic array of Oregon wildlife. There's no admission and it's open during university hours.

State Capitol

If visiting the state capitol building (tel. 378-4423) strikes you as the kind of saccharine excursion best reserved for a first-grade class trip, you're in for a pleasant surprise. The marble halls of Oregon government are adorned with attractive mu-

rals, paintings, and sculptures of the seminal events in this state's inspiring history. These incidents are given eloquent voice by on-site tour guides whose commentary is sure to fill in any gaps in your understanding of this pioneer saga. The capitol is located on Court Street between W. Summer and E. Summer streets, just north of the Willamette University campus.

Atop the capitol dome is a gold-leafed bronze statue of a bearded, axe-wielding pioneer. Massive marble sculptures flank the main entrance, *Covered Wagons* on the west side and *Lewis and Clark by Sacajawea* on the east. Maps of the Oregon Trail and the route of Lewis and Clark are

© MOON PUBLICATIONS, INC.

visible on the backs of the statues. The symbolism is sustained after you enter the double glass doors to the rotunda. Your eyes will immediately be drawn to an eight-foot bronze state seal on the floor juxtaposing an eagle in flight, a sailing ship, a covered wagon, and forests. The marble steps beyond the cordoned-off emblem lead up to the House and Senate chambers. Four large murals adorning the rose travertine walls of the rotunda illustrate the settlement and growth of Oregon: Robert Gray sailing into the Columbia estuary in 1792; Lewis and Clark at Celilo Falls in 1805; the first white women to cross the continent being welcomed by Dr. John McLoughlin in 1836; and the first wagon train on the Oregon Trail in 1843. Bronze reliefs and smaller murals symbolic of Oregon's industries also are here.

Near the ceiling in the Senate and House chambers are friezes depicting an honor roll of people who influenced the growth and settlement of Oregon. Included are Thomas Jefferson, who sanctioned the Lewis and Clark expedition, and native son and naturalist extraordinaire Thomas Condon. Among the names you will find those of six women, headed by Lewis and Clark's interpreter-guide Sacajawea. The biggest surprise in this array might be John Quincy Adams, who determined the southern boundary of Oregon when he was secretary of state. In both legislative chambers look for forestry, agricultural, and fishing symbols woven into the carpets; murals about the coming of statehood are behind the speakers' rostrums.

Architecturally eye-catching in the capitol are the rotunda's black marble, golden oak House chamber walls and furnishings, black walnut room appointments in the Senate, a walnut-paneled governor's office and bronze doornobs inlaid with the state seal throughout the building. All this was paid for with part of the two million dollars it took to build the capitol in 1938.

If you don't want to roam independently, half-hour free building **tours** are given on the hour beginning at 9 a.m. weekdays and 10 a.m. on Saturdays with a lunch break on all days from 12-1 p.m. The last tour starts at 4 p.m. Mon.-Fri. and 3 p.m. on Saturday.

A tower at the top of the capitol dome gives a superlative view of the valley and surrounding Cascade peaks and is worth the 121-step walk from the fourth floor. It's open from Memorial Day

PHOTO BY OREGON DEPT. OF TRANSPORTATION

The bearded, axe-wielding pioneer stands tall on top of the capitol rotunda.

to August but is closed off during this time when the temperature reaches 90°. Tours to the top go up during the same weekday building tour hours cited above. On weekends the tower tour hours are Sat. 9:30 a.m.-3:30 p.m. and 12:30-3:30 p.m. Sunday. Both tours run Memorial Day through August and other times of the year by appointment. Also worth a look in the building is the ongoing exhibit of outstanding Oregon artists in the governor's ceremonial office upstairs. Upstairs is a fine gift shop of Oregon-made crafts, food, and other indigenous items.

Capitol Grounds

At each end of the building are parks. Between the capitol and the State Executive Building on the corner of Court and Cottage streets is **Wilson Park.** Lush lawns, a gazebo for concerts, and a wide variety of trees including sequoia, Port Orford cedar, Asian cedar, blue spruce, mountain ash, dogwood, and incense cedar invite a picnic. There are also two large multicolored rose gardens which bloom through much of the year to garnish your spread; a trio of bronzed beavers make the perfect lunch companions. Also to the west of the building are the beautiful E.M. Waite Memorial Fountain and a replica of the Liberty Bell. To the east is **Capitol Park,** where you can admire Corinthian columns salvaged from the old capitol (destroyed by fire in 1935) and statues of Dr. John McLoughlin, Reverend Jason Lee, and the circuit rider. The latter honors horseback evangelists to the pioneers during the era of missionary zeal.

The oldest government building in Salem is the **Supreme Court Building** (1147 State St.), dating back to 1914. It's located to the east of the capitol on the southern half of the block across Waverly Street, facing State Street and bounded by 12th Street. The building's facade is white terra cotta and the marble interior has tile flooring. Visual highlights include an ornate stairwell and a stained-glass skylight in the third-floor courtroom framing a replica of the Oregon State Seal. Above all, don't miss the public restrooms. Tastefully appointed in marble, oak, and tile, these facilities were described in *Oregon Magazine* as "doing justice to public needs."

South of the legislative building and the campus are some other places that encourage a step back in time. The historic **Deepwood Estate** (1116 Mission St. S.E., tel. 363-4825) features tours of an elegant 1894 Queen Anne-style home with gorgeous stained-glass windows and a well-marked nature trail. English formal gardens here evoke a more genteel era, and the Pringle Creek Trail's native flora and the public greenhouse's tropical plants have a timeless appeal. Parking is at 12th and Lee streets near the greenhouse. The Deepwood Estate is open May through September noon-4:30 p.m. everyday except Saturday. Winter hours are 1-4 p.m. Sun., Mon., Wed., Fri., and the grounds are closed on holidays. Admission is $2, discounts for children and seniors. Sit in Deepwood's pagoda-like gazebo with the scent of boxwood heavy in the air on a spring afternoon and you'll soon forget the hue and cry of political proceedings at the capitol.

Bush House And Park

Bush House Museum (600 Mission St., tel. 363-4714) is located in Bush Pasture Park off Mission, High, and Bush streets. This 1877 Victorian, with many original furnishings, is the former home of a pioneer banker and newspaper publisher. Even if you're not big on house tours, the Italian marble

fireplaces and elegant walnut and mahogany staircase are worth a look. The museum is open Sept.-May, Tue.-Sun. 2-5 p.m. and June-August, Tue.-Sun. noon-5 p.m. The last tour begins at 4:30 p.m. Adults pay $1.50, with discounts for students and seniors. The house is part of the 80-acre **Bush Pasture Park.** Besides being a sylvan retreat for picnickers and sports enthusiasts, the park is home to the **Bush Barn Art Center** (write c/o the Bush House, tel. 581-2228). Located next to the Bush House Museum, this center features two galleries with monthly exhibits. On the grounds there's also the Bush Conservatory Greenhouse and rose gardens. The Bush Barn hours are 10-5 p.m. Tue.-Fri and Sat. 1-5. The conservatory is open Mon.-Fri 8-4 p.m. and Sat. 2-4:30. Both have free admission.

Honeywood Winery

Of the half-dozen local vintners, Honeywood Winery (501 14th St. S.E., tel. 362-4111) is the largest and the most easily reached with a location a block from Mission Mill Village. It also bills itself as Oregon's oldest winery, having begun in 1934. Honeywood produces a full line of fruit (try the blackberry) and varietal wines and offers free tasting Mon.-Fri. 9-5; Sat. 10-3, and Sun. 1-5 p.m. all year long. Tours leave 10 a.m. and 2 p.m. Mon.-Friday.

The Reed Opera House Mall

At the corner of Court and Liberty is the Reed Opera House Mall. This one-time venue of minstrel shows and other pioneer cultural activities still retains a brick facade and long windows but has new tenants—the boutiques and restaurants of a tastefully rendered shopping mall. After you admire the restoration which helped this atrium gain admittance to the Natural Register of Historic Places, peek inside a shop which does justice to the creative traditions of the frontier—**Made In Salem** (189 Liberty St. N.E., Salem 97302; tel. 399-8197). This is a crafts co-op of four dozen local artisans. Creations made from stained glass, Oregon's "exotic woods," and many other mediums are featured, along with artists working on-site. It's open 10-9 p.m. Fri., noon-3 p.m. Sun., and 10-6 weekdays.

The Enchanted Forest

Seven miles south of Salem off I-5 on Exit 248 is the Enchanted Forest (8462 Enchanted Way,

Turner 97392; tel. 363-3060), one man's answer to Walt Disney. An enterprising Oregonian has single-handedly built a false-front Western town, an Old West village, a haunted house, and many more attractions. Whether it's the old woman who lived in the shoe, the seven dwarves' cottage, or Alice-in-Wonderland's rabbit hole, these and other nursery-rhyme, fairy tale re-creations will get thumbs up with anyone under 99 years of age. It's open daily 9:30 a.m.-9 p.m. March 15 through September 30. Adults pay $4 and ages 3-12 pay $3.50, with admission to the bobsled ride and haunted house each 75 cents extra.

Gardens

Both **Schreiner's Iris Gardens** (3625 Quinaby Rd. N.E., Salem 97303; tel. 393-3232) and **Cooley's Gardens** (11553 Silverton Rd. N.E., Silverton 97381; tel. 873-5463) bill themselves as the world's largest iris growers. Both claims are correct based on different criteria, but the important thing to remember is that from mid-May through the first week of June these are the places to visit. Schreiner's is seven miles north of Salem next to I-5, and Cooley's is on the way to Silver Falls State Park. Both places can be visited 8 a.m.-dusk.

DAY-TRIPS FROM SALEM

Silver Falls State Park

If Silver Falls State Park (22024 Silver Falls Highway, Sublimity 97385; tel. 873-8361) were in California instead of a remote part of the Willamette Valley, it would probably be designated a national park and be flooded with visitor facilities and people year-round. Instead, one of Oregon's largest and most spectacular state parks remains relatively quiet except during the summer. At that time, hordes seeking relief from the heat of the valley head up to this cool enclave of waterfalls in the foothills of the Cascades. They come to see 10 major waterfalls 30 to 178 feet in height cascading off canyon walls in a forest filled with old-growth Douglas fir, ferns, and bigleaf and vine maple. The best time to come is during fall foliage season when there are few visitors here, just before icy roads and trail closures inhibit travel. The east winds of autumn sometimes make the falls here appear like ice sculptures.

To get there from Salem, drive east on ORE 22 towards Stayton and take the turn toward Sublimity on ORE 214 , which heads 10 miles north to the town of Silverton. Here signs divert you east up steep, windy Silver Creek Drive (an extension of ORE 214) above the town. After several miles, this route levels out into gently undulating hills and Christmas tree farms as it loops south. A dearth of signs and a distance which seems longer than the posted 15 miles from town will have you second-guessing these directions until you come to the Silver Falls parking lot. Walk across the bridge over Silver Creek on the east side of the lot where a trail map located by the restrooms outlines several hiking options. Serious hikers will want to take on the seven-mile **Silver Creek Canyon Trail** which heads down into a fern-lined basalt gully. The profusion of trees and moisture gives the air a special freshness here, and when the sun hits some of the ten falls just right you can see rainbows.

The highlight of this Civilian Conservation Corps trail from the 1930s is 177-foot-high **South Falls.** This cascade is the second highest in the park (one foot lower than Double Falls) and an easy mile from the parking lot, but there are other reasons for its popularity. The opportunity to walk behind a waterfall attracts a lot of visitors here who follow the trail through a basalt overhang in a cleft of the cliff. This enables them to view the "underside" of South Falls without getting wet.

Bikers and horseback riders also enjoy specially designated trails in this 8,300-acre paradise. A $1 day-use fee per vehicle is charged on summer weekends and on holidays.

Mount Angel Abbey And Oktoberfest

Four miles northwest of Silverton off ORE 214 is a retreat of a different sort. High above the rest of the Willamette Valley is the Mt. Angel Abbey (St. Benedict 97373; tel. 845-3066 and 800-365-5156). The Benedictine abbey sits on a 300-foot hill overlooking cropland and Cascades vistas. From the bluff, look northward at Mt. Hood, Mt. St. Helens, Mt. Adams, and according to locals, Mt. Rainier on exceptionally clear days. Further inspiration can be gained from an ancient manuscript library and the landscaped serenity of the abbey's hilltop quadrangle.

Regarding meditative retreats, the price is $35 per day for lodging and meals ($20 for just the room). While the creature comforts are ascetic, the peace of the surroundings and the beauty of the monks' rituals brought from Switzerland in

A couple relaxes in a soothing hot spring pool at Breitenbush.

PHOTO BY TED LONG ISHIKAWA

1880 will make the cares of the world go away no matter what your spiritual orientation (or lack thereof). Weekend retreats begin Friday at 7:30 p.m. and end on Sunday at 1 p.m. For further information and reservations write Mt. Angel Abbey Retreat House, St. Benedict, or call 845-3025.

Mt. Angel's other claim to fame is **Oktoberfest,** which takes place in mid-September down in the town itself. Over the quarter century of its existence, many hundreds of thousands have come to guzzle brews in the beer garden ($2 admission), enjoy the oompah-pah of German traditional music, monastery tours, stage shows, art displays, yodeling, and street dancing amid beautiful surroundings. The biggest attraction of all, however, is the food. Stuffed cabbage leaves, strudels, and an array of sausages are the stuff of legend in the Willamette Valley. Call 845-9440 for details or write Box 1054, Mt. Angel 97362.

Bikers relish the foothills and farmland around Mt. Angel, which are nearly devoid of traffic. Fall color is exceptional here and a varied topography ensures an eventful ride whatever the season. Lowland hop fields and filbert orchards give way to Christmas tree farms in the hills. On the way up, pumpkin and berry patches also break up the predominantly grassy terrain.

Peoples Of The Central Valley

Even if you don't have time for in-depth exploration, you'll probably find the diverse ethnic makeup of the north central valley fascinating. In the town of **Woodburn** (located eight miles northwest of Mt. Angel) for example, local school classes are taught on a multilingual basis to accommodate the large concentration of Mexican migrants and Russian Old Believers here. The latter fled religious persecution in the 1960s by traveling to Brazil and New Jersey and then to the Willamette Valley. A small museum devoted to their history is located on the grounds of the Mt. Angel Abbey. Down in the town of Mt. Angel, signs in Spanish add further evidence of a rich cultural mix. In addition, many residents proudly point to French-Canadian backgrounds bespeaking their connections to the region's first pioneers.

Breitenbush Hot Springs

Salem residents have traditionally taken to the hills via ORE 22 along the North Santiam River to enjoy the fishing and camping at **Detroit Lake** as well as skiing at **Hoodoo Ski Bowl** (see "High Cascades"). Lately, the traffic to the mountains includes those seeking a different kind of renewal. Breitenbush Hot Springs Retreat and Conference Center (Box 758 Detroit 97342; tel. 854-3314 or in Salem, tel. 371-3754) offers mineral springs baths, trails forested with old growth, as well as a wide variety of programs aimed at healing body, mind, and spirit. Whether or not new-age bodywork and meditation appeal to you, the peace and beauty of the Breitenbush complex will enchant and edify. Set in the Cascade foothills, this one-time Indian encampment's artesian-flow hot springs have attracted people for healing throughout the ages. The pools, set variously in forest and meadow, have curative effects thanks to 30 freely occurring minerals, including the salutary chemical lithium. Music, storytelling, theater, and superb vegetarian cuisine are also part of the experience. Finally, a special sanctuary with a vaulted glass pyramid roof lets you watch the stars or winter storms through the canopy of trees.

The retreat cabins are spartan but sufficient. All have electricity and heat, and most have indoor plumbing. Rates range between $35-45 per person (bring your own bedding or pay $7 extra) and include three sumptuous vegetarian meals and use of the facilities and waters during your stay at Breitenbush. Day-use fees for hot springs and other facilities are $10 for a full day and $5 for a half-day. Individual meals for daytime visitors are $5, all-you-can eat, and the food is sure to make converts of those who still think of vegetarian fare as mostly rice and slime. Guided (arrange at the reception desk) or individual hikes through an old growth forest are highly recommended here. This is a good opportunity to see that bird in the head-

PHOTO BY OREGON DEPT OF TRANSPORTATION
Some of Oregon's finest hikes are found on and around 10,495-foot Mt. Jefferson.

lines, the spotted owl (see "Fauna" in the general Introduction).

To get to Breitenbush from Salem, take ORE 22 to the town of Detroit. Turn at the gas station (the only one in town) onto Forest Service Road 46. Drive 10 miles to Cleator Bend Campground. Go past the campground 100 feet and take a right over the bridge across Breitenbush River. Follow the signs, taking every left turn after the bridge, to the Breitenbush parking lot. If you have to rely on mass transit, it's possible to get here Monday, Wednesday, and Friday. First, catch a Greyhound from wherever to the Salem Bus Center. Arrive in time to catch the 1:30 p.m. Resort Bus Lines Salem-Bend scheduled run. After getting off in Detroit, call Breitenbush to pick you up. This must be arranged prior to arrival and costs $5. Getting back to Salem from Detroit by bus is possible Tuesday, Thursday, and Saturday. Because Detroit is a "flag" stop, call Greyhound so they can alert the driver to look for you.

Mount Jefferson

After a soak in the pools at Breitenbush, your muscles will be primed to hike up Mt. Jefferson, Oregon's second highest peak at 10,497 feet above sea level. This snowcapped symmetrical volcanic cone dominates the Oregon Cascades horizon between Mt. Hood to the north and the Three Sisters to the south. Unlike Mt. Hood, Mt. Jefferson is rarely visible to motorists approaching from the west.

The mountain comes into view a short distance up Whitewater Road 1044, about 12 miles east of Detroit and five miles east of Idanha. The seven-mile Forest Service Road off ORE 22 leads to the five-mile **Whitewater Creek Trail** to **Jefferson Park** at 5,800 feet in elevation. This is the northern base of the mountain and features a plethora of lakes and wildflowers. The alpine meadows here are full of purple and yellow lupine and red Indian paintbrush in July. On the way up, wild strawberries and red huckleberries can provide a delectable snack. For a special experience during the summer, start up the trail after 5 p.m. on the night of a full moon and enjoy this trail bathed in soft lunar light.

Above Jefferson Park, the ascent of the dormant volcano cone is a precarious endeavor and should only be attempted by the best in the business. You'll reach the bottom of Whitewater

Glacier at 7,000 feet. Thereafter, climbing routes steepen to 45° and snow and rock ridges destruct upon touch. Near the top, the rocks aren't solid enough to allow use of ropes or other forms of climbing protection, forcing what climbers refer to as "death moves," particularly because going down is even more dangerous than going up. Even if you head up the more sedate south face you can expect difficulties due to the instability of the final 400 feet of rock on the pinnacle.

Those who elect not to make the ascent may run into other problems. Sometimes the mosquitoes in Jefferson Park are bloodthirsty enough to pierce thick clothing. On occasion, the area is so crowded with day-use visitors and folks moving along the Pacific Crest Trail nearby that this place seems more like a city park than a mountain wilderness. No matter . . . the sight of Mt. Jefferson in alpenglow at sunset or shrouded in moonlight will make you forget the intrusions of man or the elements.

PRACTICALITIES

Accommodations
Coming into town off the Interstate you'll see cut-rate motels advertised with loud billboards. Need we say more? If you think so, please consult the following chart.

SALEM ACCOMMODATIONS

Name	Address	Telephone	Price	Features
Salem Grand Motel	1555 State St.	581-2466	$29-65	wheelchair access, cable TV, pets, pool, nonsmoking rooms, very close to capitol complex and Willamette University
City Center Motel	510 Liberty St. S.E.	364-0121	$37-39	cable TV, pets, nonsmoking rooms, complimentary continental breakfast
Tiki Lodge	3705 Market St. N.E.	581-4441	$40-45	cable TV, pool, pets, kitchenettes, laundry, restaurant/lounge, nonsmoking rooms
Salem Super 8 Motel	1288 Hawthorne N.E.	370-8888	$42	wheelchair access, pets, covered pool, laundry, nonsmoking rooms
Best Western Pacific Highway Inn	4526 Portland Rd. N.E.	390-3200	$45-56	wheelchair access, cable TV, pool, restaurant/lounge, nonsmoking rooms
State House Bed and Breakfast	2146 State St.	588-1340	$45-50	cable TV, meals available, laundry, nonsmoking rooms, river view

SALEM ACCOMMODATIONS, cont.

Name	Address	Telephone	Price	Features
Shilo Inn	1855 Hawthorne N.E.	581-9410	$48-50	cable TV, pets, pool, nonsmoking rooms, complimentary continental breakfast
Execulodge	200 Commercial St. S.E.	363-4123	$51-73	cable TV, pool, restaurant/lounge
Chumaree Hotel and Convention Center	3301 Market St. N.E.	370-7888	$56-103	wheelchair access, pets, covered pool, restaurant/lounge, laundry, nonsmoking rooms, live entertainment

Food

Salem is blessed with an unusually large amount of Mexican restaurants for a city this size in the Northwest. Many of these establishments boast regional specialties from the state of Jalisco that cater to the large influx of agricultural workers who've come to the Willamette Valley from northwestern Mexico. Some ubiquitous entrees in these places include carne asada and camarones al mojo de ajo. Carne asada is grilled beefsteak, often tough but flavorful. Camarones al mojo de ajo is shrimp coated with garlic and butter. An example of a typically unpretentious but tasty "estilo Jalisco" restaurant is **La Estrellita** (1111 N.W. Edgewater, Salem, tel. 362-0522). With a name that translates as "The Little Star," this place shines with the aforementioned specialties as well as such other classics as camarones à la Diabla (shrimp cooked in red sauce with onions and mushrooms) and chile verde (chunks of pork, green pepper, onions, and spices in a green tomatillo sauce). Dinners run about $8 and can be washed down by a dozen different kinds of Mexican beer. La Estrellita's north Salem location makes it a perfect stopover en route to Silver Falls State Park. Despite a fast-food ambience this place serves the real stuff and you needn't be afraid to drink the water.

An ethnic restaurant in a more centralized location is **Pilar's** (in the Reed Opera House, 189 Liberty St. N.E., tel. 371-1812). In addition to being convenient to downtown shopping and sightseeing, this restaurant manages to be elegant, informal, and affordable. Fresh pasta, Oregon wines, and gelato and European pastries are the focal points of the menu, but there are seafood and vegetarian specialties as well. Salmon lasagna, bouillabaisse, Greek salad, and Spanish paella (available with two hours' notice) are also featured; Pilar's affordable lunches with Mediterranean flair have the secretaries in the government buildings talking.

Another secretarial pool favorite is **Croissant Co. Bakery and Cafe** (190 High St. S.E., tel. 36-BREAD). This is the best bread in Salem, and the bagels, croissants, pumpernickel, and sourdough wheat are especially popular. Coffee and lunch are served in the bakery, plus items like pasta salads and ham and cheese croissants. Finish things off with scrumptious homebaked cookies.

Two places to kill hunger pangs in a hurry are **Los Baez** (12920 Lancaster Dr. N.E., tel. 371-3867 and 2920 Commercial St. S.E., tel. 363-3109) and **North's Chuckwagon** (694 Lancaster Dr. N.E., tel. 581-7311). Los Baez is the home of the legendary Wally Burrito, more than a meal-in-itself with chicken, beef, pork, cheese, refried beans, guacamole, cheese, and sour cream wrapped in a flour tortilla and topped with green enchilada sauce. It might not be estilo Jalisco, but at $4, it's one of the best deals you'll find north of the border.

North's Chuckwagon is an all-you-can-eat buffet with food that's good and ample enough to attract long-haul truckers. In addition, the prices here are in line with the budget of fixed-income retirees. The fare at lunch is not substantially different from the selection at dinner, but it's a buck cheaper.

When you hear that **Mazzi's** (4250 Commercial St. S.E, tel. 364-3374) is a chain with other outlets in Eugene, Portland, Anchorage, and Corvallis, you might think it's just another formula pizza joint. The only thing cliché about the restaurant, however, are the red-checkered tablecloths. You immediately sense quality when you sample a handful of Parmesan cheese from the bottle on your table. Instead of the usual heavily salted stale-tasting condiment-from-a-can which passes for cheese, these tasty morsels are as fresh as the hot French bread that accompanies every meal. The best deal for dinner is the $8.95 pasta special—a large salad, minestrone soup, spaghetti and ravioli, with spumoni ice cream for dessert. Although we know it's not the case, everything here seems homemade from scratch. Except perhaps for a pizza crust that's too doughy, Mazzi's is every traveler's Italian food fantasy.

Camping

Many of the previously mentioned Salem and vicinity excursions are close to campsites. **Silver Falls State Park** (20024 Silver Falls Highway, Sublimity 97385; tel. 873-8681) lets campers escape the summertime heat of the valley. There are 53 tent sites and nine sites for trailers or motor homes up to 35 feet long. From mid-April to early October this facility operates with electricity, piped water, and picnic tables. Showers, firewood, and a laundromat are available. Campsites are $7 and electricity and water use are $8. In addition to hiking, swimming, and biking, there are stables near the park's entrance.

On the way to Breitenbush Hot Springs, **Cleator Bend** (write: Willamette National Forest, ORE 22, Detroit 97360; tel. 854-3366) offers a campground close enough to the Breitenbush Hot Springs Retreat Center and facilities to permit day use there. Nearby, the Breitenbush River has good fishing. There's nine sites for trailers or motor homes up to 16 feet long as well as picnic

tables and firegrills. Fees are $3 a night from mid-May to late September. On Forest Service Road 46, you'll pass several other campgrounds between ORE 22 and the retreat center.

Recreation And Activities

Salem's recreational mix belies its reputation for being a town dedicated to legislation and little else. Cultural life revolves around the **Pentacle Theatre** (Box 186, Salem 97303; tel. 364-7121) located five miles west of downtown Salem. This large attractive log building set in a wooded area hosts a 10-play season that has won awards. Those who prefer more active pursuits should head to **Leierer's Outdoor LTD** (934 Hylo Rd. E, Salem, tel. 581-2803). This store offers canoe rentals on the Salem waterfront each weekend. One-day guided Santiam and Willamette river trips are also available. Rafting and kayaking equipment can be rented from **Santiam Whitewater Outfitters** (1595 Cottage St. NE, Salem, tel. 585-2628). They also provide guide service.

The **Salem Golf Club** (2025 Gold Course Rd., tel. 363-6652) is one of the best public courses in the state. Another alternative is **Santiam Golf Course** (ORE 22 and Golf Club Rd., Stayton, tel. 764-3485). If you drive 15 mintues east on ORE 22 you can look forward to combining a round of golf with a walk in the country. Low greens fees and a full-service restaurant and bar add to the pleasure.

U-pick farms are a delight from spring through fall in and around Salem. Cherries, strawberries, apples, peaches, plums, and blackberries are some of the bounty available at area farms. Early in June, the Salem *Statesman Journal* (tel. 399-6622) puts out a list of local outlets in the area (what's available where and when) entitled "Oregon Direct Market Association." The *Statesman Journal* is sold throughout the Willamette Valley and has a "weekend planner" section with entertainment listings and reviews every Friday. Although these listings focus on Salem, some attention is also given to events throughout the Willamette Valley.

The **Oregon State Fair** (2330 17th St. NE, tel. 378-3247) is an annual celebration held in Salem during the 11 days prior to Labor Day. The fair showcases Oregon agriculture, industries, tourist attractions, natural resources, government, and cultural activities. Big-name entertainment, amusement park rides, an international photography show, and a horticultural exhibit are also included in this blend of carnival and commerce.

The Salem Art Association (see "Bush House" above for address and phone) puts on the **Salem Art Fair and Festival** for several days the third week of July. The event includes 200 artists, performing arts, food, childrens' activities, a five-km run, an Oregon authors' table, wine and cheese tasting, and art techniques demonstrations.

Information And Services

The **visitor center** (1313 Mill St., tel. 581-4325) is in the first building of the Mission Mill complex. While there are no shortage of pamphlets and the volunteers are pleasant, don't expect too many authoritative answers to your questions. The staff refrains, however, from making specific recommendations for restaurants, lodging, and attractions. It's open Mon.-Fri. 9-5 p.m.

Salem provides a lot of ways to get in and out of town. The **Greyhound** station (450 Church St. NE, tel. 362-2428) is open daily 6:45 a.m.-8:45 p.m. **Amtrak** (13th and Oak streets, tel. 588-1551) sits across from Willamette University. The Salem **airport** (tel. 588-6314) is located a few miles east of downtown. Flights to Portland and the coast are provided by **Horizon Airlines** (tel. 800-547-9308). A Salem-to-Portland airport shuttle is run by **Hut Limousine Service** (tel. 362-8059). For short hops to town, there's Salem **Yellow Cab** (tel. 362-2411). Car rental companies include **National** (745 Liberty St. NE, tel. 585-4226 or 800-CAR-RENT). Mass transit in town means **Cherriotts** (216 High St., tel. 588-2877). Terminals are in front of the courthouse. Fares range from 25 to 50 cents, depending on the length of your trip, and originate from High Street. Hours of service are 6 a.m-6:15 p.m. (with buses every half hour during rush hours) Mon.-Fri. On Sat., they run every hour 7:45 a.m.-6:15 p.m.

The **post office** (1030 25th St., Salem, 97301) is open Mon.-Fri. 8-5 p.m. Other useful numbers include the **Salem Hospital Memorial Unit** (tel. 370-5701) and the **Women's Crisis Center** (tel. 399-7722).

CORVALLIS AND VICINITY

The name Corvallis refers to the city's pastoral setting in the "heart of the valley." But this appellation just tells part of the story. The influence of Oregon State University looms so large here that it might as well be called "College Town U.S.A." In fact, Cascadia, the quintessential college town in Bernard Malamud's novel *A New Life*, was modeled on Corvallis. Everything from the coffee houses and used bookstores to the pizza joints and network of biking trails seems to owe their existence to the ivy-covered walls of academe here. Beyond the campus neighborhood, the vast acreage of Oregon State University's agricultural extension complex contains facilities ranging from lambing barns to experimental forests in the Coast Range. Agriculture and engineering are emphasized in OSU's course offerings, attracting a less flamboyant student body than the more liberal arts-oriented University of Oregon in Eugene. As such, the Corvallis institution is sometimes characterized as "Oregon Straight" or "Moo U." Call it what you will, but the existence of this campus is essential to the economic base of the city, supplying recruits for local companies as well as assistance to agricultural endeavors. After gazing upon the grass seed farms surrounding the town or at the sprawling Corvallis division of the electronics industry-giant Hewlett Packard, it's evident that OSU is the straw that stirs the drink for this city of 50,000.

Corvallis is not so much a place to sightsee as a place to live. While it lacks a Golden Gate Bridge or a Space Needle, this community was selected as the second best "micropolitan" city in the country (according to the *Rating Guide to Life in America's Small Cities*, Prometheus Books, 1990). This list of 219 "mega-towns" considers environment, economics, education, housing, transportation, sophistication, recreation, public safety, and urban proximity. Aesthetic beauty, tranquility, and Corvallis's centralized location in the heart of the valley also recommend it as a base from which to explore the bird sanctuaries, the Coast Range, and nearby historic communities. In town, you'll be struck by the abundance of stately old trees, some dating back to the first pioneers who came here in 1847. Streets with wide bike lanes and scenic routes for cyclists that parallel the Willamette and Mary's rivers also contribute to the feeling of an idyllic time warp here. This is especially the case in summer when many students leave town.

SIGHTS

Campus And Downtown

In springtime, the "daffodiled" approach to Corvallis on ORE 99W is made even more glorious by the Coast Range and its highest mountain, **Mary's Peak** (4,097 feet), to the west over the hay meadows. Much of the winter, this summit is obscured by rain or fog. Your first stop should be the 500-acre Oregon State campus (follow the signs to Jefferson or Monroe streets, tel. 737-0123), home to 15,200 students. The park-like campus of this 1868 land-grant institution is the hub of activity in town, with a slew of eateries, bookstores, and craft boutiques on its periphery. Cultural activities on campus include lectures, concerts, theater productions, films, and art exhibits. Many are free and open to the public. Oregon State University publishes an activities calendar, obtainable at no cost by writing the Office of University Relations, Oregon State University, Corvallis, OR 97331.

Come to OSU mid-January through mid-March and you can watch ewes giving birth in the lambing barns. To get there from downtown Corvallis, take Harrison Street to 35th and turn left. Continue four blocks and turn right on Campus Way. Look for the white barn just up the road on the right. The campus also maintains 11,500 acres of woodlands, **McDonald Experimental Forest,** eight miles west of town just off ORE 20 (look for signs) that feature hiking trails as well as the chance to see the rare Fender's blue butterfly. The latter had been thought extinct for the last 50 years until a habitat was rediscovered here in 1990. This ecosystem serves primarily as a living laboratory for the OSU Forestry Department (for more information on the Dunn and McDonald forests, check the forest research office on campus, tel. 737-4452).

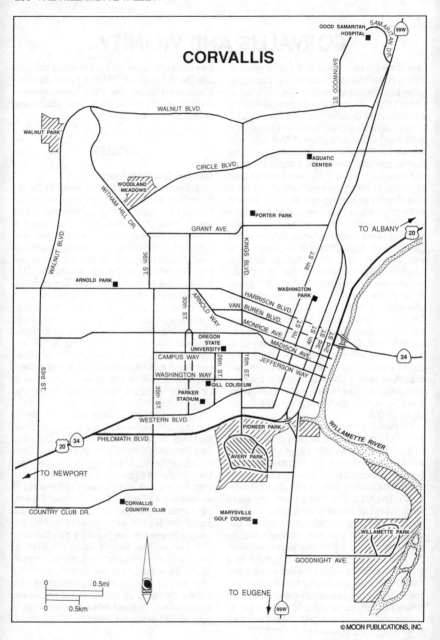

CORVALLIS

GOOD SAMARITAN
HOSPITAL

SAMARITAN DR.

SATINWOOD ST.

99W

WALNUT BLVD.

WALNUT PARK

CIRCLE BLVD.

AQUATIC
CENTER

WOODLAND
MEADOWS

WITHAM HILL DR.

PORTER PARK

TO ALBANY

20

GRANT AVE.

36th ST.

KINGS BLVD.

9th ST.

WALNUT BLVD.

ARNOLD PARK

WASHINGTON
PARK

30th ST.

ARNOLD WAY

HARRISON BLVD.

VAN BUREN BLVD.

MONROE AVE.

7th ST.

4th ST.

3rd ST.

2nd ST.

34

53rd ST.

OREGON STATE
UNIVERSITY

MADISON AVE.

CAMPUS WAY

26th ST.

15th ST.

JEFFERSON WAY

WASHINGTON WAY

35th ST.

GILL COLISEUM

PARKER
STADIUM

WESTERN BLVD.

20

34

PHILOMATH BLVD.

PIONEER PARK

WILLAMETTE RIVER

AVERY PARK

TO NEWPORT

CORVALLIS
COUNTRY CLUB

COUNTRY CLUB DR.

MARYSVILLE
GOLF COURSE

WILLAMETTE PARK

GOODNIGHT AVE.

0   0.5mi

0   0.5km

TO EUGENE

99W

© MOON PUBLICATIONS, INC.

The university facility to visit is the **Horner Museum** (in the basement of Gill Coliseum on 26th Street off Washington Street and Western Boulevard on the southwest portion of the OSU campus, tel. 754-2951). Taxidermic displays of regional animals, Oregon mineral exhibits, and pioneer and Indian artifacts (including sagebrush sandals, see "Fort Rock" in the Lake County section) highlight Oregon's largest state-owned collection of human and natural history. Although the focal point of the exposition is Oregon, the "Other Worlds" exhibits expand the scope of what many refer to as "Oregon's Smithsonian." Hours are 10 a.m.-5 p.m. Tues.-Fri., 10-2 p.m. Sat., and 2-5 p.m. Sunday. Admission is free. Before you leave, pick up the museum's pamphlets about Oregon history. These can aid you in exploring this part of the Willamette Valley. The major historic landmark in the city is the **Benton County Courthouse** (near 4th, 5th, and Monroe), the oldest functioning courthouse in the state. You can't miss its large white clock tower.

Also downtown is the **Corvallis Art Center** (7th and Madison streets, tel. 654-1551), located in the renovated 1889 Episcopal Church near Central Park. It sells local crafts and hosts weekly lunchtime concerts. Hours are noon-5 p.m. daily except Monday.

Houses, Heritage, And Hospitality

The chance to visit Oregon's greatest concentration of historic homes and covered bridges near Corvallis make it more than just another college town. In addition to the surrounding heritage-conscious communities, artifact collections and pageantry also liven up the historical landscape of Linn and Benton counties.

Three miles west of Corvallis on ORE 20 is the town of **Philomath** with the **Benton County Historical Society** (1101 Main St., Philomath, 97370; tel. 929-6230). Looms, carriages, printing presses, and other pioneer history exhibits are mildly diverting here but the real star is the 1867 Georgian-style brick structure housing the collection. Just look for the imposing building on the right-hand side of the highway on your way to the coast. Hours are 10 a.m.-4:30 p.m. Tues.-Sat. and 1-4:30 p.m. Sunday. Admission is free.

South of town one mile east of Shedd off I-5 on the banks of the Calapooia River is the **Thompson Feed Mill.** This is one of only two water-powered mills (see "Grist For The Mill" under "Medford") still operating in Oregon. Drop-in visitors can't be accommodated, but on the third weekend of each month, you'll have the opportunity to tour this 1862 landmark. Ask the Corvallis Area Chamber of Commerce for more information.

Albany

Twelve miles east of Corvallis on ORE 20 is Albany, a city which has more historic homes than any other city in Oregon. More than 350 Victorian houses here are left over from Albany's golden

Oregon State University, Corvallis

PHOTO BY HENNING LARSEN

age, 1849 to the early 20th-century, when steamships and railroads exported Willamette Valley produce and flour. Wheat was the primary crop. In 1910, 28 trains departed Albany daily and the town was a commercial hub. The **Albany Visitors Association** (435 W. 1st Ave., Albany, 97321; tel. 926-1517 or 800-526-2256) and an information gazebo (corner of 8th and Ellsworth streets) have maps and pamphlets about the three historic districts covering 100 square blocks here.

Pick up another pamphlet which lays out a self-guided **covered bridge tour**. These canopied crossings protected the wooden trusses from rain, extending the life of the bridges by several decades. By the late '30s, many of the 300 or so covered bridges in the state had fallen into disrepair or were replaced by modern steel and concrete spans. Statewide, 54 remain, with 30 in the Willamette Valley. The Albany visitors association pamphlet lays out a tour of eight bridges reachable by a 20-30 minute drive from the Albany-Corvallis area. All of these are within an eight-mile radius of **Scio**, a town 13 miles northeast of Albany on Ore 226.

The **Fire Museum** (120 34th St. S.E., tel. 967-4302) is another place in town you might want to tour independently. Call the fire department for hours and be sure to check out the 1907 steam-driven, horse-pulled engine. Tree-lovers will want to ask at the visitors association or information gazebo for the flyer on old plantings around town. These include copper beech, catalpa, elm, and sycamore trees in various gardens, and the old-fashioned rose and herb gardens near the gazebo.

Prime time for a stroll down Albany's memory lane is during the Christmas holiday season. On the second Sunday in December, annual old-fashioned **parlour tours** lets you revel in eggnog, snapping fires, and frontier hospitality as a guest at a number of Victorian homes. Visitors are welcomed by hostesses at each home and are permitted to walk through the parlor and other open rooms. Entertainment and homemade refreshments are part of the festivities. Pick up tickets at the United Presbyterian Church (330 S.W. 5th Ave.), $7.50 for adults, children under 12 free. On most Fridays and Saturdays in December, a historical district **haywagon caroling tour** (reservations, tel. 928-9634) can get you in the holiday spirit. The $3 charge includes hot beverages. Tickets are available at Flinn's Block (222 1st Ave.), where tours depart every half hour.

Other organized house tours take place every Sunday in July and August from 1-5 p.m. These are conducted by guides dressed in Gibson girl costumes. Tours leave in horse-drawn carriages from the gazebo and cost $3 per person. The summer interior tour is held on the last Saturday in July from 11 a.m.-5 p.m. Visitors are invited to walk through the gardens and complete interiors of several homes; background anecdotes are supplied by guides. Old-fashioned quilts and dolls complement the tour, as do many people in turn-of-the-century dress strolling the avenues. Admission is $6 for adults, $4 for seniors and children. At all times of the year, more than a dozen antique shops also lure visitors here. A list of these stores is available at the information gazebo.

Brownsville And Vicinity

When Albany's air is befouled by August field-burning and a pulp mill located near the I-5 entrance to town, a more pristine version of the pioneer experience awaits in Brownsville. Drive south on ORE 99E (or I-5 and take Exit 216) where ORE 228 will take you five miles east into this small town located between the Calapooia River and the Cascade foothills. This 1846 settlement began to prosper in 1862 with a woolen mill and shortly thereafter the coming of the railroad. Today, the **Linn County Historical Museum** (101 Park Ave., Brownsville, 97327; tel. 466-3390) is located in a turn-of-the-century train depot flanked by freight cars and a circus train. Inside these structures are displays focusing on the lifestyle of the area's first settlers (a barbershop, kitchen, post office, etc.), the Calapooya tribe, and local natural history. After viewing exhibits, pick up a self-guided tour brochure here Mon.-Sat. 11 a.m.-4 p.m., Sun. 1-5 p.m. May through September.

The museum also coordinates wagon ride-interludes into the past. Known as **Carriage Me Back Days,** these excursions reenact daily life from days of old. This pageant takes place the third weekend of April. Check here too about tours of the **Moyer House,** an elegant 1881 Italianate home whose high-ceilinged interior features a Carrera marble fireplace, ornate wood trim, hand-painted floral patterns, stencils on the ceilings, and oil-painted outdoor scenes on the upper panels in the bay windows. Come in June to see the strangely twisted wisteria tree on the front lawn in full bloom.

Brownsville and vicinity has other worthwhile attractions. A **pioneer cemetery** on the east end of Kirk St. shelters the grave of the last Calapooya descendant and headstones dating to 1846. A collection of rocks, Indian arrowheads, and wood carvings are housed in an interesting stone structure at the **Living Rock Studio** (ORE 228 west of town, tel. 466-5814). Admission is free and hours are Tues.-Sat. 10 a.m.-5 p.m., Sun. 2-5 p.m. The state's oldest celebration takes place here in June with the **Pioneer Picnic.** Northeast of Brownsville between Sweet Home and Lebanon is the **Council Tree,** a huge Douglas fir which served as the site of the annual gathering of the Calapooyas. This 400-year-old tree can be reached by taking ORE 228 to Sweet Home and heading north a few miles on ORE 20 to Liberty Road, which goes a mile to the turnout. The Sweet Home area is famous among rockhounds for petrified wood and agates. Finally, Brownsville and vicinity might evoke a deja vu, having provided big-screen backdrops for such recent films as *Isn't It Shocking, The Flood, The Body,* and *Stand By Me.*

Natural Attractions
West of Corvallis, two spots have drawn seekers of natural beauty and solitude for millennia. Mary's Peak and Alsea Falls are each a short drive from ORE 34, a scenic route to Waldport, which branches off of ORE 20 southwest of Philomath.
Mary's Peak (for information write: Siuslaw National Forest supervisor's office, 4077 Research Way, Box 1148, Corvallis, 97333; tel. 757-4480) sits about 12 miles southwest of Corvallis. A sign north of the highway points the way to a 10-mile drive to the top of the Coast Range's highest peak. Along the way, pretty cascades and interesting rock outcroppings and over-the-shoulder views of the Cascades on the eastern horizon intensify your anticipation of this moutaintop Calapooyan vision-quest site. When you get to the parking lot at the end of the road, the view is impressive but don't stop there. If it's a clear day, take the short walk across the meadows to either of the two summit lookouts for perspectives on Mounts Hood and Jefferson, the Three Sisters to the east, and the Pacific Ocean at the base of the Coast Range to the west. In the foreground of the Cascades, agricultural plots patchwork the verdant Willamette Valley, site of 83% of Oregon's

prime farmland. During August, huge smoke plumes rise off the valley floor, making it look like a war zone. And it is, in a sense. Despite no shots being fired, you're looking at an environmental battleground. The state's 300 million-dollar-a-year grass seed industry burns the fields here in order to kill off such diseases as ergot and nematodes. In addition, these fires kill weeds which compete with rye grass and reduce herbicide use. Field-burning also recycles nutrients back into the soil.

Nonetheless, the respiratory distress incurred upon valley residents has compelled several serious attempts to ban the practice. When smoke from grass seed fields was implicated in a 20-car pile-up on I-5 in 1989, the anti-burning campaign gained impetus. While farmers have been able to head off opposition by pointing to the agricultural benefits and cost effectiveness of field-burning, they also have been working with opponents to find alternative uses for the straw. There is optimism on both sides that straw-fueled power plants and using excess straw to make paper, fiber board, composting materials, kitty litter, and animal feed will eventually eliminate the need to burn the fields.

The outlook is not so sanguine for opponents of clearcutting on the flanks of Mary's Peak. The Forest Service claims its hands are tied, despite potential damage to watershed when erosion on denuded slopes spills into streams. The summit, thank goodness, remains untouched. A biome unique to the Coast Range exists up here with such flora as alpine phlox, purple lupine, and the noble fir. Snow, an infrequent visitor to Coast Range slopes, can often be found here in winter, even at lower elevations. In fact, the road is sometimes impassable without chains from late fall till early spring.

Farther down ORE 34 is the town of **Alsea.** The adjoining Lobster Valley area drew many countercultural refugees here in the '70s, a portion of which have remained to become farmers and craftspeople. The work of some of these local artisans is sold at **Farmer's Kitchen and Herb Garden** (185 W. Main, Alsea, 97314; tel. 487-4384). Besides the work of potters, basketmakers, and fly-fishing "tie-ers," the gardens which surround the rustic dining room here provide herbs and edible flowers for the restaurant. The greenness of the valley surrounded by Coast Range foothills recalled the lower alpine regions of Europe enough to inspire the nickname "Little Scotland."

South of here, a paved-over logging road through the tall timbers of the Coast Range can take you back to the Willamette Valley on a remote scenic byway. Look for a sign that says Alsea Falls, South Fork Road/Monroe. You'll follow the Alsea River much of the way until you come to the sloping parking lot near Alsea Falls on the east side of the road. A short trail leads you to a picturesque cascade, ideal for a picnic. (See "Willamette Bird Sanctuaries," p. 245.) The road continues through once active logging towns into farming country and the Finley Wildlife

Refuge south of Corvallis. From here, ORE 99W goes north to Corvallis or south to Junction City and Eugene.

PRACTICALITIES

Accommodations

The following accommodations chart covers area lodgings which are pretty much what you'd expect for a midsized Willamette Valley college town—lots of garden-variety motels with an occasional upscale unit for visiting parents of OSU students.

CORVALLIS ACCOMMODATIONS

Name	Address	Telephone	Price	Features
Model Motel	1480 S.W. 3rd St.	752-8756	$20-48	cable TV, pets, kitchenettes, restaurant/lounge, nonsmoking rooms
Jason Inn Motel and Restaurant	800 N.W. 9th St.	753-7326	$32-75	cable TV, pets, pool, restaurant/lounge, nonsmoking rooms, live entertainment
Valu-Inn by Nendels	101 N.W. Van Buren	752-9601	$32-65	cable TV, pets, restaurant/lounge, nonsmoking rooms
Shanico Inn	1113 N.W. 9th St.	754-7774	$37-43	wheelchair access, cable TV, pets, pool, nonsmoking rooms
Huntington Manor	3555 N.W. Harrison Blvd.	753-3735	$47	bed and breakfast, cable TV, fireplace, laundry, nonsmoking rooms
Nendels Inn	1550 N.W. 9th St.	753-9151	$47-77	wheelchair access, cable TV, pool, restaurant/lounge, laundry, nonsmoking rooms
The Hanson Country Inn	795 S.W. Hanson St.	752-2919	$50	bed and breakfast, nonsmoking rooms

late spring in the Willamette Valley, a prime camping time

PHOTO BY OREGON DEPT. OF TRANSPORTATION

Bed And Breakfast

Bed and Breakfasts can provide a dollar-wise alternative to an impersonal hotel room. There are some good choices in the Corvallis area.

Lilla's Bed and Breakfast and Cafe (206 7th Ave. S.W., Albany, tel. 928-9437) is a century-old house rich in Victorian nuance. The rates are $45-55 for two, including a full breakfast. Lilla's is also reputed to be a good place to have Sunday brunch or dinner (not included with lodging).

In Corvallis, the **Madison Inn Bed and Breakfast** (660 S.W. Madison Ave., Corvallis, 97333; tel. 757-1274) is a 1903 vintage home on the National Register of Historic places; it's across from Central Park and within walking distance of OSU and downtown. For $41-44 double occupancy, you can enjoy such comforts of home as patchwork quilts, antique furniture, fresh flowers, sitting rooms filled with books, complimentary wine, and breakfast with home-baked goodies. Reserve this one a month in advance.

Camping

Camping in this part of the Willamette Valley can be delightful, especially in late spring and early autumn.

In Corvallis, your best best from April to late October is **Willamette City Park** (Corvallis Dept. of Parks and Recreation, Box 1083, Corvallis, 97339; tel. 757-6918). To get there drive a mile south of the city on ORE 99W, then go a half mile east on S.E. Goodnight Road to the park. For $4 a night, you can enjoy one of the 25 sites for tents and RVs serviced by vault toilets, piped water, and a small outdoor kitchen. If you need civilized comforts, a store, cafe, and laundromat are a mile away. Trails to the nearby Willamette River yield birdwatching and fishing opportunities in this 40-acre park.

Food

Just because *Pacific Northwest Magazine* in its 1990 restaurant poll mentioned several Corvallis area-eateries as among the elite of the state, don't get the impression that the town is full of prohibitively priced dining spots. The city's Eden-like setting is ideal for picnics, and there's no shortage of places to get good grub no matter what your tastes or budget might be. In addition to the sub shops, Chinese takeout places, and pizza joints opposite the campus, the eat 'n' run for lunch bunch will especially appreciate the **Albany Farmer's Market** (Water and Broadalbin streets, Albany), a short drive from Corvallis. From 9 a.m.-noon on Saturdays, June through Thanksgiving, enjoy the Willamette Valley's bountiful harvests of corn, fruit, garlic, peppers, or whatever else happens to be in season. There are also cut flowers on sale as well as such regional specialties as the mild-tasting large-cloved elephant garlic, marionberries (a blackberry, raspberry, and gooseberry hybrid developed by OSU with a tart taste), and dried jumbo Brooks prunes. Best of all, you're buying direct from the grower at a fraction of supermarket cost.

Another Albany tradition is **Novak's Hungarian Paprikas** (2835 Santiam Highway, Albany, tel. 967-9488). Authentic kolbasz (a spicy sausage), stuffed cabbage, and chicken paprika exemplify the earthy eastern European fare. Try chocolate cake with apricot preserves for dessert. Lunch and dinner are served Sun.-Fri., dinner only on Saturday from 4-9 p.m.

Back in Corvallis, start the day at **Cafe Croissant** (215 S.W. 5th, Corvallis, tel. 752-5111) with croissants (selected as the best in town by a local publication) or homemade granola. For lunch there's quiche, soups, salads, and lasagna. Fresh vegetables from the owner's garden are a special treat in summer as are the array of muffins and pastries from the in-house bakery any time of the year.

Another place guaranteed not to go against the grain is the **New Morning Bakery** (231 S.W. 2nd St., Corvallis, tel. 754-1081 and 1870 S.W. 3rd, tel. 757-1821). Try the honey cinnamon rolls here or choose from over a dozen varieties of cookies. It's close enough to Riverfront Park on the Willamette for a picnic, which is a good idea given New Morning's limited seating. Take along some Italian flat bread or French bread for your outing. Oregon-made jams and homemade soups are also available here.

Near Central Park behind the Benton County Courthouse is **Oscar's** (559 Monroe Ave., tel. 753-7444), another picnic-in- the-park and breakfast favorite of the locals. Design-your-own-omelettes can be ordered throughout the day and quiche, salads, and sandwiches are served after 11 a.m.

Perhaps the best place to provision a picnic is **First Alternative Co-op** (1007 S.E. 3rd St., Corvallis, tel. 753-3115), which you'll encounter as you come into town via ORE 99W from the south. The organic produce section is a marvel and the largely volunteer staff can give excellent leads on what's happening in the area. Across from the co-op, **Papa's Pizza** is a better-than-average chain. The best pie in town, however, is at **Woodstock's Pizza Parlor** (945 N.W. Kings Blvd., Corvallis, tel. 752-5151).

Another spot for those who place a premium on wholesome fare is **Nearly Normal** (corner of Monroe and 15th, Corvallis, tel. 753-0791), whose mismatched kitschy decor does justice to its name. Low prices and huge helpings reflect the predominantly student clientele who savor egg and stir-fry dishes, burritos, and falafels. There's live music on Wednesday, Thursday, and Saturday, and an entertaining waitstaff every day of the week.

Two Corvallis restaurants which were tops in their respective categories in the aforementioned magazine poll were the **Gables** (1121 N.W. 9th St., Corvallis, tel. 752-3364) and **Papagayo's** (550 N.W. Harrison, Corvallis, tel. 757-8188). The Gables is full of students and parents on graduation day enjoying prime rib, fresh seafood, lamb chops, and other traditional standbys. This is the most expensive place in town (though early-bird specials can make things more affordable), but the understated home-like elegance and venerable cuisine make it perfect for an occasion. To get there, follow Harrison to 9th Street; the restaurant is located a half mile west of ORE 99W.

Exquisite Mexican paintings and hand-woven tapestries on the walls prepare you for something unique even before you sit down at the table at Papagayos. The menu itself features weekly specials rarely seen north of the border to complement permanent entrees like enchiladas and chile rellenos. Whether it's pozole (a stew with hominy, chicken, and pork covered with shredded cabbage, lettuce, and salsa) or black bean chili, there's always something for the Mexican food maven with a sense of adventure. Often what might seem innovative here actually draws from the *real* cuisine of the country as opposed to the Tex-Mex-influenced fare found in the majority of U.S. places.

In this vein, Papagayo's uses a delicious gruyere-like cheese from Chihuahua in their chile rellenos. This is the way it's done in most of Mexico where they've never heard of monterey jack, and after one bite of queso Chihuahua, you'll see why. Fresh locally grown peppers, barbecuing over mesquite, and serving the traditional mole (a chocolate and chile sauce over turkey or chicken) in honor of the Christmas holiday season are also noteworthy. Not only is the food extraordinary, but the portions are sufficiently ample to inspire disbelief at the $10 average dinner tab.

Events

Of the many events in Corvallis, the premier celebration has to be the **Corvallis Fall Festival.** This gathering of exceptional artists and craftspeople is now in its second decade. Nonstop varied entertainment and a block of food concessions, including an Oregon wine garden, backdrop this hotbed of creative ferment from 10 a.m.-6 p.m. the last weekend in September. Contact the chamber of commerce for more information about this event which takes place in Central Park between 6th and 8th, Monroe and Madison).

The OSU **basketball** season at Gill Coliseum (26th and Washington, tel. 754-2951) is a favorite wintertime activity here because the Beavers are a perennial PAC-10 championship contender. Tickets begin at $6.50.

On the first full weekend of June, **Lebanon** celebrates its **Strawberry Festival** (for information write: 104 Park St., Lebanon, 97355; tel. 258-7164). This town southeast of Albany off ORE 20 has become famous for its annual *Guinness* world record-sized strawberry shortcake whose 17,000 pieces are dished out at the climax of the event.

On the third weekend in June, the 100-year-old **Brownsville Pioneer Picnic** features an old-time fiddlers jamboree and a tug-o-war involving large local teams. There's also a parade, a carnival, crafts fair, a foot race, and a tour of historic homes (for information see "Linn County Historical Museum" above). The three-day celebration is held near the spot where a ferry plied the Calapooia in 1846, now part of ten-acre Pioneer Park, located off Main Street at the end of Park Avenue. This event begins every morning with a wagon train breakfast.

Albany's **World Championship Timber Carnival** takes place from July 1-July 4. Contact the visitors association for more information. Admission is $6 for adults and $4 for children to see three days of logging-related competition. While such events as speed-climbing, springboard-chopping, and logrolling have little place in the increasingly mechanized world of modern timber management, they're still fun to watch.

Information And Services

The **Corvallis Area Chamber of Commerce** (420 N.W. 2nd, Corvallis, 97330; tel. 757-1505) has a driving tour brochure of the area to supplement this section. **Greyhound** and **Valley Retriever** (153 N.W. 4th, Corvallis, tel. 757-1797) operate every day with routes north, south, and west to the coastal town of Newport.

The main **post office** (311 S.W. 2nd St., Corvallis, 97330) is open 9-5 weekdays. The **Parks and Recreation Department** (tel. 757-6418) can steer you to numerous recreation facilities in and around the area, including an indoor rock-climbing gym, tennis courts, and city parks. **Trysting Tree Golf Course** (ORE 34 and N.E. Electric Rd., tel. 752-3332) is located across the river from downtown Corvallis. **Good Samaritan Hospital** (3600 Samaritan Dr., tel. 757-5111) has 24-hour emergency room service.

To catch up on local events, read the *Corvallis Gazette Times* (Box 368, Corvallis, tel. 753-2641). KOAC 550 on the AM dial is an excellent public radio station with a top-notch news team and excellent classical music offerings. It serves much of western Oregon and can be picked up in remote coastal and mountain communities.

Corvallis has many fine bookstores. Among them, the **Book Bin** (351 N.W. Jackson, Corvallis, tel. 752-0040 and 2305 Monroe, tel. 753-TEXT) and **Avocet Used Books** (614 S.W. 3rd) have good selections of regional titles.

EUGENE AND VICINITY

The pioneers who established Eugene's townsite in 1864 were motivated by visions of material prosperity derived from thick forests and good soil for farming. By contrast, many of the modern emigrants over the last few decades haven't come here primarily to get rich. The local job market, even when big timber is booming, is cyclical at best. Instead, a garden-like setting, good schools, and a recreational and cultural mix unsurpassed by any other city of comparable size explain Eugene's present-day allure.

The Willamette River curves around the northwest quarter of the community and abundant trees and flowers dot the cityscape. From an elevated perch you can see the Coast and Cascade ranges beckoning you to beach and mountain playgrounds little more than an hour away. In town, a world-renowned Bach Festival and other big-time cultural events are showcased in the Hult Center, praised by the *L.A. Times* as having the best acoustics on the West Coast. The University of Oregon campus provides another forum for the best in art and academe while its Hayward Field track has been the site of the U.S. Olympic Trials several times.

Outdoor gatherings such as Saturday Market and the Oregon Country Faire bring the community together in a potlatch of homegrown edibles, arts, and crafts. You'll also see Eugenians outside indulging in such local passions as jogging, biking, basketball, and gardening. Less evident to those passing through might be the huge network of environmental organizations and other outlets of political and social activism. In this vein it should be mentioned that Eugene has more human service organizations per capita than any city in the United States. The 110,000 people who live in Eugene combine with neighboring Springfield's population of 41,000 to make up the second largest residential center in the state. Visitors from rural Lane County flock to the Eugene/Springfield area on weekends to shop at Valley River Center, see a movie, attend a convention or simply go "garage saleing" (this place seems to have more flea markets than just about anywhere!).

Eugene has also earned the reputation as the timber capitol of the world. Situated between the Willamette and Siuslaw national forests, the area is the major point of origin for domestic lumber sales. The mill-choked main drags of Springfield once compelled writer Janice Rule to deride the city as Eugene's "ugly half-sister," but the traveler can appreciate some good dining spots and city parks there as well as the gateway to the scenic McKenzie River National Recreation Area. In addition to the timber industry, the region's fortunes rise and fall with the University of Oregon, the single largest employer and a leading recipient of federal government grants.

The activities of another economic mainstay, the multimillion-dollar grass seed industry, contributes to summertime air-quality emergencies with field-burning and allergy-causing pollens. Air pollution from this source, woodstoves, automobiles, and industrial emissions constitute the major noticeable excess in a town noted for a

PHOTO BY BRUCE BUSH

The Eugene Skinner cabin sits under a canopy of fall foliage at Skinner's Butte.

Evening falls over Spencer's Butte and Eugene.

PHOTO BY JURETTA NIDEVER

health-conscious, progressive outlook. More often than not, a cleansing rain saves the day here for those with sensitive respiratory systems.

In an era when expressions like "livability" and "quality of life" exist primarily as media buzzwords, these elusive entities have taken tangible form in Eugene, Oregon.

SIGHTS

Skinner's Butte

A good place to get oriented in Eugene visually as well as historically is Skinner's Butte. If you look north from most anywhere downtown you'll see this landmark. A beautiful park is located at the butte's northern base fronting the Willamette River. It's reachable by following the Scenic Drive signs to the river via High Street. This riverfront site served as a dock for pioneer sternwheelers and was where founding father Eugene Skinner ran a ferry service for farmers living north of the river. Eugene tried to become a major shipping port, but the upper Willamette was uncharted, as well as too shallow and meandering. In addition, sunken logs, gravel bars, and submerged trees and rocks made steamboat navigation difficult. As a result, Ben Holladay's Oregon and California Railroad became Eugene's most effective mode of transport in 1871.

By following the Scenic Drive signs from the park or driving north on Lincoln Street (you can

also walk up from the south side in 15 minutes), you can get to the top of the butte and enjoy the vantage point from which Eugene Skinner surveyed the landscape in June, 1846. Calapooya Indians called this promontory "Yapoah," meaning "High Place," and used it for ceremonial dances. While a city of 110,000 people (261,000 in the greater Eugene-Springfield area) has grown up in the once pristine valley below, you can still see the Coastal and Cascade ranges on a clear day as well as pockets of greenery throughout the city. You can also spot another good reference point in your orientation, **Spencer's Butte,** looming above the southern hills four miles away. Eugene Skinner, like so many Oregon Trail-era migrants, wanted to take advantage of the federal government's 640-acre land giveaway offer to pioneers, so he staked a claim from the banks of the Willamette to present-day 8th Avenue and from Monroe Street to the river on Hilyard Street. He built his shelter on 2nd and Lincoln streets and later opened up Lane County's first trading post here.

Another historic house in the area is the 1888 vintage **Shelton McMurphey House** (perhaps the inspiration for the name of local author Ken Kesey's main character in *One Flew Over the Cuckoo's Nest)* on the lower south slope of the butte. The aqua-colored Victorian is the most eye-catching of some 2,000 designated historic properties in the city. During the third week of May the interior of this and other landmarks in the east Skinner's Butte neighborhood may be toured

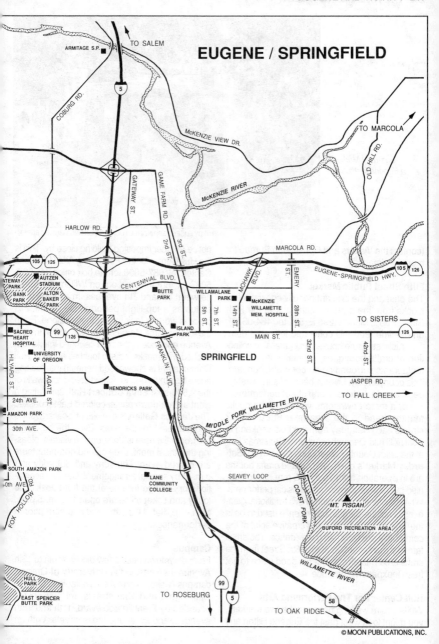

EUGENE / SPRINGFIELD

TO SALEM

ARMITAGE S.P.

COBURG RD.

5

McKENZIE VIEW DR.

GATEWAY ST.

GAME FARM RD.

HARLOW RD.

2nd ST.

3rd ST.

McKENZIE RIVER

TO MARCOLA

OLD HILL RD.

MARCOLA RD.

105 126

CENTENNIAL BLVD.

EUGENE-SPRINGFIELD HWY.

105 126

GATEWAY PARK

BANK PARK

AUTZEN STADIUM

ALTON BAKER PARK

BUTTE PARK

WILLAMALANE PARK

MOHAWK BLVD.

EMERY ST.

28th ST.

32nd ST.

42nd ST.

TO SISTERS

126

McKENZIE WILLAMETTE MEM. HOSPITAL

5th ST.

7th ST.

14th ST.

SACRED HEART HOSPITAL

99 126

ISLAND PARK

MAIN ST.

SPRINGFIELD

JASPER RD.

TO FALL CREEK

UNIVERSITY OF OREGON

HILYARD ST.

AGATE ST.

FRANKLIN BLVD.

HENDRICKS PARK

24th AVE.

AMAZON PARK

30th AVE.

MIDDLE FORK WILLAMETTE RIVER

SOUTH AMAZON PARK

50th AVE.

FOX HOLLOW RD.

LANE COMMUNITY COLLEGE

SEAVEY LOOP

COAST FORK

MT. PISGAH

BUFORD RECREATION AREA

99

5

TO ROSEBURG

WILLAMETTE RIVER

HULL PARK

EAST SPENCER BUTTE PARK

58

TO OAK RIDGE

Saturday Market, a Eugene institution

PHOTO BY EUGENE SPRINGFIELD CONVENTION AND VISITORS BUREAU

(contact the Visitors and Convention Bureau for more information).

Fifth Street Public Market

The past and the present happily coexist a few blocks from the butte's south flank at the Fifth Street Public Market (296 E. 5th, tel. 484-0383), an old-time feed mill converted into an atrium. This rustic structure houses an impressive collection of crafts boutiques, specialty stores, and restaurants surrounding an open-air courtyard. This courtyard is a favorite haunt of sun worshippers, people-watchers, and street performers.

For a more downhome version of the public market, head to the area near 8th and Oak streets each Saturday from the first weekend in April until mid-December (when a Christmas Fair at the Lane County Fairgrounds takes over). **Saturday Market's** open-air food and crafts booths are in operation from 10 a.m.-5 p.m., accompanied by "new vaudeville" and musical performers. While the latest incarnation of this traditional gathering is not the bargain basement it used to be in the '70s, the good vibes and creative spirit of the community are still in ample evidence. The small farmer's market set up across 8th Street from the crafts area has always been a good place to get fresh inexpensive produce.

Hult Center For The Performing Arts

While you're walking between the two markets, you might look west past the Eugene Hilton and notice another imposing building close by. This is the Hult Center for the Performing Arts (1 Eugene Center, tel. 687-5000 for the box office, tel. 687-5087 for tour information) on Willamette Street between 6th and 7th avenues. In addition to its status as a top-flight performance venue, this place is worth a look for aesthetics alone. From the frog and troll statues that greet you at the 6th Avenue entrance to the high-ceilinged interior bedecked with masks, artistic touches abound. Hult Center talent is showcased beneath interlocking acoustic panels on the domed ceiling and walls of the 2,500-seat **Silva Concert Hall**, simulating a giant upside-down pastel-colored Easter basket. The **Jacobs Gallery**'s exhibits of local artwork is another feast for the eyes. Even the building's bathroom tile here is done up in a visually pleasing theatrical motif. Free guided one-hour tours are offered every Thursday and Saturday at 1 p.m. or by special arrangement. Call for reservations or arrange for one at the front desk. The lobby and ticket office are open 11 a.m.-5 p.m., Mon.-Fri., Sat. 11-3 p.m., and one hour prior to performances.

Campus

From downtown head a few blocks south to 13th Avenue then east to the **University of Oregon** campus (visitor information available at Oregon Hall, Agate and 13th streets, tel. 346-3814) bounded by Franklin Boulevard, 11th and 18th avenues, and Alder and Moss streets. With an enrollment around 20,000 students plus multimillion-dollar federal endowments in the upper echelon of American university funding, you might be expecting a bureaucratic, impersonal feeling here. Instead, the grounds of the campus are graced by architecturally inviting buildings dating back to the school's creation in the 1870s as well as 400 varieties of trees. **Deady Hall**, the oldest building on campus, was built in 1876. This bucolic campus has often been selected by Hollywood to portray the ivy-covered halls of academe, most notably in the campus comedy *Animal House.* The quiet and tranquility of the campus is sustained by banning vehicular traffic beyond 13th and Kincaid streets.

If you wander the north part of the U of O complex toward Franklin Boulevard, in between the schools of law and journalism majestic and rare trees (including a Chinese dawn redwood) dot the landscape. Interesting outdoor sculptures also liven up a stroll of the campus.

Deady Hall, the oldest building on the U of O campus

A "must" on any campus tour is the **Museum of Art** (next to the U of O library, tel. 346-3027). The highlight is a second-floor nationally renowned Oriental collection, but the revolving paintings and photography exhibits on the first floor are also usually worthwhile. A secret hideaway on the first floor is a courtyard which could have been taken out of a charming older neighborhood in Paris. You might also stop at the excellent crafts gift shop to the left of the door as you enter the museum. There's no admission charge to the museum and the hours are noon-5 p.m. Wed.-Sun, Sept.-June. If you're so inclined, call the museum office about free one-hour tours. Speaking of tours, you can get a free **campus tour** weekdays 10:30 a.m. and 2:30 p.m. from Oregon Hall. You're better off, however, just picking up the free map and setting your own pace.

Another museum here is dedicated to natural history (between Agate and Moss and 15th streets, tel. 686-3024). Oregon prehistory is showcased here with artifacts from digs in eastern Oregon and bird and mammal fossils from around the state.

Next to the Museum of Art is the **U of O Library.** On the second floor the **Oregon Collection** (tel. 346-3468) has books and periodicals about the state in open stacks—a great place to plan trips or learn about the region.

PARKS

Hendricks Park

Beyond the campus and downtown, Eugene and vicinity has five parks which rank among its preeminent attractions (other parks are mentioned in "Activities And Recreation"). About two miles east of the campus on a forested ridgeline is Hendricks Park, home to 850 naturally occurring rhododendrons and azaleas and around 10,000 hybrids. There are several ways to get to the park, but the easiest route is turning from Fairmount Boulevard onto Summit Drive, or take Lane Transit bus #27/Fairmont, disembark at Summit Drive, and hike on up the hill a quarter mile. Two parking lots accommodate cars; one near the picnic area of stoves and tables, the other at the upper entrance on Sunset Boulevard. The rhododendron gardens are in their glory during May with 15-20-foot-high plants in shades of pink, red, yellow, and purple. Even though the display declines by late June, it's always a great place to stroll. Gorgeous views of the city can be enjoyed from the west end of the garden, and tree-shaded footpaths lead to benches located in secluded cul-de-sacs of the hillside.

The Rose Garden

Another floral display is located at the Jesse Owens Memorial Rose Garden at the end of Jefferson Street along the banks of the Willamette River. Thirty varieties of roses here peak in June and last until fall. Along with 3,000 roses, tremendous old cherry and oak trees also command attention.

Ridgeline Trail

The South Hills Ridgeline Trail is only minutes from downtown Eugene and offers wildlife-watching opportunities (look for deer, tree frogs, garter snakes, and all kinds of birds) and more species of fern than perhaps any single spot in Oregon. In addition, old growth Douglas fir and the lovely and increasingly hard to find Calypso orchid grow here. A pamphlet listing all the trailside flora and fauna and their months of bloom is put out by Eugene Parks and Recreation Cultural Services (22 W. 27th Ave., Eugene, 97401; tel. 687-5333). The trail is seldom steep and has some spectacular views of the city through clearings. A spur route leads up to the highest point in Eugene, **Spencer's Butte,** (elevation 2,052 feet) via a steep and often muddy trail (If you like seclusion, however, this route might be preferable to the ones outlined in the next paragraph). The Ridgeline Trail can be reached from several points, including Dillard Road; near the corner of Fox Hollow and Christenson roads; near Willamette and 52nd; from Spencer's Butte parking area (see below); and off Blanton Road near 40th.

Spencer's Butte

The Spencer's Butte parking lot is nearby. Just drive south on Willamette Street until you see the signs on the left side of the highway. According to one legend, the butte was named after a 19th-century English trapper killed by Indian arrows. The Calapooyan name "Chamate" meant "Rattlesnake Mountain." An 1848 account (from Batterns DeGuerre's *Ten Years In Oregon*) of the view from the summit reads as follows:

On one hand was the vast chain of Cascade Mountains, Mt. Hood looming in solitary grandeur far above its fellows; on the other hand was the Umpqua Mountains, and a little farther on the coast ridge. Between these lay the whole magnificent panorama of the Willamette Valley, with its ribbon streams and carpet-like verdure.

The view today has all of the above but there are some differences. Below the north summit you look down on Eugene/Springfield with Fern Ridge Reservoir in the northwest toward Junction City. Beyond the reservoir you can sometimes see Mary's Peak. Other Cascade mountains not noted in the previous account include Mt. Jefferson, Mt. Washington, the Three Sisters, and Mt. Bachelor. To the southeast Creswell and the hills around Cottage Grove are visible.

The two main trails to the top vary in difficulty. If you bear left immediately after leaving the parking lot, you'll come to the route known among the locals as "The Face." This trail is shorter in distance than its saddleback counterpart, but much steeper and littered with boulders and, sometimes, muddy spots. It can be scaled in forty minutes by anyone in reasonable health. The main trail is a straight shot from the parking lot, looping up and around the steep hills. These inclines are broken up by flat stretches. Allow about an hour for the ascent. While signs caution against rattlesnakes, falling limbs, and poison oak, the only one to really worry about is the three shiny leaves of the notorious poison oak, particularly on the flanks of the summit. A mixed conifer forest featuring old growth Douglas fir with an understory of numerous ferns and wildflowers will usher you along. Die-hard hikers equipped with Sorel boots or other durable footwear will enjoy "shooting the butte" in the snow. A "snow-shoot" takes you up into a winter wonderland with trails wreathed by old growth fir dusted with snowflakes.

Mount Pisgah

Mt. Pisgah (Box 5601, Eugene, 97405; tel. 747-3817) features a mile hike to a marvelous viewpoint and an arboretum on the lower slopes. The arboretum (plants and bird lists are often available at the visitor center, open weekends) sponsors such events as a fall fair dedicated to area mushrooms and a spring wildflower show and plant sale (dates vary so call ahead). Mt. Pisgah

WILLAMETTE BIRD SANCTUARIES

Several bird sanctuaries were established in between Salem and Eugene by the federal government in the mid-1960s because of the encroachment of urbanization and agriculture on the winter habitat of the dusky Canada goose. This species now comes to **Baskett Slough National Wildlife Refuge** (N.W.R.) west of Salem, **Ankeny N.W.R.** southwest of the capitol, and **Finley N.W.R.** south of Corvallis each October after summering in Alaska's Copper River Delta. Refuge ecosystems mesh forest, cropland, and riparian environments to attract hummingbirds, swans, geese, sandhill crances, ducks, egrets, herons, plovers, sandpipers, hawks and other raptors, wrens, woodpeckers, and dozens of other avian ambassadors. A pamphlet, *Birds of Willamette Valley Refuges,* details the best months to birdwatch, frequency of sightings, and location of hundreds of kinds of birds. It can be obtained by writing the Refuge Manager, Western Oregon Refuges, 26208 Finley Refuge Rd., Corvallis, 97337; tel. 757-7236.

In the interest of maintaining the sanctity of the birds' habitat, the refuges restrict birders by closing some trails in winter; other trails farther from feeding grounds are kept open year-round. While Finley and Baskett N.W.R.s along 99W are more user-friendly to hikers than Ankeny (Ankeny Hill Exit, off I-5, six miles south of Salem, then drive Buena Vista Road through the refuge), it's still advisable to pick up refuge maps in the drop boxes at each locale to find your way.

A hike which can be enjoyed any time of year is Finley N.W.R.'s one-mile **Woodpecker Loop.** A variety of plant communities exist here due to Calapooyan field-burning followed by pioneer logging and cattle grazing; the loop's diversity is also attributable to its location on the border between the Coast Range and the Willamette Valley. Forests of oak, Douglas fir, and a mixed deciduous grove combine with marshes to provide a wide range of habitats. Look for the rare pileated woodpecker in the deciduous forest. The loop's trailhead is reached by taking 99W to Refuge Road. Look for the footpath on the right after driving three miles. A drop box has a pamphlet with pictures and information on the birds, wildlife, and plant communities here.

Another trail that's always open is the one-mile **Baskett Butte Loop.** Along with birdwatching, Willamette Valley views can be enjoyed from an elevated perch. To get there from the junction of ORE 22 and ORE 99W, drive north on 99W almost two miles and turn left onto Colville Road and drive one mile to the trailhead on the right. The path climbs gently above the Morgan Lake trailhead.

can be reached by following East 30th Avenue from Eugene past Lane Community College to the I-5 interchange. Cross the bridge over the freeway, turn left, and take the next right onto Seavey Loop Road. You'll cross the coast fork of the Willamette River and then turn left onto a gravel road (look for the Mt. Pisgah signs) which leads to the trailhead; the arboretum is just beyond the parking lot.

The path to the 1,514-foot-high Mt. Pisgah summit has a dearth of trees, enabling hikers to enjoy vistas of the Willamette Valley on the way up. At the top an unforgettable perspective of the valley in the foreground and the Three Sisters and other Cascade peaks in the distance awaits. In addition, installation of a monument is underway on the summit honoring, author Ken Kesey's son and other members of the ill-fated U of O wrestling team who perished in a van accident (two miles to the east in **Pleasant Hill** is the home of Oregon's most celebrated author). This memorial consists of a sculpture with a relief map depicting the mountains, rivers, towns, and other landmarks in the Eugene area. Supporting the map are three five-sided bronze columns upon which the geologic history of Oregon over the past 200 million years is portrayed, using images of more than 300 fossil specimens.

Those making the climb in August will find blackberry bushes for browsing along the way. If you're perspiring from the climb, when you're back on the valley floor head south of the trailhead to the adjoining **Buford Recreation Area** for a dip in the cool waters of the Willamette River. The banks of the coast fork here also have a great profusion of blackberry bushes.

ACTIVITIES AND RECREATION

Eugene's identity is rooted in its reputation as "Tracktown U.S.A.," and also in its superlative

Parks and Recreation Department. Articles in *Money* and *Self* magazines in 1988 cited such recreational priorities when ranking the city as America's sixth best place to live and the best place to work out in the country respectively. The *Self* article went into depth about the 100 miles of bike paths, back-country cycling minutes from downtown, and track events.

But wait, there's more. Hiking trails, whitewater rafting, golf courses, and other outdoor pursuits are complemented by more sedate activities like wine-tasting, scenic drives, and museums. The following listings scratch the surface of this array: More detailed information can be culled from the Eugene/Springfield Convention and Visitors Bureau or Eugene Parks and Recreation (see "Information and Services" below).

Highbrow Haunts
Maude Kerns Art Center (1910 15th Ave., Eugene, tel. 345-1571) is near the U of O campus.

Alton Baker Park offers miles of biking along the Willamette River.

Set in an old church, this gallery is dedicated to contemporary art of nationally known as well as regionally prominent artists. The center is open 10 a.m.-5 p.m. Mon.-Sat., 1-5 p.m. Sunday. Admission is free.

Hinman Vineyards (27012 Briggs Hill Rd., Eugene, tel. 345-1945) is a perfect place to spend a summer's afternoon. The winery is 15 miles southwest of downtown and is open noon-5 p.m. daily. Drive west on 11th Avenue, turn left on Bertelson Road, then right on Spencer Creek Road. A left down Briggs Hill Road takes you to the tasting room located on a hillside overlooking a valley.

The Lane County Historical Museum (740 W. 13th Ave., Eugene, tel. 687-4239) can be found next to the fairgrounds. Just look for the steam donkey on the front lawn. There are other 19th-century logging vehicles on display and period rooms. Hours are 10 a.m.-4 p.m. Tues.-Fri., 11-4 p.m. Sat.-Sunday. Admission is $1, seniors 75 cents; children under 18 pay 50 cents.

Water, Water, Everywhere
Alton Baker Park along the Willamette, and the **Millrace Canal** which parallels the river for three or four miles, provide escapes from Eugene's main downtown thoroughfares. The millrace is easily accessed from the U of O campus by crossing Franklin Boulevard. Rent canoes or kayaks from **EMU Waterworks Company** (1395 Franklin Blvd., tel. 346-4386), run by U of O students. The rental rates are $3.60 an hour on the millrace, $14 a day off the millrace with a $30 deposit. Hours are Mon.-Fri. 12:30-dusk; Sat.-Sun. 11 a.m.-dusk, March through October. Alton Baker Park can be entered from below the Ferry Street Bridge. In addition to running and biking paths, there's also **Autzen Stadium,** home of the U of O football ducks (and occasionally rock concerts) and the **Willamette Science and Technology Center** (2300 Centennial Blvd., tel. 484-9027). The highlight of the revolving exhibits at the center is the planetarium shows given at 3 p.m. Due to a financial crisis (explaining a $4 admission fee), the museum might be closing temporarily or cutting back in hours, so call ahead. Further west on the Willamette is the **Riverhouse Outdoor Program** office (301 N. Adams St., tel. 687-5329), headquarters of the Parks Department outdoor program and a roped-off swimming area.

(top left) the Oregon Caves (Oregon Tourism Division); (top right) Hat Rock, Umatilla County (Oregon State Highways Division); (bottom) the painted hills of eastern Oregon (Frank Long)

Reservoirs (for information contact the U.S. Army Corps Public Information, Box 2946, Portland, 97208-2946) beyond downtown Eugene provide a wide range of recreation. The one closest to town is **Fern Ridge.** Camp, picnic, swim, water-ski, sail, or watch wildlife here. In addition, fishing for crappie, cutthroat trout, large-mouth black bass, and catfish is excellent in early spring. When the Long Tom River was dammed in 1941, Fern Ridge Lake was created. Its southeast shore was designated a wildlife refuge in 1979. To reach the lake drive 10 miles east of downtown on W. 11th Avenue (ORE 126) towards Veneta, or take Clear Lake Road off of ORE 99W. There are marinas on the south or north shores especially coveted by sailboaters and sailboarders. The lake is drained in winter to allow for flood control, but the resulting marsh (and wildlife refuge) hosts tree frogs, newts, ospreys, rare purple martins (in spring), blacktailed deer, red foxes, beavers, muskrats, minks, pond turtles, and great blue herons. The wildlife area is closed to the public from January 1 to March 15 for the protection of wintering birds.

Dorena Reservoir is 30 minutes south of Eugene and has camping, fishing, and boating. The Army Corps dammed the Row River to create the facility, which can be reached by driving south on I-5 or ORE 99 for 20 miles to Cottage Grove. Then head under the bridge below I-5's Cottage Grove Exit and pick up on Mosby Creek Road (this is a mountain road, so check snow conditions) which goeseight miles east to Dorena Lake. En route several covered bridges in this area can be visited. In addition, Dorena Lake is the gateway to the **Bohemia mining district** (see "Events" below) where there are old abandoned mines. Check the Cottage Grove Pioneer Museum (Buch and H streets, no phone) for more information on these attractions or contact the Cottage Grove Chamber of Commerce (710 Row River Rd., Box 487, Cottage Grove, 97424; tel. 942-2411). The ranger station in Cottage Grove (tel. 942-5591) has a map of a 70-mile Bohemia driving loop as well as updates on snow conditions.

An hour to the east of **Fall Creek Reservoir** off ORE 126 is **Cougar Reservoir and hot springs.** Take ORE 126 to Cougar Reservoir Road and drive a few miles down and park. The springs can be reached by hiking to the end of a short trail.

PHOTO BY ANGELA ENGLERT
An angler tries his luck at Dorena Lake.

This trail overlooks a steep drop-off so be careful. The several pools in this tranquil forest setting can be overcrowded on weekends.

Off The Beaten Track
Along with the well-known hiking areas described above, the nearby Cascade and Coast ranges also have some recently developed hidden gems thanks, paradoxically, to such extractive industries as logging and gravel. The industrial "cat" trails which once cut a swath in these forest are today maintained (and sometimes paved over) by the Forest Service for access to natural wonders. Two such places are Kentucky Falls and a grove of the tallest trees in the Northwest.

Picturesque **Kentucky Falls** is set in an old growth forest on the upper slopes of the Coast Range. To get there from downtown Eugene, drive 35 miles west on ORE 126 to the Whiteaker Creek Recreation Area on the south side of the road, approximately six miles west of the Walton Store and post office. The route to Kentucky Falls

(top) fishing a quiet Oregon lake, early morning (Oregon Tourism Division); (bottom left) Cannon Beach (Oregon Tourism Division); (bottom right) Natural Bridges Cove (Ted Long Ishikawa)

winds through the clear-cut lower slopes of 3,700-foot-high **Roman Nose Mountain** (the highest peak in this part of the Coast Range).

From Whiteaker Creek Recreation Area drive one mile south and make a right turn. Then in another one mile bear left on Dunn Ridge Road. In about seven miles you'll turn left onto a back road to Reedsport. Several miles later veer right onto Forest Service Road 23 and go about one mile to Forest Service Road 2300-919. Several miles later, you'll arrive at the Kentucky Falls trailhead marked by a sign on the left side of the road. An old growth Douglas fir forest on gently rolling hills for the first half mile gives way to a steep descent into a lush canyon. The upper falls is visible a little over a mile down the trail. You'll hear the water before you actually get a full cross-section of a broad cascade pouring out from over the rim of this green canyon. On your drive back to ORE 126, retrace your route carefully to avoid veering off on a hair-raising spur route to Mapleton.

A chance to see what may be the **Northwest's tallest trees** is possible northeast of **Lowell**. This recently discovered grove's 500-year-old Douglas firs average close to 300 feet in height. The tallest tree has been measured at 322 feet, which places it in the rarefied atmosphere of the giant Sequoia. Be sure to take along a forest map from the Lowell Ranger Station (Lowell, 97452; tel. 937-2129) or the Forest Service headquarters in Eugene (211 E 7th Ave., Eugene, 97405; tel. 687-6521).

To get there from Eugene, take ORE 58 to Lowell. From Lowell, follow the Jasper-Lowell Road two miles to the Unity Covered Bridge and turn right onto Big Fall Creek Road. Proceed down Big Fall Creek Road for 11 miles, where it becomes Forest Service Road 18. Turn left onto Forest Service Road 1817 and continue on for 10 miles until you reach Forest Service Road 1806, at which point you will turn left. Go down 1806 for three miles and then turn left onto Forest Service Road 427. The trailhead is a half mile down the road on the left-hand side, but park on the right.

Sports Facilities And Outoor Programs

The U of O and Eugene Parks and Recreation provide the community with a wide-ranging smorgasbord of recreational facilities and programs.

University sport facilities are open to the public year-round for $2 per day. Covered tennis courts and racquetball courts are found on 15th Ave. east of the physical education building. There are also gyms, weightrooms, a swimming pool, and more racquetball courts inside the physical education building. Pick up schedule information at the physical education building on the corner of University and 15th streets or at the U of O recreation desk (103 Gerlinger Hall, tel. 346-4113).

Headquarters for the U of O **outdoor program** (tel. 346-4365) are located in a southeast corner basement room of the Erb Memorial Union (corner of 13th and University), festooned with maps, photos, and bulletins covering every sport from biking to hiking. The program sponsors more whitewater activities than any other group in town as well as backpacking trips outside the state to supplement area hikes. Outings are run on a cooperative shared-expense basis with the participants customizing the trip to their needs. In addition to these activities, you can also connect with people on your own through the office exchange bulletin board. The outdoor program also has camping equipment on loan for free. In addition, it's an excellent resource center for statewide travel information with books, maps, pamphlets, and videos about Oregon wilderness locales and outdoor activities. You're privy to all this and more for a $5 membership fee.

Eugene Parks and Recreation (22 W. 7th Ave., Eugene, 97401; tel. 687-5333) puts out free seasonal publications about their offerings which include bus tours, hikes, arts and special interest classes as well as a heavy dose of fitness activities. These are largely coordinated through four community centers wherein staffed recreational facilities and bulletin boards offer programs for all ages. Sports equipment is rented inexpensively out of these offices. Especially popular are the pools and fitness centers at **Echo Hollow** (1560 Echo Hollow Rd., Eugene, tel. 687-5525) and **Sheldon** (2445 Willakenzie Rd., Eugene, tel. 687-5314). The drop-in user fee is $2, which gets cut in half with a one-month pass for $25. These pools have fitness centers equipped with weights and exercise paraphernalia. Consult Parks and Recreation literature or call for the schedule.

Lane County Ice (Lane County Fairgrounds, 13th and Monroe streets, Eugene, tel. 687-4ICE) offers ice-skating lessons and open public skating. Admission is $3 and adult skate rental is $3, $2 for students.

Golf

Laurelwood Golf Course (2700 Columbia St., Eugene, tel. 687-5521 for info or 484-4653 for tee times) is a regulation-length golf course owned by the City of Eugene. Greens fee (around $12) and rentals are reasonable and there's a 250-yard driving range here.

Of the many courses in Lane County, **Tokatee** (54947 ORE 126, Blue River, tel. 822-3220 or 800-452-6376) is the best. In fact, *Golf Digest* once rated it among the top 25 courses in the nation and another publication, *Back Nine,* rated it the best public course in the Pacific Northwest. To get there, drive 47 miles east of Eugene on the McKenzie Highway (ORE 126). The 18 holes here are set in a mountainous landscape patrolled by elk and other forest creatures. It's always a good idea to call ahead for reservations.

Tennis, Jogging, And Horseback Riding

Of the many public tennis courts throughout Eugene, the best-lit facilities are at the U of O and on 24th and Amazon Parkway near Roosevelt Middle School.

Near the Amazon courts, runners will enjoy the bark-o-mulch trail which follows Amazon Creek in a one-mile loop. The best jogging of all, however, is found at the four-mile **Prefontaine Trail** along the Willamette River east of Alton Baker Park. Named after Steve Prefontaine, whose world-record times and finishing kicks used to rock the Hayward Field grandstands before his untimely death in 1974, this soft path meanders along the river not far from the University. To get there, follow the bikepath from Alton Baker Park east towards Springfield. Another route is the road behind Oregon West Fitness (1475 Franklin Blvd.) that's closed off to motorized traffic. This leads to the footbridge that takes bikers, hikers, and joggers to the Prefontaine Trail, Willamette bike path, Autzen Stadium, and other facilities found along the Willamette River Greenway. Exercise equipment can break up your run on the "par course" section of the Prefontaine Trail.

If you're more interested in taking to the trails on your trusty steed, **Bow Wow Ranch** (33435 Van Duym Rd., tel. 345-5643) is located off I-5 at Exit 199, four miles north of Beltline. Rentals and lessons are also available at **Pruitt's Equestrian Center** (83260 Rattlesnake Rd. Crow, tel. 726-1545) southwest of Eugene. Call ahead for schedule and reservations.

ENTERTAINMENT

Keeping up with Eugene's multifaceted entertainment offerings involves previewing the listings put out by two local newspapers, the weekly *What's Happening* and the daily *Eugene Register Guard.* Calling the U of O ticket office for athletic event information (tel. 346-4461) and reading the bulletin boards on the ground floor of the 5th Street Public Market or at Sundance Natural Foods can supplement these sources.

Spectator Sports

Each spring, the U of O track team, a perennial contender for the best team in the nation, has meets at **Hayward Field** (Agate and 15th streets). This site has hosted world-class events like the NCAA Finals and the United States Olympic Trials in addition to the U of O schedule. Track fans come here each June to enjoy the **Twilight Meet**, where the elite of the sport compete. Tickets to all U of O sporting events will usually cost you a little more than seeing a first-run movie, but at least the money goes toward a fine educational institution.

Fall means Duck football at **Autzen Stadium** (Centennial Blvd. on Day Island). To get there, head north on Ferry Street. Just after crossing the Willamette River, take a hard right on Centennial Boulevard. The U of O football team has produced several NFL players of note including Dan Fouts and Ahmad Rashad. In winter, the townsfolk cram into **MacArthur Court,** located just south of the physical education building on University Street, which is a funky anachronism from 1939, the year the Ducks won the first NCAA basketball championship. Even if you're not a fan, you're bound to get caught up in the frenzied decibels of "quacker backers" who support a team known for its never-say-die attitude.

In summer, the **Eugene Emeralds** play ball at Civic Stadium (2077 Willamette Street, tel. 342-5367) for honor, glory, and a chance to break into the big leagues. This AA team is most famous for once having all-time great Mike Schmidt on its roster and for serving some of the best concession food you'll ever taste at a ballpark. Barbecued chicken along with hot dogs and burgers are grilled outside, and microbrews are on hand to help wash it all down. Tickets cost $3.50 for adults, $2 for kids. Come July 4th to see the best fireworks display in town (or watch it free from Amazon Park or College Hill).

Dancing And Music

If you tire of watching other folks in action, the best spot for frenetic dancing in town is the **W.O.W. Hall** (291 W. 8th St., tel. 687-2746). This is an old Wobblie (International Workers of the World) meeting hall and has remained as a monument to Oregon's activist past in labor history. Today, this place, despite having all the ambience of a junior high school gym, hosts some surprisingly big names, including the likes of Queen Ida, Taj Mahal, and other venerated rock and blues performers. The W.O.W. bills itself as having the best hardwood dance floor in the Pacific Northwest. In any case, it's probably the most crowded and features an interesting cross section of Eugenians. Beer and wine are served downstairs.

Another major concert venue which features dancing to live bands is the **Erb Memorial Union Ballroom** (13th and University streets, tel. 346-4000, tickets 346-4362). Local-guy-who-made-good Robert Cray, Los Lobos, and other nationally known performers have played here. The dance floor is more spacious than the W.O.W. Hall, but can actually exceed its downtown counterpart in B.T.U.s generated by the mass of writhing bodies.

The **Eugene Hilton Ballroom** (66 E. 6th, tel. 342-2000) has a ballroom which also hosts big names, including John Lee Hooker, Asleep at the Wheel, and other acts running the gamut of popular music. For more sedate, the **Hult Center** (see "Hult Center" under "Sights" above) is next door to the Hilton. The Eugene Symphony under the dynamic direction of Marin Alsop and other estimable local groups like the Chamber Singers perform here along with a wide-ranging array which has included the Neville Brothers, George Winston, Merle Haggard, Andre Watts, and George Carlin.

Live jazz in the basement of **Jo Frederigo's** (295 E. 5th Ave., Eugene, tel. 343-8488) is made more enjoyable by crayons, paper, and one of their famous Long Island ice teas. Decent Italian food is served upstairs.

The Hult Center's summer series, **Eugene Festival of Musical Theater** (834 Pearl, Suite 240, tel. 345-0028) puts on shows like *The King and I* and *Peter Pan* under the direction of Ed

Ragazzino. At Christmas, the *Nutcracker* is always a treat at the Hult.

Down the block the **Oregon Electric Station Restaurant and Lounge** (5th and Willamette, tel. 485-4444) hosts live jazz. This historic landmark features excellent dinner (best prime rib in town) and lunch entrees, a full bar as well as a backroom with couches, wing chairs, and the ambience of an English club.

In the same neighborhood, **Allan Brothers Coffeehouse and Bakery** (152 W. 5th St., tel. 342-3378) has live folk and blues at night and the same excellent coffee as its Corvallis outlets. This spacious coffeehouse is in a charming old building across from the Lane County Jail and attracts everyone from off-duty cops to madmen playing speed chess. Home-baked goodies and breakfast, lunch, and dinner entrees can be ordered at the counter.

Another coffeehouse hangout is the **Coffee Corner** (28th and Oak streets, tel. 342-7238). The entertainment might be limited to an occasional magician or pianist, the coffee prices may be a tad higher than elsewhere, but there's a bright cheery ambience thanks to windows on all sides and a staff who dispense good vibes along with cups of ambition. In addition to quality java, this place is quietly one of the better places to eat in town. The Mexican scramble for breakfast ($4.75) is filling, and the fresh fish, quiche, and homemade soup during the rest of the day are top-notch. Leave room for dessert.

Theaters

While there's no shortage of movie screens in this town, the real cinematic gems are usually found at the University (consult the *Oregon Daily Emerald,* the U or O student newspaper which is distributed free at Fifth Street Market, the U of O Bookstore, and Sundance Natural Foods) and the **Bijou Theatre** (492 E. 13th Ave., Eugene, tel. 686-2458). The University series favors cult classics (*Yellow Submarine, The Last Wave, The Bicycle Thief, King of Hearts,* etc.) and the $1-2 admission helps you forget the oppressiveness of the lecture halls which serve as theaters. The Bijou is the place to see foreign films, art flicks, and less commercial mainstream movies. This old converted church is intimate, has great munchies, and late-night presentations.

If you want first-run motion pictures, chances

are you can find whatever flick you're looking for at **Movies 12** (Gateway Mall, 2850 Gateway St., Springfield, tel. 741-1231). A dozen features, a $5 admission for adults, $3 for children, and discounted admissions before 6 p.m. make this Eugene's leading moviehouse.

PRACTICALITIES

Accommodations
A few bed and breakfasts and an A.Y.H. Hostel provide the best values for the dollar in town. Seniors, however, can use various discount cards (AARP et. al) to offset the high prices of such upscale accommodations as the Valley River Inn and the Eugene Hilton. Otherwise, you just have a choice of cheap motels on E. Broadway, moderately priced ones on Franklin Boulevard, as well as others detailed in the following chart. The best bets for the budget traveler are the campsites and rustic digs east of town on the McKenzie River Highway (see "ORE 126—The McKenzie Highway").

The **Eugene Green House A.Y.H. Hostel** (1117 W. 11th, Eugene, 97402; tel. 344-5296) is located in west Eugene close to city buslines, bike paths, grocery stores, and the U of O. In addition, it is 10 miles equidistant to the downtown terminals of Greyhound and Amtrak and the airport. The hostel is currently being transformed into an "eco-home" where alternative energy and recycling are utilized. This is appropriate given its status as headquarters for the environmentally activist Southern Willamette Greens. There's an $8.50 per night charge for members, $10 for nonmembers. With room for only five guests, reservations must be made well in advance.

Visiting parents of U of O students, college lecturers, and folks willing to spend a little for quality head for the **Campus Cottage Bed and Breakfast** (1136 E. 19th, Eugene, 97403; tel. 342-5346). Bedroom amenities like down comforters, antiques, and fresh flowers are in keeping with rates around $75 a night. The three bedrooms have private baths, and guests can also enjoy a living room with a fireplace, an outside deck, two cats, and a dog. A full breakfast of special egg dishes, fresh fruits, and pastries is included. As its name implies, the Campus Cottage is located one block south of the U of O.

Twenty minutes south of Eugene, **Ivanoff's Inn** (3101 Bennett Creek Rd., Cottage Grove,

97424; tel. 942-3171) is a more moderately priced alternative for those seeking the best of the country near the city. To get to Bennet Creek Road, take the Cottage Grove Exit off I-5. This will run into ORE 99, which leads into River Road in a quarter mile. Bennett Creek is an eighth of a mile down on the right. Beautiful trees and lush greenery line Bennett Creek Road, which is paralleled by the Hidden Valley Golf Course on one side and hills leading up to the Willamette National Forest on the other. Ivanoff's is set on five hilly acres with forested trails. These appealing surroundings are only five minutes (three miles) from Cottage Grove downtown shopping and close to covered bridges and the Bohemia mining country (see "Dorena Lake"). Three rooms (one with private bath) run between $35-65 a night. This includes a full breakfast featuring Swedish specialties.

Eugene Cuisine
While there are a number of good restaurants in Eugene, you'll probably be more impressed by the staggering array of locally made gourmet products and natural foods available at markets here. Whether its Tsunami sushi, Toby's tofu pate, or Euphoria chocolate truffles, it's not hard to find exotic munchies right on the grocer's shelves. Even less arcane local fare offers surprises as one taste of Nancy's honey yogurt, Humble bagels, Prince Puckler's ice cream, Genesis juice, or Metropol French bread will confirm. As you might have guessed, many of these delectables come free of chemicals and often with nutritional concerns foremost. Produce labels in many Eugene specialty food stores intone "fresh," "home-grown," and "organic" with the constancy of a mantra, and meat and poultry markets carry products that are rabinically pure.

Two of the leading purveyors of Eugene cuisine began as hippie health food stores around 20 years ago. Today, **Sundance Natural Foods** (748 E. 24th, tel. 345-6153) and the **Kiva** (125 W. 11th, tel. 342-8666) stock more than just grains, sprouts, and vitamins and feature some of the best selections of wine and organic produce in the state. Such relatively recent arrivals upon the scene as **Friendly Foods** (2757 Friendly, tel. 688-3944) and **Oasis Fine Foods** (2489 Willamette, tel. 345-1014) have expanded the largely vegetarian inventory of their hippie forefathers with more meat and takeout items.

EUGENE ACCOMMODATIONS

Name	Address	Telephone	Price	Features
Budget Host Motor Inn	1190 W. 6th Ave.	342-7273	$20-24	cable TV, pets, nonsmoking rooms
Executive House Motel	1040 W. 6th Ave.	683-4000	$20-50	cable TV, nonsmoking rooms
Red Carpet Motel	1055 W. 6th Ave.	345-0579	$24-26	cable TV
Motel Six	3690 Glenwood Drive.	687-2395	$25-35	cable TV
Sixty Six Motel	755 E. Broadway	342-5041	$26-29	cable TV, nonsmoking rooms
Pacific Nine Motor Inn	3550 Gateway St. (Springfield)	726-9266	$27	cable TV, wheelchair access, pool
Campus Inn	390 E. Broadway	343-3376	$28-34	cable TV, wheelchair access, pool, pets, nonsmoking rooms
Eugene Motor Lodge	476 E. Broadway	344-5233	$28-34	cable TV, pool, kitchenettes, non smoking rooms
Timbers Motel	1015 Pearl St.	343-3345	$29	cable TV, pets, nonsmoking rooms
Eugene Travelers Inn	540 E. Broadway	342-1109	$32-36	cable TV, pool, pets, nonsmoking rooms
Downtown Motel	361 W. 7th Ave.	345-8739	$34-38	laundry, nonsmoking rooms, complimentary continental breakfast
Friendship Inn	1857 Franklin Blvd.	342-4804	$38-39	cable TV, restaurant, kitchenettes, pets, nonsmoking rooms, complimentary continental breakfast
Angus Inn Motel	2121 Franklin Blvd.	342-1243	$40-52	cable TV, wheelchair access, pool, restaurant/lounge, exercise room, non-smoking rooms

EUGENE ACCOMMODATIONS, cont.

Name	Address	Telephone	Price	Features
Barron's Motor Inn	1859 Franklin Blvd.	342-6383	$41-48	cable TV, wheelchair access, pets, restaurant/lounge
Best Western Greentree Motel	1759 Franklin Blvd.	485-2727	$45-60	cable TV, wheelchair access, pets, restaurant/lounge, pool
Best Western New Oregon Motel	1655 Franklin Blvd.	683-3669	$45-65	cable TV, wheelchair access, pets, restaurant/lounge, covered pool, laundry, nonsmoking rooms
Nendels Inn	3540 Gateway St.	726-1212	$47-85	wheelchair access, pets, restaurant/lounge, pool, laundry, live entertainment, nonsmoking rooms
Shilo Inn	3350 Gateway St. (Springfield)	747-0332	$52-58	cable TV, wheelchair access, pets, restaurant/lounge, pool, laundry, nonsmoking rooms, complimentary continental breakfast
Red Lion Inn Eugene/Springfield	3280 Gateway St.	726-8181	$64-67	cable TV, pool, restaurant/lounge, tennis courts, nonsmoking rooms
Red Lion Inn Eugene	205 Coburg Road	342-5201	$67-78	cable TV, wheelchair access, pets, restaurant/lounge, pool, live entertainment, non-smoking rooms
Valley River Inn	1000 Valley River Way	687-0123	$75-103	wheelchair access, restaurant/lounge, pool, sauna, jacuzzi, non-smoking rooms, river view

EUGENE BED AND BREAKFAST

Name	Address	Telephone	Price	Features
B & G's Bed and Breakfast	711 W. 11th Ave.	343-5739	$29-49	cable TV, lunch/dinner available, laundry, nonsmoking rooms, breakfast included
Wheeler's Bed and Breakfast	404 E. McKenzie (Coburg)	344-2276	$34-39	cable TV, lunch/dinner available, pets, laundry, nonsmoking rooms, breakfast included
Shelly's Guest House Bed and Breakfast	1546 Charnelton St.	683-2062	$45-55	meals available, fireplace, cable TV, laundry
Lorane Valley Bed and Breakfast	86621 Lorane Highway	686-0241	$69	wheelchair access, meals available, nonsmoking rooms
Campus Cottage Bed and Breakfast Inn	1136 E. 19th Ave.	342-5346	$78-93	meals available, fireplace, nonsmoking rooms

Campus Area

The eateries on the campus periphery are a cut above those found in most college towns.

Start the day at **Campus Glenwood** (1340 Alder, tel. 687-0355) or at the southside **Glenwood** (2588 Willamette St., tel. 687-8201). The menu is standard American breakfast fare with a few entrees paying deference to eclectic college-town tastes. Try the turkito, a turkey burrito with melted cheese that comes with hash browns for $3.75, or various tofu dishes. Many folks will tell you that the huevos rancheros here ($4.50) are the best in town. You can also get good and reasonably priced lunches (like the veggie burger) and dinners (seasonal specials like fresh salmon) here.

If your tummy can only handle coffee and a croissant in the morning, head to **Espresso Roma** (825 E. 13th Ave., tel. 484-4848) or **Fall Creek Bakery** (881 E. 13th Ave., tel. 484-1662) Espresso Roma has a delightful outside courtyard which fills up when the rain stops. The Fall Creek Bakery is distinguished for award-winning cinnamon rolls and chocolate chip cookies. The latter is supplemented by **Valentine's** wine, coffee, and to-go snacks in the rear of the bakery.

Oriental lunchtime favorites include combination lunch specials (dim sum on Sunday) at **China Blue** (879 E. 13th, Eugene, tel. 343-2832 and also 2307 N.W. 9th St., Corvallis, tel. 757-3088). The **Bamboo Pavilion** nearby could well be the best dollar value around thanks to huge portions for under $3. **Sy's New York Pizza** (1211 Alder, tel. 686-9598) would make his mentor, Original Ray's of New York, proud with a by-the-slice operation that lines 'em up at lunch and dinnertime.

Also in the shadow of the campus is one of the best restaurants in town, the **Excelsior Cafe** (754 E. 13th Ave., tel. 485-1206). Set in a charming old colonial home, the menu changes monthly, highlighting what's in season. It can be spendy but lighter "bistro dinners" and hors d'oeuvres let you appreciate the restaurant's innovative approaches to seafood, veal, game, and salads at a cheaper price. While lunch and dinner are served here every day, there's also a Sunday brunch and service till 2:30 a.m. on Saturday. Despite a reputation for fine food, it's their wonderful decadent assortment of desserts and cozy bar that pulls in the lion's share of the clientele.

Rennie's Landing (1214 Kincaid, tel. 687-0600) serves breakfast, gourmet burgers, homemade soups, beer, and wine. Late-night and predawn hours, a second floor outside deck, and a location right across from the U of O campus make this a favorite with the campus crowd—particularly after Duck games.

Farther away from campus, the McNemanin brothers have two brewpubs. One is on the corner of Agate and 19th streets, the other on High Street (1243 High St., tel. 345-4905). Each repeat the successful formula of the establishments discussed in the Portland chapter. The High Street pub is ensconced in a comfy converted old house in back of which a tree-shaded brickwork patio makes the perfect hangout on a hot afternoon.

5th Street Market Eateries
A local newspaper once gave the nod to **Terry's Diner** (5th Street Market, tel. 683-8190) for the best burgers and best omelettes (thanks to the lemon in the eggs which makes them extra fluffy) in town. Old advertising billboards and jukebox tunes from the '50s, thick malteds that come in the metal mixing container like they did at old soda fountains, and laugh-a-minute waitresses stylishly reinvent the all-American diner for those born too late. Terry's is open for all meals till 10 p.m. except Sundays, when it closes at 6 p.m.

Upstairs in the market is **Mekala's** (tel. 342-4872). Despite elegant decor and exotic Thai dishes (try the duck, pad thai, any of the curries, and coconut ice cream for dessert), prices are reasonable. Because few people smoke in Eugene, request the smoking section for intimate dining and a window on 5th Ave., a people-watching perch extraordinaire.

Downstairs in the market, **Casablanca** (tel. 342-3885) has Middle Eastern cuisine with pita sandwiches, babbaghanoush hummous, and other regional specialties. This restaurant was voted Eugene's favorite lunch spot in a local poll.

Downtown Dining
In the heart of downtown are two other popular restaurants. **Anatolia** (992 Willamette, tel. 343-9661) features Greek and Indian food par excellence. Spicy curries and vindaloo chicken are complemented by Saganaki (fried cheese), spanakopita (spinach cheese pie), and gyro sandwiches here. The best baklava in town for dessert and a shot of ouzo or retsina can finish off a richly flavored and moderately priced repast. Folks who remember Poppi's, a fabled Greek taverna in the campus district that was forced to close when Sacred Heart hospital expanded, will especially relish Monday nights here when the menu of one of Eugene's all-time favorite restaurants is re-created. Anatolia's is quickly gaining the following of Poppi's, so get there early.

Dominating the first floor of the Atrium building, **De Frisco's** (99 W. 10th, tel. 494-2263) has built its reputation on the more than 20 microbrews, imports, and domestic beers it has on tap. A pool table and big-screen TV, a wall paneled with books, and live jazz on Wednesday nights also explain De Frisco's enthusiastic following. A variety of hearty soups and barbecued chicken sandwiches are lunchtime mainstays here.

A few blocks east is downtown's gourmet gulch. Two places stand out from the pack. **Cafe Zenon** (898 Pearl St., tel. 343-3005) has a multi-ethnic menu which is constantly changing. Despite this challenge, the Zenon manages to pull off dishes ranging from Italian to Thai in fine style. The only problems you'll run into here are getting in without a wait since there are no reservations, and when you're ready to leave, walking out past the eye-popping dessert display without stopping.

Across the street is a spacious two-story Italian restaurant, **Ambrosia** (174 Broadway, tel. 342-4141). Antique furnishings and stained glass set the stage for old-world cuisine prepared to suit contemporary tastes. The individual-sized gourmet pizzas (cooked slowly in a wood-burning oven), a wonderful squid-in-batter appetizer, and northern Italian specialties will make spaghetti and meatballs seem like old hat here.

Some of the best restaurant values are located on the fringes of downtown. Pushed up against the railroad tracks, the **Kestrel Cafe** (454 Willamette, tel. 344-4794) features lots of inventive dishes like tofu fajitas and Creole specialties like jambalaya. The atmosphere is cozy, the food good, and the prices reasonable. Try the curried chicken and rice for $6. A few blocks away from the Kestrel down on 5th Street, the **Keystone**

Cafe (395 W. 5th St., tel. 342-2075) is also known for huge portions, low prices, and its support of community activism. Home-style breakfast features eggs and potatoes and whole grain pancakes. Highly recommended are side orders of Mexican chorizo (a spicy sausage) made by a local butcher shop specializing in chemical-free meat. Mexican dinner specials on Friday and Saturday are particularly good. The chicken mole or chile rellenos with black beans and rice are as tasty as you'll find in many area Mexican restaurants and only cost around $5.

Perhaps the busiest neighborhood during lunchtime is around Willamette and 16th. The biggest reason for this is the **French Horn** (1891 Willamette, tel. 343-7473). For $2.25, the restaurant's soup of the day with fresh french bread is the salvation of scores of people with little time and a taste for home cooking. Hot entrees and salads with homemade mayonnaise round out the menu. At breakfast, the $2 scrambled eggs come with your choice of additional ingredients (bacon, cheese, spinach, etc.), each 25 cents. The French Horn's baked goods are also scrumptious.

Across Willamette in a large white colonial building is the **Vets Club**, where you can sit in the same dimly lit vinyl booths where such visiting literati as Willam S. Burroughs, Gregory Corso, and Hunter S. Thompson have raised a glass with local writer/god Ken Kesey. Drinks here are inexpensive and quite strong.

A block south from the Vets Club on the corner of Willamette is **Euphoria Chocolate Co.** (6 W. 17th, tel. 343-9223), a chocolatier of national repute. Their Grand Marnier truffle and other confections are sold around town. Come here after holidays and buy the bite-size Santas, hearts, and bunnies at reduced price.

Though the corner of 15th and Willamette may not conjure up the "gunfight at the OK Corral," **Tino's** (tel. 342-8111) is fighting off a most unlikely challenger across the street. The **Bread Stop** (1478 Willamette St., tel. 345-4811), a small whole-grain bakery, has managed to commit the ultimate heresy and get away with it—a pizza with an organic whole wheat crust that actually tastes good. Compounding the felony, condiments like artichoke hearts and chopped raw garlic grace these nontraditional pies. By contrast, Tino's straight-ahead approach emphasizing a crisp crust, copious amounts of cheese, and a

low grease factor has made it a Eugene tradition for 40 years. If pizza isn't your bag, Tino's does a fine job on calzone and fresh pasta dishes. The Bread Stop is also known for sandwiches, microbrews, cookies, scones, and the ultimate survival food—hiker's bread. This yeast-free bread contains amaranth, which when combined with other ingredients, provides a complete protein.

Close by the public library is a place often touted as the best in town. The **Cafe Central's** (382 W. 13th, tel. 343-9510) "nouvellish" and traditional entrees are light and flavorful dishes centered around local ingredients. A complete bar with microbrews and creative desserts are also notable. While prices here are considered high for Eugene, they are actually modest in comparison with what a restaurant of this ilk would charge elsewhere. Budget travelers will appreciate the "roll-up" sandwiches (meat, cheese, watercress, and tomatoes) for $1 and a full line of Euphoria chocolate truffles (under the same ownership as the restaurant).

Beyond the downtown are two of Eugene's better ethnic restaurants. **Hilda's** (400 Blair Blvd., tel. 343-4322) specializes in South American food. Brazilian marinated flank steak strips with black beans and rice typifies this hearty cuisine, reminiscent of Mexican cooking but not as hot or as greasy. The restaurant is small enough to create long waits on weekends. **Tom's Tea House** (788 W. 7th, tel. 343-7658) is *the* place for Sichuan and Hunan stir fry. Kung pao chicken and mu shu pork are reliable choices here.

Events

There is a lot happening in this south Willamette Valley hub of culture and athletics. Several events, however, impart the flavor of the area best.

Of these, only one enjoys international acclaim. The **Oregon Bach Festival** (write: U of O Music School, 18th St., Eugene, 97403; tel 867-5000 for tickets, 346-5666 for business office) takes place over two weeks in late June into early July under the baton of famed Bach interpreter Helmuth Rilling from Germany. *New York Times* critic Harold Schonberg once rated the festival the best of its kind in the country, and an influx of renowned visiting opera and symphonic virtuosi guarantees this will remain the case. Over two dozen separate concerts are featured, with musical styles ranging from the baroque era to the 20th century.

THE OREGON COUNTRY FAIRE

Time warp: 1969-1991

If you've been too busy to follow the growth of the '60s counterculture, put on your paisley and follow an eclectic caravan of handpainted schoolbuses, Volkswagon beetles, Volvos, and BMWs to the Oregon Country Faire.

After buying your ticket at the gatehouse, join the crowds of tie-dyed, fringed, and lovebeaded fairgoers. Entering, you wander through a kaleidoscope of natural fabrics, graceful ceramics, stained glass, rainbow candles, and thousands of other variously sculpted wares. Manufactured items are simply unavailable. Every aspect of the fair, its booths, and participants are, in a sense, art.

What? Two hours gone by already? You need a cup of espresso and a piece of torte if you're going to make it through this day. Ah, the **Hilltop Bakery** is just around the corner with all the caffeine and sweet treats necessary. Or perhaps you want a **Rita's** burrito bulging with avocado, salsa, and sprouts. The choices are mouthwatering: get fried rice, Tsunami sushi, blazing salads, or even a tofuless tofu burger (100 % ground beef) and more!

All fed up and ready for a little entertainment? Overwhelmed by the constant parade of costumed stiltwalkers, strolling musicians, winged "country fairies," children in face paint, bare-breasted women, and other ambient wonders? Not far from any burnout point is a stage.

Shady Grove is a quite venue for acoustic folk, classical, new age, and other music.

The **Daredevil, W.C. Fields,** and **Energy Park** stages host contemporary New Vaudeville stars and other rollicking performances.

See the **Royale Famille du Carniveaux** debut a unique musical comedy.

Marvel as the **Reduced Shakespeare Company** performs *Romeo and Juliet* backwords in one minute flat.

Shake your head and mutter as **Up For Grabs** juggles circular sawblades and/or small children.

But wait, there's more. Try **The Circus** with its parade, orchestra, and veteran virtuosos. Ogle snake charmers and belly dancers at the **Gypsy Stage.**

Or dance to the national and international stars of rock and roll, reggae, and alternative music on the **Main Stage.**

Starting to sound less like a "hippie fair" and more like a well catered and established art convention? Don't worry; there's always a sojourn into geo-socio-polictical-eco-consciousness at **Community Village**. Several booths here and in **Energy Park** teach and demonstrate the latest in new and matured '60s activism and environmental awareness.

Tired already? So are we, but there's a whole year to rest up and reminisce before the next Oregon Country Faire.

To get there, head west from Eugene on ORE 126 and follow the signs. Additional information can be acquired by contacting the Oregon Country Faire, Box 2972, Eugene, 97402; tel. 343-4298.

The Oregon County Faire is where Renaissance-era arts and crafts meet sixties activisim and whimsy.

PHOTO BY MARIA THOMAS

Pianist Marian McPartland, dubbed the First Lady of Jazz by the *Chicago Sun Times,* and Polish composer/conductor Penderecki, critically acclaimed for his modern liturgical pieces, were guest performers in the 1990 series. The centerpieces of the festival, however, are Bach works like St. Matthew's Passion, numerous cantatas, and the Brandenburg Concertos.

Tickets range from $5-25 with performances taking place in the Hult Center and at the Beall Concert Hall at the U of O Music School. Free events, including "let's talk with the conductor," jazz and bluegrass concerts, and children's activities take place at these venues during the Festival. The schedules are available at the U of O Music School and are also published in the *Eugene Register Guard* and *What's Happening.* A scheduled series of brunches, lunches, and dinners with the musicians also add a special touch to the festival.

Just after the Bach Festival in late July, the **Oregon Country Faire** takes place (see callout) as the second major cultural event of the summer. This annual fantasyland is staged among the trees west of Noti on ORE 126; for more information, contact the faire at Box 2972, Eugene 97402; tel 343-4298.

The fall is ushered in with the **Eugene Celebration.** This two-week fete in late September and early October includes such events as the mayor's Fine Art Show, readings by Oregon authors at the Hult Center, the Fifth Avenue Jazz Festival, and the coronation of the Slug Queen. Street performers all over town and food booths in the parking lot on 8th Avenue and Willamette also help the community put its best foot forward. Contact the Lane County Visitors and Convention Bureau for more details.

The University sponsors the **Eugene Folk Festival** (tel. 686-INFO) in the spring which has attracted the likes of Tom Paxton and blues harpist James Cotton. Call for the schedule of the upcoming concerts. It generally takes place behind the student union on the second weekend of May.

On the second weekend in August, the **Junction City Scandinavian Festival** (Greenwood St., between 5th and 7th, Junction City) celebrates the town's Danish founding fathers. Folk dancing, traditional crafts, and food make up the bulk of the activities. Skits of Hans Christian Anderson folk tales are enacted during the four-day event, along with guided bus tours into the city's Scandinavian past. The latter are an hour long and take you by Scandinavian pioneer farmsteads built in the 1800s. Tour tickets are available at the info windmill for $2.50. Swedish, Finnish, Norwegian, and Icelandic ethnicities also exert a presence in this festival. Junction City is located 12 miles northwest of Eugene off ORE 99. Contact the local chamber of commerce (Box 3, Junction City, 97484; tel. 998-6154) for more information on the festival. They can also tell you how to get to the **daffodil display** on Ferguson

last-minute arrivals to the Oregon Bach Festival

PHOTO BY JURETTA NIDEVER

Road west of Junction City that peaks in mid-March.

In the other direction from Eugene, **Bohemia Mining Days** (contact the Cottage Grove Chamber of Commerce, 710 Row River Road, Box 587, Cottage Grove, 97424; tel. 942-2411) convenes in mid-July. The five-day event highlights the grand miner's parade, the prospector's breakfast, and gold-panning demonstrations. In addition to events showcasing the region's mining heyday, a half-marathon, a bake-off, a flower show, an ugly-dog contest, and other competitions keep folks busy here. Many of the events take place at re-created **Bohemia City** near the chamber of commerce on Row River Road. Don't miss the grand miner's parade, which happens on Saturday afternoon. Floats, horse teams, drill teams, and color guards make their way from Harrison Avenue to Row River Road with colorful costumes and the kind of enthusiasm last seen around here after turn-of-the-century lucky strikes.

Information And Services
The following list scratches the surface of Eugene's many service institutions and information outlets. A bevy of literature befitting Oregon's second most populated area can be obtained at the **Eugene-Springfield Convention and Visitors Bureau** (305 W. 7th Ave., tel. 484-5307 or 800-452-3670 in Oregon, 800-547-5445 outside Oregon).

Eugene Parks and Recreation have the following switchboard numbers: tel. 687-5333 for general information, 687-5360 for athletics, 431-5850 for arts, and 687-5311 for disabled recreation.

The **U of O Switchboard** (795 Willamette St., tel. 346-3111) is a multipurpose referral line. Rides, housing, and emergencies can be taken care of Mon.-Fri. 8-5. The main **post office** is located at 5th and Willamette (tel. 341-3611) and is open Mon.-Fri. 8-5. and Sat. 9 a.m.-noon.

Sacred Heart Hospital (1255 Hilyard, Eugene, tel. 686-6962) is one of the leading institutions of its kind in the state. Emergency-room care is available 24 hours daily. A cheaper alternative is the **Whitebird Clinic** (341 12th St., Eugene, tel. 342-8255).

Across the street from Sacred Heart, the **Smith Family Bookstore** (768 E. 13th, Eugene, tel. 345-1651) and (525 Willamette St., Eugene, tel. 343-4717) is an excellent used bookstore.

The **U of O Bookstore** (13th and Kincaid) and the **Bookmart** (865 Olive, tel. 484-0512) have the best selection of new titles and periodicals. For travel books, you can't beat the **S.S. Adventure** (888 Pearl St., Eugene, tel. 485-7348). This store also carries U.S. Geological Survey maps and camping guides.

The **Eugene Public Library** (100 W. 13th, tel. 687-5450) has the most user-friendly periodical section in the state.

Eugene's network of outdoor clubs and environmental organizations is extensive enough to preclude a thorough listing, but the vortex of the environmental community, the **U of O Survival Center** (Suite 1, Erb Memorial Union, U of O campus, tel. 346-4356), can steer you to the right adventure.

Getting Around
Amtrak at 4th and Willamette (tel. 485-1092), **Greyhound** at 9th and Pearl (tel. 344-6265), and **Green Tortoise** which picks up passengers in front of the U of O library at 15th and Kincaid (tel. 937-3603) are the major modes of long-distance public transport. Around town, **Lane Transit District** (tel. 687-5555) has canopied pavilions which post the bus timetables downtown. Their business office on 10th and Willamette has pocket-sized schedules. Fares are 75 cents (children and seniors half price) and about a third less on weekends. The **ride board** on the bottom floor of the Erb Memorial Union at the U of O has a list of rides available for those willing to share gas and driving. **Emerald Taxi** (tel. 686-2010) is fast, reliable, and reasonably priced.

If you're in your own car, just remember that the campus is in the southeastern part of town; 1st Avenue parallels the Willamette River; and Willamette Street divides the city east and west. Navigation is complicated by lots of one-way roads and dead-ends. Look for alleyways to avoid getting stuck.

The Eugene **airport** (tel. 687-5430) is a 20-minute drive northwest from downtown. Just get on the Delta Highway off Washington Street and follow the signs. It's served by Alaska (tel. 800-426-0333), American (tel. 800-547-7000), Northwest (tel. 800-692-7000), United and United Express (tel. 800-241-6552), and U.S. Air (tel. 800-428-4322). This new facility has food service on the second floor.

Media

Public radio stations are all clustered near the bottom of the FM dial with the dominant presence being KLCC 89.7 FM. The station's programming ranges from new wave jazz and "Blues Power" (Saturday afternoons) to a dynamic news department. The University of Oregon station KWAX 90.1 FM can be heard in eastern Oregon and on the coast and provides continuous classical music. On Sunday nights between 8-11 p.m., the campus and countercultural communities tune into three hours of all-Grateful Dead programming on KLCX, 104.7 FM. Perhaps the most popular radio show in the area is KUGN's (59 AM) morning show, which mixes news and local gossip with good music of different genres.

What's Happening (1251 Lincoln St., tel. 484-0519) carries on Eugene's proud tradition of alternative weeklies. Hard-hitting investigative reporting, entertaining features, insightful reviews, travel articles, and the best entertainment listings in Eugene make it a "must" for the Eugene traveler. Particularly compelling are the environmental articles done by Dave Johnson, who is largely responsible for the eastern Oregon chapters in this volume. *What's Happening* is free and can be picked up all over town.

The *Eugene Register Guard* (975 High St., Eugene, tel. 485-1234) was mentioned in the general Introduction. Travelers should especially look for *Guard* columnist Mike Thoele's coverage of offbeat Oregon locales, personalities, and local color.

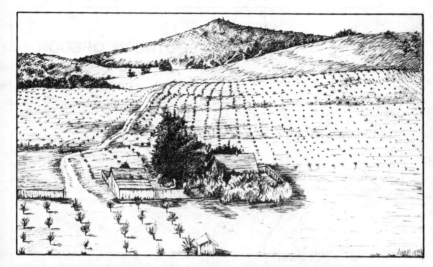

SOUTHERN OREGON

South of the Willamette Valley and east of the Cascades is a corridor of the state most residents call southern Oregon. To be more precise, this label refers to cities along Interstate 5 below Cottage Grove as well as towns in the shadow of the Siskiyou Mountains' eastern flank. What the coast range is to the Willamette Valley, the Siskiyou's rugged V-shaped canyons, wild rivers, and serpentine rock formations are to southern Oregon. The outstanding features of this region include world-class kulturfests, the biggest chunk of remaing wilderness on the Pacific coast, and California retirees who've come in search of cheap real estate and more sun than they'll see anywhere else west of the Cascades.

Initially it was gold finds on the Rogue River which drew prospectors into the territory in the 1850s. Settlers following a southern alternative to the Oregon Trail, the Applegate Trail, also migrated here around this time. A stagecoach line in the 1870s and a railroad a decade later established commerce with California markets. Forest products, orchard crops, and precious metals went south on these modes of transport until interstate trucking supplanted the iron horse in the 1930s.

Recently, attention has been focused on the northern part of the Siskiyou Range's 440,000 acres of old growth Douglas fir. Many timber company contracts to clearcut these trees are being contested by environmental groups. The environmentalists claim the forest represents one of the world's most botanically diverse regions with eight different soil types and more living matter per hectare than any other forest on the planet. As always, timber companies see the trees as a renewable resource and suggest logging would create minimal damage to the ecosystem.

The region is no stranger to activism and aberration in general. Back-to-land refugees came into the tiny hamlet of Takilma on the Smith River to pursue alternative lifestyles decades ago and are still keeping the dream alive. So-called survivalists have chosen the Rogue Valley as the place to make their last stand in the Armageddon they say is inevitable. Several religious and new-age communities have also established themselves here.

Adding to this eclectic mix are whitewater rafters, fishermen, and culture vultures who are drawn to southern Oregon's Shakespeare Festival in Ashland and the Peter Britt Music Festival in Jacksonville. Travelers enjoy this dynamic region where Oregon's past, present, and future come together.

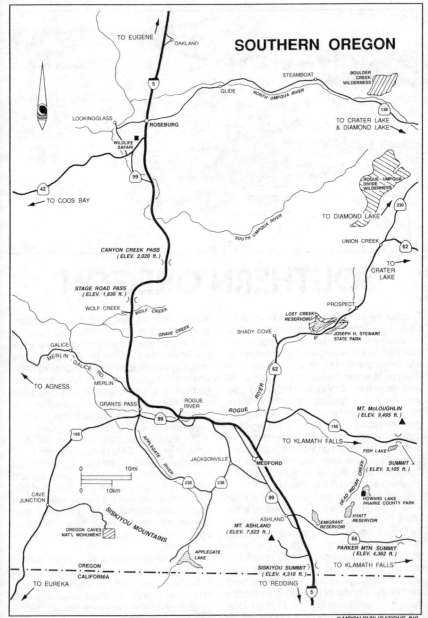

SOUTHERN OREGON

TO EUGENE
OAKLAND

STEAMBOAT
BOULDER CREEK WILDERNESS

GLIDE
NORTH UMPQUA RIVER

138
TO CRATER LAKE & DIAMOND LAKE

LOOKINGGLASS
ROSEBURG

WILDLIFE SAFARI

ROGUE - UMPQUA DIVIDE WILDERNESS

42
TO COOS BAY

99

TO DIAMOND LAKE

230

SOUTH UMPQUA RIVER

UNION CREEK

62
TO CRATER LAKE

CANYON CREEK PASS
(ELEV. 2,020 ft.)

STAGE ROAD PASS
(ELEV. 1,830 ft.)

PROSPECT

LOST CREEK RESERVOIR

WOLF CREEK
WOLF CREEK

GRAVE CREEK

SHADY COVE

JOSEPH H. STEWART STATE PARK

GALICE
MERLIN
GALICE RD

TO AGNESS

MERLIN

62

GRANTS PASS

ROGUE RIVER

ROGUE RIVER

MT. McLOUGHLIN
(ELEV. 9,495 ft.)

99

140

199

APPLEGATE RIVER

TO KLAMATH FALLS

FISH LAKE

SUMMIT
(ELEV. 5,105 ft.)

JACKSONVILLE

MEDFORD

0   10mi
0   10km

238   238

99

DEAD INDIAN CREEK

HOWARD LAKE PRAIRIE COUNTY PARK

CAVE JUNCTION

ASHLAND

MT. ASHLAND
(ELEV. 7,523 ft.)

EMIGRANT RESERVOIR

HYATT RESERVOIR

66

OREGON CAVES NAT'L MONUMENT

SISKIYOU MOUNTAINS

APPLEGATE LAKE

PARKER MTN. SUMMIT
(ELEV. 4,362 ft.)

TO KLAMATH FALLS

OREGON
CALIFORNIA

SISKIYOU SUMMIT
(ELEV. 4,310 ft.)

TO EUREKA

TO REDDING

5

© MOON PUBLICATIONS, INC.

ASHLAND AND VICINITY

With the possible exceptions of Stratford-on Avon's Shakespeare presentations and Oberrammergau, Switzerland and its Passion play, there is no town as closely identified with a cultural event as Ashland and the Oregon Shakespeare Festival. You can immediately sense that this is not just another timber town from a Tudor-style McDonald's and some of the highest prices you'll encounter anywhere in the state. The newcomer will also be struck by the dearth of neon and obtrusive signs in this population center of 18,000 people. Theater tickets are the coin of the realm here, with contemporary classics and off-off Broadway joining presentations of the Old Bard.

Blessed with a bucolic setting between the Siskiyous and the Cascades, Ashland embodies the spirit of the Chataqua movement of a century ago, which was dedicated to bringing culture to the rural hinterlands. Up until the 1930s, however, entertainment was mostly confined to the traveling vaudeville shows that came into the Ashland/Jacksonville area to entertain the residents of a gold rush country in decline. Then Southern Oregon University started up the Shakespeare Festival under the direction of Professor Angus

Bowmer. Such noted thespians as George Peppard, Stacey Keach, and William Hurt have graced Ashland's stages early in their careers, and the festival has garnered its share of Tonys and other awards.

Ashland's tourist economy is also sustained by an auspicious location roughly equidistant from Seattle and San Francisco. Closer to home, day-trips to Crater Lake, Rogue River country, and the southern Oregon coast have joined the tradition of "stay four days, see four plays" as a major part of Ashland's appeal.

SIGHTS AND DAY-TRIPS

Lithia Park

The centerpiece of Ashland is Lithia Park. Recognized as a National Historic Place, the park was designed by John McLaren, landscape architect of San Francisco's Golden Gate Park. A walk through 100-acre Lithia Park along Winburne Way's beautiful tree-shaded trail, is a must on any itinerary here. This trail follows Ashland Creek up into the foothills. The park owes its existence to Jesse Winburne, who made a fortune from ad-

the Oregon Shakespearean Festival's outdoor Elizabethan stage

PHOTO BY HANK KRANZLER

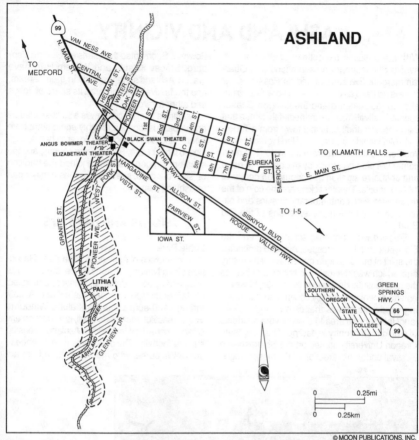

ASHLAND

© MOON PUBLICATIONS, INC.

vertising on the New York subways and tried to develop a spa around Ashland's Lithia Springs, which he said rivaled the venerated waters of Saratoga Springs, New York. Although the spa never caught on due to the Depression, Winburne was nevertheless instrumental in landscaping Lithia Park with one of the most varied collections of trees and shrubs of any park in the state. Winburne is also responsible for piping the famous Lithia water to the plaza fountains so all may enjoy its beneficial minerals. While many visitors find this slightly sulfurous, effervescent water a bit hard to swallow, many locals have acquired a taste for Ashland's acerbic answer to Perrier, and happily chug-a-lug it down.

The hub of the park in the summer months is the Bandshell, where concerts, ballets, and silent movies are shown. Children love to play at the playgrounds, or feed the ducks in the ponds. Big kids enjoy tennis, volleyball, horseshoes, or traversing one of the many trails in the park. Every Tuesday on Water Street next to Lithia Creek the **Farmer's Market** is held. Rogue Valley farmers, craftspeople, and ranchers sell arts and crafts, fruit and produce, and dried flowers.

Another way to enjoy the park is by taking a nostalgic ride in a horse-drawn carriage through it. **Lithia Carriage Company** (tel. 482-5319) offers 25-minute excursions that begin at the information booth on the plaza near the park entrance.

Schneider Museum Of Art

The Schneider Museum of Art (Southern Oregon State College campus, Ashland, 97520; tel. 482-6245) features contemporary art forms from national and international artists. Hours are 11-5 p.m. Tuesday through Friday and 1-5 p.m. Saturday.

Up Up And Away

Rogue Valley Balloon Flights (474 N. Main, Ashland, tel. 482-4310) takes up to four passengers on an hour excursion high over the Rogue River Valley. Liftoff is shortly after dawn, but you'll be wide awake as you soar skyward with your FAA-approved pilots and aircraft. The valley wind blows gently one way, and then gradually changes direction as the earth is warmed by the heat of the sun. A ground chase crew is following the balloon at all times, just in case the thermals are a little uncooperative that morning. Bring your Visa/MasterCard, because this is a spendy sort of attraction at well over $100 a person. Reservations required. Another high-flying outfit is **Big Al's** (tel. 482-4310), which also features balloon trips over the Rogue Valley. Upon landing, the adventure is commemorated with a certificate, photographs of your flight, and a champagne brunch. Call ahead for reservations and additional information.

A slightly cheaper alternative to lighter-than-aircraft is a 30-minute flight over the valley in a vintage biplane with **Ashland Air** (403 Dead Indian Road, Ashland, 97520; tel. 488-1626). The planes may be old-fashioned, but they are newly built and equipped with the latest in modern technology to ensure your trip is both safe and enjoyable. Flightseeing includes downtown Ashland and Lithia Park, Emigrant Lake, and Pilot Rock. To get to the airstrip, go a mile past the Ashland Hills Inn on ORE 66. Be sure to call ahead for reservations.

Day-trips

Jackson Hot Springs (ORE 99, tel. 482-3776) is two miles north of Ashland on the old highway and has a naturally heated public swimming pool as well as private mineral baths. Lighted tennis courts are found in Lithia Park, Hunter Park (on Summit Street), and on the Southern Oregon State College campus.

Meyer Memorial Pool (Hunter Park, Summit St., Ashland, 97520; tel. 488-0313) includes a wading pool for infants and toddlers under age five as well as a large swimming pool for grownups. The season kicks off with a splash Memorial Day weekend with lap and open swimming sessions 1-6 p.m. Saturday and Sunday. Summer hours start mid-June with open swimming 1:30-4:45 p.m. Monday through Friday, 7:30-8:45 p.m. Monday and Wednesday, and the regular weekend hours of 1-6 p.m. Saturday and Sunday. Admission is 50 cents per session.

Six miles east of Ashland on ORE 66 is **Emigrant Lake.** In addition to water-skiing, sailing, fishing, and swimming, a 270-foot twin flume waterslide ($3.75 for 10 rides, plus $2 admission, open 10-7 p.m. Mon.-Thurs., 10-8 p.m. Fri.-Sun.; tel. 776-7001), rental hobie cats, and windboards add to the fun in the sun. Sailing lessons and boat rentals are available from the lake's **Hobie House Marina** (tel. 488-0595). Further down ORE 66 on the summit of the Greensprings Highway about a half hour outside of Ashland is **Enchanted Rabbit Mountain** (tel. 488-1913). Here you can enjoy horse-drawn wagons, and in winter, sleigh rides, which wind leisurely through the mountaintop pine forests, taking in great views of the Rogue Valley and wildlife. Afternoon rides with an English picnic are $20; romantic moonlight rides are $10. Be sure to call ahead for reservations.

East of Ashland 20 miles on Dead Indian Road is **Howard Prairie Lake Resort** (tel. 482-1979). This 4,500-foot-high, six-mile-long lake has facilities for all water sports, horseback riding, and golf. A general store, restaurant, lodging, and 250-acre campground are also found at this retreat.

ASHLAND DRAMA

Shakespeare

While Lithia Park is the heart of Ashland, Shakespeare is the soul of this community. The festival began when Angus Bowmer, an English professor at Southern Oregon College, decided to celebrate Independence Day weekend in 1935 with a performance of *As You Like It.* He wasn't sure if the people *would* like it, so he scheduled cockfights and a boxing match during the show's intermission to ensure a large enough box office draw. By the time he retired as artistic director of the festival in 1970, his Fourth of July dream had grown up into an internationally acclaimed drama company with three theaters, one named in his honor. Nowadays, the Shakespeare festival contributes 45-million dollars annually to the area's economy, and four million people have purchased tickets over the last 55 years.

The three festival theaters are located at the southeast end of Lithia Park. Take the Shakespeare steps up the small hill by the Lithia water fountains to get to the complex known as the Shakespeare Plaza. The **Elizabethan Stage**, built on the site of Ashland's Chautauqua Dome, was modeled after the Fortune Theatre of London, 1600. This outdoor summer-only theatre is the largest of the three, and is primarily the domain of the Old Bard. While Shakespeare under the stars is incredibly romantic ("I knew she would be my wife after we saw the play together"—true story), it can also get very cold after sunset. Dress warmly, and consider investing a few bucks in the rental lap blankets and pillows for extra comfort. Also, be aware that the AA and BB rows are so close your neck gets sore peering up at the action. In addition to the physical discomfort, the large sets can be overwhelming and you not only hear the thespians say it, but you feel them spray it as well.

The second-largest playhouse is the 600-seat **Angus Bowmer.** This indoor complex is a masterpiece theater, with excellent acoustics, computerized sound and lighting, and nary a bad seat in the house. The echoes of Shakespeare's immortal prose fill this hall during the wetter winter months when the outdoor stage is closed. Finally, the 150-seat **Black Swan** is the actors' and directors' theater, where modern works and experimental productions are the norm.

Tickets

Getting tickets to the **Shakespeare Festival** (15 South Pioneer St., Box 158, Ashland, 97520; tel. 488-5406) is as much a part of the show as the performance. Due to its tremendous popularity, seats will sell out months in advance, especially for the comedies. Your best strategy is to plan ahead and order well in advance. All seats are reserved, with the best seats up front (but not too close) commanding top dollar ($20) and prices going down for seats further from the stage ($18, $16, and $12.50). If you are unable to get tickets ahead of time, your best bet is to get to the

Shakespeare Plaza an hour or two before the show with a sign requesting what show you want to see. If you are lucky, you will score tickets from someone with extras. Avoid bidding wars with other would-be theatergoers, as ticket scalping is frowned upon here. Be at the ticket window at 6 p.m. for any available seats that will then be released. There are usually standing room only tickets ($9) if all else fails.

If you would like to get a behind-the-scenes look at the action, visit the box office on the Shakespeare Plaza to find out when the backstage tours are scheduled. These tours are given by the actors and actresses and lend an interesting inside perspective to the magic of the theater.

That's Show Biz

Shakespeare isn't the only act in town. Some of the other local companies include the **Actors Workshop,** the **Lyric Theatre, Studio X, Children's Theatre,** the **Oregon Caberet Theatre,** and **Southern Oregon State College** productions. Ashland is also home to the **State Ballet of Oregon,** which gives many summer performances. The Ashland Visitor Information Center

PHOTO BY HANK KRANZLER

Sir John Falstaff is a basket case in
The Merry Wives of Windsor.

PHOTO BY OREGON STATE HIGHWAYS

*7,525-foot-high Mount Ashland is
Oregon's southernmost ski area.*

(tel. 482-3486) has complete information on all the goings-on, as does the Southern Oregon Reservation Center, tel. 488-1011 or (800) 547-8052.

A few miles north of Ashland is the town of **Talent.** The **Minshall Theatre** melodrama has been a popular favorite there for over 20 years, mainly because audience participation is openly encouraged. Here you get to cheer for the hero and boo and hiss the villain, and a splendid time is guaranteed for all.

SPORTS AND RECREATION

Skiing

Perched high atop the Siskiyou range and straddling the California/Oregon border is the highest point west of the Cascade mountains, 7,235-foot-high **Mt. Ashland** (tel. 482-2897 for info, 482-2754 for the snow report). To get there, take the Mt. Ashland exit off of I-5 and follow the road for a few miles to the complex. Skiers of all levels enjoy the 22 different runs and breathtaking vistas. An average 325 inches of snow fall on the mountain, making it possible to ski Thanksgiving through Easter. Night skiing Thursday through Saturday.

It is a good idea to check with the Southern Oregon Reservation Center (see"Information And Services" below) about any special ski packages available. Also, the spring and fall are a good time to come to Ashland, as the rates are lower than during the peak summer tourist season. Many proprietors include free Mt. Ashland ski lift tickets with the price of the room. When the snow has melted off, the walk to the top of Mt. Ashland is an easy one, with good views of the Siskiyous and Mt. Shasta. It's prudent to bring along a sweater, as it gets fairly windy up there.

Pedal Power

If you like to ride a bike but are not big on pedaling, contact the **Adventure Center** (40 N. Main, Ashland, 97520; tel. 488-2819 or 800-444-2819) for information about their Mt. Ashland downhill bike cruise. This half-day morning or picnic lunch ride descends 4,000 feet on 16 miles of quiet paved roads through the countryside to Emigrant Lake. The three-hour morning cruise departs at 8 a.m., costs $24, and includes fruit, pastries, and drinks. The four-hour picnic cruise departs at 11 a.m., costs $30, and includes a great lunch in a beautiful mountain glade. Bicycles, safety equipment, roundtrip transfer from Ashland, and a friendly, experienced guide are also provided. All you really have to do is steer! The Adventure Center also has mountain bikes for rent that include helmet, lock, and maps for $4 an hour $12 for a half day, and $20 for a full day.

The **Bicentennial Bikepath** crisscrosses through town before going down the valley to Medford along Bear Creek.

Horseback Riding

To graduate from a two-wheeled coast to a four-legged gallop, **Mountain Gate Stables** (tel. 482-8873) has many horseback riding packages to choose from. Short trail rides take in scenic views of the mountains and valleys, and longer rides deep into the woods of the Greentree Mountains include a saddlebag lunch prepared by the Greentree Restaurant. Another option features an overnight stay in creek-side cabins at Buckhorn Springs. And in the event of inclement weather, you can always practice your walk, post, and canter form in the arena. To get there, take Ashland

Street (ORE 66) two miles east of the Ashland Hills Inn. Call ahead for additional information and reservations.

Equipment, Guides, And Golf

You can rent outdoor recreation equipment from **Ashland Mountain Supply** (31 N. Main St., Ashland, 97520; tel 488-2749) for reasonable rates. The Bicentennial Bikepath crisscrosses through town before going down the valley to Medford along Bear Creek. **Headwater River Adventures** (31 N. Main St., Ashland, 97520; tel. 488-0583) operates river-running trips daily. **Four Seasons Adventures** (290 Helman St., Ashland, 97520; tel. 482-8352) also organizes rafting trips. **Ashland's Whitewater Rafting Co.** (1257 Siskiyou Blvd., Ashland, 97520; tel. 482-4721) offers full-day guided trips with lunch and transfers included. Choose between paddle rafts, rowing rafts, or inflatable kayaks.

A few miles outside of Ashland on ORE 66 is **Oak Knoll Golf Course** (3070 ORE 66, tel. 482-4311). Get into the swing of things before the play; at $6 for nine holes and $10 for 18 holes, even if you triple bogy, you can't miss. For weekend rates, add a dollar or two onto the greens fee.

PRACTICALITIES

Bed And Breakfast

The warm traditions of England are represented in Ashland not only by Oregon's leading Shakespearean festival, but also by the town's having the most bed and breakfasts of any locale in the state. Although they cost a bit more than a plastic, carbon-copy motel unit, you get so much more for your money. In addition to fresh flowers in your room, antique brass beds with down comforters, and complimentary evening aperitifs, hearty morning meals are also included. The romantic ambience of these homes away from home is ideal for a special occasion.

Another plus is that most of these establishments are within easy walking distance of the the theaters. Chances are good you will be home after the show way before many other patrons of the arts are getting to their parked cars. The properties are small, with usually only a handful of rooms, but they are also quite popular, especially during the summer. Advance planning and reser-

vations are crucial, for the odds of strolling in off the street and and finding accommodations at an Ashland bed and breakfast are remote.

Ashland Guest Villa (634 Iowa St., Ashland, 97520; tel. 488-1508, $50-65) is run by the Lamb family. Fresh flowers, gourmet breakfast, and a grand piano in the living room are a few of the features of this well-regarded establishment. **Ashland's Main St. Inn** (142 N. Main, Ashland, 97520; tel. 488-0969, $55-70) is a Victorian-style home stocked with period furnishings. A continental breakfast is brought up to your room. **The B Street House** (111 B St., Ashland, 97520; tel. 482-4217) is an entire house available for families or groups. With three bedrooms that can comfortably sleep eight, and a fully equipped kitchen, it's a steal at $135 a night.

Chanticleer (120 Greshan, Ashland, 97520; tel. 482-1919, $55-75) rules the roost with six romantic rooms replete with fluffy comforters and private baths. The **Coach House Inn** (70 Coolidge, Ashland, 97520; tel. 482-2257, $45-50) is one of Ashland's best bed and breakfast bargains. The cozy guest rooms in this restored 1890s farmhouse have beautiful mountain views. **The Country Walrus Inn** (2785 E. Main, Ashland, 97520; tel. 488-1134, $50-60) is out in the countryside, a short five-minute drive from downtown. Two spacious guest rooms are available in this restored 1880s farmhouse. Danish pancakes are the specialty for breakfast.

The six rooms of the **Edinburgh Lodge** (586 E. Main, Ashland, 97520; tel. 488-1050, $55-70) have handmade quilts and private baths. **The Hersey House** (451 N. Main, Ashland, 97520; tel. 482-4563, $65-75) is an elegantly restored Victorian with antique furniture and private baths. **The Iris Inn** (59 Manzanita, Ashland, 97520; tel. 773-7700, $50-60) is a cheerful Victorian with a fitting decor. After a walk through the Iris's gardens, you'll probably agree with Shakespeare when he wrote, "of all the flowers, methinks a rose is the finest."

The McCall House (153 Oak St., Ashland, 97520; tel. 482-9296, $55-70) is a restored Victorian built in 1883 by Ashland pioneer John McCall. It's a block away from restaurants, shops, theaters, and Lithia Park. Iron beds and handmade quilts underscore the **Miners Addition** (737 Siskiyou Blvd, Ashland, 97520; tel. 482-0562, $50-60). Children are welcome here, and

ASHLAND ACCOMMODATIONS

Name	Address	Telephone	Price	Features
Ashland Hostel	150 N. Main	482-9217	members $7 nonmembers $10	reservations highly advised
Ashland Motel	1145 Siskiyou Blvd.	482-2561	$24-30	pets, pool
Manor Motel	476 N. Main	482-2246	$25-32	kitchenettes
Vista 6 Motel	535 Clover Lane (I-5 Exit 14)	482-4423	$25-35	pool
Columbia Hotel	262 E. Main	482-3726	$30-50	European-style inn
Knight's Inn Motel	2359 Ashland St. (I-5 Exit 14)	482-5111	$30-45	cable TV, pool
Palm Motel	1065 Siskiyou Blvd.	482-2636	$32-100	wheelchair access, pool
Curl Up Motel	50 Lowe Rd.	482-4700	$34-46	pool
Timbers Motel	1450 Ashland St.	482-4242	$36-40	kitchenettes, pool
Ashland Super 8	2350 Ashland St.	482-8887	$45	wheelchair access, covered pool
Hillside Inn	1520 Siskiyou Blvd.	482-2626	$47-49	wheelchair access, pool
Valley Entrance Motel	1193 Siskiyou Blvd.	482-2641	$48-50	nonsmoking rooms, pool
Best Western	132 N. Main	482-0049 or	$50-85	heated pool
Mark Anthoy Hotel	476 N. Main	482-2246	$50-90	National Historic Landmark
Windmill's Ashland Hills Inn	2525 Ashland St.	482-8310	$60-90	free theater shuttle, many amenities
Stratford Inn	555 Siskiyou Blvd.	488-2151	$67-107	wheelchair access, covered pool

a babysitter is available. **The Morical House** (668 N. Main, Ashland, 97520; tel. 482-2254, $50-70) is a restored 19th-century home tastefully decorated with antiques. Flower gardens surround a putting green.

Five miles out of town is the **Neil Creek House** (341 Mowetza, Ashland, 97520; tel. 482-1334, $70-85). It's more than just a place to stay; it's a five-acre country retreat with pool, creek, and duck pond that help create an atmosphere of relaxed elegance. Although **Romeo Inn** (295 Idaho St., Ashland, 97520; tel. 488-0884, $78-88) is eight blocks from the Shakespeare Plaza, the large bedrooms with private baths and the patio with a heated pool and jacuzzi make it worth the walk. The **Royal Carter House** (514 Siskiyou Blvd., Ashland, 97520; tel. 482-5623, $50-80) has rooms with private baths, antiques, and a special breakfast fit for a king.

Three miles south of town is a real farm Bed and Breakfast, the **Shutes Lazy S** (200 Mowetza, Ashland, 97520; tel. 482-5498, $50-65, two-day minimum, nonsmokers). In addition to down comforters, antiques, and a drama library where you can read up on the evening's play, an organically grown feast is elegantly presented for you. The **Spiridon House** (353 Haragadine St., Ashland, 97520; tel. 488-1362, $100-130) is another place where you can bring the tribe—three bedrooms sleep eight in this light and airy home three blocks from downtown. The **Winchester Inn** (35 S. 2nd St., Ashland, 97520; tel. 488-1113, $55-80) is a six-room Victorian with private baths and a gourmet restaurant. Breakfast is served out on the patio at the **Wisteria House** (133 N. Main, Ashland, 97520; tel. 488-1598, $60-70), and the adjacent carriage house has two-room suites that can comfortably sleep six.

Food

The **Wizard's Den** (59 N. Main St., Ashland, 97520; tel. 482-4867) is a bakery/restaurant that features wonderful breads, gourmet lunches, and enormous salads. The back room overlooking Lithia Creek is the best place to sit. Good pita sandwiches can be had at **Toonerville Deli and Wine Shop** (Orchid Lane Mall, Ashland, 97520; tel. 482-1233). The **Back Porch Barbecue** (88 N. Main, Ashland, 97520; tel. 482-4131) lives up to its name. In addition to chicken, ribs, and the like, live music on summer weekends and extra

tables outside the building along the creek round out the cookout motif. The **Bakery Cafe** (38 E. Main St., Ashland, 97520; tel. 482-2117) makes a mean breakfast, and the buckwheat pancakes come with real maple syrup. **Theresa's Cantina** serves "heart smart" Mexican cuisine without all of the MSG, salt, and lard. **Omar's**, (1380 Siskiyou Blvd., Ashland, 97520; tel. 482-1281), Ashland's oldest restaurant, is noted for its seafood. **Michael's Fine Hamburgers** (457 Siskiyou Blvd., Ashland, 97520; tel. 482-9205) not only has the best burgers in town, but Texas-style barbecue and chili as well. **Geppetto's** (345 E. Main, Ashland, 97520; tel. 482-1138) is the place to go for Italian cuisine. Nothing fancy, just real food prepared and served by real people at real prices. If you're in the mood for crepes filled with your choice of fresh ingredients, try **Banbury Cross Crêperie** (55 N. Main, Ashland, 97520; tel. 482-3644). **Brothers Restaurant and Deli** (95 N. Main, Ashland, 97520; tel. 482-9671) specializes in kosher-style foods. **Rosie's Sweet Shop** (303 E. Main, Ashland, 97520; tel. 488-0179) and **Second Hand Rose Ice Cream Parlor** (40 N. Main, Ashland, 97520; tel. 482-9962) both feature hot dogs, burritos, and customized sandwiches, as well as gourmet ice cream. **Frank's Pizzeria** (92 N. Main, Ashland, 97520; tel. 482-4531) offers New York-style pizza by the slice or by the pie.

Chata (1212 S. Pacific Highway, Talent, 97540; tel. 535-2575) is a few miles away from Ashland but worth the trip. Reflecting the warm traditions of Poland, *bigos* (hunter's stew), *golabki* (cabbage balls), and *mamaliga* (sautéed cornmeal with cheeses) are a few of the well-prepared dishes you'll find here. The only buffet champagne brunch in town is at the **Ashland Hills Inn** (2525 Ashland St., Ashland, 97520; tel. 482-8310). An abundant array of salads, pastries, entrees, and a seafood bar are featured here 1-2 p.m. The brunch is held outside on the patio in warm weather. A decent list of Oregon and California wines adds to the variety of dishes.

The menu at **Crystal** (212 E. Main, Ashland, 97520; tel. 482-1721) is as elaborate as the huge chandelier that looms over the dining room. A Paris-trained chef prepares sumptuous entrees, artful soups, and elegant desserts. **Chateaulin** (150 E. Main St., Ashland, 97520; tel. 482-2264) looks the most Shakespearean, with its dark wooden interior and lighted stained glass behind the bar. Traditional French and nouvelle cuisines are offered in a menu that changes weekly. If you go there after the play for one of their 25 specialty coffee drinks, be careful what you say about the performance—Hamlet or Falstaff may show up wearing blue jeans.

Nightlife

Rogue Brewery and Publichouse (31 S. Water St., Bluebird Park, Ashland, 97520; tel. 488-5061) is southern Oregon's only microbrewery and brewpub. A full selection of handcrafted ales is complemented by a unique menu designed to enhance the flavor of the beer. Another particularly pleasant feature is that this is a smokeless pub. The only rock 'n' roll club in the valley is **Soc Hop** (1700 Ashland St., Ashland, 97520; tel. 488-1780). A live DJ plays your favorites of the '50s, '60s, and '70s. The standard soda fountain menu keeps you fortified and rockin' around the clock. What else can you say? Some of us never grow up!

Allann Brothers (1602 Ashland St., Ashland, 97520; tel. 488-0700) is a cozy coffeehouse with live music Friday and Saturday nights. Gourmet coffee drinks, soups and sandwiches, and fine desserts are available. During the summer, **Brooklyn A Nightclub** (33 Water St., Ashland, 97520; tel. 488-2867) has nightly rock and rhythm 'n' blues, except Sunday and Tuesday. **The Vintage Inn** (31 Water St., Ashland, 97520; tel. 482-1120) is right next door and features a potpourri of nightly entertainment. Jazz, classical, folk, and bluegrass are some of the musical strains you may hear here. Something always seems to be happening at the **Mark Anthony Hotel** (212 E. Main, Ashland, 97520; tel. 482-1721), whether it be music in the lounge, piano bar in the lobby, or a play in the ballroom. Call ahead to find out what's scheduled on the program. **Jazmin's** (180 C St., Ashland, 97520; tel. 488-0883) has a dance floor and live music Thur.-Sat. evenings; cover $1 and up. The cheapest beer in town can be found at the **Log Cabin Tavern** (41 N. Main St., Ashland, 97520; tel. 482-9701).

Services And Information

Ashland's Visitor Information Center (110 E. Main St., Ashland, 97520; tel. 482-3486) offers brochures, play schedules, and other up-to-date information on what's happening. The chamber has two booklets in particular (available upon request for a small fee) that will help you appreciate the unusual variety of trees and shrubs in Lithia Park: *Woodland Trails* and *Lithia Park—The History.* Another excellent source of information is the **Southern Oregon Reservation Center** (Box 477, Ashland, 97520; tel. 488-1011 in Oregon, 800-547-8052 in U.S.A.). This agency specializes in arranging Shakespearean vacation packages with quality lodging, choice seats for performances in all three theaters, and other tour and entertainment extras.

The **post office** (Lithia Way and 1st St., Ashland, 97520; tel. 482-3986) is open during regular business hours, Monday through Friday; for **police** call 482-5211 or 911. **Ashland Community Hospital** (280 Maple St., Ashland, 97520; tel. 482-2441) has 24-hour medical service.

Getting There And Getting Around

Greyhound (91 Oak St., Ashland, 97520; tel. 482-2516) serves Ashland with a handful of daily north and southbound departures. Local connections between Medford and Ashland are possible through **Rogue Valley Transportation** (tel. 799-BUSS). The #10 bus leaves every half hour from 5 a.m. to 8 p.m. Contact **Ski Ashland** (Box 220, Ashland, 97520; tel. 482-2897) for information on the Mt. Ashland daily bus runs to and from Medford and Ashland. Twenty-four-hour **taxi** service is available from **Ashland Taxi** (tel. 482-3065). **Executive Rent-a-Car** (Butler Ford, 1977 U.S. 99, tel. 482-2521) picks up and delivers anywhere in the Bear Creek Valley. Used cars for $10 a day plus mileage are possible through the **Ashland Hills Inn** (2525 Ashland St., Ashland, 97520; tel. 482-8310).

MEDFORD AND VICINITY

In the 1850s, gold discoveries drew people and commerce to the Rogue River Valley. The seat of the prosperity was Jacksonville, whose boom went bust in the 1880s when the new railroad line bypassed this major stagecoach stop for a train station known as Middle Ford. Middle Ford became shortened to Medford and was incorporated in 1885.

Today, along with a resource-based economy revolving around agriculture and timber products, Medford is becoming established as a retirement center. Proximity to Ashland's culture, Rogue Valley recreation, and Cascade getaways, as well as rainfall totals half those recorded in the Willamette Valley, are some of the enticements. Unfortunately, if the current population of 40,000 grows much larger, the already poor air quality here will become worse. Already smog alerts brought on by heat and inversions have folks calling the city "Dreadford."

Call it what you will, but for cost of living, location, and employment opportunities, there is no better place to live in southern Oregon than Medford.

SIGHTS

Table Rocks

About 10 miles outside of Medford to the northeast are two eye-catching basaltic mesas, Upper and Lower Table Rock. These mesas are composed of sandstone with an erosion-resistant lava cap that was deposited during a massive Cascade eruption about four to five million years ago. Over the years, the wind and water have undercut the sandstone. Stripped of their underpinnings, the heavy basalt on top of the eroded sandstone is pulled down by gravity, creating nearly vertical slabs that we see today.

Table Rocks was the site of a decisive battle in the first of a series of Rogue Indian Wars in the 1850s. Major Kearny, who later went on to distinguish himself as the great one-armed Civil War general, was successful in routing the Indians from this seemingly impervious stronghold. A peace treaty was signed here soon afterwards by the Rogue (Takilma) Indians and the American government. For a time, this area was also part of the Table Rock Indian Reservation, but the reservation status was terminated shortly thereafter.

For nearly a century, the Table Rocks were the domain of vultures and rattlesnakes until the **Lower Table Rock Preserve** was established in 1979. This 1,890-acre preserve is near the westernmost mesa that towers 800 feet above the surrounding valley floor. Initially established by the Nature Conservancy and later turned over to the government, the preserve protects an area of special biologic, geologic, historic, and scenic value. Pacific madrone, white oak, manzanita, and ponderosa pine grow on the flank of the mountain, while the crown is covered with grasses and wildflowers. Park checklists show that over 140 different kinds of plants reside here, including dwarf meadow foam, which grows no place else on earth. One reason is because water doesn't readily percolate through the lava. Small vernal ponds collect on top of the mesa, nurturing the wildflowers that flourish in early spring. The wildflower display reaches its zenith in April. A dozen different kinds of flowers cover the rock-strewn flats with bright yellows and vivid purples.

Hikers who take the two-mile trail to the top of Lower Table Rock are in for a treat. Be on the lookout for batches of pale lavender fawn lilies peeking out from underneath the shelter of the scraggly scrub oaks on the way up the mountain. The trail takes you to the top of this crudely U-shaped mesa. You'll want to walk over to the cliff's edge, which will take you past some of the mima "mounds" or "patterned ground" that distinguishes the surface of the mesa. How the mounds were formed is a matter of scientific debate. Some scientists believe they represent centuries of work by rodents, others think they are accumulated silt deposits, while still others maintain that they have been created by the action of the wind. However they got there, the mounds are the only soil banks on the mountain that support grasses that are unable to grow on the lava. Lichens and mosses manage to grow on the lava, however, painting the dull black basalt with luxuriant greens and fluorescent yellows during the wetter months.

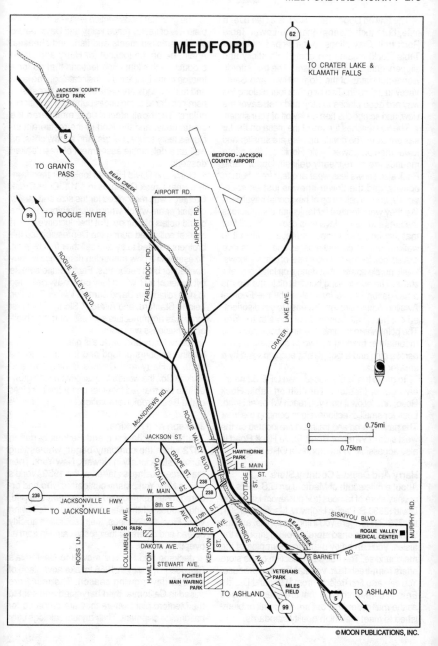

MEDFORD

TO CRATER LAKE &
KLAMATH FALLS

JACKSON COUNTY
EXPO PARK

MEDFORD - JACKSON
COUNTY AIRPORT

TO GRANTS
PASS

TO ROGUE RIVER

BEAR CREEK

AIRPORT RD.

AIRPORT RD.

TABLE ROCK RD.

ROGUE VALLEY BLVD.

McANDREWS RD.

CRATER LAKE AVE.

0   0.75mi

0   0.75km

JACKSON ST.

HAWTHORNE
PARK

E. MAIN
ST.

GRAPE ST.

OAKDALE
AVE.

W. MAIN
ST.

COTTAGE
ST.

JACKSONVILLE HWY.

TO JACKSONVILLE

8th ST.

10th ST.

RIVERSIDE
AVE.

SISKIYOU BLVD.

BEAR CREEK

MURPHY RD.

ROGUE VALLEY
MEDICAL CENTER

UNION PARK

MONROE

ROSS LN.

COLUMBUS
AVE.

HAMILTON

DAKOTA AVE.

KENYON
ST.

BARNETT RD.

STEWART AVE.

FICHTER
MAIN WARING
PARK

VETERANS
PARK

MILES
FIELD

TO ASHLAND

TO ASHLAND

© MOON PUBLICATIONS, INC.

The trail up Upper Table Rock is a little over a mile, but much steeper than the Lower Table Rock trail. Clay clings to the slopes of Upper Table Rock, making the going both sticky and slippery during the wet season. The trail affords wonderful vistas of the Rogue River and Sams Valley to the north. Two benches found along the way are good places to stop and rest, savor the view, and scrape the heavy clay off of your shoes.

The trail reaches the top of the mesa on the far eastern side. The ponds up here are smaller and fewer than on Lower Table Rock, but the mima mounds are more clearly defined. Upper Table Rock also shows less wear and tear from human activity, and the flower show is just as spectacular. Long black strips of hexagonal basalt look like they were formed by tanks marching across the mesa while the lava was cooling. You'll find that this irregular, knobby surface is difficult to walk on, but the colorful mosses and lichens love it. Also look for the tiny bouquets of grass widows, lovely purple flowers that dangle on long, graceful stalks. The odd-looking building off to the west is a navigation device maintained by the Federal Aviation Administration. It's easy to get disoriented out here, with hundreds of acres to explore. The point where the trail descends back down the mountain is marked by two large trees, a ponderosa pine and a Douglas fir, accompanied by a smaller cedar.

To get to the Table Rocks, take ORE 62 northeast out of Medford. Turn left on Table Rock Road, and follow it until you reach Wheeler Road. Look for small directional signs pointing the way. The parking area and trailhead are located on the west side of Wheeler Road. Table Rock Road is also accessible to the north via ORE 234.

Harry And David's Country Store

About a mile south of Medford on U.S. 99 is the country store of famous fruit purveyors Harry and David (2836 S. Pacific Highway, Medford, 97501; tel. 776-2277). Here you'll find food, gifts, and fun in their old-fashioned store. Strolling through the aisles, you can enjoy many free samples of the merchandise. The fruit-stand section of the store offers farm-fresh fruit, vegetables, and produce. You can also find "rejects" from Harry and David's Fruit-of-the-Month Club that are nearly as good as the mail order fruit, but are too small or blemished to meet their high quality standards.

The gourmet foods section features their complete line of freshly made Harry and David baked goods, smoked meats and fish, and cheeses. Again, be on the lookout for Harry and David products with slight imperfections that go for a fraction of the cost listed in their catalog. The jams and fruit spreads are particularly less expensive here compared to the prices published in their circulars. Their deli stacks up a multitiered ice cream cone, and the food in the restaurant includes tasty soups, salads, and sandwiches, as well as a delectable assortment of fresh-baked desserts.

Harry and David Holmes took over their family's Bear Creek Orchards in 1914. Bear Creek Orchards was recognized for the size and quality of their pears which where were shipped to the grand hotels of Europe. But their lucrative export market collapsed during the Depression, so the brothers decided to try and sell their fruit by mail. To establish a new reputation domestically, they headed for both seaboards. Each carried sample gift boxes of fruit, which they personally delivered to high rollers like David Sarnoff, Walter Chrysler, Leland Stanford, and Alfred P. Sloan. Their first foray was an immediate success, and their mail-order business was born.

Today, Harry and David's is one of the world's leading shippers of food and fruit gifts. To the north of Harry and David's is Jackson and Perkins Co., the world's largest private rose grower. The two merged together under the auspices of the Bear Creek Corporation.

Jackson And Perkins

The history of Jackson and Perkins began in 1872 when the company began wholesaling nursery stock locally in Newark, New York. Their mail-order business started at the 1939 World's Fair in New York. Many customers who had ordered roses appreciated having them shipped, and requested the same service the following year. From this nucleus, their reputation quickly spread and orders for their roses came in from all over the country.

Jackson and Perkins moved to California's San Joaquin Valley in 1966 to take advantage of the 262-day growing season. The roses are raised in California, then harvested and sent to the Medford plant where they are prepared for nationwide shipment. Their annual catalogs offer bulbs, seeds, and plants of all kinds as well as their award-winning roses. Take a walk down the primrose path of their 43,000-square-foot Test and Display Garden next to the warehouse anytime between May and October to enjoy the colorful sights and sweet smells of the floral displays.

Grist For The Mill

About 15 minutes away from Medford on ORE 62 is Oregon's last original water-powered grist mill that's still in operation, the **Butte Creek Mill** (Box 561, 402 Royal, Eagle Point, 97524; tel. 826-3531). To get there, take ORE 62 about 10 miles north to Eagle Point and follow the signs to the mill. Built in 1872, you can see that the foundation pillars were hand-hewn with an axe and that wooden pegs and square nails hold up the rest of the structure. The two 1,400-pound millstones were quarried in France and assembled in Illinois. From there, they were shipped around the Horn and then transported over the mountains by wagon. Listen to the harmonious discord of the belts clapping, pulleys creaking, and grindstones groaning. Genuine stone-ground products are available in the mill shop. The list of fresh-ground items is extensive: 12 kinds of flours, four kinds of meal, four cracked grains, six cereals, four mixes (pancake, waffle, cornbread, and biscuit), and other grain products. The mill also makes many kinds of pasta and old-fashioned peanut butter. A variety of health food products rounds out the nutritious collection of edibles here. Open from 9-5 p.m. daily (except Sunday and major holidays), the admission is free.

Adjacent to the mill is the **Oregon General Store Museum.** This museum is a re-creation of a late 1800s typical general store. Home remedies, giant coffee grinders, pickle barrels, and other common goods of the day are exhibited. A working music box, antiques and collectibles, and old advertising signs add to the decor. Open 11-4 p.m. on Saturdays.

Ridin' The Rails

Just about anyone who likes trains will enjoy **Medford Railroad Park** (tel. 770-4586 or 779-7979). The park is located on Berrydale Avenue off of Table Rock Road, a few blocks away from the Rogue Valley Mall. The park features miniature steam railroad trains that run the second and fourth Sundays of each month, April through October, from 11-3 p.m. Locomotives and other railway equipment are faithful reproductions of full-size trains, only one-inch here equals a foot out in the real world. Coal, wood, oil, and propane fire the steam boilers that propel the trains around a mile-long track. Passengers are carried in small cars across bridges, culverts, and over a small grade. Admission is $2 for adults, $1 for children.

SPORTS AND RECREATION

Take Me Out To The Ball Game

Medford's **Miles Field** (tel. 770-5364) is located about a mile south of town near the Armory on U.S. 99, and is the home turf of the Medford Athletics baseball team, a farm club of the 1989 World Champion Oakland Athletics. Here you get the opportunity to watch budding hopefuls round the bases on their way up to the bigs and might-have-beens shuffle back unnoticed to the dugout. Jose Canseco, Oakand's home-run slugger and American League Rookie of the Year in 1985, used to play here. And while it's not exactly Major League action, you can sit closer to the field and the admission is definitely minor: it costs $3.50 for adults and $2.50 for seniors and children. The season runs from mid-June through Labor Day. Call ahead to see what team is in town.

Golf

Near Miles Field is **Bear Creek Golf Course** (2325 South Pacific Highway, Medford, 97501; tel. 773-1822). This is a compact little nine-hole course that's both a challenge and a bargain at $5 a round. If you would rather go for a regulation-sized field, **Cedar Links Golf Course** (3144 Cedar Links Dr., Medford, 97501; tel. 773-4373) in northeastern Medford has 18 holes waiting for you. To get there, take ORE 62 north towards White City. Turn right on Delta Waters Road, right again on Springbrook Road, and then left on Cedar Links Drive. The greens fee is $9 for nine holes and $14 for 18 holes; add a dollar or two more on weekends.

Splish Splash

When the mercury heats up into the 90s and 100s during the summer, it's time to cool off in one of Medford's several public swimming pools. **Jackson Pool** (815 Summit, Medford, 97504; tel.

770-4586) is a popular family place to get wet. In addition to the 100-foot-long water slide, a concession stand there sells popsicles, ice cream bars, soft drinks, and other snacks. The swimming season starts June 11 and runs on into early September. An open recreational swim is held from 1-3 p.m. Monday through Wednesday and also on Friday. Thursday evenings are reserved for family swims, 7:30-9:15 p.m. Admission is $1 for adults, 50 cents for people 18 and under. **Hawthorne Pool** (505 E. Main St., Medford, 97504; tel. 770-4586) features an open swim from 1-3 p.m. and 3:30-5:30 Sunday through Friday.

The indoor **YMCA Pool** (1522 W. 6th St., Medford, 97504; tel. 772-6295) offers several open swim sessions all year around. Open swims are 3-4:30 p.m. Monday, 3-3:45 and 8-9 p.m. Tuesday, 3-3:45 Wednesday, 8-9 p.m. Thursday, 10-11 a.m. and 3-4:30 Friday, and 1-4:15 p.m. Saturday. Admission is $1.50 per session; be sure to call ahead to confirm scheduling.

PRACTICALITIES

Bed And Breakfast

A romantic bed and breakfast with a park-like ambience is the **Greenwood Tree** (3045 Bellinger Lane, Medford, 97501; tel. 776-0000). The rooms and suites here have private baths and are decorated with antiques, Persian rugs, and fabric art collections. A lavish breakfast and afternoon tea in the parlor, on the porch, or out in the garden as well as chocolate truffles on your pillow at night further enhance the atmosphere. In addition to a hand-hewn and hand-pegged building dating

MEDFORD ACCOMMODATIONS

Name	Address	Telephone	Price	Features
Valli Hai Hotel	1034 Court St.	772-6183	$20-25	clean and cheap
Harvey's Motel	1510 S. Central Ave.	779-6561	$20-25	
Motel 6	950 Alba Dr.	773-4290	$24-30	pool
City Center Motel	324 S. Central Ave.	773-6248	$24-30	pool
Cedar Lodge Motor Inn	518 N. Riverside Ave.,	773-736	$26-31	pool, nonsmoking rooms
Pine Tree Inn Motel	525 S. Riverside Ave.	772-6133	$27-32	pool, nonsmoking rooms
Sierra Inn Motel	345 S. Central Ave.	773-7727	$27-32	kitchenettes
Millwood Inn Motel	1034 N, Riverside Ave.	773-1152	$28-34	pool. lounge
Windmill Inn of Medford	1950 Biddle Rd.	779-0050	$41-59	wheelchair access, pool
Horizon Motor Inn	1154 E. Barnett Rd.	779-5085	$42-48	wheelchair access pool, lounge
Shilo Inn of Medford	2111 Biddle Rd.	770-5151	$45-55	wheelchair access, pets
Pony Soldier Motor Inn	2340 Crater Lake Highway (ORE 62)	779-2011		wheelchair access, pets, pool
Red Lion Inn	200 N. Riverside Ave.	772-9099	$62-75	everything

LA BURRITA

If you are an aficionado of Mexican food, make sure that you plan for a lunch or dinner at La Burrita. The original La Burrita Restaurant is on ORE 238 between Jacksonville and Medford, and recently outlets of this popular establishment have opened up in Medford and Grants Pass. But as with many replicas, the copies never seem to be quite as good as the original, so visit the *genuine* La Burrita (2715 Jacksonville Hwy.—same as ORE 238— tel. 770-5770) if possible.

Half of this restaurant is a store that carries authentic Mexican foodstuffs and beverages. This is where you order your food at the counter. The chile rellenos here are the best in Oregon, and generous two item combination plates with rice, beans, and chips go for under $3. The accompanying homemade salsa is hot enough for most people, but if you really want to do the Oregon version of the "Mexican Hat Dance," ask for the extra hot salsa: this legendary green mixture is pure ground jalapenos. The dining room is also a throwback to old Mexico, with day-glo felt paintings on the walls that are "so bad that they're good." Enjoy your food along with the toe-tapping gay-sad strains of a distant accordion, gracias to the Norteño music that is always playing in the background. This is where the migrant workers come to fortify themselves and socialize in between gigs in the fields and orchards. The place may be funky, but its great food at a great price, as well as being a bite-sized slice of southern Oregon life.

back to the Civil War, a willow swing in a three-story barn, a hammock suspended between enormous 300-year-old oaks, and a gazebo beneath shady apple trees overlooking the rose garden also grace the grounds.

Another popular bed and breakfast is found at the **Holly Street Suites** (304 North Holly St., Medford, 97501; tel. 779-4716). Three historic structures here offer unique accommodations. The five-room Waverly Cottage was built around the turn of the century and is one of southern Oregon's most ornate Queen Anne-style homes. A magnificent red cedar archway with gold-leafed carvings and antique etched glass is between the dining room and parlor. The kitchen and pantry are tastefully painted to bring out the oak cabinets, counters, and plaster gingerbread. The bathroom is equipped with a clawfoot bathtub and a European temperature-controlled shower sprayer. The master bedroom has a canopied king-sized bed, the other bedroom has a double bed, and both rooms have antique dressers. All five of these rooms are yours to enjoy privately.

The Edwardian is a private three-room suite featuring a bedroom with a queen-sized brass bed, private bath, living room with cable TV, kitchen, and laundry room. Plants, flowers, a wraparound porch, and breakfast-in-a-basket delivered to your door add the finishing touches.

The Holly House is broken up into two suites, the King and Queen. The King suite is a spacious three-room unit fit for royalty. The king-sized bed, private bath, and a kitchen/dining room featuring African mahogany and a rosewood wet bar will make you feel like the lord of the manor. The other half of the building houses the Queen suite. The bedroom is large with two queen-sized beds separated by an oak divider. The kitchen has an antique wood cookstove, and the solarium is bright and comfortable. Both suites have private entrances and breakfast is delivered between 7:30-9:30 a.m. at your convenience.

Rates for these digs are $75 for singles and $80 for double accommodations Sunday through Thursday, and $95 for singles and $100 for doubles Friday and Saturday. Additional guests are $20 each. Reservations are advised, and the Waverly Cottage has a two-day minimum-stay requirement on weekends and holidays.

Food

The **Alpine Restaurant** (1011 Spring St., Medford, tel. 772-2481) offers cuisine that reflects the traditions of old Germany. Open for breakfast, lunch, and dinner, the German apple pancake is a popular way to start the day. For dinner try some sauerbraten served with red cabbage and spaetzle (homemade German noodles). Dinners are accompanied with soup, salad, and fresh baked bread.

A family restaurant where you can find some elegance on a budget is **Apple Annie's** (1021 S. Riverside, Medford, tel. 776-0711 and 900 Alba Dr., Medford, tel. 779-4472). Many specialty items are featured on the menu here, as well as some of the more traditional favorites. Breakfast specials like the French toast combo (two pieces of French toast, two breakfast meats, and one egg) and the deluxe pancake sandwich (Two eggs, two meats, and two pancakes) go for $3.35. Dinner specials range from $5-10.

Deli Down (406 E. Main St. #6, Medford, tel. 772-4520) makes its own pasta every day. Specialties include pasta salads, meat pastries, overstuffed sandwiches, all you can eat pasta bar, and homemade cheesecake. You'll find the restaurant in the Main Street Market. For some Italian cuisine and atmosphere, try **Ruffino's** (730 E. Main, Medford, tel. 770-5539). Many types of pastas are featured here, including spaghetti and meatballs, lasagna, and cannelloni. Wash down some spicy buffalo wings with a good selection of beer and wine.

Mr. Pauls (1922 N. Pacific Highway, Medford, tel. 776-0711) is a full-menu restaurant offering family-style food. Daily breakfast specials like a Denver omelette, French toast and bacon, or ground sirloin steak and eggs are $2.99. Lunch soup and sandwich specials are $3.50. Dinner specials like roast turkey and dressing or Italian spaghetti with meatballs and garlic toast are $3.99. All dinners include choice of potato or rice pilaf, vegetable, soup or salad, and roll and butter.

Stanley's (510 N. Riverside, Medford, tel. 772-5114) is open for breakfast, lunch, and dinner. Lunch specials like Caesar salad with chicken tenders and quiche Lorraine go for $4.25, with dinner specials ranging from $5-8. **The Sandpiper** (1841 Barnett Road, Medford, tel. 779-0100) is open weekdays for lunch and dinner and for dinner only on weekends. Early-bird dinners

like teriyaki chicken, petite sirloin, prime rib, or the fresh catch of the day are served with soup, rice, and vegetables for $9.95. Full chicken, beef, and seafood dinners that range from $12-20 come with choice of soup, salad or salad bar, potatoes or rice, vegetables, and bread. Turtle boats and mud pie are among the variety of sweet treats on the dessert tray.

The Wild Plum (1528 Biddle Road, Medford, tel. 772-5200) features fresh salads, soups, and sandwiches as well as light and full dinners. You may go "plum crazy" trying to decide which one of their 33 flavors of pie to enjoy. A favorite with loggers and truckers, **Withams** (2339 Biddle Road, Medford, tel. 772-9307) has inexpensive daily lunch and dinner specials that include soup or salad for $2.95 and $3.95 respectively. The food's pretty good, and the price is right, even though you might think you're on the set for *Convoy*.

Events

The **Jackson County Fair** is held at the county fairgrounds just north of town the third weekend of July. Admission is $5 for adults, $2 for children, and parking is an additional $2. Frequent shuttle bus departures from Medford relieve you of fighting the crowds for limited parking spaces. The buses leave from downtown Medford, Poplar Square, Crater High School, and other points around town. The trip back from the fair is free, and the shuttles run approximately every 15 minutes. This service is provided by **Rouge Valley Transportation** (3200 Crater Lake Ave., Medford, 97504; tel. 799-2988).

Cowboys, ranchers, and farmers all come in with their families for fun and top-name entertainment. Country music seems to dominate the stage, with performers like Ricky Skaggs, Waylon Jennings, and Charlie Pride drawling out their tunes. If the kids are going to spend the day at the midway, consider purchasing their ride tickets in advance and saving 50% off (except Saturday) the regular $7.95 "one price for all rides." Check with the Medford Chamber of Commerce (see "Services And Information" below) for presale ticket outlets.

Free rides on a 40-foot sternwheeler are offered on the south pond. Professional fishing guides will teach kids tricks of the trade at Huck Finn's Fishing Pier, which is also located on the pond. And in addition to the normal selection of

sunset views of Harris Beach (both Frank Long)

jams, fruits, and vegetables, fly-tying and contemporary collections (like baseball cards) are other judged categories that are worth a closer look.

Services And Information

The **post office** (333 W. 8th, Medford, 97501, tel. 776-3604) is open Mon.-Fri. 8:30-5, and can also help with passport information in addition to selling stamps and envelopes. **Providence Hospital** (1111 Crater Lake Avenue, Medford, 97501; tel. 773-6611) has 24-hour emergency care. This is where the flying angels of Air Medivac speedily bring in people from remote areas for immediate treatment. From basic home health services to intensive care, the staff of **Rogue Valley Medical Center** (2825 Barnett Road, Medford, 97501; tel. 773-6281) is ready around the clock to help you when you need help. **Medford Physicians and Surgeons Clinic** (1025 E. Main St., Medford, 97501; tel. 773-6271) offers 24-hour pediatrics, surgery, and cardiology care as well as specialists for a host of other ailments.

The **police** (tel. 770-4783 or 911 for emergencies only) and state police (2700 N. Pacific Highway, Medford, 97501; tel. 776-6111 or 911 for emergencies only) can help out in case there's trouble. The **Medford Visitors and Convention Bureau** (304 S. Central Ave., tel. 772-6293) and **Log Cabin Information Center** (88 Stewart Road, Medford, 97501; tel. 776-4021) have all kinds of useful maps, directories, and information for the asking. Both offices are open Monday through Friday 9-5. Additional information on recreational sites and parks of interest in the Medford area can be acquired from the **Bureau of Land Management** office (3040 Biddle Road,

Medford, 97501; tel. 770-2200). The Medford library (413 W. Main, Medford, 97501; tel. 776-7287) has one of the best collections of books, magazines, and periodicals in southern Oregon.

Out of a half dozen coin-operated laundries in Medford, **B.J.'s Homestyle Laundromat** (1712 W. Main, Medford, 97501; tel. 773-4803) is the most pleasant establishment. With games, television, and a snack bar, it's almost like doing your laundry at home. Open seven days a week from 8 a.m. to 9 p.m., an attendant is always on duty and dry-cleaning and drop-off washing services are available.

Getting There And Getting Around

The **Greyhound** (212 Barlett Rd., tel. 779-2103) depot is open 6 a.m. to midnight daily. **Rogue Valley Transportation** (3200 Crater Lake Ave., tel. 799-2988) provides connections to Jacksonville, Phoenix, White City, Talent, and Ashland. Most buses depart Medford at 6th and Bartlett, Mon.-Fri. 8-5, Sat. 9-5, no service Sundays. Linkages to Eagle Point and White City are courtesy of **Cascade Bus Lines,** but call 664-4801 for the schedule, as it fluctuates. **Courtesy Yellow Cab** (tel. 772-6288) has 24-hour service in the Medford area. A wheelchair van, senior citizen discounts, and special rates on airport transfers are all available on request.

Medford/Jackson County Airport (administrative office tel. 776-7222) is the air hub for southern Oregon and is served by United, Horizon, and other carriers. Two rental car agencies are out at the airport, **Budget** (tel. 773-7023) and **National** (tel. 779-4863).

(top) Deep Creek Falls, Lake County, eastern Oregon; (bottom left) Sahalie Falls, Linn County, Cascades; (bottom right) Vidae Falls, southern Oregon Cascades (all Oregon Tourism Division)

JACKSONVILLE

Oregon's pioneer past is tastefully preserved in Jacksonville. Located five miles west of Medford and cradled in the foothills of the Siskiyou Mountains, Jacksonville retains an atmosphere of tranquil isolation. This small town of 2,100 residents with about 90 original wooden and brick buildings dating back to the 1850s was the first designated National Historic Landmark District in Oregon and the third such site in the nation to receive this distinction.

In early 1852, two itinerant prospectors, Cluggage and Poole, were returning to a northern California mining camp with supplies from the Willamette Valley. They camped by a creek in the area for a night's rest. The next morning, they found a good-sized gold nugget in a hoof print made by one of their pack animals in what became known as Ruth's Gulch. They continued on to California with their goods for the other miners, but in the excitement of their discovery, the secret slipped out. They hurriedly backtracked their way to southern Oregon and staked their claims along Ruth Gulch and Daisy Creek. Within a matter of weeks, the mining camp population grew from two to 2,000. Tents, wooden shacks, and log cabins were hastily erected, and the town of Table Rock City was born. The name was changed to Jacksonville the following year, in honor of President Andrew Jackson and the town's namesake county.

The town grid was surveyed in September, 1852 into 200-foot-square blocks. California and Oregon streets were then as well as now the hub of business and social life in Jacksonville. But the city's tightly packed wooden structures proved to be especially prone to fire. Between 1873 and 1884, three major fires reduced most of the original building to ashes. These harsh experiences prompted merchants to use brick in the construction of a second generation of buildings, and the practice was further substantiated by an 1878 city ordinance requiring same. Most of the building blocks were made and fired locally. To prevent them from returning to the earth during the damp seasons, the porous bricks were painted to protect them from the elements; cast iron window shutters and door frames further reinforced the structures.

Boomtown Jacksonville was the first and largest town in the region and was selected as the county seat. It was even nominated and briefly considered as the state capitol. The prominence of Jacksonville was made manifest with the 1883 erection of a 60-foot-high courthouse with 14-inch thick walls. But like the gold finds that quickly played out, Jacksonville's boisterous exuberance began to subside when the Oregon and California Railroad bypassed Jacksonville in the early 1880s in favor of the nearby hopeful hamlet of Medford. Businesses were quick to move east to greet the coming of the iron horse, and Jacksonville's stature as a trading center diminished. When the county seat was finally moved to Medford in 1927, the heady days of Jacksonville had long since vanished.

During the Depression, families with low incomes took up residence in the town's unmaintained buildings, taking advantage of the cheap rents. Gold mining enjoyed a brief comeback, with residents digging shafts and tunnels in backyards, but it was not enough to revive the derailed economy. However, the following decades saw a gradual resurgence of interest in Jacksonville's gold rush heritage. The Southern Oregon Historical Society was created after World War II and took up residence in the former Jacksonville County Courthouse building. Individuals began to take interest in the many unaltered late 1880s buildings and restore them to their former glory. The **Beekman Bank** was one of the first structures to be spruced up, and the prominent **United States Hotel** was rehabilitated in 1964. The restoration movement was rewarded when the National Park Service designated Jacksonville as a National Historic Landmark in 1966.

Today, Jacksonville paints a memorable picture of a Western town with its historic buildings, excellent museum, and a beautiful pioneer cemetery. In addition, a renowned music festival, colorful pageants, and a rich local folklore all pay tribute to Jacksonville's golden age.

Jackson County Museum

A good place to start your explorations is at the museum (206 N. 5th St., Jacksonville, 97530; tel. 773-6536). This imposing two-story brick-and-stone Italianate building was completed in 1883, and served as the county seat of government until it was moved to Medford in 1927. For more than two decades, the structure didn't have any permanent tenants, but then became the Jackson County Museum and headquarters of the Southern Oregon Historical Society in 1950.

Nowadays, in addition to pioneer artifacts, a mock-up of Peter Britt's photo studio, and interesting old pictures, the museum also has a good walking tour map of the other historical sites in the city. Another bonus is that admission is free, although donations are greatly appreciated. The stucco building next door to the courthouse used to be the county jail, but today it serves as the **children's museum.** Kids of all ages will enjoy the hands-on experience of seeing old-fashioned toys close up. A small bookstore is located here as well, specializing in local and regional historical publications.

Peter Britt Gardens
Peter Britt came to Jacksonville not long after gold was first discovered in Ruth Gulch in 1851. After briefly trying his hand at prospecting for color, he redirected his efforts towards painting and photography. The latter turned out to be his specialty, and for nearly 50 years he photographed the places, people, and events of southern Oregon. He also incorporated new techniques and equipment in his studio as photographic advances were developed. Hence, you'll find his ambrotypes, daguerrotypes, stereographs, and tintypes on display at the Jackson County Museum attesting to his willingness to incorporate technological changes. His pioneer spirit is also manifest in his being the first person to photograph Crater Lake.

The Swiss-born Peter Britt was also an accomplished horticulturalist and among the first vintners in southern Oregon. In addition to experimenting with several varieties of fruit and nut trees to see which grew best in the Rogue River Valley, he kept the first recorded weather data records in the region. Another testimonial to his love of plants is the giant redwood tree you see on the western edge of the Britt Gardens (located on S. 1st and W. Pine Streets) which he planted 130 years ago to commemorate the birth of his first child, Emil.

His house was a beautifully detailed Gothic Revival home that was first built in 1860 and then enlarged in the 1880s. Unfortunately, it was destroyed by fires in 1957 and 1960, and can now only be remembered through photographs. The stone and mortar wall visible today marks the site of the original foundation. Some of the remaining plantings are part of the original gardens and many others were lovingly put in place in 1976 by Robert Lovinger, a landscape architecture professor from the University of Oregon. The Peter Britt Music Festival was held on the grounds of the estate from 1962 until 1978 when the new Britt Pavilion was built just south.

A short half-mile hike begins 15 yards uphill from the Emil Britt redwood tree. A fairly level path follows the abandoned irrigation ditch that used to divert water from Jackson Creek to the Britt property. Soon you will notice Jackson Creek below the trail, as well as several overgrown sections of a nearly forgotten logging railroad bed. This is a particularly nice walk in the spring when the wildflowers are in bloom and the mosses and ferns are green.

Peter Britt Music Festival
On a hillside near the home site of pioneer photographer Peter Britt is where a small classical music festival began in 1962. Nearly 30 years later, the scope of the **Britt Festival** (offices at 614 Medford Center, Medford, 97504; tel. 773-6077 or 800-88-BRITT) has developed into a musical smorgasbord encompassing such diverse styles as jazz, folk/country/bluegrass, music theater, and dance in addition to the original classical repertoire. Mel Torme, B.B. King, Jean Pierre Rampal, and the Nitty Gritty Dirt Band are just a few of the big-name artists who have performed here over the years.

The festival runs from the last week of June through the first week of September with a series of nearly 40 concerts. The prices for tickets range from $10-16 for general admission, depending on the show and the seating section you occupy. Seating is as much an integral part of the atmosphere of the Britt Festival as the music. Concertgoers often bring along blankets, small lawnchairs (allowed only in designated areas), wine, and a picnic supper to enjoy along with entertainment on balmy summer evenings. Reserved seating was added in 1987, a move many thought would destroy the intimate ambience. However, these seats are built somewhat down into the ground, so the patrons on blankets and lawn chairs behind them are still able to see the action, while those with bad backs and tired bones are able to enjoy the show too. The reserved seats run $2-4 more than general admission. A large area in front of the seats is for those who like to sit on the grass or on blankets.

Wherever you decide you might like to sit, be sure to call well in advance to order your tickets to avoid having to stand outside. As with the Oregon Shakespeare Festival, the shows sell out months in advance, especially for the well-known performers.

Hello, Dolly

The comprehensive collection of dolls on display at the **Jacksonville Doll Museum** at the corner of 5th and Jacksonville streets contains nearly every doll pictured in the *Blue Book of Dolls*. The oldest one on display here is a fragile 1640 Italian creche doll with carved ivory head and hands. Carved wooden Queen Anne, Dutch or penny woodens, and papier-mâché types are representative of the 1770s and early 1880s styles. China heads, Parian, and stone bisques which were popular from 1830 on are also lined up for your inspection. But whatever your fancy—bisque, celluloid, cloth, composition, metal, plastic, or rubber—you'll find it here. Open daily 11 a.m.-3:30 p.m. May 30-September 30, with admission $1 for adults, 50 cents for children under 12, and free for kids under six.

Tours And Tastings

During the summer, **Trolley Tours** (tel. 535-5617) offers 50-minute narrated tours every hour on the hour from 10-4 p.m. A motorized trolley car picks up passengers at the corner of 3rd and California streets for an informative and entertaining excursion into Jacksonville's pioneer past. Adult fares are $3.50, children under 12 are $1.50.

For a taste of some of the best of the Pacific Northwest, head for the **Tasting Room** (ORE 238, Jacksonville, 97530; tel. 899-1001). Here you can sample fine food and wine for free. After the tastings, you'll have a better idea of what to choose from in their store. Oregon wines, hickory smoked meats and jerky, and cheeses are some of the goodies you'll want to take home with you. The Tasting Room packs special Britt Festival picnic baskets too.

Pioneer Days

The Wild West returns to life in mid-June in Jacksonville with the town's annual **Pioneer Days.** A parade in old-time regalia down the main streets of Jacksonville kicks off the party. Following the parade, a street fair featuring arts, crafts, and food booths is held along California Street for the rest of the day. A street dance follows in the afternoon with live music, as well as an old-time fiddlers performance. Children's games and activities are also scheduled for the afternoon. One of the most popular kiddie games is the haystack search, where tots grub around in the straw for over $200 in hidden currency. At 2 p.m., another fun annual event takes place called the Ugly Legs Contest. Contestants wear paper sacks over their heads so they are judged solely on how bad their legs look. Mud, sandals, worn out sneakers, and other cosmetic/artistic touches are allowed. Other special events are also planned for seniors, and bingo games are held all day long. Call the chamber of commerce (tel. 889-8118) for details.

PRACTICALITIES

Bed And Breakfast

The **Jacksonville Inn** (175 E. California St., Jacksonville, 97530; tel. 899-1990, $75-85) lies in the heart of the commercial historic district. In addition to eight air conditioned room furnished with restored antiques and private baths, the inn has an excellent dining room with gourmet fare and an extensive wine list with well over 700 selections. Reservations are highly recommended, especially during the summer. A block further down California St. is the **McCully House Inn** (240 E. California St., Jacksonville, 97530; tel 899-1942, $60-80). Built in 1861 in the classical revival style, this mansion has four beautifully decorated bedrooms with private baths. European and American antiques, oriental rugs, delicate lace curtains, and a magnificent square grand piano (tuned a half step lower than today's "A 440") add to the historical ambience. A full "country continental" breakfast is included with the price of your room.

The **Touvelle House Bed and Breakfast** (455 N. Oregon St., Jacksonville, 97530; tel. 899-8223, $55-75) was built in 1916, in the craftsman style of archecture, distingushed by its broad, over-hanging eaves, shingled exterior walls, and thick-tapered porch posts. Frank Touvelle, an affluent Easterner, came here in the early 1890s and invested heavily in the fledgling pear and apple orchard industry. Nowadays, his 15-room antique-furnished house welcomes visitors year-round. Their hearty breakfast starts the day on the right foot, and the pool and hot tub are the perfect things for unwinding tired muscles after exploring the sights of Jacksonville.

The **Colonial House Bed and Breakfast** (Box 1298, 1845 Old Stage Road, Jacksonville, 97530; tel. 770-2783) is a beautiful Georgian colonial revival home built in 1917. The five-acre grounds have graceful old oaks, well-maintained lawns, and a shady pond. Two suites are available, both tastefully decorated and with private baths. A full breakfast that includes gourmet omelettes, homemade muffins, and seasonal local fruits or a traditional English breakfast is also included. Afternoon tea is served at 4 p.m. Rates are $95 per night for one to two people; each additional person is $25. No smoking is allowed, and reservations are recommended.

The **Reames House** (Box 128, 540 E. California St., Jacksonville, 97530; tel. 899-1868) is a spacious Victorian built in 1868. Listed on the National Historic Register, the house is furnished with antiques and is complemented by lovely flower gardens and a covered patio. The carved antique walnut double bed, lace curtains, and period lamps of the Victoria Room ($80) transport you back into the last century. The private bath features a pull-chain toilet and a clawfoot tub. The Peachtree Room ($80) also has a private bath, as well as twin mahogany sleigh beds, dresser, and armoire with stenciled walls and curtains. The Colonial Room ($75) shares a bath with the Gold Strike Room ($75). All guests receive a full breakfast of seasonal fruits, fresh baked goods, gourmet egg dishes, and other breakfast entrees served with freshly ground coffee. The Reames House also offers the use of bicycles, frisbees, tennis rackets, and even a gold pan if you care to try your luck at Ruth's Gulch.

Food

The Jacksonville Inn (175 E. California St., Jacksonville, tel. 899-1900) has consistently been rated one of the top restaurants in Oregon by *Oregon Magazine* and *Pacific Northwest Magazine.* Distinctive cuisine, served a la carte or table d' hôte, is prepared by master chefs for your enjoyment. While the gold-rich mortar sparkles in the walls of the dining room and lounge, the menu is what offers some real treasures. Steaks, seafood, and specialties of the inn like veal, duck, and prime rib are among the offerings. A selection of vegetarian dishes is also available upon request. A connoisseur's wine cellar of over 700 vintages further enhances your gourmet meal. Open every day for lunch and dinner; reservations are suggested.

The **Bella Union Restaurant and Saloon** (170 West California St., Jacksonville, tel. 899-1770) is another popular spot in town. Soups, salads, chicken, steaks, pasta, and pizza are some of the items you'll find on the menu here. Vegetarians can enjoy fare like steamed vegetables with cashews and three cheeses or spaghetti with a tangy marinara sauce, both of which include soup or salad and homemade bread for $7.95. The patio in back of the restaurant is a pleasant place to enjoy luncheon on a fine summer day.

If you're in the mood for some Mexican food, try **Munchies** (105 S. Oregon St., Jacksonville, tel. 899-1029). The food here is made mostly from scratch and has no MSG or lard. The also make their own vegetarian refried beans and offer eight vegetarian specials. An especially popular favorite here is the Munchie burrito, a large tortilla stuffed with beef or chicken and beans, and topped with melted cheese, lettuce, onions, olives, tomatoes, salsa, sour cream, and guacamole. The largest of these delectables costs $5.95. Burgers, sandwiches, and all-day breakfast are also on the menu, as well as beer and wine. Try to save some room for the homemade pie ($1.75).

Trombino's Restaurant (605 N. 5th, Jacksonville, tel. 899-1340) serves up a tasty lunch and dinner. Since they make their own fettucine, lasagna, and manicotti noodles, pasta dishes are among the fortes of the house. Lunch specials, including soup or salad and garlic bread, range from $3-6. Chicken, steak, and seafood dinners that include soup, salad, side of spaghetti or baked potato, garlic bread, and ice cream range from $8-17. All food is cooked with traditional Italian ingredients like provimi veal, imported cheese, and olive oil. Mama mia!

The budget-conscious will appreciate **The Claimjumper** (115 W. California St., Jacksonville, tel. 899-8193). This establishment offers sandwiches, burgers, soups, and salads at a price you can afford. The burrito with cheese, sour cream, and onions costs $2.05. The chili and beans with cheese, sour cream, and onions is a popular local favorite here; a large bowl with homemade cornbread costs $3.20. Vegetarians will enjoy the veggie sandwich (jack cheese, tomato, mushrooms, sprouts, and mayo) for $3.75. You may want to savor your food out on the back patio with some beer or wine.

Another possibility for lighter fare is the **Apache Junction Coffee House and Deli** (165 S. Oregon St., Jacksonville, tel. 899-7884) This is the home of the 25-cent cup of coffee that tastes like it costs a dollar. They also feature sandwiches stuffed with veggie fillings and your choice of cold cuts. Complementing the sandwiches is the soup of the day for 95 cents a cup and $1.25 a bowl.

Services And Information

The Jacksonville **library** (170 S. Oregon St., Jacksonville, 97530; tel. 899-1665) is open Monday and Tuesday 12-6 p.m., Wednesday and Thursday 11-5 p.m., Friday 10-4 p.m., and is closed on weekends. The **Jacksonville Chamber of Commerce** (Box 33, 185 N. Oregon St., Jacksonville, 97530; tel. 889-8118 or 800-332-7488 in Oregon or 800-882-7488 out of state) is open 10-4 p.m. daily and has the scoop on events and activities. The Jacksonville **post office** (175 N. Oregon St., Jacksonville, 97530; tel. 899-1563) is open 8:30-5 p.m. weekdays. Public transportation connecting Jacksonville with Medford is available on the 30A and 30B buses. Call 799-BUSS for scheduling information.

GRANTS PASS AND VICINITY

The banner across the main thoroughfare in town proudly proclaims, It's the Climate. But while the 20-inches-a-year precipitation average and 52° yearly mean temperature might seem desirable, the true allure of Grants Pass is the mighty Rogue River that flows through the heart of this community. More than 25 outfitters in Grants Pass and the surrounding villages of Rogue River and Merlin specialize in fishing, float, and jetboat trips. Numerous riverside lodges, accessible by car, river, or footpath, yield remote relaxation in the shadow of the nearby Klamath-Siskiyou Wilderness.

It was the climate that attracted back-to-the-land refugees of the '60s in nearby Takilma, a planned utopian community. More recently, the survivalists, in expectation of nuclear Armageddon, have established a network of shelters in the area. They believe that forests filled with game and foraging opportunities coupled with prevailing winds that will keep radioactive fallout away improve their odds . . . good luck!

The climate is also responsible for the once thick forests in the surrounding mountains, timber source for the numerous mills which in turn provided many jobs. However, decades of overcutting by the lumber companies has dramatically diminished the supply of saw timber, resulting in mill shutdowns and high unemployment rates. In response, the economic base has been gradually shifting away from wood products, and now keys on the natural beauty of the area, the recreational opportunites, and of course, the benign weather.

SIGHTS

Oregon Vortex

About ten miles south of Grants Pass on I-5 is the House of Mystery at the Oregon Vortex (4303 Sardine Creek Rd., Gold Hill, 97525 tel. 855-1543). Called the "Forbidden Ground" by the Rogue Indians because the place spooked their horses, it is actually a repelling magnetic field where objects tend to move away from their center of alignment and lean in funny directions. For example, a ball at the end of a string would not

hang straight up and down at a 90-degree angle, and people would seem taller when viewed from one side of the field as opposed to the other. Visitors may bring balls, levels, cameras, or any other instrument they wish to test the vortex for themselves. Guided tours through the house built on this curious site are $3.50 adults, $2.50 children. Open March 1st-Oct. 14th, 9-4:45, except on Sundays and sometimes Thursdays.

Gold Gulch

In the same area as the Oregon Vortex is Gold Gulch (contact address 8785 Blackwell Road, Central Point, 97502; tel. 664-2847). To get there, take I-5, U.S. 99, or the Old Stage Road (ORE 228) north from Jacksonville and look for the brightly colored billboards around Gold Hill pointing the way.

Gold Gulch is a re-created early-day mining town that borders on being hokey but provides some worthwhile attractions. Mining and logging exhibits, antique mining equipment and tools, and an authentic Arrastre gold mill offer insights into the rigours and dangers of the industries that first opened up the Oregon frontier. A gambling den, mining and assay office, blacksmith shop, Wells Fargo Express Depot, and, of course, the hangman's tree round out the picture of life in the gold country. One of the highlights of Gold Gulch is a walk down into the Millionaire Mine to see a true quartz gold vein and learn how gold is recovered from the depths of the earth. Open June 1 through Labor Day, the admission is $1.50 for adults and 50 cents for children.

Wolf Creek Tavern

Approximately 20 miles north of Grants Pass on I-5 in Wolf Creek is Oregon's oldest hostelry, the Wolf Creek Tavern (tel. 866-2474). Originally a hotel for the California and Oregon Stagecoach Line, this historic property is now owned by the state and operated as a restaurant and hotel. President Rutherford B. Hayes visited the tavern in the late 1880s, and you can view the small room where author Jack London stayed and wrote part of his famous novel, *The End of the Story.* The staff wears early 19th-century clothing

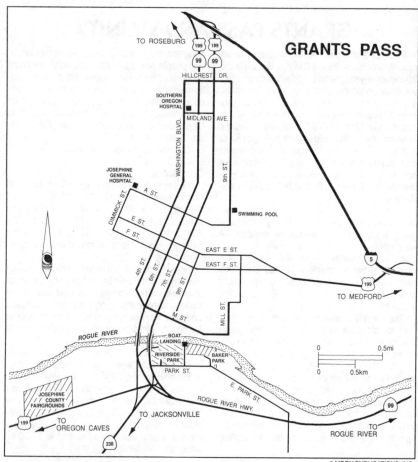

GRANTS PASS

TO ROSEBURG

HILLCREST DR.

SOUTHERN OREGON HOSPITAL

MIDLAND AVE.

WASHINGTON BLVD.

9th ST.

JOSEPHINE GENERAL HOSPITAL

A ST.

DIMMICK ST.

E ST.

F ST.

SWIMMING POOL

EAST E ST.

EAST F ST.

4th ST.

6th ST.

7th ST.

9th ST.

M ST.

MILL ST.

TO MEDFORD

ROGUE RIVER

BOAT LANDING

RIVERSIDE PARK

BAKER PARK

PARK ST.

JOSEPHINE COUNTY FAIRGROUNDS

E. PARK ST.

ROGUE RIVER HWY.

TO OREGON CAVES

TO JACKSONVILLE

TO ROGUE RIVER

0   0.5mi

0   0.5km

© MOON PUBLICATIONS, INC.

in keeping with the ambience of this famous road-house. Some of the food in the restaurant is a little more modern, with such fare as hamburgers, hot dogs, and grilled cheese sandwiches on the menu, mainly to keep the kids happy. However, other entrees are more like what you might have found a hundred years ago when taking a road trip through southern Oregon, and are quite good. And should the lure of tradition pall, fans of haute cuisine can enjoy such dishes as shrimp scampi and house-cut steaks here.

Big Pine

About an hour outside of Grants Pass is the tallest ponderosa pine in the world. Standing a whopping 246 feet high and sporting a 57-inch girth, Big Pine lives up to its name with an estimated volume of 12,500 board feet of wood. This 300-year-old giant lives in a grove of large pines, cedars, and Douglas firs at **Big Pine campground.**

To get there, take the Merlin Exit off of I-5 just north of Grants Pass and proceed towards Galice. Just beyond Morrison's Lodge on the Rogue River, turn left onto Taylor Creek Road #25. Big Pine campground is about 10 miles further. Another routing option is via U.S. 199. About 20 miles south of Grants Pass on U.S. 199, look for Onion Creek Road on the north side of the highway. Follow Onion Creek Road for another 20 miles and it will take you to Big Pine.

The campground features 12 picnic sites and 14 campsites. Picnic tables, fire rings, and vault toilets are provided. Water is available from a hand pump between campsites seven and nine. A small playground and primitive softball diamond are tastefully incorporated into the grounds. Many trails take hikers to the Big Pine and beyond for a short hike or an all-day adventure. A lazy creek meanders through the area, with alders, hazelnuts, and an array of colorful wildflowers growing along its banks. Deer and other wildlife are frequently spotted grazing in the fragrant meadows nearby. Foragers can pick their fill of blackberries in July and August. Cost is $5 a night.

The Oregon Caves

About 30 miles southwest on U.S. 199 to Cave Junction and then 20 miles up winding ORE 46 are the Oregon Caves. The cave itself, as there is really only one which opens onto successive caverns, was formed over the eons by the action of water. As rain and snowmelt seeped through cracks and fissures in the rock above the cave and percolated down into the underlying limestone, huge sections of the limestone saturated and collapsed much how a sand castle too close to sea level always caves in. When the water tabled eventually lowered, these pockets were drained of water and the process of cave decoration began.

THERE'S GOLD IN THEM THAR HILLS

Geologists estimate that the prospectors of the 1850s and commercial mining operations that followed found only 25% of the potential take. With the wild gyrations of the timber-dependent economy and the price of gold fetching several hundred dollars a troy ounce, it's no wonder that many out-of-work loggers and other people have taken to gold panning in the waterways of southern Oregon.

Almost all streams in Coos, Curry, Douglas, and Jackson counties are good sources of "color." "Color" refers to the flecks and bright chips of metal sometimes called gold dust; larger odd-shaped lumps of gold are nuggets. The gold originally comes from veins in the mountains, where it is washed out by winter weather. Spring floods and heavy rains carry the gold further downstream. The density of gold causes it to settle in obstructions (like moss), in quiet water behind boulders, or at the foot of waterfalls. These deposits of gold can vary from fine gold flecks to a bonanza of nuggets.

But before you head for the hills, you will need some basic equipment. Specially designed gold pans with flaring sides three to four inches deep are available at many hardware stores. Width sizes range from six to 24 inches; pick one that is comfortable for you to handle. Keep in mind that a pan full of water and gravel can get pretty heavy! Your pan must also be "blued" before panning, otherwise the layer of oil on it will stick to the gold and cause the stuff to float out with the other lighter materials. Heat the pan on your stove until it is a deep blue color and the oils are burned off. Other useful tools include tweezers, a small vial or two, a trowel, and a small shovel or pick.

Panning takes finesse, but with practice quickly becomes easier. Put some dirt from a likely location in your pan with some water. Pick out the larger pieces of rock and gravel or squeeze out the moss and discard. Swirl the pan gently around from side to side. This causes the gold to sink to the bottom, making it possible to scoop out more gravel from the top. Tilt the pan at a slight angle, and the gold will now fall to the bottom of the lower edge. Remember that gold is 19 times heavier than water and most other minerals contained in the gravel of streams. Continue to dip, shake, and remove sand until you have only a small amount left. This is the stage where you have to be extra cautious not to wash away your gold. When you have taken out as much sand as possible, you will have (if you hit "pay dirt") small strands of black sand and gold in your pan. Extract the color with tweezers, grab a beer, and start the process all over again. With some work and a little luck, you'll soon be singing the old refrain, "We're in the money."

PHOTO BY FRANK LONG
The marble halls of the Oregon Caves attract thousands of visitors.

First, the limestone is dissolved by the water and carried in solution into the cave. When the water evaporated, it left behind a microscopic layer of calcite. This process was repeated countless times, gradually creating the beautiful formations visible today. When the minerals are deposited on the ceiling, a stalactite begins to grow. Limestone-laden water that evaporates on the floor might grow up to be a stalagmite. When a stalactite and a stalagmite meet, they become a column. Other cave sculptures you'll see include helicites, hell-bent formations that twist and turn in crazy directions; draperies, looking just like their name implies, only they're cast in stone instead of cloth; and soda straws, stalactites that are hollow in the center like a straw, carrying the building drops of moisture to their tips.

First discovered in 1874, the Oregon Caves attract thousands of visitors annually. During the Depression, walkways and turnoffs were built to make the cave more accessible. Unfortunately, tons of rock and rubble were stashed into nooks

and crannies in the cave, instead of being transported out. This had the ironic effect of burying the very formations that the trail was being constructed to see. However, the National Park Service started to remove the artificial debris in 1985, exposing the natural formations once again. Little by little, the cave is looking much more like nature made it, as opposed to the man-made passageways that were viewed by previous visitors.

The River Styx, another victim of Depression era "improvements," is also enjoying a similar resurrection. This stream used to run through the cave but was diverted into pipes to aid trail and tunnel construction, and the pipes ended up buried underneath tons of pulverized rock. The Park Service is hard at work undoing the hand of man and letting the stream flow where God intended it to go.

Tours of the cave are conducted year-round by well-informed National Park Service interpreters. Their presentations are both informative and entertaining, and you will leave the cave with a better understanding of its natural, geologic, and human history. Admission is $6 for adults and $3 for children ages 6-11. The tour takes a little under an hour, and requires some uphill walking. Good walking shoes are recommended as well as warm clothing. It may be warm and toasty outside, but the cave maintains a fairly consistent year-round temperature of 41 degrees. Passageways can be narrow, ceilings low, and the footing slippery. Due to federal regulations, children under the age of six are not permitted inside the cave. However, a babysitting service is available. Tour times can be obtained by calling 592-3400.

Oregon Caves Chateau

During mid-June through early September, the six-story Oregon Caves Chateau (Box 128, Cave Junction, 97523; tel. 592-3400) offers food and accommodations. Built in 1934, this rustic building blends in with the forest and moss-covered marble ledges. The rooms feature views of Cave Creek canyon, waterfalls, or the Oregon Caves entrance. Rates range from $55-75 per night for two to four people. Special "lovers' retreat" weekend packages including discount dinners and cave admissions are also available, but make reservations early, as the number of packages is limited. The chateau has been nicknamed the "Marble Halls of Oregon," and you can see the huge marble fireplace in the lobby for yourself while you thaw out after your spelunking expedition. The food at the chateau is surprisingly good, and having Cave Creek running through the center of the dining room definitely adds to the unique atmosphere.

ROGUE RIVER TRIPS

There are about as many ways to enjoy the Rogue as there are critters around its natural confines. Some people prefer the excitement and challenge of maneuvering their own craft down the treacherous rapids. Oar rafts, where the guide rows for you, paddle rafts, where you provide the propulsion, and one-man inflatable kayaks are the most widely used boats for this sort of river exploration. The 40-mile section downstream from Graves Creek is open only to these types of non-motorized vessels, and river traffic is strictly regulated by the U.S. Forest Service. The limited number of float permits (25 a day) are prized by rafters around the world, as the Rogue not only has the best whitewater in America, but also guarantees a first-rate wilderness adventure. And yet, it can be a civilized wilderness. Hot showers, comfortable beds, and sumptuous meals at several of the river lodges tucked away in remote quarters of this famous waterway welcome boaters after a day's voyage. Excellent camping facilities are available for those who want to directly experience nature.

But you don't have to risk life and limb in a fancy inner tube to see the Rogue, because several local companies offer jetboat tours. On a jetboat, powerful engines suck in hundreds of gallons of water a minute, and shoot it out the back of the boat through a narrow nozzle, generating the necessary thrust for navigation. With no propeller to hit rocks and other obstacles, these 20-ton machines can carry 40 or more passengers in water only six inches deep. This makes the jetboat an ideal way to enjoy the beauty of the Rogue and at the same time keep your feet dry. Finally, many outfitters charter drift boats to secret fishing holes for anglers to try their luck landing supper.

Float Trips
Paul Brooks Raft Trips (Box 638 Merlin, 97532; tel. 476-8051) offers a one-day guided trip that gives you the choice of oar raft, paddle raft, or in-flatable kayak. Enjoy an excellent lunch at one of the river lodges. **Eagle Sun Inc.** (Box 611, Ashland, 97520; tel. 482-5139) has half-, full-, and multi-day trips on oar or paddle rafts. Their adventures range from the mild to the wild, and child care can be arranged through their office. **Galice Resort and Store Raft Trips** (11744 Galice Rd., Merlin, 97532; tel. 476-3818) offers full-day raft or inflatable kayak trips. All-day trips depart at 9 a.m., and half-day departures are at 9 a.m. and 1 p.m. respectively. **Noah's World of Water** (Box 11, Ashland, 97520; tel. 488-2811) has been providing quality rafting and fishing trips since 1974. They have half-day and one- to four-day excursions that vary from exciting whitewater rafting highs to kinder, gentler floats. From late March to early October, they depart Ashland for the Rogue three times daily, and a roundtrip transfer from your lodging is always included in the price. **Orange Torpedo Trips** (Box 1111-S, Grants Pass, 97526; tel. 479-5061/800-635-2925) has half- and one- to three-day raft or inflatable kayak (also affectionately known as orange torpedoes because of their color and shape) adventures. They also offer a unique VIP two-day package that combines the best on the river: jetboat tour, wagon ride, gourmet dining, lodging, wildlife park, and float trip all rolled into one unforgettable extravaganza.

Otter River Trips (12163 Galice Rd., Merlin, 97532; tel. 476-8590) caters to families with one-day whitewater rafting trips. They also operate fishing excursions year-round and special gold-panning trips. **River Adventure Float Trips** (Box 841, Grants Pass, 97526; tel. 476-6493) has summer raft and fall fishing trips that vary from a half day to several days. **River Trips Unlimited, Inc.** (4140 Dry Creek Rd., Medford, 97504; tel. 779-3798) has been guiding trips on the Rogue for over 30 years. They have one- to four-day raft, Tahiti, or summer-run steelhead fishing trips that include meals and overnight stays at some of the river lodges.

Rogue/Klamath River Adventures (Box 4295, Medford, 97501; tel. 779-3708) has one to three-day whitewater rafting and inflatable kayak trips that give you the option of camping out under the stars or roughing it in style at a river lodge. **Rogue/Klamath Whitewater Co.** (1202 E. Main St., Medford, 97504; tel. 772-8467) has personalized high-quality trips for the lowest available rates. Exciting half-, full-, and two-day over-

One of the most popular ways to see the Rogue is by jetboat.

nighter raft, inflatable kayak, and guided salmon fishing trips are among the offerings. **Rogue Wilderness, Inc.** (Box 1647, Grants Pass, 97526; tel. 336-1647) is here to tailor-make just about any length of trip you may care to take. Whitewater rafting, inflatable kayaking, and salmon and steelhead fishing are some of the available options. For more information on scenic whitewater raft and fishing trips, contact the Rogue River Guides Association (Box 792, Medford, 97501 tel. 772-5194).

Jetboat Trips
Rogue Jetboat Excursions (935 S.E. 7th, Grants Pass, 97526; tel. 476-2628/800-648-4874) is the most popular jetboat company on this end of the river. Their boats are the newest and the most quiet around, and their friendly and skillful guides have grown up on the Rogue. They proudly share their "home" with their guests, telling them inside stories about local lore and interesting tidbits of information on the scenery and wildlife. The jetboat trips include a two-hour tour to Hellgate Canyon, a five-hour whitewater lunch trip, a champagne brunch cruise, and a four-hour dinner excursion. The dinner trip is particularly enjoyable, as the wildlife tends to come out more in the late afternoon and early evening. When the boat finally docks at the OK Corral for dinner, you can expect home-grown home-cooked food, and lots of it. Be sure to call ahead for reservations, as space on all of their runs books up fast.

Hellgate Excursions (Box 982, Grants Pass, 97526; tel. 479-7204) mimics Rogue Jetboat's offerings, with a two-hour tour, five-hour whitewater trip, and four-hour dinner cruise. They also have a champagne brunch any day of the week, provided that 20 or more adults sign up. **Jet Boat River Excursions** (Box 658, Rogue River, 97537; tel. 582-0800) has two-hour scenic trips and four-hour dinner cruises. Based in Rogue River about 10 miles upstream from Grants Pass (Exit 48 off of I-5), this company tours a different section of the river than the other outfits—the waters above the impassable Savage Rapids Dam.

EVENTS

Boatnik Festival
The Boatnik Festival starts on Memorial Day weekend at Riverside Park in Grants Pass. A carnival, parade, and softball tournament are featured, but the top event is the whitewater boat races. Over two dozen modified speedboats and jetboats compete in a 46-mile course of the Rogue River. Warm-ups begin on Memorial Day morning followed by the race at 1 p.m. The competition starts at the boat docks in Riverside Park.

Josephine County Fair
The Josephine County Fair normally takes place in mid-August at the fairgrounds in Grants Pass. In addition to the usual fair attractions such as the

carnival, concessions and 4-H livestock, entertainers like Johnny Cash and Three Dog Night perform for the enthusiastic crowds. A popular annual competition held here is the four-wheel tractor pull. Souped-up farm vehicles attempt to drag a bulldozer with its blade down 100 yards as fast as possible.

Rooster-crowing Contest

The nearby city of **Rogue River** southeast on I-5 has something to crow about. On the last day of June, the Rogue River Rooster Crow is held at the Rogue River Elementry School grounds, beginning with a parade and followed by live music and entertainment. A street fair featuring arts, crafts, and food is also set up on the premises. But the big event takes place early in the afternoon. Farmers from all over Oregon and northern California bring their roosters to strut their stuff and wing out a song to the enthusiastic crowds. A fowl tradition since 1953, the rooster to crow the most times in his allotted time period wins the prize for his proud owner.

Grants Pass Downs

Horse racing aficionados can pick up their heels and get down to Grants Pass Downs. The season opens Memorial Day weekend with races on weekends through the Fourth of July. Place your bets on your favorite steeds to place, win, or show ($2 minimum). The cash-sell betting is all computerized, allowing for more exotic bets like the quiniela and the trifecta. The latter are "wheel" bets in which you get to choose one of every possible combination of two or three horses ($1 minimum) to win. Even if you're not the betting sort, it's a kick watching the horses thunder around the bend and down the home stretch.

Campgrounds

Many fine campgrounds are found along the banks of the Rogue River near Grants Pass. The privately owned and operated RV parks in the KOA genre tend to be more expensive than their public counterparts but also offer more amenities like swimming pools, laundromats, and other conveniences. They range from about $10-15 a night and are found along U.S. 99 between Gold Hill and Grants Pass. The four county parks listed below cost $8 for hookup sites, $7 for tent sites. Contact the **Josephine County Parks Dept.** (Rogue River 97537; tel. 474-5285) for reservations and additional information.

Indian Mary Park is the showcase of Jose-

THE CHRISTMAS FLOOD OF 1964: POSTSCRIPT TO DEVASTATION

Passing through the serene Rogue River Valley today gives little indication of the ravages of the Christmas Flood of 1964. The winter of that fateful year seemed to augur the coming of a peaceful winter in Rogue country. With the white snow on the mountains, and a ring around the harvest moon, the only thing that seemed missing was ol' Saint Nick himself, riding through the night sky.

But then the rains came. Slowly at first, then little by little, almost imperceptibly, the downpour transformed into a deluge. The warm rains quickly melted the snowpack, and the swollen streams spurred the foaming Rogue on its course to the sea. Logjams and abnormally high tides contributed to raising the water levels to record heights.

Whole towns had to be evacuated from the onslaught of water. Many families saw their hopes and dreams wash away, with their tears, in the rain, victims of the impartial hand of nature. However, the inundation was not confined to the Rogue, as the killer storm turned almost every western Oregon river into a frighteningly efficient generator of destruction. Governor Hatfield declared the region a disaster area. The damage statewide was in the millions of dollars, and many lives were lost by the time the muddy waters receded a week later. To avert a similiar castastrophe.here in the future, the Army Corps of Engineers constructed Lost Creek Reservoir on the upper Rogue not long afterwards.

And while time has healed the effects of the Christmas flood of 1964, you can still find high water marks here and there in the valley. Tacked high up on trees and bridges, perched over 100 feet above the now placid waters of the Rogue, they silently tell you the magnitude of this great disaster.

phine County parks. To get there, go about eight miles east of Merlin on the Merlin-Galice Road. Located on the banks of the Rogue River, this campground has 89 sites, several with sewer hookups and utilities, as well as showers, flush toilets, and piped water. A boat ramp, beautiful hiking trails, a playground, and one of the best beaches on the Rogue make this one of the most popular county campgrounds on the river.

Griffen Park is a smaller campground with 24 sites for tents and trailers. To get there, take the Redwood Highway (U.S. 199) to Riverbanks Road, and then turn onto Griffen Road and follow it about five miles to where it meets the Rogue. The park has a boat ramp, showers, flush toilets, piped water, and RV dumping facilities. **Schroeder Park** is another complete campground near town. Located on Schroeder Lane off of Red-

GRANTS PASS ACCOMMODATIONS

Name	Address	Telephone	Price	Features
In Town				
Flamingo Inn	728 N.W. 6th St.	476-6601	$22-32	pool, pets, kitchenettes
City Center Motel	741 N.E. 6th	476-6134	$24-36	kitchenettes
Fireside Motel	839 N.E. 6th St.	474-5558	$25-35	pool
Motel 6	1800 7th St.	474-1331	$25-30	pool and air conditioning
Hawks Inn	1464 N.W. 6th St.	479-4057	$25-30	pool and air conditioning
Uptown Motel	1253 N.E. 6th	479-2952	$25-30	pets
Rogue River Inn	6285 Rogue River Highway (old Hwy. 99)	582-1120	$30-38	
Redwood Motel	815 N.E. 6th St.	476-0878	$32-40	playground, pool, pets
Golden Inn	1950 N.W. Vine St.	479-6611	$33-40	pool, food, pets
Knight's Inn Motel	104 S.E. 7th	479-5595	$35-38	laundromat, pets
Motel de Rogue	2600 Rogue River Highway	479-2111	$40-55	on the river
Shilo Inn of Grants Pass	1880 N.W. 6th,	479-8391	$45-60	pool, pets
Best Western Grants Pass	111 Agness	476-1117)	$45-75	many amenities

GRANTS PASS ACCOMMODATIONS, cont.

Name	Address	Telephone	Price	Features
Rogue River Retreats				
Rogue Valley Resort	7799 Rogue River Highway	582-3762	$35-55	reservations required
River Shore Resort Highway	2520 Rogue River	476-6203	$35-55	reservations required
Riverside Motel Restaurant	971 S.E. 6th St.	456-9753	$55-75	home port of Rogue Jetboat Excursions
Paradise Ranch Inn	700 W. Monument Dr.	479-4333	$65-93	reservations recommended
Morrison's Rogue River Lodge	8500 Galice Rd.	476-3825	$150-240	the super-deluxe treatment

wood Avenue, the park has 31 sites, some with hookups and utilities. Showers, flush toilets, and a boat ramp make this a favorite spot for fishing enthusiasts. In addition to a picnic area and an excellent swimming hole, a rope tied to a huge cottonwood on the opposite bank of the river near the park is waiting for any swingers who like to make a big splash.

Whitehorse Park is six miles west of Grants Pass on Upper River Road. Purchased by the county in 1958 from the Rogue Rovers Trail Club, this park has 44 campsites, many with hookups and utilities. Showers, piped water, lighting, and good hiking trails developed by the previous owners are found here. The river channel shifted away from the park in the wake of the Christmas flood of 1964, and it's only about a half-mile walk to a fine beach on the Rogue.

The only state park in the area is **The Valley of the Rogue.** Located about halfway between Medford and Grants Pass off of I-5, the park is set along the banks of its namesake river. Although there are 97 trailer/motor home sites and 77 tent sites, this place fills up fast, so reservations are recommended during the warmer months. Hookups, utilities, showers, laundromat, and

some wheelchair-accessible facilities make this campground worth the $9-a-night fee.

Food

Although it's not the gourmet capital of Oregon, Grants Pass is a town where many travelers pull in for a bite. Its proximity to Rogue River recreation and fishing together with a wide range of dining alternatives explain this popularity.

Billy D's Western BBQ (211 N.E. A St., Grants Pass, 97526; tel. 476-7165) is noted for "Okie"-style catfish seasoned with Billy's special sauce. There's BBQ pork, beef, and chicken too. The **Blue Heron Dinner House** (330 Merlin Ave., Merlin, 97532; tel. 479-6604. Wed.-Sun 4-10) serves everything from seafood fettucine to chicken piccata. Dinner theater with the Col. Edwards Traveling Troupe, performing what can best be described as frontier vaudeville, is also featured in a separate dining room.

The **Blue Parrot Grill** (117 Main, Rogue River, 97537; tel. 582-4086) sounds and looks like something out of *Casablanca,* and for Rogue River, the food is almost as exotic. Some of the nightly specials include Oriental prime rib, fresh seafood, and choice steaks. For home cooking and local color, **Buzz's Wheel-in Cafe** (450 Merlin Rd., Merlin, 97532; tel. 476-3912) is a safe bet. Breakfasts are the most popular, featuring a mean stack of pancakes that would satisfy even Paul Bunyan. The menu at **China Hat** (1434 N.W. 6th, Grants Pass, 97526; tel. 476-3441) features interesting entrees such as vegetarian chow yuk, Mandarin pineapple duck, and ma po tofu. Even if you don't always understand the lingo, don't worry; all you really need is a big appetite to finish their large portions.

El Vaquero Cantina (111 N.E. Hillcrest, Grants Pass, 97526; tel. 479-0823) serves crispy chips and tangy salsa, huge chicken fajitas, and 16-ounce margaritas to help wash it all down. **Erik's** (1067 Redwood Spur, Grants Pass, 97526; tel. 479-4471) is for the serious eater. The 22-foot long salad bar is a meal in itself, and there's a hot dinner buffet where you can fill any extra space left on your plate. A wide range of steak, seafood, chicken, and pasta dinners are also available. **Fare with Flair** (831 N.E. 7th, Grants Pass, 97526; tel. 474-0182) offers an ever-changing selection of European and Oriental gourmet creations. This ambitious restaurant also turns out original soups and sandwiches.

Granny's Kitchen (117 N.E. F St., Grants Pass, 97526; tel. 476-7185) has great breakfast omelettes, a full lunch menu that includes everything from pot pie to quiche, and all-American dinners. Their bakers are busy during the wee hours of the morning producing extraordinary pies that sell like hot cakes the rest of the day. To satisfy your craving for non-meat burgers and vegetarian fare, try the **Grayback Cafe** (120 Cedar Flat Rd., Williams, 97544; tel. 846-6900). Located about 20 miles south of Grants Pass in Williams on the back road to the Oregon Caves, they also have ribs, chicken, and regular burgers. The **Skinny Spot** (126 N.E. F St., Grants Pass, 97526; tel. 479-6234) is one of the few restaurants in Oregon that caters to those with special dietary needs. Restricted calorie, low cholesterol, and minimal sodium and sugar are emphasized on their menu.

The **Hong Kong** (820 N.W. 6th, Grants Pass, 97526; tel. 476-4244) has a family-pack dinner to go that at $8.95 for two people is one of the best deals in town. **Herb's La Casita** (515 S.E. Rogue River Highway, Grants Pass, 97526; tel. 476-1313) has a little bit of everything, including one of the largest Sunday brunches in southern Oregon for only $6.25, or $5.50 seniors. **Little Italy** (201 S.W. 6th, Grants Pass, 97526; tel 479-1066) was rated one of the top 200 restaurants in the state by *Oregon Magazine*. In addition to down-home Italian dishes like saltimbocca, there's an ample selection of American food too.

Maria's Mexican Kitchen (105 N.E. Mill, Grants Pass, 97526; tel. 474-2429) uses hand-made tortillas and a special family recipe to make some of the best burritos around. **Pongsri's** (1571 N.E. 6th, Grants Pass, 97526; tel. 479-1345) is an Oriental restaurant with good vegetarian and seafood dinners. The price is right, and the helpings are generous. **R-Haus** (2140 Rogue River Highway, Grants Pass, 97426; tel. 476-4287) is a formal dining room in a turn-of-the-century house. A local favorite dinner spot, check to see what the nightly early-bird specials are.

We Ask U Inn (5560 Rogue River Highway, Grants Pass, 97426; tel. 470-0596) was purchased in 1927 by "Rainbow" Gibson and became the stomping grounds for many Hollywood movie moguls like Ginger Rogers and Clark Gable back in the '30s and '40s. Today, the restaurant's homey atmosphere and prime location on the Rogue make it a fine breakfast or lunch getaway. The waitresses dress in Victorian style at **Yankee Pot Roast** (720 N.W. 6th, Grants Pass, 97426; tel. 476-0551), but the menu will bring you back to the future. Light dinners are only $6.95, and all other dinner selections are $7.95 and $8.95 respectively.

Services And Information
Josephine Memorial Hospital (715 Dimmick, Grants Pass, 97526; tel. 476-6831) offers community-one ambulance service around the clock. **Southern Oregon Medical Center** (1505 N.W. Washington, Grants Pass, 97526; tel. 479-9717) is a participating member of Blue Cross health service and also features 24-hour emergency care. The **police** (tel. 474-6370) and state police (tel. 474-3175) are only a phone call away.

The **post office** (132 N.W. 6th, Grants Pass, 97526; tel. 479-7526) is open 8:30-5 weekdays. The **Grants Pass Chamber of Commerce** (1501 N.E. 6th, Grants Pass, 97526; tel. 476-7717) is open from 9-5 p.m. daily.

A pleasant air-conditioned and carpeted laundromat is **Maytag Laundry and Dry Cleaners** (1620 Williams Highway Plaza, Grants Pass, 97526; tel. 479-1743). Located on the south side of Safeway in the Plaza, it's open seven days a week from 7:30 a.m. to 10 p.m. **Classic Auto** (414 N.E. F St., Grants Pass, 97526; tel. 476-8938) features new and used rental cars. Pick up and delivery is free anywhere within the city limits, nonsmoking cars are available, and all cars are air conditioned.

ROSEBURG AND VICINITY

Many people just passing through the Roseburg area would probably quickly dismiss it as a hick town of lumberjacks and country bumpkins. A closer look, however, reveals many more interesting layers beneath the mill-town veneer. While about half of the folks here rely upon the woods as a workplace (and this fact is reflected in the no-nonsense cafes and businesses meeting their needs), growing pockets of refinement are found in between the pickup trucks and lumber mills. An award-winning museum, Oregon's only drive-through zoo, and some fine restaurants are a few examples of culture in the hinterland.

And yet, the true allure to Roseburg is not really in town, but in the surrounding countryside. The Mediterranean-like climate of the Umpqua Valley has proven ideal for producing world-class wines and contributes to wonderful winetasting tours. The beautiful North Umpqua River to the east offers rafting, camping, hiking, and fishing. In addition to trout, salmon, and bass, anglers come from all over to enjoy one of the world's last rivers with a native run of summer steelhead. Numerous waterfalls along the river and the frothy whitewater make the Indian word Umpqua ("Thunder Water") an appropriate name. And if you are really interested in a closer look at a lumber mill, you can visit the world's largest particle board plant.

In short, there's more here than a hasty visual appraisal would suggest, and it's worth more time than it takes to top off a tank of gas and wolf down a hamburger. Check it out—you'll be glad you did.

SIGHTS

Art And Culture
The **Douglas County Museum of History and Natural History** (Box 1550, Roseburg, 97470; tel. 440-4507/800-452-0991) is located at the Douglas County Fairgrounds (Exit 123 off of I-5). This nationally acclaimed museum has four wings of exhibits that range from a million-year-old saber-toothed tiger to 19th-century steam logging equipment. Indian artifacts, a re-creation of the 1882 Dillard Oregon and California Railroad depot, an imaginative forest industry exhibit, and an extensive collection of historical photos make your visit both entertaining and educational. Open Tue.-Sat. 10-4; Sun. 12-4.

The **Umpqua Valley Arts Center** (1124 West Harvard, Roseburg, 97470; tel. 672-2532) has two galleries. The main gallery features monthly rotating shows of local, regional, and Northwest artists. The Gift Gallery offers one-of-a-kind gifts made by a wide variety of Oregon artists.

Flower Power
The **Lotus Knight Memorial Gardens** are in Riverside Park. Located between Oak and Washington streets on the banks of the South Umpqua River, these gardens feast the eyes with colorful azaleas and rhododendrons in the spring. Open 5 a.m.-10 p.m. daily.

Something Fishy
The **Winchester Fish Ladder** is just off I-5 on Exit 129 on the north bank of the North Umpqua River. Here visitors can watch salmon and steelhead in their native environment as they swim by the viewing window at Winchester Dam. The North Umpqua and the Columbia are the only rivers in Oregon that offer this attraction. Spring chinook and summer steelhead migrate upriver May through August and during September through November, coho, fall chinook, and more summer steelhead swim on by. From December through May, winter steelhead are the primary species going through the fish ladders and on past the window.

Mill Tours

The world's largest particle board plant, **Roseburg Forest Products** (tel. 679-3311, ext. 392), south of Roseburg in nearby **Dillard**, offers tours by appointment only (with 24 hours' advance notice required) Wednesday and Friday at 1:30p.m. This plant runs around the clock, seven days a week, producing this versatile building material. You'll see the entire process, from wood chip to finished product, accompanied by a cacophony of bells and whistles. The tour lasts approximately two hours, with some uphill walking and stair climbing. Dress appropriately, as no open-toe shoes or high heels are allowed. Visitors must be 10 years of age or older. Contact the Roseburg Visitors and Convention Bureau for info on other local mill tours.

Wildlife Safari

Tucked away in a 600-acre wooded valley is **Wildlife Safari** (Safari Rd., Winston, 97496; tel. 679-6761), Oregon's drive-thru zoo. To get there, take Exit 119 off of I-5, and follow ORE 42 for four miles. Turn right on Lookingglass Road, and right

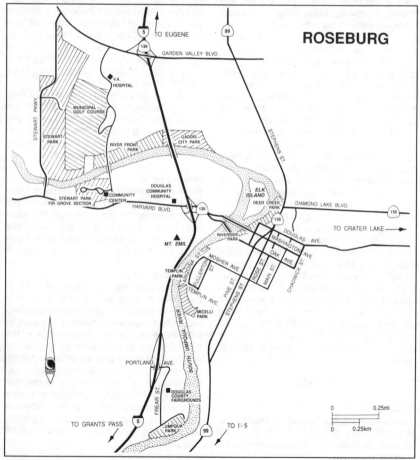

© MOON PUBLICATIONS, INC.

DOUGLAS COUNTY

A good look at just about any local mountainside tells the story of Douglas County. For years, the economy here has revolved around *Pseudotstuga menziessi* ("false hemlock"), the Douglas fir. Named after David Douglas of the English Botanical Society, who visited Oregon in the 1820s to research Northwest flora and fauna, the Douglas fir has enabled her namesake county to rank near the top of the state's timber production levels. This distinction has given it the nickname of the "Lumberjack County."

After all of this fanfare, you probably think that the Douglas fir and Douglas County is named after David Douglas, right? Wrong! It's really named after Illinois Senator Steven A. Douglas, who gained fame for de-

bating Abraham Lincoln in 1858 on the "peculiar institution" of slavery. Although Lincoln lost the senatorial election to Douglas, the debates helped Lincoln to gain national prominence and polarized the issue, which James Madison called "a firestorm in the night." Douglas's notoriety out West, however, was due more to his ardent advocacy in congress of Oregon statehood. It was no small honor to choose his name to grace this county where stagecoaches passed en route to Jacksonville gold country, where California-bound steamships plied the Umpqua, and where Oregon's most esteemed pioneer family, the Applegates, chose to settle.

again on Safari Road. Once inside the park gates, the brightly colored birds and semi-exotic game animals transport you to other lands, despite an oddly appropriate Oregon backdrop. Be that as it may, every possible step has been taken at Wildlife Safari to re-create African and North American animal life zones. Lest this conjure the image of lions, tigers, and bears eating Bambi and company for supper before your very eyes, rest assured that these critters are kept apart from their natural enemies. Similar precautions are taken with humans. People must remain inside their vehicles except in designated areas, and windows and sunroofs must be kept closed in the big cats and bears areas.

The first loop takes you to see the tigers and cheetahs. These giant felines loll lazily about or catch catnaps in the tall grass. The next link takes you through the heart of "Africa," where the deer and the antelope play. Wildebeests, zebras, and other creatures scamper freely about, seemingly oblivious to the slow parade of cars and people watching them. Elephants, rhinoceroses, and other African big game are also represented here. Soon you are in "North America." Bears, bighorn sheep, pronghorns, moose, and buffaloes are just a few of the animals who live down in the valley. Perhaps the most popular attraction is the petting zoo, where children get "hands-on" experience. When the weather is good, play sheik or sultan and take a memorable ride on the

camel or the elephant. Open at 8:30 a.m. in the summer, and 9 a.m. the rest of the year, the park closes at dusk regardless of the season.

WINERIES

There are nine wineries in the Roseburg vicinity that offer tastings and tours. The dry, Mediterranean climate and rich variety of soils in the area are ideal for chardonnay, pinot noir, gewürztraminer, riesling, zinfandel, and cabernet sauvignon varietals. A good wine tour pamphlet with a fine map showing the location of the wineries is available from the Roseburg Visitors and Convention Bureau.

Hillcrest Vineyard, Callahan Ridge Winery

Hillcrest Vineyard (240 Vineyard Lane, Roseburg, 97470; tel. 673-3709) is one of the oldest established vineyards in Oregon (since1963). Their first batch was a humble 240 gallons, but production has since grown to over 20,000 gallons annually. The winery is noted primarily for its rieslings but also produces cabernet sauvignon, pinot noir, and small quantities of other varieties. Open daily 10-5 for tastings, tours, and sales, Callahan Ridge Winery (340 Busenbark Lane, Roseburg, 97470; tel. 673-7901) is the Umpqua Valley's newest vintner. They offer a very dry gewürztraminer, white zinfandel, and white riesling, as

Camels smile at passing motorists at Wildlife Safari.

PHOTO BY OREGON STATE HIGHWAYS

well as barrel-aged chardonnay and a late-harvest gewürztraminer. The tasting room hours are open daily 11:30-5:30, April-October.

Umpqua River Vineyards, Davidson Winery, Giradet Wine Cellars

The Umpqua River Vineyards (451 Hess Lane, Roseburg, 97470; tel. 673-1975) offers tastings daily from 11:30-5:30. Davidson Winery (2637 Reston Rd., Roseburg, 97470; tel. 679-6950) produces estate-bottled wines that range from pinot noir and cabernet sauvignon to lighter, fruity table wines. Visitors are welcome, but *by appointment only*. Down the road from Davidson Winery is Girardet Wine Cellars (895 Reston Rd., Roseburg, 97470; tel. 679-7252). Philippe Girardet, from a town at the headwaters of the Rhone River in Switzerland, brings to Oregon European wine-blending techniques. This process produces unique chardonnay, pinot noir, cabernet sauvignon, and riesling wines. Tastings, tours, and sales daily 12-5 from May-September; Sat. 12-5 Oct.-April, and the winery is closed Dec. 20-January 30.

Bjelland And Jonicole Vineyards

The Bjelland Vineyard (Bjelland Vineyard Lane, Tenmile, 97481; tel. 679-6950) is located 22 miles southwest of Roseburg. Established in 1969, this winery offers cabernet, semillon, pinot noir, and Johannesburg riesling as well as blackberry, raspberry, and other fruit wines. Open daily 11-5. Jonicole Vineyards (491 Vineyard Lane, Roseburg, 97470; tel. 679-5771) offers cabernet sauvignon, chardonnay, pinot noir, and rosé. Open daily 12-5:30.

Lookingglass And Henry Wineries

The Lookingglass Winery (6561 Lookingglass Rd., Roseburg, 97470; tel. 679-8198) endorses a philosophy of winemaking that includes quality fruit, strict temperature control, and the limited use of antioxidants like sulfites. Their first release in January, 1990 was a rare Botrytised late-harvest white riesling. Open daily 12-5, April-December. The Henry Winery (Box 26, ORE 9, Umpqua, 97486; tel. 459-5120/459-3614) has produced a string of award-winning varietals from chardonnay, gewürztraminer, and pinot noir grapes. Their 1984 pinot noir won the double gold award at the prestigious San Francisco Expo National Wine Competition, proving that Oregon wines can compete with California's best. Recent newcomers to their outstanding lineup include pinot noir blanc and Muller-Thurgau. In addition to tasting and tours daily from 12-5 p.m., lunch at their shaded picnic tables near the vineyard and the Umpqua River can heighten your enjoyment of the fruit of the vine.

SPORTS AND RECREATION

Two area golf courses are open to the public. **Sutherlin Knolls** (tel. 459-4422) is 12 miles north of Roseburg to the west of Sutherlin on ORE 138. Golf nine holes for $7, 18 holes for $13. For a dollar or two more, you can use an electric golf cart to get you and your irons over the hills and dales. A coffee shop and lounge provide sustenance and lubricants to keep you putting happily around. **Roseburg Municipal Golf Course** (1005 Stewart Park Dr., Roseburg, 97470; tel. 672-4592) is closer to town. It costs $6 for nine holes, and $10 for 18 holes; knock off a buck or two during winter. In addition to power carts, a lighted driving range, and rental golf clubs, a complete pro shop offers lessons and any peripherals you may need.

Tennis buffs will find free courts at the Douglas County Fairgrounds, Roseburg High School, and Umpqua Community College. Twelve lighted courts are located at Stewart Park off of the Stewart Parkway, but they require fees and reservations (tel. 673-8650). The YMCA (tel. 440-9622) is also located in Stewart Park and has racquetball and basketball courts as well as an indoor swmming pool. Umpqua Community College (tel. 440-4600, ext. 686, $1.50) has a pool that's open to the public during the summer from 1-4 and 7-9 p.m. Roseburg also has two bowling alleys and two movie theater complexes.

DOUGLAS COUNTY FISHING

The Umpqua River system is home to a dozen species of popular eating fish that range from the big chinook salmon to the tiny silver smelt. The following overview will help you decide where and when to go and what to take to land some supper.

Chinook Salmon

Spring chinook enter the North Umpqua River from March to June, work their way upstream during July and August, and spawn from September to October. The average size is about 15 pounds, though occasionally people hook some big ones two to three times that weight. You'll need a stout rod, sturdy reel, drifting eggs or sand shrimp for bait, and some type of spinner.

Fall chinook are mainly found in the warmer South Umpqua River. Their migration starts in midsummer and peaks in September when the rains increase water flow and lower the river's temperature. Bait and tackle for fall chinook fishing is pretty much the same as spring chinook gear.

THE GOATS OF MOUNT EMIL

There's a saying that only a dude or a fool will predict the weather. But the folks here in Roseburg, however, were able to tell with 93% accuracy if it was going to rain. Their system was simple enough. A basalt mountain called Mt. Emil that rises up from the west bank of the South Umpqua River near downtown had been home to a herd of goats for as long as anyone could remember. When the goats came down from the top of Mt. Emil, that meant it was going to rain.

In the early 1960s, Mother Nature's barometer had to make way for the wheels of progress. Road-building crews blasted out huge chunks of Mt. Emil to make room for Interstate-5. The goats endured this incursion into their domain, and still managed to faithfully make their pilgrimage down from the mountaintop when inclement weather was imminent. However, the entrance to the freeway on the sharp corner around the base of Mt. Emil was deemed too dangerous by the highway engineers. Twenty years later, in the early 1980s, the men and machines once again assaulted the goats' territory.

This time, the citizenry of Roseburg came together to protect their weather soothsayers. They circulated petitions to "save our goats," and sent them to Salem with an emotional plea to the governor to halt the construction, but to no avail. With their turf dynamited into oblivion and the gentle grassy glade metamorphosed into a steep cliff, the goats departed for points unknown. Today, Mt. Emil survives in the form of an ugly rock escarpment that echoes with the 24-hour roar of traffic, while the plaintive bleating of the goats of Mt. Emil is only a fading memory.

PHOTO BY FRANK LONG

The South Umpqua River, an angler's mecca, winds through wooded southern Oregon hills.

Steelhead

The best fishing for summer steelhead on the North Umpqua is from June to October; the fish spawn from January to March. This fish averages only six to eight pounds, but it will make you think that you are trying to reel in a chinook by the way it struggles. Fly-fishing for summer steelhead is extremely popular—so much so that the 31-mile stretch from Rock Creek upriver to Soda Springs is for fly-angling only. Elsewhere on the North Umpqua, spin-casting with drift eggs, plugs, lures, or shrimp are allowed. There are no summer steelhead on the South Umpqua because there are no deep pools for them during the hot summer months.

Winter steelhead are found in both the North and South Umpqua rivers. They begin their migration upriver in November, so December and January are the best fishing months. The fish spawn from February to April. The success of the winter steelhead runs is in great part determined by the weather, which affects important variables

like water temperature, water level, and water color. Generally speaking, if it's cold and wet (but not too wet), the fishing tends to be better. This makes it important to dress warmly in appropriate raingear so you don't turn as blue as the fish you're trying to catch.

Coho And Sockeye Salmon

The coho, alias "silvers," are found throughout the Umpqua River system. The coho cycle is about three years. They spend their first year in fresh water, head for the ocean to spend one to two years, and then return to fresh water to spawn. The adults weigh an average 10 pounds.

Far more rare in the Umpqua River system is the crimson sockeye, affectionately nicknamed "reds" by local guides and everyone else. These river denizens usually weigh about five pounds. You will need lightweight gill nets and purse seiners for tackle; eggs are the preferred bait. Possessing more oil than the chinook, the sockeye is regarded as the number-one salmon for quality and flavor.

Rainbow Trout

You'll find this brightly speckled fish in nearly all rivers and streams of the Umpqua River system where the water is relatively cool and gravel bars clean. They don't like warm water and avoid the lower South Umpqua and Cow Creek for this reason. Rainbows do like the riffles at the entry or exit of pools. This is the most common fish in the water, mainly because the rivers, lakes, and streams of the Umpqua are routinely seeded with over 100,000 legal size (eight inches) rainbows. The fishing season opens in April, with the best fishing in early summer when the fish are actively feeding. The best bait is salmon eggs, worms, or small flies; lures can also be used with success. The most popular tackle is spin-casting gear with a light leader.

Brown And Brook Trout

In the rapids of the upper North Umpqua you'll find browns, particularly around Soda Springs. Browns seem to like faster-moving water than rainbows. The average size is about a foot long, but sometimes 20-inchers are landed. Midsummer is the best time to fish for browns. Worms and salmon eggs prove effective, but the best lure is one that resembles a small fish.

High in the icy blue upper reaches of the North Umpqua is a small population of brook trout. The adult brook averages about six inches, which is also the legal minimum size, so light tackle is best. Mid- to late summer is when the brook trout are biting, and they go for eggs and worms.

Smallmouth, Largemouth, And Striped Bass

The smallmouth is the most numerous of the three bass species commonly found in the Umpqua River system. The largest concentration of them is near Elkton, and they average between one and two pounds. The best time to fish for this species is when the water warms up to a high 50s-low 60s temperature range during spring and summer. Spinning gear with three-pound test line and a four-inch plastic worm are the most popular, with smaller deep-diving plugs right behind. So plentiful are smallmouth bass on the Umpqua that the river has its own set of guidelines that are more generous than the regulations governing other Oregon waterways. You are allowed 12 bass a day with no more than five over 17 inches.

Largemouth bass are found mainly in valley lakes and reservoirs. These fish average two pounds, with some big ones now and then tipping the scales at four pounds. The bait, tackle, and regulations are the same as smallmouth. The key difference is that fishermen should have a boat to keep moving with the school.

Striped bass are found in the main Umpqua, and seem to roam back and forth from brackish to sweet water continuously. The striped bass is the largest of the bass species found here, and the Umpqua has produced some world-record catches of the fish over the years. You'll need a boat to fish for "stripers" as the guides call them, as well as a stout rod, 20-30 pound test line, and a variety of bait. Minnow or eel imitations are good for trolling, herring or smelt work for bottom-fishing, and try hooks or plugs for surface casting.

Shad

Commerical fishing interests have been fishing for shad in the Umpqua River since the 1920s. Light gill nets are used to catch shad, with a 12-pound breaking strength that allows striped bass and salmonids to escape. Since 1964, about 60,000 shad a year are taken from the Umpqua. Shad eggs or roe are considered a delicacy, particularly on the East Coast.

Smelt

Smelt are found on the lower Umpqua near Reedsport around Dean Creek. They have no set timetable for their migrations, moving about the ocean and into the river whenever they deem it necessary. Smelt are usually caught with a small mesh net.

PRACTICALITIES

Bed And Breakfast

Alice's Bed and Breakfast (1753 N.W. Estelle, Roseburg, 97470; tel. 673-7249, $45-55) has beautiful, spacious bedrooms in a 1919 house conveniently located close to shops and restaurants. **Oak Hill Guest House** (2184 N.W. Andrea St., Roseburg, 97470; tel. 672-0059, $45-55) is a comfortable home in the west hills of town. A full breakfast, fresh flowers in your room, and afternoon tea with homemade cookies make for a relaxing stay. Although the house is in a country setting, it is only two miles away from town.

Fort Sugar Pine B&B Inn (613 Colwell Hill Lane, Roseburg, 97470; tel. 679-8658, $45-60) is located 12 miles southwest of Roseburg in the wine country. This old-fashioned single-story log cabin is surrounded by tastefully landscaped grounds that include shade trees, decorative shrubs, and wildflowers. There are many hiking trails nearby to walk off the delicious, homemade meals. **The Umpqua House** (7338 Oak Hill Rd., Roseburg, 97470; tel. 459-4700, $55) is located 13 miles northwest of Roseburg. The owners of this country home rent out the entire bottom floor to guests, which includes a private entrance and bath, as well as a fine view of the Umpqua Valley. Home-baked breads and vegetarian dishes for those who prefer them are among the amenities.

The Wood's Bed and Breakfast (428 Oakview Dr., Roseburg, 97470; tel. 672-2927, $45-60) is located six miles northwest of town near scenic River Forks Park. Their guest suite overlooks a pond on their seven-acre wooded spread. Judy Wood, the hostess, has published her own cookbook, and gourmet meals are always featured.

Campgrounds

Armacher County Park (tel. 672-4901, $5-10) is five miles north of town off I-5 on Exit 129. The park is situated on the North Umpqua and has 10 tent sites and 20 RV/trailer sites with full hookups.

ROSEBURG ACCOMMODATIONS

Name	Address	Telephone	Price	Features
Rose City Motel	1142 N.E. Stephens St.	673-8209	$18-35	cable, pets
Casa Loma	1107 N.E. Stephens St.	673-5569	$20-50	cable, jacuzzi
City Center Motel	1321 S.E. Stephens St.	673-6134	$20-46	basic
Hilltop Motel	978 N.E. Stephens St.	673-6223	$20-40	cable
Town House Motel	525 N.E. Stephens St.	672-4526	$21-35	cable, pets
Vista Motel	1183 N.E. Stephens St.	673-2736	$22-50	showtime, HBO, pets
Budget 16 Motel	1067 N.E. Stephens St.	673-5556	$22-30	pool
Holiday Motel	444 S.E. Oak	672-4457	$25-45	pool, pets
Motel Orleans	427 N.W. Garden Valley Blvd.	673-5561	$25-65	pool, restaurant, lounge
Pine Motel	2821 N.E. Stephens St.	672-4063	$25-30	kitchenettes, pool
Sycamore Motel	1627 S.E. Stephens St.	672-3354	$26-30	restaurant
Shady Oaks Motel	2954 Old 99	672-2608	$27-30	air conditioning
Roseburg Travelodge	315 W. Harvard	672-4836 (800) 255-3050	$35-55	pool
Dunes Motel	610 W. Madrone	672-6684	$40-45	lounge, pets
Best Western Douglas Inn Motel	511 S.E. Stephens St.	673-6625	$40-50	restaurant
Windmill Inn of Roseburg	1450 N.W. Mulholland Dr.	673-0901 OR (800) 452-5315 U.S.A. (800) 547-4747		everything
Best Western Garden Villa Motel	760 N.W. Garden Valley Blvd.	672-1601 (800) 547-3446	$43-50	pool, pets, nonsmoking rooms

A bathhouse and picnic area are also found here. **Twin Rivers Vacation Park** (433 Rivers Forks Rd., Roseburg, 97470; tel. 673-3811, $6-15) is six miles out of town (via I-5, take Exit 125) where the north and south forks of the Umpqua converge. Water, electricity, waste disposal, and a coin-op laundry are available at this 85-site park. **Fairgrounds RV Park** (210 Frear St., Roseburg,

97470; tel. 440-45505, $6) has 50 hookups, water, and a drive-thru dump station. **U-Haul RV Center** (1182 N.E. Stephens, Roseburg, tel. 672-6864) has a dumping station for self-contained vehicles.

Food

Roseburg is not exactly the fine-dining capital of Oregon. Most of the folks here are more interested in getting a big plate of food than titillating their palates. Since there is no shortage of fast-food joints, greasy spoons, and truck driver restaurants, let's focus instead upon a few unique eateries in town.

Old family southwestern-style recipes are used for tamales, chile rellenos, salsa, and much more at **Abuelita's** (815 S.E. Oak Ave., Roseburg, 97470, tel. 673-9772). From the four varieties of salsa (mild red, hot red, salsa fresca, and salsa verde) to the sopaipillas for dessert (served with honey butter or blackberries and ice cream) almost everything here is made fresh. Chicken and beef fajitas, burritos, tostadas, enchiladas verde, and chili rellenos are all on the menu. The tamales, made fresh daily with a hundred-year-old recipe, come wrapped up in corn husks and stuffed with pork, beef, or chicken fillings. The black bean soup with grated cheese, diced tomatoes, green onions, and sour cream is also quite good. In fact, all of the food is delicious, but be forewarned that everything tends toward the spicy side and packs a punch. Beer, wine, and margaritas are available to help put out the fire. Lunches start at $2.95, dinner combinations range from $3.95-7.95.

Another highly regarded Tex-Mex establishment is **La Hacienda** (940 N.W. Garden Valley Blvd., Roseburg, 97470; tel. 672-5330). You'll know the place when you see it. In front of the cream-colored stucco building with green and orange stripes are tall arches of typical Spanish design. The food inside is equally inviting. In addition to the usual assortment of tacos, tostadas, and tamales, you'll find some dishes that break away from the Mexican food norm. The shrimp and chicken fajitas are good, as are the combination dinners and seafood dishes. One of the latter you may care to try is langostinos jalisco, prawns sautéed in butter, garlic, and white wine. A big basket of chips with green tomatillo salsa or the more traditional red salsa comes with your meal.

La Hacienda also features a wide selection of Mexican beers to enhance your lunch or dinner.

If you're in the mood for some good, cheap, and plentiful Italian cuisine, head for **Momma's Home Cookin'** (834 N.W. Garden Valley Blvd., Roseburg, 97470; tel. 672-4361). Spaghetti, linguine, fettucine, canneloni, and manicotti are among the "pastabilities." Momma's also features calzone as well as a full line of pizzas. Open seven days a week for lunch and dinner. You'll find good deli sandwiches at **Between the Buns** (214 S.E. Jackson, Roseburg, 97470; tel. 672-8633). "Dagwood-style" sandwiches piled way too high with fillings come at a low price that makes them easy to swallow. Open Monday through Friday 11-5 p.m., call the night before to order a picnic lunch.

Brutke's Wagon Wheel (227 M.W. Garden Valley Blvd., Roseburg, 97470; tel. 762-7555) is the place to go for prime rib. The chef's prime rib recipe dates back over 30 years and accounts for over a third of the food sales at the restaurant. But if you don't fit the beefeater's shoes, chicken and "heart smart" entrees are also featured on the menu. The restaurant has a colorful, homey atmosphere. You might see loggers wearing flannel shirts and denims while other folks sport formal wear and furs. It's not uncommon for couples to come by here for special occasion and families to drop in for a good, wholesome meal. Open Monday through Friday for lunch and dinner, and Saturday and Sunday for dinner only.

Those who enjoy the full fanfare of sumptuous soups and salads, flambé dinners, and sinfully rich chocolate desserts, consider a meal at **P.B. Clayton's Fine Food and Spirits** (968 N.E. Stephens, Roseburg, 97470; tel. 672-1142). This contemporary restaurant specializes in fresh seafood, chicken, and pastas. A dance floor and a live DJ in one section of the restaurant make P.B. Clayton's a popular night spot. Open for lunch and dinner Monday through Saturday, with dinner only Sunday.

Chin's Cafe (1614 S.E. Stephens, Roseburg, 97470; tel. 673-3291) has Chinese food worth crossing over the mountains for. Chin's makes a wide selection of beef, pork, chicken and seafood specialties. Open for lunch and dinner Sunday through Friday, with dinner only Saturday. **Ku-raya's** (5096 Old Highway 99 South, Roseburg, 97470; tel. 679-9701) features Thai food that is guaranteed to spice up your evening. A popular dish here Pad Thai, which features noodles, sprouts, and scallions beneath a sauce blending hot, sweet, and peanut flavors. Their homemade coconut ice cream will soothe your stomach if you overdosed on the hot stuff. Open seven days a week for lunch and dinner.

For a lumberjack-sized breakfast, the **Timber Mill** (2455 Diamond Lake Blvd., Roseburg, 97470; tel. 672-0705) will fill you up without breaking the bank. Open seven days a week from 4 a.m. to 9 p.m., early risers should be prepared to share the restaurant with mill workers fortifying themselves for the day's work. An old log-truck driver adage is "Never eat at a place called Mom's," but you can make an exception at **Mom's Place** (634 E. Cass, Roseburg, 97470; tel. 672-8459). Open seven days a week from 3 a.m. to 3 p.m., large platefuls and low prices make this place another workingman's friend.

Events
Roseburg's big event is the **Douglas County Fair,** held annually out at the fairgrounds the second week of August. In addition to the usual assortment of 4-H prize bulls, mom's marmalade, and grandma's-secret-recipe apple pie, the bright lights of the midway rides, food booths, and horse and stock-car races add to the festive atmosphere. In the afternoon, big-name singers entertain the crowds with toe-tapping country music. While it's seven days of fun, and well worth seeing if you're in the neighborhood, high temperatures compel an early start.

Services And Information
The **Roseburg Visitor and Convention Bureau** (410 S.E. Spruce St., Roseburg, 97470; tel. 672-9731) has all kinds of useful information free for the taking. One particularly useful pamphlet is a driver's guide to historic places. And while the staff here is courteous and can offer decent travel planning suggestions, they are tight-lipped when it comes to specific recommendations on food and lodging. Open Mon.-Fri., 8-5:30.

The **Douglas County Library** (1036 S.E. Douglas, Roseburg, 97470; tel. 440-4305/800-452-0992 ext. 311) is in the west wing of the Douglas County Courthouse. Hours are Mon. 12-9, Tue.-Wed. 10-9, and Thur.-Sat. 10-6. From September-May, the library is also open Sun. 12-4. The **Douglas County Museum Lavola Bakken Research Library** (Douglas County Fairgrounds, Roseburg, 97470; tel. 440-4507) is a reference library on the first floor of the museum. It has a good collection on the historical and cultural development of Douglas County as well as botanic, geologic, and zoological information.

Douglas Community Hospital (735 W. Harvard Blvd., Roseburg, 97470; tel. 673-6641) offers a 24-hour physician-staffed emergency room treating everything from colds to major trauma. **Harvard Urgent Care Clinic** (1813 W. Harvard Blvd., Suite 110, Roseburg, 97470; tel. 673-1503) is the place to drop in for minor medical problems.

The Roseburg **police** (774 S.E. Rose, Roseburg, 97470; tel. 673-6633 or 911 for emergencies only) and the state police (tel. 440-3333) are always available should any trouble occur. The **post office** (519 S.E. Kane, Roseburg, 97470; tel. 673-5326) is open 8:30-5 p.m. Monday through Friday. If you're recycling your dirty clothes, **Wash and Dry Laundry** (1820 N.E. Stephens, Roseburg, 97470; tel. 673-7701) and **Clothes Hamper Launderette** (2428 W. Harvard Blvd., Roseburg, 97470; tel. 672-0240) both feature coin operated machines.

Getting There And Getting Around
The **Greyhound/Trailways** bus depot (835 S..E. Stephens, Roseburg, 97470; tel. 673-5326) is open weekdays 7:30 a.m.-6:30 p.m., Saturday 8-5 p.m., and is closed on Sunday. Routes connect Roseburg with California, the Willamette Valley, and Washington as well as the Oregon coast. **Pal Auto Rental** (1410 S.E. Stephens, Roseburg, 97470; tel. 673-5210) features new and late-model car rentals at reasonable rates. **The Mobile Tune** (1400 S.E. Stephens, Roseburg, 97470; tel. 673-5210) has vehicles ranging from compacts and economy cars to luxury sedans and pickup trucks in addition to trailers and RVs. **Roseburg Sunshine Taxi Express** (tel. 672-2888) can chauffeur you around the city.

OAKLAND

Many travelers drive by the exit marked "Oakland" on I-5 joking that maybe they made a wrong turn somewhere and ended up in California. But the curious who venture a few miles off the freeway to explore this National Historic Landmark discover that *this* Oakland is an interesting voyage into Oregon's past. Established in the 1850s, this hamlet today gives little indication of the caprices of fate and fortune it has experienced in its 140-year history.

Oakland was a stopover point for the main stagecoach line linking Portland and Sacramento until the Oregon and California Railroad came to town in 1872. With these two transportation linkages, Oakland's economy thrived as a trading center for outlying hop fields and prune orchards. In the early 1900s, millions of pounds of dried prunes were shipped all over the world from Oakland. In the 1920s and '30s, raising turkeys became the prominent industry in the area, and Oakland became the leading turkey-shipping center in the western United States. During the '40s through the '60s, the lumber industry dominated the local economy. Today, livestock ranching, farming, and tourism are the economic mainstays.

While not as built up as its counterpart restoration further south in Jacksonville, Oakland still provides a good place to pull off the interstate and reflect on the passing of time in a one-time boomtown turned rural hamlet.

SIGHTS

Old Town Oakland is a good place to start your tour, because this is where it all began. An excellent free history and walking tour pamphlet is available at city hall (117 3rd St.). The original wooden buildings were destroyed by fires in the 1890s, and most of the present structures of brick and stone in the historical district date back to this era of reconstruction. There are many antique stores, art galleries, and curio shops to browse through as well. The **Oakland Museum** (136 Locust) is worth visiting. The exhibit in the back recreates Oakland during its boom times. Open daily 1-4:30; closed on holidays; admission is free.

PRACTICALITIES

Accommodations
Situated on a bluff overlooking Old Town, **The Pringle House Bed and Breakfast Inn** (114 N.E. 7th St., Oakland, 97462; tel. 459-5038, $35-55) is Oakland's only available lodging. This 1893 Victorian, warmly furnished with antiques, features wing chairs in front of the fireplace as well as an interesting doll collection. Guests are treated to a breakfast of fresh juice, coffee or tea, fruits, cheeses, croissants, homemade jams and jellies, and a "house specialty." Check-in time is between 2-10 p.m.; reservations are recommended.

Food
The **Lamplighter Inn** (126 Locust, Oakland, 97462; tel. 459-4938) opens at 6 a.m. for breakfast, and serves basic American food like omelettes, sandwiches, and burgers. The lounge in the back of the restaurant is the "hot spot" in town where locals come to tilt glasses and play video poker. Even if you're not in the mood for a drink, go inside and check out their huge Maxfield Parrish-like painting of a naked lady petting a swan. It is based on William Butler Yeats's 1923 poem "Leda and the Swan." Leda was ravished by Zeus in the form of a swan, and subsequently gave birth to Helen of Troy. Oakland is noteworthy for these leftover touches of refinement from its golden age, which seem almost incongruous against its present-day small-town facade

Fancier fare is found across the street at **Tolly's** (115 Locust, Oakland, 97462; tel. 459-3796). Lunch is served 10-6, and features deli, croissant, and Scandinavian sandwiches (like the Svensk Farsk Frukt, which is cream cheese, peanut butter, dried apricots, prunes, and bananas, guaranteed to give you that "get up and go" feeling), as well as creative entrees and salads. Elaborate gourmet dinners are served 5:30-10 (except Mondays) and are complemented by a fine wine list and mellow piano music. Whichever meal you are having, be sure to save some room for the homemade desserts proudly shown off in the lobby display case. The well-illuminated upstairs room is the nicest place in which to sit. Here, you can admire the sturdy 25-foot-long, 4 by 20-inch Douglas fir roof supports that tell of another era when lumber was king.

Services And Information
The small but quaint **Oakland Public Library** (100 N.E. 7th) is in the historic Washington School Building (1910). Open Mon. 2-8, Tues. 10-2, Wed. 10-12/2-6, and Fri. 1-5. The **post office** (109 Locust St., Oakland, 97462) is open Mon.-Fri. 8:30-5, closed one hour for lunch. The **chamber of commerce** is at city hall (117 3rd St.). The **police** can be reached at tel. 440-4471, and for **emergency medical care**, dial 911.

THE HIGH CASCADES
INTRODUCTION

The Cascades comprise one of the most magnificent natural playgrounds in the world. This collage of green forest and black basalt outcroppings is topped by extinct volcano cones covered with snow. Plenty of lakes, rivers, and waterfalls provide a pleasing contrast to the earth tones here. There are over 160 parks in the High Cascades, providing easy access to hiking, camping, climbing, and other recreational pursuits. Many of these parks are linked together by the Pacific Crest Trail, which traverses the entire range border to border. The famous thoroughfare is the backbone of an extensive network of trails that wind through this spectacular region. In addition, six national forests, six federal wilderness areas, and Oregon's only national park, Crater Lake, are also found in the Oregon Cascades. Add to the bevy of luxury resorts nine developed ski areas, hundreds of miles of cross-country skiing and snowmobiling trails, and numerous waterways teeming with fish, and you have all the accouterments for roughing it in style.

THE LAND

What fault scarps are to the California landscape, lava fields and snowcapped volcano cones are to Oregon. While remnants of the state's not-so-distant volcanic past abound, the most impressive and dramatic examples are found in the High Cascades, a chain of icy peaks stretching from northern California to British Columbia. The Oregon Cascades lie in the heart of this great range, and many have been named after former military commanders and heads of state. Given their stature and commmanding presences, Mounts Hood, Jefferson, and Washington rate such distinction. Mt Hood (11,239 feet) is the tallest in the state, and many others top out at over 10,000 feet. Oregon's peaks are part of the great "Ring of Fire" which encircles the Pacific. Cotopaxi (Equador), Fuji (Japan), and Krakatoa (Indonesia), as well as the Cascades' notorious sister volcanoes Lassen (California) and St. Helens

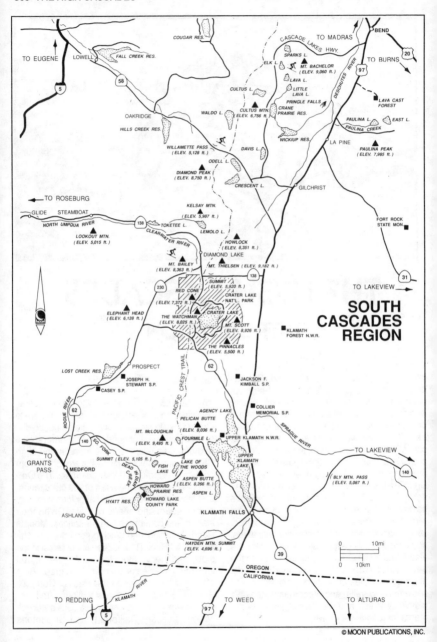

© MOON PUBLICATIONS, INC.

(Washington) are said to belong to this group, each peak sharing common roots with the others.

They are linked together by the theory of continental drift and plate tectonics. According to the theory, the land masses force the ocean floor to slip underneath the continental plate. This creates heat-generating friction, causing rocks to melt. The resulting hot, soupy subterranean mass feeds inland volcanoes with magma and molten rock 20-plus miles beneath the earth's surface. When water is added to this hellish brew, the melting point of the rocks is lowered by 1000° F or more. Water also acts as the major explosive agent of volcanic eruptions, primarily due to the steam created in the reaction. Eventually, the vapors can no longer be confined, and the plugged vent is pierced by the tremendous pressures of the steam and other gases produced from the magma. The lighter materials are ejected first—ash, cinders, and pyroclastic debris, and oftentimes the earth spits up mouthfuls of its fiery interior as well. Once the water supply is spent, the lava usually becomes too viscous to flow, and the vent is once again sealed up by the cooling rock to start the process anew.

The Cascade Range is said to be approximately 25 million years old. However, geologists are uncertain when the Cascade volcanoes began to form, but "guesstimates" put them at several million years of age, during the Pleistocene epoch. And while the mountains appear to be dormant, keep in mind that nature's timeclock is unpredictable. Although the odds of Oregon becoming a Pompeii in our lifetime seem remote, the recent worldwide increase in earthquakes and volcanic eruptions suggest that the earth's internal burners are heating up again, and one of Oregon's slumbering giants may awaken soon.

There are four major types of volcanoes, and all of them are found in the Cascades. Cinder cones, like Lava Butte and Black Butte, are formed by the explosive ejection of ash and particles of lava, and rarely exceed 1,200 feet. Shield volcanoes, like Washington and Three Fingered Jack, form a gently sloping dome that tends to be wider than it is high. Erosion is responsible for their present ragged-edged appearance. Plug-dome volcanoes, like Beacon Rock in the Columbia River Gorge, is the result of lava cooling until it's too thick to flow beyond the vent, creating a massive dome. Finally, there are composite volcanoes, making up the bulk of the majestic Cascades, which are formed layer by layer from ash, cinders, and lava.

CLIMATE

The Cascades, never more than 100 to 150 miles from the Pacific, effectively divide the state into dramatically different biomes. The moisture-laden westerlies dump prodigious amounts of precipitation on western Cascade slopes, up to 150 inches a year in some locations. Having thus purged themselves, the clouds then pass over the east side of the range, retaining what little moisture they have left. While the wet-siders are busy picking the moss out from between their toes and enduring the seemingly endless succession of rainy days, the dry-siders enjoy an average 200 days of sunshine and about 12 inches of precipitation a year.

When it's not raining in the Cascades, it's usually snowing. Willamette Pass, for example, gets an average 300 inches of snow a year. Crater Lake, oftentimes the coldest place in the Cascades, has recorded a chilly -21° F. Mt. Hood has experienced over 100 feet of snowfall in a year. The snow nourishes glaciers on the major peaks leftover from the last ice age 11,000 years ago, and feeds rivers, lakes, and streams with summer runoff as well. The snowpack also makes for some of the finest skiing in the Northwest.

Lest you think folks living on the western Cascades' flanks are confined to their log cabins all year by the lavish amounts of precipitation, the good news is that the weather is secretly hot and dry most of the summer and into the early fall. Sweltering summer temperatures that can push the mercury up into the 80s also usher in conditions favorable for a variety of outdoor recreational pursuits. The flip side of the benign weather is that it brings higher numbers of visitors and dry, tinderbox conditions to the forest. The latter, along with frequent thunderstorms, makes forest fires a reccurring seasonal menace.

FLORA AND FAUNA

Flora

The wet western slopes of the Cascades are dominated by the state tree, the Douglas fir. This towering evergreen requires abundant moisture and plenty of sunshine. The drier east side is comprised mostly of ponderosa and lodgepole pine forests. The trees often meet with almost no transition zone, because the changes in rainfall are so marked on Cascade summits. However, in southern Oregon, where precipitation levels are generally lower, pine trees have stolen over the crest into the Klamath, Rogue, and Umpqua river basins.

Fires and the hand of man can have more effect on the natural balance of a forest than fluctuations in weather. The changes in groundcover, shade, and soil make conditions more favorable for one species of tree over others. The aggressive Oregon oak is one such example, an easily established tree that can quickly challenge the kingdom of the Douglas fir. The oak's reign is often cut short by the bitter cold, deep snow, and dry summers. Eventually, the Douglas fir is able to usurp the oak and regain its former rule over the forest.

The lodgepole pine is the primary benefactor in the southern Cascades, where frequent summer lightning storms take their annual toll of other species. The tough little cones of this tree endure fires and other adversities such as climatic extremes and barren soils, sprouting when favorable conditions return. The tree colonizes an area rapidly, growing up straight, true, and fine. As their name implies, these forthright trees were often used in the construction of lodges by the Indians and pioneers. But the lodgepole pine usually meets the same fate as the Oregon oak, sooner or later choked out by the larger and longer-lived climax species like Douglas fir, cedar, balsam fir, Engelmann spruce, white pine, and hemlock.

But the lodgepole pine is not entirely free of competition for turf in the wake of a fire. Oftentimes low brush quickly moves in, firmly establishing its territorial dominance over young pine seedlings. The tenacious manzanita, sticky laurel, and varieties of ceanothus, currants, and other miscellaneous shrubs generically labeled as buckbrush or snowbrush are the predominant examples of this type of chaparral.

Wild rhododendrons, dogwoods, and myriad wildflowers are the smile of spring in the Cascades as Old Man Winter releases his frozen grip upon the land. Summer foragers can find blackberries, huckleberries, and salmonberries, as well as many exotic types of mushrooms in the damp recesses of the forest. Fall color from hardwoods

PHOTO BY THE OREGON TOURISM DIVISION
Bear grass, a common sight in the Cascades, blooms under Mt. Hood's shadow.

is limited on Cascade slopes. Bright splashes of gold are provided by ash, aspen, cottonwood, tamarack, and bigleaf maple, but the heavy hitters are the brilliantly colored Douglas and vine maples. The vine maples in particular can make the otherwise lackluster fall foliage of the Cascades come alive with vivid reds and yellows.

Fauna

The Cascades is Oregon's forest primeval. The black bear, wolf, mountain lion, lynx and bobcat compete with each other as well as man in the hunt for beavers, deer, elk (Wapiti), and snowshoe hares. The smaller predators such as foxes, weasels, and martens prey upon chipmunks, squirrels, porcupines, and rats. Other commonly encountered forest creatures include the coyote, raccoon, and skunk. A half dozen species of bats add to the diversity of mammals present in the Cascades. Indeed, this is where the wild things are.

The mountains are also home to a wide range of amphibians and reptiles. Generally speaking, most amphibians, such as frogs and salamanders, are found in cool and damp habitats west of the Cascades, whereas their cold-blooded reptilian fellow travelers (especially the lizard) prefer the warm and dry eastern flank. However, there always seem to be exceptions for every rule. Several of these critters are found on both sides of the Cascades, seemingly oblivious to the inherent climatic discrepancies.

The most widespread example of Cascade herpetofauna is the Pacific tree frog, *Hyla regilla*. It has been found on both sides of the range at elevations up to 7,000 feet. One secret to the frog's success is its versatility in using available breeding water for egg-laying and larval development. While many mountain pools are strictly temporary or seasonal, they nonetheless allow enough time for the rapid growth and subsequent proliferation of the species. Also, the frogs are able to adapt to their terrestrial existence. During the dry summer months, tree frogs absorb moisture from the night air through their skin. The moisture is collected in their bladder and then excreted through the skin during the day to keep the frog cool. Furthermore, the frogs seem to have enough sense to take refuge during extreme weather conditions in abandoned rodent burrows or rock/log crevices and sit it out.

In addition to the Pacific tree frog, a handful of other species of frogs and toads hop around the Cascades. If you are camping near a Cascade lake in the summer, you may be surprised at how loudly the frogs croak at night. While this deep-throated chorus may leave some campers tossing and turning on their air mattresses, others will undoubtedly rest assured that the frogs are also busy consuming an inordinate amount of insects, especially the pesky mosquito.

Visitors to the high country come upon many a giant Pacific salamander in mountain waterways. Common in high to low elevations, the timing of their metamorphosis into adults coincides with the seasonal flucuations of their home stream. In addition to the Pacific giant, six other species of salamanders also call the Cascades home.

Reptiles prefer to slink around the warmer and drier east side. Over a dozen species of snakes and lizards are common to the Cascades. The most dangerous member of the family is *Crotalus viridis*, the western rattlesnake. Able to strike with blinding quickness and inject potentially lethal amounts of venom into its victim, this diamond-headed snake should be avoided at all costs. They like to sun themselves in warm open spots and can be difficult to spot until you step on them, as they tend to coil up. Listen for the telltale rattle of the snake's tail, and give them a wide berth.

Baby rattlers, while smaller than the adults, are just as deadly, and more dangerous to wilderness adventurers because their rattles have not yet developed enough to make any noise. And while you may be tempted to smash a rattlesnake to smithereens with a handy rock or tree branch, keep in mind that these reptiles effectively police the exponential growth of rodent populations.

The Cascades have over 70 species of birds, ranging from the great horned owl to the pewee. The successional stages of forest management in the mountains play an important role in the habitat and territory of many species. When an area is first logged over, the subsequent grasses and small shrubs that grow soon afterward are a favorite haunt of the state bird, the western meadowlark. The mountain quail prefers thicker brush and small trees, the second phase of forest regeneration. The mixed deciduous woods that comprise the next stage is the ideal habitat for warblers. Finally, when the conifers are once again the climax species of the forest, sharp-shinned hawks will move in. Thus, changes in habitats often increase certain species of birds at the expense of others.

SKIING THE CASCADES

The Cascades are a haven for winter sports that range from Alpine and Nordic skiing to smowmobiling and snowshoeing. There are nine developed ski areas and hundreds of miles of backcountry trails for these wintertime recreational pursuits. And while other ski areas in Colorado, Idaho, and California have been hard hit by drought due to the global warming trend, Oregon is still blessed with an abundant annual snowpack that makes for nearly year-round skiing. It is no wonder that ski pros like Billy Kidd and the famous Mahre brothers hold racing camps in Oregon, or that the Cascades is the official training ground for the U.S. Olympic Ski Team.

Mount Hood

In addition to being the highest mountain in the state, Mt. Hood also boasts the most ski areas, five in all. A popular destination for families and beginners is **Copper Spur** (1335 Columbia St., Hood River, 97031). Located on the northeastern flank of the mountain, it usually offers protection from storms and prevailing westerlies, and yet has more than enough snow for a good time. Operating hours are Wed.-Sat., 9 a.m.-10 p.m.; Sun., 9-4. Call 386-5900 for holiday hours and the snow report. You can also find out about the Cloud Capes auto tour, an 11-mile scenic loop in the area. Also on the east side is **Mt. Hood Meadows** (Box 470, Mt. Hood, 97028; tel. 337-2222), the peak's largest ski area. Ten miles from Government Camp on ORE 35, hundreds of acres of groomed slopes, and seven double chairlifts plus one triple and one quad ensure plenty of room for all. Hours are Mon.-Tues., 9-4:30; Wed.-Sat., 9 a.m.-10 p.m.; Sun., 9-7. Call 227-SNOW for the snow report.

Ski Bowl

Ski Bowl (Box 280, Government Camp, 97028; tel. 272-3206) is only 53 miles away from metropolitan Portland on ORE 26 and features the most extensive night skiing in the country. The upper bowl also has some of the most challenging skiing to be found on the mountain. Hours are Mon.-Thur., 9 a.m.-10 p.m.; Fri., 9-11; Sat., 8:30-11; Sun., 8:30-10. Call 222-BOWL for the snow report. A mile further down ORE 26 is **Summit Ski Area** (Box 385, Government Camp, 97028; tel. 272-3255), the place for families, beginners, and people who just like to play in the snow. Affectionately called "Snow Bunny" by many locals, this small 62-year-old ski area may have only one chairlift, one rope tow, and three half-mile trails, but it is always big on fun. Open only on weekends and holidays 8-4:30, call 272-3351 for the snow report.

Timberline

The undisputed king of the mountain is Timberline (Timberline Ski Area, Timberline Lodge, 97028; tel. 272-3311). Located 60 miles east of Portland on ORE 26, the skiing starts where the trees end. With the highest vertical drop of any ski area in Oregon (3,600 feet) as well as the mountain's highest elevation accessible by chairlift (8,600 feet), 60% of Timberline's ski runs are in the intermediate-level category. Given this terrain, it should come as no surprise that the U.S. Olympic Ski team trains here on the Palmer Glacier during the summer months. Hours are Sun.-Tues., 9-4; Wed.-Sat., 9 a.m.-10 p.m. Call 222-2111 for the snow report. This is the mountain's only year-round ski area.

Attractive midweek ski packages are available that include lodging at the hall of the mountain king, **Timberline Lodge.** This National Historic Site was built in the 1930s as a Works Progress Administration project. Billed as the most magnificent wooden structure ever built, the lodge also features fine dining and a heated outdoor swimming pool. For lodging reservations and info on special packages, call 231-5400 from Portland; (800) 452-1335 from the rest of Oregon; and (800) 547-1406 from Nevada, northern California, Idaho, Utah, and Washington. Transportation direct from Portland airport to Timberline can be arranged through **Mt. Hood Express** (tel. 250-4379). This van service ranges from $14/person for six to as high as $54 for one person.

Hoodoo Ski Bowl

The state's oldest ski area, Hoodoo Ski Bowl, (Box 20, ORE 20, Sisters, 97759; tel. 342-5540) has the dual distinction of also being the least expensive. Located between Salem and Bend on ORE 20, this family-oriented resort is evenly divided into beginner, intermediate, and advanced terrain and also offers night skiing. Hours are Tues.-Sun., 9-4; night skiing Wed.-Sun., 4-10. For the snow report, call 345-7416 from Eugene, 585-8081 from Salem, or 752-8887 from Corvallis.

Willamette Pass

Willamette Pass (1899 Willamette St., Suite 1, Eugene, 97401; tel. 484-5030) has some of the most challenging runs in the state as well as a multitude of beginner and intermediate trails. Since Willamette Pass plows its own parking lot, you will not need a snow park permit here. Hours before Jan. 1: Wed.-Sun., 9-4. After Jan. 1: Wed.-Sat., 9-9; Sun., 9-4. Call 345-SNOW for the ski report.

Mount Bachelor

The Northwest's largest and most complete ski area is Mt. Bachelor (Box 1031, Bend, 97709; tel. 800-547-6858 outside Oregon, 382-8334 inside Oregon). Located 22 miles southwest of Bend on Century Drive, 10 ski lifts and trails that range from beginner to expert make for some of the most popular skiing in the state. This is the winter training grounds for the U.S. Olympic Ski Team. With a top elevation over 9,000 feet, skiing here can run well into the summer months. Hours are weekdays 9-4, weekends and holidays, 8-4. Call 382-7888 for the snow report.

Mount Bailey

Limited to only 12 skiers a day, Mt. Bailey Snow-cat Skiing (Diamond Lake Resort, Diamond Lake, 97731; tel. 793-3311) is a unique backcountry adventure for the experienced skier. Located north of Crater Lake on ORE 138, Mt. Bailey does not have crowds and lines, but does have virgin slopes of powder and dynamite scenery. Snowcat skiing tours begin at 7 a.m., by reservation only.

HEALTH

Tick Talk

While relevant Cascade health hazards have already been discussed in the Introduction of this book (see "Health And Help"), a few words about ticks are also in order. The deer tick, found throughout the Cascades, has been fingered in the spread of Lyme disease. First discovered in Lyme, Connecticut in 1975, this strain of disease is now extant in western Oregon. The first sign of an infected bite is a rash called erythema chronicum migrans. It starts at the site of the bite, and gradually enlarges, clearing up at the center while staying red around the edges. The rash is accompanied by flu-like symptoms, and the rash spreads all over the body in one out of two cases.

The second stage of the illness effects only about 15% of those infected, but the consequences are no less severe. Inflammation of the nerves and covering tissues of the spinal cord/brain can often result in headaches and memory and concentration problems. The heart can also be affected, resulting in decreased heart function and fainting spells.

The last stage occurs weeks to years from the rash. It is characterized by aching joints, and the knees appear to be particularly vulnerable. It is suspected that the illness also can contribute to arthritis in the victim's future.

The good news is that the disease can be cured with a 10-day dosage of Tetracycline. If you see the telltale red rash weeks after your romp in the woods, see a doctor. Another prescription for prevention would be to lay the insect repellant on real thick.

KLAMATH FALLS

"One person's conservation is another's unemployment." This fact underscores life in Klamath County, which has one of the highest unemployment rates and lowest per capita incomes in the state, largely due to recent cutbacks in logging. Klamath Falls, or "K Falls," as locals call it, is the county's population hub with 17,000 people. It's used to hard times after witnessing the decline of its previous economic base, the railroads. In an attempt to build a viable economic future, the Salt Caves Dam Project was proposed on the Klamath River. In addition to producing enough megawatts in hydroelectric power to fuel a city the size of Medford (50,000 people), Klamath Falls stands to make tens of millions of dollars from paybacks on the sale of bonds.

But there was one snafu. The Bureau of Land Management's designation of the Klamath as a Federal Scenic River gave environmentalists, hikers, fishermen, and whitewater rafters a legal leg to stand on in a prolonged battle against the project. They allege reduced fish runs and diminished scenic and recreational values along the Klamath will result from the coming of the dam. The orientation of the local populace is made evident by the fact that there isn't one whitewater rafting company listed in the Klamath Falls phone directory, despite the approximate half-million-dollar yearly take of commercial rafters on the Upper Klamath River.

Whatever happens with the project, everyone hopes that the locals can somehow determine and improve their economic destiny without compromising the aesthetic and biological integrity of the Klamath River.

SIGHTS

Favell Museum

A fine collection of Indian artifacts and Western art is found at the Favell Museum (125 W. Main St., Klamath Falls, 97601; tel. 882-9996). Here you'll find beautiful displays of Indian stonework, bone and shell work, beadwork, quilts, basketry, pottery, and Northwest coast carvings. A collection of

KLAMATH FALLS

©MOON PUBLICATIONS, INC.

over 60,000 mounted arrowheads, including an exquisite fire-opal arrowhead, also help get the point across that this is no ordinary museum. Other exhibits of note include the Cougar Mountain Cave Collection, the Nicolarsen Cache Find, and Monte Sherman's silver treasure from an abandoned wagon train. Another attraction is the collection of miniature working firearms ranging from Gatling guns to inch-long Colt 45s displayed in the museum's walk-in vault.

If artifacts aren't your bag, you're bound to appreciate one of the best collections of Western art in the state. Oils, acrylics, and watercolors are featured here, as well as bronzes, dioramas, pho-

tography, taxidermy, and woodcarvings. Over 300 artists are represented, including eight from Oregon, 13 members of the Cowboy Artists of America. The museum's gift shop and art gallery specializes in limited-edition prints and original Western art. Open Monday through Saturday from 9:30 a.m.-5:30 p.m.; admission is $4 for adults, $3 for seniors, $1 for children 6-16, and kids under age six get in for free.

Klamath County Museum

A good background on the region can be gained from a visit to the free Klamath County Museum (1451 Main St., Klamath Falls, 97601; tel. 883-

4208). The natural history section of the museum has exhibits on fossils, geology, minerals, and indigenous wildlife of the Klamath Basin. The exploration and settlement area depicts the hardships of pioneer life and the events leading to the Modoc Indian War. The general history section takes you through the world wars and on up memory lane to the present. Those who really want to revel in local history can make an appointment to pour through one of the largest regional collections of primary sources on Captain Jack and the Modoc Indian War, available in the museum's research library. During the summer, a restored 1906 trolley will give you free transportation from the Klamath County Museum to the Favell Museum and the historic Baldwin Hotel. The Klamath County Museum is open daily from 10-6 p.m., June through Labor Day.

Mares Eggs Springs
Not far west of Klamath Falls off of ORE 140 W is Mares Eggs Springs. This shallow pond, about an acre in size, is one of the few places on earth where *Nostoc amlissimum gard,* also known as Mares Eggs, grows. This blue-green unicellular algae is actually groups of minute cells that are joined together in chains by a gelatinous substance, forming a spherical colony in a rusty-green sac. When the colony, or mares egg, reaches maturity, it breaks up into small fragments which in turn form new colonies. The mares eggs found in this locale can range in size from a pinhead to an extra large potato.

Nostoc thrive here in the cold, clear water. Snowmelt and icy springs feed this pond, and temperatures never exceed 40 degrees. Mares eggs have also been called witch's butter, star jelly, and spittle of the stars. They are considered a delicacy in China and Japan.

To get to Mares Eggs Springs, take ORE 140 W to the first paved road past the Rocky Point turnoff marked To Fort Klamath. Turn right, and go past a marsh to a wooded area. The pond is on the right and marked by a sign, but look carefully because it can be easy to miss if you are not paying attention.

Collier Memorial State Park
About 30 miles north of Klamath Falls on U.S. 97 is Collier Memorial State Park. Donated to the state in 1945 by Alfred and Andrew Collier as a memorial to their parents, this 146-acre park documents the history of logging's technological improvements. The first building at the south end of the parking lot in the park's Pioneer Village is the logger's homestead cabin stocked with a wide variety of tools and artifacts on display inside. Near the homestead cabin is the blacksmith shed, representative of the type of shop found in early logging camps. The next building houses an assortment of logging machinery that ranges from log wagons with wheels made of cross-cut sections of logs bound in iron to chain-drive trucks with hard rubber tires. Also on display are steam-propelled devices including tractors, a narrow-gauge locomotive, and a one-person handcart.

Thunderbeast Park
About 40 miles north of Klamath Falls on U.S. 97 is Thunderbeast Park. For the price of admission ($2.50 for adults, $1.50 for students, and kids under age five get in for free), you can see life-sized replicas of the giant mammals that roamed western Oregon 50 million years ago. Two-horned rhinoceroses, zebra-like horses, and large saber-toothed tigers are just a few of the critters that haunt this place. The size and shapes of these animals are based upon skeletons from the American Museum of Natural History in New York, and their outward appearances are based on paintings from nationally known paleontologists. Placards are placed in front of each exhibit that give the name and a concise history of the animal. While some are quick to scoff at the park as a hokey tourist trap, many people, especially youngsters, enjoy this well-presented glimpse into the past when the land was semitropical.

KLAMATH BASIN WILDLIFE REFUGES

The Klamath Reclamation Project
One hundred years ago, about 185,000 acres of the Klamath Basin consisted of shallow lakes and marshes. These wetlands used to be a fall stopover for over six million waterfowl migrating south for the winter. In addition to the wide variety of birds winging their way through the territory, large concentrations of marsh birds like pelicans, cormorants, egrets, and herons resided here as well. The fertile web of life created by the wet-

lands further supported a host of other animals like mink, otter, beaver, deer, bear, and elk. Lunker trout and other species of fish grew fat in the nutrient-rich waters, providing an abundant food source for the largest concentration of osprey and bald eagles in the contiguous United States.

But our national bird didn't get to rule the roost for long. Many people believed that keeping the wetlands in their natural state was a waste of space. In 1905, the U.S. Bureau of Reclamation began to pull the plug on many of the lakes and marshes here with the initiation of the Klamath Reclamation Project. The drained land was converted to irrigated agricultural endeavors, which now support a major facet of the basin's economy. However, while this was good for ranchers and farmers, it was not so good for the birds. Faced with a habitat reduced over 75%, the peak fall concentrations of migratory Pacific Fyway waterfowl have dwindled over 80%. Fortunately, some of the basin's original habitat has been saved and protected as national wildlife refuges that are managed by the **U.S. Fish and Wildlife Service** (1400 Miller Island Rd. W., Klamath Falls, 97603; tel. 883-5732). There are currently six such refuges, three in Oregon and three more just across the state line in California. Coniferous forests, grassy meadows, marshes, open water, sagebrush and juniper grasslands, and cliffs and rocky slopes are some of the habitats found in the parks. This variety of terrain and vegetation supports an abundant population of wildlife; park checklists show 411 different species present at the refuges.

Fall is the best time of year to observe waterfowl migrations. Starting in late August with the arrival of pintails and white-fronted geese, the numbers of ducks and geese swell to nearly one million by early November. Canada, Ross', and snow geese, mallards, green-winged teals, tundra swans, and pigeons are some of the other major migratory species represented. August and September are also good times to view marsh birds like cormorants, egrets, grebes, gulls, herons, pelicans, and terns. The latter group generally moves out of the basin by late October.

Eagles

From December through February, the Klamath Basin is home to the largest wintering concentration of bald eagles in the lower forty-eight states. The thousands of winter waterfowl that reside here provide a plentiful food source for over 500 of these raptors. While bald eagles can and do take live birds, they feed primarily on waterfowl that have died from hunting injuries, diseases like fowl cholera, or natural causes.

Oregon's largest lake, Upper Klamath, is also home to large bird populations

PHOTO BY THE OREGON DEPT. OF TRANSPORTATION

In addition to a readily available food supply, the eagles require night roosting areas. The **Upper Klamath National Wildlife Refuge** and the **Bear Valley National Wildlife Refuge** both have mature stands of timber that can support the weight of up to 300 eagles a night. The eagles prefer trees on northeastern-facing slopes that protect them from the cold southwest and westerly winds. They also like trees that have large open-pattern branches that give them easy landing and takeoff points. However, the eagles *don't* like it when people bother them. Hence, the roosting areas are closed from early November through March 30.

The good news is that there are still ample viewing opportunities of our national bird, especially when it is very cold. When ice covers the shallow lakes and marshes, the waterfowl are forced to congregate in the few areas of remaining open water. With the food source concentrated like this, it doesn't take long for an eagle to swoop down out of the sky and grab some supper. Contact the Fish and Wildlife office for the latest information on the best eagle-watching locations.

A world-renowned eagle conference is held in February with lectures, a film festival, art and photography shows, road racing, field trips, and workshops. The highlight is a pre-dawn field trip to the nearby Bear Valley roost. For more information, contact the Audubon Society of Portland (5151 NW Cornell Rd., 97210; tel. 292-0661).

Water Birds

March through May is when waterfowl and shorebirds stop over in the basin on their way north to their breeding grounds in Alaska and Canada. They rest and fatten up during the spring to build up the necessary strength and body fat to carry them through their long migration. This time of year is also the nesting season for thousands of marsh birds and waterfowl. The **Klamath Forest National Wildlife Refuge** north of Klamath Falls on U.S. 97 is a good place during spring to observe sandhill cranes, shorebirds, waterfowl, and raptors.

The summer months are ideal for taking the self-guided auto tour routes and canoe trails. Descriptive leaflets are available for both attractions from the Oregon Fish and Wildlife office. Among the most prolific waterfowl and marsh bird areas

in the Northwest, over 45,00 ducks, 2,600 Canada geese, and thousands of marsh and shorebirds are raised here each year. You may also see American white pelicans, *Pelecanus erythrorhynchos,* at the Upper Klamath National Wildlife Refuge during the summer. Unlike the brown pelican found on the Oregon coast, white pelicans prefer freshwater or estuarine areas. Another distinction that separates them from their sea-bound counterparts is that they paddle and dip their bills for food, whereas brown pelicans will dive into the water for fish.

The refuges are open during daylight hours, except when nesting and hunting seasons dictate schedule modifications. Overnight camping is not permitted at any of the refuges.

PRACTICALITIES

Bed And Breakfast

The **Klamath Manor** (219 Pine St., Klamath Falls, 97601; tel. 883-5459) is a beautifully decorated turn-of-the-century home with French doors, period furnishings, and oak floors. The master bedroom is the most luxurious bedroom available, with a fireplace and private bathroom. Afternoon tea and a full English-American or vegetarian breakfast are included; rates are $40-60 per night double occupancy. No pets or small children please.

Located on the southern shore of Klamath Lake is a rustic home called **The Stone House** (803 Front St., Klamath Falls, 97601; tel. 883-8317). The bedrooms are modest yet cozy and stocked with antiques. A full country-style or continental breakfast is included, and the Stone House is happy to oblige special dietary considerations. The nicest thing about the property is its location on Oregon's largest lake, Upper Klamath Lake. From the front porch, several species of ducks, Canada geese, great blue herons, white pelicans, and bald eagles can be observed. The lucky visitor here in the spring can be treated to the spectacle of the courting dance of the western grebe. Rates are $45-60 per night double occupancy; reservations are recommended.

Campgrounds

Most of the campgrounds you'll find in the vicinity of Klamath Falls are privately owned operations.

KLAMATH FALLS ACCOMMODATIONS

Name	Address	Telephone	Price	Features
Maverick Motel	1220 Main St.	882-6688	$22-25	pool
Pony Pass Motel	75 Main St.	884-7735	$22-25	a/c
Hill View Motel	5543 S. 6th St.	883-7771	$23-30	restaurant/lounge, pets
La Vista Motor Lodge	ORE 97 or P.O. Box 761 Klamath Falls 97601	882-8844	$24-30	pool, laundry
North Entrance Motel	3844 ORE 97	884-8104	$24-30	covered pool, pets
High Chaparral Motor Lodge	5440 ORE 97	882-4675	$24	pool, pets
Malatore's Motel	100 Main St.	882-4666	$25-40	pool
Oregon Motel 8	1348 ORE 97	883-3431	$26-32	pool, kitchenettes, laundry
Value 20 Motel	124 N. 2nd St.	882-7741	$27-32	wheelchair access, river views
Klamath Falls Super 8 Motel	3805 ORE 97	884-8880	$35-40	wheelchair access, restaurant, laundry
Best Western Klamath Inn	4061 S. 6th St.	882-1200	$44-72	covered pool, continental breakfast
Thunderbird Motel	3612 S. 6th	882-8864	$58-63	pool, pets

These facilities cater mostly to RVs with electric, water, and sewer hookups as well as other creature comforts like swimming pools, laundromats and recreational halls. These properties also tend to be in prime locations, which accounts for rates that are steeper than their public counterparts. Fortunately, there's several places to pitch a tent in both types of parks without having to deal with someone parked right next to your sleeping bag in a 40-foot-long mobile home watching *Wheel of Fortune* instead of the night sky.

On the north end of Upper Klamath Lake adjacent to the Upper Klamath National Wildlife Refuge lies **Harriman Springs Resort and Marina** (Harriman Route, Box 79, Klamath Falls, 97601; tel. 356-2323). The campground features six tent and 17 RV sites with electric, water, and sewer hookups. Flush toilets, showers, firewood, and a laundromat are also available. Open from April to late October, the fee is $7 per night. To get there, go 27 miles northwest of Klamath Falls on ORE 140 W and take a right onto Rocky Point Road. Proceed another two miles and you will see the resort on the right.

Another mile down Rocky Point Road is **Rocky Point Resort** (Harriman Route, Box 92, Klamath Falls, 97601; tel. 356-2287), which also enjoys close proximity to the Upper Klamath National Wildlife Refuge. This resort has five tent and 28 RV sites with electricity, water, and sewer hookups. Flush toilets, showers, firewood, a laundromat, recreation hall, and other summer-camp trappings are available. Open April to mid-November, the camp charges $10 per night.

Several other campgrounds are also found on Upper Klamath Lake. The best deal around is **Hagelstein County Park** (County Parks Dept., Klamath Falls, 97601; tel. 882-2501). The park can accommodate five tent campers and five RVs in sites that feature picnic tables and fire-grills, with flush toilets and water nearby. In addition to being the only campground on the east shore of the lake, it's the only free campground in the area. Open April to late November, reservations in this small park are advisable. To get there, head north of Klamath Falls for nine miles and look for the signs on the left side of the road.

About four miles north of Klamath Falls on U.S. 97 on the southeastern shore of Upper Klamath Lake is **Mallard Campground** (Route 5, Box 1348, Klamath Falls, 97601; tel. 882-0482). Here you'll find 10 tent and 43 RV sites with power, water, and sewer hookups. Showers, flush toilets, laundromat, and pool are also on the premises. Open all year, the fee is $10 per night.

Approximately seven miles further north of Mallard campground on U.S. 97 is **KOA Klamath Falls** (3435 Shasta Way, Klamath Falls, 97601; tel. 884-4644). Set along the shore of Upper Klamath Lake, the park features 18 tent and 73 RV sites complete with power, water, and sewer hookups. In true KOA style, flush toilets, showers, a pool, laundromat, recreation hall, and other amenities are available, Open all year, the fee is $10 per night.

Food
Klamath Falls is a small, unpretentious town that doesn't try to be anything more than what it is (which isn't much). As such, some locals suggest that visitors come here for the birds, not necessarily for the food. Fowl jokes aside, sandwiched in between the obligatory fast-food joints are some eating establishments worthy of a brief mention.

You can get just about anything you want at **Alice's** (1012 Main St., tel. 884-1444) restaurant. Open for breakfast, lunch, and dinner, Alice's recalls a San Francisco bill of fare. Fresh pasta, steaks, seafood, and fresh baked goods are complemented by good coffee, espresso, and import-

ed beers and wines. Vegetarian meals are also available here.

For something Italian, try **Fiorella Italian Ristorante** (6139 Simmers, tel. 882-1878). Open for dinner Tues.-Sat., the restaurant specializes in pasticcio (Venetian-style lasagna). Seafood and vegetarian meals are also found on the menu as well as imported beers and wines. **Malatore's** (100 Main St., tel. 884-6298) also features Italian cuisine, with moderately priced steak and seafood rounding out the offerings.

If you're in the mood for some Chinese food, head right for **Wong's** (421 Main St., tel. 884-6578). In addition to an assortment of Chinese combination dinners and vegetarian dishes, you can also find American-style steak and seafood here. **King Wah** (2765 Pershing Way, tel. 882-0489), specializing in Cantonese cuisine and thick-cut steaks, is another option for oriental fare.

The **Bagelry Company** (2542 Shasta Way, tel. 882-3419) produces fresh breads, bagels, and pastries. They make great sandwiches on bagels or deli breads stuffed with meats and cheese, ideal for birdwatching picnics. The veggie sandwich with avocado, cheese, sprouts, and tomato provides respite from meat between the buns. **Grampa Bailey's** (2838 South 6th St., tel. 883-7369) is a full-service family-style restaurant. In addition to giant hamburgers loaded with all the trimmings and accompanied with thick homestyle fries, the fresh baked pies and cinnamon rolls also come highly rated.

Services And Information
The **post office** (317 S. 4th, tel. 884-9226) is open 9-5 p.m. weekdays. You can find additional information about the region by visiting the **Klamath County Library** (126 S. 3rd, tel. 882-8894). The **police** (5th and Walnut, tel. 883-5336 or 911 for emergencies only) and state police (2525 Biehn, tel. 883-5711) are always on call to assist. **Greyhound** (1200 Klamath Ave., tel. 882-4616) can take you to California and the Willamette Valley. You can find the hard stuff at the **State Liquor Store** (4309 S. 6th, tel. 884-3313). For health problems, the men and women of **Merle West Medical Center** (2865 Dagget Ave., Klamath Falls, 97601; tel. 882-6311 or 883-6176 for emergencies only) can help put all the pieces together again.

ORE 62: THE CRATER LAKE HIGHWAY

Many locals who live near the Crater Lake Highway sport bumperstickers on their vehicles that read, I Survived Highway 62. The challenges of successfully navigating this challenging precipitous and circuitous thoroughfare, with its horrific winter weather and slow-moving summer crowds, help give it a killer reputation. With it all, there always seems to be traffic on this winding conduit between Crater Lake and southern Oregon. This isn't surprising when you consider the scenic appeals of the Rogue River and Cascade Mountains. Add excellent fishing on the Rogue below Oregon's largest fish hatchery, Eagle Creek, along with the swimming, boating, and rafting opportunities, and you too will be taking to the hills along Highway 62.

HIKES

Many choice hikes are found along the 50-mile stretch of the Rogue River Trail from Lost Creek Lake to the river's source at Boundary Springs just inside Crater Lake National Park. Tall waterfalls, deep gushing gorges, and a natural bridge are all easily accessible. Those interested in more than just a short walk from the parking lot to the viewpoint can design hikes of two to 18 miles with or without an overnight stay. Travelers with two cars can arrange shuttles to avoid having to double back.

Mill Creek Falls

One of the more scenic recreation spots is owned by Boise Cascade, a timber conglomerate. Boise Cascade has constructed paths through its land to a series of three waterfalls and an impressive, rock-choked section of the Rogue River called the Avenue of the Giant Boulders. The largest of the three waterfalls is Mill Creek Falls, which plunges 173 feet down into the river. A sign along the highway and Mill Creek Drive (a scenic loop out of the community of **Prospect**) directs visitors to the trailhead. Boise Cascade has also posted a large map that further details the trail routes. The hike is short, but steep.

Takelma Gorge

A particularly wild section of the river is found at Takelma Gorge. Located one mile from River Bridge Campground on the upper Rogue River, the trail offers vistas of sharp, foaming bends in the river with logs jammed in at crazy angles on the rocks, and ferns growing in the mist of the waterfalls. Although the river's course is rugged, the grade on the trail is an easy one.

Natural Bridge

Even if you're in a hurry, you should take 15 minutes to get out of your car and stretch your legs at the Natural Bridge. Located a quarter mile from Natural Bridge Campground a mile west of Union Creek on ORE 62, here the Rogue River drops down into a lava tube and disappears from sight, only to emerge later a little way downstream. A short paved path takes you to a man-made bridge that fords this unique section of the river. Several placards along the way explain the formation of the natural bridge and other points of interest.

Rogue River Gorge

Just outside of **Union Creek** on ORE 62 is the spectacular Rogue River Gorge. The narrowest point on the river, the action of the water has carved out a deep chasm in the rock. A short trail with several well-placed overlooks follows the rim of the gorge. Green mossed walls, logjams, and a frothy torrent of water are all clearly visible from the trail. Informative placards discuss curiosities like the living stump and the potholes carved in the rock by pebbles and the action of the water.

National Creek Falls

Another short hike for hurried motorists is National Creek Falls. An easy half-mile walk down a trail bordered by magnificent Douglas firs leads to this tumultuous cascade. To get there, take ORE 230 to Forest Service Road 6530. Follow the road until you reach the trailhead marked by a sign.

Boundary Springs

A two-mile hike down a cool and shady trail takes you to the source of the mighty Rogue River,

PHOTO BY TED LONG ISHIKAWA
the narrow confines of the Rogue River Gorge

Boundary Springs. Situated just inside Crater Lake National Park, it's a great place for a picnic. About a mile down the path from the trailhead, hang a left at the fork to get to Boundary Springs. Once at the springs, you'll discover small cataracts rising out of the jumbled volcanic rock that's densely covered with moss and other vegetation. While the temptation to get a closer look is great, the vegetation here is extremely fragile, so please refrain from walking on the moss. To get there, take ORE 230 north from ORE 62 to the crater rim viewpoint, where parking can be found on the left-hand side of the road.

Camping
For those who like roughing it in style with all of the amenities in their RVs, there are a couple of well-maintained trailer parks in the Rogue country that can accommodate large vehicles. **Fly-Casters Campground and Trailer Park** (Box 1170, Shady Cove, 97539; tel. 878-2749, $8 per night) and **Shady Trails RV Park and Campground** (Box 1299, Shady Cove, 97539; tel. 878-2206, $10 per night) are both located about 23 miles north of Medford on ORE 62. Situated on the banks of the Rogue River, these parks feature electricity, piped water, sewer hookups, and picnic tables. Flush toilets, bottled gas, grey wastewater disposal, and showers are also available. A grocery store and restaurants are in the nearby town of **Shady Cove.** Both these parks are good home bases for RV owners who like to fish and hike.

Five miles below Lost Creek Lake on ORE 62 is **Rogue Elk County Park** (Jackson County Parks and Recreation, 10 South Oakdale, Medford, 97501; tel. 465-2241). This campground features 20 sites for tents and RVs (15 feet maximum) with picnic tables and firegrills. Piped water and vault toilets are also on the premises. Open July to late October, the camp fee is $8 per night. The kids will enjoy swimming in Elk Creek which in addition to being adjacent to the campground is warmer and safer than the Rogue. A rope swing tied to a tree adds to the fun at the swimming hole.

Along the shore of Lost Creek Lake is **Joseph Stewart State Park** (35251 ORE 62, Trail, 97541; tel. 560-3334). Here you'll find 50 tent and 151 RV sites (40 feet maximum). Electricity, sewer hookups, firegrills, and picnic tables are provided. Flush toilets, water, grey wastewater disposal services, showers, and firewood are also available. Boat launching facilities for Lost Creek Lake are located nearby. Open all year, the fee is $7 per night. Eight miles of hiking trails and bike paths crisscross through the park. Lost Creek Lake also has a marina, beach, and boat rentals.

If you want to get away from the highway, head for **Abbott Creek** (Rogue National Forest, Prospect Ranger Station, Prospect, 97536; tel. 560-3623). One of the few backwoods camps in the area that has potable water, it's located seven miles northeast of the town of **Prospect** on ORE 62 and three miles down Forest Service Road 68. Situated at the confluence of Abbot and Woodruff creeks and not far from the upper Rogue River, this campground has nine tent and 12 RV sites (22 feet maximum) with picnic tables and firegrills. Hand-pump water and vault toilets are also available. Open from late May to late October, the camp charges is $4 per night.

Set along the bank of Union Creek where it merges with the upper Rogue River is **Union Creek** (Rogue National Forest, Prospect Ranger Station, Prospect, 97536; tel. 560-3623). Located 11 miles northeast of Prospect, you'll find 72 tent and RV sites (16 feet maximum) with picnic tables and firegrills at the campground. Piped water and pit toilets are also available. Open from late May to early September, the fee is $5 per night. Many fine hikes on the Rogue River Trail (see "Hikes" above) are within close proximity of the campground.

A half mile further past Union Creek Campground on ORE 62 is **Farewell Bend** (Rogue National Forest, Rogue Prospect Ranger Station, Prospect, 97536; tel. 560-3623). Located near the junction of ORE 62 and ORE 230, the camp has 61 tent and RV sites (22 feet maximum) with picnic tables and firegrills. Piped water and flush toilets are also within the campground boundaries. Open from late May to early September, the fee is $6 per night. This campground is situated along the banks of the upper Rogue near the Rogue River Gorge (see "Hikes" above).

A nice little campground tucked off the highway and yet fairly close to the Rogue River and Crater Lake National Park is **Huckleberry Mountain** (Rogue National Forest, Prospect Ranger Station, Prospect, 97536; tel. 560-3623). To get there, go about 18 miles northeast of Prospect on ORE 62 and then four miles down Forest Service Road 60. There you'll find 15 tent and RV sites (21 feet maximum) with picnic tables and firegrills. Water and vault toilets are also available. Open July to late October, the campground is free of charge (14-day maximum stay). This campground is at an elevation of 5,400 feet, so be sure to have the proper gear to ensure a comfortable visit (see "Camping And Wilderness Travel" in the general Introduction).

Accommodations

The types of accommodations you'll find on ORE 62 are rustic and simple, catering mainly to fishermen and lovers of the great outdoors. The abundance of excellent campgrounds and RV parks also explain the dearth of lodgings.

The **Maple Leaf Motel** (20717 ORE 62, Shady Cove, 97539; tel. 878-2169) has kitchenettes, cable TV, and a picnic and barbecue area to grill the day's catch or some burgers if the fish weren't

biting. Rates range from $30-40. The **Two Pines Motel** (Box 182, 21331 ORE 62, Shady Cove, 97539; tel. 878-2511) features kitchenettes with cable TV and runs $20-35 per night. The **Royal Coachman Motel** (Box 509, Shady Cove, 97539; tel. 878-2481) has kitchenettes, cable TV, and HBO for $35-48 per night. Rooms with decks overlooking the river run from $48-53.

The **Prospect Hotel and Motel** (391 Mill Creek Road, Prospect, 97536; tel. 560-3664) gives you a choice between something old and something new. The hotel, built in 1889 and listed on the National Register of Historic Places, has several small but comfortable rooms with bath. The rooms are named after local residents and famous people who have stayed at the hotel like Zane Grey, Teddy Roosevelt, and Jack London. Because the hotel is small and old, no children, smoking, or pets are permitted. Rates are $50 a night per room. The adjacent motel features clean, spacious, and modern units that range from $35-50 with some kitchenettes available. You can smoke and bring the kids and family dog along, too.

Not far away from Prospect on the Crater Lake Highway is the **Union Creek Resort** (Prospect, 97536; tel. 560-3339 or 560-3565). Built in the early 1900s, the Union Creek is listed on the National Register of Historic Places. Open year-round, it has rooms available in the original lodge, in cabins, and housekeeping cabins. The lodge rooms, which range from $29-38, have washbasins in them and lodge guests share the bathrooms down the hall. The sleeping cabins with bath range from $35-42. The housekeeping cabins with bath and kitchen range from $40-60. The **Union Creek Country Store**, located at the resort, carries groceries and other essential items. Fishing licenses and snow park permits can also be purchased here.

Food

Loli's Hacienda (21666 ORE 62, Shady Cove, tel. 878-2144) is open for lunch and dinner. Though the Santa Fe pink-and-green interior and faux adobe may cause you to shake your head, the food gets a nod. Broasted chicken, pizza, and Mexican cuisine are some of the items you'll find on the menu here. Lunches range from $4.50-7.50, dinners range from $6.50-10. Perhaps part of Loli's charm is the old coin-operated puppet show machine located in the dining room. For two bits, brightly dressed senoritas dance about as the band plays on.

Down the road a little bit is the finest restaurant on this section of the Rogue River, **Beldi's.** From the cloth napkins to the crystal wineglasses, you're assured a first-class dinner from start to finish. The dining room is perched on a bluff overlooking the river, further enhancing the visual appeal of the meal presentation. Chicken, veal, steak, and seafood dinners range from $10-17. Be sure to call ahead (tel. 878-2010) for reservations.

About halfway between Medford and Crater Lake in the vicinity of Prospect are a few eateries worth a mention. The **Prospect Cafe** (31 Mill Creek Road, Prospect, tel. 560-3641) is open for breakfast, lunch, and dinner seven days a week. Breakfast with two eggs, hash browns, toast, and jam costs $2.50. Omelettes are cooked the way you like them with your choice of a dozen fillings. Best buys include the Mini Logger (one hotcake, one egg, two strips of bacon, and two links) and the Timber Feller (two hotcakes, two eggs, two strips of bacon, and two links for $3.25).

While the names of the sandwiches on the menu (like Cougar Catch and Beefy Bobcat) match many of the stuffed critters adorning the walls, lunch is basic lumberjack fare and lots of it. All sandwiches are accompanied with fries and choice of potato, cole slaw, or green salad.

Dinner entrees range from $6-11 and include soup and salad, vegetable, choice of potato, and fresh baked bread. Be sure to ask about the nightly special. Big wedges of home-baked pie are $1.50 a slice, or $2 with ice cream melting down the sides.

The dinner house at the **Prospect Hotel** (391 Mill Creek Road, Prospect, tel. 560-3664) also comes recommended. Dinner is served family style with the works Tuesday through Saturday from 5-9 p.m. The menu offers a choice of two main courses that are different each night, and the menu changes monthly. One very special treat you can enjoy year-round here is huckleberry pie. A generous slice accompanied with a good strong cup of coffee costs $2.75.

Beckie's (Union Creek Resort, tel. 560-3339) is an intimate place to stop for a bite to eat. One-half of the building is an old log cabin; the other half is a modern design with plenty of windows. Breakfast runs from $3-5 with all the trimmings. The lunch menu features sandwiches and burgers in the $2-5 bracket. Dinners that include chicken, pork, or steak entrees range from $8-12. If you simply want to cool off on a hot day, the thick soda fountain-style shakes or malts ($1.95) at the ice cream parlor next door to the restaurant will do the trick.

CRATER LAKE

INTRODUCTION

High in the Cascades lies the crown jewel of Oregon, Crater Lake. America's deepest lake (1,962 feet) glimmers like a polished sapphire in a setting created by a mountain blowing its top and collapsing thousands of years ago. Crater Lake's extraordinary hues are produced by the depth and clarity of the water and its ability to absorb all the colors of the spectrum except the shortest light waves, blue and violet, which are reflected and refracted skyward. Kodak used to send their apologies along with customers' photographs of Crater Lake, because they thought that they had goofed on the processing, so unbelievable are the colors of the water. In addition to a 33-mile rim drive around the main attraction, Oregon's only national park also features 210 campsites, dozens of hiking trails, and boat tours on the lake itself.

THE LAND

Geologically speaking, the name Crater Lake is a misnomer. A crater is an elliptical or circular depression in the surface of the earth that is surrounded by an inward-facing rim. Many craters are volcanic in origin, their walls formed by ash and lava fragments that were expelled explosively from the volcano's vent. Technically, however, Crater Lake lies in a caldera, which is produced when the center of a volcano caves in upon itself; in this case, the cataclysm occurred 6,600 years ago with the destruction of formerly 12,000-foot-high Mt. Mazama.

Oregon's crown jewel, Crater Lake

PHOTO BY TED LONG ISHIKAWA

Klamath Indian legend has it that Mt. Mazama was the home of Llao, King of the Underworld. The chief of the world above was Skell, who sometimes would stand upon Mt. Shasta, 100 miles to the south. A fierce battle between these two gods took place, a time marked by great explosions, thunder, and lightning. Burning ash fell from the sky, igniting the forest, and molten rivers of lava gushed 35 miles down the mountainside, burying Indian villages. For a week the night sky was lit by the flames of the great confrontation. The story climaxes with Skell's destruction of Llao's throne, as the mountain collapsed upon itself and sealed Llao beneath the surface, never again to frighten the Indians and destroy their homes. Although the lake became serene and beautiful as the caldera filled with water, the Indians believed that only punishment awaited those who foolishly gazed upon the sacred battleground of the gods.

The aftereffects of this great eruption can still be seen. Huge drifts of ash and pumice hundreds of feet deep were deposited over a wide area, up to 80 miles away. The pumice deserts to the north of the lake and the deep, ashen canyons to the south are the most dramatic examples. So thick is the pumice that water percolates through too rapidly for plants to survive, creating reddish pockets of bleakness in the otherwise green forest. The eerie grey hoodoos in the southern canyons were created by hot gases bubbling up through the ash, hardening it into rock-like towers.

These formations have withstood centuries of erosion by water that long since washed away the loosely packed ash, creating the steep canyons visible today. **Wizard Island**, a large cinder cone that rises 760 feet above the surface of the lake, and the **Phantom Ship**, located in the southeastern corner, offer evidence of volcanic activity since the caldera's formation.

The lake is confined by walls of multicolored lava that range from 500 to 2,000 feet above the water. Although it does not have a drainage outlet, Crater Lake is not saline because it is fed entirely by snow and rain, and the surrounding volcanic rocks are nearly salt-free. And yet, the level of the lake fluctuates only one to three feet a year, as evaporation and seepage keep it remarkably constant. Another surprise is that while Crater Lake often records the coldest temperatures in the Cascades, the lake itself has only frozen over once since records have been kept. The water stays around 38°, although scientists have discovered hot spots 1,400 feet below the lake's surface that are 66°. Rainbow trout and kokanee (a landlocked salmon) were introduced to the lake many years ago by man. Too small and scrawny to eat due to the lack of proper food, the fish manage to eke out a meager existence in the frigid waters. There are some types of mosses and green algae that grow more than 400 feet below the lake's surface, a world record for these freshwater species.

HISTORY

Accounts differ on who "discovered" Crater Lake, but most sources agree that it was John Wesley Hillman, a prospector looking for the Lost Bucket Mine. He christened his find Deep Blue Lake. Successive discoverers named it Blue Lake, Lake Majesty, Great Sunken Lake, and finally, Crater Lake. Peter Britt first photographed it in the 1880s, bringing widespread attention to the lake. This, coupled with the tireless work of William Gladstone Steel, culminated in Crater Lake's establishment as a national park in 1902.

SIGHTS

Visitor Centers

The new visitors center is located below Rim Village near park headquarters and is a good place to start. Open daily from summer into fall (depending on snowfall), the center provides information, maps, and publications as well as backcountry permits and first-aid. If the lake is socked in by lousy weather, you can still see it anyway: excellent films about Crater Lake are shown in the center's theater every half hour and by special arrangement. For additional information, contact the superintendent (Crater Lake National Park, Box 7, Crater Lake, 97604; tel. 594-2211).

The original visitor center is on the rim. A rock stairway behind the small building leads to Sinnot Memorial and one of the best views of the lake. Perched out on a rock outcropping, accompanying interpretive placards help you identify the surrounding formations and savor the vista.

Boat Tours

There are over 100 miles of hiking trails in the park, and yet only one leads down to the lake itself. This is because the 1.1-mile-long **Cleetwood Trail** is the only part of the caldera's steep, avalanche-prone slope safe enough for passage. The trail drops 700 feet in elevation and is recommended for those in good physical condition. There is no other alternative transportation to Cleetwood Cove dock located at the end of the trail where the Crater Lake **boat tours** (tel. 594-2511) begin. These narrated excursions depart at 10 a.m., 11 a.m., noon, 1, 2, 3, and 4 p.m. and

cost $10 for adults, $5.50 for children under 12, (kids under 18 months ride for free). In addition to cruising around the lake and giving you a close-up look at the Phantom Ship and other geologic oddities, the tour includes a 10-minute stop on Wizard Island. Passengers electing to hike the steep, one-mile spiral path to the top of the island volcano can catch a later boat back to the dock. However, keep in mind that boats have limited space available, which means your return trip could be as late as 5 p.m., depending upon availability And while it's a great place for a picnic, please be careful to leave this unique island paradise in an unspoiled condition for the use and enjoyment of future visitors.

Hikes

July and August are the most popular months. Colorful flowers and mild weather greet the summer throngs. One of the best places to view the mid-July flora is on the **Castle Crest Wildflower Trail.** The trailhead to this half-mile-long loop trail is a half mile from the park headquarters. Stop there for directions to the trailhead as well as a self-guiding trail booklet that will tell you what the flowers along the trail are called.

A suitable challenge of brawn and breath is the **Garfield Peak Trail.** The trailhead to this imposing ridge is just east of Crater Lake Lodge. It is a steep climb up the 1.7-mile-long trail, but the wildflower displays of phlox, Indian paintbrush, and lupine as well as frequent sightings of eagles and hawks give ample opportunity to stop and catch your breath. The highlight of the hike is atop Garfield Peak, which provides a spectacular view of Crater Lake 1,888 feet below.

When snow again buries the area in the wintertime, services and activities are cut to a minimum. However, many cross-country skiers, snowshoe enthusiasts, and winter campers enjoy this solitude. Park rangers lead snowshoe hikes (weather permitting) at 1 p.m. weekends, daily during Christmas week. Ski and snowshoe rentals are available at Rim Village.

PRACTICALITIES

Campgrounds

Mazama Campground, eight miles south of the rim, has 198 sites, restrooms, and a dump station. **Lost Creek Campground,** located on the eastern section of Rim Drive, has 12 sites, water, and pit toilets. Neither campground has showers or hookups. They are opened when the snow melts, and closed for the season when the snow returns. Contact the park superintendent (tel. 594-2211) for more information.

Accommodations And Food

One of the nicest things about 183,180-acre Crater Lake National Park is that it's not very developed. The services are concentrated on the southern edge of the lake at **Rim Village.** The Crater Lake Lodge has been condemned by state inspectors and is shut down and boarded up. Plans for removal or renovation of the lodge are currently being considered by the National Park Service. From May 19 to October 14, the only accommodations in the park, **Mazama Cabins** (tel. 954-2511), are found next to Mazama Campground. Each room features two queen beds and a bath, and two are designed for wheelchair access. Be sure to call ahead for reservations.

Although there are now no accommodations on the rim, you can at least still get a hot meal at the **Cafeteria** and the **Watchman Deli Lounge.** The Cafeteria is open all year, serving traditional breakfasts, with lunch and dinner offerings including a salad bar, cook-to-order entrees, and deli sandwiches. The Watchman Deli Lounge is located upstairs above the Cafeteria and is open from noon to 11 p.m. June 11 through Labor Day. The menu includes hamburgers, deli sandwiches, pizza, and snacks as well as beer, wine, and spirits. Even though it's called a lounge, families are always welcome. The adjoining gift shop is stocked with postcards, knickknacks, and trinkets. A small grocery section there sells various foodstuffs and beverages in case you've run out of peanut butter and beer.

Getting There And Getting Around

The only year-round access to Crater Lake is from the south via ORE 62. This highway makes a horseshoe bend through the Cascades, starting at Medford and ending 20 miles north of Klamath Falls. The northern route via ORE 138 (Roseburg to ORE 97, south of Beaver Marsh) is usually closed by snow mid-October through July. The tremendous snowfall also closes down 33-mile-long Rim Drive, although portions are opened when conditions permit. Rim Drive is generally opened to motorists around the same time as the northern entrance to the park.

ORE 138: THE UMPQUA HIGHWAY

One of the great escapes into the Cascade Mountains is via the Umpqua Highway. This road runs along the part of the Umpqua River coveted by Zane Grey and Clark Gable as well as legions of less balleyhooed nimrods during steelhead season. The North Umpqua is a premier fishing river full of trout and salmon as well as a source of excitement for whitewater rafters who shoot the rapids. Numerous waterfalls, including the second highest falls in Oregon, **Watson Falls,** feed this great waterway and are found close to the roadbed. Tall timbers line the road through the Umpqua National Forest, and many fine campgrounds are situated within its confines. Mountain lakes like **Toketee Reservoir, Lemolo Lake,** and **Diamond Lake** offer boating and other recreational opportunities. The Umpqua National Forest also boasts challenging and yet accessible mountain trails up the flanks of **Mt. Bailey** (8,603 feet) and **Mt. Thielson** (9,182 feet). And when snow carpets the landscape in winter, you can go cross-country skiing, snowmobiling, and snowcat skiing on Mt. Bailey free from the crowds at other winter sports areas.

The main reason this place is still so wild is because of the ruggedness of the terrain. The first road was built in the 1920s, a crude dirt trail that ran from Roseburg to Steamboat. Travelers of the day who wanted to get to the Diamond Lake Lodge spent three days traversing this road by car, and then had to journey another 20 miles on horseback to reach their final destination. The North Umpqua Road was expanded to Copeland Creek by the Civilian Conservation Corps during the Depression, but the trip to Diamond and Crater Lakes were still limited to a trailwise few.

It wasn't until the late 1950s, when President Dwight D. Eisenhower pushed for development of the nation's interstate freeways and state highways, that road improvement began in earnest. Douglas County responded to the president's call by allocating 2.76 million dollars toward federal matching funds to construct the Umpqua Highway. The all-weather thoroughfare was completed in the summer of 1964, opening up the North Umpqua basin to timber interests, sportsmen, and tourists.

The economy of Douglas County feeds upon the timber of the Umpqua National Forest. Approximately three-fourths of all workers in the county are directly or indirectly dependent on the timber industry. Timber receipts from federal lands generate 60 million dollars annually for county coffers, providing money for roads, schools, and other services. But with over a quarter million truckloads of logs rolling out of the

a whitecapped portion of the Umpqua River

PHOTO BY FRANK LONG

Numerous Indian rock
paintings are found in
the Umpqua region.

PHOTO BY FRANK LONG

Umpqua National Forest each year, it's no wonder that the timber boom is going bust. The reasons include the dwindling supply of trees after 25 years of unabated cutting and huge cutbacks in the allowable harvest of old-growth timber due to endangered species like the spotted owl. Thus, the lumberjack county is in for a major transition in the near future.

The good news is that there are still many unspoiled areas that were spared the lumberman's axe and that are easily accessible to the traveler. Come and enjoy a beautiful green section of the Oregon Cascades on a road less traveled.

SIGHTS

Colliding Rivers
Just off of ORE 138 on the west side of the town of **Glide** is the site of the colliding rivers. The Wild and Umpqua rivers meet head on in a bowl of green serpentine. The best time to view this spectacle is after winter storms and when spring runoff is high. If the water is low, check out the high water mark sign from the Christmas Flood of 1964. Water levels from that great inundation were lapping at the parking lot.

Waterfalls
Visitors can get an unusual perspective of **Grotto Falls** because there's a trail in back of this 100-foot cascade. If you venture behind the shimmer-

ing water, watch your step because the moss-covered rocks are very slippery. To get there, take ORE 138 for 18 miles east of Roseburg to Glide. Follow the Little River Road to the Coolwater Campground where you'll find the turnoff to Forest Service Road 2703 nearby. Take Forest Service Road 2703 for five miles until you reach the junction of Forest Service Road 2703-150. Proceed down Forest Service Road 2703-150 for another two miles until you reach the trailhead. It's only a short hike in to view Grotto Falls.

About 10 miles west of the town of **Steamboat** is 50-foot-high **Susan Creek Falls** whose trailhead sits off ORE 138 near the Susan Creek picinic area. A one-mile trail winds through a rainforest-like setting to the falls. The cascade is bordered on three sides by green mossy rock walls that never see the light of the sun and stay wet 365 days a year. Another quarter mile up the trail are the **Indian Mounds.** One of the rites of manhood for Umpqua Indian boys was to fast and pile up stones in hopes of being granted a vision or spiritual powers. Also called the Vision Quest Site, you can see many different stacks of moss-covered stones in an area protected by a fence.

Four miles west of Susan Creek Falls is **Fall Creek Falls.** Look for the trailhead off of ORE 138 at Fall Creek. A good walk for families with young children and older people, the mild one-mile trail goes around and through slabs of bedrock. Halfway up the trail is a lush area called **Job's Garden.** Stay on the Fall Creek Trail and in another half mile you'll come to the falls. It's a double falls with each tier 35 to 50 feet in height. Back at Job's Garden, you may care to explore the Job's Garden Trail, which will lead you to the base of columnar basalt outcroppings.

During fish migration season, it's fun to venture a little way off of ORE 138 at Steamboat and go up Steamboat Creek Road 38 to see the fish battle two small waterfalls. The first, **Little Falls,** is a mile up the road. It's always exciting to see the fish miraculously wriggle their way up this 10-foot cascade. Four miles further down Steamboat Creek Road is **Steamboat Falls.** A viewpoint showcases this 30-foot falls, but not as many fish try to swim up this one because of the fish ladders nearby.

Back on ORE 138 about three miles east of Steamboat is **Jack Falls.** Look for the trailhead sign and follow the trail along the brushy bank of Jack Creek to a series of three closely grouped falls ranging from 20 to 70 feet in height.

Two big waterfalls are another 19 miles down ORE 138 near the Toketee Ranger Station. To get to **Toketee Falls,** follow Forest Service Road 34 at the west entrance of the ranger station, cross the first bridge, and turn left. There you'll find the trailhead and a parking area. The half-mile trail ends up at a double waterfall with a combined height of over 150 feet. The word Toketee means "graceful" in the Indian dialect, and after viewing the water plunge over the sheer wall of basalt you'll probably agree it's aptly named.

Double back to ORE 138 and take Forest Service Road 37 near the east entrance of the Toketee Ranger Station. This road will take you to the trailhead of **Watson Falls,** a 272-foot-high flume of water. A moderate half-mile trail climbs through tall stands of Douglas fir and western hemlock and is complemented by an understory of green salal, Oregon grape, and ferns. A bridge spans the canyon just below the falls, giving outstanding views of this towering cascade. The cool spray that billows up to the bridge always feels good on hot days after the hike uphill.

Another falls worth a visit is **Lemolo Falls.** *Lemolo* is an Indian word meaning "wild and untamed," and you'll see this is the case with this thunderous 100-foot waterfall. To get there, take Lemolo Lake Road off of ORE 138, then follow Forest Service Road 2610 and 2610-600, and look for the trailhead sign. The trail is a gentle one-mile path that drops down into the North Umpqua Canyon and passes several small waterfalls on the way to Lemolo Falls.

Umpqua Hot Springs

The Umpqua Hot Springs is mostly unknown and far away enough from civilized haunts not to be overused, and yet is accessible enough for those in the know to enjoy. The springs have been developed with wooden pools and a crude lean-to shelter. It's best to go during midweek, as weekends tend to have more visitors, forcing you to wait your turn for a soak. To get there, go north from the Toketee Ranger Station and turn right onto County Road 34, which is just past the Pacific Power and Light buildings. Proceed down 34 past Toketee Lake about six miles. When you cross the bridge over Deer Creek, which is clearly noted by a sign, you will be a little less than a half-mile from the turnoff. The turnoff is a dirt road to the right that goes a mile and ends at a small parking area. Please note that in wet weather, this road may be impassable and is not recommended for low-slung cars at any season. From the parking area, it's a half-mile down the blocked road to the hot springs trailhead and another half-mile to the pool.

SPORTS AND RECREATION

Fishing Outfitters

"Fishing is our only business," proclaims the sign at **Umpqua Angler** (420 S.E. Main, Roseburg, 97470; tel. 673-9809), and their staff is always eager to help you sink your hooks into some supper. This full-service shop features licensed and insured guides for spring and fall salmon as well as summer and winter steelhead. They have all kinds of fishing equipment, bait and tackle, and boats and boat supples. If you have trouble with your rod and reel, this is the place to bring it in for repairs. Open at 7 a.m. seven days a week.

Gary's Guide Service (607 Fawn Dr., Roseburg, 97470; tel. 672-2460) has been in the fishing business for over 20 years and can teach you tried and true secrets of the trade. Licensed, bonded, and insured, all equipment is provided for fly- or drift-fishing on the North Umpqua for salmon and steelhead. Rates are $150 for a one- to two-person full-day trip. **Bill Conners Guide**

Service (Box 575, Glide, 97443; tel. 496-0309) offers trips on the North Umpqua River for winter steelhead January-April, for chinook salmon May-June and September-October, and for summer steelhead June-October. He uses drift boats and gives you a choice of fly-, bait-, or lure-fishing. Rates are $150 for a day-trip with one to two people and includes bait, tackle, and a snack. With either outfitter, be sure to call ahead for reservations.

Rafting

It's no secret that the fishing is excellent on the North Umpqua River. And yet, the river has only recently been "discovered" and gained popularity with whitewater rafters and kayakers. But fishing and floating are not always compatible, so guidelines for boaters and rafters have been established by the Bureau of Land Management and the Umpqua National Forest. The area around Steamboat has the most restrictions, mainly because of the heavy fishing in the area that boaters would disturb. Be sure to check with the Forest Service (tel. 498-2531) prior to setting sail to make sure that you are making a legal trip. A good way to get started rafting and avoid the hassle of rules, regulations, and gear is to go along with an experienced whitewater guide. They provide the safety equipment, the boats, and the expertise; all you have to do is paddle. There are, however, a few things to know before you go.

Don't bother to bring a camera; your hands will be too busy paddling to have time to take pictures. Besides, keeping a camera dry in a raft is not an easy task and often requires special protective equipment. Short pants are preferable, because a little water that splashes up on your leg can be brushed off easily, whereas soaked jeans will remain wet and continue to draw out heat from your body for the duration of your voyage. Ponchos can be effective at keeping the water off of your upper body, but they breathe poorly. This means your perspiration from the exertion will get you nearly as soaked as any souse hole. Another thing to remember is to bring along a pair of worn-out sneakers that you don't really care about and leave the Gucci sandals at home. There always seems to be a little bit of water in the bottom of the boat, and shoes are always required for safety reasons. Finally, a hat and liberal layers of sunscreen are recommended to protect your skin from the ravages of the mountain sun.

Rafting Outfitters

North Umpqua Outfitters (Box 1574, 368 N.E. Garden Valley Blvd., Roseburg, 97470; tel. 673-4599) offers raft, kayak, and drift boat trips. Half-day raft trips are $30 per person, full-day raft trips with lunch are $45 per person. This company operates the North Umpqua Kayak School, which gives classes on how to paddle safely, to roll and handle surfing waves, and survive souse holes (exhilarating pools of foaming water that can be equally dangerous because of their strong eddies). Half- and full-day kayak lessons include all necessary equipment. Half- and full-day drift boat trips are available for those who like to troll their fishing line in the water on their way downstream. They also rent boats, rafts, kayaks and the appropriate accouterments. If you make your reservation in advance, you are given a discount, and you can also knock off 10% on certain packages if you bring in their brochure, available at the Roseburg Visitors and Convention Bureau (see "Services And Information" under "Roseburg").

Located halfway up the river is **Mazama Outdoors, Inc.** (ORE 138, HC 60, Box 64-A, Idleyld Park, 97447; tel. 498-2235). This company runs the North Umpqua exclusively and has a variety of packages available. Half-day ($30), full-day ($45), and overnight trips ($75) are among the offerings. If you want to rent your equipment, a good place to check out is **North Umpqua Equipment Rental Sales and Service** (14168 ORE 138, Roseburg, 97470; tel. 673-5391). You'll find it 12 miles east of Roseburg on ORE 138 next to the Whistlers Park Mercantile Store. They feature one- and two-person inflatable kayaks (also called "orange torpedos") and whitewater rafts for two to six people.

Hikes

Over 570 miles of trails crisscross through the one-million-acre **Umpqua National Forest**. With elevations that range from 1,000 to over 9,000 feet, there are hikes to please families and mountain climbers alike. Wildlife and wildflowers, mountain lakes and mountain peaks, old-growth forest and alpine meadows are some of the attractions visitors see along the way.

If you're camping along the North Umpqua River, many pleasant day hikes are possible on the **North Umpqua Trail.** Slated to be completed by the mid-1990s, this projected 76-mile thoroughfare will stretch from Rock Creek just east of Idleyld Park all the way up to the Pacific Crest Trail at Windigo Pass. The trail connects many of the campgrounds, and has many access points from ORE 138. Check with the Umpqua National Forest Ranger Station (Diamond Lake Ranger District, HC 60, Box 101, Idleyld Park, 97447; tel. 498-2531) for a map and brochure to plan your expedition along this beautiful walkway.

One completed segment of the North Umpqua Trail is **Panther Trail.** This gentle one-mile hike begins near Steamboat at the parking lot of the former ranger station. Many wildflowers are seen in late April through early June on the way up to the old fish hatchery. One flower to look for is the bright red snow plant, *Sarcodes sanguinea,* that grows beneath Douglas fir and sugar pine trees. Also called the carmine snowflower or snow lily, the snow plant is classified as a saprohpyte, a plant that contains no chlorophyll and derives nourishment from decayed materials. Growing eight to 24 inches in height, the red flowers are crowded at the crown of the stem.

A **five-mile hike** that ranges from easy to moderate is found on the south slope of 8,363-feet-high Mt. Bailey. Bring plenty of water and good sturdy hiking shoes because the last half-mile of the ascent is steep with many sharp rocks. To get to the trailhead, take ORE 138 to the north entrance of Diamond Lake. Turn off onto Forest Service Road 4795 and follow it five miles to the junction of Forest Service Road 4795-300. Proceed down 4795-300 another mile until you see the trail marker.

The easy two-mile **Diamond Lake Loop** takes hikers through a mix of lodgepole pine and true fir to Lake Creek, Diamond Lake's only outlet. There are many views of Mt. Bailey along the way, as well as some private coves ideal for a swim on hot days. But while the grade is easy, keep in mind that the elevation is nearly a mile high, and pace yourself accordingly. To get to the loop, take Forest Service Road 4795 off of ORE 138 on the north entrance to Diamond Lake, and look for the trailhead sign on the west side of the road.

For those who like to climb mountains for reasons other than just because they are there, the **Mt. Thielsen Trail** offers a million-dollar view from the top of the mountain. This four-mile moderate to difficult trail winds to the top of Mt. Thielsen's spire-pointed volcanic peak 9,182 feet high. Bring

along water and quick energy snacks, and hiking boots are also recommended due to the sharp volcanic rocks which could easily damage ordinary shoes. Extra care should be taken getting up and down the last 200 feet since the rocks weaken from ice and erosion during the winter and are prone to crumbling underfoot. If you make it to the top, be sure to enter your name in the climbing register found there. Then take a look at the view which stretches from Mt. Shasta to Mt. Hood and forget all the silly preoccupations that plague us mortals. You'll find the trailhead on the east side of ORE 138 one mile north of the junction of ORE 230.

Mount Bailey Snowcat Skiing

Located 80 miles east of Roseburg off of ORE 138 in the central Cascades is Mt. Bailey (tel. 793-3333). Snowcats transport no more than 20 skiers up the mountain from Diamond Lake Resort to the summit of this 8,363-foot-high peak. Experienced guides then lead small groups of skiers down routes that best suit the abilities of each group. The skiing is challenging and should only be attempted by those who can ski advanced runs at major ski areas in various snow conditions. Open bowls, steep chutes, and tree-lined glaciers are some of the types of terrain encountered during the 3,000 foot drop in elevation back to the resort.

The prices may also seem steep at $90 a day, but it's worth it given the pristine beauty of the area, dearth of crowds, and superlative skiing. You can save some money with the Powder Pass—six days of skiing for the price of five. Other attractive packages include overnight lodging in fireside cabins at Diamond Lake Resort as well as an "alpine lunch" of breads, meats, cheeses, vegetables, homemade pie, and coffee served up on the mountain. Rates are $240 for the two-day package, $345 for the three-day, and $550 for the five-day. Only a limited number of skiers can be booked, so be sure to call ahead for reservations.

Slip Slidin' Away

If you fit the bunny hill category, you might enjoy inner-tubing at **Sliding Hill** (tel. 793-333) near Diamond Lake Resort. A rope tow takes "tubers" to the top of the hill seven days a week, 9-5 for nonstop thrills and spills on the way back down. The hill has a ticket system similar to other ski lifts, with full-day, half-day, and two-hour passes available. Passes including an inner tube cost $9 for the full-day, $7 for the half-day, and $6 for the two-hour. A $5 refundable deposit is required for the equipment, and many sizes of inner tubes are available. If you bring your own inner tube, you can save some money. Passes cost $6 for the full-day, $5 for the half-day, and $4 for the two-hour.

Cross-country Skiing

Over 56 miles of designated Nordic trails are found in the Diamond and Lemolo lakes area along the upper reaches of ORE 138. The trails range from 4,200 feet to over 8,000 feet at the top of Mt. Bailey. Some of the trails are groomed, and all of them are clearly marked by blue trail signs. Contact the Umpqua National Forest Service (Diamond Lake Ranger District, HC 60, Box 101, Idleyld Park, 97447; tel. 498-2531) and request maps and information on these trails.

The **Nordic Center** (tel. 793-3333) at Diamond Lake Resort has equipment, waxes, and rentals, and is open 8-5 daily. It costs $12 per day for skis, boots, and poles rental packages. Lessons are also available. A great option to cross-country buffs is to take a snowcat from Diamond Lake to the north rim of Crater Lake for $40 per person. You have the option to ski the 10 miles back to Diamond Lake (which is mostly downhill) with a guide, or to ride back on the snowcat for an additional $30. A hardy lunch is included in the package.

Motorized Snow Trails

Approximately 133 miles of designated motorized snow trails are concentrated around the Lemolo and Diamond lakes area. The trails are usually open in late November, when snow accumulations permit, and range from 4,000 to over 8,000 feet in elevation. Many of these trails are groomed on a regular basis, and all are clearly marked by orange trail signs and diamond-shaped trail blazers pegged up on trees above the snowline. Contact the Umpqua National Forest Service (see "Cross-country Skiing" above) for maps and additional information.

One of the more exotic runs is into Crater Lake National Park. Snowmobiles and ATVs (All Terrain Vehicles) must register at the north entrance of the park and stay on the road. The trail climbs up about 10 miles from the park gates to the north rim of the lake. Be aware that the mountain weather here can change suddenly, creating dangerous subzero temperatures and white-out conditions. Also, watch for Nordic skiers and other people sometimes found on motorized vehicle trails.

Snowmobile Tours

If you've ever wanted to ride on one of these motorized snow broncs, then this is the way to go. Each person is furnished with their own snowmobile and all the fuel they'll need. A half dozen tours are available ranging from $25 for the one-hour, 17-mile ride around Diamond Lake to $110 for the eight-hour, 100-mile trip to Crescent Lake. The most popular trip is the Crater Lake rim tour. It costs $55, takes four hours to cover the 50 miles of snowbound terrain, and a hearty lunch is also included. Make your reservations at the **Diamond Lake Resort Hilltop Shop** (tel. 793-3333). The only catch to the offer is that you must be a guest of the resort due to the liability insurance clauses carried by the concessionaire.

PRACTICALITIES

Camping On The Little River

If the thought of a campground with good shade trees and a waterfall with a swimming hole sounds idyllic, head for **Cavitt Creek Falls** (Bureau of Land Management, 777 N.W. Garden Valley Blvd., Roseburg, 97470; tel. 672-4491). To get there, head east of Roseburg on ORE 138 to Glide, take Little Creek Road (County Road 17) for seven miles, then continue three miles down Cavitt Creek Road. Eight sites for RVs (20 feet maximum) with picnic tables and firegrills are provided, with piped water, pit toilets and firewood available on the premises. Open May to late October, Cavitt Creek runs $5 per night.

Another campsite five miles up Little River Road is **Wolf Creek** (North Umpqua Ranger District, 18782 ORE 138, Glide, 97443; tel. 496-3532), which features five sites for tents and RVs (16 feet maximum) and three tent-only sites. Picnic tables and firegrills are provided, vault toilets and piped water are available. Open mid-May to late October, the fee is $3 per night. The grounds also have a group picnic site with a pavilion sheltering 14 picnic tables, plus barbecue grills, flush toilets, and chlorinated water. This facility is booked on a reservation-only basis for $30 per day. A softball field, horseshoe pits, and swimming in the Little River make this a fine place for family get togethers.

An easy way to keep your cool is at **Coolwater** (North Umpqua Ranger District, 18782 ORE 138, Glide, 97443; tel. 496-3532). Seven tent and RV sites (16 feet maximum) with picnic tables and firegrills are available; vault toilets and well water from a hand pump are also on the grounds. Open mid-May to late October, the campground charges $3 a night. To get there, follow Little River Road 15 miles out of Glide. There are many good hiking trails nearby, including **Grotto Falls, Wolf Creek Nature Trail,** and **Wolf Creek Falls Trail.**

One of the best deals on the Little River is at **White Creek** (North Umpqua Ranger District, 18782 ORE 138, Glide, 97443; tel. 496-3532). Open from mid-May to late September, this small five-site campground accommodates tents and RVs (31 feet maximum) free of charge. Picnic tables and firegrills are provided, and piped water and vault toilets are available. Situated at the confluence of White Creek and Little River, there is a good beach and shallow water that provide excellent swimming for children. The only catch to this oasis of tranquility is that you can only stay here for two weeks at a time. To get there, take Little Creek Road 17 miles to Red Butte Road, and proceed a mile down Red Butte Road to the campground.

Tucked away at 3,200 feet in elevation on the upper reaches of the Little River is **Lake in the Woods** (North Umpqua Ranger District, 18782 ORE 138, Glide, 97443; tel. 496-3532). Here you'll find nine sites for tents and RVs (16 feet maximum) with picnic tables and firegrills provided and vault toilets and hand-pumped water available. Open from June to late October, the camp charges $3 per night. Set along the shore of four-acre, man-made Little Lake in the Woods, motorized craft are not permitted in this eight-foot deep pond. Two good hikes nearby go to either **Hemlock Falls** or **Yakso Falls.** To get there, head 20 miles up Little River Road to where the pavement ends; proceed another seven miles until you reach the campground.

North Umpqua River Camping

Set along the bank of the North Umpqua River 15 miles east of Roseburg on ORE 138 is **Whis-**

tler's Bend (Box 800, Winchester, 97495; tel. 673-4863). Picnic tables and firegrills are provided at this county park, as are piped water, flush toilets, and showers. No reservations are necessary, and the fee is $6 per night. The fishing is good here, and even though it's fairly close to town, it doesn't usually get too crowded.

About 30 miles east of ORE 138 is **Susan Creek** (Bureau of Land Management, 777 N.W. Garden Valley Blvd., Roseburg, 97470; tel. 672-4491). This campground has 33 tent and RV sites (20 feet maximum) with picnic tables and firegrills. Flush toilets, piped water, and firewood are also available. Open May to late October, the fee is $6 per night. Situated in a grove of old-growth Douglas fir and sugar pine next to the North Umpqua River, a fine beach and swimming hole complement the setting.

Within easy access to great fishing (fly-angling only), rafting, and hiking, **Bogus Creek** (Diamond Lake Ranger District, HC 60 Box 101, Idleyld Park, 97447; tel. 498-2531) offers you the real thing. Here you'll find five tent sites and 10 tent and RV (20 feet maximum) sites with picnic tables and firegrills. Flush toilets, iodinated water, and grey waste water sumps are available. Open May 1-October 31, the fee is $4 per night. As the campground is a major launching point for whitewater expeditions as well as being within a few miles of Fall Creek Falls and Job's Garden Geological Area (see "Waterfalls), it's hard to beat the feeling here.

About 38 miles east of Roseburg on ORE 138 near Steamboat is **Canton Creek** (Diamond Lake Ranger District, HC 60 Box 101, Idleyld Park, 97447; tel. 498-2531). Take Steamboat Creek Road (38) of off ORE 138 and proceed 400 yards to the campground. This campground features 12 sites for tents and RVs (16 feet maximum) with the standard picnic tables and firegrills. You'll find piped water, flush toilets, and grey waste water sumps in the campground too. Open from mid-May to late October, Canton Creek costs $4 per night. Close to good fly fishing on the North Umpqua, this site gets surprisingly little use.

Horseshoe Bend (Diamond Lake Ranger District, HC 60 Box 101, Idleyld Park, 97447; tel. 498-2531) is 10 miles east of Steamboat. There are 34 sites for tents and RVs (22 feet maximum) with picnic tables and firegrills. Flush toilets, piped water, grey waste water sumps, laundromat, and general store are also available. Open mid-May to late September, the fee is $6 per night. Located in the middle of a big bend of the North Umpqua covered with old-growth Douglas firs and sugar pines, this is a popular base camp for rafting and fishing enthusiasts.

Campsites At Diamond Lake

Several campgrounds are in the vicinity of Diamond Lake. Set along the shores of this beautiful 5,200-foot-high lake, boating, fishing, swimming, bicycling, and hiking are among the popular recreational options here. The trout fishing is particularly good in the early summer, and there are also excellent hikes into the Mt. Thielsen Wilderness, Crater Lake National Park, and Mt. Bailey areas. While technically no reservations are necessary, sites in the campgrounds here can fill up fast, so it's always a good idea to book a space ahead of time.

Though ORE 138 twists and turns most of the 80 miles from Roseburg to Diamond Lake, many people head straight for **Broken Arrow** (Diamond Lake Ranger District, HC 60 Box 101, Idleyld Park, 97447; tel. 498-2531). This 142-site campground with standard picnic tables and fire-grills has plenty of room for tents and RVs (30 feet maximum); flush toilets, piped water, and grey waste water sumps are available. Open from early May to late September, the fee is $5-10 per night, depending upon the site. Premium lakeshore sites command top dollar.

The next campground bears the name of its raison d'être, **Diamond Lake** (Diamond Lake Ranger District, HC 60 Box 101, Idleyld Park, 97447; tel. 498-2531). Here you'll find 160 campsites for tents and RVs (22 feet maximum) with picnic tables and firegrills. Piped water, flush toilets, and firewood are also available. Open from May 15 to Oct 31, the fee is $6 per night. Numerous hiking trails lead from the campground, including the Pacific Crest National Scenic Trail. Boat docks, launching facilities, and rentals are nearby at Diamond Lake Lodge.

On the east shore of Diamond Lake is **Thielsen View** (Diamond Lake Ranger District, HC 60 Box 101, Idleyld Park, 97447; tel. 498-2531). It features 60 tent and RV sites (30 feet maximum) with picnic tables and firegrills. Piped water, vault toilets, grey waste water sumps, and a boat ramp

PHOTO BY FRANK LONG

Many Umpqua River campgrounds are close to Eagle Rock.

are also available. It's open late May to late September, and the fee ranges from $5-7 per night depending upon the site. As the name implies, this campground has picturesque views of Mt. Thielsen.

Accommodations

The number of lodgings on the North Umpqua is limited to a few properties that range from rustic lodging to full-service resorts. The abundance of campgrounds and wilderness getaways accessible via the Umpqua Highway partially explain the dearth of motel units. In short, most people come here to get close to nature's teachings and leave the trappings of civilization behind. However, if the weather takes a turn for the worse or you'd rather rough it in style, you have several options available that will give you shelter from the storm.

Near Idleyld Park is the **North Umpqua Resort** (Box 177, Idleyld Park, 97447; tel. 496-

0149). Situated on ORE 138 along the north bank of the Umpqua, the place is not fancy but it is at least clean. The rooms range from $27-50, and good fishing can be had from the private bank of the property on the river. About four miles east of Idleyld Park is the **Dogwood Motel** (HC 60, Box 19, Idleyld Park, 97447; tel. 496-3403). Here you'll find clean modern units with or without kitchenettes located on tidy, well-kept grounds. Room rates range from $40-50.

Near the summit of the Cascade Mountains about 75 miles east of Roseburg is **Lemolo Lake Resort** (write HC 60, Box 79 B, Idleyld Park, 97447; tel. 496-0900). Formed by a Pacific Power and Light dam, Lemolo Lake has native German brown trout, as well as kokanee salmon, eastern brook, and rainbow trout. The lake is sheltered from wind by gently sloping ridges, and there are many coves and sandy beaches found along the 8.3 miles of shoreline. Water-skiing is permitted on the lake. Boats and canoes can be rented, and many miles of snowmobiling and cross-country skiing trails are nearby.

The resort itself has cabins and rooms available. The housekeeping Swiss chalet cabins are equipped with a furnished kitchen, bathroom with shower, and wood-burning stoves. They can sleep up to five and they cost $55 per night. The Swiss chalet cabins with bathroom sleep six in two double and two single beds for $50. Rooms with two double beds go for $45 and rooms with one double bed cost $35.

Food

If you've got a craving for some junk food, the **Colliding Rivers Drive-In** (19162 ORE 138, Glide, tel. 496-3205) can satisfy you. Nothing fancy: burgers, chicken, and spuds. For the ulti-

STEAMBOAT INN

In the late 1800s, a steamboat chugged up the Umpqua River from Reedsport to Roseburg. Based upon this sole voyage, the Umpqua is still listed as a navigable river by the U.S. Coast Guard and all river traffic is regulated. While no vessels made it to the area 38 miles upriver from Roseburg that's called Steamboat today, the name comes from the common practice of unscrupulous gold speculators who would overestimate the value of the holdings to buyers and after the sale would catch the first available steamboat out of the region.

The gold mines are worked out now, but the real treasure of the North Umpqua can still be found at the **Steamboat Inn** (Steamboat, 97447; tel. 496-3495 or 498-2411). This is the premier dining and accommodations property on the river. Lodging rates run $80 for small individual rooms, $130 for condo cottages with kitchens and hot tubs, and $165 for suites with Japanese-style tiled soaking tubs. The Inn is extremely popular and there are only 15 units, so reservations are a must. The grounds are beautifully maintained and blend in with the natural surroundings. It's an ideal getaway from civilization that's near the hiking trails, waterfalls, and fishing holes that the Umpqua is famous for.

The food here is also top-notch. The sweet and cold water served here is devoid of chemicals and comes right out of the ground the way God put it in for your enjoyment. The breakfast specialty are the sour cream roll-ups (one for $2.25, two for $3.75, three for $4.50). These delectable concoctions are big pancakes stuffed with homemade jam and sour cream. Omelettes, French toast, hotcakes, and eggs are other featured eye openers, and homemade cinnamon rolls and bran muffins round out the offerings. The health conscious will enjoy the homemade granola with yogurt and fresh fruit ($4.50).

Lunch features burgers, sandwiches, soups, and salads. The veggie burger ($3.75) made with beans and lentils and topped with a thick slice of cream cheese, lettuce, tomatoes, and onions is delicious. It also comes with the homemade soup of the day. The fresh-baked selection of pies ($2.25) makes for a perfect dessert.

In addition to a regular dinner menu, the special Fisherman's Dinner ($25) is served nightly during the summer and on weekends the rest of the year. The elaborate presentation begins about a half hour after dusk with champagne and hors d' oeuvres. The entree of the day (vegetarian entrees are available upon advance request), freshly baked bread, vegetables, and other dishes are served up family style on the Inn's big wooden slab tables. An elegant dessert and hot beverage conclude the meal. Reservations are required for the Fisherman's Dinner.

mate gut bomb, try the Overload, a three-quarter-pound hamburger with bacon, cheese, and ham for $5.99. Chicken dinners with spuds and dinner rolls are $15 for 15 pieces and $22 for two dozen pieces. Sixteen flavors of ice cream offer a sweet alternative to fried food.

Munchies (20142 ORE 138, Glide, tel. 496-3112) features Mexican food made mostly from scratch with no lard or MSG. They make their own vegetarian refried beans and offer eight vegetarian specials on the menu. Omnivores will enjoy the Munchie burrito, a large tortilla sutffed with beef or chicken and beans and topped with melted cheeses, lettuce, onions, olives, tomatoes, salsa, sour cream, and guacamole. The large burrito will fill you up in a hurry and costs $5.99. Burgers, sandwiches, and all-day breakfasts can be found here as well as homemade pie ($1.75). Open seven days a week from 9-9.

Another option in Glide is **The Red Barn** (20641 ORE 138, Glide, tel. 496-0246). Breakfast here ranges from $2-6, and lunches featuring burgers or sandwiches come with fries or chips and potato or green salad. Vegetarians will enjoy the garden veggie sandwich with swiss cheese, lettuce, tomato, cucumber, alfalfa sprouts, and cream cheese that comes garnished with cottage cheese or potato salad for $4.50. Moderately priced steaks, poultry, and seafood are the primary dinners featured which include salad, fries, rice or baked potato, and a light dessert ranging from $7-14. Lighter fare is available as well, and the best seats in the house are in the back room overlooking the Umpqua River. Open Monday through Thursday 7:30 a.m.-8:30 p.m., Friday through Saturday 7:30-4 p.m., and Sunday 7:30 a.m.-8:30 p.m.

In nearby Idleyld Park is **Dave and Ellen's** (Box 177, Idleyld Park, tel. 496-0855). This full-service restaurant makes its food from scratch and piles your plate high with lots of it. Breakfast ranges from $3-6, lunches from $3-7, and dinners from $7-14. Homemade rolls and stir-fried vegetables accompany all dinners.

Services And Information
The **post office** (18404 ORE 138, Idleyld Park, 97447; tel. 496-3412) is open 8-1 p.m. and 2-5 p.m. Monday through Friday. If you're looking for additional information on hikes, campgrounds, and fishing, you can get it from the **Forest Service** (North Umpqua District Ranger Station, 18782 ORE 138, Glide, 97443; tel. 496-3532).

ORE 58: OAKRIDGE AND VICINITY

Halfway between Eugene and the Cascades' summit on ORE 58 lies the town of Oakridge. Originally a railway stop on the Southern Pacific called Hazeldel, the named was changed in 1912 to fit the topography. Known also as the "Gateway City to the Willamette National Forest," lumber, recreation, and tourism support this small community (pop. 4,000) tucked away in a foothill valley of the Cascades. The surrounding Willamette National Forest turns out billions of board feet of lumber each year, while it still retains some of the finest wilderness areas in Oregon. There are over 100 lakes and streams near here, waiting for just about any nimrod to pull out his or her quota of rainbow, German browns, and cutthroat and Dolly Varden trout from the cool waters. A short drive from town are **Waldo Lake** and **Diamond Peak Wilderness Area**, as well as summer sailing and water-skiing at **Odell Lake**. Winter sport enthusiasts can find excellent downhill skiing at Willamette Pass, and there are plenty of beautiful trails available for Alpine skiers too. If you like to fish, hike, camp, sail, ski, or just hang out in the woods, it's all only minutes away from Oakridge.

SIGHTS

The **Oakridge Pioneer Museum** (76433 Pine St., Oakridge, 97463; tel. 782-2666/782-2703) is open Saturdays 1-4 p.m., or by special request. Pioneer artifacts that range from tools to toys are on display here. Two colorful exhibits in particular re-create the 1880s—a grocery and typical kitchen of the early Oregon settlers. A large collection of old dolls and children's toys fills up a showcase that today's kids still find fascinating. The Chain Saw Tree, an interesting presentation on the evolution of the saws that conquered the forest, is worth taking a look at too.

McCredie Hot Springs is found ten miles southeast of Oakridge on ORE 58 near mile marker 45. A short walk down to Salt Creek brings you to a small hot spring that is adjacent to the river. This location allows the visitor to enjoy the rush of simultaneously hot and cold water. Depending on how you position yourself, you can take a bath at any temperature you choose. There are plans to develop McCredie Hot Springs into a resort, so it is recommended that you par-

Clear Creek in winter finery

PHOTO BY THE OREGON TOURISM DIVISION

take of this experience while it's still in its raw, natural state.

HIKES

Fall Creek National Recreation Trail

The Fall Creek National Recreation Trail is about 30 miles southeast of Eugene. To get there, take ORE 58 about 15 miles to **Lowell**. From Lowell, go north for two miles to the covered bridge at Unity Junction. Take a right onto Forest Service Road 18 (Fall Creek Road), and stay to the left of the reservoir. Follow the road for 11 miles to Dolly Varden Campground, where the trail starts.

The 14-mile long Fall Creek Trail is ideal for short day hikes or longer expeditions; several national forest entry/exit points crop up along the way. Another plus is the low elevation of the trail, which makes it accessible year-round. Strolling through the wilderness, you will pass many deep pools, whitewater rapids, and over a dozen small streams. Giant Douglas firs, bigleaf maples, vine maples, dogwoods, and red alders are some of the predominant vegetation you'll see along the way. In the spring, visitors are treated to shooting stars, trillium, bleeding heart, and other vibrant wildflowers.

There are five campgrounds and three other spur trails that merge into the Fall Creek Trail. **Bedrock Campground** is a particularly popular spot for swimming. Those without a fear of heights can jump off the bridge into the deep waters of the creek 40 feet below, or perhaps attempt a dive off of the adjacent rock escarpment.

Larson Creek Trail

The Larison Creek Trail (3646) is less than 10 minutes away from Oakridge. To get there, take

WILLAMETTE NATIONAL FOREST

In the middle of Oregon's Cascade Range is the Willamette National Forest. Encompassing 1,675,407 acres of land stretching from the Mt. Jefferson area east of Salem to the Calapooya Mountains northeast of Roseburg, this forest is about the size of New Jersey.

One quarter of this enormous area lies within eight wilderness areas, containing seven major peaks of the Cascades. In addition to three national recreation trails (Fall Creek, McKenzie River, and South Breitenbush Gorge) and the famed Pacific Crest Trail, there are over 1,300 miles of developed trails throughout the Willamette National Forest.

Recreational opportunities abound. There are two developed ski areas, Willamette Pass and Hoodoo Ski Bowl. Near each ski park are snowmobile areas, at Waldo Lake and Big Lake respectively. Cross-country skiing is also available on many of the National Forest Service roads and trails. Precipitation in the Willamette National Forest ranges from 40-150 inches a year, providing the Willamette and McKenzie rivers with excellent conditions for whitewater rafting, driftboat fishing, canoeing, and kayaking. Dozens of lakes and reservoirs round out the boating picture with sailing, rowing, and water-skiing. Big-game hunters can stalk black bear, Roosevelt elk, and deer (blacktailed deer west of the Cascades, mule deer east). Anglers can try their luck catching dinner in one of the forest's many lakes, rivers, and streams.

And yet, this playground in the woods is also the workplace for a significant percentage of the population in the six counties that occupy the Willamette National Forest. The area is usually the top timber producer of all 159 national forests in the United States. Supplying approximately eight percent of the total cut on national Forest Service lands in the country, the Willamette National Forest generates over 130 million dollars annually in timber receipts. In addition to providing a steady source of employment for thousands of people, 25% of the forest's timber revenues go to local coffers to help fund public schools and roads.

There are four major highways that lead to the Willamette National Forest: ORE 58 (the Willamette Highway), ORE 126 (the McKenzie Highway), U.S. 20 (the Cascadia Highway), and ORE 22 (the Santiam Highway). We have organized the information along these thoroughfares. Whatever route you choose to follow, the truth of William Cullen Bryant's words should apply: " . . . Go forth, under the open sky, and list to Nature's teachings. . . .The hills rock-ribbed and ancient as the sun—the vales stretching in pensive quietness between; the venerable woods—rivers that move in majesty, and the contiguous woods where rolls the Oregon . . . "

ORE 58 to Oakridge. Turn onto Kitson Springs County Road and proceed for a half mile. Turn right on Forest Service Rd. 21 and follow it three miles to the trailhead, which you'll find on the right side of the road.

Multicolored mosses cover the valley floor and its walls simulate a brush-stroked backdrop to stands of old growth fir. Further contrast is supplied by waterfalls and swimming holes. The mild grade and low elevation of this trail make it accessible year-round.

Tufti Creek Trail

Another good hike close to Oakridge is the Tufti Creek Trail (#3624). To get there, take ORE 58 to Oakridge. Turn onto Kitson Springs County Road and proceed for about a mile. Turn left onto Forest Service Road 23 and follow it for six miles. This will take you along the northeast bank of Hills Creek Lake and on past Kitson Hot Springs (which is also worthy of investigation). Look for the trailhead sign on the right, about a mile past the hot springs.

This short and friendly half-mile trail winds through large Douglas firs and cedars and overlooks Hills Creek Gorge. There are many small waterfalls and deep swimming holes along the way. This trail is also accessible year-round.

Rigdon Lakes

A more ambitious hike would be up to Rigdon Lakes (trails 3590 and 3583). To get there, follow ORE 58 for 24 miles southeast of Oakridge. Take a left on Forest Service Road 5897. Follow it 10 miles to North Waldo Campground; the trailhead is to the right of the restrooms. This three-mile walk starts at North Waldo Lake Campground on trail 3590. The trail is mild and scenic, paralleling the north shore of Waldo Lake for about two miles until the Rigdon Trail junction (trail 3583). Head north (turn right) at the trail intersection for another mile to get to the first of the three Rigdon Lakes, which has several peninsulas that are ideal for a picnic, and several small islands that might tempt swimmers who don't mind cold water. A hike afterwards up to the top of Rigdon Butte is highly recommended. You will have to bushwack, as there is no clear trail, but it is not a difficult climb if you follow the saddle of the ridge. From this vantage point, you can see all three Rigdon Lakes as well as many other nearby Cas-

cade landmarks. If you want to take a closer look at the two other Rigdon Lakes, it is only another mile or so down trail 3583 from the first lake.

PRACTICALITIES

Accommodations

Three reasonable options in the area are **Hall's Motel and Mobile Home Park** (48229 ORE 58, Oakridge, 97463; tel. 782-2611); **Silver Star Motel** (47487 ORE 58, Oakridge, 97463; tel. 782-2602); and the **Best Western Oakridge Inn** (47433 ORE 58, Oakridge, 97463; tel. 782-2212), which has 30 nice units that during the June 1-Oct 30 summer season range from $40-$45. Winter rates are about $3 less.

Odell Lake, 30 miles southeast of Oakridge on ORE 58, deserves a special mention. There are two resorts, several summer homes, and five campgrounds around this 3,582-acre lake. Located in a deep glacial trough, the lake probably filled with water about 11,000 years ago when a terminal moraine blocked the drainage of Odell Creek. Due to the depth of the lake and the nearly perpetual west-to-east winds that blow through Willamette Pass, the water averages a cold 39°. Those breezes, however, help to keep the pesky mosquitos and other obnoxious insects away, and make for some of the best sailing in the Cascades. The premier property on Odell Lake is the **Odell Lake Lodge** (P.O. Box 72, Crescent Lake, 97425; tel. 433-2540). To get there, take the East Odell exit off of ORE 58 and follow the road a couple of miles. The hotel rooms range from $34-$38 a night, with the cabins going for $42-$65. Skiers may want to take advantage of large cabin 12 that comfortably houses as many as 16 people. As the lodge is extremely popular, reservations are strongly recommended, as much as a year in advance for weekends.

Moorages are available for rent, as are canoes, powerboats, and sailboats. The lodge has a complete tackle shop to help outfit you to catch the kokanee and mackinaw that inhabit the icy waters, and rental equipment is also available if you don't bring your own. The restaurant at the lodge will cook your bounty for you and serve it along with soup or salad, potatoes, vegetables, and bread for $7 per person. The lodge also maintains its own system of trails, which provide

mile-high Waldo Lake

PHOTO BY TED LONG ISHIKAWA

good biking in the summer and cross-country skiing in the winter. Both bikes and ski equipment can be rented from the lodge. In addition to these outdoor pursuits, basketball, volleyball, badminton, and horseshoes round out the fun. Tots and toddlers will enjoy the sandbox, the toy library, and the swings. Every Sunday afternoon, the lodge restaurant features Cajun food, which is accompanied biweekly throughout the summer by hot licks from the Étouffee Cajun Band.

Campgrounds

Blue Pool Campground on the banks of Salt Creek is 10 miles from Oakridge on ORE 58. During the summer, water is available for flush toilets and general use. Each of the 18 sites features a picnic table and a fireplace grill. It costs $5 a family per site, or $10 for two families on one site. Golden Age passports grant the holder a 50% discount. Contact the Oakridge Ranger Station (46375 ORE 58, Westfir, 97492; tel. 728-2291) for information.

Six miles west of Oakridge on the banks of the Willamette River and not too far from Lookout Point Lake is **Black Canyon Campground.** Open May through late-October, there are 72 sites for tents, trailers, or motorhomes up to 22 feet long for $5 a night. Picnic tables and fireplace grills are standard; piped water, firewood, and vault toilets are also available. Boat docks and launching facilities are nearby on the south end of Lookout Point Lake. For additional information,

write to Willamette National Forest (46375 ORE 58, Westfir, 97492; tel. 782-2291).

There are two very nice campgrounds up at Waldo Lake called **Shadow Bay** and **North Waldo.** To get there, take ORE 58 for 24 miles southeast of Oakridge. Take a left on Forest Service Road 5897. It is five miles to FSR 5896, which takes you to Shadow Bay, and 10 miles down FSR 5897 to North Waldo.

Since there are 150 campsites between the two campgrounds, this usually ensures enough views of this mile-high lake for everyone to enjoy. Open June to late-September, the fee is $6 a night. Boat docks and launching facilities are available, plus good sailing and fishing at Waldo. There are many trails that lead to small backcountry lakes from here; this is a good place to establish a base camp. Contact the Oakridge Ranger District for additional information.

If you want to get away from the traffic of ORE 58 and don't mind bouncing down forest service roads for over half an hour, you might consider **Blair Lake Campground.** To get to Blair Lake, head east out of Oakridge on County Route 149 for one mile. Turn left onto Forest Service Rd. 24 and go eight miles until you hit 1934. It's another seven miles down FSR 1934 to Blair Lake. For further information, contact Willamette National Forest (46375 ORE 58, Westfir, 97492; tel. 782-2291).

On the shore of little Blair, a picturesque setting at 4,800 feet with nine tent sites awaits the determined explorer. Open June through mid-October, the fee is $4 per night, no reservations necessary. Picnic tables and fireplace grills are provided, with piped water, firewood, and pit toilets available. Boat docks are nearby, but no motorized craft are permitted on the lake.

Food
Sandwiched in between the roller rink (where the tri-state competition is annually held) and the bowling alley is **Taco Villa** (47961 ORE 58, Oakridge, tel. 782-2935). You might think the artwork and decor are funky, but one look at the menu and you'll see that the price is right. For example, the fajita dinner (chicken or beef, grilled onions/bell peppers on a tortilla spread with guacamole, cheddar cheese, lettuce, and tomato) that comes complete with potatoes, beans, salsa, and sour cream is only $4. You can complement your meal with a fresh old-fashioned milkshake from the soda fountain or top it off with one of sixteen different ice creams for dessert.

After a hard day skiing, head on down the hill to **Timber Jim's** (45727 ORE 58, Oakridge, tel. 782-4310). This restaurant can best be described as the house that Jack built—lumberjack, that is. Huge rough-hewn wooden beams provide the roof support, the walls are paneled with latticework, and thick slabs of wood provide tables and benches for eating. Misery whips (a two-man crosscut saw), pictures of logging crews from over 50 years ago, and other lumber paraphernalia round out the decor. A barroom piano sits proudly in the middle of the room, and sing-alongs after a ski party are not uncommon. Big Jim serves beer and wine, and the salad bar is decent. Try the Logger's Favorite pizza with works, $11.95. Dinners range from $3.75 for spaghetti to $7.75 for steak and prawns.

If you're in the mood for a home-cooked meal, go to **Manning's Cafe** (47460 ORE 58, Oakridge, tel. 782-3366). In addition to good coffee that's only a nickel, they offer a selection of $6 dinners that satisfy lumberjack-sized appetites. Homemade soups thaw out that chill for $.80 a cup, $1 a bowl, and $1.30 for a large bowl. Not only do the Mannings make their own bread and rolls that come with soup and dinner, they also make delicious homemade pies and cakes for dessert.

Latecomers or early risers should remember that the **Sportsman Cafe** (48127 ORE 58, Oakridge, tel. 782-2051) is open 24 hours a day (except Christmas Eve/Day). This is where you can hear many a fish story about the day's catch or the big one that got away. If the fish weren't biting, you can still find something good on the menu to get your hooks into here. Dinners that come with salad, fries, and toast range from $3.50 for veal cutlets to $5.25 for grilled halibut or batter-dipped jumbo prawns.

Services
The **Liquor Store** (48019 Hwy 58, Oakridge, 97463; tel. 782-3405) is open Mon-Sat, 11-7; closed on holidays. The **chamber of commerce** (47811 ORE 58, Oakridge, 97463; tel. 782-4146) offers a wide assortment of info on the area.

The **post office** (48264 E.1st, Oakridge, 97463; tel. 782-2730) is open during business hours. To get there, turn at the town's only traffic light, cross over the bridge, and go right. The post office is about a half mile down. The **Oakridge Medical Clinic** (47815 ORE 58, Oakridge, 97463; tel. 782-2221) offers family and emergency medicine. Hours are 9-5 Mon.-Fri., 9-noon Saturday For after hours emergencies, call 911.

Getting There
Greyhound serves ORE 58 to Klamath Falls and points beyond and stops at the Taco Villa restaurant (47961 ORE 58, Oakridge, 97463; tel. 782-2935). **Amtrak**'s *Starlight Express* services Oakridge. The southbound train arrives/departs at 6 p.m., the northbound at 10:45 a.m. Be sure to call ahead (800-USA-RAIL) for reservations.

ORE 126: THE MCKENZIE HIGHWAY

The best way to get to this scenic road from the Willamette Valley is to take I-105 east from I-5 near Eugene. Take a left at the end of the interstate near the outskirts of Springfield, and you will be on the McKenzie River Highway. There are four lanes for a couple of miles, and this is one of your best chances to ease by any slow-moving vehicles. However, beware of The Man, who often patrols the road here—he loves to write those tickets!

In any case, just past where the four lanes merge into two is a sign that reads McKenzie River Recreation Area Next 60 Miles. For the next 60 miles, you will not see any major population centers, as most of the towns out here are little more than a post office. However, you will see beautiful views of the blue-green McKenzie River with heavily forested mountains, frothy waterfalls, jet-black lava beds, and snowcapped peaks as a backdrop.

The first 15 miles of the McKenzie Highway passes through many fruit and nut orchards (primarily apples, cherries, and filberts), Christmas tree farms, and berry patches (blueberry, raspberry, and marionberry). McKenzie River farmers enjoy plentiful water supplies from the McKenzie diversion canal, as well as fertile soils and a mild climate. **Walterville** is located in the middle of this agricultural section of the McKenzie Recreation Area.

The Leaburg Dam on the right signals your entry into the middle section of the McKenzie, where there are many vacation homes. There are a total of six dams on the McKenzie that provide power, irrigation, and what the Army Corps of Engineers call "fish enhancement." A favorite haunt of fishing enthusiasts, the mellow waters of the middle McKenzie teem with trout, steelhead, and salmon. You'll notice many driftboats parked in driveways. These boats have double bows to prevent water inundation from either front or back. Mild whitewater rafting and driftboat fishing are popular here, and there are many local guides and outfitters ready to help you float your expeditions (see "Guides And Outfitters" below).

The Willamette National Forest boundary is near Blue River. Huge, old growth Douglas firs usher the clear blue waters of the McKenzie on through the mountains. In addition to the McKenzie River National Recreation Trail, waterfalls, mountain lakes, and lava formations are all a short trek from the road.

SIGHTS

Proxy Falls
To get to Proxy Falls, follow the old McKenzie Pass (ORE 242) from the new McKenzie Pass

Oregon produces most of the world's supply of filberts.

PHOTO BY TED LONG ISHIKAWA

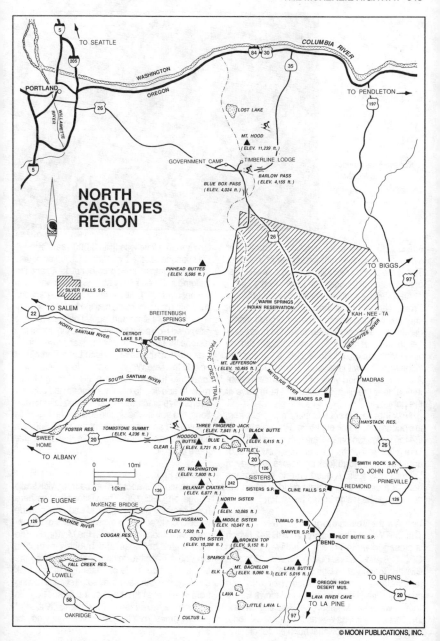

TO SEATTLE

COLUMBIA RIVER

WASHINGTON

OREGON

PORTLAND

TO PENDLETON

LOST LAKE

MT. HOOD
(ELEV. 11,239 ft.)

GOVERNMENT CAMP

TIMBERLINE LODGE

BARLOW PASS
(ELEV. 4,155 ft.)

BLUE BOX PASS
(ELEV. 4,024 ft.)

NORTH CASCADES REGION

SILVER FALLS S.P.

TO SALEM

PINHEAD BUTTES
(ELEV. 5,585 ft.)

WARM SPRINGS INDIAN RESERVATION

TO BIGGS

KAH - NEE - TA

BREITENBUSH SPRINGS

NORTH SANTIAM RIVER

DETROIT LAKE S.P.

DETROIT

DETROIT L.

PACIFIC CREST TRAIL

MT. JEFFERSON
(ELEV. 10,495 ft.)

METOLIUS RIVER

DESCHUTES RIVER

MADRAS

SOUTH SANTIAM RIVER

GREEN PETER RES.

MARION L.

PALISADES S.P.

FOSTER RES.

TOMBSTONE SUMMIT
(ELEV. 4,236 ft.)

THREE FINGERED JACK
(ELEV. 7,841 ft.)

BLACK BUTTE
(ELEV. 6,415 ft.)

HAYSTACK RES.

SWEET HOME

HOODOO BUTTE
(ELEV. 5,721 ft.)

BLUE L.

SUTTLE L.

TO ALBANY

CLEAR L.

MT. WASHINGTON
(ELEV. 7,800 ft.)

SISTERS

SMITH ROCK S.P.

TO JOHN DAY

0   10mi

0   10km

BELKNAP CRATER
(ELEV. 6,877 ft.)

SISTERS S.P.

CLINE FALLS S.P.

REDMOND

PRINEVILLE

TO EUGENE

MCKENZIE BRIDGE

MCKENZIE RIVER

NORTH SISTER
(ELEV. 10,085 ft.)

THE HUSBAND
(ELEV. 7,520 ft.)

MIDDLE SISTER
(ELEV. 10,047 ft.)

TUMALO S.P.

COUGAR RES.

SOUTH SISTER
(ELEV. 10,358 ft.)

BROKEN TOP
(ELEV. 9,152 ft.)

SAWYER S.P.

BEND

PILOT BUTTE S.P.

SPARKS L.

FALL CREEK RES.

ELK L.

MT. BACHELOR
(ELEV. 9,060 ft.)

LAVA BUTTE
(ELEV. 5,016 ft.)

TO BURNS

LOWELL

LAVA L.

OREGON HIGH DESERT MUS.

LAVA RIVER CAVE

TO LA PINE

LITTLE LAVA L.

OAKRIDGE

CULTUS L.

Koosah Falls thunders on the Mckenzie.

PHOTO BY BRUCE BUSH

(ORE 126) for 10 miles. Look for a small hiker symbol sign on the right-hand side of the road. This is the only marker for the trail to a spectacular pair of waterfalls, Upper and Lower Proxy Falls.

An A+ trail, it's an easy half-mile walk to Upper Proxy. The trail goes through a lush forest that changes with the season. There are giant rhododendrons that bloom in late spring, tart huckleberries in summer, and brilliant red foliage from the vine maples in the fall. Take a left at the first fork in the trail. This will take you to Upper Proxy Falls. A particularly good view of the falls can be obtained near the giant Douglas fir at the base of the pool.

Now that you've seen Upper Proxy Falls from the bottom up, check out Lower Proxy Falls from the top down. Go back to the fork in the trail, and take a left. In less than a half mile, you will suddenly be on a ridge looking across a valley at Lower Proxy falls. A good time to photograph both of these falls is around midday when the sun's angle best illuminates the water.

Dee Wright Observatory

The Dee Wright Observatory on ORE 242 (which is closed in winter) is about halfway between ORE 126 and Sisters. Built in the early '30s as a Civilian Conservation Corps project, it was christened after the building's supervisor who died prior to its completion. The tower windows line up with views of Mt. Jefferson, Mt. Washington, and the Three Sisters, as well as the eight-mile-long, half-mile wide lava flow that bubbled out of near-

by Yapoah a little less than 3,000 years ago.

Unfortunately, the Dee Wright Observatory was struck by lightning in September of 1989, and the building suffered heavy structural damage from the ensuing fire. Built mostly out of lava rock, the supporting timbers sustained the bulk of the damage. With tight state and federal budgets and the estimated high price tag for repairs, the fate of this historic landmark remains unclear. However, all was not lost: the half-mile long **Lava River Trail** next to the Dee Wright Observatory offers a fine foray into the surrounding hills of rolling black rock. In addition to helpfully placed and concise interpretive placards explaining the lava formations, the trail is wheelchair-accessible. But while the walk is an easy enough one, the 5,300-foot elevation can sometimes make it seem a little more difficult.

Koosah Falls

This cascade is about 20 miles from McKenzie Bridge on ORE 126. The visitor facilities here have recently been improved and now provide wheelchair access and excellent views of this impressive 70-foot-high falls on the McKenzie. The blue water bounces and bubbles over and through a basalt formation that flowed into the McKenzie thousands of years ago. If you look carefully, you can see many small springs flowing from crevices at the base of the falls. The blue water may have inspired the name "Koosah," which comes from the Chinook Indian word for sky.

Sahalie Falls

Another beautiful waterfall is only a half mile further east on ORE 126 from Koosah Falls. It is only a few yards from the parking lot to the viewpoints of the falls. Also the result of a lava dam from the Cascade Range's not-so-distant volcanic past here, the river tumbles 100 feet into a green canyon. The highest falls on the McKenzie river, *sahalie* means "high" in the Chinook Indian dialect. It's said that this waterfall churns out the highest volume of water of any falls in the state. Anyone who might want to take a shower is welcome to hike the slippery, unimproved trail to the base of the roaring cascade. Most people, however, are content to enjoy the view from benches and observation posts along the paved path.

Sawyer's Cave

This ice cave is on the right just past the junction of ORE 126 and U.S. 20, near mile marker 72. You'll need a flashlight and a sweater to explore Sawyer's Cave; watch your head and watch your step. Classified as a lava tube, it's the result of a lava flow that cooled faster on the top and sides, forming a crust. Underneath, the hotter lava continued to drain downhill, leaving the lava tube behind. There are also small stalactites hanging down from the ceilings, formed from lava drippings. The basalt rock is a poor heat conductor, and like a natural refrigerator, keeps the coolness of winter and night inside the cave. Ice can be found on the floor of the cave during the hottest summer months.

HIKES

McKenzie River National Recreation Trail

The Mckenzie River National Recreation Trail runs for 26 miles. It starts just outside the small town of **McKenzie Bridge** and goes to the Old Santiam Wagon Road, about three miles from the junction of ORE 126 and U.S. 20. But don't let that scare you. There are enough access points to design treks of three, five, eight, or more miles along this beautiful trail. It is hard to say which section of the footpath is the best, as each portion has its own peculiar charms; the following highlights give you a sample of what to expect.

Start up at the top of the McKenzie River Trail at the **Old Santiam Wagon Road.** Completed in

the early 1860s, this was the first link of the mid-Willamette Valley to central and eastern Oregon. Way stations were established a day's journey apart to assist the pioneers along their weary way. While most of these primitive establishments are no more, some of these historic buildings have survived and are still used today by packers. There isn't much left of the Old Santiam Wagon Road either, as much of it was destroyed with the construction of ORE 126. However, a seven-mile stretch remains from ORE 126 through the rugged lava country to the Pacific Crest Trail. A short walk on this former road to the promised land helps you to both appreciate the hardiness of the pioneers and the comforts of modern travel.

From the Old Santiam Wagon Road, the McKenzie River Trail surveys many remarkable volcanic formations. Lava flows over the last few thousand years have built dams, created waterfalls, and even buried the river altogether. At the northern end of **Clear Lake,** you can see the remains of an ancient forest preserved for nearly 3,000 years in the lake's cool waters. When nearby Sand Mountain erupted, the lava dammed up the McKenzie River and created Clear Lake. Koosah and Sahalie falls were also created by lava dams, and the perspective of these whitewater cascades from the McKenzie River Trail is much different than the accessible version from the highway. Another interesting sight is the **Tamolitch Valley,** where the McKenzie gradually sinks beneath the porous lava, disappearing altogether until it reemerges three miles later at Tamolitch Pool. This area is accessible only on the National Recreational Trail.

If at all possible, arrange your McKenzie outing with friends and take two cars. This way you can have a car stationed at the begining and ending segments of your hike, and thus avoid doubling back. Also keep in mind that hikes starting at the upper end of the trail take advantage of the descending elevation.

Robinson Lake Trail

The quarter-mile-long Robinson Lake Trail takes you to a heart-shaped lake with some fishing and swimming. To get there, turn off of ORE 126 onto Robinson Lake Road. Be on the lookout for logging trucks and rocks on the gravel road. Follow the signs marked Forest Service Road 2664. At the unmarked junction, go straight onto the red pumice road (FSR 2664) and continue until you reach the parking lot. It takes about 10 minutes to drive the four miles in. The trail is in good condition; the left fork takes you to the center shore of Robinson Lake. The shallow lake warms up considerably during the summer, making a swim all the more inviting.

Guides And Outfitters
McKenzie River Adventures (Box 567, Sisters, 97759; tel. 549-1325/822-3806 evenings) has half-day, full-day and two-day whitewater rafting trips May-September. The half-day (four hour) trip (lunch included) is $40 per person, $25 per child, the full-day (six-hour) trip (lunch incl.) is $50 per person, $30 per child, and the two-day overnighter (meals incl.) is $150 per person, $100 per child The cruises range from seven to18 miles, and take in some Class II and III rapids. Reservations are recommended.

Jim's Oregon Whitewater (56324 ORE 126, McKenzie Bridge, 97413; tel. 822-6003) charters whitewater rafts April-September and fly-fishing driftboats April-Oct. The half-day whitewater rafting trip (lunch included) costs $40 per person, the full-day (lunch incl.) is $50 per person, and the two-day overnighter (meals incl.) is $120 per person. For those interested in some serious fly-fishing, it's $150 per boat (one to two people) per day. A more mellow fishing trip is the Scenic Drift Boat for $100 per boat (one to two people) per day. Reservations are recommended..

Spencer Outfitters and Guide Service (656 N. 71st Street, Springfield, 97478; tel. 747-8153) charters white-water rafting, fishing, and hunting trips. The half-day raft trips (lunch included) are $25, the full-day raft trip (lunch incl.) is $35, and the one- to three-day overnighters (meals incl.) are $50 per day. Fishing and hunting trips (one to two persons) are $150 a day. Fly-fishing is Bob Spencer's specialty, and all fishing equipment is provided.

Prince River Outfitters (Box 116, Vida, 97488; tel. 896-3941) charters whitewater rafting trips May-September. The half-day raft trips (no lunch) cost $25, the full-day (lunch included) is $40, and the two-day overnighter (all meals) is $129. Fishing for spring chinook or summer steelhead (April 15-Oct. 31) costs $90 per person, fly-fishing for rainbow trout (May 1-Oct. 31) is $50

half-day, $75 all day. Food, tackle, and raingear provided on all fishing charters.

PRACTICALITIES

Accommodations
Fry's Double JJ Motel (Ore 126, Vida, 97488; tel. 822-5304) is a small family operation that rents out two housekeeping cabins. Depending upon the time of year and the number of people, the units range between $25-$45. Reservations required.

Sleepy Hollow Motel (54791 Ore 126, Blue River, 97413; tel. 822-3805) is located within walking distance of one of the finest public golf courses in the country, Tokatee. This property is open from April 1-Nov. 1. The motel has 14 air-conditioned units that range from $30-$45, $5 each additional person. Reservations are recommended.

The Cedarwood Lodge (Ore 126, McKenzie Bridge, 97413; tel. 822-3351) is tucked away in a grove of old cedars just outside of the town of McKenzie Bridge. The lodge has nine vacation housekeeping cottages that feature fully equipped kitchens, bathroom (with shower), fireplaces (wood provided) and portable BBQ's. Rates vary from $43-75 for two people, depending on the cabin and the season, $7.50 each additional person. Pets are allowed, but only by advance arrangement. Minimum three-day advance reservations are required July-Sept. and holidays.

The **Sportsman's Lodge Resort** (56228 Delta Dr., McKenzie Bridge, 97413; tel. 822-3243) is a popular retreat for golfers who come here to enjoy the award-winning Tokatee Golf Course. The lodge has two small cabins that cost $50 and $70 each, plus the huge Delta House. The Delta House can comfortably take in up to eight people, as there are four bedrooms, four bathrooms, a kitchen, dining room, living room, and a fireplace. Delta House rates decrease with the length of the stay: $240 for one night, $188 per night for two nights, $178 per night for three to six nights, and $160 per night for a week's visit or longer.

The historic **Log Cabin Inn** (ORE 126, McKenzie Bridge, 97413; tel. 822-3432) is an excellent bed and breakfast. Built in 1906, President Hoover, Clark Gable, and the Duke of Windsor are among the many notables who have stayed here over the years. With its homey decor, wrap-around porch, and cedar-paneled dining hall, the Log Cabin Inn would make a wonderful label on a bottle of maple syrup. There are also nine guest cottages, each one of them boasting a fireplace, a porch, and a view of the McKenzie River. For $4 per person, the Inn will bring a continental breakfast to your cabin in the morning for you to enjoy along with the scenery. Room rates range from $35-45 d, each additional person $5. Reservations required.

Belknap Springs Lodge (Box 1, McKenzie Bridge, 97413; tel. 822-3512) offers rooms, cabins, and camping. The rooms range from $35-$50 per couple, $5 each additional person. The five cabins range from $22-$38, $3 each additional person. Camping sites are $3.50 per person per day, or $20 per person per week. The main attraction on the property is **Belknap Springs.** The water (which incidentally contains 26 different minerals) is gently filtered piping hot into a swimming pool on the south bank of the McKenzie. The property is clean, the scenery is beautiful, and the price is right. For $2, you can use the mineral pool facilities, just what the doctor ordered to ease the aching muscles from that killer hike or the ski marathon. But don't wait too long to fill this prescription—the pool closes at 9 p.m. If you forget your towel, you can rent one for $1.

Campgrounds

The following campgrounds are under the jurisdiction of the **Willamette National Forest** (McKenzie Ranger District, McKenzie Bridge, 97413; tel. 822-3381). Contact the office for reservations and additional information. Many of these campsites connect with the beautiful McKenzie River National Recreation Trail. The fishing is also quite good on the McKenzie and the many lakes and reservoirs within this balliwick. Its prime location halfway between Eugene and Bend also helps make the area a popular vacation spot during the summer, so advance reservations are recommended.

A mile west of McKenzie Bridge on ORE 126 is **McKenzie Bridge Campground.** As the name implies, this 20-site multi-use park is along the banks of its namesake river. Open late-May to early September, the fee is $4 a night. Piped well water, vault toilets, and a boat launch are provid-

ed. East of McKenzie Bridge, about three miles on ORE 126, is **Paradise Creek Campground.** Although there are 54 tent/RV (up to 22 feet) campsites, flush toilets, and piped water, only 20 of them are premium riverside sites. The summer trout fishing here can be very good, and the fireplace grills and wooden tables that are provided make it easy to cook and eat a fresh-caught meal. Welcome to paradise! Open late May to early September, the fee is $8 a night and reservations are recommended.

Olallie Campground is 11 miles outside of McKenzie Bridge on ORE 126 and has 17 multi-use sites. Olallie is situated on the banks of the McKenzie River; boating, fishing, and hiking are some of the nearby attractions. Piped water, vault toilets, and picnic tables are provided. Open late May to early September, the fee is $3 a night. A couple more miles past Olallie on ORE 126 is **Trailbridge Campground.** Located on the north shore of Trailbridge Reservoir, piped water, vault toilets, and picnic tables are provided at this 24-site multi-use campground. Boat docks are close by, and the reservoir is noted for its good trout fishing.

Another ideal campground for boating enthusiasts is **Lake's End** on nearby Smith Reservoir. One of the few boat-in campgrounds in Oregon, the only way to reach this park is via a two-mile sail across the lake. To get there, take ORE 126 for 13 miles northeast of McKenzie Bridge and turn right on Forest Service Road 1477. Follow the road for three miles to the boat ramp, and bon voyage! Be sure to take along plenty of water, because the campground does not provide any. You will, however, find picnic tables, vault toilets, and plenty of peace and quite away from the cars and traffic of the other mainstream parks. Open late-May through early September, there is no fee for this escape from the ordinary.

On the south shore of Clear Lake, 14 miles northeast of McKenzie Bridge on ORE 126, is **Coldwater Cove Campground.** Piped water, vault toilets, and picnic tables are provided at this 34-site multi-use park. Open late May to early September, the fee is $4 a night. **Crocket Lodge** (no phone) is adjacent to the campground, and does have a store, cafe (serving breakfast 6:30-10 a.m. and lunch 11-2), and cabins, as well as boat docks, launches, and rentals. But before you haul your 426-horsepower Glastron jetboat up

McKenzie Pass to cut some mean 20-foot high "rooster tails" with your CX-202 competition water-skis, keep in mind that small electric fishing boat motors are the only mechanical means of propulsion allowed by the Forest Service here.

A handful of campgrounds dot ORE 242, the old McKenzie Pass, but only **Alder Springs** has piped water. This remote campground with seven tent sites is open late-May to early September; the fee is $2 a night.

Food

It's easy to zip by a tiny restaurant near Vida called the **Village Cafe** (Vida, 97488, tel. 822-3891). But if you have a sweet tooth, be on the lookout for milepost 35 and a small red building nearby with a sign on top that reads Mom's Homemade Pies. This place has established quite a reputation, as the hundreds of business cards pinned to the ceiling will attest. The food is simple and straightforward; hamburgers, hot dogs, grilled-cheese sandwiches, and the like. However, Mom's pies are the main attraction that keep the parking lot full and the customers coming back for more.

Fifteen minutes up the road is the **Forest Glen Restaurant** (51774 Cascade Street, Blue River, tel. 822-3714). This is the place to go if you want a fine-dining experience in the wilderness. Chicken, steak, seafood, and pasta are among the elegant offerings here. Ranging from $10-22, dinners come with a shrimp appetizer, bread, soup and salad bar, and your choice of brown rice with vegetables, baked potato, or french fries. There are also reasonably priced burgers and fries for the kids to keep your budget balanced.

If you've been camping out in the woods for a few days and you're getting tired of freeze-dried food, you might want to time your return to civilization with the Forest Glen's Sunday brunch buffet. This all-you-can-eat extravaganza includes such delectables as custom-made omelettes, crab and shrimp crepes, French toast with fresh strawberries and whipped cream, eggs Benedict, and roast top sirloin. Add this to a smorgasbord of homemade pastries, bagels, and croissants, a soup and salad bar, and the chef's choice entrees, you'll understand why reservations are recommended. It's a good place to bring a hungry brood, because it costs only 50 cents per year through age 11; adults are $8.95.

If you're in the mood for a good lunch or dinner served with a generous helping of historical ambience, head for the **Log Cabin** (see "Accommodations" above). Built in 1906, the inn's cedar-paneled dining room reflects the soft hues of a different era. Their sandwiches range between $3-5 and are served with potato salad. For $2 extra, you can wash lunch down with a glass of smooth port. Dinners range from $6-16 and come with all the trimings. Whatever meal you choose to take in, try the beer-cheese soup, and save some room for one of their homemade cobblers or pies.

Getting There

The best way for carless travelers to get to the McKenzie National Recreation Trail from Eugene is via Lane Transit District (tel. 687-5555). Their bus starts at downtown Eugene and goes up the McKenzie River Highway, stopping at many small communities along the way. The terminus point is the McKenzie River Ranger Station at McKenzie Bridge, and the fare is $4. The schedule changes with the season and weather conditions, so be sure to call ahead first to plan your trip and return.

SISTERS

Sisters, established in 1888 when nearby Camp Polk was deactivated, is named after its backdrop to the south, the Three Sisters. These over 10,000-feet-high peaks were the last major obstacle for the pioneers to circumnavigate on their journey to the fertile Willamette Valley. The emigrants named the mountains after some of the virtues that helped propel them through the hardships of the frontier: faith, hope and charity. Over the years, no one could agree upon exactly which mountain was named what, so the Oregon Legislature settled the dispute by labeling the mountains as the North, Middle, and South sister respectively.

In any case, while most of the Old Santiam Wagon Road has long since been replaced by asphalt and forest overgrowth, the 19th-century flavor of that era has been preserved in the town of Sisters. Wooden boardwalks, 1880s-style storefronts, and plenty of good-ol'-fashioned Western hospitality grace this small town of about 1,000. Some people are quick to lambast the thematic zoning ordinances of Sisters as cheap gimmicks to lure tourists, while others seem to enjoy the lovingly recreated ambience. As well as being a food, fuel, and lodging stop, Sisters is also a jumping-off point for a wealth of outdoor activities.

Skiing at Hoodoo Ski Bowl, fly-fishing and rafting on the Metolius River, and backpacking into the great Three Sisters Wilderness are just a few of the popular local pursuits available. Nearby luxury resorts such as Black Butte, an annual rodeo, and North America's largest llama ranch add to the appeal of this vintage 1888 village.

SIGHTS

Dick Patterson's Arabian Ranch
Dick Patterson's Arabian Ranch (15425 U.S. 20, Sisters, 97759; tel. 549-3391) is located just outside the city limits. In addition to a large herd of these fine-looking horses, the ranch is also home for over 500 llamas. These critters are used for pack animals on expeditions into the mountains as well as for pets and wool production. Sheep ranchers in particular like to have a llama or two around their livestock because predators like wolves and coyotes abhor their scent. The Pattersons do not have guided tours of the ranch. However, they will try to accommodate people who would like to visit and see the animals *if* you call ahead and make an appointment.

the Three Sisters Wilderness, backyard to the vintage town of Sisters

PHOTO BY BRUCE BUSH

Metolius River

About ten miles from Sisters is the second largest tributary of the Deschutes River, the Metolius. To get there, take the Camp Sherman Highway off of ORE 20 five miles west of Sisters. This road will take you around Black Butte. On the north face of this steep, evergreen-covered cinder cone lies the source of the Metolius. Known simply as "The Spring," the water wells up out of the earth at a constant 48°. The warm, spring-fed waters of the upper Metolius are ideal for insect egg and larval development, which in turn provides an abundant food source for rainbow, brown, brook, and bull trout, kokanee salmon, and whitefish. Consequently, some of the best fly-fishing in the state is found on the upper Metolius. This was no secret to the Indians. The name Metolius derives from the Indian word for "white fish," after the lightly colored salmon found in the river. A beautiful riverside trail that follows the Metolius as it meanders through the ponderosas passes many excellent fishing holes. Driftboats are used to tackle the harder-to-reach places along this 25-mile-long river.

Other streams merge with the Metolius, lowering the water temperature to an average 35°. While the fishing isn't as good as the warmer upper reaches of the river, the whitewater rafting is actually better downstream. The increased water volume coupled with steeper flow gradients provide plenty of exciting rapids for river-runners to splash around in.

Hoodoo Ski Bowl

A little over a half hour west of Sisters on ORE 126 is one of Oregon's most family-oriented skiing areas, Hoodoo Ski Bowl (tel. 342-5540). Generally operating from Thanksgiving to Easter (snow conditions permitting), it's open every day (except Monday) from 9-4 p.m. Hoodoo features 17 ski runs serviced by three chair lifts and a rope tow. The maximum vertical drop is 1,035 feet, and the runs are fairly evenly divided between advanced, intermediate, and beginner. The rates at this 55-year-old ski bowl are equally attractive. Adult all-day passes are $14, seniors (65 and over) and children under six accompanied by a paying adult ski free. The rates on the rope tow are $7 per day. The "sno-fone" (tel. 354-7416 from Eugene, 585-8081 from Salem, 753-8887 from Corvallis, and 342-5540 to reach Hoodoo) has the latest information on weather and snow conditions.

Inexpensive lodging is found across the highway from the ski area at **Santiam Lodge** (tel. 342-5540). Built by the Civilian Conservation Corps during the Depression, this facility offers dormitory-style accommodations for groups of 15-75. A fully equiped kitchen, dining room, and large lounge with a fireplace are upstairs; the rooms and bathrooms are downstairs. The rates are quite reasonable, as little as $12 per night per person. "Lodging and three meals" packages start at $25, and reduced rates on lift tickets and rental equipment are also available to groups making advance reservations. After a weekend at Santiam Pass, there will be no doubt "Hoodoo" you love.

PRACTICALITIES

Food

The **Ranch House** (310 S.E. Hood St., Sisters, tel. 549-8911) specializes in sandwiches and take 'n' bake pizza and also has a good selection of domestic and imported beers and wines. The **Lonetree Restaurant** (160 E. Cascade, Sisters, 97759; tel. 549-8940) features good old American food. Check the board for the daily specials.

The **Gallery Restaurant** (230 W. Cascade, Sisters, tel. 549-2631) offers chuckwagon dinners that range from $6.25-$7.25. Surprisingly tasteful paintings on Old West themes as well as flintlocks and other ancient armaments pay homage to the area's pioneer past. Many eastern Oregonians will tell you that **Papandrea's** (325 S.W. Hood, Sisters, tel. 549-6081) makes the best pizza in the state. While such claims are highly subjective, outlets in Bend and Oregon City attest to this small chain's dedicated following.

The hot spot in town is undoubtedly the **Hotel Sisters and Bronco Billy Saloon.** Built in 1912, the upstairs rooms of this historic structure have been refurbished into intimate mini-dining rooms. BBQ ribs are the specialty of the house, but you can also find fresh seafood, steaks, chicken dishes, and Mexican fare here. In one corner of the building, on the other side of the Western-style saloon doors, is Bronco Billy's. This funky watering hole must look much the same as it did 80 years ago. A racy painting that used to grace the local brothel is proudly displayed behind the bar, and cowboy hats on most heads complete the picture of a town whose Old West ambience gets better with age. For the price of a beer, you can get one of the local Stetson-hatted good-ol'-boys to tell you the inside scoop on where to go and what to do in this neck of the woods.

Accommodations

Sisters Motor Lodge (600 W. Cascade, Sisters, 97759; tel. 549-2551) is within easy walking distance of the shops and boutiques of Sisters. Bedrooms and kitchenettes go for $30-40 a night, and you can bring the dog along too. The **Best Western Ponderosa Lodge** (505 ORE 20, Box 218, Sisters, 97759; tel. 549-1234/800-528-1234) is a new, ranch-style resort motel. Rooms ($45-60) feature private balconies with views of the mountains and the adjacent Deschutes National Forest, as well as dial-direct phones and cable TV. Other amenities include a spa, heated pool, and free continental breakfast.

The **Fourth Sister Lodge** (Box 591, Sisters, 97559; tel. 549-6441) offers bedrooms and bedroom suites ($35-100). The bedroom suites have a fully equipped kitchen, a dining room, and a large living room with a fireplace as well as one or two bedrooms. The recreation room in the center of the lodge complex has a sauna, spa, and swimming pool. Reservations are requested two weeks in advance, but since this property is popular and fills up fast, extra lead time is advised.

The **Metolius River Lodge** (P.O. Box 110, Camp Sherman, 97730; tel. 595-6290) is a 12-unit complex featuring six pine-paneled cabins. The latter vary in price ($54-75) depending on room configuration and accouterments. The most coveted pair have decks extending over the river, and the majority have fireplaces. The price includes continental breakfast, brought to your door, and all the firewood you need.

Campgrounds

A handful of campgrounds open only in summer are near Sisters on the old McKenzie Highway, ORE 242. **Cold Springs** (Contact Sisters Ranger Station, tel. 549-2111, $5) is five miles west of town on ORE 242. This campground 3,400 feet high in elevation has 23 sites for tents and small trailers (22 feet maximum). Picnic tables, firegrills, pits toilets, and water are provided. It's a pretty spot, near the source of Trout Creek.

Six miles further down the road is Whispering Pine (same contact). No fees are charged at this primitive campground with six tent sites, mainly because there is no water available. Another six miles up the pass at 5,200 feet is **Lava Camp Lake** (same contact). Two tent sites and 10 RV sites (22 feet maximum) are available at this rustic campground. There is no fee, but there's also no water. The main allure is its close proximity to the Pacific Crest Trail and the Three Sisters Wilderness.

Events

The **Sisters Rodeo** annually opens the second weekend of June. In addition to the normal assortment of calf-roping and bronco-bucking, country dances, a "buckaroo breakfast," and a 10-kilometer **Stampede Run** rounds out the fun. Contact the Sisters Chamber of Commerce (Box 476, Sisters, 97759; tel. 549-0251) for the schedule of events.

Services

The Sisters **post office** (160 1st St., Sisters, 97759; tel. 549-3561) is open for service Mon.-Fri., 9-5. The office is also open Sat., but without window service. The mail goes out at 4:30 p.m. Monday through Saturday. The **liquor store** (216 Cascade, Sisters, 97559; tel. 549-9841) is open Mon.-Sat., 10-6, Oct. 1-May 31; Mon.-Sat., 10-7, June 1-Sept. 30. Three miles outside of Sisters, the area's **laundromat** is found at the KOA campground (67667 U.S. 20, Bend, 97701; tel. 549-3021) which is open 9 a.m.-10 p.m. all week long.

BEND AND VICINITY

Since 1980, Deschutes County has been the state's fastest growing population center, largely due to its hiking trails, fishing streams, golf courses, whitewater runs, and ski slopes. Proximity to this recreation has made the city of Bend Oregon's number-one destination for the active traveler. While the resulting increase in traffic and prices can sometimes make you forget that you're in Oregon, Bend's location in between the eastern flank of the Cascades and the desert provides respite from what the locals call "Californication."

The seeds of growth were planted several decades ago when a one-time military encampment a dozen miles south of town was transformed into the Sunriver Resort community. Black Butte Ranch, the Inn of the Seventh Mountain, and other destination resorts soon followed. South of the city is some of the best skiing in the

© MOON PUBLICATIONS, INC.

PHOTO BY FRANK LONG

the Deschutes River

state on Mt. Bachelor; to the north, world-class rock-climbing routes at Smith Rock State Park and famed fishing holes on the Metolius River await. Add Cascade hiking, Deschutes River rafting and fishing, and other nearby locales for rockhounding, golf, horseback riding, and water sports, and you'll understand why it's often hard to find a place to bed down for the night here on weekends.

AREA SIGHTS

Drake Park
The Deschutes River has a dam and diversion channel just above downtown Bend. It provides valuable irrigation water for the farmers and ranchers of the dry but fertile plateau to the north, and creates a placid stretch of water called Mirror Pond that is home to Canada geese, ducks, and other wildlife. Drake Park is on the east bank of this greenbelt and is a nice place to relax, have a quiet lunch, or maybe toss a frisbee around.

However, you had better be careful where you step, as the birds leave behind numerous land mines. The folks living in those nice houses on the west bank of Mirror Pond got tired of scraping the guano off of their shoes, but unfortunately for them, they were legally unable to do anything against their fowl neighbors due to their protected status. They came up with a rather ingenious solution for the geese and their offensive droppings. The residents chipped in $1,500 to buy a pair of swans from Queen Elizabeth's Royal Swannery in England. Since geese and swans do not get along, the citizens reasoned that the blue-blooded swans would chase away the common Canada geese. While the geese are still here, you will notice that they tend to congregate in Drake Park, while the swans have a decided preference for the private estates.

Pilot Butte
On the east side of town is Pilot Butte. A road barber-poles its way up to the top of this 511-foot-high volcanic remnant. Here, you can enjoy a sweeping view of nine snowcapped Cascade peaks and their green forests from the lookout. It is also pretty at night with the twinkling lights of the city below and the stars above. Full moons are especially awesome, illuminating the ghostly forms of the mountains in icy light-blue silhouettes.

Pine Mountain Observatory
Another peak experience worth investigating is the Pine Mountain Observatory (tel. 382-8331), which is located about 40 miles east of Bend on U.S. 20. Take the road out of Millican to the top of 6,395-foot-high Pine Mountain to reach the installation. Three Cassegrain telescopes with 15-, 24-, and 32-inch mirrors are used by University of Oregon teachers and students to unlock the secrets of the universe. The friendly astronomers here will oftentimes allow visitors an intriguing peek at the neighboring stars and planets. Please be sure to call ahead first for information and weather conditions before making the trip.

Petersen's Rock Garden
What began as one man's flight of fancy over the years metamorphosed into a full-fledged rock fantasy. Petersen, a Danish immigrant farmer, created four acres of intricately detailed miniature

castles, towers, and bridges made of agate, jasper, obsidian, malachite, petrified wood, and thunder eggs. The rock garden (7930 S.W. 77th St., Redmond, 97756; tel. 382-5574) is free of charge, and open 365 days a year, 7 a.m.-9 p.m. (or till dusk in winter). To get there, take Gift Road off of U.S. 97 seven miles south of Redmond and 10 miles north of Bend. Follow the signs; it's only three miles off the highway. There is a very nice museum and gift shop in the rear of the complex that features many types of rocks, crystals, and semiprecious gemstones. In the back of the museum is the Fluorescent Room in which little castles made of zinc, tungsten, uranium, and manganese glow in the dark. The staff will help direct rockhounds to promising sites in the vicinity to further their own collections. The admission is $1.50, 50 cents for children 6-16.

Lava Lands Visitor Center, Lava Butte

About 11 miles south of Bend on U.S. 97 is the Lava Lands Visitor Center (tel. 593-1221) and Lava Butte. The center has some interpretive exhibits that explain the volcanic history of the region, as well as a small but good selection of local geology books and an assortment of free pamphlets on local attractions; their bulletin board has the latest activities and goings-on posted. Open 9-4 daily.

After your orientation at the visitor center, hop back into your buggy and cruise on up to the top of 500-foot-high **Lava Butte,** located just behind the visitor center. The observation platform on top of the fire lookout established here in 1928 offers the best viewpoint. Nearly a mile high (elevation 5,020 feet), the butte affords a commanding panorama of the Cascade Range. On a clear day you can see most of the major peaks, from Mt. Shasta to the south in California to Mt. Rainier north in Washington.

A short trail circumnavigates the 150-foot-deep crater on Lava Butte and is complemented by informative placards that help you interpret this otherwordly environment. From the trail you can see how the lava flow from the butte changed the course of the Deschutes River. You can also see the "kipukas," small islands of green trees surrounded by a sea of black lava. Along the trail, look for some of what geologists call "splatter." You'll know it when you see it, because it looks exactly like what it sounds like. Pick up a couple of red pumice rocks for the children, who will be fascinated by the way the stones float in the bathtub.

Lava River Cave

About 12 miles south of Bend on U.S. 97 is Oregon's longest known lava tube, the Lava River Cave (tel. 593-2421). Open from mid-May to mid-September, the admission is $1.50 and lantern rentals (available at the Lava Lands Visitor Center) are also $1.50. The cave is a cool 40° year round, so dress warmly. Since the walking surface is uneven, flat-heeled shoes are recommended. Bring a flashlight to guide you through this lava tube, or rent one at the entrance for 50 cents. The trail is an easy 2.4-mile roundtrip from the parking lot.

The first chamber you enter is called the Collapsed Corridor. Volcanic rocks that fell from the roof and walls lie in jumbled piles. Freezing water in cracks pries a few rocks loose each winter, which is why the cave is usually closed during the cold months. Stairs take you out of the Collapsed Corridor into a large void called Echo Hall. Here the ceiling reaches 58 feet high and the cave is 50 feet wide. Conversations from the opposite side of the hall return as eerie noises in the dark. The lateral markings you see etched on the walls here show the various levels of past volcanic flows.

At Low Bridge Lane, watch your head because the ceiling dips down to five feet. Look for the "lavacicles" in this and other areas of the cave. This term comes from a geologist's 1923 publication on the cave called *The Lava River Tunnel*, and there are two kinds of them found here. One type is the hollow cylindrical "soda straws" that were formed by escaping gases. The cone-shaped formations were created by remelted lava dripping down from the ceiling.

The next curiosity you'll come across is a cave inside the cave, the Two Tube Tunnel. Here two tubes are found running for 95 feet with intermittent connections between them. The smaller tube was formed when the level of the lava flow dropped, and the cooling lava created a second roof and tube inside the existing cave.

The terrain changes again in the Sand Gardens. Rain and snowmelt carry volcanic ash down through cracks and openings in the cave and deposit them here. The process continues today with the nearly constant dripping water carving out spires and pinnacles in the sand. These formations take hundreds of years to grow, so please stay behind the fenced-off area. The sand gets thicker and thicker until it completely blocks off the lava tube, forcing an abrupt about-face. The walk back to the light of the sun affords a different perspective of this remarkable natural attraction.

It is important to avoid littering the cave, collecting samples, or other acts which mar this national treasure. Don't light flares, paper, or cigarettes, because the fumes kill off insects, the food source of the cave's bat population. Roosting bats should not be disturbed, because waking them from hibernation results in certain death for these winged mammals. In short, "Leave nothing but footprints, take nothing but pictures, and kill nothing but time."

Benham Falls

Four miles down Forest Service Road 9702 from the Lava Lands Visitor Center is Benham Falls. Give other cars a wide berth and plenty of following distance, as the road's pumice and fine dust are hard on paint jobs and engines. The road leads to a small picnic area in a grove of giant Ponderosa pines on the bank of the Deschutes River. With tables, pit toilets, firegrills, and plenty of shade, this is a nice place for a picnic. Be sure to tote your own fluids though, because there is no water. Day use only, no fees and no camping.

The hike to the falls is an easy one-mile jaunt downstream. Take the footbridge across the river, and enjoy your stroll past a spectacular section of untamed whitewater. While the water here in the Deschutes is much too cold and dangerous for a swim (except perhaps on very hot days), it's always ideal for soaking your feet a little after you've completed your hike.

High Desert Museum

Six miles south of Bend on U.S. 97 is the High Desert Museum (59800 South U.S. 97, Bend, 97702; tel. 382-4754). This five-million-dollar center for natural resources, native animals, and cultural history of the intermountain, western high desert is well worth the price of admission (adults $3, seniors $2.50, children ages 6-12 $1.50, and kids under five get in free). Along the many trails that wind through the 150-acre facility, visitors can observe river otters at play, porcupines sticking it to each other, and birds of prey dispassionately watching over the whole scene. Replicas of a sheepherder's cabin, a settler's cabin, forestry displays, and other historical interpretations are also along the museum walkways.

Inside the museum's main building, a unique array of exhibits, slide and movie shows, galleries, and pioneer history demonstrations are presented. The Orientation Center has lizards, snakes, and toads on display, and other animals can be seen at the Wildlife Observation Pavilion. The **Earle A. Chiles Center** exhibit on the Spirit of the West features eight "you are there" life-sized dioramas. This walk through time begins 8,000 years ago beside a still marsh and takes you to a fur brigade camp, into the depths of a gold mine, and down Main Street of a boisterous frontier town.The **Spirit of the West Gallery** has representative arts and artifacts of the early American West, as well as tools, clothing, and other personal belongings from the 19th century.

Newberry Volcano

Lava Butte is one of over 400 cinder cones in a family of over 1,000 other smaller volcanoes that comprises Newberry Volcano. This vast shield volcano covers 500 square miles of land. In the caldera of this immense million-year-old mountain lie two alpine lakes called Paulina and East lake respectively.

Composed of rocks ranging from basalt to rhyolite, the black obsidian flow that's found at Newberry Volcano has been the source of raw material for Indian spearpoints, arrowheads, and hide scrapers for thousands of years. Prized by the original inhabitants of the area, the obsidian tools were also highly valued by other Indian nations and were a medium of exchange for blankets, firearms, and other possessions at the Taos Fair in New Mexico. These tools and other barterings helped to spread Newberry Volcano obsidian all across the West and into Canada and Mexico.

Paulina And East Lakes

South from Bend 27 miles on U.S. 97 is the turnoff to Paulina and East Lakes. The 16-mile paved but ragged County Road 21 twists and turns its way up to the lakes in the caldera of Newberry Crater. Several campgrounds and two resorts are located along the shores of these lakes noted for their excellent trout fishing. Be sure to take the drive (summer only) to the top of 7,985-foot-high Paulina Peak. Towering 1,500 feet over the lakes in Newberry Crater, the peak also allows great views of the surrounding area.

The Paulina Peak drive is one of the highest in the state.

PHOTO BY TED LONG ISHIKAWA

Richardson's Recreational Ranch

If you're a rockhound, you'll want to visit Richardson's Recreational Ranch (Gateway Route Box 440, Madras, 97741; tel. 475-2680). This family owned and operated enterprise has extensive rock beds loaded with thunder eggs, moss agates, jaspers, jasper-agate, Oregon sunset, and rainbow agates. If you want to chip agates out of one of the many exposed ledges on the ranch, you will need to brings chisels, wedges, and other necessary hard-rock mining tools. Once you've completed your dig, you drop your rocks off at the office and pay for them by the pound. And if you don't care for dirt under your fingernails, you can always find rocks for sale from all over the world in the ranch's rock shop.

The motto here is "fun for everyone," and you're sure to meet many interesting "rocky fellers" back at the ranch. To get there, take U.S. 97 north of Madras for 11 miles and turn right at the sign near milepost 81. Follow the road for three miles to the ranch office.

Smith Rock State Park

The majestic spires towering above the Crooked River north of Redmond on U.S. 97 are part of this 623-acre state park. Named after a soldier who fell to his death off of the highest promontory (3,230 feet) in the configuration, the park is a popular retreat for hikers, rock-climbers, and casual visitors. Seven miles of well-marked trails follow the Crooked River and wend up the canyon walls

to emerge on the ridgetops. Because the area is delicate and extremely sensitive to erosion, it's important not to blaze any trails because they may leave visible scars for years. Picnic tables, drinking water, and restrooms can be found near the parking area. The more adventurous can camp out in the park's primitive walk-in camping area.

While it's not exactly Yosemite, some of the climbing routes at Smith Rock are as difficult and challenging as any you'll find in the United States. Chocks, nuts, friends, and other clean-climbing equipment and techniques are encouraged here to reduce damage to the rock. On certain routes where these methods would prove impractical, permanent anchors have been placed. Climbers should use these fixed bolts (after testing them first for safety, of course) to minimize impact on the face. *Oregon Rock: A Climber's Guide* by Jeff Thomas has listings of all the routes at Smith Rock that do not require mounting of additional fixed protection. Climbers should never disturb birds of prey and their young in the lofty aeries.

SPORTS AND RECREATION

Horsing Around

Several public stables are found in the vicinity of Bend which offer horseback rides that satisfy everyone from the dude to the experienced equestrian. Whether it be a mild-mannered pony for young children or a lively steed for the wannabe buckaroos, you'll find appropriate mounts and trail rides for all ages and skill levels.

Black Butte Stables (Box 402, Sisters, 97759: tel. 595-2061 or 595-1297) at Black Butte Ranch has several packages that take you down trails in the shadow of the Three Sisters. The Big Meadow pony ride for children is $5 for 15 minutes and $10 for a half hour. The one-hour Big Loop trail ride costs $17, the one-hour Gobblers Knob trail ride costs $21, the two-hour Glaze Meadow trail ride costs $25, and the Hole-in-the-Wall Gang ride (for experienced riders only) costs $30. The half-day Reata trail ride costs $45, and the full-day Oregon Trail ride costs $65.

If you want a box lunch on the Oregon Trail ride, it's an additional $5. Evening meal rides include the Buckaroo Barbecue for $28 and the Steak ride for $35. If you want to start your day in the saddle, consider the Buckaroo Breakfast ride for $28. Reservations are suggested for the short rides, and are required on the half-day, full-day, and meal rides. Riding lessons are also available.

Located 15 minutes west of Sisters on ORE 126 is **Blue Lake Corrals** (tel. 595-6681). The

PHOTO BY OREGON STATE HIGHWAYS

Rock-climbers will enjoy the diverse terrain of Smith Rock.

half-hour pony ride for children on Jeepers costs $5. The one-hour Crater Rim ($20) ride takes you through alpine meadows to the top of the crater that holds 314-foot-deep Blue Lake. The two-hour Waterfalls trail ride ($25) incorporates views of several waterfalls as well as Three Fingered Jack. The two-hour Lakes Loop trip ($25) meanders through the forest past three crystal clear mountain lakes. The two-hour Twilight ride ($26) offers cooler temperatures, lovely sunsets and skyscapes, and views of wildlife coming out of the woods to feed.

Blue Lake Corral's three half-day packages, the Discovery Trail, Meadow Lake Trail, and Cache Mountain Trail, all cost $45. The all-day Alpine trip ($60) goes into the Mt. Jefferson Wilderness. Summer is the best time to go on this trip due to the abundance of wildflowers, and lunch is also included. Meal rides, like the Cowboy Breakfast and the Chuck Wagon Supper, are also available and run from $26-36. Two-day wilderness pack trips are featured too. Reservations are requested at least one hour before the trail rides, and the meal rides need 24 hours' advance notification.

Five miles west of Redmond at the Eagle Crest Resort is **Eagle Crest Equestrian Center** (Box 1194, Redmond, 97756; tel. 923-2072. The half-hour kids' pony ride on Geronimo costs $6. The one-hour Juniper trail ride takes you through the junipers and sagebrush of the high desert and costs $15. The two-hour Cline Butte trail ride ($29) goes to the top of Cline Butte, where you get a good view of the interface between Cascade and desert life zones. The half-day Skyline trail ride takes you out into the wilds of the desert, where you and your guide blaze your own trails (reservations required). Wagon rides, cookout rides, and riding lessons are also available.

About 15 miles south of Bend on U.S. 97 at Sunriver Resort is **Sunriver Stables** (Box 3254, Sunriver, 97709; tel. 593-2538). The 15-minute Smallest Buckaroo pony ride costs $7. A good ride for beginners is the half-hour Bald Eagle Loop ($12) that goes along the Deschutes River. The one-hour Nature's Cove trail ride ($18) takes in views of the Deschutes River, wildlife, and wildflowers. The two-hour Ramsey Ridge ride climbs to a panoramic viewpoint overlooking the resort. For those who want to do some serious riding, you can create your own ride (three hours' minimum) into the Deschutes National Forest for $34 for the first two hours, then $12 per additional hour. Private lessons, surrey, covered wagon, and sleigh (winter only) rides are also available.

Fishing

With over 100 mountain lakes and the Deschutes River within an hour's drive of Bend, your piscatorial pleasures will be satisfied in central Oregon. The high lakes offer rainbow, brown, and brook trout as well as landlocked Atlantic and coho salmon. The Deschutes River is famed for its red-sided rainbow trout and summer steelhead. You will need appropriate fishing gear like chest waders, rod 'n' reel, and fishing license/steelhead tags. All gear and permits are available locally.

A full-service pro shop with everything for the fly fisher is **The Fly Box** (923 S.E. 3rd. St., Bend, 97701; tel. 388-3330). Custom-tied flies and a full selection of fly-tying tools and materials provide you with the goodies to keep the fish biting. Fly-fishing classes, fishing guide services, and equipment sales, rentals, and repairs can also be found here.

Lacy's Whitewater and Wild Fish (57 Pine-crest Court, Bend, 97701; tel. 389-2434) offers guided float trips on the Deschutes and John Day rivers, fly-fishing on the high Cascade lakes, and walk-in river treks on Fall River, Crooked River, and the Upper Deschutes River. Lacy's floats nearly 100 miles of the Deschutes River on a year-round basis. Stable water temperatures from the spring-fed river and abundant water hatches of baetis, midges, and stoneflies, prolific summer hatches of stoneflies, salmonflies, and golden-stones, and excellent mayfly and caddis hatches in summer keep the fish here in top condition. The wild red-sided trout of the Deschutes River are there all year, and the summer steelhead are found in the river from July through December. The John Day River is noted for being the only river in the state that hosts an all-wild run of summer steelhead. All-day float trips on either river cost $200 for one person, $285 for two, and $335 for three people. A deli-style lunch is also included. Rates for multi-day trips (minimum two people, three days) run $145 per person per day and include all meals.

Guided trips to High Cascades lakes are $155 for one person and $205 for two. Walk-in river treks reach the good fishing holes not accessible

by boat, and are good for beginners. Half-day treks cost $75 for one person and $100 for two, and the full-day treks with a deli-style lunch cost $100 for one person and $150 for two.

High Desert Drifter (721 N.W. Ogden, Bend, 97701; tel. 389-0607) also offers guided fly-fishing float trips on the Deschutes River. The full-day trip that includes lunch and the necessary river boater pass and Warm Springs Indian Reservation fishing permit costs $200 for one person, $275 for two, and $375 for three. Multi-day trips including all meals run $350 for two days, $525 for three days, $700 for four days, and $875 for five days.

Both outfitters require completion of a trip application form and a deposit.

Whitewater Rafting

The Deschutes River offers some of the finest whitewater in central Oregon. The numerous lava flows have diverted the river to create tumultuous rapids that attract raft, kayak, and canoe enthusiasts. From short rafting trips to multi-day adventures, you'll find many options available to enjoy the exciting Deschutes River.

Hunter Expeditions (Box 346, Bend, 97709; tel. 389-8370) features several rafting packages. The two-hour Mini Expedition ($25) takes you down a three-mile section of the Deschutes River that has Class I-IV rapids. Six daily departures from Bend include transfer to and from the river. The all-day trip ($60) takes in 12 action-packed miles of whitewater including some exciting Class IV rapids like Box Car, Oak Springs, and Elevator. A deli-style lunch and plenty of drinks are included. The transfer pickup point for the day-trips is in the town of **Maupin**, 80 miles north of Bend on U.S 97 and U.S. 197 in front of the Oasis Cafe, and leaves promptly at 11 a.m.

The Inn of the Seventh Mountain (18575 Century Dr., Bend, 97701; tel. 389-2722) offers a short two-hour raft trip ($27) down a three-mile section of the Deschutes that takes in some Class I-IV rapids. With names like Pinball Alley and the Souse Hole, you can be assured a good ride! Transfer to and from the Inn of the Seventh Mountain and the river is included.

Rapid River Rafters (60107 Cinder Butte Road, Bend, 97702; tel. 382-1514 or 800-962-3327) offers a series of full- and multi-day packages on the Deschutes River. The one-day trip ($65) takes in 13 miles of the river between Wapinitia Rapids and Sherar's Falls. A deli-style lunch with fresh fruit and beverages is provided. The two-day trip ($170) floats 29 miles of exciting whitewater. The three-day trip ($250) runs 44 miles between Trout Creek rapids and Sherar's Falls. The four-day trip ($330) takes in 55 miles of the Deschutes and is designed to allow you free time for additional options like hiking, sunbathing, swimming, and fishing. On all of the multi-day trips, the camping and meal preparations at pleasant riverside locations are taken care of by your guides.

Sun Country Tours (Box 771, Bend, 97709; tel. 382-6277) is based at the Sunriver Resort. Their three-hour, three-mile whitewater adventure takes in Class I-IV rapids on the the Deschutes River. It costs $23 for children 8-12 and $25 for adults. The full-day trip ($65) runs 13 miles through a dozen minor rapids and seven major ones including Wapinitia, Train Hole, and Oak Springs. A deli-style lunch is included. Multi-day packages that vary from 29 to 55 miles are also available. The two-day trip costs $170, the three-day costs $250, and the four-day costs $330. All meals on multi-day trips are included, and the transfer from Sunriver to Maupin is also part of the day-trip packages.

If you would rather shoot the rapids on your own, you can rent canoes, kayaks, and rafts from **Bend Whitewater Supply** (Box 461, 2245 N.E. Division, Bend, 97709; tel. 389-7191). This locally owned and operated full service whitewater store can provide you with everything necessary for a safe and enjoyable whitewater experience. Bend Whitewater Supply also offers canoe and kayak lessons.

Juniper Aquatic And Fitness Center

One of the finest aquatic and fitness centers east of the Cascades is found at Juniper Aquatic and Fitness Center (800 N.E. 6th Street, Bend, 97701; tel. 389-7665). Part of the Bend Metro Park and Recreation District, the center is located in 20-acre Juniper Park and features two indoor pools and a large 40-yard outdoor pool providing plenty of space to splash around in. Serious swimmers can enjoy frequent lap swims and adults-only swim times daily. An aerobics room, weightroom, jogging trail, and tennis course offer other exercise options. A sauna and jacuzzi provide you with yet another way to sweat it out. Call ahead to see what's on the schedule for the day's activities.

Cycle Coasting

If you like to bike but would rather have gravity do all of the work, consider the Paulina Plunge with **High Cascade Descent** (333 Riverfront, Bend, 97702; tel. 389-0562). They provide quality 15- and 18-speed mountain bikes, helmets, experienced guides, and the shuttle transfer from Bend and back. The action starts at Paulina Lake, where you begin your coast down forested trails alongside Paulina Creek. You'll pass by 50 waterfalls on your 3,000-foot descent as well as abundant wildlife and varied vegetation. A deli-style lunch (vegetarian meals available upon request) and numerous opportunities for photography and fishing round out the fun. The tour costs $35 per person, $30 for children under 12. Large groups of over 10 people can receive discounts if they book trips in advance. If you have your own bicycle, you can deduct $5 from the tour price.

Flying High

For a morning lighter-than-air experience, take off with **Morning Glory Balloon Company** (7843 S.W. 77th Street, Redmond, tel. 389-8739). One-hour flights in Oregon's largest passenger balloon soar high in the sky, affording spectacular vistas of the high desert and Cascade Mountains. Celebrate your adventure upon landing with champagne. Balloon fare is $150 per person; reservations are required.

Golf

Central Oregon has recently gained recognition for world class golfing. And no wonder. With a dozen courses and six more slated for construction, you can find just about every kind of golf challenge here. The warm sunny days, cool evenings, and spectacular mountain scenery make every shot a memorable one.

Two well-groomed courses, Big Meadow and Glaze Meadow, are found at **Black Butte Ranch** (tel. 595-6689). Big Meadow is more open and forgiving, while Glaze Meadow demands precise shots. Both have tall trees and lush fairways from tee-to-green. Greens fees are $17 for nine holes and $30 for 18. Reservations for weekdays must be made at least one day in advance, while weekend bookings must be made no later than the Monday before.

A good course for the ladies, average players who want to score, and good players who want to shoot birdies is at the **Crooked River Ranch** (tel. 923-6343). This nine-hole par 32 course is wide open with few trees, but that doesn't detract from the challenge or the scenic vistas. Rates are $8 for nine holes and $13 for 18. Weekend reservations must be made by Thursday.

A blend of open and tight holes can be found on the popular course at **Eagle Crest Resort** (tel. 923-4653). The two nine-holes of this par 72 course differ in character. The first set allows you to swing away whereas the second places a premium on club and shot selection. The stand of 1,000-year old junipers in mid-fairway and excellent greens add to the challenge and enjoyment. The greens fee is $15 for nine holes and $24 for 18 for visitors, $12 for nine holes and $18 for 18 for registered guests. Weekend reservations must be made by Thursday.

Nine new holes just opened up for play this summer at the **Inn of the Seventh Mountain** (tel. 382-8711). Designed by Robert Muir Graves, strategically placed trees, lakes, and sand traps have already given this place the reputation as the "mean green" golf course of central Oregon.

A true desert course found in Redmond that requires shot accuracy is the **Juniper Golf Club** (tel. 548-3121). This is a 18-hole par 72 course that snakes through the juniper and lava of the high desert. The prevailing winds and abundance of rocks off of the fairway challenges the golfer's shot-making abilities. Rates are $10 for nine holes and $18 for 18. Reservations are required at least one day in advance.

Sixty miles north of Bend is the well maintained 18-hole par 72 course at **Kah-Nee-Ta Resort** (tel. 553-1112, ext. 371). While shorter than many other resort courses in the area, it's nonetheless both a challenge and a delight to play. In addition to water to contend with from the Warm Springs River that meanders through the course, several holes have elevated greens that require blind shots to reach. The greens fees are $12 for nine holes and $21 for 18. Reservations can be made at anytime.

A beautiful course in Bend with tight fairways, large greens, sand, and water, water everywhere is **Mountain High Golf Club** (tel. 382-1111). Two tricky par four dogleg holes, three par fives, and the necessity of placing shots over and around the junipers add to the test. Rates are $12.50 for nine holes and $25 for 18. Reservations can be made anytime for weekdays, but must be made

at least four days in advance for weekends.

About 45 miles north of Bend on U.S. 97 at the Madras Golf and Country Club is **Nine Peaks** (tel. 475-3511). This short par 36 nine-hole course is flat and more forgiving than most courses in the area. The name comes from the nine Cascade peaks that provide a stunning visual backdrop. Rates are $5 for nine holes and $10 for 18 on weekdays; $7 for nine holes and $14 for 18 on weekends. Reservations are required at least one day in advance.

A course popular with seniors, ladies, and beginners is found at **Orion Greens** (tel. 388-3999) in Bend. This short executive course with no homesites lining the fairways can be deceptively tough. Water comes into play on four holes and shot accuracy is a must. Rates are $8 for nine holes and $14 for 18. Reservations are required at least one day in advance.

The hilly, rocky terrain of **River's Edge** (tel. 389-2828) in Bend makes it both beautiful and an extreme challenge. This testy nine-hole par 36 course has tiered greens and one of the region's most demanding water holes. Shot accuracy is more important here than at any other course in the vicinity. Rates are $12 for nine holes and $20 for 18 on weekdays; $12 for nine holes and $22 for 18 on weekends. Reservations are required one week in advance.

Two distinct 18-hole courses are found at **Sunriver Resort** (tel. 593-1221) 15 miles south of Bend on U.S. 97. The South Course is long with fast greens that require a soft touch. The North Course is the premier course in the area, has been rated among the top 25 courses in the country, and is the site of the annual Oregon Open. Water, abundant bunkers, and constricted approaches to the greens make club selection and shot accuracy very important. South Course rates are $15 for nine holes and $25 for 18 for registered guests; $21 for nine holes and $35 for 18 for visitors. The North Course is $18 for nine holes and $30 for 18 for registered guests; $24 for nine holes and $40 for 18 for visitors.

PRACTICALITIES

Accommodations

Bend has exploded into the largest full-fledged resort town in the state. On holiday or ski weekends, it's hard now to find a decent room here if

BEND ACCOMMODATIONS

Name	Address	Telephone	Price	Features
Chalet Motel	510 S.E. 3rd St.,	382-6124	$18-22	TV, a/c small rooms
Edelweiss Motel	2346 N.E. Division	382-6222	$18-22	clean
Sonoma Lodge	450 S.E. 3rd St.	382-4891	$21-24	pets
Royal Gateway Motel	475 S.E. 3rd St.	382-5631	$21-24	HBO
Hill Crest Motel	61405 ORE 97	389-5910	$24-35	kitchenettes, pets
Rainbow Motel	154 N.E. Franklin Ave.	382-1821	$25-27	kitchenettes, nonsmoking rooms
Tom Tom Motor Inn	3600 ORE 97	382-4734	$26-30	pets, laundry
Palmer's Motel	645 N.E. Greenwood Ave.	382-1197	$28-32	covered pool
Cascade Lodge Motel	420 S.E. 3rd St.	382-2612	$28-30	pool, pets, restaurant
Sportsman's Motel	3705 ORE 97	382-2211	$28-35	kitchenettes, pets
Motel West	228 N.E. Irving	389-5577	$30-36	kitchenettes, pets
Westward Ho Motel	904 S.E. 3rd St.	382-2111	$31-35	covered pool, fireplaces, pets
Maverick Motel	437 N.E. 3rd St.	382-7711	$33-35	pool, pets, restaurant/lounge
Cimarron Motel	201 N.E. 3rd St.	382-8282	$33-35	pool, pets
Dune Motel	1515 N.E. 3rd St.	382-6811	$33-35	pool, pets
Bend Super 8 Motel	1275 ORE 97	388-6888	$38-40	wheelchair access, covered pool, laundry
Best Western Woodstone Inn	721 N.E. 3rd St.	382-1515	$38-45	pool, jacuzzi, pets
Best Western Entrada Lodge	19221 Century Dr.	382-4080	$38-45	pool, jacuzzi, pets, restaurant

you don't have reservations, and it's bound to get worse. As such, expect many of the prices in this chart to be significantly higher than what was listed at press time.

Campgrounds
With the Three Sisters Wilderness and the Deschutes National Forest flanking the western edges of Bend, there are many wonderful spots

to enjoy a night camping out under the stars. But for those who want to stay within a two-mile radius of civilization, there are four decent RV parks near Bend. **Bend Keystone** (305 N.E. Burnside, Bend, 97701; tel. 382-2335, $11), **Crown Villa** (60801 Brosterhous, Bend, 97701; tel. 388-1131, $14), **Lowe's Trailer Park** (61416 U.S. 97 South, Bend, 97701; tel. 382-6206, $11), and **KOA Bend** (63615 U.S. 97 North, Bend, 97701; tel. 382-7728, $12) offer all of the major amenities. However, while a swimming pool, recreation room, and cable TV hookups are pleasant enough, this can ultimately take the spotlight away from the main attraction: around Bend, nature is the star.

Tumalo State Park (tel. 382-2601, $8) provides a middle ground between the rugged wilderness and tamed RV parks. Located five miles northwest of Bend off of U.S. 20 along the banks of the Deschutes River, 68 tent sites and 20 sites for RVs up to 35 feet long are available here. Showers, flush toilets, hookups, utilities, and a laundromat are also accessible. Open mid-April to late-October.

A more secluded setting would be **Tumalo Falls** (contact Deschutes National Forest, 1230 N.E. 3rd St., Bend, 97701; tel. 388-5664, no fee). Located 16 miles west of town down Forest Service roads 4601 and 4603, this small campground is situated along Tumalo Creek. Many fine hiking trails are in the area, including a short one to 97-foot-high Tumalo Falls. However, the facilities are primitive—pit toilets and no water.

Another exceptionally beautiful but equally rustic National Forest Service campground is **Todd Lake** (also contact the Forest Service for more info). To get there, take Century Drive toward Mt. Bachelor. About a mile or two past the ski area, take the first Forest Service Road on the right. While this road eventually arrives at Sisters, it is not recommended for passenger cars. However, you will only have to venture less than a mile on a well-maintained section to reach the parking area for Todd Lake. It is a short walk up the trail to the campsites on this 6,200-foot-high alpine lake. While there are tables, firegrills, and pit toilets, you will need to pack in your own water and supplies, as no vehicles are allowed. It's a good thing, because the drone of a Winnebago generator into the wee hours of the night would definitely detract from the grandeur of this pristine spot. You'll find good swimming and wading on the sandy shoal on the south end of the lake, and you can't miss the captivating views of Broken Top to the north.

Food

The scenery around Bend feeds the soul and restaurants here do the rest. While area restaurants run the gamut from fast-food franchises to elegant dinner houses, many travelers also want something in between these extremes. Here are some alternatives for every budget.

Beef and Brew (Bend River Mall, Bend, tel. 388-4646) is a good dinner house for choice beef, seafood, and a tall cool one. Reservations are recommended. For lunch and dinner, **Brandy's** (197 N.E. 3rd, Bend, tel. 382-2687) features fresh seafood, poultry, and a good salad bar. They have light and children's menus that cater to smaller-sized appetites. The best place to sit is in the solarium; live entertainment and dancing is featured here evenings.

Many locals concur that **Cyrano's** (119 N.W. Minnesota Ave., Bend, tel. 389-6276) is one of central Oregon's premier dining experiences. With a reputation built around thick-cut steaks that are grilled to perfection over red oak, the menu also features fresh seafood and other gourmet specialties. If the weather is pleasant, enjoy lunch outside at their sidewalk cafe. Wholesome home-cooked food (90% from scratch) is available at **D & D Bar and Grill** (927 N.W. Bond Street, Bend, tel. 382-4592). Open every day (except Christmas) for breakfast, lunch, and dinner, the Grill has reasonably priced breakfasts and a good selection of hamburgers.

A popular Portland chain has opened up an outlet in Bend. **De Nicola's** (811 N.W. Wall Street, Bend, tel. 389-7364) offers a fine selection of Italian dishes, pizza, soups, and salads. If you love Italian food but are trying not to add more notches to your belt, ask for their special low-fat menu. Bend also boasts central Oregon's first brewery and brewpub, **Deschutes Brewery and Public House** (1044 N.W. Bond Street, Bend, tel. 382-9242). This is the place to come and relax with fresh, handcrafted ales and good homemade food. Large viewing windows in the pub enable you to watch next month's batch being concocted in the brewery.

A good place for families and fun is **Deschutes Station** (61219 South U.S. 97, Bend, tel. 389-7574). In addition to pizza and 26 varieties of hamburgers, they have games, video machines, and giant slides that keep the children entertained. The **Desert Deli** (118 N.W. Minnesota, Bend, tel. 382-3559) is good for a quick "fix" with salads, sandwiches, and home-baked desserts. Decent Chinese cuisine is found at the **Hong Kong Restaurant and Lounge** (580 S.E. 3rd, Bend, tel. 389-8880). A wide selection of Cantonese, Szechuan, and American food as well as many vegetarian and "health food" dishes are prepared here.

Giuseppe's Ristorante (932 N.W. Bond Street, Bend, tel. 389-8899) brings the taste of northern Italy to Bend. Dinner specialties include chicken, veal, and 17 pasta dishes. Another Italian fine-dining experience is available at the **Italian Cottage** (1564 N.E. Division Street, Bend, tel. 382-5062). You can choose from over 30 entrees here, and their pastas and breads are made fresh daily. For some of the largest portions in central Oregon, head down to **Jake's Diner** (61260 South U.S. 97, Bend, tel. 382-0118). Hardy breakfasts are served here 24 hours a day, and they have tasty giant cinnamon rolls. Truckers everywhere in the West sing the praises of this place.

Le Bistro (1203 N.E. 3rd Street, Bend, tel. 389-7274) is consistently rated the region's best French restaurant by the American Automobile Association and the Mobile Guide. Situated in an old church and designed with an open kitchen, the European chef/owner treats you to fresh seafood, chicken, lamb, veal, and steak dinners. Complement your fare with a bottle off the impressive wine list. **Mexicali Rose** (301 N.E. Franklin, Bend, tel. 389-0149) has the best Mexican food around Bend. Open every evening for dinner, be sure to ask for their special black beans with your entree. Call ahead for reservations, because the restaurant is very popular with locals.

The **Pine Tavern Restaurant** (967 N.W. Brocks Street, Bend, tel. 382-5581) has been in business since 1919, so they must be doing something right. Overlooking Mirror Pond, prime rib, lamb, and sourdough scones are among the many specialties here. Reservations are recommended. **Yoko's Japanese Restaurant** (1028 N.W. Bond Street, Bend, tel. 382-2999) is Bend's preeminent Japanese restaurant and sushi bar. While the teriyaki, tempura, and sukiyaki dinners are prepared to suit American tastes, it's not uncommon to see Japanese visitors here enjoying their native cuisine.

Finally, located at the Inn of the Seventh Mountain, **El Crab Catcher** (18575 Century Drive, Bend, tel. 389-2722) rates an especially ardent recommendation. This restaurant chain first got its start on Maui, and now has come to Bend to share regional delights with a Polynesian flair. Try the flash-frozen-and-flown-in-fresh king crab legs with lemon butter, salad (go for the house dressing topped with crumbled bleu cheese), vegetables, and hot sourdough rolls. Fresh seafood, steaks, poultry, and a variety of light suppers are also featured here. The staff is extremely friendly and goes out of its way to ensure you a prompt and delicious repast. Be sure to call in your reservations early, as this restaurant is as popular with the après-ski crowd as it is with the clientele of luxury motorcoach tours.

Services And Information

The **police** (720 N.W. Wall Street, Bend, tel. 388-5530 or 911) and the state police (63319 U.S. 20 West, Bend, tel. 388-6300 or 911) are at your beck and call. The **post office** (2300 N.E. 4th, Bend, 97701; tel. 388-1971) is open from 8:30-5:30 p.m. Monday through Friday. If you like to make your own cocktails, the **liquor store** (939 N.W. Bond, Bend, tel. 382-6450) is open 12-8 p.m. For additional information on the Bend area, the **chamber of commerce** (63085 U.S. 97 North, Bend, tel. 382-2777) is open Mon. through Thurs., 9-5 p.m., Fri., 8-6 p.m., Sat., 8-5 p.m., and Sun. 11-4 p.m. The **Deschutes County Library** (507 N.W. Wall Street, Bend, tel. 388-6677) is open 9-6 p.m. Mon. through Saturday.

St. Charles Immediate Care Center (1302 U.S. 97, Bend, tel. 388-7799) can be of assistance for minor medical problems and emergencies. The parent hospital, **St. Charles Medical Center** (2500 N.E. Neff, Bend, tel. 382-4321 or 382-4321 ext. 7100 for emergencies only) treats major trauma and other health care problems. If you're out in the boondocks and time is of the essence, **Air Life of Oregon** (tel. 800-621-5433 or 911) can get you to the medical center in a hurry. The **Bend Memorial Clinic** (1501 N.E. Medical Center Drive, Bend, tel. 382-2811) is another option to remedy minor aches, pains, and ailments.

Events

The **Cascade Festival of Music** is held the third week of June on the banks of the Deschutes River. In addition to world-class performances of classical, pop, and jazz in the pavilion tent, children's concerts, music workshops, and strolling minstrels round out the pageant. Tickets and information are available through the Cascade Festival of Music office (tel. 382-8381).

The **Sunriver Music Festival,** held in the log structure called the Great Hall at Sunriver Resort, has been pleasing capacity crowds since the festival's inception in 1977. The five-concert series feature top performers from around the world. Highlights include the Gala pops concert and the Gourmet Dinner as well as four traditional classical concerts and two children's concerts. Tickets and information are available through the Sunriver Music Festival office (tel. 593-1084).

GETTING THERE AND GETTING AROUND

By Air

The air hub of this section of the state is in Redmond, located 16 miles north of Bend on U.S. 97. **Alaska Air** (tel. 800-426-0333) has nonstop jet flights out of L.A. and Seattle; **Horizon Air** (tel. 800-547-9308) services the region from Portland and Seattle; and **United Express** (tel. 800-241-6522) provides trips from Portland and San Francisco. Taxi, limo, and bus transfers connect the traveler to Bend at nominal costs.

By Bus

Greyhound (1068 N.W. Bond St., Bend, 97701; tel. 382-2151) is open 8-5 p.m. and 9-10 p.m. weekdays and 8-4 p.m. on weekends. Bus service connects Bend with Klamath Falls to the south and Biggs, Maupin, and The Dalles to the north. **Resort Bus Lines** (767 S.E. Glenwood Drive, Bend, tel. 389-7755) handles service to most outlying areas not serviced by Greyhound. **Central Oregon Shuttle Service** (tel. 382-0800) serves Bend to and from Portland International Airport. **Redmond Airport Shuttle** (tel. 382-1687 or 800-955-8267) offers door-to-door service to and from the Redmond airport. A free **ski shuttle** is run by Mt. Bachelor (tel. 382-2442) that links downtown Bend to West Village on the mountain.

Yellow Cab (tel. 382-3311) can always haul you around if you need a ride.

By Train

The closest you can get to Bend via Amtrak (tel. 800-872-7245) is Chemult, 60 miles to the south on U.S. 97. Amtrak will assist you in scheduling your transfer to Bend.

By Car

The automobile is still the vehicle of choice for exploring this quadrant of the state. Highways 97 and 20 converge on Bend, much as the Indian trails and pioneer wagon roads did 150 years ago when this outpost on the Deschutes was called Farewell Bend. Portland is three hours away via U.S. 97 and ORE 26, Salem is two hours away via ORE 20 and ORE 22, and Eugene is two hours away via ORE 20 and ORE 126. Crater Lake National Park is about two hours south down U.S. 97. There are also many loops worth investigating, like the Cascade Lakes Highway and the Newberry Crater Lava Lands and other touring corridors.

You can rent a car for $19.95 per day with 50 free miles daily from **Dorn Bothers Rentals** (148 N. 6th, Redmond, 97756; tel. 923-2027 in Redmond, tel. 382-2783 in Bend). They offer compacts, midsize, passenger vans, four-by-fours, and pickups. Ski racks are also available. **Hertz** (1057 S.E. 3rd St., Bend, tel. 382-1711) and **Budget** (2060 U.S. 20 East, Bend, tel. 389-3031) are two national rental outfits also represented here.

Tours

Caprine Express Tours (65315 N. U.S. 97, Bend, 97701; tel. 389-7800 or 800-552-7577) has half a dozen tour packages of central Oregon, Cascade Mountains, and the high desert. The Cascade Lakes Highway Loop tour takes you past Mt. Bachelor and the many beautiful lakes of this scenic thoroughfare, allowing for frequent stops for pictures and fresh air. A chair-lift ride to the top of Mt. Bachelor is the high point of the day. Fare is $20 for adults, $15 for children under 12.

The four-hour Lava Lands tour takes in some of the highlights of the Newberry volcano area. The trip includes the Lava Lands Visitor Center, the Lava Cast Forest, and the High Desert Museum. Fare is $18.50 for adults and $13.50 for children under 12. The six-hour Metolius River/Sisters tour first goes to the headwaters of the Metolius River at the base of Black Butte and then visits the Wizard Falls Fish Hatchery further downstream. A lunch and shopping break is next in the quaint village of Sisters, and the afternoon is topped off with a visit to the largest llama ranch in Oregon, Dick Patterson's. Fare is $20 for adults, and $15 for children under 12.

The eight-hour Crater Lake tour circumnavigates the entire caldera of the lake, allowing lots of time for pictures. Lunch and ranger talks are available at Rim Village. Fare is $25 for adults and $20 for children under 12. The four-hour Smith Rock tour takes in Smith Rock State Park, the Ogden Gorge of the the Crooked River, and Petersen's Rock Garden. Fare is $18.50 for adults and $13.50 for children under 12.

The eight-hour Painted Hills tour takes you to the John Day Fossil beds and the colorful desert. Plenty of time is allotted for photography and exploring, and a box lunch is included. Fare is $27 for adults and $22 for children under 12.

MOUNT HOOD

HIKING AND CAMPING

Mount Hood Climbs
Mt. Hood, the highest mountain in Oregon at 11,239 feet, has the dual distinction of being the second most climbed glacier-covered peak in the world. Nicknamed the "Fujiyama of America," there are hikes up Mt. Hood that cater to everyone, from beginners to advanced climbers. Another similarity to its Japanese counterpart is that there are only about two months out of the year that are safe for climbing, from May to mid-July. Since the summer heat brings on the threat of avalanche danger and rockfall hazards, the time of day of your departure is just as important as the time of year. Most expeditions depart in the wee hours of the morning when the snow is firm and rockfall danger is lessened. Though you won't get as much sleep, you will be able to enjoy beautiful sunrise scenery as you venture to the top of the world—in Oregon, that is. Nonetheless, remember there are beginner's routes to the summit, too.

There are a few short and easy hikes from Timberline Lodge that require basic day-hiking equipment—hiking boots, water, snacks, sunglasses, sunscreen, and warm, waterproof clothing, since the weather can change rapidly, even in midsummer. Those intent upon reaching the top of the mountain, however, had best go prepared. In addition to the previously mentioned supplies, an ice axe, crampons and extra straps, extra clothing and food, first-aid kit, at least a quart of water, CB radio, topographic map and compass, and a 120-foot rope are necessary. Your boots should be waterproof and well insulated, because the final 3,000 feet in elevation is over glaciers and snowfields. Wool is the best material for keeping warm; wool socks (take an extra pair for emergency mittens), mittens, hat, sweater, and pants will keep you warm even when wet. A warm, water-resistant jacket is also a good idea.

While the climb looks like only a few miles on the map, it takes 10-15 hours to make the trip from Timberline Lodge to the top and back. The four primary routes up Mt. Hood—Hogsback, Mazama, Wyeast, and Castle Crags—are all *technical climbs;* there is no hiking trail to the summit. Having the right equipment means little if you don't know how to use it. It takes a minimum of three people to compose a safe party (and many solo adventurers here have ended up decomposing), and you should have a competent and experienced leader in command. Always register at the lodge before climbing and check out when you return. Most climbing deaths and injuries are avoidable. Dangers like falling ice, rock, and snow, gaping crevasses, and the temperamental mountain weather can all be surmounted with planning, preparedness, and common sense. Be one of the hundreds of thousands of happy hikers who have successfully reached the summit and back, not another unfortunate statistic claimed by Old Man Mountain.

Hogsback
Of the four routes to the summit departing from Timberline Lodge, Hogsback is the most climbed.

A good trip for beginners, the climb takes an average 10-12 hours roundtrip. The first mile ascends 1,000 feet and ends at the Silcox Warming Hut. Built in 1939, this rustic stone and timber shelter used to house the upper terminal of the original Magic Mile chairlift. This was the second chairlift built in the country, the first to use steel towers, and the nation's oldest operating chairlift until it was discontinued in 1962. This first leg of the climb is a good short hike for those who want to stay in the mellow zone.

The trail continues on up the Palmer glacier and onto the White River glacier. You climb up the glacier between Crater Rock and the Steel Cliffs and soon reach the saddle above Crater Rock. From here you stay on the saddle and head for the chute which leads to the summit. **Mazama** is a variation on Hogsback, and is a good route for your second climb. You would cross the saddle above Crater Rock and reach the summit going up the chute on the far left of the rock outcroppings.

Wyeast

An intermediate route for experienced climbers is Wyeast, which averages 12-14 hours roundtrip. About a half mile above Silcox Warming Hut, you would cross over the White River glacier and reach the saddle of the Steel Cliffs. From there you follow the saddle on up to the top. It doesn't go over as much snow, but the rocks on the ridge of the Steel Cliffs are dangerous and require expertise.

Castle Crags

Castle Crags offers an advanced route for experienced climbers. Because this trail goes over Illumination Rock and the Hot Rocks, climbers must go when the ice and rock are solid during January through April. Adding to the dangers of bonafide rock-climbing is the everpresent threat of winter weather. Disorienting whiteout conditions, frigid cold, and wicked gale-force winds compound the hardships already imposed by the grueling trail. This 12-14 hour roundtrip should only be attempted by serious climbers when the weather conditions are right.

Buried Forest Overlook

If the snowbound summit is not for you, an easier one-mile roundtrip hike is the Buried Forest Overlook. This overlook provides a dramatic view of the White River Canyon, where a thick forest was buried during one of the mountain's major eruptive periods about 200-250 years ago. Superheated gases blew down giant trees like matchsticks, and in the next instant, it was all buried underneath a mixture of water, ash, and mud. The ero-

glacier-covered Mt. Hood, above Trillium Lake

PHOTO BY OREGON STATE HIGHWAYS

THERE SHE BLOWS!

In the past, Mt. Hood and Mt. St. Helens in Washington have shared many periods of volcanic activity. Although the 1980 eruption of Mt. St. Helens has given her more name recognition and public awareness than her Oregon counterpart, Mt. Hood is nonetheless a slumbering giant that occasionally snores loudly. Consider that six eruptions were recorded on Mt. Hood in the mid-1800s, with the last one in 1907. According to a carbon dated four- to six-inch layer of ash found on the northeast and southeast flanks of the mountain, Lewis and Clark just missed the 1804 eruption. And with smoky emissions coming out of Mt. Hood fumaroles in the 1980s, scientists have placed sensitive seismic monitoring equipment to keep tabs on the volcano.

While Old Man Mountain still appears to be sleeping, the Portland Office of Emergency Management has drafted contingency plans for worst-case scenarios. Portland is located far enough away to be out of range of most volcanic debris, but its water source would be cut off. Portland relies upon the bountiful Bull Run watershed located on Mt. Hood, and ash and mudflows from a major eruption would have devastating effects upon the city's water supply. Giant mudflows into the Columbia River present another threat, which could precipitate downstream flooding.

The federal government has also gotten involved by developing complex evacuation plans for the foothill communities of Sandy and Hood River. The residents may be lucky enough to escape with their hides intact, but the lush fields and well-groomed orchards on the northeastern side of the mountain would very likely be blanketed with ash and debris and sound the death knell to their way of life. The loss of this major agricultural resource would have statewide repercussions. The timber industry would also be hard hit by a major eruption. In addition to the scores of acres of forest destroyed by mud, ash, and lava flows, scientists suggest that there's a high probability of forest fires as well. Like the fruit growers of the Hood River Valley, the timber industry would also be severely constrained for many years.

The good news is that, like a spurned lover, the aftereffects of a volcanic eruption are eventually softened with time. In the wake of the Mt. St. Helens blast, insects, vegetation, and wildlife returned to the area within a year or two. Farmers in eastern Washington who saw their crops destroyed in 1980 are now enjoying bumper yields due to the soil's increased fertility. Nonetheless, in an era of worldwide earthquakes and volcanic eruptions, many locals look to the mountain and wonder if it will soon be Mt. Hood's turn to roar.

---

sional forces of wind and water have since exposed the remains of the Buried Forest. To get there, follow one of the trails behind Timberline Lodge up the mountain about a quarter mile until you reach the Pacific Crest National Scenic Trail. Turn east (right) onto the Pacific Crest Trail and follow it another quarter mile or so to the overlook.

Camping

Set along the banks of the Salmon River is **Green Canyon** (Zigzag Ranger District, 70220 East ORE 35, Zigzag, 97049; tel. 622-3191 or 666-0704 from Portland). Here you'll find 15 campsites for tents and RVs (31 feet maximum) with picnic tables and firegrills, piped water, pit toilets, and firewood available. Green Canyon is open from May to late September, and the fee is $5-7 per night depending upon the site. Nearby is a trail that goes through the old-growth forests lining the Salmon River and past several water-

falls. A store, ice, and cafe are about five miles away. To get there, go to Zigzag on U.S. 26 and take Salmon River Road (2618) four miles to the campground.

Near the replica of the Barlow Road Tollgate is **Tollgate** (Zigzag Ranger District, 70220 East ORE 35, Zigzag, 97049; tel. 622-3191 or 666-0704 from Portland). Set along the banks of the Zigzag River, this campground has 23 tent sites and nine RV sites (22 feet maximum) with picnic tables and firegrills. Water, pit toilets, and firewood are also available. Open from late May to late September, the campground costs $4 per night. While it's one of the more primitive campgrounds in the area, it's close to the Mt. Hood Wilderness and many hiking trails. Take U.S. 26 one mile past Rhododendron to get there.

Situated on the Clear Fork of the Sandy River, **McNeil** (Zigzag Ranger District, 70220 East ORE 35, Zigzag, 97049; tel. 622-3191 or 666-0704 from Portland) has a good view of Mt. Hood. The campground has 34 sites for tents and RVs (22 feet maximum) with picnic tables and firegrills. Piped water, vault toilets, and firewood are also available. Open May to late September, McNeil charges $4 per night. To get there, turn onto Lolo Pass Road (County Route 18) at Zigzag and follow it for four miles. Turn right onto Forest Service Road 1825 and follow signs to the campground, about a mile further.

A popular place for a night out in the woods is **Camp Creek** (Zigzag Ranger District, 70220 East ORE 35, Zigzag, 97049; tel. 622-3191 or 666-0704 from Portland). This campground has 30 sites for tents and RVs (22 feet maximum) with piped water, picnic tables, and firegrills. Flush toilets and firewood are also available. Open from late May to late September, Camp Creek charges $3 per night. Situated along Camp Creek not far from the Zigzag River, the campground has double campsites that two parties can share. To get there, go three miles east of Rhododendron on U.S. 26 and turn south to the campground.

About a mile down the road from Timberline Lodge is **Alpine** (Zigzag Ranger District, 70220 East ORE 35, Zigzag, 97049; tel. 622-3191 or 666-0704 from Portland). The high-elevation setting here lives up to its name, with snow remaining on the ground until late in the summer during heavy snow years. There are 16 campsites for tents and trailers (22 feet maximum) plus piped water, picnic tables, and firegrills. Alpine is open July to late September, and the fee is $5 per night. In addition to summer skiing up at Mt. Hood, the Pacific Crest Trail passes by very close to the camp.

Near the junction of U.S. 26 and ORE 35 is **Still Creek** (Zigzag Ranger District, 70220 East ORE 35, Zigzag, 97049; tel. 622-3191 or 666-0704 from Portland). Here you'll find 27 sites for tents and RVs (30 feet maximum) with picnic tables and firegrills. Piped water, pit toilets, and firewood are also available. Open from mid-June to late September, Still Creek costs $4 per night. The campground has many large trees, and is close to the Old Swim Hot Springs Resort, a pioneer cemetery, and Trillium Lake.

A good place for a base camp for those who like to canoe is at **Trillium Lake** (Zigzag Ranger District, 70220 East ORE 35, Zigzag, 97049; tel. 622-3191 or 666-0704 from Portland). there are 30 sites for tents and RVs (30 feet maximum) with picnic tables and firegrills. Piped water and vault toilets are also available, boat docking and launching facilities are nearby, but no motorized craft are permitted on the lake. Open from late May to late September, $6-8 per night, depending upon the site. To get there, take U.S. 26 two miles southeast of Government Camp, and then right onto Forest Service Road 2656. Proceed for one mile to the campground.

A spot that offers good fishing, swimming, and windsurfing is **Clear Lake** (Bear Springs Ranger District, Route 1, Box 222, Maupin, 97037; tel. 328-6211). Here you'll find 28 tent and RV sites (22 feet maximum) with picnic tables and firegrills. Piped water, vault toilets, and firewood are also available. Clear Lake is open late May to early September, and the fee is $5 per night. Boat docking and launching facilities are nearby, and motorized craft are allowed on the lake. To get there, go nine miles southwest of Government Camp on U.S. 26, then one mile south on Forest Service Road 449 to the campground.

The east side of Mt. Hood is the kind of place where you'd almost expect Robin Hood and his band of merry men to come bounding out of the forest. While you may not come across these characters in your travels, you can nonetheless appreciate their spirit at **Sherwood** and **Robinhood** campgrounds (Hood River Ranger District, 6780 ORE 35, Parkdale, 97041; tel. 352-6002 or 666-0701 from Portland). Both feature about two dozen sites for tents and RVs set along the banks of Hood River, with picnic tables and firegrills. Piped water, pit toilets, and firewood are also available. Open from mid-May to early September, the two campgrounds charge $5 per night. The campgrounds are both set along the banks of Hood River.

A midsized county park called **Toll Bridge** (7360 Toll Bridge, Parkdale, 97041; tel. 352-6300) is located 18 miles south of Hood River on ORE 35. This campground has 18 tent and 20 RV (20 feet maximum) sites with electricity, piped water, sewer hookups, and picnic tables. Flush toilets, showers, firewood, a recreation hall, and a playground are also featured. Open April to November (and weekends during the off-season, weather permitting), $8 per night. Set along the banks of Hood River, this campground includes bike trails, hiking trails, and tennis courts.

PRACTICALITIES

Accommodations

Since Mt. Hood is only an hour away from Portland, most people return to the city instead of staying at one of the commercial properties on the loop. But if you do want to make a night of it on Mt. Hood, forgo the ersatz Swiss ski chalets, follow the signs from ORE 26, and step into history at **Timberline Lodge** (Timberline, 97208; tel. 800-452-1335 from outside Oregon, 231-7979 instate). This is Oregon's Hall of the Mountain King whose alpine setting and W.P.A.-commisioned interior decor make it a cherished landmark of the Northwest. Room rates ranging between $50-150 make it as affordable as a garden-variety ski condo, and numerous bargain ski packages also help lay out the welcome mat. Minutes away from Timberline's 1,100-pound door is a ski lift, your magic carpet to the slopes and, during the summer, an array of wildflowers and superlative views. Another Timberline claim to fame are pioneer and Indian motifs to match the mountain. Hand-forged wrought-iron light fixtures and hand-woven draperies and upholstery complement the 92-foot-high fireplace and floor-to ceiling windows in the lobby.

The food in the award-winning Cascade Dining Room is outstanding, particularly the pine-smoked salmon. Spirits can be purchased there, in the Ram's Head bar, and the Blue Ox bar. After a long day skiing the challenging slopes here, you'll relish a soak in the outdoor heated pool, especially enjoyable in the middle of a snowstorm or on cold clear nights under a full moon.

Food

It doesn't really matter what you've been up to on the mountain. Whether you've been skiing, hiking, climbing, or biking, the end result is usually the same by the time you get down the hill . . . you're hungry. The Mt. Hood corridor is blessed with several eateries that fit most any mood and pocketbook. From fast-food-on-the-fly to leisurely gourmet dining, it's all here on the loop.

Twenty years ago, chef Kurt Mezger got tired of cooking for the Benson Hotel in Portland, so he bought the **Chalet Swiss** (U.S. 26 at Welches Road, Welches, tel. 622-3600). The formality and high prices of his alma mater are left far behind, but the quality of the cuisine remains outstanding.

Ten Swiss and continental entrees are backed up with Northwest seafood specialties and premium cuts of beef. The Chalet also boasts one of the best wine lists on the mountain. Full-course meals range from $10-25 and can take an hour or two from appetizer to aperitif. A la carte selections ranging from $4-12 and wine by the glass provide a quicker and lighter alternative. Open for dinner only Wednesday through Saturday 5-10 p.m., 5-9 on Sunday.

One mile west of Zigzag on U.S. 26 in Wemme is **The Inn Between.** Open for lunch and dinner, here you can tour the taps (a dozen draft beers are available) and enjoy a steak cooked just the way you like it, because you supervise how it's cooked yourself. Tuesday night is when steak prices drop to $6.95 for the 12-ouncer and $5.95 for the smaller version. If you've got a beef against red meat, the Inn can prepare a feast to suit even the most discriminating of vegetarian palates. Seafood specialties, teriyaki chicken, and gourmet sandwiches are also among the many offerings. For lighter appetites, a variety of salads and delicious homemade soups are also available. On Monday nights, in addition to the football game on the big-screen TV, the Inn features 75-cent tacos that will fill you up in a hurry. If you're only here for the beer, try some barbecued ribs in the Inn's secret zesty sauce or perhaps the "Macho Nachos" to keep your blood alcohol level reasonable.

For some good, downhome cooking at a down-to-earth price, head to **Mary McCrank's at the Ivy Bear** (U.S. 26, tel. 622-3476), located eight miles east of Sandy. You'll know the food is good when you walk through the door, with a packed house and nonsmoking environment further enhancing the rich aromas. Open daily for dinner, a dozen rib-sticking entrees on the menu here that include salad, beverage (coffee, buttermilk, or tea), and dessert range from $7-12. Try the iron-skillet fried chicken, accompanied by mashed potatoes and gravy and tender carrots baked in cream and brown sugar. Finish your meal off with sour cream raisin pie, the most popular dessert in the restaurant.

One of the best family budget eateries on the loop is at the **Carnivorous Cantaloupe** (U.S. 26, Wemme, tel. 622-3055). Look for the blinking roadside sign about a mile west of Zigzag mounted on an old Ford pickup that points the way to some of the best pizza this side of ski heaven.

Pick-your-own combination pizzas are built on a tasty crust that is neither too thick nor too thin. Other additions to the menu include fish that's always fresh, never frozen, deep-fried Oregon-grown chicken, and burgers, shakes, and old-fashioned malts.

Another popular eatery in the shadow of Mt. Hood is the **Barlow Trail Inn** (9580 East U.S. 26, Zigzag; tel. 622-3877). Open from 6 a.m. to 2 a.m., the Inn features excellent three-egg omelettes that will keep you energized all day long. Vegetarians are sure to enjoy the marinara spaghetti ($5.25) or the veggie garden burger made with mushrooms, nuts, oats, and low-fat mozzarella. Homemade chili, chicken dinners, and moderately priced steak and seafood round out the menu.

The Store Natural Foods and Cafe (U.S. 26, Welches; tel. 622-3130) is located about a mile west of Zigzag in Welches; look for the sign of the carrot on the highway. This is a homey sort of place where the soup pot is always on, the fire flickering in the woodstove, and the atmosphere warm and relaxed. A wide variety of fruits, snacks, wholesome cookies, bread, and crackers are available at the store. The chalkboard lists hot/cold sandwiches, soups, and salads of the day. Fresh-roasted coffee and fresh-squeezed juices complement the other freshly made surprises on the menu. The collection of local arts and crafts and old lunchboxes from the golden days of children's television displayed here provide additional color to the decor.

If you want to spice up your evening, consider **Los Amigos Spanish Restaurant** (46881 S.E. U.S. 26, Sandy; tel. 668-5444). You won't need a cast-iron stomach to eat here, because the food is cooked Spanish style, not jalapenos-by-the-truckload Tex-Mex style. The sauces, tamales, and chorizo are all prepared on the premises, delicately seasoned with chili powder, Mexican oregano, cumin, garlic, and onions. Try the enchilada grande, a flavorful blend of ground beef and chorizo rolled in a corn tortilla and topped with a delectable sauce. The Los Amigos sopaipilla also differs from what other south-of-the-border greasy spoons provide. Instead of a flat, oily, and overly sugared concoction, the sopaipilla here is a yeast-risen bread that's grilled up fresh for you. Prepare to feast in a pleasant, smoke-free environment without having to mortgage the homestead to pay for it.

SOUTHEASTERN OREGON
LAKE COUNTY

One of Oregon's three largest counties, Lake County covers 8,359 square miles and yet has only a smidgen over 8,000 inhabitants. In other words, there's lots of elbow room, with the population density working out to about one person per square mile. This land of open spaces and geologic marvels is home to a hardy breed who cling to the traditions of the Old West. Cowboys herd cattle on horseback, itinerant prospectors dig for color in the Quartz Mountains, and homesteaders tend to their farms in the remote outback. The county is called the Gem of Oregon because of the stark beauty of wide-ranging vistas beneath skies of pastel blue, and because the region is the best place to find Oregon's official gemstone, the "Plush diamond," a type of spangled glass also called aventurine.

Visitors can climb the ancient citadel of Fort Rock, camp along a high mountain stream in the Fremont National Forest, soak their bones in the soothing mineral waters of Hunter Hot Springs, or watch the graceful strides of antelopes as they cross the uplands of the Hart Mountain Wildlife Refuge. In addition to enjoying outdoor activities year-round, the people of Lake County are an active bunch with a busy calendar of rodeos, fairs, and celebrations.

The climate here is generally cool and semiarid with 250 days of sunshine a year. Summer temperatures stay in the mid-80s, winter temperatures drop to the low 30s with precipitation averaging about 16 inches a year. This area can be a harsh land with little tolerance for the foolish, so take sensible precautions like toting extra water and gas. Despite a low density of creature comforts, you'll enjoy exploring this high desert country loaded to its sandy brim with wonders found nowhere else.

HISTORY

The history of human occupation here has been dated back to 13,200 years through Dr. Luther

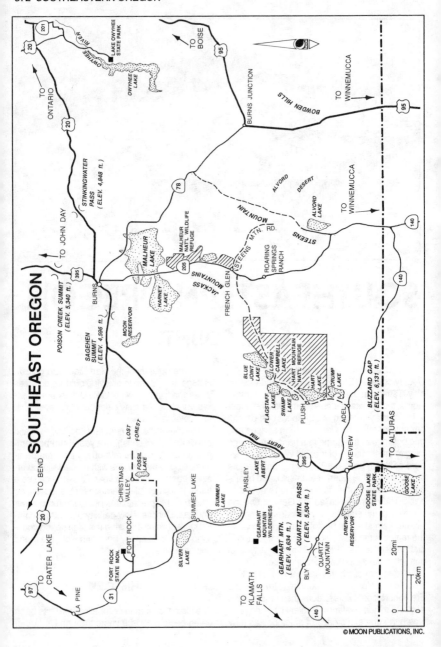

SOUTHEAST OREGON

© MOON PUBLICATIONS, INC.

Cressman's exploratory work at Fort Rock Cave. Early desert dwellers who roamed the Great Basin in search of game and food witnessed the eruption of Mt. Mazama 6,000 years ago. Their descendants, the Northern Paiutes, were also hunter-gatherers. This Lake County tribe was known as the "Groundhog Eaters."

The first Europeans to venture into the area were French Canadian trappers working for the Hudson Bay Company in the early 1800s. The guard hairs of America's largest rodent were used in the manufacture of felt hats, much coveted by the aristocracy of the time. Seeking out beaver pelts for the fashion trade back East and in Europe, these trappers were eventually joined by American mountain men. It wasn't until 1825 that Peter Skene Ogden, chief trader for the HBC, made an "official" tour of the area when he sensed the threat of an American incursion. John Fremont and a party guided by Kit Carson marched through here in 1843, naming Summer and Abert Lakes.

The journals kept during these expeditions noted broad valleys with grasses "belly-high to a horse." This information attracted a new cast of players to the Great Basin, the cattle and sheep barons. With the passage of the Homestead Act in 1862, homesteaders moved in and started up more modest spreads. The white influx resulted in frequent tensions with the original occupants, which often culminated in bloodletting on both sides. But after the Bannock-Paiute uprising in 1878, the local natives were herded up and banished to a reservation.

This predictable quick-fix eased the trouble on the frontier and led to a growth spurt. The town of Lakeview was chartered in 1889; it burned to the ground the following year and was rebuilt with brick and corrugated iron roofs. Other hopeful hamlets with names like Arrow, Buffalo, and Loma Vista sprang up around the county. Many of these tiny burghs dried up and blew away after the two-year drought of 1918-20. However, the larger communities like Lakeview, Paisley, and Summer Lake held on. With the advent of refrigerated railroad cars, big ranchers prospered, selling beef to our "hamburger nation." Local farmers figured out how to irrigate and cultivate this ornery land, and those tough enough to survive eventually came to terms with life on the dry side. Nonetheless, because riparian rights are still being clarified, many underground water tables are being drained, raising the spectre of another prolonged dry spell here.

SIGHTS: LA PINE TO LAKEVIEW

Lake County has some of the most intriguing geological formations in the Northwest. The following is a tour of a few of these marvels, starting at the junction of U.S. 97 and ORE 31 at La Pine.

Cracks And Caves
Twenty-six miles down ORE 31 is **Hole-in-the-Ground,** a curiosity located a mile off the highway. Although this 500-foot-deep indentation looks like a meteor crater, scientists believe that molten lava came into contact with water, causing a massive explosion that quarried out the quarter-acre pit. About five miles further down the road is **Fort Rock Cave.** Sandals over 9,000 years old

The 325-foot-high Fort Rock is visible from miles away.

PHOTO BY THE OREGON DEPT. OF TRANSPORTATION

woven from sagebrush were found here in 1938 by anthropologist Luther Cressman.

Not far from the cave is **Fort Rock,** which towers 325 feet above the sagebrush plains. **Fort Rock State Park** offers trails and amenities for climbers and sightseers. The nearby town of Fort Rock has an old-time flavor that has been accentuated by the recent restoration of homestead cabins in a pioneer village managed by the **Fort Rock Valley Historical Society** (tel. 576-2327).

An interesting journey down into the bowels of the earth is offered at **Derrick Cave,** located 22 miles north of Fort Rock. This large lava tube is a half-mile long with rooms up to 40 feet wide and 60 feet high. During the Cuban missle crisis of the early 1960s, the cave was turned into a fallout shelter. Metal doors were installed and provisions for 1,000 people were stockpiled. Fortunately, cooler heads prevailed and a nuclear confrontation was avoided. The supplies were plundered by vandals and the cave's civil defense status was eventually dropped. Another good place to cool off on a hot day is **South Ice Cave,** three miles past Derrick Cave. This quarter-mile long cavern has many rooms filled with stalagtites.

Eight miles north of Christmas Valley is another break in terra firma which will keep your imagination working overtime. **Crack-in-the-Ground** is about two miles long, 10-15 feet wide, and up to 70 feet deep. According to geologists, this dramatic fissure has been open for at least 1,000 years. A Bureau of Land Management picnic area is at one end of this curious landmark.

Fossil Lake

Fossil Lake is two miles east of Christmas Valley. This was once a watering hole for camels, elephants, and miniature horses during wetter times thousands of years ago. The water and animals disappeared when the climate changed, but their fossilized remains are still unearthed by paleontologists on sanctioned digs. Be aware that it is illegal to remove *any* fossils from the beds without proper authorization. Unfortunately, unscrupulous profiteers, many of them connected with the drug trade, have been looting these timeless treasures from the lake and other fossil-rich sites in eastern Oregon. Be sure to notify the authorities immediately if you see any suspicious characters pilfering these valuable relics.

Lost Forest

An unusual sight in this area is located ten miles northeast of Christmas Valley on a rough but passable BLM road. A 9,000-acre stand of Ponderosa pines intermixed with the largest juniper trees in Oregon is all that is left of an ancient grove that dates back thousands of years. This island of green is 40 miles away from the nearest forest, accentuating the isolation and solitude of these stately sentinels. Many of the junipers here are over a thousand years old. On hot summer days, this place is a source of shade. Any time of year, the sound of the desert wind through the trees can stir contemplation.

Summer Lake

Summer Lake lies 15 miles beyond Silver Lake. The old Harris school on ORE 31 in the town of Summer Lake is worth a picture. This classic one-room schoolhouse, complete with bell tower, is straight out of *Little House on the Prairie*. The highway also passes through the **Summer Lake Wildlife Area,** home to 170 species of migratory birds. Spring is the best time to see snow geese, avocets, black-necked stilts, and snowy plovers. Summer Lake Hot Springs, on the southern tip of Summer Lake, is a private operation open seven days a week from 9-9 during summer and Sat.-Thur. 9-6 during winter. A dip in the concrete pool costs $1.50 for people six and over, free to children under six.

Paisley

A few miles south of the lake is the cowtown of Paisley. At the **Paisley Ranger Compound** there are several structures built by the Civilian Conservation Corps during the Depression. Check out the dugout canoe carved from a pine tree by CCC workers for Forest Service personnel to use in nearby mountain lakes.

If you're getting a little hungry, there are a couple of eateries in Paisley that will satisfy your cravings. The **Homestead Restaurant** (tel. 943-3187) is the full-service establishment in the locale, serving breakfast, lunch, and dinner. The soup de jour complemented with a sandwich makes a good lunch, and be sure to save room after dinner for the homemade cobbler. The local watering hole, **Pioneer Saloon** (tel. 943-3289), doubles as a family eating place. Pizza, steaks, and Mexican food are among the offerings on the menu here.

Lakeview

The "big city" of the county (population 1,800) is Lakeview, and it's where you will find some interesting repositories of history. The **Schminck Memorial Museum** (128 S.E. Lakeview, 97630; tel. 947-3134) has over 5,000 antiques assembled by the American chapter of the Daughters of the American Revolution, and is open Tues.-Sat. 1-5 or by appointment. **Indian Village** (508 N. 1st, tel. 947-2833) boasts one of the West's largest arrowhead collections. The complex also has a restaurant and lounge which features eye-opening specials like scrambled eggs with diced mushrooms, toast, and coffee for $2. The gift shop offers turquoise and silver jewelry and, oddly enough, is where many working people buy their flannel shirts and cowboy hats. If you're in the mood for something different, cruise 15 miles south of Lakeview on U.S. 395 to **Stringer's** (tel. 947-4112). In addition to fine gifts, they produce the world's only wild plum wine and wild plum jam.

Abert Rim

Fifteen miles north of Lakeview on U.S. 395 is the Abert Rim, the highest fault escarpment in the United States. The rim rises 2,000 feet above Lake Abert. This unusual body of water has no outlet and is rich in brine shrimp which attract countless waterfowl and shorebirds. Due to its high salinity, it is hazardous to swim in the lake. Forest Service roads (see "Lakeview Ranger Station" under "Information" for routing on obscure byways) lead through the North Warner Mountains to BLM trails up to the back side of Abert Rim. While it is an arduous journey down bumpy back roads and a steep hike up the mountain, the view from the rim is spectacular.

Gearhart Mountain Wilderness Area

About 40 miles west of Lakeview off of ORE 140 is the 22,000-acre roadless Gearhart Mountain Wilderness Area. Accessible only by foot or by horseback, two major trails take adventurers into a challenging outdoor environment. **Gearhart Trail** (#100) incorporates 12 of the area's 16 miles of improved trails. This trail runs from **Look-out Rock** on the southeast corner of the wilderness, up over the mountain, down to **Blue Lake,**

and to a trailhead on North Creek. The **Boulder Springs Trail** (#100A) runs from the west side of the wilderness to a junction with the other trail a half-mile from the mountain summit. For maps and more information, contact the U.S. Forest Ranger offices in Lakeview, Paisley, or Silver Lake (see "Servies And Information" below).

While you're in the neighborhood, you might want to visit the **Mitchell Monument** on ORE 140 between the wilderness area and Bly that commemorates a tragedy that occurred on May 5, 1945. Reverend Archie Mitchell and his wife were escorting five children on a picnic near Corral Creek when one of the kids discovered a bomb dropped by a balloon from a Japanese plane. Unfortunately, the child triggered the bomb, and all but the good reverend were killed. This is the only recorded incident of World War II fatalities in the 48 contiguous states.

Hart Mountain National Antelope Refuge

At the far eastern end of the county is a wildlife

PHOTO BY FRANK LONG

Lake County is where the deer and the antelope play.

refuge that stretches across a high plateau rising above Warner Lakes. To get there from **Adel,** the first town east of Lakeview on ORE 140, go northeast 29 miles to **Plush** and take the road to the refuge headquarters. The station has information and a display describing this 275,000-acre sanctuary for pronghorns. The refuge is also home to bighorn sheep, mule deer, 213 species of birds, and many small mammals. A dunk in the hot springs a short distance from the station is highly recommended to take out the stiffness from bouncing down the dirt roads to get there. A campground is near the hot springs.

SPORTS AND RECREATION

In Town
The **Lakeridge Country Club** (ORE 140, tel. 947-3855) has a nine-hole golf course with a pro shop, putting green, lessons, golf cart rentals, and a pro shop. **Christmas Valley Golf Course** (Christmas Valley, tel. 576-2333) is another nine-holer next to a 130-acre man-made lake that's served by a pro shop in the nearby Christmas Valley Lodge. The restaurant here is the only full-service dining room in these parts.

On Friday, Saturday, and Sunday, the **Alger Theatre** (22 F St., Lakeview, tel. 947-2023) shows top-name films for $3.75 adults, $2 children ages 2-11.

Fishing
With a name like Lake County, you'd be right in thinking that there is all kinds of fishing here. Known for excellent trout fishing in the mountainous areas, the region is also gaining a reputation for bass crappies, catfish, and other warm water fishing. **Crump, Flagstaff, Anderson,** and **Campbell** lakes in eastern Lake County provide the hottest action for crappies. **Friday Reservoir,** located between Adel and Plush, is stocked with Lahontan cutthroat trout, and **Rock Creek,** which flows out of the Hart Mountain National Wildlife Refuge, has red-banded trout. In western Lake County, **Goose Lake,** half in California, half in Oregon off U.S. 395, is also home to the native red-banded trout, but it's hard to fish for this unique subspecies in the shallow water. **Drews Reservoir,** 25 miles west of Lakeview on ORE 140, offers excellent fishing for channel catfish—some as large as 10 pounds. In the northern sec-

tion of the county, **Thompson Valley Reservoir,** reached by driving south from Silver Lake on County Road 4-12, has yielded large rainbows. The **Chewaucan River,** which flows into Abert Lake, is heavily stocked with native trout.

Skiing
Winter sports play a major role in Lake County's recreational schedule. **Warner Canyon Ski Area,** seven miles east of Lakeview on ORE 140, can accommodate almost any level of Alpine and Nordic skier, with 14 runs and three miles of cross-country trails. Thanks to a mile-high base elevation and the dry southeastern Oregon climate, excellent dry powder conditions are common. The area has a day lodge near the base of the hill with a snack bar that serves breakfast and lunch. The season may start as early as mid-December and run through the end of March. During this time the hill is open from 1-4 p.m. Thurs.-Fri., 10-4 Sat.-Sun.

Rockhounding
Rockhounding is a popular hobby in Lake County. Best known for its abundance of sunstones (known as "Plush diamonds"), the area also has jasper, agates, petrified wood, fire opal, wonder stones, thunder eggs, and obsidian. To get to the sunstone hunting grounds, go east on ORE 140 to the Plush junction and turn north. At the first junction take Valley Falls Road and follow the signs. Another spot for rockhounding can be reached by taking Hogback Road just north of the upper section of the Abert Rim; the Hogback junction is about 50 miles north of Lakeview on U.S. 395.

PRACTICALITIES

Campgrounds
Junipers Reservoir RV Resort (tel. 947-2050) is 10 miles west of Lakeview on ORE 140. This private reservoir with campgrounds is situated on a working cattle ranch that's open April 15-Oct. 31, depending on the weather. Designated as one of six private wildlife viewing areas in the state, a visit to this spread offers an excellent chance to view longhorn cattle, deer, eagles, ospreys, and coyotes.

Goose Lake Campground is a large facility 15 miles south of Lakeview on U.S. 395. The campground has tent sites, RV hookups, and a

LAKE COUNTY ACCOMMODATIONS

Name	Address	Telephone	Price	Features
Desert Inn	Christmas Valley	576-2262	$17-23	kitchenettes with refrigerators
Rim Rock Motel	U.S. 395, Lakeview	947-2185	$22-30	cable TV, air conditioning, complimentary continental breakfast
Lakeside Terrace Motel and Restaurant	Christmas Valley	576-2309	$20	
Hunter's Hot Spring Resort	U.S. 395, Lakeview	947-2127	$23-32	pool, kitchenettes, restaurant/lounge, live entertainment
Interstate 8 Motel	354 N. K St., Lakeview	947-3341	$26-36	pets, kitchenettes, restaurant, laundry, complimentary continental breakfast
AA Motel	411 N. F St., Lakeview	947-2201	$28-30	modern, air conditioned units
Hart Mountain Store & Bed & Breakfast	Plush	947-2491	$30-40	
Lakeview Lodge Motel	301 N. G St., Lakeview	947-2181	$32-40	pets, kitchenettes, air conditioning, nonsmoking rooms
Best Western Motor Lodge	Skyline 414 N. G St. Lakeview	947-2194	$42-52	covered pool, air conditioning, laundry, nonsmoking rooms, complimentary continental breakfast

boat launch on the shore of this huge lake which dips down into California. **Corral Creek Campground** is a good headquarters for an exploration of the Gearhart Mt. Wilderness, an area of high meadows, cliffs, and worn-down volcanoes. To get to the campsite turn off ORE 140 at Quartz Mountain, 24 miles west of Lakeview, and drive north on Forest Service Road 3600. **Wildlife Refuge Campground** is on the Ana River just north of Summer Lake on ORE 31. Birdwatchers like to camp here and walk the dikes of Summer Lake looking for waterfowl and swamp mammals.

Food

Like most parts of the sagebrush side of Oregon, Lake County isn't known for its nouvelle cuisine. Be prepared for basic American food with an emphasis on hearty, home-cooked meals. Here's a list of eateries that won't enchant your palate, but they will refuel your tank.

The **AA Restaurant** (Lakeview, tel. 947-2563) has dinners that range from $4.25 for liver and onions to $9.95 for steak and shrimp combo. **Papa Dan's** (1217 N. 4th, Lakeview, 97630; tel. 947-2248) serves Mexican food, pizza, and sandwiches. Complete dinners range between $4-5 with a la carte available, including chile rellenos for $2 and tostada supreme for $4. They also deliver for a $2 fee unless the order is over $15, in which case the service is free.

For authentic Chinese cuisine, try the **King's Cafe** (27 N. F St., Lakeview, 97630; tel. 947-2217). For homemade grub like chicken baskets, pizza, burgers, and Mexican food, **Dan's Chuckwagon** (N. P St. and ORE 140, Lakeview, 97630; tel. 947-3436) is the place to go. Whenever you're hungry, **Jerry's** (508 N. 2nd, Lakeview, 97630; tel. 947-2600) is always open. The **Safeway** in Lakeview is also open 24 hours and is a good place to stock up on groceries prior to heading out into the boondocks. The **Duck Inn Restaurant** at Hunter's Hot Springs Resort offers steaks, seafood, and Chinese food. Many locals consider the best place in the county to be **Plush West** (9 N. F St., Lakeview, 97630; tel. 947-2353). They are open for dinner only from 5:30 p.m.

Entertainment And Events

The **Christmas Valley Rodeo** runs the last weekend in May. Local cowboys and cowgirls compete in bareback riding, roping, and races. The following weekend is the **Silver Lake Rodeo** with more of the same. During the last weekend in June, the **Lake County Junior Rodeo** is held at the Lake County Fairgrounds in Lakeview. Finally, the fall **Lake County Round-Up** and fair held Labor Day weekend at the Lakeview county fairgrounds includes a carnival, several parades, a barbecue, buckaroo breakfast, and the annual rodeo.

Many of the earliest pioneers in Lake County were Irish immigrants who worked as sheepherders, some of whom turned to cattle ranching. To celebrate St. Patrick's Day, Lakeview merchants hold **Irish Days,** with a parade led by the Grand Leprechaun, usually the town's oldest Irishman. Other popular events are the potato stick races and the cowchip fling. The community of Paisley prides itself on having some of the largest mosquitos in the state. To raise funds for controlling these pests, the town stages the **Mosquito Festival** in late July. The action includes a parade, a raft race, turkey shoot, spitting, lying, cussing, and hollering contests, and the crowning of Ms. Quito.

Around Christmas time people flock to the town's little blue post office to request a timely postal cancellation (done by hand and larger than machine-franking symbols). Collectors send a letter addressed to themselves with a request for a Dec. 24 or 25 cancellation. Such noel niceties can be obtained by addressing an envelope to Christmas Valley, Oregon 97641 and enclosing instructions.

In case you're interested, this nondescript alfalfa-farming town got its romantic name by accident. Southeast of here, John C. Fremont spent Christmas at a lake during one of his mid-nineteenth-century treks and called it Christmas Lake. A turn-of-the-century mapmaker mistakenly affixed this name to a lake adjacent to the present-day town site, which also took on the merry monicker.

Services And Information

The **Lake District Hospital and Nursing Facility** (700 S. J St., Lakeview, 97630; tel. 947-2114) has 24-hour emergency services. The **Lake County Chamber of Commerce** (tel. 947-2249) is located at the Lake County Courthouse. The **Lakeview Ranger Station** (U.S. 395 North, Lakeview, 97630; tel. 947-3334) has info on the nearby wildernesses. The **post office** (18 S. G St., Lakeview, 97630; tel. 947-2280) is open 9-5. The Lakeview **police** (525 N. 1st St., Lakeview, 97630; tel. 947-2029) are here if you have any trouble. **Fire and Ambulance** service is available by calling 947-2345.

Finally, should you ever need to call on someone here, be aware that the code of the frontier is fully operative. People gladly help each other out and expect nothing in return. Although the small population in a harsh land is extremely close-knit, people passing through need not ever fear being shunned as outsiders.

Getting There And Around

Buses depart twice a day from the **Red Ball Stage Lines Depot** (619 Center St., Lakeview, 97630; tel. 947-2255) for Klamath Falls and other connecting points. The depot is open from 9-11 a.m. for the 9:15 departure (10 a.m. on Saturday), and 4:15-5:15 p.m. for 5:05 departure. Public **airports** are located in Lakeview, Paisley, Christmas Valley, and Alkali Lake with private and government strips at Silver Lake, Fort Rock, Adel, and Wagontire. There are no regular commercial flights, but **Goose Lake Aviation** (tel. 947-4222) provides air taxi service and an air ambulance at the Lakeview field.

BURNS AND VICINITY

Harney County occupies 10,185 square miles of sagebrush, rimrock, and grassy plains that are shared by only 7,100 inhabitants. With an average elevation of 4,000 feet above sea level, this northern edge of the Great Basin has a short growing season, a yearly snowfall of 36 inches, and clear skies at least 250 days per year. The main industries are logging, milling, and cattle ranching, with farming limited to hearty grains and hay.

For travelers, the towns of Burns, Hines, and a few wide spots along U.S. 20 hold few points of interest—just places to refuel your rig and yourself. But off the main thoroughfares traversing the southeastern portion of the state are recreational retreats worthy of closer investigation. The Malheur Wildlife Refuge is nationally recognized as one of the best birdwatching sites in the country; the Steens Mountain Recreation Area is also famous for its stunning scenery; and the Ochoco and Malheur National Forests are renowned for their fishing, boating, camping, backpacking, and hiking opportunities.

HISTORY

Oregon's high desert county was first inhabited by Bannocks, Northern Paiutes, and Shoshone Indians. When French Canadian trappers arrived in the area, they were promptly ripped-off by the natives. After losing horses and supplies, the trappers named the nearby river "Malheur" ("unhappiness" or "bad hour," depending on what source you use).

Explorer Peter Skene Ogden scouted the area in 1826 while leading a fur brigade for the Hudson Bay Company. He wasn't impressed with the region as a place for settlers, but the Idaho gold rush of 1860 brought prospectors through the area on their way to the gold fields who told stories of rich grasslands, plentiful water, and broad forests.

Pony soldiers under the command of General William Harney explored the region in 1848 and again in 1858, opening up southeastern Oregon to settlement. The most noted military adventure was a wagon road built between Harney County and Eugene. The leader of this work party, Enoch Steen, gave his name to Steens Mountain.

In 1878, 2,000 Bannocks, fed up with their loss of territory and poor treatment, took to the warpath. Troops from forts all over the West were sent to fight the natives in a war that dragged on until 1880.

The town of **Burns**, named after the Scottish poet Robert Burns, was founded on January 22, 1884. By 1889 it had a population of 250, which has since grown to over 3,000. A significant boost to the town's economy came in 1924 when a rail line reached Burns. It's sister city, **Hines**, was incorporated in 1930. Named after Chicago lum-

Steens Mountain, rising abruptly above Mann Lake

PHOTO BY OREGON STATE HIGHWAYS

berman Edward Hines, this town of 1,400 residents is primarily a bedroom community for Burns.

SIGHTS

Sagehen Hill Nature Trail

The Sagehen Hill Nature Trail is 16 miles west of Burns at the Sagehen Rest Stop on U.S. 20. This half-mile nature trail has 11 stations on a route that takes you around Sagehen Hill through sagebrush, bitterbrush, and western juniper. Other plants found along the way include lupine, larkspur, owl clover, and yellowbell. The lucky visitor in the spring (early May) may also catch the sage hen courtship ritual. The male will display his plumage and make clucking noises to attract the attention of the ladies. If these feathered friends are not visible, the views of Steens Mountain (elevation 9,733) to the southeast can make the hike worthwhile.

THE CATTLE KINGS OF EASTERN OREGON

Cattle barons, those imperious characters in old Western movies, and more recently, the "crusty but benign" Ben Cartwright of television's "Bonanza," have given us an image of those early-day entrepreneurs who ran the huge livestock operations of the 19th century. They were two-fisted, hardheaded men who brooked little interference in their affairs. Redskins, sheepherders, and homesteaders beware! A quick look at the lives of three Eastern Oregon cattle kings confirms some of this stereotype, yet John Devine, Pete French, and Bill Brown were unique individuals with personalities that are still talked about today.

John Devine came to Oregon in 1686 and started snapping up land by the simple method of squatting on it. He grabbed U.S. government land, Indian territory, and acreage ostensibly owned by road companies which he quickly covered with vast herds of cattle. Part of his holding included the Alvord and the Whitehorse ranches on the east side of the Steens. After the devastating winter of 1889-90, during which he lost 75% of his stock, Devine's fortunes plummeted. He was bought out by another cattle baron, Henry Miller, and only held on to the Whitehorse Ranch until his death in 1901 at the age of 62.

Another rancher whose fate is still debated in this arid country is Pete French, an arrogant, forceful man with a bushy mustache that gave him the appearance of Wyatt Earp. Born in Red Bluff, California in 1849, French moved to Oregon in 1873 to manage the stock ranch of Dr. Hugh Glenn, in the Blitzen Valley. French married the boss's daughter, and after Glenn was murdered by his bookkeeper, French built the French-Glenn Livestock Company into one of the largest spreads in the West. At its peak, the ranch had 100,000 acres on which roamed 30,000 head of cattle

and 3,000 horses. Five hundred miles of barbed wire defined this empire stretching from the Blitzen River to Harney Lake.

While he was developing the P Ranch, French earned the enmity of hundreds of local homesteaders, many of whom were evicted from their squatter's shacks. One of his enemies, homesteader Ed Oliver, rode up to French one day and shot him dead. Oliver was arrested but later acquitted by a jury of settlers.

Bill Brown was a more popular and certainly more eccentric rancher than Pete French. His Gap Ranch, headquartered a few miles east of Hampton, halfway between Brothers and Riley, was at its largest 38,000 acres spread throughout four counties. Bill Brown didn't start out rich and he died penniless. In between he earned and lost a number of fortunes. His first enterprise was running a flock of 400 sheep. During that era he was so hard up he only owned one sock which he switched to the other foot every day. Brown added horses to his holdings with such zeal that by the advent of World War I, he owned 25,000 head, many of which he sold to the U.S. Cavalry. After the war and with the advent of mass production of automobiles, Brown lost his shirt and his land. Many stories have been told about this balding six-footer with a square jaw and a mild manner. He never cussed, drank, or gambled, unless his faith in his store customers could be considered gambling. The operator of a mercantile, Brown was seldom behind the counter, relying instead on the honesty of his customers, who were asked to toss their cash in a cigar box. Another quirk was Brown's legendary habit of writing checks on anything available, from tomato can labels to wooden slats. Local bankers had no problem cashing the "checks" for Brown's hired help or suppliers.

Harney County Museum

The Harney County Museum (18 W. D Street, Burns, 97720; tel. 573-2636) started its career as a brewery and then became a laundry and a wrecking yard. Local pioneer families have donated its displays of quilts, furniture, complete kitchen, a wagon shed, and machinery. Of special interest are artifacts from Pete French's ranch. The museum is open June through September, Tue.-Fri. 9-5, Sat. 9-noon. Admission is $1.50 adults, $2 for a family, and 50 cents for children.

Diamond Craters

Diamond Craters have been described by scientists as the most diverse basaltic volcanic features in the United States. To tour these unique formations, drive 55 miles south of Burns on ORE 205 until you reach the Diamond Junction. Turn left and begin a 40-mile route ending at New Princeton on ORE 78. On the way you'll see why this area is called "Oregon's Geologic Gem." There are craters, domes, lava flows, and pits that give an outstanding visual lesson on volcanism. To aid your self-guided tour, pick up the Diamond Craters brochure at the BLM office in Hines.

Round Barn

While on the road to New Princeton, stop at the Round Barn, a historic structure built by rancher Pete French to break his saddle horses. Located 20 miles northeast of Diamond, the barn is 100 feet in diameter with a 60-foot circular lava rock corral inside. Twelve tall juniper poles support a roof covered with 50,000 shingles. Hundreds of cowpokes have carved their initials in the posts of this famous corral.

Malheur National Wildlife Refuge

Malheur and Harney lakes, fed by the mountain snow runoff from the Blitzen and Silvies rivers, have been major nesting and migration stopovers since prehistoric times. The contrast between the stark, dry basin land with its red sandstone monoliths and mesas, and the lush green marshes is startling. These vast marshes, meadows, and riparian areas surrounded by the eastern Oregon desert attract thousands of birds and hundreds of birdwatchers. Bring binoculars and take time to pull over and observe Canada geese, pelicans, avocets, teals, mallards, and other waterfowl.

Refuge officials say that 250 species have been counted within its boundaries.

In the late 1800s, settlers enjoyed unrestricted hunting here and at the turn of the century, plume hunters killed thousands of swans, egrets, herons, and grebes for feathers for the millinery trade. In 1908, President Theodore Roosevelt put a stop to the slaughter by protecting the area as a bird sanctuary. The Blitzen Valley and P Ranch were added to the refuge in 1935. Today, 185,000 acres are protected.

To get to the refuge drive 25 miles south from Burns on ORE 205 and then nine miles east on the county road to Princeton. The last six miles to the refuge headquarters are gravel surfaced. Of interest at the headquarters are a museum, an information center, and a charming park on the edge of the lake. For information on the refuge, call 493-2612.

Frenchglen

Named for Pete French and his father-in-law, Dr. Hugh Glenn, who bankrolled the famous rancher, the town of Frenchglen was originally known as P Station and was part of the nearby P Ranch. Today, this historic community with its hotel, store, corral, and post office remains essentially the same as it was 50 years ago. To get there, drive about 60 miles south on ORE 205 from Burns.

Steens Mountain

Steens Mountain, named after Major Enoch Steen, an army officer assigned to the task of building a military road through Harney County, is one of the great scenic wonders of Oregon. A 30-mile fault block, the mountain rises straight up from the Alvord Desert to a row of glacial peaks. On the western side, huge gorges carved out by glaciers a million years ago descend to a gentle slope drained by the Donner and Blitzen River, which flows into Malheur Lake. Steens Mountain has five vegetation zones ranging from tall sage to alpine tundra. The best way to see the transition is to drive the **Steens Mountain Road** out of Frenchglen to the top of Steens Mountain. This is the highest road in Oregon, rising 9,720 feet in elevation. The first 15 miles of the road are gravel and the last nine miles are dirt. The last portion of this road is not recommended for low-slung passenger cars.

Steens Mountain Loop

A good way to see the Steens area is via the Steens Mountain Byway, a 52-mile adventure starting and ending at Frenchglen. The first four miles of the trek lead across the Malheur Wildlife Refuge and up to the foothills of Steens Mountain. **Page Springs,** the first campground on the route, is a popular spot offering campsites along the bank of the Donner and Blitzen River. Approximately 13 miles beyond Page Springs is **Lily Lake,** a good place for a picnic. This shallow lake has an abundance of water lilies, frogs, songbirds, and waterfowl. After Lily Lake, you really start to climb up the mountain to **Fish Lake, Jackman Park** (both with campsites), and viewpoints of Kiger Gorge and the East Rim. **Kiger Gorge** is a spectacular example of a wide, U-shaped path left by a glacier. The **East Rim** is a dramatic example of earth-shifting in prehistoric epochs. The lava layers which cap the mountain are thousands of feet thick, formed 15 million years ago when lava erupted from cracks in the ground. Several million years later, the Steens Mountain fault block began to lift along a fault below the east rim. The fault block tilted to the west, forming the gentler slope that stretches to the Malheur Lake Basin.

The area has off-highway vehicle restrictions to protect the environment. Five gates controlling access to the Steens are located at various elevations and are opened as road and weather conditions permit. Normally, the Steens Byway is not open until mid- to late July and is closed by snow in Oct. or November. Gas is available only in Burns, Frenchglen, and Fields. Take reasonable precautions when driving the loop: sudden storms, lightning, flash floods, and extreme road conditions can be hazardous to travelers. The loop returns to ORE 205 about 10 miles south of Frenchglen.

Catlow Valley/Alvord Desert Loop

Another equally ambitious loop is the drive around Steens Mountain along the Catlow Rim and Alvord Desert and back to Burns. Starting at Burns head south on ORE 205 through the Malheur Wildlife Refuge, past Frenchglen, and up over the divide into the Catlow Valley, which was once a massive inland lake. A side trip to the ghost town of **Blitzen** starts at a right turn (to the west) four miles south of the Steens Loop Road. This eight-mile jaunt will take you to the ruins (a half-dozen dilapidated buildings) of a little town

founded in the late 1800s. Blitzen was named after the Donner and Blitzen River which flows nearby. *Donner und blitzen* is German for thunder and lightning, the label given this stream by Captain George Curry, who tried to cross it during a fierce thunderstorm.

The next point of interest on the loop is **Roaring Springs Ranch,** tucked under the west rim of Steens Mountain. Originally homesteaded by Tom Wall, the ranch was sold to Pete French and in later years developed into the largest cattle operation in the county. The dramatic backdrop, well-kept classic ranch building, and the surrounding meadows makes Roaring Springs Ranch an ideal Western movie set.

After driving 33 miles through the Catlow Valley you'll come to **Fields,** the largest community on the east side of Steens. Homesteaded by Charles Field, the town was established as a supply station in 1881. Fields now has a gas station, store, cafe, and motel. Fields's original stone cabin is across the road from the store and cafe.

From Fields head north into the Alvord Desert, site of the dry Alvord Lake and home to the Alvord Ranch. Along the way you'll pass through **Andrews,** a small community at the edge of the alkali flats. Another stop worthy of attention, particularly if you're in need of revitalization after your travels, is the **Alvord Hot Springs** a few miles north of Andrews. This rustic spa is recognizable from its corrugated steel shack on the east side of the road. Two pools of hot mineral water piped in from spring runoff will cook your bones and soak away your aches and pains at no charge. The road continues on until it connects with ORE 78, which leads back to Burns or south to Burns Junction. The panorama of the east side of Steens Mountain alone is worthy of a trip, but views of the **Pueblo Mountains** to the south and the Great Basin country to the east are also impressive.

Oard's Free Museum

Oard's Free Museum (tel. 493-2535) is located 23 miles east of Burns on U.S. 20. The museum has antique guns, clocks, barbed wire, spinning wheels, and dolls as well as native artifacts, including a Yakima chief's costume. Hours are 7 a.m. to 8 p.m. every day.

Paiute Reservation

If you want a livelier encounter with Native American culture, visit the Burns Paiute Reservation.

Contact the tribal headquarters first for information; either call them at 573-2088 or write to HC-71, 100 Pa' Si' Go Street, Burns, 97720.

SPORTS AND RECREATION

Golf

Harney County's "Oasis in the Desert" is the nine-hole **Valley Golf Club** (345 Burns-Hines Highway, Burns, 97720; tel. 573-6251). This challenging course is open to the public, but clubhouse facilities are reserved for members and guests.

Rockhounding

Harney County is rockhound country. Each year, thousands of these enthusiasts flock to this far-flung corner of the state to collect fossils, agates, jasper, obsidian, and thunder eggs. The **Stinking Water Mountains**, 30 miles east of Burns, are a good source of gemstones and petrified wood. Thunder eggs can be dug up four miles south of Oard's Museum on U.S. 20 after getting permission from the Don Robbins family. Contact them through the museum. **Warm Springs Reservoir**, just east of the Stinking Water Mountains, is popular with agate hunters. **Charlie Creek** and **Radar**, west and north of Burns respectively, produce black, banded, and brown obsidians. Be sure to collect only your limit—be a rockhound, not a rockhog. Also keep in mind that it is illegal to take arrowheads and other artifacts from public lands.

Fishing

Rainbow and red-banded trout occur naturally in most streams in this area and many lakes and rivers are also stocked. Good fishing is available on the Donner and Blitzen and Malheur rivers, Emigrant Creek, Chicahominy Reservoir, Delintment Lake, and Yellowjacket Lake. Krumbo Reservoir on the Malheur Wildlife Refuge is a good bet for trout or largemouth bass.

PRACTICALITIES

Accommodations

If you're seeking shelter in Burns, you'll find that the properties here are generally inexpensive, have air conditioning to help you beat the heat, and allow you to bring the family dog along too. The **Orbit Motel** (Highways 20/395, Burns, 97720; tel. 573-2034) features a pool, nonsmoking rooms, cable TV, and wheelchair access; their rates range from $24-40. Another bargain is the **Silver Spur Motel** (789 North Broadway, Burns, 97720; tel. 573-2077) which offers nonsmoking rooms, a weight workout room, and a complimentary continental breakfast for $23-33. You get treated like a king at the **Royal Inn** (999 Oregon Ave., Burns, 97720; tel. 573-5295). Enjoy the tennis courts, two swimming pools, and a decent restaurant without paying a king's ransom. Rates range from $34-36. The **Best Western Ponderosa Motel** (577 W. Monroe, Burns, 97720; tel. 573-2047) features a swimming pool, nonsmoking rooms, and large spacious rooms for $34-39.

The **Frenchglen Hotel** (tel. 493-2825) is 60 miles south of Burns and is an excellent place to

The Frenchglen Hotel is a restored turn-of-the-century hotel.

PHOTO BY OREGON DEPT. OF TRANSPORTATION

stay while visiting the Steen Mountains or Malheur Wildlife Refuge. Built in 1914 as a stage stopover in historic Frenchglen, the hotel has rooms from $30-40 and ranch cooks ready to fix you a family-style breakfast, lunch, or dinner. The hotel's season runs March to November.

Campgrounds
There are three high-elevation campgrounds along the Steens Mountain Loop Road. **Page Springs,** four miles southeast of Frenchglen, is open all year. Close to the Malheur Wildlife Refuge, the campground is a good headquarters for birdwatching, fishing, hiking, and sightseeing. **Fish Lake** is the next campground, located 17 miles east of Frenchglen. Open July 1-November 15, the lake is stocked with eastern brook, cutthroat, and rainbow trout. **Jackman Park** is three miles east of Fish Lake and is particularly popular with backpackers who use it as a takeoff point. There is no potable water at the site so be sure to tote your own. All of these campgrounds cost $3 per night for each vehicle. Write the BLM, Burns District HC-74 P.O. Box 12533 Hwy. 20 West, Hines, 97336; tel. 573-5241.

A couple of campgrounds to the north of Burns up in the Malheur National Forest are **Yellowjacket** and **Idlewild.** Yellowjacket is on the shore of Yellowjacket Lake, 30 miles northwest of Burns on Forest Service Road 2170. As the name implies, be sure to keep your food under wraps, especially meats, if you want to avoid being visited by the namesake hosts of the lake. Idlewild is 17 miles north of Burns on U.S. 395. There is no charge for overnighting in either spot, but don't expect amenities either.

Food
Steens Mountain Cafe (195 Alder, Burns 97720; tel. 573-7226) is an anomaly—a first-rate restaurant in a town known for its lousy chow. Chef Tony is proud of his sourdough breads, pancakes, waffles, and pizza crust. He also has a big selection of deli sandwiches from $2.95-4.95, and chicken parmesan or spaghetti dinner for $4.95. His deep-dish and regular pizzas run from $8.95-11.95.

Silver Sage (239 North Broadway, Burns 97720; tel. 573-7878) has both American and Mexican meals, a salad bar, and beer, wine, and cocktails. Their buckaroo burger with ham, cheese, fries, and salad is $4.30. Dinner entrees include fajitas for $7 and rib steaks with salad bar and homemade bread for $10.75.

Entertainment And Events
In mid-April, the **John Scharff Migratory Waterfowl Festival** held in Burns celebrates the spring return of waterbirds to the region with lectures, movies, slides, and guided birdwatching tours. For information on the festival call 493-2612. Harney County, once the trapping territory of mountain men like Peter Skene Ogden and Joe Meek, has two blackpowder clubs which relive those days with a yearly **Blackpowder Shoot and Rendezvous.** The **Steens Mountain Men** hold their shoot in September and the **Harney Free Trappers** hold theirs in June. These rendezvous attract colorful gatherings of folks in buckskin talkin', shootin', lyin' and renewing friendships "afore last winter." For information on dates and locations call Bigfoot at 573-7814 or Silver Fox at 573-7554.

Steens Mountain Days is held in early August. Centered in Frenchglen, the fun includes a 10-km run along the Steens rim, sagebrush roping contest, barbecue, street dance, and beer garden. During the last weekend in June, the sky is filled with lighter-than-air ships for the **High Desert Hot Air Balloon Rally** at the Burns Union High School. Burns is also the site of **Obsidian Days** in mid-June, as well as the **Harney County Fair** and the Rodeo and Race Meet held in early September.

Information
For general information on the region, contact the **Harney County Chamber of Commerce** (18 W. D Street, Burns, 97720; tel. 573-2636). For information on recreation, stop by the **Bureau of Land Management** office (12533 West U.S. 20, Hines, 97738; tel. 573-5241). The **Burns and Snow Mountain Ranger District** is also nearby (Box 12870, U.S. 20, Hines, 97738; tel. 573-7292).

If you need the law, the Burns and Hines City **police** (tel. 573-6028) and the Harney County **sheriff** (tel. 573-7281, or after 5 p.m. and weekends, 573-6028) are there to help. The **post office** (222 North Broadway, Burns, 97720, tel. 573-2931) is open 9-5 weekdays.

Burns is serviced by **Trailways Bus Lines** (682 North Broadway, Burns, 97720; tel. 573-2736). The Burns Airport (87A, Rural Route HC 71, Burns, 97720; tel. 573-6139) is five miles from town.

U.S. 26: PRINEVILLE TO SUMPTER

Prineville, the geographic center of Oregon, is a fitting starting point for this route across the north-central section of the state. Coming from the west, you drop down from tall bluffs into the Crooked River Valley and nearing the city, cruise through hills dotted with juniper. White and black magpies dart in front of your car and redwing blackbirds observe your passing from their fence-posts. A thriving community and the county seat of Crook County, Prineville has a population of 5,000, gets a meager 10 inches of rain a year, and relies on agriculture, wood products, and tourism for its economy. The town is also known as the Gateway to the Ochocos, a heavily wooded mountain range that runs east-west for 50 miles. One of Oregon's least known recreational areas, the Ochocos are still ruggedly pristine. Beyond these mountains stretches the long valley of the John Day River. In the vicinity are also the famous John Day Fossil Beds, the historic goldmining camps of Canyon City and Sumpter, and another wild country called the Strawberry Mountain Wilderness.

Just as the fossil beds provide a cross section of the earth's history, a trip down U.S. 26 will give you a feel for the leather-tough countryside of central eastern Oregon and the people who settled here: the second-generation pioneers from the Willamette Valley, the Basques, Scots, and Irishmen from the old countries, and the Chinese who came to pick over the tailings left by goldminers in a hurry. Their combined heritage is here for the finding, along with night skies unobscured by city lights and diverse wildlife roaming the surrounding plains and forests.

HISTORY

The Ochocos

The Ochoco country, named after a Paiute Indian word for willows, was heavily populated by natives who lived off a bounty of deer, elk, fish, and camas roots. The first significant passage of Europeans other than trappers through the area was the Lost Wagon Train of 1845. Led by Stephen Meek, brother of the Oregon Territory spokesman Joe Meek, the pioneers were seeking an easier route to the Willamette Valley than the arduous trek over the Blue Mountains. Instead, they found hardship, starvation, thirst, and death on a tortuous journey through the deserts of Malheur and Harney counties and along the rugged ridges of the Ochoco Mountains. Their hardships finally ended when they found the Crooked River and followed it north to The Dalles. Somewhere during the trek, members of the party scooped up gold nuggets and kept them in a blue bucket. Though the legend of the Blue Bucket Mine has since captivated fans of Oregon history, its actual site has never been found.

In 1860, Major Enoch Steen led an expedition through the region, which resulted in a number of geographic areas being named after him, including Steens Mountain and Stein's Pillar. Eight years later, Barney Prine built a blacksmith shop, a store, and a saloon near the bank of Ochoco Creek which grew into the city of Prineville, the only town in 10,000 square miles. It was settled by the sons of the pioneers who came West in the wagon trains. It was their turn to carve out a life from the wilds.

At the turn of the century, cinnabar, the raw ore in which mercury is found, was discovered in the Ochocos, which brought an influx of miners. About the same time, a range war broke out between the cattlemen and sheepherders. Groups like the Ezee Sheep Shooters and the Crook County Sheep Shooters Association bragged that they had slaughtered 8,000 to 10,000 sheep in 1905 alone. Incensed by this lawlessness, the citizens of Oregon moved to stop the killing, but troubles continued for cattle and sheep ranchers and farmers. Harsh winters took their toll on livestock, and the hope that the plains would be receptive to wheat farming didn't work out.

During World War I, many homesteaders gave up and moved to the cities to work for the war effort. In 1917, Prineville made a decision that would boost the local economy. They built a railroad to Redmond, linking their line with the Union Pacific. Used primarily to haul ponderosa pine logs, the railroad remains the only city-owned railroad still in operation in the United States. In the

1950s a new industry was added to the main-stays of logging, ranching, and farming. Gem-stones of high quality were discovered in the Ochocos, prompting a rockhound/tourism boom that continues to this day.

One peculiar historical note of interest: ever since its establishment in 1882, Crook County has proved a bellwether county, giving the majority of its vote to the winner of every presidential race.

John Day Region

A string of communities runs east from Prineville, beginning with Mitchell, followed by Dayville, Mt. Vernon, John Day, Canyon City, and Prairie City. The early history of this stretch of the John Day Valley centers around the discovery of gold in 1862. According to most estimates, 26 million dollars in gold was taken out of the Strawberry Mountain Wilderness. At the peak of the gold rush, Whiskey Flat, later called Canyon City, was populated by 5,000 miners, which made it larger than Portland at the time. Thousands of Chinese immigrated to the area to work the tailings, or left-overs, from the mines. The impact of the Chinese miners is celebrated every year during Kam Wah Chung Days (see "Entertainment And Events") in John Day.

One of the more colorful denizens of Canyon City was the celebrated poet Joaquin Miller, who served as the first elected judge in Grant County. Known as the "Byron of Oregon," this dashing fig-ure dressed like Buffalo Bill and orated his florid sonnets to a baffled audience of miners.

Lastly, the area generated an irony common in history: John Day, the man whose name was at-tached to a river, a valley, and a town, never saw any of them. A hunter from Virginia, Day was hired to provide meat for the Pacific Fur Compa-ny Expedition led by Wilson Price Hunt. Thirty miles east of The Dalles, near what was then known as the Mau Hau River, Day and another mountainman were attacked by Indians and left naked and injured. The river soon became known as Day's River; mapmakers later changed it to the John Day River.

SIGHTS

Prineville

A good place to begin your travels in Ochoco country is at the **A.R. Bowman Museum** (246 N. Main St., Prineville, 97754; tel. 447-3715), open 10-5, Mon.-Fri. and Sat. 12-5. This museum's two floors of exhibits and displays are a notch above most small-town historical museums. Fans of the Old West will enjoy the tack room with saddles, halters, and woolly chaps. Rockhounds will be delighted with the displays of Blue Mountain pic-ture jasper, thunder eggs, and fossils. Other clas-sic displays are a campfire setup with a granite-ware coffee pot and pound of Bull Durham tobac-co, a moonshine still, a country store, and an up-stairs parlor of the early 1900s.

Stein's Pillar

Once out of town, the country east of Prineville starts to shift from juniper flats to pine ridges. One landmark that stands out is Stein's Pillar, a 300-

---

ADOPT-A-WILDERNESS PROGRAM

Most of eastern Oregon is public land under the ju-risdiction of the Bureau of Land Management. One of the laws that governs the BLM's management of these millions of acres of semiarid steppes is the Federal Land Policy and Management Act (FLPMA) of 1976, which mandates a review of all BLM roadless areas for possible inclusion in the Wilderness Preservation System. Of the five mil-lion acres inventoried, the BLM is recommending protection of 1.1 million acres. Conservationists are calling for twice that amount. To convince Congress to meet the conservationists' acreage requests, an Adopt-A-Wilderness Program has been initiated with the goal of preparing a collec-tion of on-site reports called the Sage Alternative. Sponsored by the Oregon Natural Desert Assoc-iation, the program invites desert-lovers to pick an area to adopt as their own. The "parents" go on field trips, gather information, take photographs, prepare slide shows, brochures, portfolios, and other profiles as evidence that their small portion of the desert needs to be preserved in its natural state.

To get involved, contact ONDA (Box 1005, Bend, 97709; tel. 385-6908), the central clearing-house for the program. Then lace up your boots, grab your hat, and get out there!

foot monolith which rises like a rocky forefinger out of the pines. To get to this impressive column of stone, take the Mill Creek Road at Ochoco Lake, six miles east of Prineville. Stein's Pillar will be on your right. The scenic route back to Prineville from the Mill Creek Wilderness on McKay Road takes you by some exquisite meadows and clear mountain streams.

Lookout Mountain

Another side trip of note is a visit to the Lookout Mountain Special Management Area. Located in the Ochocos, it's a unique biosphere with 28 plant communities and one of the finest stands of ponderosa pines in the state, lots of elk and deer, and creeks full of rainbow and brook trout. A seven-mile trail starts at the Ochoco Ranger Station 22 miles east of Prineville on County Road 22, and ends at the summit of Lookout Mountain from which 11 major peaks are visible. Friends of Lookout, a coalition of environmental and recreational groups, invites you to visit the area and lend your support to efforts to secure legislation protecting this unique habitat.

John Day Fossil Beds

The next sights as you travel east are among the most prominent tourist stops in eastern Oregon. In the 1860s, self-taught geologist Thomas Condon discovered what is now known as the John Day Fossil Beds. These archives of stone provide a paleontological record of the 70 million years and five geologic epochs of life on this planet. The days of 50-ton brontosaurs and 50-foot crocodiles as well as the delicate imprints of ferns and flowers are captured in the rock formations of the three beds, easily visited in a day's excursion.

The first stop, the **Painted Hills,** is 50 miles east of Prineville on U.S. 26. Turn left at the sign and go six miles to the site. Although the view from the road is impressive, you really have to get out and hike the trails to literally get the picture. The **Fossil Leaf Trail** will lead you to remnants of a 30-million-year-old hardwood forest. The **Carroll Rim Trail** takes you to the top of Carroll Rim for a spectacular view of the Painted Hills. The **High Desert Trail** is a three-mile loop out into the desert for those seeking the quiet and solitude of the big empty.

The next bed, the **Clarno Formations,** can be reached by taking ORE 207 north of Mitchel to Service Creek, then ORE 19 to Fossil and ORE 218 to Clarno. After passing through Fossil, the Clarno Formations are 18 miles west. The **Clarno Arch Trail** will get you up into the formations to the base of the Eroded Palisades, the Petrified Logs, and the Clarno Arch. A scenic little side loop through the ghost town of Twickenham will take you down through a canyon with sandstone pillars looming like gargoyles, huge juniper trees, and green creek-bottom meadows—just follow the signs through this little wayside. The banded cliffs are so close you can almost reach out and touch them! The road connects with ORE 19 at Butte Creek Pass.

The third area of the John Day Beds, the **Sheep Rock Unit,** can be reached by driving back down ORE 19 to Service Creek, where you turn east and follow the John Day River to **Spray** and **Kimberly** and then south for 20 miles. The trails here include the **Sheep Rock Overlook Trail, Island in Time Trail,** and the **Blue Basin Trail.** The Sheep Rock Unit is also home to the **Cant Ranch Visitor Center,** headquarters for the National Park Service which maintains the John Day Fossil Beds National Monument. The center has an excellent interpretive exhibit, books and informational pamphlets, and a knowledgeable staff who will answer your questions.

The address is John Day Fossil Beds National Monument, 420 W. Main, John Day, 97845; tel. 575-0721. There's not much camping here but "Selected Local Campgrounds of Grant County," put out by the Grant County Chamber of Commerce (281 W. Main, John Day, 97845; tel. 575-0547), lists what's available.

Where East Meets West

After visiting the John Day Fossil Beds, head east to the town of John Day. A must stop while in town is the **Kam Wah Chung and Company Museum** (250 N.W. Canton, tel. 575-0028). It's open from May to October, Mon.-Thurs. 9-noon. Weekend hours are 1-5, and the museum is closed Friday. No admission is charged to this collection of numerous artifacts; also featured are replicas of a general store, a pharmacy with over 500 herbs, a doctor's office, Chinese temple, and home. The building was constructed as a trading post on the Dalles Military Road in 1866-67. It soon became the center of Chinese life in the John Day area, serving as a general store, herbal pharmacy, hotel fortuneteller's studio, casino, assay office, and Taoist shrine. When you consid-

Sheep Rock looms over the John Day Fossil Beds.

PHOTO BY OREGON STATE HIGHWAYS

er that John Day had twice as many Chinese residents as Caucasian in the 1880s, it's clear that this museum is not some arcane exhibit but rather an important window on the past.

Museums

Another repository of local history is the **Grant County Historical Museum** in Canyon City, a couple of miles south of John Day on U.S. 395. The museum is open June 1 through September 30, Mon.-Sat., 9:30-4:30, Sun. 1-5. Centered in the heart of Oregon's mining and ranching country, the facility's wealth of memorabilia depicts the early days of Grant County and includes an extensive rock collection plus Chinese and Native American items.

The **Dewitt Museum** (South Main, Prairie City) is housed in the old western terminus of the Sumpter Valley Railroad, which operated between Baker and Prairie City from 1909 until 1947. The depot was restored in 1979 and today has ten rooms full of artifacts from Grant County's early days. Open from May 15 to October 15, the museum hours are Thurs. to Sat., 10-3 p.m.

While not an official museum, the ghost town of **Whitney,** located 12 miles up ORE 7 from its junction with U.S. 26 (about 15 miles east of Prarie City), has a story to tell to those who visit its ruins. Whitney was the terminus for stage lines to the mining and cattle towns of Unity, Bridge-port, and Malheur City. Now abandoned buildings are all that remain of this bustling community of the early 1900s. An interpretive sign just off ORE 7 explains the local history.

Sumpter

Traveling north of Whitney, you come to the **Sumpter Valley Wildlife Area,** a 158-acre site located between Phillips Reservoir and Sumpter on ORE 7. Canada geese, ring-necked ducks, bitterns, and Virginia rails can be seen in the wetlands and gravel dredge remains along the Powder River.

A few miles north of the refuge is Sumpter, a gold mining town in the Elkhorn Mountains. To get there, turn off U.S. 26 at Austin and drive 22 miles on ORE 7 through the Sumpter Valley to this historic little town. The first settlers were five Southerners who built a stone cabin and christened it Fort Sumter after the South Carolina garrison which was shelled in April of 1861, signaling the start of the Civil War. In 1883, the U.S. post office rejected the name, so locals changed it by dropping the "Fort" and adding a "p." The heyday of gold mining in the area was 1900-05, when over 3,000 miners worked the hardrock mines and dredged the Powder River. By 1905, most of the gold was gone, but dredging continued until 1954.

One of the attractions of the Sumpter area is the **Sumpter Valley Railroad Excursion.** Passengers ride in two observation cars pulled by a wood-burning, narrow-gauge steam engine originally used to haul logs, ore, and people. The seven-mile run from Phillips Lake to Sumpter costs $4 for adults, $3 for children under 16. The railroad is open from Memorial Day weekend through the last weekend in September with four runs daily at 10 a.m., noon, 2 p.m. and 4 p.m. From July 7 through September 2, the railroad adds a moonlight ride that departs at 8 p.m.

When you're ready to leave Sumpter, there are three travel options. You can retrace your route back to U.S. 26 and continue east to Vale and Ontario or head west toward U.S. 97 and Bend. Another possibility is to drive 19 miles east on ORE 7 to ORE 245, and then north nine miles to Baker. The third choice, the **Elkhorn Drive National Scenic Byway**, takes you northwest from Sumpter through the gold mining territory to Granite, across the north fork of the John Day, past Anthony Lake, and on to Baker.

SPORTS AND RECREATION

Lakes
Prineville Reservoir, 17 miles south of Prineville on ORE 27, was built for irrigation and flood control and covers 310 acres. A popular year-round boating and fishing lake, it is famous for its huge bass. **Ochoco Lake,** six miles east of Prineville on U.S. 26, is a favorite recreational spot for locals, with year-round fishing, boating, and camping (see"Camping" under "Practicalities").

Rockhounding
The Ochocos are prime rockhound territory, with free public collecting areas operated by the Rockhound Pow-Wow Association. Two good sites are off of U.S. 26. **Whistler Springs** is between mileposts 49 and 50. Turn left on Forest Service Road 27 for about six miles, then turn right onto Forest Service Road 500 and follow it to the springs. The collection area is near the campground. **White Fir Springs** is a good spot for jasper-filled thunder eggs. To get there, drive to milepost 41, turn left on Forest Service Road 3350, and follow it five miles to the diggings.

Riding The Ranges
Ever dreamed of going on a cattle drive? You can do it for real in the John Day River Valley with the cowboys of the **Cottonwood Ranch** (Box 334, Dayville, 97825; tel 987-2134). The two-day trip includes camping in tipis, chuckwagon dinners and breakfast, a hayride, and a barbecue. The cost is $250 per person.

A more civilized way to spend the day might include a round of golf at the **Mountain View Country Club** (tel. 575-0179). Located just west of John Day on U.S. 26, this nine-hole golf course accepts greens fees from nonmembers.

PRACTICALITIES

Accommodations
The **Rustlers Roost Motel** (960 W. 3rd, Prineville, 97754; tel. 447-4185) was designed in the Old West style. Art by local artists and antique furniture grace the rooms. Rates start at $29.95 for a single and $34.25 for a double. The **Prineville Reservoir Resort** (HC 78, Box 1300, Prineville, 97754; tel. 447-7468) is on the shoreline of Prineville Reservoir, 17 miles southeast of Prineville on the Paulina Highway (ORE 27). This resort offers motel accommodations with kitchenettes starting at a double for $48. Camping units go for $12. The resort also rents fishing and paddleboats and motors.

The **Elliot House Bed and Breakfast** (305 W. 1st, Prineville, 97754; tel. 447-7442) is a classic Queen Anne-style home which was entered on the National Register of Historic Places in 1989. In keeping with the 19th-century flavor of the house, the hosts serve a sumptuous breakfast and later a formal tea at 3 p.m.. Not as fancy, but handy if you find yourself in Fossil for the evening, is the **Fossil Motel and Trailer Park** (Box 282, Fossil, 97830; tel. 763-4075). Owner Nancy Grimm invites you to "sleep in a fossil bed." Rates are $20-35. If you find yourself in a similar situation in John Day, try the **Dreamer's Lodge** (144 Canyon Blvd., John Day, 97845). There's air-conditioning and a fridge in every room. Rates are $28-32. **Bed and Breakfast by the River** (Route 2, Box 790, Prairie City, 97869; tel. 820-4470), located on a working ranch by the John Day River, is a good takeoff spot for hiking in the nearby Strawberry Mountain Wilderness, fishing or rafting on the river, or just basking in country hospitality. Rates are $25 and $50 per day for double occupancy.

Camping

For good campsites in the Ochocos, take the Ochoco Creek Road approximately 10 miles east of Ochoco Lake. Choices include **Ochoco Camp, Walton Lake** (where you can fish, boat, or hike the trail to Round Mountain), **Wildwood,** and **Ochoco Divide.** Open from mid-April to late October, these campsites cost $7 per night. While on this loop, stop at the mining ghost town of **Mayflower.** Founded in 1873, the community was active until 1925. A stamp mill is still visible.

Strawberry Fields Forever

The **Strawberry Mountain Wilderness,** a pocket mountain range southeast of John Day, offers a good system of trails, seven lakes, volcanic rock formations, and if you're lucky, glimpses of bighorn sheep. Set up your base camp at **Strawberry Campground,** eight miles south from Prairie City on County Route 60, then two miles on Forest Service Road 6001. Open from June to mid-October, Strawberry's fees are $4 per night. The campground is next to Strawberry Creek and is the trailhead for jaunts to Strawberry Lake, Strawberry Falls, and Strawberry Mountain. As you might guess, chances are good you'll find some of these wild berries along the way!

If your travels find you in this neighborhood in winter, try the groomed snowmobile and cross country ski trails which run from the Austin House in Bates (at the junction of U.S. 26 and ORE 7) to Sumpter, a distance of 23 miles. For more information on the trails, contact this roadhouse (Box 8, U.S. 26, Bates, 97817; tel. 488-2387).

Food

If you get hungry while in Prineville, you can try a folksy little spot called **Barr's Cafe** (887 N. Main, Prineville, 97754; tel. 447-5897). It's open 24 hours with breakfast served around the clock. The top-of-the-line restaurant in town is the **Ochoco Inn and Cinnabar Restaurant** (123 E. 3rd, Prineville, 97754; tel. 447-3888) You'll find the ubiquitous Western motif in a building built on the site of the Jackson Hotel, which burned in 1922, and the Prineville Hotel, which went up in flames in 1966. The restaurant makes generous bunkhouse deli sandwiches from $4.50-6.50 and features a hazelnut pesto fettucine dish for $7.75. The eclectic menu is highlighted by a seven-ounce steak marinated in whiskey, worchester-

shire sauce, red wine, and herbs for $8.95. Cheers!

A more traditional approach to beefsteak is favored by the **Grubsteak Mining Company** (149 E. Main St., John Day, 97845; tel. 575-1970). Their best deal is an eight-ounce rib-eye steak for $11.50. Thirteen miles east of John Day you come to **Prairie City,** currently going through a transition into a tourist town similar to Sisters in central Oregon. One of the prime examples of this renovation is **Ferdinand's** (128 Front St., Prairie City, 97869; tel. 820-9359). This colorful watering hole in a refurbished butcher shop built in 1902 has a carving of a bull over the front door, and inside sports a collection of antiques, cougar hides, and old photos on the walls. Be sure to check out the two carved maidens, called the Twin Virgins, over the classic long bar. The figures were sculpted in Milan, Italy in 1879, and they and the bar furniture made the trip around the Horn, up the Columbia River on a sternwheeler, and then to Prairie City by wagon. Ferdinand's has a full menu of surprisingly urbane fare which can be washed down with microbrewery beer and ale from Portland.

Finally, if you have a car full of hungry children, you might want to fill them up in the **Elkhorn Saloon and Family Restaurant** (tel. 894-2244) in Sumpter. The claim to fame here is a homemade combo pizza, weighing in at five pounds, for $16.95.

Entertainment And Events

The **Central Oregon Timber Carnival** is held in Prineville during the second week in May with a parade, equipment display and logging show, men's and women's logrolling, and a tug-of-war between loggers and Forest Service workers. For more information call 447-5031. Another popular Prineville get-together is the **Annual Prineville Rockhound Show and Pow-Wow** (Box 671, Prineville, 97754; tel. 447-6760), held in mid-June. The powwow attracts prospectors and rockhounds from all over the country. The first week in July is the time and Prineville is the site for the **Crooked River Roundup,** with pari-mutuel horse racing. The restored cars of the Prineville Railroad make special trips during the summer, including a **4th of July barbecue run.** Check with the Prineville Chamber of Commerce for details.

Down the road a ways, Mt. Vernon holds its **Cinnabar Mountain Rendezvous** May 26-28. The rendezvous includes a parade, dance, community potluck, and lumberjack contest. **Kam Wah Chung Days** in John Day are held in late April to celebrate the Chinese heritage of the area. A full schedule of events includes rickshaw races, a Chinese checkers tourney, flower arranging demos, puppet theater, and a Chinese parade. Another midsummer festival is **'62 Days** in Canyon City, just south of John Day on U.S. 395, which celebrates the local discovery of gold in 1862 with a medicine-wagon show, can-can girls, and a reenactment of the opening of historic Sel's Brewery. The **Elkhorn Crest Sled Dog Races** in January and the **Rooster Crowing Contest** in July are two popular Sumpter events. On the first weekend of August the town sponsers the **Old Time Fiddler's Contest** and the **Sumpter Valley County Fair and Flea Market,** one of the largest crafts shows and flea markets in the Northwest.

Services
The **Pioneer Memorial Hospital** (1201 N. Elm, Prineville, 97754; tel. 447-6254) has 24-hour emergency services. In John Day, medical help is available at the **Blue Mountain Hospital** (170 Ford Road, John Day, 97845; tel. 575-1311). The **3rd St. Shell and Food Mart** (550 W. 3rd, Prineville, 97754; tel. 447-4476) is open 24 hours. The **Laundry and Dry Cleaners** (250 E. 4th St., Prineville; tel. 447-3126) is also open 24 hours, with dry cleaning available, 9-5, Mon.-Fri. In John Day, you can get your clothes clean at the aptly named **Weary Traveler Laundromat** (755 S. Canyon Blvd., John Day, 97845; tel. 575-2076).

Information
Here's how to get in touch with people who can help you in case of trouble or direct you down the right trail.

For general information, the **Prineville-Crook County Chamber of Commerce** (390 N. Fairview St., Box 546, Prineville, 97754; tel. 447-6304) is a valuable resource. If you need the law,

the **Prineville City Police** (400 E 3rd St., Prineville, 97754; tel. 447-4168), the **Crook County Sheriff's Office** (308 E. 2nd St., Prineville, 97754; tel. 447-6398), and the **state police** (400 E. 3rd St., Prineville, 97754; tel. 447-4168) are always ready to serve you. In the next county over, the **John Day Police** (240 S. Canyon Blvd., John Day, 97845; tel. 575-0030) and the **Grant County Sheriff's Office** (200 S. Canyon City Blvd., Canyon City, 97820; tel. 575-1131) are also at your beck and call. Out here in the wide open spaces, these numbers can sometimes prove useful.

The two newspapers in the area are the *Central Oregonian* (558 N. Main, Prineville, 97754; tel. 447-6205), which publishes twice a week, and the *Blue Mountain Eagle* (714 E. Main, John Day, 97845; tel. 575-0710) that's circulated weekly on Thursdays.

The Prineville **post office** (155 Court, Prineville, 97754; tel. 447-5652) is open Mon.-Fri. 6:30 a.m.-5:15 p.m., Sat. 6:30 a.m.-4:30 p.m. The John Day post office (151 Canyon Blvd., John Day, 97845; tel. 575-1306) keeps similar hours.

The Ochoco National Forest is administered from the following offices: **Prineville Ranger District** (2321 E. 3rd., Prineville, 97754; tel. 447-3825), **Paulina Ranger District** (6015 Paulina Star Route, Paulina, 97751; tel. 447-3713), **Big Summit Ranger District** (Box 225K, Mitchel Start Route, Prineville, 97754; tel. 447-3845), **Snow Mountain Ranger District** (Star Route 4, Box 12870, ORE 20, Hines, 97738; tel. 573-7292), and the **Malheur National Forest Office** (139 N.E. Dayton St., John Day, 97845; tel. 575-1731).

Getting Around
Prineville Airport (tel. 447-2833), two miles west of Prineville, is a fixed-base operator facility serviced by Rimrock Aviation. The **John Day Airport** (Airport Road, John Day, 97845; tel. 575-1151) has no commercial flights but does have a charter service. Prineville is served by **Greyhound** (1825 E. 3rd., Prineville, 97754; tel. 447-5516), and no buses serve John Day and vicinity.

NORTHEASTERN OREGON
ALONG THE OLD OREGON TRAIL

The pioneer trek along the Oregon Trail, a tide of migration starting in 1841 and lasting over 20 years, is one of this country's great epochs celebrated in novels, films, books, and songs. The wagon trains started in Independence, Missouri as soon as the spring grass was green. Then the race was on to get across the far mountains before the winter snows. Although the first few hundred miles were easy traveling across the plains, the hardships were not long in coming. Indian attacks, cholera, exhaustion, drownings, and in some cases, bad directions gave this 2,000-mile journey the nickname of "The Longest Graveyard."

At Fort Hall in eastern Idaho, there was a fork in the trail and a sign which read To Oregon. It was here that the pioneers had to make a key decision. They could head south to California and the gold fields shining with the promise of instant wealth, or they could continue west to Oregon where the fertile valley of the Willamette offered its own allure as a New Jerusalem for serious farmers and homesteaders. Those who chose Oregon crossed the Snake River near Ontario,

the Malheur River at Vale, and followed the wagon ruts north to lose sight of the Snake at Farewell Bend. The route is now paralleled by I-84 through Baker, La Grande, Pendleton, and on down the Columbia River Gorge to Portland. The towns along this modern Oregon Trail reflect the heritage of the pioneer era. The character and tenacity of those who chose Oregon over California can be seen in the sunburned, wind-creased faces of these sagebrush citizens. The following section offers a tour of this region, starting with Ontario and traveling northwest.

Located midway between Portland and Salt Lake City in Oregon's "far east," Ontario is where "Oregon's day begins." It's the biggest city in Malheur County with a population of 9,750. Ontario ships over five percent of the nation's onions and provides a good portion of the sweet russet potatoes used for french fries. Other local crops include sugar beets and peppermint.

Baker, set in a valley between the Wallowas and the Blue Mountains, is the jumping-off spot for Hells Canyon, the deepest gorge in the world.

Ranchers still drive their herds down the highways here, and folks wave howdy to passers-by. It's a friendly place that has held on to its pioneer spirit.

La Grande, located in what the indigenous peoples called Copi Copi (the surrounding "Valley of Peace"), is now known as the Grande Ronde Valley. Home of Eastern Oregon State College, La Grande enjoys a brisk economy based on beef ranching, wheat farming, and timber.

HISTORY

Ontario, the town at the beginning of the Oregon section of the Oregon Trail, began as a cattle-shipping depot. The 1883 completion of the Oregon Short Line Railroad connected it to the Union Pacific and markets in the East. In 1939, man-made reservoirs began irrigating the Snake River Valley, turning it into a rich agricultural region. During World War II, relocation centers for Japanese Americans were built here. The only crime these citizens committed was having the wrong ancestry. Stripped of their rights by a single executive order signed by President Roosevelt, about 5,000 Americans of Japanese ancestry were forced to liquidate their property and move into prison-like barracks in remote sections of the West. This serious breach of constitutional freedoms remains one of the saddest chapters in American history. It's also worth noting that many of of these unjustly incarcerated pariahs fought in the European theater of war in some of the most decorated units in the American Armed Forces.

In any case, a good percentage of the internees stayed in the area and now are well represented in the local business and agricultural communities. As in the Columbia Gorge, Japanese surnames grace many a ranch or farmstead in eastern Oregon. The U.S. Senate has appropriated money for a museum here documenting the internment. It's expected to be built at Treasure Valley Community College and should be open by the time you read this book. An influx of Hispanic migrant workers who came to work the crops in the 50s and 60s also stayed to start new lives, adding yet another ethnic flavor to the cultural stew in Ontario.

Baker, the next major town up the line, was named after Col. Edward Baker, Oregon's first senator and a one-time law partner of Abraham Lincoln. Baker City got its charter in 1874 and soon became known as the "Queen City," for all roads led to this commercial center. In 1861, it became the hub of the eastern Oregon gold rush and its population swelled to 6,600, making it bigger than Boise. Stop by the U.S. National Bank there and check out the 80.4-ounce "Armstrong" gold nugget found in 1913 on display. Pioneer cattleman Herman Oliver recalls his visits to Baker as a young boy. He remembers the trolley car that ran the length of Main Street for a nickel. When the conductor reached the end of the line, he pulled a pin holding the horse and led the animal to the other end of the trolley and hooked it up for the return trip.

La Grande, the third city on the Oregon Trail, is in a valley where the Nez Perce once gathered

Leslie Gulch in Malheur County

PHOTO BY OREGON TOURISM DIVISION

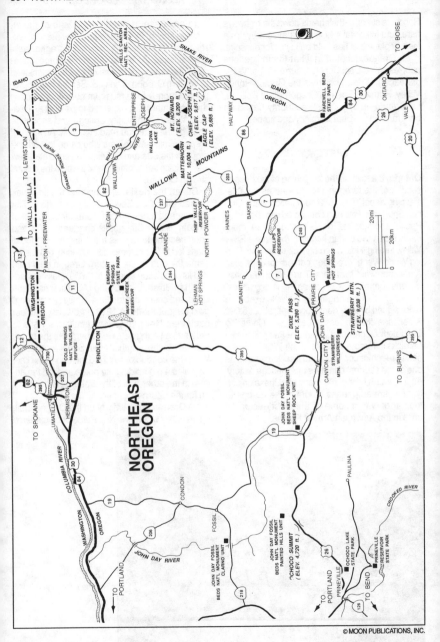

© MOON PUBLICATIONS, INC.

OREGON'S NEW GOLD RUSH

California's "Days of '49," and other historic gold rushes in Alaska, Colorado, and Oregon have given us a colorful image of gold mining, with bushy-bearded miners in plaid shirts and red long johns panning for the glitter in sparkling mountain streams. But a new gold rush in Oregon has a less romantic edge to it—the use of cyanide to leach gold dust from pulverized earth.

At Grassy Mountain near Vale in Malheur County, Quartz Mountain in southern Lake County, Farewell Bend north of Ontario, and the Bohemia Mountains near Cottage Grove in the Willamette Valley, mining corporations are investing millions in a new process that promises to extract the last flakes of the yellow stuff which is now worth between $400-500 an ounce. The process is called heap leach-mining and it's a lot cheaper than underground mining. A gridwork of ammonia nitrate and diesel fuel is detonated, and the tons of earth loosened by the explosion are ground up and spread out in huge plastic-lined ponds. Then a solution of cyanide and water is sprayed over the ore. The solution leaches out the gold and other metals. The mining corporations expect to get $370 million from the Grassy Mountain project and up to $1.5 billion from the Quartz Mountain mine. The jobs that these operations bring to local areas will be welcomed in a time of uncertain employment in rural Oregon. But there is a definite down side.

Gary Brown of Ontario is a member of Concerned Citizens for Responsible Mining. He states that the cyanide leaching is dangerous and destructive. It contaminates the water table, attracts and poisons birds and animals, and uses up 50 times more the amount of earth as underground mining.

Like offshore oil exploration, the harvesting of ancient forests, and the damming of scenic rivers, this new gold rush will be another battleground for the ongoing conflict between environmentalists and natural resource-dependent industries.

---

for their summer encampments until the Oregon Trail cut through their territory. More than a few of the pioneers were impressed with the possibilities of the Grande Ronde country. They stayed to build a town that became the market center for a broad stretch of wheat and grass seed farms. Lumber from the Blue Mountains and livestock which fattened easily on lush fields of tall grass also helped the Oregon Trail pioneers' dreams come true.

SIGHTS

Vale And Oregon Trail Sites

Vale, the county seat of Malheur County, is located on the Malheur River at the spot where the wagons crossed the river, 28 miles west of Ontario on U.S. 20/26. If you're intrigued by the drama of the pioneers, this little town offers an abundance of historic insight. On your visit to Vale, look north to **Malheur Butte** at mile marker 254. This long-extinct volcano was used as a lookout point by Indians watching for the wagon trains. The next historical site is **Malheur Crossing** on the east edge of Vale. The pioneers stopped here to take advantage of natural hot water from underground thermal springs to bathe and do their laundry. The **Keeney Pass Oregon**

Trail Historic Site, on the southern outskirts of Vale, has a display of the deep ruts cut into the earth by iron-tired wagon wheels. This exhibit marks the most used route of the wagon trains as they passed through the Snake River Valley on their way to Baker Valley to the north. Another site of interest is the **Stone House,** one block east of the Courthouse on Main Street. Built in 1872, it replaced a mud hut way station on the trail.

National Historic Oregon Trail Interpretive Center

On a small promontory called **Flagstaff Hill** near Baker is the 23,000-square-foot Oregon Trail Interpretive Center (Box 854, Baker, 97814; tel. 523-6391) that houses a theater, artifacts, photographs, and diaries of Oregon Trail pioneers. Exhibits on Native Americans, the fur traders, and the soul seekers round out the historical perspective. Outside the building you see the panorama of the Blue Mountains, the Lone Pine Valley, and the Oregon Trail itself. A re-creation of living history is featured at the **Pioneer Encampment,** where interpretive demonstrations life give you an up-close view of what life was like on the trail. Your next stop is an authentic **mining camp,** site of one of the earliest gold strikes along the trail. Get a taste of gold fever through the exhibited remnants and depictions here. There are five miles of nature walks and trails that have much the same flora and fauna that the pioneers saw, compounding the impression that the sky and the land were the only signposts along the 2,000-mile-long Oregon Trail. At last, you come to the famous thoroughfare itself and you can follow the footsteps of the 227,000 people who made the epic transcontinental trek. Some say that if you are out here alone, close your eyes, and tilt your head to one side, you can still hear the grunts and groans of man and beast as they wearily slog along their way to the promised land.

Oregon Trail Regional Museum

The Oregon Trail Regional Museum (Campbell and Grove Streets, Baker, 97814; tel. 523-9308) is open daily from 10-4 from the second weekend in May through the third weekend in September. As well as exhibits depicting the great migration, the museum houses an extensive collection of seashells and corals and one of the most comprehensive exhibits of rocks, minerals, and semiprecious stones in the West.

Crossroads Center

Crossroads Creative and Performing Arts Center (2020 Auburn Ave., Baker, 97814; tel. 523-3704) is in the old Carnegie Library. It has monthly exhibits, a gift shop, and an Arts and Crafts Fair held July 17-19. While you're at the Crossroads Center, ask for a pamphlet describing the **Baker's Dozen,** a tour of the town's historic homes.

Eastern Oregon Museum

The Eastern Oregon Museum (3rd and School, Haines, 97833; tel. 856-3568) is open every day from 9-5 from April 15 to October 15 and has an outstanding collection of farming, mining, and pioneer artifacts.

Geographical Center Of The United States

According to local wags, the geographical center of the United States shifted dramatically with the addition of Hawaii and Alaska, to a spot 12 miles north of Medical Springs, where ORE 203 meets Catherine Creek. (Apologies to Port Orford on the south coast which also claims this title; obviously, different frames of reference are being used or someone is trying to hype the public.) As with claims by several places in the state for being the westernmost location in the continental lower 48

or the only place to have sustained a shelling in World War II, another dubious distinction is up for grabs out here in the desert.

Hot Lake

Hot Lake Mineral Hot Springs (tel. 963-5587) was considered "Big Medicine" by the western tribes who camped near its healing waters. The lake, located five miles east of La Grande on ORE 203, was also a popular spot for explorers and emigrants. In 1864, Samuel Newhart built a hotel and bathhouse here. A hospital was added at the turn of the century and it soon became known as the Mayo Clinic of the West, a polite euphemism for one of the Northwest's first "fat farms." During that era, the healing waters here were also thought to give relief from arthritis and rheumatism. Recently, the resort has reopened, with a soak in its 80-year-old porcelain-lined cast iron tubs costing $7. Hot Lake is open Wed.-Sun from 1-4 p.m.

North Powder Elk Views

North Powder Elkhorn Wildlife Management Area is a winter elk feeding station open for visits (by permit) from December 1 to April 15, but viewing is possible from nearby county roads in late afternoon and evening. To get there, go west 10 miles from Exit 285 off I-84. Viewpoints are one mile south of the headquarters on River Road and two miles north of headquarters on Tucker Flat Road. These Rocky Mountain elk are somewhat smaller than the Roosevelt elk commonly seen on the west side of the Cascades.

Deadman's Pass

Deadman's Pass, at Exit 228 on I-84, led emigrants out of the Blue Mountains into the Umatilla Valley. This was the last big hump they had to cross before the raft trip down the Columbia. The name comes from three incidents during the Bannock Indian War of 1878 in which seven men were killed. Look for a sign directing you up a trail to a sampling of still visible wagon ruts.

SPORTS AND RECREATION

The country through which the Oregon Trail passes is filled with recreational choices. Here's a short rundown of possibilities. **Ontario-Shadow Butte Golf Course** (tel. 889-9022) is an 18-hole municipal course with pro shop and lounge two miles west of Ontario. **Bully Creek Reservoir,** 30-minutes' drive west of Ontario near the small town of Vale, has boat launch facilities, picnic and camping areas, swimming, and water-skiing. The fishing includes crappie, bass, trout, and perch. **Anthony Lakes Ski Area** (tel. 800-762-7941) is between Baker and La Grande, 18 miles west of North Powder and Haines on I-84. Open November through April from 9-4, this ski resort has a chairlift, Nordic trail system, day lodge, ski shop, and ski lessons. All day tickets are $16.50; children under 10 pay $11.

Camping
Of the many campsites in the Wallowa Whitman National Forest, here are four of the best. **Grande Ronde Lake Campground** along the shore of the lake has all the amenities and good trout fishing as a bonus. The fee is $3 per night. To get there drive 17 miles northwest of Haines on ORE 411, then eight miles west on Forest Service Road 73. The camp is one-half mile northwest on Forest Service Road 43. **Sherwood Forest Campground** is a small site on the banks of the Grande Ronde River. There is no fee for this campground which is open late May to late November. Go nine miles northwest of La Grande on I-84, then 13 miles southwest on ORE 244. From there, drive six miles south on Forest Service Road 51. A third site, **Hilgard Junction State Park,** is also on the Grande Ronde River, at the foot of the Blue Mountains. Fees for this full-service campground are $5 per night. To get there drive eight miles west of La Grande on I-84 to Starkey Road. The fourth site is **Emigrant Springs State Park,** a large facility with flush toilets, a laundromat, and playground right off I-84. The fee is $8 per night. This park has a display on the Oregon Trail and is a good spot to stop while traveling on the interstate.

PRACTICALITIES

Accommodations
These lodgings, ranging from affordable to fancy, should make your own trek along the Oregon Trail far more comfortable than it was 150 years ago. The **Fireside Motel** (1737 N. Oregon, Ontario, 97914; tel. 889-3101) will run you $18-28. The **V Motel** (64 N.E. 3rd Street, Ontario, 97914; tel. 889-2631) costs $17.95.

Closer to the other end of the scale, the **Grant House Bed and Breakfast** (2525 3rd Street, Baker, 97814; tel. 523-4364) charges $50. This large, four-story inn boasts an outdoor hot tub and five sleeping chambers, including the Gore Vidal and Cybill Shepherd rooms. The **Sunridge Inn** (1 Sunridge Lane, Baker, 97814; tel. 523-6444) has a heated pool and private patios and is this town's high-priced spread with rates from $40-50. The **Western Motel** (3055 10th Street, Baker, 97814; tel. 523-4646) is a more economical choice with rates from $22-26. If you don't feel like dining in their restaurant, you can whip something up in your own kitchen. **Stange Manor** (tel. 963-2400) is a Georgian colonial mansion built by a timber baron. Period furniture and views of the mountain make this a steal at $50 for two.

The **Union Hotel** (326 N. Main, Union, 97883; tel. 562-5417) will take you back to another era with a room and bath for $14. The town of Union is 11 miles southeast of La Grande on ORE 203. Lots of great old brick buildings and oldtime atmosphere. The **Moon Motel** (2116 Adams Avenue, La Grande, 97850; tel. 963-2724) is the most affordable lodging in town with rates from $18-20. Lastly, the **Pitcher Inn Bed and Breakfast** (608 N. Street, La Grande, 97850; tel. 963-9152) is a 1925 Georgian home with a honeymoon suite with private bath and three more rooms sharing two baths. It's open all year except Jan. 2-15. Rates are $50-75.

Food
Not too many recommendations on this route, but here's a few worth tucking in your napkin for. The **Cheyenne Social Club and Lounge** (11 S.W. 1st, Ontario, 97914; tel. 889-3777) was named after a bawdyhouse run by Jimmy Stewart in a 1970 Western. Lunches run from $4.25-9, and dinners from $9-25, primarily steak and seafood entrees, all in a late 19th-century setting.

Blue and White Cafe (1825 Main, Baker, 97814; tel. 523-6792) is an institution. For nearly 40 years this cafe has been selling coffee for a dime and cinnamon rolls for 25 cents. You'll have to vie for counter space here with a bunch that calls itself the Main Street Nearly Honest Senile Businessmen. For a more hearty breakfast try the biscuits and gravy!

A sure bet for a good all-American meal is the **Farm House Restaurant** (401 Adams, La

Grande, 97850; tel. 963-9318). Sandwiches cost $3 and dinners $6. If you appreciate "gourmet" (by La Grande standards) Mexican food try **Mamacitas** (110 Depot, La Grande, 97850; tel. 963-6223). Entrees run from $4.25-6.25 including a Guadalajara tostada for $5.25, flautas for $4.50, and arroz con pollo for $6.25. **Ten Depot Street** (10 Depot Street, La Grande, 97850; tel. 963-8766) might be a harbinger of things to come. Such interesting plates as teriyaki tofu for $7.95, Oregon-raised lamb chops for $12.95, and a delicious salmon pâté for $3.95 will evoke bistros west of the Cascades. To complete the effect they also serve Portland microbrewery beer and ale.

Entertainment And Events

Like every town in America, the towns on our route each have a special festivity in which the locals whoop it up in their own way. The **Obon Odori Festival** celebrating Ontario's Japanese heritage is held the third week in July at the Buddhist Temple. On the schedule are tours of the temple, a dinner featuring oriental cuisine, Asian arts and crafts displays, and an evening of dancing with audience participation.

The **Vale Rodeo** is a four-day fete that takes place July 1-4. It's highlighted by the Suicide Race, an event held at nearby Vale Butte in which cowboys race their horses off a steep slope into the arena. The **Miner's Jubilee,** the big shivaree in Baker, is traditionally celebrated during the third week in July. On the bill are a fiddle festival, arts and crafts fair, bed and raft races, cowbelles' breakfast, and the World Championship Porcupine Sprint Race. On the Fourth of July in Haines, a wide spot on ORE 30 between Baker and North Powder, they have a competition to name the oldest working cowhand in the Northwest. If you think you qualify call 856-3211. La Grande's major celebrations of the year are the **Oregon Trail Days and Rendezvous** in mid-August and **Blue Mountain Days** in late June with a parade, rodeo, and motorcycle rally.

Health

Ontario's hospital is **Holy Rosary Medical Center** (381 S.W. 9th, Ontario, 97914; tel. 889-5331). It has a 24-hour emergency service. **St. Elizabeth Hospital** (3325 Pocahontas Road, Baker, 97814) has a 24-hour emergency room. **Grande Ronde Hospital** (900 Sunset Drive, La Grande, 97850; tel. 963-8421) has an air ambulance service called Blue Mountain Aeromedical (tel. 800-426-5554).

Information

The Malheur County **Chamber of Commerce** office (173 S.W. 1st Street, Ontario, 97914; tel. 889-8012), the Vale County Chamber of Commerce (272 North Main, Vale, 97918; tel. 473-3800), the Baker County Chamber of Commerce (490 Campbell Street, Baker, 97814; tel. 523-5855) and the La Grande-Union County Chamber of Commerce (1502 N. Pine , La Grande, 97850; tel. 963-8588) all have useful information to aid your explorations along the Old Oregon Trail.

You can find a **post office** in Baker (1550 Dewey Avenue, Baker, 97814; tel. 523-4237) and in La Grande (1202 Washington, La Grande, 97850; tel. 963-2041). The **state police** have offices in Baker (1050 South Bridge, Baker, 97814; tel. 523-5866) and La Grande (3014 Island Avenue, La Grande, 97850; tel. 963-7174). The **local police** also have offices in Baker (tel. 523-3644) and La Grande (tel. 962-1017).

Getting Around

There is very little public transit in this land of large distances and small population. Here's what is available. **Greyhound** has terminals in Baker (515 Campbell, Baker, 97814; tel. 523-5011) and in La Grande (2108 Cove Avenue, La Grande, 97850; tel. 963-5156). **Grande Ronde Transportation Company** (1901 Jefferson, La Grande, 97850; tel. 963-6119) has a bus charter service. **La Grande Aviation** (Route 2, Box 2546, La Grande, 97850; tel. 963-6572) will fly you where you want to go. **Amtrak** (tel. 800-872-7275) has two unmanned stations, in Baker (2803 Broadway) and La Grande (Depot and Jefferson).

THE WALLOWAS

Acclaimed as the "Switzerland of America," the Wallowa Mountains and the broad valley to the north of this range is not just another spectacular alpine region. Thanks to the outdoor recreation boom and a publicity mill fueled by magazines like *Outside* and *Backpacker,* these mountains have become the new hot mecca for lovers of life on the wild side. Come now, before the word gets out any more about this backpackers' paradise where snowcapped Teton-like spires and blue-green glacial lakes are still relatively unvisited.

Ask most any Oregonian who has been there and they will tell you that the Wallowas is one place in Oregon "you gotta see—you just gotta." With 17 of the state's 29 mountains over 9,000 feet and 50 glacial lakes sprinkled throughout 300,000 acres, the **Eagle Cap Wilderness** is a recreational area that should figure prominently in your travel plans. Here, campers and cross-country skiers are regularly treated to glimpses of bighorn sheep, mountain goats, elk, and mule deer, as well as snow-streaked granite peaks rising above meadows dotted with an artist's palette of wildflowers.

The Wallowa Valley, formed by the drainages of the Wallowa, Minam, and Grande Ronde rivers, has lots of open space. Area economy is fueled by the traditional eastern Oregon triad of timber, farming, and cattle ranching. Enterprise is the commercial center of it all, while Joseph is the hub of a growing arts community and the gateway to Wallowa Lake, a recreational haven at the end of the road. After a visit to this "larger than life" countryside, it is easy to see how it sustained the proud and indomitable Nez Perce, the native people who once roamed its river canyons, glacial basins, and grassy hills.

HISTORY

The Wallowa Valley, set apart by deep river canyons and mountain ranges, is the ancestral home of the Nez Perce, a tribe known for its horse-raising skills and fierce independence. This regal people, astride their spotted Appaloosas, first encountered Europeans when mountain men wandered onto their land. At first they were friendly, feeding and caring for the Bonneville Party which had struggled up out of the Snake River Canyon in 1834. Later, when a dry spell in the Grande Ronde Valley to the south prompted homesteaders to give the Wallowas a try, the two cultures clashed. A tense era followed in which various drafts of different treaties added to the confusion. The settlers later successfully lobbied the United States government to evict the natives, which led to the Nez Perce War of 1877. Chief Joseph and his people fought a running battle that covered 1,700 miles and ended with his surrender in the Bear Paw Mountains, 50 miles from the Montana-Canada border. Meanwhile, back at the ranch in the Wallowa Valley, the toughest of the settlers endured the winters, droughts, and other hardships of life on the frontier. One bachelor, in an attempt to ease his loneliness, sent the following note to a friend in Missouri: "Send at once C.O.D. a good-looking maid or widow, 30 years or under. Widow with a few children preferred."

In 1908, a passenger train steamed into Wallowa on a newly laid track from Elgin, thus expanding a route that had previously seen only horsemen and wagons. Not much has changed since those early days. The people of the Wallowa Valley believe that they inhabit paradise, and they seem to enjoy sharing it with visitors drawn by its natural beauty and vivid history.

SIGHTS

Wildlife
Two wildlife viewing areas await you as you sweep down into the Wallowa Valley. The **Spring Branch Wildlife Area,** a woodland marsh, is two miles east of Wallowa on ORE 82, on the north side where the road leaves the Wallowa River. The eight-acre viewing area, managed by the Oregon Department of Fish and Wildlife, has beaver dams and lots of waterfowl, including the black tern, an insect-eating bird found in eastern Oregon marshes. The **Enterprise Wildlife Area** is two miles west of Enterprise off ORE 82. To get there, turn south on Fish Hatchery Road to this

CHIEF JOSEPH

The Nez Perce Indians had lived in peace with white explorers and neighboring tribes of the Northwest for generations. They gave the Lewis and Clark Expedition much needed horses and promised that they'd never make war on the white man. But with the incursion of miners and settlers and because of misunderstandings surrounding the annexation of Indian land through a series of treaties never signed by Chief Joseph, tension increased to the breaking point. White disregard of native property spurred on some rash young Nez Perce to retaliate. The ensuing 11 week conflict, during which the Nez Perce engaged 10 separate United States military commands in 13 battles (the majority of which the Nez Perce won), guaranteed Chief Joseph's fame as a brilliant military tactician. However, after many hardships, Chief Joseph surrendered with the following words to Generals Miles and Howard on October 5, 1877, only 30 miles from the sanctuary of the Canadian border.

Tell General Howard I know his heart. What he told me before, I have in my heart. I am tired of fighting. Our chiefs are killed. Looking Glass is dead. Too-hool-hool-suit is dead. The old men are dead. It is the young men who say yes and no. He who led on the young men is dead. It is cold and we have no blankets. The little children are freezing to death. My people, some of them, have run away to the hills and have no blankets, no food; no one knows where they are, perhaps freezing to death. I want to have time to look for my children and see how many I can find. Maybe I shall find them among the dead. Hear me, my chiefs. I am tired; my heart is sick and sad. From where the sun now stands, I will fight no more forever.

In 1879, Chief Joseph spoke to the Department of Indian Affairs in Washington D.C., detailing the broken promises of the government, the suffering of his people, and the unjust treatment of the Indians by white society.

I have heard talk and talk, but nothing is done. Good words do not last long unless they amount to something. Words do not pay for my dead people. They do not pay for my country, now overrun by white men. They do not protect my father's grave. They do not pay for all my horses and cattle. Good words will not give me back my children. Good words will not make good the promise of your War Chief General Miles. Good words will not give my people good health and stop them from dying. Good words will not get my people a home where they can live in peace and take care of themselves. I am tired of talk that comes to nothing. It makes my heart sick when I remember all the good words and all the broken promises. There has been too much talking by men who had no right to talk. Too many misrepresentations have been made, too many misunderstandings have come up between the white men about the Indians. If the white man wants to live in peace with the Indian he can live in peace. There need be no trouble. Treat all men alike. Give them the same law. Give them all an even chance to live and grow. All men were made by the same Great Spirit Chief. They are all brothers. The earth is the mother of all people, and all people should have equal rights upon it. You might as well ex-

pect the rivers to run backward as that any man who was a free man should be contented when penned up and denied liberty to go where he pleases. If you tie a horse to a stake, do you expect he will grow fat? If you pen an Indian up on a small spot of earth, and compel him to stay there, he will not be contented, nor will he grow and prosper. I have asked some of the great white chiefs where they get their authority to say to the Indian that he shall stay in one place, while he sees white men going where they please. They cannot tell me.

I only ask of the government to be treated as all other men are treated. If I cannot go to my own home, let me have a home in some country where my people will not die so fast. I would like to go to Bitter Root Valley. There my people would be healthy; where they are now they are dying. Three have died since I left my camp to come to Washington.

When I think of our condition my heart is heavy. I see men of my race treated as outlaws and driven from country to country, or shot down like animals.

I know that my race must change. We cannot hold our own with the white men as we are. We only ask an even chance to live as other men live. We ask to be recognized as men. We ask that the same law shall work alike on all men. If the Indian breaks the law, punish him by the law. If the white man breaks the law, punish him also.

Let me be a free man—free to travel, free to stop, free to work, free to trade where I choose, free to choose my own teachers, free to follow the religion of my fathers, free to think and talk and act for myself—and I will obey every law, or submit to the penalty.

Whenever the white man treats an Indian as they treat each other, then we will have no more wars. We shall all be alike—brothers of one father and one mother, with one sky above us and one country around us, and one government for all. Then the Great Spirit Chief who rules above will smile upon this land, and send rain to wash out the bloody spots made by brothers' hands from the face of the earth. For this time the Indian race are waiting and praying. I hope that no more groans of wounded men and women will ever go to the ear of the Great Spirit Chief above, and that all people may be one people.

32-acre site located just before the fish hatchery. Walk down the dike that goes through a grove of trees to view marsh wrens, snipe, mink, beavers, and muskrats.

Culture In The Hinterland

If you have an afternoon to spare in **Enterprise**, the Wallowa County Centennial Committee has organized a **walking tour** for you. Stop by the chamber of commerce booth in the Enterprise Mall and pick up their brochure. It has descriptions and locations of many of the historic buildings in the area like the Wallowa County Courthouse, the Enterprise Hotel, the Oddfellows Hall, and a number of private homes. After an hour of edification and exercise, take a break at the **Bookloft-Skylight Gallery** (107 E. Main, Enterprise, tel. 426-3351), just across the street from the county courthouse. This gathering spot for artists and community activists sells best-sellers and local history books and offers monthly shows of guest artists as well as freshly brewed coffee and home-baked cookies.

Joseph

Cruising farther into the valley, you reach the lively community of Joseph, named after the famous Nez Perce chief. A must-stop for history buffs is the **Wallowa County Museum** on Main Street (tel. 432-6095). The museum is open from the last weekend in May to the third weekend in September. Hours are 10-5, seven days a week. Built in 1888, the museum building served as a bank and a newspaper office. In 1913 it was converted into a private hospital and in 1927 the city of Joseph acquired the property for a meeting hall. Its current incarnation as a museum started in 1960. The theme of the museum is Wallowa history, including displays of pioneer life and the Nez Perce tribe, the valley's original inhabitants.

Joseph is also the center of a blossoming art community in the Wallowas. Take a walk down Main Street and you'll find a number of art galleries and antique stores, among them the Wallowa Lake Gallery, Wild Goose Antiques, and the Edge of the Wilderness Gallery. The Gene Hayes Gallery specializes in the outdoors and the Old

West, and Eagle Mountain Gallery and Valley Bronze is a casting foundry which uses the lost-wax casting process to create monumental sculptures.

Wallowa Lake

The brightest gem in the Wallowas setting is Wallowa Lake, which at 5,000 feet in elevation is the highest body of water in eastern Oregon. This classic moraine-held glacial lake is a few miles south of Joseph on ORE 62. The lake is ringed with lodges, amusement rides, a large state park with an overnight campground, pack horse corrals, boat launches, and marinas. It is also home to the **Wallowa Lake Monster,** a creature with a gentle disposition and a length varying from 30-100 feet, depending on the sighting. Reports of the critter go back several centuries to Native American tales and are also the current focus of the Monster Observation and Preservation Society (MOPS). A real treat for visitors is a ride in the **Mt. Howard Gondola.** Open during the summer from 10-4, the gondola route is the steepest and longest in North America, lifting passengers from the edge of Wallowa Lake 3,200 feet up to the 8,200-foot summit of Mt. Howard. As the lift floats upward, the pastureland and wheatfield views near Wallowa Lake give way to forests of lodgepole pine, tamarack, and quaking aspen. The 15-minute trip in the closed gondola car costs $9 for adults, $8 for seniors, and $5 for children 10 and under. The ride ends at a snack bar and gift shop on top of the peak. But forget about the snacks, knickknacks, and trinkets; the best reason for taking the trip is the view of 26 mountain peaks, including the Wallowa Range, snake River Country, and Idaho's Seven Devils area.

SPORTS AND RECREATION

Camping

Camping out in the Wallowa Valley and the Eagle Cap Wilderness can be as easy as pulling off ORE 82 just 15 miles east of Elgin and pitching your tent at **Minam State Recreation Area** ($5), or as rigorous as using one of the following three campsites as a jumping-off point for backpacking into the high country.

Boundary Campsite is five miles south of Wallowa on County Route 515, then two miles south on Forest Service Road 163. There's no

fee for this site set along the banks of Bear Creek, but there's also no water. A trailhead provides access to the dazzling grandeur of the Eagle Cap basin.

The next campsite/trailhead is **Two Pan,** one of the most popular gateways into the Wallowas. To get there, head south from Lostine on County Route 551 for seven miles and down Forest Service Road 5202 for 11 miles. This is a rough and rocky washboard grade, so take your time. Firewood and vault toilets are available; there are no fees or water. Trails leave Two Pan for the Lostine River Valley and the glacial lakes at the base of Eagle Cap.

The third campsite is **Hurricane Creek,** three miles southwest of Joseph. There's no charge for overnight camping, and piped water and firewood are available. The Hurricane Creek trailhead leads to a hike along the east slope of the Hurricane Divide past Sacajawea Peak and the Matterhorn to the glacial lakes basin. An ambitious trek would start at Two Pan and end at Hurricane Creek.

Then there's always Wallowa State Park campground (Wallowa Lake, Rt. 1, Box 323, Joseph, 97846). This is one of 13 Oregon campgrounds that operate on a reservation system (see the general

PHOTO BY OREGON DEPT. OF TRANSPORTATION
Wallowa Lake is the largest lake in northeastern Oregon.

At Eagle Cap you can hike where eagles soar.

PHOTO BY OREGON TOURISM DIVISION

Introduction). Lake views, large campsites (89 tent and 121 RV sites), clean bathhouses, and covered kitchen shelters make it worth the $13 nightly fee. A marina and a sports field (home to the Jazz at the Lake Festival in July) also recommend an early reservation.

Skiing

The recreational delights of the Wallowas are not reserved for summer only. The skiing in this alpine wonderland is excellent. **Ferguson Ridge Ski Area** (tel. 426-3493) is a good example. To get there, drive east from Joseph about five miles on the Wallowa Loop Highway, then follow signs south on Tucker Down Road. This small facility has a rope tow and T-bar that climb from a 5,100-foot base to 5,800-foot-high Ferguson Ridge. Lift tickets are $7 a day. Nordic skiers can try a mile loop trail or take an eight-mile marked and packed route to the Salt Creek Summit.

Another popular spot is **Salt Creek Summit,** about 20 miles southeast of Joseph on Wallowa Loop Highway. The facility has five miles of marked but ungroomed ski trails and a plowed snow park. A European approach to a skiing adventure is a tour of **Wallowa Alpine Huts.** Three- to five-day hut-to-hut tours of the Eagle Cap Wilderness cost $185-465. Also available are lessons, helicopter skiing, and telemark camps.

For information write to Alpine Huts (Box 9252, Moscow, Idaho 83843; tel. 208-882-1955).

For cross-country skiers, the **Wallowa Lake Nordic Center** (Wallowa Lake State Park, tel. 426-4611) maintains 13 miles of Nordic ski trails around Wallowa Lake. Finally, **Sacajawea Park Cross-Country Ski Trail** challenges the ambitious. Take the Hurricane Creek Road west from Joseph to the Hurricane Creek trailhead. This cross-country ski route will take you up into a basin on the northeast side of Sacajawea Peak. After two steep miles through the forest, the trail opens up into a clear area with a view of the surrounding glacial peaks. For more information on this trek call the Eagle Cap Ranger District office at 426-3104.

Outfitters

If your budget allows for a guided adventure into the Wallowa wilds, here are two excellent services. The **Eagle Cap Wilderness Pack Station** (Route 1, Box 416, Joseph, tel. 432-4145) fees start at $7 an hour for short trips to lakes and streams in the Eagle Cap high country and go up to $750 for deluxe excursions to Hells Canyon or along the Imnaha River. **Wallowa Llamas** (Route 1, Box 84, Halfway, 97834; tel. 742-2961) will show you a unique way to adventure into the wilderness. Surefooted, even-tempered llamas carry 20 pounds of each guest's gear; you carry the rest. The outfit offers trips to Hells Canyon, Imnaha Falls, Eagle Meadows, and across the rugged Wallowas. The expeditions are designed for those with some backpacking experience or anyone in reasonably good shape. Costs range from a three-day jaunt for $225 to a seven-day journey for $595.

Fishing

Fishing in this high country is a matter of choosing your favorite game fish. You can catch kokanee (landlocked salmon) and mackinaws in **Wallowa Lake,** trout and steelhead in the streams that flow out of the ice-capped mountains, or bass, crappie, and sturgeon in the **Snake River.** According to experts, the **Imnaha River** is one of the best late-season fishing streams in the Pacific Northwest.

PRACTICALITIES

Accommodations

Rather than list the usual motel information, here are lodgings in the Wallowas that reflect the special flavor of this unique outback.

On the Imnaha River 14 miles south of Imnaha is **Diamond W Ranch** (Route 1, Box 466, Imnaha 97842; tel. 577-3157). Their rates start at $60 for adults and $30 for children and include meals and horses. The **Flying Arrow Resort** (Route 1, Box 370, Power House Road, Joseph 97846; tel. 432-2951) not only has a great name but a chocolate shop, a bookstore, and a village market. Rates start at $40 for one- and two-bedroom cottages.

Red's Wallowa Horse Ranch (Box 26, Joseph, 97846; tel. 432-9171) is one of Oregon's best-known retreats. The lodge is tucked away in a high mountain valley with no phones or electricity and is famous for its home cooking and hospitality. You either fly in or arrive by an eight-mile pack trip. Guests stay in the lodge or log cabins equipped with hot water, kerosene lamps, and fireplaces. Horseback rides, hiking, fishing, snowshoeing, and cross-country skiing trips can be arranged. Package rates are $75-100 a day for the whole shootin' match.

Other accommodations near Joseph are **Eagle Cap Chalets** (Route 1, Box 419, Wallowa Lake Highway, 97846; tel. 432-4704). Tucked into the pines, this cluster of cabins and condos has all you need to visit Wallowa Lake in comfort and style. Rates run from $30-60. The folks at the **Wallowa Valley Guest House** (Box 843, Joseph, 97846; tel. 432-9765) have rooms for $35 and up for two. Close to Nordic and downhill ski areas, this B&B can also arrange pack trips and llama treks.

A couple of hostelries on the shore of Wallowa Lake are good bets for those who want comfort rather than campouts. The **Wallowa Lake Lodge** (Box 1, Joseph, 97846; tel. 432-4082/winter phone Jan 1-April 15 426-4336) is a renovated 1923 hotel with a mix of accommodations ranging from a single room without bath for $21 to a large cabin near the river for eight at $62. The Nordic center is a five-minute walk away and there are a store and gas station on the grounds. **Matterhorn Swiss Village** (Route 1, Box 350, 97846 Joseph, tel. 432-4071) has rates from $32-60. In keeping with the notion that the Wallowas are the "Switzerland of America," this facility has six cottages with names like the Alpenhof and Berghof, a gift and sports shop, and water-ski, bike, and windsurf gear rentals.

Food

Like most frontier outposts in the American West, the Wallowa Valley has lots of standard takeout joints and few eateries worth a special stop. However, the following restaurants will not only keep you going during your visit, but give you a few tasty surprises as well.

The **T'N'T Kitchen** in Wallowa (tel. 886-7705) grills a mean buffalo burger with soup, salad, and fries for $4.20. They also sell stuffed buffalo toys in case the kids would rather play with their food than eat it. **Cloud Nine** (105 S.E. 1st, Enterprise, tel. 426-3790) serves up deli sandwiches and homemade soups in an informal atmosphere. Sandwiches run from $2.99-3.99. **A Country Place on Pete's Pond** (Box 459, Montclair St. South, Enterprise, tel. 426-3642) is a charming lunch spot on the edge of a five-acre lake. Pete invites you to feed the fish, enjoy the swans, and eat indoors or out on the lawn. Their sandwiches run from $3.50-4.25, are made with homemade bread, and come with fries, salad, or soup. Another spot in Enterprise with good food is **Sonita's Cafe Ole** (107 S.W. 1st St., tel. 426-4888). Located in the Enterprise Mall, the cafe has both Mexican and American dishes with combination dinners running from $5.95-12.95. Specialties include the Burrito Del Mar with shrimp and monterey jack for $10.95 and chimichangas for $6.95.

Your best bet in Joseph is **Pam's Country Inn Restaurant** (500 N. Main, tel. 432-1195). Pam's has an ambience reminiscent of a French country inn. Their "country cooking" menu features dinners starting at $5 and house specialties like beef Wellington and chicken teriyaki from $9-10. Their eight-ounce filet mignon runs $12.95.

Entertainment And Events

Most of the local celebrations here center around cowboys and Indians and the arts community.

The **Wallowa Valley Festival of the Arts** held at the Joseph Civic Center happens in the third week of April. Along with awards for Northwest artists, there are wine-tasting parties, a silent auction, and a quick-draw competition. A recent addition to the festivities is a reading by cowboy poets. For information on the festival call the Wallowa Valley Arts Council at (800) 635-2000. The **Wallowa County Fiddlers' Contest** brings fiddlers from throughout the Northwest to mix it up with music, good grub, and the spirit of the pioneer days. Held in Enterprise on the third weekend in July, the contest is a treat for both the performers and their appreciative audiences.

The tiny town of **Lostine** celebrates the **Fourth of July** with artists, craftspeople, and collectors plying their wares in the Lostine Sidewalk Flea Market.

Chief Joseph Days is a week-long cowboy and Indian festival hosted by Joseph, the little town near Wallowa Lake. Held in late July, the list of events includes dances, a carnival, a Grand Parade, a ranch-style breakfast, and a three-day rodeo which has grown to be one of the largest in the Northwest. For tickets and information call 432-1015. Another echo of the Wild West can be witnessed at 1 p.m. every Wednesday, Friday, and Saturday during the summer as four outlaws ride into town and rob the First Bank of Joseph. This dramatic re-creation of a historic robbery is played out on the spot of the original heist. The bank building now houses the Wallowa County Museum.

Alpenfest is a three-day festival held the third weekend after Labor Day in Edelweiss Hall next to the tramway at Wallowa Lake. This gala return to the old country and all that's Bavarian sends echoes into the mountains with the gay-sad strains of accordion music, alpenhorn blowing, and yodeling competitions; dancing, sailboat racing, and a bounty of Northern European cuisine

are also featured. For reservations and information call the Wallowa Lake Tourist Committee at 432-6325.

Hell's Canyon Mule Days, held the second weekend after Labor Day at the Enterprise Fairgrounds, is where pack-animal fanciers can get their kicks. The action includes mule races, a parade, a speed mule-shoeing contest, and endurance races.

Information

If you need to mail a letter, call the cops, get medical attention, check out the local hotspots, or just read all about it, here's the information you'll need.

The Wallowa **post office** is at 104 N. Stories, tel. 886-3422, and at 201 W. North, tel. 426-3555 in Enterprise. The local office of the **Oregon State Police** is 522 River, Enterprise, tel. 426-3036. Contact the Wallowa sheriff's office at tel. 426-3131, Wallowa police at tel. 886-2422, Enterprise police at tel. 426-3755, and Joseph police at tel. 432-3832. The only hospital in Wallowa County is the **Wallowa Memorial Hospital** (410 E. 1st, Enterprise, tel. 426-3111).

The **Wallowa County Chamber of Commerce** (Box 427A, Enterprise, 97828; tel. 426-4622) has a booth in the Enterprise Mall with a full complement of brochures, maps, and other information on the area. The county has two newspapers, the *Wallowa County Chieftian* (106 N.W 1st, Enterprise, tel. 426-4567) and the *Joseph Eagle* (Box 549, Joseph, tel. 432-5585). If you need to get in touch with the **Forest Service,** the Eagle Cap Ranger District office is at 612 S.W. 2nd, Enterprise, tel. 426-3104; the Wallowa Valley Ranger District is one mile north of Joseph on ORE 82 (tel. 432-2171).

Getting There And Getting Around

Moffit Brothers Transportation (Lostine, tel. 569-2284) makes a daily roundtrip between La Grande and Wallowa Lake. **Wallowa Valley Stage** (tel. 432-3531) leaves from Paul's Chevron in Joseph. Don't worry about finding this gas station; it's the only one in town.

Two air services operate in Wallowa County. **Joseph Air Service** (Airport Rd., Joseph, tel. 432-6305) and **Spence Air Service** (Box 217, Enterprise, tel. 426-3288) are both listed in the *Oregon Pilot's Guide,* and are available for charter flights.

HELLS CANYON

Hells Canyon, carved out by the Snake River, is the deepest gorge in the world, averaging 6,600 feet in depth. A 67-mile stretch of the Snake at the bottom of this canyon is one of the nation's protected Wild and Scenic Rivers. In 1975, Congress established the **Hell's Canyon National Recreation Area** comprised of 650,000 acres of stunning vistas, archaeological sites with petroglyphs and native ruins, as well as a mighty river thundering through rugged canyon lands. It is a hard place to get to so be sure you check the local weather and road conditions before visiting the area. Also, it's a good idea to pack a snakebite kit. There are rattlesnakes in this country!

There are two ways to get to Hells Canyon from the Oregon side. The first route is easiest and on paved roads. From Baker take ORE 86 for 50 miles east to **Halfway**. Stop here to stock up on groceries and gas and then continue on ORE 86 another 16 miles to Oxbow Dam and then another 20 miles to Hells Canyon Dam. This site affords a spectacular view of the canyon. The other approach is via ORE 82 through the Wallowa Valley to Enterprise, Joseph, and Imnaha. From Imnaha, one of the most isolated towns in America, take a tough road for 24 miles to Hat Point Lookout. Once you get there you'll be convinced that the view was worth the hassle.

Sights

As you motor through Halfway on your way to Hell's Canyon, stop at the **Old Church** on Main Street. Inside you'll find a sumptuous array of handmade flower wreaths, bouquets, and baskets made from Oregon wildflowers. Owner/manager Sandy Kennedy's phone number is 742-6474.

The interior of Hells Canyon is a rugged wilderness framed by basalt cliffs. Cheatgrass, primroses, sunflowers, and prickly pear cactus are included in the canyon's varied botany. Bear, deer, big horn sheep, eagles, otters, and chukhar partridges are frequently seen here. Many outfitters can steer you to the canyon's pictographs which some sources place at 10,000 years of age. In addition to Chief Joseph and his Nez Perce tribe, the area was also occupied by miners and pioneers, as turn-of-the-century log cabins and shacks attest.

SPORTS AND RECREATION

Backpacking

Over 900 miles of trails provide hikers with a wide variety of recreational choices in the Hells Canyon Recreation Area. Major trails are maintained but others are difficult to follow. There are 12 campgrounds on the Oregon side of Hells Canyon. Here are a few of the better ones.

Lake Fork Campground is 18 miles northeast of Halfway on Forest Service Road 39. There are ten sites, drinking water, and good fishing at nearby Fish Lake. **Indian Crossing** is located 45 miles southeast of Joseph on Forest Service Road 3960 and has drinking water as well as a trailhead for backpacking into the Eagle Cap Wilderness. On the northern end of the recreational area, **Buckhorn Springs** is 43 miles northeast of Enterprise and features a great view, spring water, and berry-picking in season.

River Outfitters

Hells Canyon Challenge (Star Route, Box 25, Lostine, 97857; tel. 569-2445) offers an excursion full of excitement and gorgeous views. You start out at the mouth of the Grande Ronde River and then power up the Snake River in a jetboat. The rates start at $45 per person for a one-day trip and go up to $150 for a two-day trip for four persons. Other river guides offering trips up and down the Snake are **Hells Canyon Adventures** (Box 159, Oxbow, 97840; tel. 785-3352) and **Anderson River Adventures** (Route 2, Box 192-H, Milton-Freewater, 97862; tel. 558-3629). They both have one-day trips for under $100. The *Oregon Guides and Packers* publication is a good resource to locate other outfitters (see the general Introduction).

PRACTICALITIES

Accommodations

Clear Creek Farm Bed and Breakfast (Route 1, Box 138, Halfway, 97834; tel. 742-2233) is in a comfy old farmhouse on 160 secluded acres with a creek and pond for swimming and a great view of the upper Hells Canyon and Eagle Cap Wilderness. Best of all, it's all yours for $45. **Birch Leaf Lodge** (Route 1, Box 91, Halfway, 97834; tel. 742-2990) is in a turn-of-the-century farmhouse on 42 acres at the foot of the Wallowa Mountains. A special feature of this B&B is a resident excursion planner who will help you plan your recreational activities. Rates are from $40-$60 double occupancy.

Food

If you're on your own, it would be prudent to pack a few picnic items. Restaurants are few and far between in this country. But there is a good restaurant in Halfway called **Wild Bill's,** named after the owner. Their dinners run from $4.95-12.95 with two specials of the house—chicken teriyaki for $7 and chicken-fried steak made with their homemade gravy for $6.50.

Information

Hells Canyon National Recreation Area Headquarters (Box 490, Enterprise, 97828; tel. 426-3151) has additional information on Hell's Canyon.

PENDLETON

The title of Sam Shepard's play *True West* is an appropriate monicker for this outpost on the prairie. People are really at home on the range here, leaving the city streets pretty quiet until a mid-September rodeo draws cowboys, cowgirls, and "wannabes" from all over the West. The transformation of Pendleton from a refueling and supply stop for surrounding ranchers to *party central* takes place in September during the Round-Up with brewtaps going full tilt and streets filled with tourists in straw cowboy hats and bright new bandanas. When you're done whooping it up with the local good ol' boys, a town rich in history and memory awaits.

With a population of 15,000, Pendleton is one of the largest towns in eastern Oregon. It's an economic force thanks to vast wheat fields, rows

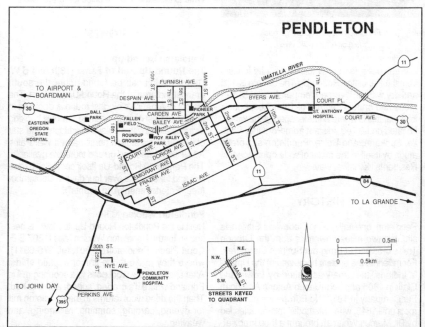

PHOTO BY OREGON TOURISM DIVISION
*Pendleton Round-up brings back
the glory of the Old West.*

tlers and 1,300 cattle to the region. The town itself, named after Senator George Hunt Pendleton, was founded in 1868 and incorporated in 1880. At that time, Pendleton consisted of a hotel and five houses. But it grew through the late 1880s to a ripsnorting cattle and farming center with 18 bawdyhouses and 32 saloons. It quickly gained the reputation of being the town that couldn't be tamed. The feistiness of the citizens here was demonstrated by the theft of the county seal and records from Umatilla Landing, thus making Pendleton the county seat.

Many of Pendleton's streets are named after Confederate generals—a legacy of hundreds of Southern emigrants who drifted West after the Civil War. Still other streets are numbered chronologically, but with confusing directional considerations. This has resulted in two 1st Streets (one southeast, one southwest.), two 2nd Streets, and so on—good luck.

Finally, Pendleton has been chosen as one of several sites for a multimillion-dollar interpretive center to celebrate the Oregon Trail in 1992. It's projected site is on the Umatilla Indian Reservation. Write to the state tourism office for further details.

of green peas, famous woolen mills, and tourism from the Pendleton Round-Up The climate is mild and dry with an average temperature of 51 degrees and annual rainfalls of 13 inches. Locals joke that this is where summer spends the winter. Located on I-84 equidistant from Portland, Seattle, Spokane, and Boise, Pendleton sits pretty much by itself in the midst of wide open spaces. Residents like it that way.

HISTORY

Pendleton, originally called Goodwin's Station, is situated two miles downriver from the Oregon Trail's crossing at Emigrant Springs State Park. For millennia the ancient homeland of the Umatilla Indians, the area was visited by Lewis and Clark in 1805 and John Jacob Astor's American Fur Company in 1812. No Europeans put down roots until 1843, when Methodist missionaries led by Dr. Marcus Whitman brought a thousand set-

SIGHTS

Pendleton Round-up
The **Round-Up Hall of Fame** (13th and S.W. Court) exhibit can be found under the south grandstand area at the Round-Up Stadium. The history of America's biggest rodeo is depicted in photos of past champions and famous bucking broncos along with displays of artifacts. The star of the show is a stuffed horse named War Paint. Admission is free and guided tours are available. The Pendleton Round-Up itself costs $5-10 dollars and takes place over four days in September (see "Entertainment And Events").

Pendleton Woolen Mills
Next to the Pendleton Round-Up, the town is best known for the Pendleton Woolen Mills (1307 S.E. Court Place, Pendleton, 97801; tel. 276-6911), where they make those immortal plaid shirts. After shearing, the wool goes to a scouring mill in Portland where it's graded, sorted, and washed. Then the dried wool returns to the Pendleton mill for dyeing, carding, spinning, rewinding, and weaving.

The business began over in the Willamette Valley in Brownsville when Thomas Kay, a Yorkshireman whose family was in the woolen business in England, started a weaving mill. His descendant, Clarence Bishop, founded the Pendleton facility. Production began in 1909 with Indian-style blankets, which are still going strong, along with men and women's sportswear.

Tours run Mon.-Fri. at 9 a.m., 11 a.m., 1:30 p.m., and 3 p.m. Large groups are asked to make tours by appointment. To get to the mills on I-84 going east, take exit 207 through Pendleton on Dorion. Do not cross the viaduct but turn left and proceed four blocks. For additional information, write Box 969, Pendleton, 97801.

Umatilla County Historical Society Museum

In 1881 the Oregon-Washington Railway and Navigation Company, a subsidiary of the Union Pacific Railroad, constructed the northern branch of their transcontinental railroad through northeast Oregon, and Pendleton served as an important stop on the route. By 1910, Pendleton had become the second largest city in eastern Oregon and merited a new railroad depot. The building (Box 253, 108 S.W. Frazer, Pendleton, 97801; tel. 276-0012), an adaptation of the California mission style, boasted multi-paneled windows, decorative brickwork, and wide, flaring eaves. The depot no longer serves railroad passengers but instead houses the museum's collection of Oregon Trail pioneer and Indian artifacts.

Tours

One of the area's liveliest attractions is **Pendleton Underground Tours** (Box 1072, Pendleton, 97801; tel. 276-0730). This visit to the wild and woolley days of the Old West takes you through the tunnels underneath Pendleton's historic district. The tour starts at S.W. First and Emigrant and continues on to the old Shamrock Cardroom filled with the bouncy sounds of honkytonk music. From there, it's on to the Cozy Rooms Bordello and other secrets of the town's past, ending with the inevitable gift shop. Admission is $5.

Hamley's Western Store (30 S.E. Court Ave., Pendleton, 97801; tel. 276-2321) is internationally known for its Western saddles and custom leathercraft. The second floor is a gallery of Native American artists. Stop by and join one of the tours of saddle-making in progress held Mon.-Sat. from 9-5:30.

A good place to learn more about the local scene is **Armchair Books** (39 S.W. Dorion, Pendleton, 97801; tel. 276-7323), a store which specializes in regional titles and authors.

SPORTS AND RECREATION

Lots of sun is conducive to such outdoor activities as golf at **Pendleton Country Club**, seven miles south of town on U.S. 395, and boating and water-skiing on **McKay Reservoir** near the country club. In a little over an hour, fishing enthusiasts can head north and arrive at the Columbia River for salmon, steelhead, and bass, or try the area's man-made lakes for bluegills, bass, and catfish. During the winter months, skiing is on tap up at **Spout Springs**, one of the oldest ski resorts in the Northwest. To get there, drive north on ORE 11 to Weston, turn east on Ore 204, and travel a few miles past Tollgate to the ski area.

PRACTICALITIES

Accommodations

The cost for lodging in this town is quite reasonable. But if you show up at rodeo time without a reservation or unprepared to pay double the room rate, you might be out of luck.

A tonic to modern life is a stay at the **Bar M Ranch**, 31 miles northeast of Pendleton on ORE 11. Built on the site of the historic Bingham Springs Resort, the ranch lies at the base of the Blue Mountains in the Umatilla National Forest. A stable of 50 horses, a natural warm springs, a recreation barn, and eight rooms in a hand-hewn log house let you rough it in style. Rates are $545 per week for a single and $505 each for double occupancy, which includes horse rides, meals, and all amenities.

Food

The Rainbow Bar and Grill (209 S. Main, Pendleton, 97801; tel. 276-4120) is a famous saloon/restaurant for rodeo fans and local buckaroos. The walls are covered with photos of Round-Up champions and Indian princesses, and the place was recently mentioned in Craig Lesley's novel *Winterkill*, the tale of a modern-day Indian bronc rider trying to scrape by. The Rainbow serves passable American diner food which you shouldn't pass up, if only for local color.

PENDLETON ACCOMMODATIONS

Name	Address	Telephone	Price	Features
Pillars Motel	1816 S.E. Court Ave.	276-6241	$15 per person	
Thrifty Motel	102 S.W. 18th St.	276-1920	$20-30	
Pioneer Motel	1807 S.E. Court	276-4521	$20-30	
Motel 6	325 Nye Ave.	276-3160	$24-34	clean and basic
Ranch Motel	7 I-84, Barnhart Exit	276-4711	$26-75	cable, wheelchair access, pets, pool, restaurant
Longhorn Motel	411 S.W. Dorion	276-7531	$28	cable, pets, restaurant, nonsmoking rooms
Travelers Inn	105 S.E. Court St.	276-6231	$28-37	cable, pets, pool, restaurant, laundry
Econo Lodge	201 S.W. Court Ave.	276-5252	$30	cable, pets, pool
Travelodge Motel	310 Dorion	276-6231	$30-45	
Chaparral Motel	620 S.W. Tutuilla	276-8654	$35-41	cable, wheelchair access, pets, kitchenettes, restaurant, nonsmoking rooms
Tapadera Motor Inn	105 S.E. Court Ave.	276-3731	$40-75	cable, pets, restaurant/lounge, non-smoking rooms
Red Lion Motor Inn	304 S.E. Nye	276-6111	$68-82	cable, wheelchair access, restaurant/lounge, pool, live entertainment, non-smoking rooms

The **Harvester Restaurant and Lounge** (2220 Court, Pendleton, 97801; tel. 276-9046) is home of the giant chicken-fried steak. **Cimmiyotti's** (137 Main St., Pendleton, 97801; tel. 276-4314) is a dark cozy spot that has both American and Italian cuisine. The **Great Pacific Wine and Coffee Co.** (403 S. Main, Pendleton, 97801; tel. 276-1350) offers evidence that "hip" has come to Pendleton. They have imported cheeses, desserts, croissant sandwiches, an espresso bar, and gourmet products.

The **Circle S** (210 S.E. 5th, Pendleton, 97801; tel. 276-9637) is a Western-style restaurant that serves up a great BBQ sandwich for $3.50. Billed as Pendleton's oldest restaurant, **A&R Burger Island** (912 E. Emigrant, Pendleton, 97801; tel. 276-3352) has carhop service after 11 a.m. **The Health Nuts** (1700 S.W. Court Place, Pendleton, 97801;

tel. 276-2251) is an oasis of natural foods in Pendleton with a complete selection of whole grains, nuts, yogurt, and organic vegetables in season.

Entertainment And Events

In 1910, Pendleton farmers and ranchers got together to celebrate the end of the wheat harvest. This was the first year of the **Pendleton Round-Up**, which now draws 45,000 rodeo fans in the grand tradition started by legendary rodeo stars like Jackson Sundown and Yakima Canutt. Usually held in mid-September at Raley Park, the fun begins with the **Westward Ho Historical Parade** with covered wagons, mule teams, buggies, and hundreds of Indians in full regalia. There's also a **Happy Canyon Pageant** which portrays the Native American culture, the coming of the emigrants, clashes between the two, and the birth of a frontier town. The Round-Up features such classic competitions as bulldogging, calf-roping, and wild horse races from Wednesday through Saturday. Tickets for each day run from $5-10 depending on location. Phone orders will be accepted for VISA or MasterCard by dialing (800) 524-2984, or you can write for an order form to Pendleton Round-Up (Box 609, Pendleton 97801; tel. 276-2553).

Services And Information

St. Anthony's Hospital (1601 Court Ave., Pendleton, 97801; tel. 278-3214) has 24-hour emergency service. The **Pendleton Chamber of Commerce Visitor and Convention Bureau** (25 S.E. Dorion, Pendleton, 97801; tel. 276-7411/800-452-9403 in Oregon or 800-547-8911 outside Oregon) can steer you to local sights and special events. If you run into trouble during the Round-Up, the **police** can be reached at tel. 276-4411. The **post office** (104 Dorion Ave., Pendleton, 97801; tel. 278-0203) is down the street and open 8:30-5.

Pendleton Airport (2016 Airport Rd., Pendleton, 97801; tel. 278-0947) is located 3$\frac{1}{2}$ miles west of town center and is served by Horizon Air (tel. 800-547-9308). Aerowest Aviation (tel. 276-3835) provides charter rentals. **Greyhound** (320 Court Ave., Pendleton, 97801; tel. 276-1551) and **Pendleton Bus Co.** (tel. 276-5621) offer charters and transportation. The main line of the Union Pacific Railroad passes through Pendleton with **Amtrak** passenger service available. However, the shelter station at S. Main and Frazer St. is unstaffed and anyone planning to catch a train here should call (800) 872-7245 in advance.

BOOKLIST

In addition to the titles cited in the text, Oregon-bound travelers would do well to acquaint themselves with these books.

Atlases

Two publications authored by Samuel Dickman make Oregon's cultural and geological landscapes come alive. *Oregon Divided* (Portland: Oregon Historical Society, 1982) and *The Making of Oregon* (Portland: Oregon Historical Society, 1979) address the human history, economics, and topography of each part of the state.

Oregon Geographic Names by Lewis Mac-Arthur (Portland: Oregon Historical Society, 1982) might physically be a weighty tome, but its alphabetic rundown of the history of the place names here makes for light and informative reading.

The Coast

There are many good books on the coast, but the only title we've found which'll give something beyond what you'll find in conventional guidebooks was written by out-of-staters. East Coast residents and former *Rolling Stone* writers Parke Puterbaugh and Alan Bisbort's *Life is a Beach* (New York: McGraw-Hill Book Company, 1988) portrays Oregon's western edge with humor, insight, and graceful prose.

Oregon Coast Hikes by Paul Williams (Denver: Mountaineers Books, 1983) is the best regional hiking guide.

Eastern Oregon

The classics for this area are *The Oregon Desert* by E. R. Jackson and R. A. Long (Portland: Caldwell Caxton, 1964) and *Steens Mountain in Oregon's High Desert Country* (Portland: Caldwell Caxton, 1967). Within the volumes, history and local color fill in the east side's wide-open spaces.

Fiction

The book to read before coming here is *Sometimes a Great Notion* by Ken Kesey (New York: Viking, 1964). This book is a fictional portrayal of what Mark Twain called the "westering spirit."

General Interest

The hottest new "read" on the region is *The Good Rain* by Timothy Egan (New York: Alfred A Knopf, 1990). The past, present, and future of the Pacific Northwest are eloquently rendered by this *New York Times* correspondent, and the chapters on the Columbia Gorge and Astoria are especially good.

Other Northwest vignettes worth perusing are found in the final chapters of the late Supreme Court Justice William O. Douglas's autobiography, *Of Men and Mountains* (San Francisco: Chronicle Books, 1985). Particularly evocative are his descriptions of the Wallowas.

The Best of Oregon by Ken Metzgler (Portland: Timber Press, 1986) is a loving look at the state.by a longtime Oregon journalist and University of Oregon professor.

Guidebooks

Ralph Friedman is Oregon's King of the Road. Of his half-dozen books, *Oregon for the Curious* (Portland: Caldwell Caxton, 1972) is most recommended. It still is the best mile-by-mile description of the state ever done.

Another writer who can stake a claim as the Dean of Oregon Travel Writers is Mimi Bell, simply on the strength of *Off Beat Oregon* (San Francisco: Chronicle Books,1983). Charming essays about travel in all four corners of the state will get you out of the armchair and onto the road.

Other excellent supplements to *Oregon Handbook* are penned by William L. Mainwaring for West Ridge Press in Salem, Oregon. His *Exploring Oregon's Central and Southern Cascades* (1979) and *Exploring the Oregon Coast* (1985) outline activities, hikes, camping, history, and local color.

History

The best concise history of Oregon can be found in the back of **Oregon Blue Book** (published biannually by the State of Oregon in Salem). This section of Oregon's political "Who's Who" is written by noted historian Terrence O'Donnell. His work in that book as well as in *Portland: An Informal History and Guide* **(Portland: Oregon Historical Society, 1964) should disabuse any notions you might have that history is boring.**

The grandaddy of them all, the *WPA Guide to Oregon* (Federal Writers' Project, 1941) was reissued a decade ago as *Oregon, the End of the Trail* (Carol Stream: Somerset Press, 1982) and is the primary inspiration for *Oregon Handbook.* The product of dozens of authors working in the Federal Writer's Project, this post-Depression guidebook still sets the standard for completeness and vividness of description. Although much of the info is dated, its rundown of pioneer history and glimpses of early twentieth-century Oregon make it a valuable tool for any modern traveler interested in understanding the Beaver State.

Photo Essays

The western part of the state is effectively profiled by Marnie McPhee in *Western Oregon: A Portrait of the Land and its People* (Helena: American Geographic Publishing, 1987). Excellent color photos make the wet-side's landscape and cultural geography come alive. In the same series, Mark Hoy's *Backroads of Oregon* (Helena: Amer-

ican Geographic Publishing, 1987) is also a winner.

Insight Guides: Pacific Northwest, edited by Hans Hoefer (Portland Graphic Arts Center Publishing Co., 1986) and featuring Oregon chapters by state residents (including the *Oregon Handbook* writers), is a cross between a coffee-table book and a guidebook. Despite the relative lack of hard information, lavish illustrations covering the whole state paint an evocative portrait in broad strokes.

The preeminent coffee-table books of Oregon photos were done by Ray Atkeson (Portland: Graphic Arts Center Publishing, 1968-1987). The once costly hard-covered editions of his *Oregon I, Oregon II,* and *Oregon III* are now available in paperback.

Statewide Hiking Guides

The best of this genre is undoubtedly *Exploring Oregon's Wild Areas* by William L. Sullivan (Denver: Mountaineers Books, 1988). Activities for hikers, backpackers, climbers, cross-country skiers, and saddlers are outlined in this well-organized book. Geology and botany are also addressed.

Finally, Doug Newman's outdoor column in the *Eugene Register Guard's* sports section is a special delight for those seeking escape to the Coast Range or Cascades.

INDEX

Boldfaced page numbers indicate primary reference. *Italicized* page numbers indicate information in maps, illustrations, charts, or callouts

ABOUT THE AUTHORS

Stuart Warren

Paradoxically, Stuart Warren's years directing tours in the Candian Rockies and Alaska as well as his work in other far-flung parts like Colombia and Guatemala fueled a resolve to write about his home state: "Oregon was always such a great place to come back to and explore." Enlisting longtime partner-in-crime Ted Long Ishikawa brought to the project a combined three decades' experience in imparting where to go and how to get the most out of a locale.

When Stuart isn't writing travel books (he has several others to his credit) or directing motorcoach tours, he's usually playing chess or hiking up and down the West Coast. He lives with his son Phineas in Portland, Oregon.

Ted Long Ishikawa

"Stu and I were working on a training manual for Tauck Tours back in 1983. The hours were long and the pay wasn't much, and many times I wanted to cash it in. After all, I'm more of a pianist than a writer. Performing for the Queen of England in Yosemite National Park and leading tours around the West seemed much more glamorous than sitting in front of a typewriter all day. But Stu kept saying, 'Someday we're going to write a book,' so I kept on typing.

"Well, I guess things haven't changed much. The hours are still long and the pay isn't much. Recording my album *Heart of Yosemite* seemed much more glamorous than writing a book. But I kept on typing, and in the process learned about the many special things my home state has to offer. It is my wish that more people will enjoy Oregon and that *Oregon Handbook* will enhance their visits."

Ted lives in Eugene, Oregon with his wife Sawako.

THE METRIC SYSTEM

1 inch = 2.54 centimeters (cm)
1 foot = .304 meters (m)
1 mile = 1.6093 kilometers (km)
1 km = .6214 miles
1 fathom = 1.8288 m
1 chain = 20.1168 m
1 furlong = 201.168
1 acre = .4047 hectares (ha)
1 sq km = 100 ha
1 sq mile = 59 sq km
1 ounce = 28.35 grams
1 pound = .4536 kilograms (kg)
1 short ton = .90718 metric ton
1 short ton = 2000 pounds
1 long ton = 1.016 metric tons
1 long ton = 2240 pounds
1 metric ton = 1000 kg
1 quart = .94635 liters
1 US gallon = 3.7854 liters
1 Imperial gallon = 4.5459 liters
1 nautical mile = 1.852 km

To compute centigrade temperatures, subtract 32 from Fahrenheit and divide by 1.8. To go the other way, multiply centigrade by 1.8 and add 32.

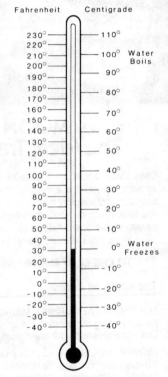

MOON HANDBOOKS
The Ideal Traveling Companions

Open a Moon Handbook and you're opening your eyes and heart to the world. Thoughtful, sensitive, provocative, and highly informative, Moon Handbooks encourage an intimate understanding of a region, from its culture and history to essential practicalities. Fun to read and packed with valuable information on accommodations, dining, recreation, plus indispensable travel tips, detailed maps, charts, illustrations, photos, glossaries, and indexes, Moon Handbooks are ideal traveling companions.

TO ORDER BY PHONE: (800) 345-5473 Monday-Friday 9 a.m.-5 p.m. PST

The Americas Series

NORTHERN CALIFORNIA HANDBOOK   by Kim Weir
An outstanding companion for imaginative travel in the territory north of the Tehachapis. Color and b/w photos, 69 maps, illustrations, booklist, index. 760 pages.   **$16.95**

NEVADA HANDBOOK   by Deke Castleman
Nevada Handbook puts the Silver State into perspective and makes it manageable and affordable. 34 b/w photos, 43 illustrations, 37 maps, 17 charts, booklist, index. 302 pages. **$12.95**

NEW MEXICO HANDBOOK   by Stephen Metzger
A close-up and complete look at every aspect of this wondrous state. 8 color pages, 85 b/w photos, 63 illustrations, 50 maps, 10 charts, booklist, index. 350 pages.   **$11.95**

TEXAS HANDBOOK   by Joe Cummings
Seasoned travel writer Joe Cummings brings an insider's perspective to his home state. 12 color pages, b/w photos, maps, illustrations, charts, booklist, index. 482 pages.   **$11.95**

ARIZONA TRAVELER'S HANDBOOK by Bill Weir
This meticulously researched guide contains everything necessary to make Arizona accessible and enjoyable. 8 color pages, 194 b/w photos, 74 illustrations, 53 maps, 6 charts, booklist, index. 505 pages. **$13.95**

UTAH HANDBOOK by Bill Weir
Weir gives you all the carefully researched facts and background to make your visit a success. 8 color pages, 102 b/w photos, 61 illustrations, 30 maps, 9 charts, booklist, index. 452 pages. **$12.95**

WYOMING HANDBOOK by Don Pitcher
All you need to know to open the doors to this wide and wild state. Color and b/w photos, illustrations, 66 maps, charts, booklist, index. Approx 450 pages. **$12.95**

ALASKA-YUKON HANDBOOK by Deke Castleman, Don Pitcher, and David Stanley
Get the inside story, with plenty of well-seasoned advice to help you cover more miles on less money. 8 color pages, 26 b/w photos, 92 illustrations, 90 maps, 6 charts, booklist, glossary, index. 384 pages. **$11.95**

WASHINGTON HANDBOOK by Dianne J. Boulerice Lyons
Covers sights, shopping, services, transportation, and outdoor recreation, and has complete listings for restaurants and accommodations. 8 color pages, 92 b/w photos, 24 illustrations, 81 maps, 8 charts, booklist, index. 425 pages. **$12.95**

OREGON HANDBOOK by Ted Long Ishikawa and Stuart Warren
Brimming with travel practicalities and insider views on Oregon's history, culture, arts, and activities. Color and b/w photos, illustrations, 28 maps, charts, booklist, index. 422 pages. **$12.95**

BRITISH COLUMBIA HANDBOOK by Jane King
With an emphasis on outdoor adventures, this guide covers mainland British Columbia, Vancouver Island, the Queen Charlotte Islands, and the Canadian Rockies. 8 color pages, 56 b/w photos, 45 illustrations, 66 maps, 4 charts, booklist, index. 396 pages. **$11.95**

GUIDE TO CATALINA AND CALIFORNIA'S CHANNEL ISLANDS by Chicki Mallan
A complete guide to these remarkable islands, from the windy solitude of the Channel Islands National Marine Sanctuary to bustling Avalon. 8 color pages, 105 b/w photos, 65 illustrations, 40 maps, 32 charts, booklist, index. 262 pages. **$9.95**

YUCATAN HANDBOOK by Chicki Mallan
All the information you'll need to guide you into every corner of this exotic land. 8 color pages, 154 b/w photos, 55 illustrations, 57 maps, 70 charts, appendix, booklist, Mayan and Spanish glossaries, index. 391 pages. **$12.95**

CANCUN HANDBOOK AND MEXICO'S CARIBBEAN COAST by Chicki Mallan
Covers the city's luxury scene as well as more modest attractions, plus many side trips to unspoiled beaches and Mayan ruins. Color and b/w photos, illustrations, over 30 maps, Spanish glossary, booklist, index. 257 pages. **$9.95**

BELIZE HANDBOOK by Chicki Mallan
Complete with detailed maps, practical information, and an overview of the area's flamboyant history, culture, and geographical features. *Belize Handbook* is the only comprehensive guide of its kind to this spectacular region. Color and b/w photos, illustrations, maps, booklist, index. 201 pages. **$11.95**

The Pacific/Asia Series

BALI HANDBOOK   by Bill Dalton
Detailed travel information on the most famous island in the world. 12 color pages, 29 b/w photos, 68 illustrations, 42 maps, 7 charts, glossary, booklist, index. 428 pages.   **$12.95**

INDONESIA HANDBOOK   by Bill Dalton
This one-volume encyclopedia explores island by island the many facets of this sprawling, kaleidoscopic island nation. 30 b/w photos, 143 illustrations, 250 maps, 17 charts, booklist, extensive Indonesian vocabulary, index. 1,050 pages.   **$17.95**

PHILIPPINES HANDBOOK   by Peter Harper and Evelyn Peplow
Crammed with detailed information, *Philippines Handbook* equips the escapist, hedonist, or business traveler with a thorough introduction to the Philippines's colorful history, landscapes, and culture. Color and b/w photos, illustrations, maps, charts, index. 550 pages.   **$12.95**

SOUTH KOREA HANDBOOK   by Robert Nilsen
Whether you're visiting on business or searching for adventure, *South Korea Handbook* is an invaluable companion. 8 color pages, 78 b/w photos, 93 illustrations, 109 maps, 10 charts, Korean glossary with useful notes on speaking and reading the language, booklist, index. 548 pages.   **$14.95**

SOUTHEAST ASIA HANDBOOK   by Carl Parkes
Helps the enlightened traveler to discover the real Southeast Asia. 16 Color pages, 75 b/w photos, 11 illustrations, 169 maps, 140 charts, vocabulary lists and suggested readings, index. 874 pages.   **$16.95**

HAWAII HANDBOOK   by J.D. Bisignani
Winner of the 1989 Hawaii Visitors Bureau's Best Guide Book Award and the Grand Award for Excellence in Travel Journalism, this guide takes you beyond the glitz and high-priced hype and leads you to a genuine Hawaiian experience. 12 color pages, 318 b/w photos, 132 illustrations, 74 maps, 43 graphs and charts, Hawaiian and pidgin glossaries, appendix, booklist, index. Approx. 870 pages.   **$15.95**

KAUAI HANDBOOK   by J.D. Bisignani
Kauai Handbook is the perfect antidote to the workaday world. 8 color pages, 36 b/w photos, 48 illustrations, 19 maps, 10 tables and charts, Hawaiian and pidgin glossaries, booklist, index. 236 pages.   **$9.95**

MAUI HANDBOOK: Including Molokai and Lanai   by J.D. Bisignani
"No fool-'round" advice on accommodations, eateries, and recreation, plus a comprehensive introduction to island ways, geography, and history. 4 color pages, 60 b/w photos, 72 illustrations, 34 maps, 19 charts, booklist, glossary, index. 350 pages.   **$10.95**

OAHU HANDBOOK   by J.D. Bisignani
A handy guide to Honolulu, renowned surfing beaches, and Oahu's countless other diversions. Color and b/w photos, illustrations, 18 maps, charts, booklist, glossary, index. 354 pages.   **$11.95**

BIG ISLAND OF HAWAII HANDBOOK   by J.D. Bisignani
An entertaining, yet informative text, packed with insider tips on accommodations, dining, sports and outdoor activities, natural attractions, and must-see sights. Color and b/w photos, illustrations, 20 maps, charts, booklist, glossary, index. 347 pages.   **$11.95**

SOUTH PACIFIC HANDBOOK   by David Stanley
The original comprehensive guide to the 16 territories in the South Pacific. 20 color pages, 195 b/w photos, 121 illustrations, 35 charts, 138 maps, booklist, glossary, index. 740 pages.   **$15.95**

MICRONESIA HANDBOOK:
Guide to the Caroline, Gilbert, Mariana, and Marshall Islands   by David Stanley
Micronesia Handbook guides you on a real Pacific adventure all your own. 8 color pages, 77 b/w photos, 68 illustrations, 69 maps, 18 tables and charts, index. 288 pages.   **$9.95**

FIJI ISLANDS HANDBOOK   by David Stanley
The first and still the best source of information on travel around this 322-island archipelago. 8 color pages, 35 b/w photos, 78 illustrations, 26 maps, 3 charts, Fijian glossary, booklist, index. 198 pages.   **$8.95**

TAHITI-POLYNESIA HANDBOOK   by David Stanley
All five French-Polynesian archipelagoes are covered in this comprehensive guide by Oceania's best-known travel writer. 12 color pages, 45 b/w photos, 64 illustrations, 33 maps, 7 charts, booklist, glossary, index. 225 pages.   **$9.95**

NEW ZEALAND HANDBOOK   by Jane King
Introduces you to the people, places, history, and culture of this extraordinary land. 8 color pages, 99 b/w photos, 146 illustrations, 82 maps, booklist, index. 546 pages.   **$14.95**

BLUEPRINT FOR PARADISE: How to Live on a Tropic Island   by Ross Norgrove
This one-of-a-kind guide has everything you need to know about moving to and living comfortably on a tropical island. 8 color pages, 40 b/w photos, 3 maps, 14 charts, appendices, index. 212 pages.   **$14.95**

The International Series

EGYPT HANDBOOK   by Kathy Hansen
An invaluable resource for intelligent travel in Egypt. 8 color pages, 20 b/w photos, 150 illustrations, 80 detailed maps and plans to museums and archaeological sites, Arabic glossary, booklist, index. 510 pages.   **$14.95**

PAKISTAN HANDBOOK   by Isobel Shaw
For armchair travelers and trekkers alike, the most detailed and authoritative guide to Pakistan ever published. 28 color pages, 86 maps, appendices, Urdu glossary, booklist, index. 478 pages.   **$15.95**

MOSCOW-LENINGRAD HANDBOOK   by Masha Nordbye
Provides the visitor with an extensive introduction to the history, culture, and people of these two great cities, as well as practical information on where to stay, eat, and shop. Color and b/w photos, illustrations, maps, charts, booklist, index. Approx 250 pages.
$15.95

IMPORTANT ORDERING INFORMATION

TO ORDER BY PHONE: (800) 345-5473 Monday-Friday 9 a.m.-5 p.m. PST

PRICES: All prices are subject to change. We always ship the most current edition. We will let you know if there is a price increase on the book you ordered.

SHIPPING & HANDLING OPTIONS:
1) Domestic UPS or USPS 1st class (allow 10 working days for delivery):
   $3.50 for the 1st item, 50 cents for each additional item.

Exceptions:
Moonbelt shipping is $1.50 for one, 50 cents for each additional belt.
Add $2.00 for same-day handling.
2) UPS 2nd Day Air or Printed Airmail requires a special quote.
3) International Surface Bookrate (8-12 weeks delivery):
   $3.00 for the 1st item, $1.00 for each additional item.

FOREIGN ORDERS: All orders which originate outside the U.S.A. must be paid for with either an International Money Order or a check in U.S. currency drawn on a major U.S. bank based in the U.S.A.

TELEPHONE ORDERS: We accept Visa or MasterCard payments. Minimum order is US$15.00. Call in your order: (800) 345-5473. 9 a.m.-5 p.m. Pacific Standard Time.

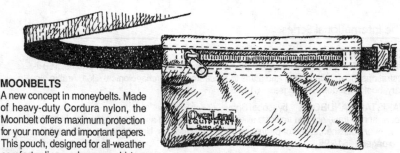

MOONBELTS

A new concept in moneybelts. Made of heavy-duty Cordura nylon, the Moonbelt offers maximum protection for your money and important papers. This pouch, designed for all-weather comfort, slips under your shirt or waistband, rendering it virtually undetectable and inaccessible to pickpockets. Many thoughtful features: one-inch-wide nylon webbing, heavy-duty zipper, and a one-inch high-test quick-release buckle. No more fumbling around for the strap or repeated adjustments, this handy plastic buckle opens and closes with a touch, but won't come undone until you want it to. Accommodates traveler's checks, passport, cash, photos. Size 5 x 9 inches. Available in black only.   **$8.95**

ORDER FORM

Name:_____Date:_____

Street:_____

City:_____

State or Country:_____Zip Code:_____

Daytime Phone:_____

Quantity	Title	Price

Taxable Total _____

Sales Tax (6%) for California Residents _____

Shipping & Handling _____

TOTAL _____

Ship to: ☐ address above ☐ other (fill in below)

_____

_____

_____

Make checks payable to:
Moon Publications, Inc., 722 Wall Street, Chico, California, 95928, USA
We Accept Visa and MasterCard
To order: Call in your Visa or MasterCard number, or send a written order with your Visa or MasterCard number and expiration date clearly written.

Card Number: ☐ Visa ☐ MasterCard

☐☐☐☐ ☐☐☐☐ ☐☐☐☐ ☐☐☐☐

expiration date:_____

Exact Name on Card: ☐ same as above ☐ other (fill in below)

_____

signature_____

WHERE TO BUY THIS BOOK

Bookstores and Libraries:
Moon Publications guides are sold worldwide. Please write sales manager for a list of wholesalers and distributors in your area that stock our travel handbooks.

Travelers:
We would like to have Moon Publications guides available throughout the world. Please ask your bookstore to write or call us for ordering information. If your bookstore will not order our guides for you, please write or call for a free catalog.

MOON PUBLICATIONS, INC.
722 WALL STREET
CHICO, CA 95928 USA
tel: (800) 345-5473
fax: (916) 345-6751